Household Production
and Consumption

NATIONAL BUREAU OF ECONOMIC RESEARCH

*CONFERENCE ON RESEARCH IN INCOME
AND WEALTH*

Household Production

and Consumption

NESTOR E. TERLECKYJ, Editor

NATIONAL PLANNING ASSOCIATION

Studies in Income and Wealth
VOLUME FORTY
by the Conference on Research
in Income and Wealth

NATIONAL BUREAU OF ECONOMIC RESEARCH
NEW YORK 1975

Distributed by COLUMBIA UNIVERSITY PRESS
NEW YORK AND LONDON

Library of Congress Cataloging in Publications Data

Conference on Household Production and Consumption, Washington, D.C. 1973.
Household production and consumption.
(Studies in income and wealth; v. 40)
Includes bibliographies and index.
1. Consumption (Economics) – United States – Mathematical models – Congresses.
2. Consumers – United States – Mathematical models – Congresses. 3. Home
economics – United States – Mathematical models – Congresses. I. Terleckyj, Nestor E.
II. National Bureau of Economic Research. III. Title. IV. Series: Conference on Re-
search in Income and Wealth. Studies in income and wealth; v. 40
HC106.3.C714 vol. 40 [HB801] 330'.08s 74-82381
ISBN 0-87014-515-0

Printed in the United States of America

*Relation of the National Bureau Directors to
Publications Reporting Conference Proceedings*

Since the present volume is a record of conference proceedings, it has been exempted from
the rules governing submission of manuscripts
to, and critical review by, the Board of Directors
of the National Bureau.

*(Resolution adopted July 6, 1948,
as revised November 21, 1949,
and April 20, 1968)*

Prefatory Note

THIS volume contains the papers presented at the Conference on Household Production and Consumption held in Washington, D.C., on November 30 and December 1, 1973. We are indebted to the National Science Foundation for its support, to the members of the Program Committee — Nestor E. Terleckyj, chairman, Robert T. Michael, and Jack E. Triplett — and to Gary S. Becker, who served as consultant. We wish to thank Elizabeth Kosciw for making local arrangements for the Conference. Our thanks are due also to Ruth Ridler who prepared the manuscript for press and to H. Irving Forman for charting.

Funds for the economic research conference
program of the National Bureau of Economic
Research are supplied by the National Science
Foundation.

Contents

Household Production
and Consumption

Introduction and Summary *

NESTOR E. TERLECKYJ

NATIONAL PLANNING ASSOCIATION

I. NEW RESEARCH ON THE BEHAVIOR OF THE CONSUMER SECTOR

THE research presented in this volume explores for the most part the observable market and nonmarket behavior of consumer units in terms of the more basic consumer objectives — objectives which can explain their choices in allocating resources among the currently purchased goods and services; between current and future consumption, investment, and leisure; and between health and personal safety and income. It explores in some detail the relationships between the particular characteristics of certain goods and services and objectives which the consumers seek to achieve by means of these goods and services. It also addresses some questions of consumer safety and information in the context of optimization through market and nonmarket processes, and includes a discussion of statistics of consumption.

The microeconomics of consumption has long been a dormant subject in economic research, perhaps because in the past the prevailing view of consumption ignored the specifics of the consumption process as distinct from expenditure.

This volume is the first in the present series to have consumer behavior as its main focus. Though, to be sure, individual papers given at the various meetings, both recent and early, addressed particular questions of consumer behavior and consumer welfare, none of the earlier meetings had the behavior of the consumer sector as its principal theme.

The present wave of research on the household sector has been given direction by the deepening and extensions of the theory of con-

* I should like to thank Robert Michael, Milton Moss, and Jack Triplett for the advice and assistance which they gave me in writing this introduction. My work in connection with this Conference was supported by research grant GS29032, from the National Science Foundation.

sumption [1] and has built on the empirical foundation provided by the hedonic price analysis. [2] Also, various social changes, including the recent growth of the consumer movement, have placed the consumer sector closer to the center of public and professional attention.

The insights afforded by the research discussed here suggest that the goods and services which consumers purchase or use can be seen as tractable inputs devoted to the achievement of personal and household objectives. Consumer behavior can be better understood in terms of specific functional relationships and objectives which goods and services and their combinations can serve by virtue of their particular properties, given the limits of consumer income, time, and other resources. The papers in this volume convey, I believe, a clear sense that the various consumer units tend to behave as competent producers in a large variety of situations often thought to be governed by irrationality or impulse responses.

The papers display a great diversity of research methods and subject matter. The subjects include determination of family size; interrelationship between education and health; allocation of work between present and future income; wage differentials in risky jobs; detailed analyses of consumption of food, automobiles, and housing; product safety; evaluation of product quality; and aggregate consumption statistics. These subjects are examined by means of a variety of research techniques including cross-sectional and sequential econometric models; benefit-cost analysis, dynamic optimization, index number analysis, estimation of utility functions, and demand analysis for product characteristics.

The papers presented in the course of the Conference are the result of a rather systematic search for advanced research in the field of consumption and household behavior. It is impossible to say how well we succeeded in representing the ongoing research, but a serious attempt in that direction was made. Two topics for which we unsuccessfully tried to find ongoing research are the role of public goods — or, more generally, of collective goods — in the consumption process, and the

[1] Gary S. Becker, "A Theory of the Allocation of Time," *Economic Journal* 75 (September 1965): 493–517; Kelvin J. Lancaster, "A New Approach to Consumer Theory," *Journal of Political Economy* 74 (April 1966): 132–157; Idem, *Consumer Demand* (New York: Columbia University Press, 1971); Robert T. Michael and Gary S. Becker, "On The New Theory of Consumer Behavior," *Swedish Journal of Economics* 75 (1973): 378–396; Richard F. Muth, "Household Production and Consumer Demand Functions," *Econometrica* 34 (July 1966): 699–708.

[2] Zvi Griliches, ed., *Price Indexes and Quality Change* (Cambridge: Harvard University Press, 1971).

interpersonal aspects of the decision processes occurring within households. Also, none of the papers deals with sources of consumer preferences or of changes in these preferences.

The first part of the volume, *Demographic Behavior of the Household*, deals with aspects of household choice of family size and with production of health. Of the two papers on family size, one reflects a cross-section model concerned with the optimum family size, and the other attempts to identify a sequential model when the decision on having one more child is considered. The health production paper is based on a recursive model, exploring the interrelationship between schooling and health.

Papers in the second part, *Market and Nonmarket Aspects of Real Earnings*, deal with two questions regarding the labor market behavior of individuals. The first paper considers the individual's allocation of working time between current income and investment in future income. Methodologically, it represents a model of dynamic utility maximization. The second paper estimates the market price of avoidance of job-related deaths, based on an analysis of wage differentials in risky occupations. The underlying model of the demand for and the supply of job safety treats jobs as multi-characteristic objects of transactions.

The third part, *Level of Aggregation in Consumption Analysis*, deals with differences and similarities of individual market goods and their characteristics. The papers explore a basic problem of consumption research: determining the appropriate level of aggregation in the definition of consumer goods and in the measurement of their prices.

One paper extends hedonic analysis by developing a two-stage estimating model for component prices of automobiles, adding a stage oriented toward performance characteristics to the one based on technical specifications. Another paper estimates cost-of-living indexes based on the parameters of eight distinct utility functions which permit substitution among goods in order to test the reliability of conventional consumer price indexes, which are based on an implicit assumption of no substitution. The third paper contains an estimation of price indexes for the components of housing, based on price estimates of detailed characteristics derived from a sample of observed price variations in a large number of houses sold within a local market over a period of time.

Papers in the fourth part, *Measurement and Policy Issues in Consumption Analysis*, deal with selected aspects of measurement of product quality and their applicability to particular policy issues. One paper discusses the measurement of risk and the setting of safety standards for consumer products, identifying relative costs and benefits of prevention of risk by consumers versus reduction of risk by producers, and illustrates the analysis by a case study. Another paper describes a subjective evaluation approach to measuring overall quality of consumer goods and retail outlets. The third paper develops a long-term quantity-consumed index of Canadian consumption, compares it with the conventional series of deflated value of consumer expenditure, and computes a residual describing the difference between the two series.

II. DEMOGRAPHIC BEHAVIOR OF THE HOUSEHOLD

Michael and Willis consider the household behavior regarding determination of family size. The authors focus on the choice of contraceptive techniques and calculate the probability distributions of conceptions as a function of the choice of techniques and the efficiencies with which they are used. Given the monthly probability of conception, the total number of children born to a couple would be determined by the length of the fertile life-span and other biological parameters. Thus, family size becomes the dependent variable, simply derivable from the monthly conception probability variable.

In the authors' model, the utility of parents depends on the number of children, the "quality" of children (which depends on the amount of time, attention, and expense which can be devoted to each child) and on other outputs of the household production processes. Its maximization is subject to lifetime income and time constraints. Given the couple's preference field, there exists an optimal number of children for the family, and deviations in the direction of excess fertility or deficit fertility reduce utility. Because the actual outcome of fertility control behavior is stochastic, utility increases can also be expected from reduction of the variance of fertility. But fertility control techniques have rising costs and consequently, for any given couple, different techniques are optimal for different family sizes. The higher the contraceptive cost, the less control will be desired, and the larger the resulting family size. The fertility control costs include not only money but also time, loss of pleasure, sacrifice of moral principles, risks to health, and other factors.

In estimating the relationships between contraception techniques used and the fertility outcome, Michael and Willis use cross-section survey data from the 1965 National Fertility Survey of 5,600 married women, grouping data by religion, race, age, and wife's education. They find substantial differences in the family size and in the estimated relationships between groups. Within homogeneous groups, they find a negative relation between fertility and the use of effective contraceptive methods. Holding other variables constant, they also find a reduction in the variance of fertility with increasing levels of wife's education.

Finally, the authors undertake a case study of the use of the pill, restricting the data to white non-Catholics and using subsamples for women who began their first, second, and third pregnancies, respectively, in 1960. They find positive effects on the use of the pill for the time trend, husband's income, wife's education, and the occurrence of prior contraceptive failure; and a negative effect for wife's age at marriage.

Rottenberg finds himself in agreement with Michael and Willis regarding their formulation of questions and their research strategy, which postulates that no contraceptive strategy is certain, that all are costly, and that households differ in their contraceptive effectiveness. He also agrees that the behavioral implications of this theory are not contradicted by the tests. Then Rottenberg points to what he considers are two shortcomings of the Michael-Willis model: it assumes that services and utility derived from children can be obtained only from own children, and treats time as a homogeneous entity.

In raising a few specific points, he argues that the data do not permit distinctions between pure and mixed contraceptive strategies, and that the fixed costs of contraceptive alternatives may be overweighted. He questions the inference that changing contraceptive techniques is uncommon, and he argues that differences in preferences rather than in the time horizon may perhaps provide a more likely explanation of why use of the pill by women married at an older age is less prevalent than it is among women who were younger when married.

Heckman and Willis develop an econometric model of fertility behavior within a sequential stochastic framework. The building of a family is viewed as a stochastic process described by a number of states with respect to fecundity and pregnancy and by the transition probabilities between these states, which depend on contraception among other things. Behavior is determined one month at a time, and the generalized equation for the expected utility is stated in terms of utility of preventing the conception of the $n + 1$st child, in month t.

In practice there are substantial components in statistical variation not included in the model. These arise from differences in health and in taste for sexual activity, as well as from differences in contraceptive efficiencies. These unmeasured components, Heckman and Willis note, pose very serious statistical problems in obtaining unbiased estimates of the effects of economic variables on the monthly probability of conception. They discuss the serial correlation problems which arise from the unmeasured variables which are assumed to be randomly distributed among individuals, but which maintain consistent levels for specific individuals over time. The authors derive estimates of the monthly probability of conception in the first pregnancy interval following marriage. The data consist of a sample of white, non-Catholic women, married once, with husband present for fifteen to nineteen years, and it is taken from the National Fertility Study for 1965. Heckman and Willis have analyzed the history of contracepting and noncontracepting couples for a maximum of 120 months, beginning with the first month of marriage. They have then proceeded to study the effects of independent variables, including wife's education, wife's age, and husband's predicted income at age 40.

Next, they have estimated the parameters of their model and the magnitude of the serial correlation. Wife's age turns out to be the only significant variable affecting probability of conception in the noncontracepting sample. Among the contraceptors, the effect of the economic variables is neither significant nor entirely trivial. Heckman and Willis convert their estimates of parameters into estimates of monthly probabilities of conception and eliminate the effect of serial correlation, which was significant. In testing the economic variables, they find, somewhat to their surprise, a substantial negative effect of husband's predicted income on completed fertility, while there is some indication of a slight positive effect of wife's education.

McFadden finds the theoretical model of Heckman and Willis very interesting and their statistical methods new and powerful. He observes that the statistical methods employed by Heckman and Willis constitute a break with tradition and provide a new method for research. He finds it particularly appropriate that instead of postulating a representative consumer who is choosing a divisible time rate of consumption, the model recognizes that the population is heterogeneous and that the number of children has to be integral. The paper introduces components of variance structure between families and within families over time.

McFadden wonders, however, whether the empirical analysis provides sufficient tests for the theory, and whether the questions raised actually lend themselves to the type of economic analysis the authors apply. The significant empirical result is that the economic variables do not explain the monthly probability of pregnancy. McFadden points out that the authors' model distinguishes only between contracepting and noncontracepting families, but some studies suggest that the socio-economic factors may influence family size through their effects on the choice of particular contraceptive techniques. He cites results from one such study showing more pronounced effects of these factors.

Grossman undertakes to explore statistically the relationship between health status and schooling. Grossman conducts econometric analysis by the application of a theoretical model he develops. In his model, health is treated as a stock of capital which is increased by investment and reduced by depreciation. Health is viewed as capital primarily determining the amount of time available to an individual. The knowledge capital produced by schooling determines the productivity of working time in the market and in the household, including time spent in production of health. Grossman discusses a recursive system of equations with schooling dependent on health and health dependent on schooling. The system is specified in three equations describing the demand for children's health, for schooling, and for adult health.

Grossman tests his model on the NBER-Thorndike-Hagen sample based on the data for the Army Air Corps cadets of 1943, who were reinterviewed in 1955 and in 1969, with a supplementary survey in 1971. Because this sample deals essentially with upper income and educational groups, the effect of schooling on health that can be examined with this data actually represents the effect of attending college. Health is measured by a self-evaluation response, but the indicator Grossman derives from it correlates with data on work-time lost.

Grossman finds that a year of school contributes about 1 per cent to the index of health, other variables held constant. Since past health is among the variables held constant, this effect presumably represents a causal relationship from schooling to health. He also finds a positive effect of wife's schooling on the husband's health. In the schooling equation, past health has a statistically significant, though not very large, effect on the years of school completed. Among other relationships explored, Grossman examines the mortality experience of the NBER-Thorndike-Hagen sample and finds a positive correlation between schooling and survival rates.

Usher discusses Grossman's model of the demand for health. He takes issue with the treatment of health expenditures as investment, arguing that many health expenditures are costs of present ill health and preconditions for preservation of life, not investments in future health. He suggests that the model is facing a paradox in the observed positive correlation between medical expenditure and occurrence of illness. Secondly, Usher questions measurement of health in units of illness-free days. He criticizes Grossman's formulation of the relationship between the state-of-health stock and the flow of illness-free days, which does not permit identifying the stock of health. Usher suggests that Grossman's empirical work probably could stand on its own, regardless of the model used, but that he would have preferred a dynamic to a static model.

Grossman, in his reply to Usher, argues that his model can accommodate negative correlation between medical care and health through an increase in the rate of depreciation, raising the shadow price of health and reducing the quantity of health capital demanded. If the depreciation rate were held constant, Grossman argues, the correlation would be positive, but because it is not held constant, the gross correlation is negative. He points out that his model can be used for defining separate demand curves for preventive and remedial medical care.

III. MARKET AND NONMARKET ASPECTS OF REAL EARNINGS

Heckman presents a model which attempts to explain the allocation of human time among work, investment, and leisure. He notes that the analysis of this subject encounters not only mathematical difficulties of dynamic models with finite time horizons, but also statistical problems, because the underlying union of the labor supply theory and the human capital theory introduces an unobservable statistical variable, i.e., work time spent investing.

In his model, Heckman assumes a utility function dependent on quantities of goods and leisure consumed at different times, a time preference rate, a budget constraint depending on the time path of hours worked, wages, and prices of consumer goods. The model also includes a conceptual division of time on the job into work and training time. Optimal investment behavior, from which the estimates of the investment time are to be derived, cannot be specified from the general model without making a series of very explicit assumptions about the model, functional forms, and values of parameters of the human capital investment. Heckman assumes a Cobb-Douglas production function for human capital and proceeds to simulate investment profiles based on the wage data. He uses synthetic cohort data, from the 1970 Census tape for white, college-educated, employed males not in school, age 23 to 65. Hourly wage rate is calculated by dividing earnings by the estimated hours worked.

Heckman develops a number of simulation models. In one model, human capital is excluded from its own production and the rate of depreciation is set at zero, while the interest rate is fixed at 10 per cent. This model yields an estimate of time spent investing which declines more or less continuously from some 25 per cent of the time at work in the market at age 23 to near zero at age 50. Since market hours increase early in the working age, the absolute amount of invested time remains constant until the early thirties and then declines until age 50. Heckman finds a sharp increase in investment time immediately after school, which contradicts the simplified model. He consequently drops the assumption of zero depreciation and zero effect of human capital on its own productivity and estimates the corresponding parameters directly. The estimated rate of depreciation is quite small, a fraction of 1 per cent, while the amount of human capital seems to have negative effect on its own production. This unconstrained model also gives much steeper decline in the time spent investing, from 30 per cent immediately after school to near zero around age 35. Heckman concludes by noting that his estimates for both models yield steeper decline in the proportion of time spent investing at each age than the amounts assumed earlier by other researchers.

Schultz finds the analytical reasoning in Heckman's paper very interesting and persuasive but raises questions about the empirical treatment. First of all, he objects to the use of synthetic cohort data in estimating a large number of parameters in a highly complicated model, especially since some time series data for individuals and actual age cohorts are becoming available. He also raises some points about specific maximum likelihood estimations. He is skeptical about the interpretation of the parameters obtained by Heckman. Even with all the restrictions made in the model in order to identify the time allocated to future income, Schultz argues, the testable empirical implications are not powerful in accounting for anomalous empirical evidence, such as a negative productivity of human capital and the jump in investment time after school.

Thaler and Rosen analyze wage differentials in risky jobs, in order to estimate the implicit market price of the avoidance of risk of death. They view safety and wage as two characteristics of jobs. Thaler and Rosen consider the workers to be selling labor, while at the same time purchasing nonmonetary aspects of jobs (safety); and assume firms to be purchasing labor, as well as selling the same nonmonetary aspects. In the theoretical model, which generalizes Adam Smith's concept of equalizing differences, the equilibrium wage differentials for risky jobs will be determined by the demand and supply functions for safety. The authors proceed to develop a theoretical model for cases of multi-dimensional risks (different injuries not comparable) and for different preferences in risk aversion among workers. Because their empirical work uses data for very risky jobs, the authors caution that their estimates of demand prices for safety may be lower than those applicable to average workers.

In their empirical estimation, the authors study a sample of male heads of households from the data in the 1967 Survey of Economic Opportunity for worker characteristics and wages, and they match this data with the risk data from the 1967 Occupation Study of the Society of Actuaries, which examines about 3 million policy years of worker experience, tabulated by occupation, over the period 1955–1964.

This actuarial data measures additional risks associated with certain occupations which are particularly hazardous, as revealed by insurance company records. The wage data the authors use is a weekly wage. For characteristics variables held constant, the authors use the regional and urban location variables, as well as personal characteristics including age, family size, race, education, and income. They also attempt to control for job characteristics by using variables representing unionization and the type of industry. With these variables, the authors estimate a number of different equations, which yield varying estimates of the actuarial equilibrium price for avoidance of one job-related fatality ranging, in 1967, from $136,000 to $260,000. This price is interpreted as the intersection of the demand curve for safety by workers and the supply curve of safety by firms.

Kosters notes that the actuarial data used by Thaler and Rosen reflect not only the risk of death on the job but also differences in the risk of death associated with characteristics of workers in various occupational categories. Their conceptual framework permits the authors to make a careful distinction between the price concept, for which they are making estimates, and the concepts involved in the demand curves for safety of the individual workers or in the cost curves of risk reduction for individual firms.

Lipsey argues that the data used by Thaler and Rosen actually measure the extra risk to the insurance company of insuring those who enter a particular occupation, rather than true occupational risks. He then points out that the associated mortality risks will not be compensated by higher wages, except to the extent that there is a correlation between risks inherent in jobs and characteristics of persons in the jobs. Consequently, the estimated coefficients for compensating wage variations are subject to bias.

IV. LEVEL OF AGGREGATION IN CONSUMER ANALYSIS

Triplett, in his role as session chairman, discusses the framework within which research on this topic is conducted. He argues that it is important to close the gap between "New Demand Theory" and empirical work on hedonic quality measurement, but he also argues that some recent attempts to do so have seriously misstated the problem to be attacked. To help illustrate his points, Triplett offers a simile comparing goods of nonhomogeneous quality, which are the object of hedonic price analysis, to preloaded grocery baskets. Under his simile, rather than placing their wares on the shelves with unit prices marked on them, the grocers have, instead, loaded various assortments into grocery baskets, attaching prices only to each of the preloaded baskets as a whole.

The hedonic research represents an attempt to find out what the prices would have been had the groceries been stocked on the shelves. Central to this research is the concept of the hedonic function, which Triplett defines as a regression in which a vector of market prices of different varieties of a product is related to a matrix describing product characteristics of these varieties. Hedonic functions cannot be derived either from preferences or from production functions, because the hedonic functions do not correspond to the demand functions, but rather to portions of budget constraints.

Ohta and Griliches present a study of automobile prices which extends the hedonic approach by distinguishing between the physical characteristics of a car and its performance variables. They postulate a two-stage hypothesis which asserts that physical characteristics of a car produce its performance. They address the question of whether the performance variables explain enough of the variation in prices to permit their substitution for the physical characteristics in hedonic regression.

The basic model relates the price of a given car, new or used, to its make, physical specification characteristics (hedonic components), and age, in a form where depreciation rates vary with make. Five physical characteristics are used: shipping weight, length of the car, maximum brake horsepower, a dummy variable for the body type, and a dummy variable for the number of cylinders. The authors study the depreciation patterns in order to establish whether the make effects persist in the used car market. They also test whether the imputed prices of physical characteristics are stable across firms and over time.

The authors find distinct make-effects which persist through the used car markets, suggesting that these are not transitory markups by manufacturers for new cars. The make-effects are greater in the used than in the new car markets. Depreciation rates, using a declining balance method, differ by make and by model year, suggesting that the hedonic method did not fully capture the vintage effect. The price of the high-priced cars is not fully explained by the physical characteristics. They conclude that the imputed prices of physical characteristics are stable over time and between makes, and that new and used cars are essentially the same good, differing only in the quantity of the good contained in them for market use. The authors interpret the systematic price differences among makes as reflecting unmeasured aspects of quality, rather than simply being pricing errors.

The performance variables based on the *Consumer Reports* data, include among others, miles per gallon, acceleration, handling, trade-in value, and frequency of repairs. Ohta and Griliches find that the performance variables correlate about as well with prices as do the physical characteristics. Performance variables with strong explanatory power are correlated with physical characteristics, such as weight and horsepower or with depreciation rates (trade-in value), while those which are not highly correlated with measured physical characteristics are not statistically significant. Comparing physical characteristics with the performance variable improves the fit somewhat but not much. The authors find that the make-effects obtained in equations using performance variables are about the same as the make-effects obtained with physical characteristics. They conclude that both sets of variables tell essentially the same story, and that the two-stage approach did not contribute much.

The authors compare the hedonic price indexes derived by the two methods and find that they are essentially similar, and that both show about the same price increase for the period 1964–1971 as does the Consumer Price Index component for new cars. Used car prices rose relative to new car prices in the early 1960s; the authors interpret this as reflecting a possible decline in the quality of new cars in that period. From the hedonic indexes, they also conclude that quality adjustments in the price indexes for new cars which treat pollution-control devices as quality improvements are not recognized as such by consumers.

Barzel notes that the selection of variables in a hedonic analysis, including the present one by Ohta and Griliches, is always incomplete. The results obtained represent a composite of the effects of the measured and of the unmeasured attributes, which would explain some of the unexplained variability. He also argues that the discontinuity in the characteristics causes discrepancies between hedonic and true cost-of-living indexes.

Ohta and Griliches, in replying to Barzel, argue that the conventional consumer price indexes are not necessarily better at complete enumeration than the hedonic indexes, and note that the hedonic indexes never aim at completeness but strive to include major variables, while permitting the rest to be included in the constant. Unless one can specify what has been left out, it is not possible to do anything about omissions. Regarding discontinuity and nonlinearity of price schedules, the authors acknowledge the seriousness of the problem but claim that it is one which afflicts all price indexes alike, with no special effect on the hedonic indexes.

Christensen and Manser construct a number of cost-of-living indexes for meat and for produce, using annual data for the period 1947–1971. Construction of cost-of-living indexes requires knowledge of the utility function representing consumer preferences. In practice, one must assume a particular utility function, estimate its unknown parameters, then use the estimates to construct a cost-of-living index. Specifically, the authors estimate the parameters of eight distinct utility functions, both for meat consumption and for produce consumption, and test the ability of these functions to explain the observed budget shares within these two groups of commodities. The translog function, the only one which does not impose either homotheticity or additivity restrictions on consumer preferences, explains the observed budget shares better than do the other forms. The different utility functions also imply quite different estimates of the price and expenditure elasticities. However, the authors find that the cost-of-living indexes computed with the translog utility function and with the other utility functions for meat and produce do not differ very much over the period studied. They also compute five price indexes using actual rather than estimated budget shares. They find that the Tornquist chain-link index which allows for substitution possibilities provides a somewhat closer approximation during the period covered to the true cost-of-living index than do fixed weight or chain-linked Laspeyres or Paasche indexes. However, the magnitudes of the numerical discrepancies between the indexes actually were not very large, suggesting that, within the range of experience covered, Laspeyres indexes (the Consumer Price Index is basically a Laspeyres index) do not differ very much from a cost-of-living index which satisfies the more demanding theoretical requirements.

Taylor, in discussing the paper by Christensen and Manser, commends the authors for their choice of an important topic and for the technical accomplishment of their work. He considers use of the translog utility function to be an important innovation in the applied demand analysis. He also considers it noteworthy that in estimating cost-of-living indexes, the authors have, in their construction and estimation, used only the indirect utility functions (functions of total expenditure and the prices of all commodities) rather than the direct function of levels of consumption of the individual commodities. Taylor suggests that the subindexes derived for the two commodity groups have to be interpreted as conditional cost-of-living indexes (conditional on the given prices and quantities for all other goods in the consumer basket). Otherwise, deriving such subindexes would not be consistent with the theoretical framework used. Finally, he voices caution that there is an inherent and unsolved problem in calculating cost-of-living indexes from parameters that have been estimated using other price indexes.

King undertakes a study of housing demand in terms of the characteristics approach. He notes that most studies have treated housing as a homogeneous commodity, while in reality many characteristics of the dwelling itself, and of its location, are important in explaining prices and consumer choices. He proposes a model of housing demand which includes a model of the residential location choice, and in which the individual characteristics of the housing bundle have their own prices. The households in his model choose their location in a three-way tradeoff among commuting costs, neighborhood quality, and advantageous characteristics of the housing itself. He further postulates that a metropolitan area would contain a series of linked submarkets, each with its own hedonic price equation for prices of the components of housing characteristics, because the existing stock of housing is fixed and can change only slowly over time.

In his empirical application, King uses data for 1,800 single-family houses sold through the multiple listing service in the New Haven, Connecticut, metropolitan region from 1967 to 1970. King also conducted a survey to collect data on such characteristics of the purchasers as income, family size, education, and place of work. He has also constructed two indicators of neighborhood quality by converting the ratings for a number of characteristics of neighborhood quality received in the questionnaire by means of a principal-components analysis.

Using political boundaries to define the boundaries of submarkets, King proceeds to derive hedonic equations for prices of housing components in which the price of the house in 1967 dollars is the dependent variable, and 31 hedonic components are the independent variables. He estimates a total of seven equations, one for each town and one for the area as a whole. King then aggregates the hedonic prices of the 31 components into prices of four characteristics of houses: basic structure, interior quality, interior space, and site. Expenditures for different components in his model can simply be added up into expenditure for a characteristic.

With these estimates of prices, King proceeds with the demand analysis, using a separable housing expenditure constraint (replacing the income constraint) and prices and quantities of the housing characteristics. With this analysis, he obtains distinct demand equations in price and housing outlay for the four characteristics, and elasticities for outlay—for own price as well as cross-elasticities. The results suggest that consumers indeed behave as if they were purchasing distinct bundles of characteristics. While this evidence suggests that purchasers behave as if they perceived the existing differences in the prices of characteristics, they do not tend to locate in the cheapest market because of location constraints. King finds that the simple tradeoff between housing price and commuting distance does not explain the departures from purchasing in the cheapest market, but by introducing a three-way tradeoff among commuting cost (distance), price of housing, and quality of neighborhood, he finds evidence that substantial tradeoffs were made between price of housing and quality of neighborhood.

King concludes by observing that an important heterogeneous good like housing can usefully be treated as a collection of specific characteristics. When analyzed in terms of characteristics, the behavior of prices and of consumers follows patterns consistent with economic rationality of choice, given income and prices.

Ingram agrees with King that the past studies treating housing as a homogeneous service have not been able to cope with the complexity of the characteristics of housing. He then discusses the variation in prices among the submarkets, observing first that the variations are included in housing expenditures, thus presenting problems for housing expenditures used as a measure of quantity consumed. He notes that spatial specifications of characteristics prices resulting in spatially tied sales differentiate analysis of housing demands from that of most other consumer goods. Ingram observes that simply adding up the products of component prices and their quantities into characteristics imposes restrictions on the utility functions of consumers, since the consumers are required conceptually to be indifferent in choosing among the combinations of components which are included in the characteristics of a given value. He also notes that the method used by King—limiting household substitutions to choices within the submarkets—raises certain issues, and he suggests some theoretical alternatives. Ingram notes that in King's analysis, the quality of neighborhood emerges as an important determinant of household location choice, and he questions the appropriateness of combining it with other attributes of the site characteristic, rather than treating it as a separate attribute.

V. MEASUREMENT AND POLICY ISSUES IN CONSUMPTION ANALYSIS

Broussalian develops a formal criterion for identifying unreasonable hazards of consumer products, and illustrates it by a case history of refrigerator doors. Unreasonable hazard is defined as possible occurrence of an undesirable event in the course of normal use of a good, in circumstances where the expected cost of the event is greater than the cost of avoiding it. Costs are defined on the social cost basis, and the benefits of avoidance are monetized. Avoidance actions can be taken both by producers and consumers.

Full market competition would tend to provide optimal risk avoidance. However, the economy may tolerate the presence of unreasonable hazards under certain conditions, such as lack of risk-insurance markets, external effects on third parties, or high transaction costs.

Broussalian illustrates his analysis by one particular case in which a physical safety standard has actually been set in order to avoid death by entrapment in a household refrigerator. In this case, there was considerable time lag in the achievement of refrigerator safety, because of the lag in replacement of old models. In fact, the degree of its actual achievement is still uncertain.

This case points to the tremendous complexity of information required in order to increase product safety. The physical safety standards set for refrigerators are an example of risk avoidance measures taken by producers. Measures which could be identified as the consumer risk-avoidance actions include following the warning literature provided by the manufacturers or the governmental warning literature, and complying with state and local criminal codes and ordinances relating to abandonment and storage of refrigerators.

In attempting benefit-cost calculation for the refrigerator case, Broussalian observes that the benefits per refrigerator were quite small because fatal accidents are rare and the discounting period long. On the other hand, the costs of the magnetic door device which proved to be most effective for easy opening were practically zero. For that reason, the producer avoidance requirement imposed by law can be considered as reducing unreasonable hazard.

Broussalian argues for the need for specific theories of accident occurrence and for careful analysis and data collection in devising helpful safety measures.

Gould notes that, in practice, benefit-cost criteria impose very difficult measurement problems on the benefit side. In the present case, the measurement problems are aggravated because benefit measurement includes monetization of injury and of loss of life, and because identification of the marginal effects of the accident avoidance actions are required. Gould also points out two serious conceptual problems in Broussalian's model. One is an inherent and implicit interpersonal utility judgment basic to the estimation of cost. In Broussalian's model, the aggregate cost for consumers is obtained by summing across individuals the costs of accident avoidance activities to the individuals. The other problem arises from minimizing social costs, rather than maximizing social welfare. Broussalian holds the level of output constant, but the changes in the level of output resulting from the imposition of hazard-avoidance costs may affect the overall consumer welfare.

Maynes proposes a general concept of quality measurement and illustrates it with the local market data for sofa beds in Minneapolis. In his concept, he includes characteristics of both the product and the seller, and deals with quality in terms of a product-brand-dealer combination.

Maynes defines quality formally as an index based on a set of characteristics scores determined by testers and weighted by a set of weights assumed to reflect the importance of the individual characteristics. Maynes uses the quality index to deflate money prices and finds in his case study that the range in the quality-deflated prices within his case sample is not much less than the range of the money prices. He further suggests that the informational effectiveness of markets can be measured by the price variation at a given level of quality, i.e., by the variation in the quality-adjusted prices.

Maynes points out that his measurement includes a cardinal scaling and requires an assumption that consumers would make uniform assessments of the quality characteristics and would attach the same weights to these characteristics. However, Maynes does not believe that it is possible to measure quality objectively, because quality is intrinsically subjective. Subjectivity persists, he continues, because different individuals in different circumstances, or with different tastes, would assign different weights, even if they all agreed on the characteristics.

Maynes also argues that because many different inputs are required to produce a given service, the definition of characteristics as services reduces the number of properties to be considered and makes measurement easier. Maynes cites automobile safety as an example where a number of specific physical properties such as stopping distance for brakes, tires, and so on have a bearing on safety, but the evaluators assess the safety characteristic as a whole.

Juster argues that there are basic flaws in the quality measurement approach that Maynes provides. He points out that whether the quality-adjusted prices show a large or only a small variation will depend largely on the scaling used to measure quality, which is itself arbitrary. It is possible to choose alternative scalings which would give very different results. If the price and the quality-scale indicator are perfectly rank correlated, then there is one way of scaling the quality indicator which will produce zero variation in the quality-adjusted prices, while other ways of scaling the quality scores of the characteristics would produce either positive or negative association between the original money prices and the quality-adjusted prices. However, if price and quality scales are not perfectly correlated, then it is not possible to find a scaling which will eliminate differences in quality-adjusted prices, and the resulting measurement would always suggest imperfect functioning of markets. But the absence of perfect rank correlation between price and quality indexes, Juster contends, could reflect interpersonal differences in the relative weights of characteristics. Therefore, in order to accept Maynes's inferences about the functioning of the markets from his quality measurements, it would be necessary to accept the scoring system he uses and the cardinal utility magnitudes inherent in it, and further to assume that there is no variation among the population in the weights assigned to characteristics. Because of the problems of deriving comprehensive quality indexes which would satisfy such requirements or avoid such difficulties, Juster expresses doubt about the value of pursuing the search for broad-gauged indexes of average product quality.

Triplett contrasts Maynes's concept of quality as a product attribute which is inherently measurable by a nonmonetary scalar indicator with the concept underlying the hedonic method. The hedonic method requires no single measure of quality as such; rather, "quality" is understood as merely a shorthand reference to the quantities in a vector of characteristics. The value of the characteristics vector can be calculated as a single number, provided one can find appropriate implicit prices for the characteristics to use as weights. Triplett argues that the concept of nonmonetary quality is not necessary for analysis because the only measure one needs is a measure of the value of quality differences (which can be obtained via the hedonic approach). Moreover, Maynes's approach cannot resolve interpersonal differences in taste; in the hedonic approach, this problem need not be addressed.

In comparing data requirements for empirical implementation of Maynes's method with the hedonic method, Triplett notes that both the hedonic method and Maynes's proposal require measurement of quantities of characteristics; however, where the hedonic technique requires only that prices be also available for different varieties in order to estimate the prices of characteristics, Maynes's method requires information on the utility of characteristics. Triplett continues that until cardinal utility can be measured, Maynes's proposal cannot be implemented but, if cardinal utility could be found, then it would not be necessary to measure characteristics, because one could then measure the utility of the entire product directly. Since utility is not measurable, Maynes's proposal, in Triplett's view, reduces to ad hoc judgment and does not contain systematic scientific measurements.

Maynes, in replying to the discussions by Juster and Triplett, defends the usefulness of his approach by citing the generally accepted usefulness of the *Consumer Reports* published by the Consumers Union and the similarity of his method to that used by the Consumers Union's scoring system. He argues that the Consumers Union scoring system is cardinal, even though in textual interpretation the Consumers Union generally has acted conservatively and taken an ordinal posture. He further argues that the quality scoring system employed by Consumers Union conforms to his model, in which the weights are relative marginal utilities associated with a given characteristic as determined by the consensus judgment of the CU testers.

Usher offers a comparison of two personal consumption time series per capita, one derived by conventional deflation of the expenditure series by a consumer price index and the other derived by revaluation of the quantities consumed by base-year prices. He computes the two series for Canada for the period 1935–1968. There is a substantial difference in their growth, which he suggests can be viewed as an analytically useful residual, possibly reflecting changes in the quality of consumption.

Usher argues that while the deflated consumption expenditure series have certain obvious advantages, such as availability of data and capacity to account for product variety, the quantities-consumed series can also illuminate trends in consumption. Usher further argues that quantity data are more closely related to the arguments of utility functions and to the social-indicator concepts than are the value data. Quantity data may also help in sorting out the types of consumption which more closely correspond to improvements in welfare from those that reflect increased costs.

Usher has constructed for consumption commodity classes, and for consumption as a whole, a revalued quantity-consumed time series using detailed data for several hundred specific items of consumption at 1961 prices. The principal empirical result of Usher's calculations is that the rate of growth of real consumption per head based on deflated value data is much higher (at 2.8 per cent per year) over the long period 1935–1968 than the per capita growth of his time series of revalued quantity data (which grew at 1.8 per cent a year). The full 1 per cent a year differential, in Usher's view, reflects the implicit adjustment for quality change, as well as conceptual differences between the series and errors of measurement. Usher views his work as experimental, but he hopes that in the future, valuable insights into the relationship between consumption growth and economic growth will be gained as better and more detailed quantity data become available.

Reid agrees with Usher's offering of his series as a tentative exploration and would emphasize this fact. Reid notes that the quality residual that Usher calculates is subject to errors in the expenditure series, in the consumer price indexes, and in the quantity indexes. She also thinks that future stimulus for improvement of quantity estimates of products is more likely to come from their contribution to knowledge of demand and welfare of specific consumption series, rather than from demand for global information. She comments that Usher offers little support for his argument that quantity indexes are more likely to be indicative of welfare than price-deflated expenditures, and also notes that none of the calculated aggregates or averages have a bearing on distributive changes. Reid also comments on the contribution to real consumption of the household economy, which Usher has not included. In view of past and future substitutions and shifts between household and market economy, quantity indexes which do not include the output of the household economy are likely to provide biased estimates of real consumption.

Mack, in her comment on the Conference as a whole, observes that the question of tastes and value systems has not been given much direct consideration. She argues that at the present levels of income and consumption in the United States, one would expect differences in tastes and in value systems to become more pronounced than they were in the earlier eras of substantial economic scarcity. Differences in tastes and value systems could be expected to have major effects on the demand for children, on the nonmarket aspects of real wages, and on product safety and quality. She points out that differences in preferences would have an important bearing on the evaluation of the informational effectiveness of markets that Maynes discusses within a single set of quality weights or, regarding the paper by Michael and Willis, on the notion that women marrying at later ages may prefer to have children sooner. She believes that explicit treatment of differences in tastes and life-styles may represent an important next step in the analyses of household production and consumption.

VI. CONCLUSIONS

What have we learned? At a general level, I think we have learned from this Conference that substantial progress is being made in the analysis of behavior of the consumer units. In large measure, but not exclusively, this progress is connected with the new theories of household production and characteristics of goods. The papers convey a sense that in many ways consumers behave as if they were producers, and that the economic models can provide useful insights into understanding consumer and household behavior.

We have also gained new knowledge and new insights regarding specific subjects. Thus, to at least some degree, consumers apparently attempt to decide on the number of family members in accordance with the economic theory of household production. Further, the years of schooling may have some effect on the efficiency with which individuals are able to take care of their own and their family's health.

Individuals apparently continue investing in their earning capacity after schooling through choice of jobs with less pay but with large training components, and this investment declines with age. Also, the wage differentials in risky occupations correspond to an actuarial premium of a magnitude which is consistent with other valuations of the financial loss from job-related deaths.

Regarding statistics, we learned that in test cases for two commodity groups, the existing price indexes are not too different from indexes which satisfy the requirements of economic theory permitting substitutions of goods. Also, based on Canadian data, physical quantity indexes of consumption showed much less long-term growth than the deflated expenditures series, even though conceptually the two indexes should provide the same results. The differences in price of different kinds of automobiles can be explained either by physical characteristics, or by consumer-related performance variables, but the two explanations are highly correlated and the second contributes little after allowing for the first. Understanding of the prices of housing and of the demand for it can be much improved by treating houses as highly complex, multi-characteristic goods, rather than single goods.

We have also learned that setting effective safety standards for consumer products imposes very demanding information requirements and that legislative and administrative practices in this regard are highly vulnerable to mistakes and oversights. We also see that some basic conceptual problems exist regarding the design and content of consumer information systems attempting overall evaluations of quality of consumer goods.

Some of the methods used in the Conference papers are complex and impose very demanding data requirements; others are more robust. Of course, the data demands depend on the specific subjects explored, as well as on the methods employed.

How much progress can be anticipated in the research on the consumer sector in the future, particularly in the near future, depends not only on the amount of interest and the number of researchers willing to enter the field, but also on the effectiveness of the techniques employed and on the quality of information available for research.

The techniques, always subject to improvement, appear to be sufficiently developed to permit further explorations along the lines pursued in the papers of this Conference. Lack of data may be a more serious though somewhat ambivalent problem. On the one hand, data appear to pose definite limits to the resolution of some of the complex issues raised in the papers, especially data dealing with the same individuals over long periods or data dealing with probabilities of events involving consumer products. On the other hand, some of the papers offer examples of fruitful utilization of data which have existed for a long time, e.g., data on the characteristics of houses and automobiles. This suggests that ingenuity in the formulation of research problems so as to utilize available information, as well as collection of own data, may provide opportunities for substantial progress.

Part I
Demographic Behavior of the Household

Contraception and Fertility:
Household Production under Uncertainty *

ROBERT T. MICHAEL

STANFORD UNIVERSITY AND NATIONAL BUREAU
OF ECONOMIC RESEARCH

AND

ROBERT J. WILLIS

CITY UNIVERSITY OF NEW YORK — GRADUATE CENTER
AND NATIONAL BUREAU OF ECONOMIC RESEARCH

I. INTRODUCTION

OVER the past century, fertility behavior in the United States has undergone profound changes. Measured by cohort fertility, the average number of children per married woman has declined from about 5.5 children at the time of the Civil War to 2.4 children at the time of the Great Depression. It is seldom emphasized, however, that an even greater relative change took place in the dispersion of fertility among these women: the percentage of women with, say, seven or more children declined from 36 per cent to under 6 per cent.[1] While students of population have offered reasonably convincing explanations for the decline in fertility over time, they have not succeeded in explaining the fluctuations in the trend and have made surprisingly

* This study has been supported by a population economics program grant to the NBER from the National Institute of Child Health and Human Development, Public Health Service, Department of Health, Education, and Welfare. We want to thank Lee A. Lillard for useful suggestions and C. Ates Dagli, Kathleen V. McNally, and Joan Robinson for their careful research assistance.

[1] These figures are taken from the report of the President's Commission on Population Growth and the American Future (see Taeuber 1972). They are indicated below in Table 1.

little effort to explain the large and systematic decline in the dispersion of fertility over time. In this paper, we attempt to study contraception behavior and its effects on fertility. One of the effects on which we focus considerable attention is the dispersion, or variance, in fertility. Our analysis is applied to cross-sectional data but it also provides an explanation for the decline in the variance of fertility over time.

The study of fertility behavior has received increasing attention by economists in the past few years. Much of this analysis has been conducted in the context of the new theory of consumer behavior pioneered by Becker (1965) and Lancaster (1966). The work on fertility behavior complements many other studies dealing with aspects of household production. One of the specific topics in the fertility literature has been the relationship between childbearing and several life-cycle production decisions, such as marriage, schooling, women's career choices, life-cycle time and money allocations, and so forth. A second and related topic of the economics of fertility behavior is the tradeoff in household production between the family's number of children and the expenditure of resources per child, particularly the expenditure of time devoted to children at the preschool age. A third focus of this research has been the fertility demand function—the form and stability over time and across groups of the household's demand function for children.[2]

Nearly all of these studies of household fertility behavior assume that the household can produce exactly the number of children it wants, costlessly and with certainty. We have previously pointed out that costly fertility control operates as a subsidy to childbearing, lowering the marginal cost of having additional children (see Willis 1971) and we have suggested a framework for analyzing the household's fertility control decisions (see Michael 1973). In this paper, we consider the household's fertility control behavior both in terms of the selection of specific fertility control strategies (the costs and benefits of specific contraceptive techniques) and in terms of the effects of different control strategies on household fertility.

One could introduce fertility control costs into a deterministic model of fertility behavior by treating these costs as transaction costs associated with acquiring any given level of fertility. In this framework,

---

[2] For a thorough model of fertility demand and the quantity-quality tradeoffs in the context of a static framework, see Willis (1973). For an extensive set of papers pertaining to topics in fertility behavior see the two NBER conference volumes, *New Economic Approaches to Fertility* and *Marriage, Family Human Capital and Fertility*, Schultz, ed., (1973) and (1974). These volumes indicate, we think, that much of observed fertility behavior is amenable to economic analysis.

TABLE 1

Mean Number of Children and Frequency Distribution
by Number of Children for Selected Cohorts
from 1835–1930 for Ever-Married Women

| Cohort | Mean Number of Children | Percent Distribution | | | | |
		0 Children	1–2 Children	3–4 Children	5–6 Children	≥ 7 Children
1835–39	5.40	7.7	17.3	20.0	18.7	36.3
1845–49	5.27	8.2	18.5	20.3	18.3	34.8
1855–59	4.97	8.9	20.6	21.3	17.9	31.3
1865–69	3.90	12.3	26.6	26.1	16.0	18.9
1875–79	3.46	15.0	30.4	25.2	14.4	15.0
1885–89	3.15	16.6	33.1	25.1	13.1	12.2
1895–99	2.71	18.6	39.0	23.9	10.0	8.4
1905–09	2.36	20.8	43.2	22.4	7.8	5.9
1915–19	2.60	13.9	43.7	28.1	8.9	5.4
1926–30	3.08	8.0	36.5	36.2	12.3	7.0

SOURCE: Taeuber 1972 (with the exception of the most recent cohort, the women were at least age 45 at the time of the enumeration; for the 1926–30 cohort the women were 40–44 at the time of the survey.)

the household can select any number of children with certainty, provided it pays the requisite costs of fertility control. Assuming that total fertility control costs are larger the smaller the number of children chosen, the positive marginal cost of fertility control raises average fertility by acting as a subsidy to childbearing. In this paper, we have treated the costs of fertility control in a somewhat different framework. We have adopted a model in which the household can select with certainty any particular monthly probability of conception,[3] but in which the household's actual fertility N is a stochastic variable. By selecting and producing a particular monthly probability of conception, the household selects a distribution of fertility outcomes. The mean of that distribution is its expected fertility; its variance indicates the uncertainty that the household faces.

As Table 1 indicates, the decline in average fertility over the past century has been accompanied by a significant reduction in the dispersion of fertility. The stochastic model of fertility control which

[3] The probability is bounded by zero and by the probability implied by natural or intrinsic fecundability, say, a probability of about 0.2 per month.

we discuss in the following section emphasizes the relationship between the mean and variance of fertility, and offers an explanation for the observed decline in the dispersion in fertility over time.

Child rearing is an exceptionally costly activity, both in terms of direct dollar outlays and forgone time and human capital.[4] Few events in one's lifetime affect subsequent behavior more extensively than having a child. While other important life-cycle decisions, such as marriage and career choice, are subject to considerable uncertainty, the uncertainty generally pertains to the quality or the characteristics of the object of choice. Of course, uncertainty about the characteristics of the prospective child exists, but in addition there is another uncertainty, the one which we are emphasizing: uncertainty about the acquisition itself.

At the individual household level, this uncertainty about the number of children affects at least three aspects of behavior. First, it may affect decisions about the expenditures of resources on existing children—if ordinary substitution between quantity and quality is relevant to children, then not knowing the final number of children may affect the household's expenditure decisions on its early children. Second, there is the possibility of substitution between expenditures on children and on other household goods and services, and also between expenditures over time. Consequently, uncertainty about the number of children, and about the timing or spacing of children, can be expected to affect the composition and timing of consumer expenditure and savings behavior. Third, because of important interactions with other household production and with the relative value of family members' time, uncertainty about the number of children may have effects on the parents' occupation choices, schooling decisions, and general orientation toward market and household activities.

At the aggregate level, positive fertility control costs and the stochastic nature of fertility behavior affect the observed mean and variance of fertility. The size and growth rate of the population affect the age distribution of the population—and the rate of growth and the composition of the economy's output.[5] The variance in fertility, on

[4] For estimates of the direct costs of children, see Cain (1971) or Reed and McIntosh (1972). Lindert (1973) presents a useful discussion of existing evidence on various aspects of the costs of children. Michael and Lazear (1971) emphasize the potential cost of children in terms of forgone human capital, and Mincer and Polachek (1974) estimate the depreciation in the mother's human capital related to her nonmarket child-rearing activity.

[5] See Kelley (1972) for a recent discussion of population growth and economic

the other hand, influences the distribution of income and of wealth. If uncertainty about fertility outcomes affects household investment and savings decisions, it may have an important influence on the distribution of inherited wealth across generations.

These considerations are not the focus of our paper, but we think the points we emphasize here—the costs of fertility control, fertility as a stochastic process, and the relationship between the mean and variance of fertility—have important implications for the level and distribution of the economy's wealth. We do not explore these aggregate relationships, nor do we resolve many of the more esoteric problems which we encounter in our analysis. We do, however, attempt to integrate into an analysis of contraceptive choice and optimum fertility behavior the constraints imposed by biological limitations and resource (or economic) limitations. We indicate how the choice of contraceptive technique affects the observed mean and variance of fertility. We also analyze the choice of contraceptive technique, in particular the adoption of the new oral contraceptive in the United States in the first half of the 1960s.

II. THE ANALYTICAL FRAMEWORK

The theory of the choice of a fertility control strategy treats the fertility goals of the household as given, while the economic theory of fertility demand focuses on the factors which determine these goals. If fertility control is costly, however, these costs, as well as the resource costs of bearing and rearing children, influence the couple's choice of fertility goals. The link between the theory of the choice of birth control technique and the theory of fertility behavior is provided by assuming that the household maximizes its lifetime utility, subject to the constraint of a fertility control cost function, as well as to the conventional economic resource constraint. The fertility control cost function is simply the combination (the envelope) of least-cost birth control strategies for all possible fertility outcomes.

In this section, we describe a stochastic model of reproduction, emphasizing the relationship between the mean and variance of fertility outcomes. We then discuss the economic benefits and costs of fertility control and conclude with an exposition of the optimal fertility control strategy.

progress. See Kuznets (1960) and other essays in *Demographic and Economic Change in Developed Countries* for discussions of the effects of population on output employment and demand.

A. Birth Control and the Distribution of Fertility Outcomes

The number of children born to a couple and the pace at which these children are born is ultimately constrained by the fact that reproduction is a biological process. The observed reproductive behavior of an individual woman over her life cycle may be regarded as the outcome of this biological process, as modified by nonvolitional social and cultural factors and by the effects of deliberate attempts to control fertility. In the past two decades, the nature of the biological constraint on fertility choices has been greatly clarified and given rigorous expression in stochastic models of the reproductive process by Henry, Potter, Perrin and Sheps, and others. The basic reasoning underlying these models and their main implications for average fertility were recently summarized by Keyfitz (1971).

These models suggest that the number of children a woman bears during her lifetime is a random variable whose mean and variance depend on her (and her partner's) choice of a fertility control strategy. In this section, we draw heavily on this literature in order to present, under simplifying assumptions, analytical expressions for the mean and variance of live births as a function of two sets of parameters, one representing the couple's biological characteristics and the other its fertility control strategy.

The simple observation that it takes a random amount of time to produce a baby provides the point of departure for recent biological models of fertility. Suppose that a woman faces a probability p of conceiving in a given month. If that monthly probability of conception is constant over time, the probability that she will conceive in exactly the jth month $(j = 1, 2, \ldots)$ is $p(1 - p)^{j-1}$, where $(1 - p)^{j-1}$ is the probability that she fails to conceive in the first $j - 1$ months. Employing the demographer's term "conceptive delay," i.e., the number of months v it takes a fecund woman to conceive, the random variable v is distributed geometrically with mean $\mu_v = (1 - p)/p$ and variance $\sigma_v^2 = (1 - p)/p^2$.[6]

Once a woman conceives, she becomes sterile during her pregnancy and the anovulatory period following pregnancy. The length of the sterile period s is also a random variable whose value depends on the type of pregnancy termination (i.e., fetal loss or stillbirth or live birth) and on the physiological and social factors (e.g., age, parity, breast-feeding practices, time until resumption of sexual activity)

[6] See Sheps (1964) for a derivation of this result. It should be noted that conceptive delay is defined to be zero months if the woman conceives in the first month.

which determine the length of the anovulatory period following each type of pregnancy termination. For simplicity, we shall assume that all pregnancies terminate in a live birth and that the length of the sterile period s is of fixed, nonrandom length.[7] The length of one reproductive cycle—the number of months it takes a fecund woman to become pregnant, give birth, and revert to a fecund, nonpregnant status—can be expressed as $t = v + s$, a random variable with mean $\mu_t = \mu_v + s$ and variance $\sigma_t^2 = \sigma_v^2$.

The number of children the woman bears during a lifetime, say a reproductive span of T months, depends on the number of reproductive cycles completed during this period. Since each cycle is of random length, the woman's fertility will also be a random variable. The probability distribution of the number of births can be represented in a simple way if the model of reproduction is represented as a Markov renewal process. In order to qualify as a renewal process, the intervals between successive births must behave as independent, identically distributed random variables (Potter 1970). To meet these qualifications, it is necessary to assume that all of the parameters of the reproductive process (i.e., p and s) are constant over time and that the reproductive period, T, is sufficiently long (i.e., infinity). Assuming reproduction to be a renewal process, the distribution of the number of births N is asymptotically normal with mean [8]

$$\mu_N = T/\mu_t \tag{1}$$

and variance

$$\sigma_N^2 = T \frac{\sigma_t^2}{\mu_t^3} \tag{2}$$

[7] See Perrin and Sheps (1964) for a model in which pregnancy terminations other than live births are allowed and the sterile period associated with each type of pregnancy is of random length. Compared with the formulas we shall present, the Perrin and Sheps model implies a smaller mean and larger variance in the number of live births a woman has over her reproductive span.

[8] See Sheps and Perrin (1966), who warn that the asymptotic normal distribution above does not adequately approximate the exact probability of N for the relevant (finite) range of T. In another paper, Perrin and Sheps (1964) suggest more accurate approximate expressions for the first two moments of N. Since the qualitative implications of these approximations are quite similar to those of the more exact approximations, it does not seem necessary to encumber the discussion with more complicated expressions for mean and variance. A more serious problem is suggested by Jain (1968), who found that the actual mean of natural fertility tends to fall progressively below the theoretical mean given by the Perrin-Sheps model as T increases, while actual variance rises progressively above the theoretical variance.

Equations 1 and 2 provide a useful way of summarizing the insights into the determinants of a woman's fertility behavior provided by mathematical demography. Her mean fertility varies in direct proportion with the length of her reproductive span T and in inverse proportion with the expected length of her reproductive cycle. The variance of her fertility outcome depends upon these same two factors and also upon the variance in the length of her reproductive cycle. The three variables which determine both the mean fertility μ_N and the variance of fertility σ_N^2 in this framework are the length of the reproductive span T, the monthly probability of conception p, and the length of the sterile period s following conception. Given T, p, and s, the mean and variance are jointly determined. Treating T and s as parameters, the mean and variance of N are related, at all values of p, as

$$\sigma_N^2 = \mu_N - k_1 \mu_N^2 + k_2 \mu_N^3 \tag{3}$$

with

$$k_1 = \frac{2s-1}{T}; \qquad k_2 = \frac{s(s-1)}{T^2}$$

where k_1 and k_2 are positive constants.

Consider, next, the determinants of the monthly probability of conception p. A woman's biological capacity to reproduce may be represented by her intrinsic fecundability $\hat{p}$, which is defined as the probability of conception from a single unprotected act of coition at a random time during the menstrual cycle (which is assumed to be one month in length). In the absence of conception, the probability p that she will conceive during a given month is then equal to the product of $\hat{p}$ and her monthly frequency of coition c.[9] Demographers frequently discuss "natural fertility" defined, following Henry (1961), as the number of live births a woman expects to have in a reproductive lifespan of T months in the absence of any deliberate attempt to control fertility. If we suppose there is some "natural" level of coital frequency $\hat{c}$ for a given couple, then $\hat{c}\hat{p} = p^*$, the couple's monthly probability of conception in the absence of any fertility control. We will generally assume $\hat{c} = 7$ and $\hat{p} = 0.03$ (see Tietze 1960), hence we will assume that $p^* = 0.2$. Given p^* and given the reproductive time span T and the length of the period of infertility s, the mean and variance of natural fertility, $\mu_{\hat{N}}$ and $\sigma_{\hat{N}}^2$, are defined by equations 1 and 2.

---

[9] Intrinsic fecundability is discussed in the demographic literature, which contains an empirical justification for expressing p as approximately proportional to c over the relevant range of variation in monthly frequency of coition.

FIGURE 1

A Theoretical Relationship between Mean and Variance of
Fertility (See Equation 3)

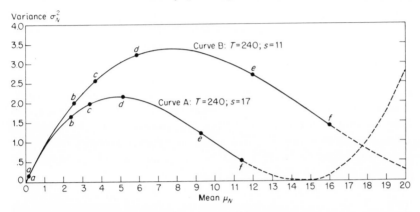

Variations across couples in the monthly probability of conception
p may result from variations in fecundity—which affect $\hat{p}$—or from
variations in coital frequency. Variations may also result from contraception. If the adoption of a particular contraceptive strategy i reduces
the monthly probability of conception by e_i per cent, then

$$p_i = p * (1 - e_i) \qquad 0 \le e_i \le 1$$

So the couple's actual monthly probability of conception p_i is determined by its fecundity, coital frequency, and contraceptive practice.

As we emphasized above, to qualify as a Markov renewal process of
reproduction the monthly probability p_i is assumed to be constant for
all fertile months in the reproductive time span of T months. Under
these circumstances Figure 1 indicates the relationship between the
mean and variance of fertility as summarized in equation 3. Curve A
assumes $T = 240$ months (a reproductive span of 20 years) and $s = 17$
months (a 17-month period of sterility following conception, see Keyfitz 1971). Each point on curve A corresponds to a different constant
monthly probability of conception ranging from $p = 0.0$ (the origin) to
$p = 0.2$ (point f on the curve).[10] Curve B in Figure 1 depicts the same

[10] For example, if $p = 0.0008$ then $\mu_N = 0.19$ births and $\sigma_N^2 = 0.18$, which is shown
as point a on curve A. The values of p which correspond to points a, b, c, d, e, f in the
figure are 0.0008, 0.0120, 0.0182, 0.0336, 0.1000, 0.2000 respectively. These values
refer to specific forms of fertility control and are discussed below.

relationship under the assumption that T equals 240 months, and s equals only 11 months.

Suppose a couple, at the time of their marriage, were characterized by the parameter values $T = 240$ months, $s = 17$ months, and $p^* = 0.2$. They would then face an ex ante distribution of fertility outcomes with a mean of 11.4 births and a variance of 0.5 (point f on curve A in Figure 1). The couple could, however, alter this expected outcome by adopting a strategy of fertility control which lowered their constant monthly probability of conception below p^*. If, for example, the couple selected a contraceptive technique with efficiency $e_1 = 0.5$, then their monthly probability would be $p_i = p^*(1 - 0.5) = 0.1$ and their ex ante distribution of fertility outcomes would have a mean of 9.2 births and a variance of 1.2 (point e on curve A). Thus, the couple affects its expected fertility and its uncertainty about the number of its births by its selection of a contraceptive strategy.[11]

Both the contraceptive technique used and the care with which it is used can affect e_i, which in turn determines p_i. In general, the couple can also affect p_i by altering its frequency of coition c and can also affect the distribution of fertility outcomes for any given p_i by altering the length of the reproductive period at risk T through decisions about the age at marriage and the age at which either partner is sterilized.[12] So the full range of fertility control strategies includes considerations other than the choice of contraceptive method, but it is the contra-

[11] In reality, it is plausible to suppose that the frequency of coition and contraceptive efficiency will tend to vary over time to accommodate a couple's preferences for child spacing as well as for total number of births, or to accommodate any changes in their fertility goals.

It is also plausible to suppose that the choices of c and e_i will be conditioned on past pregnancy and birth outcomes. Thus, in general, the values of p in a given month will tend to be a function of time (i.e., age), past reproductive history (i.e., parity), and random fluctuations in variables that determine fertility goals.

Unfortunately, the analytical simplicity of considering the stochastic model of reproduction as a renewal process is lost under these conditions. While it is possible to write out probability statements in which a couple's contraceptive strategy (i.e., its choices of c and e_i) is defined conditional on all possible fertility outcomes at each period of time, it is not possible to derive the implications of the resulting stochastic process for completed fertility outcomes using analytic methods. Moreover, the dynamic optimization problem involved in selecting a contraceptive strategy that maximizes a couple's expected utility under conditions of uncertainty may itself be analytically intractable. At this stage, it appears wiser to minimize the formal difficulties, thus the contraceptive parameters c and e_i, as well as the biological parameters, $\hat{p}$ and s, are assumed to remain constant over time.

[12] Interruptions of exposure within the time span T caused by cessations of sexual relations due to divorce or separation are ruled out by the assumption that the parameters of the process remain constant over time.

ceptive choice on which we will focus. By selecting contraceptive strategy *i*, which yields a monthly probability of conception p_i, the couple has, in effect, selected a particular ex ante distribution of its fertility outcomes. The mean of that distribution is μ_{N_i} and its variance is $\sigma_{N_i}^2$. We will assume for now that the couple is constrained to a pure contraceptive strategy, defined as the adoption of some form of fertility control which sets *p* at some fixed level (during fertile periods) for the entire reproductive span.

From studies of the average contraceptive failure rates of various contraceptive techniques, the efficiency-in-use of each technique can be computed. Table 2 lists the contraceptive efficiency e_i and the implied monthly probability of conception p_i for several contraceptive techniques.[13] The table also computes for each technique the mean and variance of the length of the reproductive cycle and the mean and variance of the fertility outcomes in a 20-year reproductive span. Thus, given the biological constraint on its fertility (e.g., curve A in Figure 1) the couple can determine the expected distribution of its fertility (its μ_N and σ_N^2) by selecting a contraceptive strategy which achieves any particular p_i. The various points labeled on curve A indicate the mean and variance of births associated with various contraceptive techniques (point *a:* pill; *b:* diaphragm; *c:* suppository; *d:* rhythm; *e:* 50 per cent reduction in coital frequency and no other contraception; *f:* no fertility control).

In this framework, the number of children born to a couple is a random variable which results from a stochastic process. Ex post, the couple has only one number of children *N*. However, the couple cannot determine its number of children with absolute certainty. Rather, it can select any particular value of *p*, the monthly probability of conception, which yields a particular distribution of fertility outcomes summarized by the distribution's mean and variance.

So long as we assume that the couple selects one value for *p* and retains that particular monthly probability of conception for all the fertile months in the twenty-year span—an assumption we will characterize as a "pure" strategy model—the couple cannot alter its expected fertility μ_N without also altering the variance σ_N^2. In short, the pure

---

[13] The estimates of contraceptive efficiency were compiled by Michael (1973) from the demographic literature (see especially Tietze (1959) and (1962)). See Michael (1973) for a discussion of the difficulties in estimating and the hazards in using this comparative list of the efficiency of contraceptive methods. In particular, note that these values represent average observed use-effectiveness and will, in general, be affected by the intensity and care with which they are used.

TABLE 2

Contraceptive Technique	Observed Use-Effectiveness R	Contraceptive Efficiency e_i	Monthly Birth Probability p_i^*	Mean Length of Reproductive Cycle μ_t	Variance of Reproductive Cycle σ_t^2	Reproductive Lifetime of 240 Months	
						Expected Number of Children μ_N	Variance of Number of Children σ_N^2
Pill	1.0	.9958	.0008	1,266	1,561,250	.19	.18
IUD	2.5	.9896	.0021	492	226,100	.48	.46
Condom	13.8	.9425	.0115	103	7,482	2.33	1.64
Diaphragm	14.4	.9400	.0120	100	6,723	2.40	1.61
Withdrawal	16.8	.9300	.0140	87	4,970	2.74	1.79
Jelly	18.8	.9217	.0157	80	4,032	3.00	1.89
Foam tablets	20.1	.9167	.0168	76	3,540	3.17	1.94
Suppositories	21.9	.9088	.0182	71	2,970	3.36	1.99
Rhythm	38.5	.8396	.0312	47	930	5.11	2.15
Douche	40.3	.8321	.0336	46	870	5.21	2.15
50% reduction in coital frequency		.5000	.1000	26	90	9.24	1.23
No method		.0000	.2000	21	20	11.42	.51

NOTE: R = (number of conceptions/number of months of exposure) $\times$ 1,200 = failure rate per 100 years of use (Source: Tietze, 1959, 1962, 1970).

$p_i = R_i \div 1,200 =$ monthly probability of conception.

$e_i = (p^* - p_i) \div p^* =$ percentage reduction in p^* where p^* is a constant equal to 0.20.

$\mu_t = [(1 - p_i) \div p_i] + s$, where $s = 17$.

$\sigma_t^2 = (1 - p_i) \div (p_i)^2$

$\mu_N = T \div \mu_t$, $\sigma_N^2 = T\sigma_t^2 \div \mu_t^3$, where $T = 240$.

38

strategy model restricts the couple to the biological constraint (curve A in Figure 1 if $T = 240$, $s = 17$). Before we relax the assumption of the pure strategy, we discuss the determinants of the couple's choice of its most preferred position along the biological constraint. We consider in turn the benefits and the costs of fertility control.

B. Benefits of Fertility Control

Recent economic theories of household behavior postulate the existence of several constraints (e.g., a money income constraint, a time constraint, production function limitations) on the household's maximization of utility. The utility is derived from a broad set of desiderata which are produced by the household itself in the non-market sector, using purchased market goods and services and the household members' own time as the inputs in the production.[14] These production functions emphasize the distinction between the household's wants (the output) and the means used to satisfy these wants (the goods and time inputs).

Willis (1973) recently utilized the household production framework to formulate an economic model of human fertility behavior. We will generalize a simple version of Willis's model to deal with imperfect and costly fertility control. The formal analysis is conducted in a static lifetime framework, although we informally suggest how the implications of the model might be altered in a more dynamic or sequential decision-making framework.[15]

In Willis's model, it is assumed that the satisfaction parents receive from each of their N children is represented by $Q_1, Q_2, \ldots, Q_N$, and the satisfaction from other sources of enjoyment is represented by S. The Q_i, or "quality," of each child, and the other composite commodity S are produced within and by the household using the family members' time and purchased market goods as inputs. The household production functions characterize the relationship between inputs of time and goods and the outputs of Q_i and S. Assuming (among other things) that parents treat all their children alike, the total amount of child services C may be written as a product of quality per child Q and the number of children N: $C = NQ$. It is assumed that Q is positively related to the amount of time and market goods devoted to each child—

---

[14] See Becker (1965) and Lancaster (1966) for early statements of this model. Several monographs and articles in recent years, notably through NBER, have utilized this framework. For a recent brief survey see Michael and Becker (1973).

[15] For a model of sequential decision making regarding contraceptive behavior in a heterogeneous population see Heckman and Willis, this volume.

Q is perhaps best considered an index of the child's human capital. The household's preferences for number and quality of children and for all other forms of satisfaction are summarized by its lifetime utility function.

$$U = U(N, Q, S) \tag{4}$$

The household's capacity to produce C and S is limited by its lifetime real income and by the quantity of its nonmarket time. Willis (1973) discusses in detail the relationship between the relative prices of N and Q, and considers how various changes in the household's characteristics and circumstances would be expected to affect its demand for N, Q, and S.

One important implication of the economic model of fertility demand should be noted. From an assumption that children are relatively time intensive as regards the wife's time (i.e., C production requires more of the wife's time per dollar of goods input than does S production), the relative cost of C rises as the wife's wage rate rises. Hence the cost of both number of children N and quality of children Q also rises with the wife's wage rate. If the relative price of N rises with the wife's wage rate, then abstracting from the change in income, women with higher wages (or higher levels of education) are expected to have lower fertility. This is the basis of the "cost of time" hypothesis (Ben-Porath 1973), which has, since Mincer's pioneering paper (1963), received much attention as an explanation for the observed negative relationship between the wife's wage and her fertility.

The household's lifetime money income constraint, its time constraint, and its production function constraints can be treated as a single constraint on the household's lifetime full real income I. Defining the marginal costs of child services π_c and the composite other commodity π_s, the formal optimization problem characterizing the household's choice is the maximization of the utility function (equation 4) subject to the full real income constraint.

$$\max \{ U(N, Q, S) - \lambda[I - \phi(\pi_c, \pi_s)] \} \tag{5}$$

where λ is the Lagrange multiplier. This optimization problem assumes that the household can costlessly and with certainty select any number of children (N) it wishes and can achieve any given level of the child's human capital (Q) it chooses.

To relax this assumption, we consider the benefits to the household of achieving any given number of children. Suppose the household had the utility function and the full real income constraint indicated in equation 5, but that the household was endowed with some arbitrary number of children N', where $N' = 0, 1, \ldots$. (To simplify the mathematics, N' will be treated as a continuous variable.) Given its arbitrary N', the household's only remaining choices would be the optimal values of child quality, Q, and other satisfaction, S, which must be chosen subject to the lifetime full real income constraint. If N and Q as well as N and S are substitutes in terms of the parents' preferences, the levels of both Q and S will tend to fall as N' is increased. This analysis implies that suboptimal values of Q and S would be chosen if fertility were arbitrarily constrained. Q and S would tend to be larger than (or smaller than) the optimal values, Q^* and S^*, as the arbitrarily constrained level of fertility N' is smaller (or larger) than the freely chosen desired level of fertility N^*.[16]

This hypothetical experiment of assigning some arbitrary N to the household is equivalent to maximizing equation 5 while treating N as a parameter, for all possible values of N. Such an exercise yields the household's net utility level as a function of its assigned level of fertility N' and the economic variables. Written as an implicit function the net utility V is

$$V = V(N; I, \pi_c, \pi_s) \qquad (6)$$

For each arbitrarily assigned value of N', there is a maximum achievable level of utility, obtained by the appropriate mix of Q and S. By definition, the maximum value of V, indicated as V^*, will be achieved at the desired level of $N(N^* = N')$, as depicted on curve A in Figure 2.

Deviations of fertility from N^* in either direction, such as N_1 or N_2, result in reduced utility levels, such as V_1 or V_2, in curve A of Figure 2. Given the emphasis in discussions of family planning on the problem of excess fertility and unwanted births (i.e., $N > N^*$), it is worth stressing that deficit fertility (i.e., $N < N^*$) may reduce welfare by at least as much as excess fertility.[17]

---

[16] It should be noted that we are implicitly assuming that the couple knows in advance what number of children it will have and can plan accordingly for its level of child quality and S.

[17] As indicated above, in the case of deficit fertility, quality per child, Q, would be higher than it would be in the case of optimal fertility or a fortiori for excess fertility. If from some ethical point of view, parents are judged to place too little weight on their children's welfare, and if we measure child welfare by the level of Q, it could be argued that the effect on Q of deficit fertility reduces or outweighs the parents' welfare loss $V^* - V_1$.

FIGURE 2

A Hypothetical Relationship between Utility and Number of Children

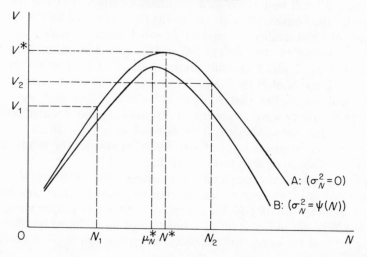

The opportunity cost of deficit or excess fertility ($V^* - V_1$ or $V^* - V_2$) is a measure of the benefits from improved fertility control. If in the absence of fertility control the household's fertility would have been N_i (yielding V_i), but with a given level of fertility control the household achieved N_j (yielding V_j such at $V_j > V_i$) then $(V^* - V_i) - (V^* - V_j) = V_j - V_i$ is a measure of the benefit from that level of fertility control. The utility benefits, then, are the gains in utility which accrue from moving nearer the optimal allocation of resources which would exist if fertility control were perfect and costless (i.e., N^*, Q^* and S^*).

We suggest above that the choice of particular values of fertility control parameters such as e_i yield particular ex ante distributions of fertility summarized by μ_N and σ_N^2. We can, therefore, formulate the discussion of the benefits of fertility control in terms of μ_N and σ_N^2. For purposes of illustration, suppose the functional form of equation 6 is quadratic in N:

$$V = a + bN + \frac{c}{2} N^2; \quad b > 0, c < 0 \qquad (7)$$

where I, π_c and π_s are held constant. Since the unconstrained maximum of V gives the desired value of fertility, N^*, it follows from equation 7 that

$$N^* = \frac{-b}{c} \tag{8}$$

We may now treat N as a random variable and take the expected value of equation 7 to obtain:

$$E(V) = a + b\mu_N + \frac{c}{2}\mu_N^2 + \frac{c}{2}\sigma_N^2 \tag{9}$$

Recall that equation 3 indicates the relationship between σ_N^2 and μ_N^2, $\sigma_{N_i}^2 = \psi(\mu_{N_i})$, where ψ is a cubic function. If $E(V_0)$ is the value of equation 9 in the absence of any fertility control, and $E(V_i)$ is its value when fertility control of e_i (yielding μ_{N_i}, $\sigma_{N_i}^2$) is employed, then the benefit from fertility control strategy i is $E(V_i) - E(V_0)$.

If we maximize the expected V (equation 9) with respect to μ_N,

$$\frac{d}{d\mu_N}(E(V)) = 0 = b + c\mu_N + \frac{c}{2}\psi' \tag{10}$$

where ψ' is a quadratic equation derived from equation 3. Noting that ψ' may be roughly approximated by a positive constant K, ($\psi' = K$) for values of $\mu_N < 5$ (see Figure 1), the optimal value of μ_N, from equation 10 is

$$\mu_N^* = \frac{-b}{c} - \frac{K}{2} = N^* - \frac{K}{2} \tag{11}$$

The optimal expected fertility μ_N^* is somewhat lower than the desired fertility N^*. Equation 9 implies that the lower the variance σ_N^2 the higher the net benefit V, ceteris paribus. Since the mean and variance are positively related at low values of N (i.e., $K = \psi' > 0$ if $N < 5$), the induced reduction in mean fertility represents the adjustment to the variance associated with N^*. This is indicated by curve B in Figure 2.[18] By subtracting an amount proportional to N from curve A, curve B peaks at a level of N below N^*.

So far, we have shown that imperfect fertility control implies that a couple's actual fertility N is a stochastic variable. The couple, by its choice of a contraceptive strategy, acquires some distribution of expected fertility outcomes, and by the nature of the biological process

---

[18] As N increases along curve A, σ_N^2 rises by K per unit of N (up to $N = 5$), thus an amount of V proportional to N, $\left(\frac{cK}{2}\right)N$, is subtracted from curve A yielding curve B.

involved, the higher the mean of the distribution the greater its variance (up to at least $N = 5$). Thus, the greater the expected fertility, the greater the uncertainty about the actual fertility, or the greater the expected deviation between the mean and the actual fertility. Since deviations from desired fertility reduce net utility V, and since higher levels of expected fertility μ_N are associated with greater uncertainty, the household is induced to reduce its optimal expected fertility μ_N^* below its desired fertility N^* in order to reduce the uncertainty or variance $\sigma_N{}^2$.

C. Costs of Fertility Control

The costs of fertility control are the amounts of other desirables forgone in achieving the control. These costs include money costs but also include forgone time, sexual pleasure, religious principles, health, and so forth. It is, at best, difficult to measure these costs empirically. We will, instead, discuss some of the determinants of these costs and seek to derive testable hypotheses about the relationship between observed fertility and contraceptive behavior.

By definition, couples which avoid all the costs of fertility control have an expected level of fertility $\mu_{\hat{N}}$, which is frequently referred to as "natural" fertility.[19] We will assume that costly fertility control strategies are limited to two dimensions: (1) the choice of contraceptive technique (including regulation of coital frequency) and (2) the care or intensity with which a given technique is used (i.e., we assume that the contraceptive efficiency, e_i, of the ith technique is a variable which may be increased at increased cost to the couple).[20] In this section, we also restrict the choice of contraception strategies to "pure" strategies. Thus, each strategy yields a different monthly probability of conception and hence a different point on the mean-variance curve (say, curve A) in Figure 1.

Associated with each contraceptive strategy is an opportunity cost measured by the utility loss associated with the change in behavior

[19] See the discussion of natural fertility in an earlier section. Throughout Section II of this paper we continue to assume that the couple's fertility control strategy is determined at the outset of the period-at-risk of conception and remains constant throughout the reproductive span. "Natural" fertility results when the age at marriage (which affects T) and the rate of coition c are determined without regard to effects on fertility.

[20] Thus, we rule out, for now, abortion and sterilization, and we assume age at marriage to be exogenous. To emphasize this restriction we will use the term "contraception" in place of "fertility control" in discussing costs, strategies, and so on. For a study of abortion as a means of fertility control see Potter (1972) or Keyfitz (1971) or for an economic analysis see a study in progress by Kramer (1973).

required to implement that strategy. Some strategies cost money, some cost sexual satisfaction, some cost real or imagined decreases in physical health. The assumption of utility maximizing behavior implies that couples will choose the least costly strategy they are aware of in order to achieve any given level of p which yields μ_N and its associated σ_N^2. Suppose the couple's cost schedule for achieving any given p_i or its fertility outcome μ_N is

$$F = F(\mu_N) \tag{12}$$

where F is the total cost of achieving μ_N, using the least costly contraceptive strategy. More specifically, let the cost of the ith contraceptive strategy be the simple linear function

$$F_i = \alpha_i + \beta_i B = \alpha_i + \beta_i (\mu_{\hat{N}} - \mu_N) \tag{13}$$

where B is the difference between $\mu_{\hat{N}}$, the couple's natural fertility, and μ_N, the mean of the distribution of its expected fertility while using strategy i. Thus, B is the expected number of births averted.

Equation 13 implies that the total cost of contraception using the ith technique may be divided into two components: (1) a fixed cost α_i, ($\alpha_i \geq 0$), which must be incurred if the ith technique is to be used at all, and (2) a variable cost $\beta_i B$, which is proportional to the number of births averted by the use of technique i.[21] The term β_i, ($\beta_i \geq 0$), is the marginal cost per birth averted.[22]

It is important to stress that the classification of the contraception costs F_i of a given technique as fixed (α_i) or variable ($\beta_i B$) is distinct from the classification of costs by their source. An economic (e.g., money or time), sociological (e.g., teachings of the Catholic church, deviation from class norms), psychological (e.g., interference with sexual pleasure, fear of adverse effects on health) or physiological (e.g., health) cost may be either fixed or variable.

Some factors, however, are more likely to affect α_i than β_i or vice versa. Lack of contraceptive knowledge, for instance, is often cited as a reason for imperfect control. To the extent that this is true, it is sensible to suppose that the acquisition of information about fertility

---

[21] Each contraceptive strategy involves both the adoption of a contraceptive technique and the care and precision in its use. The adoption of technique i and its careless use results in less efficient contraception, a lower e_i, higher p_i and fewer births averted. Nearly all contraceptive techniques are capable of achieving a low e_i with careless use or a high e_i with proficient use.

[22] The linearity of the cost functions in equation 13 is not a particularly crucial assumption in the sense that the implications to be derived could be obtained under less restrictive assumptions.

control methods is costly. A characteristic of the cost of information is that it does not depend on the amount of use to which the information is put. It follows that the costs of information tend to influence the fixed costs of contraception (the α_i's), but not the marginal costs (the β_i's).[23] The cost to a Catholic of violating the church's precepts with respect to the use of a contraceptive, for example, might be a once-and-for-all cost, in which case α_i is higher for Catholics than non-Catholics for all forbidden contraceptive techniques. Alternatively (or additionally), a Catholic may experience greater guilt the more intensively the technique is used, in which case β_i is higher to Catholics than to non-Catholics.[24]

The loss of sexual pleasure occasioned by contraception almost surely affects only the marginal costs of contraception and not the fixed costs. Thus, the number of births averted by condoms depends on how frequently and with what care condoms are used. The most ancient contraceptive techniques – abstinence or reduced coital frequency, and withdrawal – probably have zero fixed cost and rather high (psychological) marginal costs. By way of example, consider the choice between reduced coital frequency or withdrawal as alternative contraceptive techniques. If a husband and wife use neither technique at all, they will expect to have $\mu_{\hat{N}}$ births and they will avert no births (i.e., $B = 0$). The more persistently either technique is used, the smaller will be the expected fertility, the larger the expected number of births averted, and the larger the total contraception costs. Which technique is least costly depends solely on which technique has the lower marginal cost. If the marginal cost of reduced coital frequency exceeds the marginal cost of withdrawal, for example, the couple would not use the former technique whatever its desired number of averted births (note that we are limiting the choice at this point to pure strategies).

---

[23] This argument should be qualified to the extent that information is acquired by a process of "learning by doing" or that information deteriorates with disuse by a process of forgetting. In this case, the marginal cost of the ith technique (β_i) would tend to shift downward as the volume of use increases. Analytically, the learning hypothesis and the once-and-for-all hypothesis have the same implication, namely, that the average contraception cost per birth averted decreases as B increases.

[24] The cost to an individual Catholic of violating the church's precepts may also be a function of the behavior of other Catholics or of other members of the society at large. Thus, the dynamics of diffusion of the pill use among Catholics might be interpreted, in part, as the progressive lowering in the cost of contraception to each individual Catholic as he or she sees others using the pill. Of course, the equivocation within the church itself also presumably lowers the costs of using forbidden techniques (see Ryder and Westoff 1971, Chapter 8, for evidence on the effect of the Papal Encyclical on the contraceptive behavior of Catholics).

FIGURE 3

Hypothetical Fertility Control Cost Functions for
Various Contraceptive Techniques

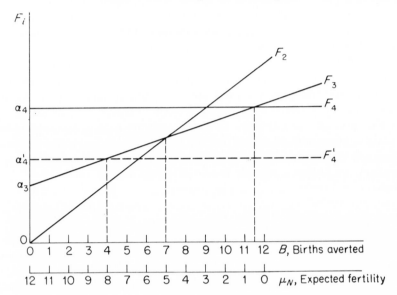

It is not always the case that one technique dominates all others for all possible fertility goals. Suppose, for example, that a third technique, condoms ($i = 3$), has a lower marginal cost than does withdrawal ($i = 2$) (i.e., $\beta_3 < \beta_2$), but that it has a positive fixed cost (i.e., $\alpha_3 > \alpha_2 = 0$). This situation is depicted in Figure 3, where line $0F_2$ indicates the total contraception cost incurred if withdrawal is used to achieve each possible value of expected births averted (reading the upper horizontal scale from left to right) or, equivalently, at each possible level of expected fertility (reading the lower horizontal scale from right to left). Similarly, line $\alpha_3 F_3$ shows the cost of using condoms to achieve each possible outcome.

To avert fewer than seven births (i.e., to have five or more children), the least cost strategy in Figure 3 is withdrawal. However, to avert more than seven births, condoms are a less costly contraceptive method. The point of equal costs (where lines $0F_2$ and $\alpha_3 F_3$ intersect) is called the "switching point": as the number of births to be averted rises, at some point (e.g., seven in the example illustrated in the figure) it becomes cheaper to incur the fixed costs or make the investment in an alternative technique—to switch to the technique with the lower marginal cost.

Additional contraceptive techniques with still higher fixed costs and lower marginal costs may have lower average cost at higher numbers of averted births. The total cost function F (equation 12) is defined as the collection of line segments which represent the least-cost method of achieving each number of averted births. It is the envelope of segments of the F_i curves in Figure 3. The limiting case would be a contraceptive with zero marginal cost (i.e., method $i = 4$ in the figure). A relatively low marginal cost appears to be a major advantage of modern contraceptive methods such as the pill and IUD. If line $\alpha_4 F_4$ represents such a technique in Figure 3, note that it represents the optimal contraceptive choice only if the couple wishes to have fewer than one child (as the figure happens to be drawn). That is, only couples wishing to avert nearly all potential births would select that high fixed cost, zero marginal cost technique.

D. Optimal Fertility Control Strategy

The preceding sections have discussed the separate elements in the determination of an optimal fertility control strategy. Using the simplifying assumption that a household must follow a pure strategy (i.e., must choose a constant value of p for the entire reproductive span), we derived a biological constraint on fertility choices illustrated by the mean-variance curve in Figure 1.

Next, we derived the expected utility of the household as a function of the mean and variance of fertility outcomes. This relationship is depicted in Figure 2. The fertility level with the highest net value N^* under conditions of certainty (i.e., $\sigma_N^2 = 0$) and costless contraception is defined as the couple's "desired fertility." If, however, the couple is constrained to choose points on the mean-variance curve in Figure 1 (but may choose any point without incurring any fertility control cost), the decrease in uncertainty associated with decreases in expected fertility makes it optimal to choose a level of expected fertility μ_N^* that is somewhat lower than its desired fertility, N^*.

Finally, we introduced the (utility) costs of controlling fertility by means of specific contraceptive techniques. We derived a fertility control cost function as the envelope of least-cost segments of the cost curves of the individual techniques, which is shown in Figure 3. Holding the couple's expected natural fertility, $\mu_{\hat{N}}$, constant, its total cost of fertility control F is larger, the smaller the level of its expected fertility μ_N.

The selection of the couple's optimal fertility control strategy involves two steps. First, for any given choice of μ_N and, jointly, σ_N^2, the couple selects the least costly contraception technique — say the ith technique — with total cost $F_i = \alpha_i + \beta_i(\mu_{\hat{N}} - \mu_N)$. Second, it selects a level of μ_N (and σ_N^2) such that total expected utility (i.e., the expected net utility from children $E(V)$, minus the total cost F_i) is maximized. That is, using the specific functional forms in equations 9 and 13

$$\max \{E(V) - F_i\} = \max \{a + b\mu_N + \frac{c}{2}\mu_N^2 + \frac{c}{2}\sigma_N^2 - \alpha_i$$
$$- \beta_i(\mu_{\hat{N}} - \mu_N)\} \quad (14)$$

The necessary condition for maximization with respect to μ_N is

$$0 = b + c\mu_N + \frac{c}{2}\psi' + \beta_i \quad (15)$$

Solving for μ_N and again approximating ψ' (see equation 10) by the constant $K > 0$

$$\mu_N = -\left(\frac{b}{c} + \frac{K}{2} + \frac{\beta_i}{c}\right) = N^* - \frac{K}{2} + \beta_i k = \mu_N^* + \beta_i k \quad (16)$$

where $k = \dfrac{-1}{c} > 0$.

Equation 16 summarizes the influence on fertility outcomes of imperfect and costly fertility control. If the couple could select any level of fertility costlessly and with certainty, it would select N^*, its "desired fertility" determined by its tastes, economic circumstances, and so forth. Since fertility outcomes involve an element of uncertainty (i.e., result from a stochastic process), there is a variance associated with each level of fertility, and since this uncertainty lowers the expected benefits or utility from each level of N, this uncertainty induces the couple to prefer an expected level of fertility μ_N^* lower than N^* ($\mu_N^* = N^* - K/2$). Furthermore, since it is costly to avert births, the costs of fertility control further modify the optimal fertility outcome, raising the optimal above the level μ_N^* ($\mu_N = \mu_N^* + \beta k$). In effect, β_i is a per unit subsidy to childbearing, because a couple may reduce its contraceptive cost by β_i with every additional birth it has.

The relationship between these various levels of fertility can be indicated by combining Figures 2 and 3 (see Figure 4). Utility would be maximized at a level of $N = N^*$ if the costs of fertility control were zero and the uncertainty about fertility outcomes were ignored

FIGURE 4

Hypothetical Fertility Control Cost and Benefit Functions
Indicating the Optimal Level of Fertility Control

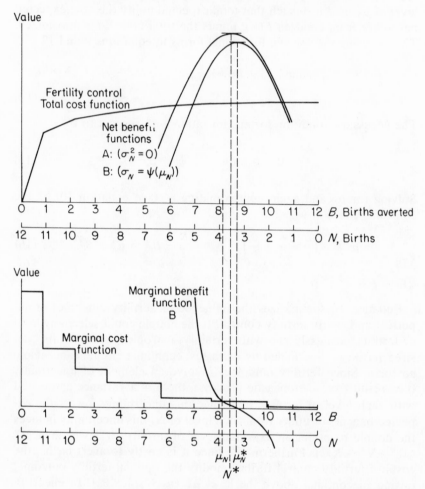

(e.g., the maximum of the net benefit function A is at a level of $N = N^*$). The presence of uncertainty modifies the optimum by raising the peak of the net benefit function (function B) to the level $N = \mu_N^*$. The presence of fertility control costs further modifies the optimum by lowering the preferred N to μ_N, the intersection of the marginal cost of fertility control and the marginal benefit from fertility control.

III. PURE AND MIXED CONTRACEPTIVE STRATEGIES

In the previous section, we restricted the discussion of contraceptive strategies to a "pure" strategy, defined as one in which the couple selects some specific contraceptive technique and uses it with some specific amount of care throughout the reproductive span of T months. The pure strategy model, in which the couple uses one technique continuously, implies a constant monthly probability of conception p over the fertile months in the reproductive span. This implication is essential for the Markov renewal process on which are based the equations for the mean and variance of fertility outcomes (equations 1 and 2) and the mean-variance curves depicted in Figure 1. So the pure strategy model lends itself to a simple analytical structure and represents a boundary on the relationship between mean and variance of fertility. As we have noted, this Markov renewal model also underlies much of the important analytical work done in the past decade in mathematical demography.

However, it is evident that, in reality, a couple is not restricted from altering its contraceptive technique over the reproductive span. Even in the context of a lifetime strategy which could be mapped out initially and carried out over time, a couple might choose to use different contraceptive techniques (including no contraception) in various segments of that span of time. Furthermore, since the discussion of the benefits of fertility control emphasized that under fairly general conditions couples prefer to reduce the variance in their expected fertility, it is economically sensible as well as technically feasible for couples to select a mixed contraceptive strategy which may result in a lower σ_N^2 for any level of expected fertility μ_N.[25]

For example, if a couple used the oral contraceptive at its average observed use-effectiveness throughout its twenty-year reproductive span, Table 2 indicates that the distribution of its expected fertility

---

[25] The economic rationale, offered in Section II, for preferring a reduced variance in fertility was that any deviation in actual fertility from the desired level of fertility implies a reduction in utility. The greater the variance σ_N^2 the greater the likelihood that the discrepancy between actual and desired fertility will be relatively large.

There is an additional economic reason for generally preferring a lower variance in the distribution of expected outcomes, risk preference aside. The more certain the couple is about the number of children it will eventually have, the more efficiently it can optimize the allocation of its resources. The couple which is more certain about the timing and number of its children can more efficiently plan its savings pattern, select an optimal size home, automobile, et cetera, plan the labor force behavior of the wife, and so forth. The same principles apply here as in the case of a firm which can achieve lower average cost of production if its rate of output is constant over the long run than if its rate of output varies significantly from season to season or from year to year.

has a mean of 0.19 births and a variance of 0.18 (point *a* on the mean-variance curve in Figure 1). If this couple wished to have about three children, it could use a less effective technique or use the pill somewhat carelessly, thereby achieving a monthly probability of conception of 0.0182 which over a twenty-year span would yield an expected fertility of 3.4 and a variance of 1.99 (point *c* on the mean-variance curve in Figure 1). The couple could also achieve a mean fertility of 3.4, however, by combining periods of pill use with periods of time in which no contraception was used. The result would be a mean of 3.4 children and a variance considerably below that indicated by point *c* on the mean-variance curve. Indeed the variance would be no greater than that indicated by point *f*, the variance associated with the use of no contraception over the entire twenty-year time span.[26]

Furthermore, the pure strategy implies that the births will arrive at random intervals over the twenty-year span, while the mixed strategy permits the couple to achieve the same number of children with considerable control over their spacing.[27] By combining the use of a highly effective technique with periods of no contraception, a couple can achieve its desired number of children with a relatively low variance σ_N^2 and relatively little uncertainty about the spacing of its children.

The mean-variance curve in Figure 1 represents the biological constraint on the distribution of expected fertility when a particular monthly birth probability persists for the entire span of T months. By using a mixed strategy, combining contraception with periods of no contraception, the biological constraint is no longer an effective constraint — the couple can move off the mean-variance curve toward the horizontal axis representing a distribution of fertility outcomes of mean μ_N and zero variance. The more efficient the contraceptive tech-

---

[26] The logical extreme would be a mixed strategy in which natural fertility (no contraception) is pursued in those segments of the reproductive span in which a birth is desired and perfect contraception (i.e., $e_i = 0$) at all other times. This strategy would enable a normally fecund couple to achieve any given number of children fewer than, say, five with virtual certainty and would also enable them to approximate many plausible desired spacing patterns fairly closely (see Potter and Sakoda 1967).

Such a strategy is not only a logical possibility, but it is also technically feasible, since the monthly probability may be set to zero at any time by reducing coital frequency to zero. The fact that couples do not appear to follow this "perfect contraception" strategy suggests that the problem of fertility control is not a matter of technical feasibility. The biological constraint on fertility choices must be considered simultaneously with other constraints on behavior, with fertility goals viewed as competing with other family goals.

[27] In the pure strategy case the variance of the interval of time between successive births, σ_t^2, is inversely related to p and hence μ_N. Thus, reduction in expected fertility along the mean-variance curve is accompanied by an *increase* in variance σ_t^2.

nique chosen during periods of contraception, the smaller is the achievable variance σ_N^2 for any given mean μ_N. Thus the more efficient the contraceptive technique chosen, the weaker is the relationship between μ_N and σ_N^2,[28] and the smaller is the incentive to lower the mean fertility as a mechanism for reducing uncertainty or variance.

The mixed strategy (defined in terms of using one specific technique while contracepting and no contraception otherwise) is feasible only when the expected number of births from the continuous use of the technique is less than the number of children the couple desires. So this form of mixed strategy is more likely to be used the greater is the efficiency of the contraceptive technique chosen.

In this discussion of mixed strategies of contraception, we have focused upon one particular type of mixed strategy – that of adopting and abandoning at intervals one contraceptive technique. Although shifting from contraceptive technique to technique is another possibility, the theoretical discussion of the costs of contraception suggested that this would not be the case. The fixed costs associated with the adoption of modern techniques would inhibit technique switching. Consistent with the model's implication, evidence from the 1965 National Fertility Survey (NFS) suggests that technique switching has not been a prevalent practice in the United States in the past two decades. Ranking contraceptive methods by their mean monthly probability of conception (as indicated in Table 2) and limiting the subsample to women who had used some contraception in each of their first three birth intervals, Michael (1973) found that the correlation among techniques used across the three pregnancy intervals was quite high (ranging from 0.57 to 0.97) for non-Catholic women partitioned by color and age cohort.[29] Ryder and Westoff (1971) study the relationship between use and nonuse of contraception across intervals and the relationship between contraceptive failures in successive intervals. They find considerable continuity of contraceptive status

[28] Some evidence that the correlation between mean and variance of fertility is positive is found in the 1960 U.S. Census of the Population. Grouping white women married once and husband present into cells defined by husband's occupation (8 categories), husband's education (5 categories) and wife's education (3 categories), the unweighted simple correlation between μ_N and σ_N^2 across cells is 0.89 for women aged 45–54 and 0.77 for women aged 35–44. If the younger cohort used better contraceptive methods on the average, then the reduction in this correlation across cohorts is consistent with the implication of a weaker correlation among users of better contraception.

[29] See Michael (1973), Table 4. One note of caution. The NFS data are oriented by the woman's pregnancy intervals, so Michael had information on only the best technique used by the woman in each interval. He could therefore identify switches in contraceptive techniques from pregnancy interval to interval, but not from technique to technique within a given pregnancy interval.

across intervals both in terms of whether a woman does or does not use contraception in successive intervals and in terms of the degree of success of use across intervals.[30]

IV. CONTRACEPTION AND FERTILITY OUTCOMES

In the model described in Section II, the household's number of children N is a random variable. The household adopts a contraceptive strategy which yields a particular value of p, the monthly probability of conception. Given p as a known and fixed parameter, the household has an ex ante distribution of fertility characterized by a mean μ_N and variance σ_N^2.

The discussion has focused on the ex ante distribution of fertility outcomes for a single household, but in our empirical analysis we focus on the corresponding distribution for relatively homogeneous groups of households. It is assumed that the observed mean and variance in births among households with relatively homogeneous demographic-economic characteristics reflect the mean and variance of the distribution of fertility outcomes faced by each of the households in that group. Recall that the equation for the variance in number of children (equation 2) assumed that the unprotected monthly probability of conception and the length of the period of infertility were constant over the couple's reproductive lifetime. To apply the model across households implies not only constancy of these parameters over time for a given household, but also constancy across households. Heckman and Willis deal explicitly with the problem of estimating the

---

[30] For example, 90 per cent of women who used some contraceptive technique in the first pregnancy interval (from marriage to first pregnancy) used a contraceptive in the second interval, while only 36 per cent of nonusers in the first interval used a contraceptive in the second interval. Similar percentages are found for each successive pair of intervals (i.e., from the fourth to the fifth interval the comparable percentages are 95 per cent and 18 per cent). See Ryder and Westoff (1971), Table IX-19, p. 255. Or, 95 per cent of the women who had used contraception in each of the first three pregnancy intervals used contraception in the fourth interval, while only 13 per cent of women who had not used contraception in any of the first three intervals used contraception in the fourth (see Ryder and Westoff (1971), Table IX-23, p. 260).

Evidence of consistency of use across intervals is indicated by the following rather remarkable statistic: of women who used a contraceptive "successfully" in the first three pregnancy intervals, 20 per cent experienced a contraceptive "failure" in the fourth pregnancy interval, while of those who had experienced a contraceptive "failure" in each of the first three intervals, 77 per cent experienced a "failure" again in their fourth interval (see Ryder and Westoff for definitions of success and failure).

This statistic and others support quite strongly, we think, the contention that couples act as if they adopt a lifetime strategy toward contraception and that that strategy involves considerable continuity in the use of a technique throughout a lifetime. (The Princeton Study begun in 1957 also suggested that across-interval changes in fertility control are "clearly not a matter of couples shifting from ineffective to effective methods" of contraception. See Westoff, Potter, and Sagi 1963 (pp. 232–235).)

average monthly probability p in heterogeneous groups of households. For our purposes, we will not pursue this issue.[31]

The model in Section II was set out in a lifetime context and considered fertility control in terms of a lifetime strategy. Accordingly, in our empirical work we frequently use information about contraceptive behavior at one point in the couple's marriage as an indication, or index, of the lifetime contraceptive strategy. As we indicated in Section III, there is considerable evidence that contraceptive behavior is not characterized by switching from contraceptive technique to technique over the life span. Consequently, in this section we will distinguish couples either by the best contraceptive technique used in the time interval from marriage to their first pregnancy or by the best technique used at any time in their marriage.[32]

[31] Consider two populations of fecund, nonpregnant women with identical mean monthly probabilities of conception, $\bar{p}$. One population is homogeneous in the sense that p is identical for all members of the population, and the other is heterogeneous in the sense that p varies across women according to some distribution with positive variance. It is known that the mean waiting time to conception in the heterogeneous population will be longer and the average birthrate lower than in the homogeneous population, and that this difference is a function of the distribution of p in the heterogeneous population (see, for example, Sheps, 1964).

[32] In addition to the evidence cited above regarding consistency of technique use between pregnancy intervals, the following table indicates the percentage of users of a specific contraceptive technique in the first interval who also used that technique in the second interval. The second column indicates the percentage who used either that same technique or no contraception in the second interval. These figures pertain to white non-Catholic women aged 40–44 from the 1965 NFS.

| First Interval | Second Interval | |
Technique Used	% Using Same Technique	% Using Same Technique or No Contraception
Diaphragm	77%	89%
Condom	72	82
Withdrawal	78	85
Jelly, foam, suppository	61	67
Rhythm	65	85
Douche	62	73

The table indicates, for example, that of those couples which used the diaphragm in the first pregnancy interval, 77 per cent also used the diaphragm in the second pregnancy interval. Furthermore, of that same group another 12 per cent used no contraception in the second pregnancy interval; thus, a total of 89 per cent used either that same contraceptive method or no method in the second interval. (The second interval here is defined as either the period of time from the first to the second pregnancy or from the first pregnancy to the time of the survey if no second pregnancy occurred.)

Since these data were collected by interview at the time these women were 40–44 years of age and pertain to periods of time shortly after marriage, there may be a tendency to give the same response for successive intervals. If so, these percentages overstate the consistency of technique selection across intervals.

In this and the following section, we use the 1965 National Fertility Survey, which was conducted by the Office of Population Research at Princeton University.[33] This cross-section survey of some 5,600 women aged 55 and under, currently married and living with their spouse, contains information on the specific contraceptive technique used in each pregnancy interval, as well as information on the couple's actual fertility outcome. In this section, we use this data set to document the relationship between contraception use and fertility outcomes. Since we are interested in studying the variance in fertility, we group the data into cells and study between-cell differences in observed behavior.

In this section we explore *how* contraception behavior is related to the observed distribution of fertility across groups of households; we do not attempt to explain *why* couples differ in their desired fertility or in the dispersion of their fertility. Although we indicated in Section II that the model is capable of treating contraception choice and fertility control choice in a simultaneous system of equations, we do not attempt to estimate the parameters of those structural equations. In the tables below, we partition the data set by household characteristics including color and religion, and we use either the wife's education or expected fertility and either age of wife or marriage duration to isolate relatively homogeneous groups of households. In the context of these homogeneous groups, we study contraception strategies as the mechanism for affecting fertility outcomes.

Figure 5 indicates the frequency distribution of live births for women aged 35–55 for groups defined by wife's level of schooling, color, and religion. Among the white non-Catholics (Figure 5(A)) the distributions appear to be less positively skewed and less dispersed (or more peaked) among women with higher levels of schooling.[34] By contrast,

---

[33] We wish to thank Charles F. Westoff and Norman B. Ryder for their help in obtaining these data. Our previously published research from this data set (Michael 1973) used a small data file obtained from Professor Westoff. Our current research uses the publicly available data tape from the 1965 NFS, which was acquired through Larry Bumpass. The data set is fully described in Ryder and Westoff, *Reproduction in the United States 1965* (Princeton: Princeton University Press, 1971).

[34] A few chi-squared tests have been performed on pairs of distributions of live births for groups of white non-Catholics with different education levels from specific 5-year cohorts. These tests imply rejection (at $\alpha = .05$) of the hypothesis that the grade-school women's distribution of live births and the college women's distribution of live births might have been drawn from the same population.

For example, $\chi^2 = 36.8$ with 12 degrees of freedom for a comparison of ≤ 8 years versus ≥ 13 years of schooling for women aged 40–44. The critical value for χ^2 with 12 degrees of freedom at $\alpha = .01$ is 26.2.

FIGURE 5

Frequency Distribution of Live Births by Wife's Education, by Color and Religion for Women Aged 35–55

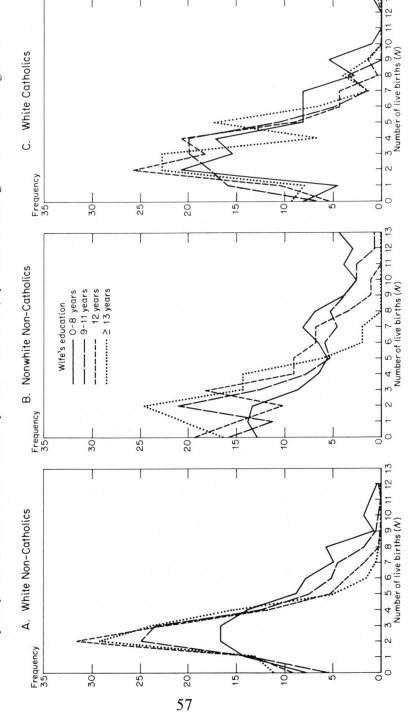

57

the distributions for nonwhite non-Catholics (Figure 5(B)) are considerably less peaked and more skewed. Among this latter group, the level of schooling does not distinguish the frequency distributions so clearly, although the percentage of households with, say, seven or more births appears to decline as the level of schooling rises. Among Catholics (Figure 5(C)) the distributions are somewhat less dispersed than among the nonwhite non-Catholics, and the level of schooling does not appear to influence the distributions systematically.

Among white non-Catholics, there appear to be distinctly different distributions of live births by wife's education. These differences are further emphasized by the following table derived from Appendix Table A.1. Also, the groups of nonwhites and Catholics appear from

Percentage of Women with Six or More Live Births:
White Non-Catholic Women
(calculated from Appendix Table A.1)

Wife's Education	Wife's Age			
	35–39	40–44	45–49	50–54
≤ 8	22.7	22.4	23.4	19.6
9–11	11.5	15.6	5.7	13.1
12	6.8	6.7	4.8	1.3
≥ 13	2.7	1.6	1.6	2.2
Total	8.8	10.1	7.9	8.7

Figure 5 to have considerably different frequency distributions than the most highly schooled white non-Catholic groups. The discussion above has suggested that different contraceptive strategies yield different distributions of fertility, so we expect to find that groups which differ in the distribution of their actual fertility also differ in their contraception behavior. The NFS data contain information on the particular contraceptive method used by each woman in each pregnancy interval. The data do not indicate how extensively, regularly, or carefully a contraceptive method was used; we know only that the woman indicated that between the time she married and the time she first became pregnant, for example, she used contraceptive method i (including no method at all).

Figure 6 indicates the percentage of women in each education, color,

FIGURE 6

Percentage Ever Using "Good" Contraception by Wife's Education for Groups by Color and Religion, Women Aged 35–55

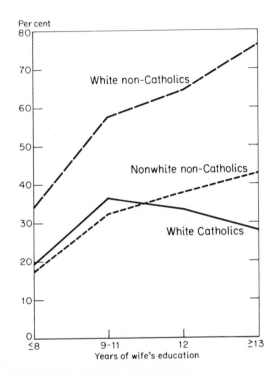

and religion group which ever used a "good" [35] contraceptive technique. The relationship between these percentages and the distributions of births indicated in Figure 5 is striking. Among white non-Catholics, the percentage of users of "good" contraceptive techniques rises significantly with the wife's level of schooling, and this is also the group for which schooling most clearly distinguishes the dis-

---

[35] Throughout this section, "good" contraception is defined to include pill, IUD, condom, and diaphragm. For older cohorts, the best available contraceptive methods were the condom and diaphragm, while for the younger cohorts the more reliable pill and IUD were also available. Since we are attempting at this time to distinguish use of highly reliable from less reliable techniques, the distinction was arbitrarily made as indicated. All contraceptive methods other than the pill, IUD, condom and diaphragm are categorized as "poor" methods. The use of no contraception is called "none" and is distinguished from the "poor" methods.

tributions of births. The percentages rise less rapidly by education among the nonwhites, and for these groups the frequency distributions of births are less clearly delineated by education. Among Catholics, neither the percentage of users of good contraceptive techniques nor the frequency distribution of births seems to be closely related to wife's education. Thus, in comparisons among and within color and religion groups, there appears to be a quite consistent relationship: groups characterized by a relatively high percentage of users of good contraception are also characterized by relatively low dispersion in fertility.

Table 3 summarizes this same relationship. The table indicates, for each education, color, and religion group, the percentage of couples ever using "good" contraception and the actual mean and standard deviation of live births. Groups characterized by a high percentage of users of good contraception are characterized by relatively lower variance and somewhat lower mean fertility. Simple correlations across these groups between the percentage of couples which ever used good contraception (at any time since marriage), "% good," and the mean fertility μ_N, and between "% good" and the standard deviation σ_N are consistently negative. As emphasized in the theoretical discussion of the mean-variance curve, the observed correlation between the mean and variance (or standard deviation) in fertility is positive in all cases:

Simple Correlation Coefficients between % Good (the Percentage of Couples Which Ever Used Good Contraception), μ_N (the Group's Mean Number of Live Births), and σ_N (the Standard Deviation in the Group's Number of Live Births)

	Simple Correlation			
	% Good, μ_N	% Good, σ_N	μ_N, σ_N	(n) [a]
White non-Catholics	−.647	−.896	.884	(8)
Nonwhite non-Catholics	−.508	−.675	.952	(8)
White Catholics	−.334	−.700	.879	(8)
All combined	−.475	−.601	.864	(24)

[a] Number of cells.

The relationship between contraception behavior and fertility outcomes indicated by Table 3 is somewhat circumstantial—groups of

TABLE 3

Percentage of Couples Using "Good" Contraception,
Mean and Standard Deviation of Live Births; by Wife's
Education, Age, Color, and Religion

		Education of Wife				
		$\leqslant 8$	9–11	12	$\geqslant 13$	Total
White Non–Catholics						
Age 35–44	% good [a]	37.4	62.9	67.4	79.9	64.9
	μ_N	3.658	3.284	2.738	2.583	2.946
	σ_N	2.635	1.942	1.567	1.472	1.849
	(n) [b]	(155)	(232)	(503)	(230)	(1,120)
Age 45–54	% good	29.9	45.4	57.2	67.8	50.9
	μ_N	3.645	2.616	2.136	2.189	2.579
	σ_N	2.459	2.004	1.593	1.415	1.962
	(n)	(121)	(99)	(206)	(106)	(532)
Nonwhite Non-Catholics						
Age 35–44	% good	21.7	35.3	41.8	46.9	32.7
	μ_N	4.968	3.613	3.493	2.531	3.980
	σ_N	3.855	3.231	2.636	1.796	3.355
	(n)	(124)	(119)	(67)	(32)	(342)
Age 45–54	% good	11.3	21.2	25.0	35.3	17.4
	μ_N	4.474	3.848	1.800	1.765	3.754
	σ_N	4.309	3.173	1.765	1.480	3.797
	(n)	(97)	(33)	(20)	(17)	(167)
White Catholics						
Age 35–44	% good	18.0	41.6	31.7	28.3	31.6
	μ_N	4.213	3.217	3.353	3.567	3.461
	σ_N	2.659	1.831	2.027	2.126	2.111
	(n)	(61)	(106)	(218)	(60)	(445)
Age 45–54	% good	20.9	23.0	39.3	26.7	28.8
	μ_N	3.646	2.564	2.705	2.133	2.896
	σ_N	2.497	1.832	1.395	1.598	1.949
	(n)	(48)	(39)	(61)	(15)	(163)

[a] Percentage of couples in the cell which ever used "good" contraception (i.e., pill, IUD, condom, or diaphragm).
[b] n indicates cell size. These figures are in parentheses.

households which had relatively high rates of use of good contraception also had relatively low mean and low variance in fertility. To relate contraception use to fertility outcomes more directly we partition the age, education groups of white non-Catholics by their contraceptive strategies. Table 4, for example, indicates the separate frequency distribution of live births for users of good contraception and users of poor contraception in the first pregnancy interval by wife's age for women with 12 years of schooling. That is, in Table 4 two of the cells in Table 3 (defined by wife's education equal to 12 years for women aged 35–44 and aged 45–54) are partitioned by the contraceptive technique used in the first birth interval.

For each of the two age groups the distribution of live births is considerably less dispersed among the users of good contraception than among users of poor contraception (e.g., the percentage of households with five or more live births was 10.3 and 3.0 among users of good contraception, while the percentages were 14.9 and 15.4 among users

TABLE 4

Frequency Distribution of Live Births for White
Non-Catholic Women with 12 Years of Education by
Contraceptive Method Used in the First Pregnancy Interval
and by Wife's Age

Contraceptive Method	Number of Live Births					Cell Size
	0	1	2–4	5–6	≥7	
Age 35–44						
Good [a]	1.4	7.0	81.2	8.9	1.4	(213)
Poor	2.0	13.9	69.3	11.9	3.0	(101)
None	15.3	14.8	55.6	11.1	3.2	(189)
Total	6.8	11.3	69.2	10.3	2.4	(503)
Age 45–54						
Good [a]	0.0	16.7	80.3	3.0	0.0	(66)
Poor	0.0	12.8	71.8	7.7	7.7	(39)
None	31.7	20.8	41.6	5.0	1.0	(101)
Total	15.5	18.0	59.7	4.9	1.9	(206)

[a] "Good" methods are defined to be pill, IUD, condom, and diaphragm; "poor" methods include all other contraceptive methods excluding abstinence.

of poor contraception). Notice, too, the large percentage of nonusers in the first interval which had zero live births. Presumably a relatively large fraction of the users of no contraception knew themselves to be sterile or subfecund. In the terminology of the model developed in Section II, couples with a relatively low natural fecundity and a low expected fertility need avert fewer births to achieve any given level of desired fertility. Consequently, these couples have less incentive to use any contraception, in general, and less incentive to adopt high-fixed-cost techniques, in particular.

Table 5 also indicates the relationship between contraception use and fertility outcomes. While Table 4 shows a frequency distribution of live births by contraception use for two of the cells of white non-Catholic women from Table 3, Table 5 indicates the mean and standard deviation of the live births by contraception use for each of the 5 cells of white non-Catholic women aged 35–44 from Table 3.

Compare the fertility behavior of the "good" and "poor" contraceptors for some given level of schooling in Table 5. In terms of mean fertility, couples which used a "good" contraceptive method (pill, IUD, condom, or diaphragm) in the first birth interval had somewhat lower mean fertility than couples which used relatively "poor" contraceptive methods. As panel B indicates, however, very few of the differences in means are statistically significant. By contrast, the comparison of differences in the standard deviation of the fertility outcomes does exhibit statistical significance: the users of poor contraception have appreciably higher variation in their fertility outcomes than do users of good contraception.[36]

The lack of a stronger association between contraception use and mean fertility in Table 5 is somewhat surprising. However, recall that equation 16 emphasized two opposing forces influencing optimal mean fertility. The marginal costs of fertility control raised optimal mean fertility ($\beta_i k$), although the positive relationship between the mean and variance lowered optimal fertility ($-K/2$) as a mechanism for reducing the uncertainty about the number of births. We showed that couples wishing to avert more births would be induced to adopt better (higher-fixed-cost, lower-marginal-cost) contraceptive techniques. We also suggested that users of better techniques are more likely to use a mixed strategy of contraception, which implies a weaker relationship between the mean and variance of fertility. So users of

---

[36] Note that in the tests of significance of the variances, the few pair-wise comparisons which were not significant involved the relatively small cells containing 40 or fewer observations.

TABLE 5

Mean Number of Live Births μ_N and Standard Deviation of Number of Live Births σ_N for White Non-Catholic Women by Wife's Education and by the Contraceptive Method (Good, Poor, None) Used in the First Birth Interval, for Women Aged 35–44

A.

Contraceptive Method Used in First Birth Interval		Education of Wife				
		≤8	9–11	12	≥13	Total
Good	μ_N	3.769	3.069	2.784	2.887	2.920
	σ_N	2.065	1.476	1.274	1.076	1.334
	(n) [a]	(26)	(72)	(213)	(124)	(435)
Poor	μ_N	3.840	3.800	2.941	2.706	3.185
	σ_N	2.444	2.028	1.515	1.488	1.802
	(n)	(25)	(40)	(101)	(34)	(200)
None	μ_N	3.587	3.242	2.577	2.000	2.872
	σ_N	2.817	2.134	1.860	1.854	2.224
	(n)	(104)	(120)	(189)	(72)	(485)
Total	μ_N	3.658	3.284	2.738	2.583	2.946
	σ_N	2.635	1.942	1.567	1.472	1.849
	(n)	(155)	(232)	(503)	(230)	(1,120)

B.

Tests of Statistical Significance of Differences in Means and Variances in Number of Live Births, for Specific Pairs of Cells

Difference by Contraceptive Method	Education of Wife			
	≤8	9–11	12	≥13
Test of Difference in Means (Student's t Test)				
Good vs. poor	0.11	2.03 [c]	0.91	0.67
Poor vs. none	0.45	1.47	1.82 [b]	2.08 [c]
Good vs. none	0.37	0.64	1.20	3.70 [d]
Tests of Difference in Variance (F Test)				
Good vs. poor	1.40	1.88 [c]	1.42 [c]	1.91 [d]
Poor vs. none	1.33	1.11	1.50 [c]	1.56
Good vs. none	1.86 [c]	2.09 [d]	2.14 [d]	2.97 [d]

TABLE 5 (concluded)

Test of Differences in Mean and Variance of Number of Live Births by Wife's Education for Users of Good Contraception Only

| | Difference in | |
Difference by Wife's Education	Means (*t* Test)	Variance (F Test)
≤8 vs. 9–11	1.59	1.95 [c]
≤8 vs. 12	2.35 [c]	2.63 [d]
≤8 vs. ≥13	2.12 [c]	3.67 [d]
9–11 vs.12	1.46	1.34 [c]
9–11 vs. ≥13	0.92	1.88 [d]
12 vs. ≥13	0.78	1.40 [c]

[a] *n* indicates cell size. These figures are in parentheses.
[b] Implies statistical difference at $\alpha = .10$ (two-tailed *t* test).
[c] Implies statistical difference at $\alpha = .05$ (two-tailed *t* test).
[d] Implies statistical difference at $\alpha = .01$ (two-tailed *t* test).

good contraception are expected to have lower marginal costs of fertility control (a lower β_i) and also a weaker relationship between mean and variance (a lower K). Consequently, if wife's education sorts couples by their desired fertility in Table 5, the further partitioning by good or poor contraception may not have a systematic effect on mean fertility. The users of good contraception have lower marginal cost of averting births, but less incentive to reduce mean fertility as a mechanism for lowering the uncertainty or variance of fertility. As the relationships in Tables 3 through 5 indicate, *across* relatively homogeneous groups there is a negative relationship between the use of good contraception and mean fertility, but *within* the homogeneous groups, the use of good contraception systematically affects only the variance of fertility outcomes. Couples wishing to avert relatively more births have greater incentives to use good contraception, and within a group homogeneous with respect to their desired fertility, those who use good contraception achieve a lower variance of fertility.

Table 5 also indicates that there is a tendency for the more educated women to have lower mean fertility and smaller variance of fertility for each contraception category. The differences in the means do not often exhibit statistical significance (see panel B), but the differences in the variances among users of good contraception are statistically significant, often at $\alpha = .01$. The observed relationships between μ_N and σ_N across education groups for good and for poor contraception users separately, mirror the observed relationship between μ_N and σ_N across good and poor contraception users, holding education constant. This observation is quite consistent with more educated couples being more proficient users of each given contraceptive method – the partitioning of the sample of women aged 35–44 by "good" and "poor" (holding education constant) yields the same qualitative differences as the partitioning by more and less education (holding contraception quality constant).

To obtain another measure of the relationships among contraception choice, the wife's education, and fertility outcomes as indicated in Table 5 a multiple regression was run using the twelve education–contraception method cells. Let $\bar{N}_j$ and $\bar{V}_j$ be the mean and standard deviation of live births in cell j, G_j and P_j be dummy variables reflecting the use of good contraception (compared to poor) and poor contraception (compared to none), and E_j be the wife's education level (assigned the values 7, 10, 12, and 14 for the respective columns). The regressions, weighted by the square root of the cell sizes, yielded:

$$\bar{N}_j = 5.23 - 0.18(E_j) + 0.34(G_j) + 0.42(P_j)$$
$$\phantom{\bar{N}_j = }(8.51) \quad (-3.63) \quad\quad (1.13) \quad\quad (1.43)$$

and

$$\bar{V}_j = 3.38 - 0.15(E_j) - 0.34(G_j) - 0.31(P_j)\,^{37}$$
$$\phantom{\bar{V}_j = }(15.45) \quad (-8.27) \quad (-3.25) \quad (-3.03)$$

(Figures in parentheses are t ratios.)

The wife's education has a significant negative effect on both the mean and the standard deviation of the number of live births. Contraception use had no significant effect on the mean number of live births, but users of poor contraception had a significantly lower standard deviation in live births than users of no contraception, and users of good contraception had a significantly lower standard deviation in live births than users of poor contraception.

Table 6 partitions this set of households, the white non-Catholics, by duration of marriage and the expected number of children, for women married only once and aged 35 and above. Since age at marriage differs systematically by several socioeconomic characteristics,

---

[37] The standard deviations of N_j and V_j were 0.559 and 0.517 and the standard errors of the estimates were 0.359 and 0.127 respectively.

TABLE 6

Mean Number of Live Births μ_N and Variance in Number of Live Births σ_N^2 for White Non-Catholic Women Aged 35 or Above and Married Once; by Marriage Duration, Expected Number of Children and Contraceptive Method (Good, Poor, None) Used in the First Pregnancy Interval

Estimated Number of Births[a]

		Marriage Duration 15–19 Years			Marriage Duration 20–24 Years				Marriage Duration 25 Years			
		2	3	Total	2	3	4	Total	2	3	4	Total
Good	μ_N	2.815	3.125	2.907	2.724	2.803	3.455	2.809	2.277	2.842	4.000	2.746
	σ_N^2	1.162	2.042	1.573	1.349	1.661	4.873	1.745	1.596	1.528	4.286	2.138
	(n)[b]	(108)	(88)	(204)	(76)	(61)	(11)	(157)	(47)	(57)	(8)	(114)
Poor	μ_N	3.300	3.095	3.301	2.952	3.000	3.200	2.946	2.864	3.333	4.636	3.383
	σ_N^2	2.537	2.283	2.713	1.948	2.455	3.700	2.326	1.933	3.121	6.655	3.464
	(n)[b]	(20)	(42)	(73)	(21)	(45)	(5)	(74)	(22)	(48)	(11)	(81)
None	μ_N	2.286	3.050	2.640	2.225	3.109	4.333	3.012	1.836	3.106	4.182	3.184
	σ_N^2	2.790	4.368	4.006	3.512	3.087	5.884	4.182	2.991	5.860	7.466	7.001
	(n)[b]	(56)	(101)	(178)	(40)	(92)	(24)	(166)	(55)	(94)	(33)	(201)
Total	μ_N	2.707	3.087	2.866	2.613	2.990	3.950	2.919	2.185	3.085	4.250	3.098
	σ_N^2	1.881	3.079	2.746	2.107	2.497	5.331	2.867	2.380	3.957	6.623	4.914
	(n)[b]	(184)	(231)	(455)	(137)	(198)	(40)	(397)	(124)	(199)	(52)	(396)

[a] Estimated from a fertility demand equation (see text footnote number 38). The cells are defined on intervals: 2 is 1.5 to 2.5; 3 is 2.5 to 3.5; 4 is 3.5 to 4.5. Total includes observations with estimated number of births < 1.5 and > 4.5 as well.

[b] n indicates cell size. These figures are in parentheses.

the partitioning by marriage duration should more adequately standardize for the length of the period of time at risk of conception. To
standardize further for the incentives to avert births, we have used a
definition of expected number of children derived by regressing the
actual number of live births on a set of economic and demographic
characteristics.[38] We used this fertility demand function to estimate
$\hat{N}$ for each household, then grouped households into cells defined by
intervals of $\hat{N}$.[39]

One observes in Table 6 that when the marriage duration and the
household's expected fertility $\hat{N}$ are held constant, users of good contraception had smaller variation in their actual fertility than did users
of poor or no contraception. Also, standardized for marriage duration
and contraception choice, households characterized by $\hat{N}$ equal to
three tended to experience a larger variation in actual fertility than
households characterized by $\hat{N}$ equal to two. That is, there appears
to be a positive association between mean fertility and the standard
deviation of fertility. Furthermore, as Figure 7 indicates, the positive
relationship between $\hat{N}$ and σ_N appears to be strongest among users of
no contraception.[40]

Since more educated women tend to marry at later ages, the total
length of time at risk of conception probably differs by education for
women of a given age. Table 5 partitions the sample by wife's age and
education; for comparison Table 7 partitions the sample by wife's
education and marriage duration for women married once and aged 35
and above. Although the cell sizes in Table 7 are smaller and the results somewhat more erratic, one again observes a tendency for users
of good contraception to have somewhat lower mean fertility and,
more systematically, lower variation in their fertility.

[38] The regression was estimated from the 1965 NFS for white non-Catholic women
aged 35 or above. The estimation yielded: $N = 10.09616 - 0.35473 \ (MAR1) - 0.00042$
$(I) - 0.34462 \quad (ED) + 0.00003 \quad (EDXI) + 0.30078 \quad (URB) + 0.09881 \quad (MARD) -$
$0.12119 \ (AGE)$, where $MAR1$ equals 1 if married more than once or equals zero otherwise; I is an estimate of the husband's income at age 40 based on an estimated earnings
function using husband's education and market experience; ED is the wife's education
level; $EDXI$ is a multiplicative interaction term using ED and I; URB equals 1 if the
household lives in a rural area or equals zero otherwise; $MARD$ is the duration of the
current marriage in years; and AGE is the wife's age.

[39] This procedure partitions the group of households into cells on the basis of the
economic and demographic characteristics which, on average, are associated with one,
two, three, or four children. For our purposes this procedure suffices, but it does not
resolve the problem of partitioning the household's actual fertility into the "desired"
and the "unwanted" components.

[40] The figure plots only cells based on 20 or more observations. Unfortunately the cell
sizes for the users of poor contraception are quite small, making generalizations difficult.

FIGURE 7

Variance in Live Births by Expected Number of Births by
Contraception Method and by Marriage Duration

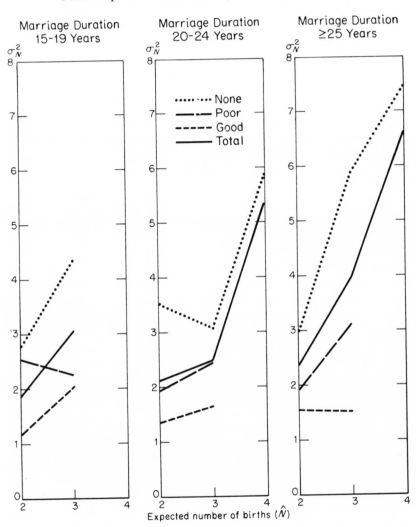

Expected number of births ($\hat{N}$)

TABLE 7

Mean and Standard Deviation of Live Births and Unwanted
Births for White Non-Catholic Women Aged 35 or Above
and Married Once, by Marriage Duration, Wife's Education,
and Contraceptive Method (Good, Poor, None)
Used in the First Pregnancy Interval

A. Marriage Duration 15–19 Years

Contraceptive Method		Education of Wife				
		$\leqslant 8$	9–11	12	$\geqslant 13$	Total
		Live Births				
Good	μ_N	3.167	3.192	2.766	3.000	2.907
	σ_N	1.722	1.833	1.202	0.984	1.254
	(n) [a]	(6)	(26)	(107)	(65)	(204)
Poor	μ_N	4.182	2.857	3.098	3.429	3.301
	σ_N	1.991	2.410	1.428	1.453	1.647
	(n)	(11)	(7)	(41)	(14)	(73)
None	μ_N	2.708	3.146	2.600	2.061	2.640
	σ_N	2.458	2.056	1.946	1.580	2.001
	(n)	(24)	(41)	(80)	(33)	(178)
Total	μ_N	3.171	3.135	2.768	2.777	2.866
	σ_N	2.290	1.988	1.543	1.327	1.657
	(n)	(41)	(74)	(228)	(112)	(455)
		Unwanted Births [b]				
Good	μ_U	0.167	0.962	0.523	0.431	0.539
	σ_U	0.408	1.587	1.049	0.770	1.052
	(n)	(6)	(26)	(107)	(65)	(204)
Poor	μ_U	2.091	1.714	0.512	0.714	0.904
	σ_U	1.921	2.563	0.952	1.139	1.474
	(n)	(11)	(7)	(41)	(14)	(73)
None	μ_U	0.667	1.268	0.837	0.455	0.843
	σ_U	1.341	2.013	1.354	0.905	1.480
	(n)	(24)	(41)	(80)	(33)	(178)
Total	μ_U	0.976	1.203	0.632	0.473	0.716
	σ_U	1.573	1.916	1.155	0.859	1.311
	(n)	(41)	(74)	(228)	(112)	(455)

TABLE 7 (continued)

B. Marriage Duration 20–24 Years

Education of Wife

Contraceptive Method		$\leqslant 8$	9–11	12	$\geqslant 13$	Total
				Live Births		
Good	μ_N	4.000	2.571	2.784	2.610	2.809
	σ_N	1.961	1.513	1.219	1.115	1.321
	(n) [a]	(14)	(28)	(74)	(41)	(157)
Poor	μ_N	2.000	3.842	2.686	2.917	2.946
	σ_N	0.926	1.642	1.430	1.379	1.525
	(n)	(8)	(19)	(35)	(12)	(74)
None	μ_N	4.114	3.366	2.701	1.609	3.012
	σ_N	2.285	2.009	1.715	1.616	2.045
	(n)	(35)	(41)	(67)	(23)	(166)
Total	μ_N	3.789	3.216	2.733	2.355	2.919
	σ_N	2.169	1.765	1.459	1.402	1.693
	(n)	(57)	(88)	(176)	(76)	(397)
			Unwanted Births [b]			
Good	μ_U	1.571	0.571	0.311	0.171	0.433
	σ_U	1.910	0.920	0.720	0.442	0.942
	(n)	(14)	(28)	(74)	(41)	(157)
Poor	μ_U	0.0	1.211	0.400	0.167	0.527
	σ_U	0.0	1.273	0.604	0.389	0.879
	(n)	(8)	(19)	(35)	(12)	(74)
None	μ_U	1.971	1.561	0.881	0.391	1.211
	σ_N	2.419	1.988	1.332	1.076	1.822
	(n)	(35)	(41)	(67)	(23)	(166)
Total	μ_U	1.596	1.170	0.545	0.237	0.776
	σ_U	2.203	1.613	1.013	0.690	1.419
	(n)	(57)	(88)	(176)	(76)	(397)

(continued)

TABLE 7 (concluded)

C. Marriage Duration ≥ 25 Years

Contraceptive Method		Education of Wife				
		≤8	9–11	12	≥13	Total
Live Births						
Good	μ_N	3.688	2.739	2.471	2.708	2.746
	σ_N	1.957	1.789	1.065	1.301	1.462
	(n) [a]	(16)	(23)	(51)	(24)	(114)
Poor	μ_N	4.105	3.400	3.152	2.667	3.383
	σ_N	2.105	2.113	1.523	1.658	1.861
	(n)	(19)	(20)	(33)	(9)	(81)
None	μ_N	4.240	3.580	1.932	1.706	3.184
	σ_N	3.004	2.548	1.680	1.359	2.646
	(n)	(75)	(50)	(59)	(17)	(201)
Total	μ_N	4.136	3.333	2.406	2.360	3.098
	σ_N	2.724	2.295	1.516	1.439	2.217
	(n)	(110)	(93)	(143)	(50)	(396)
Unwanted Births [b]						
Good	μ_U	1.063	0.435	0.392	0.208	0.456
	σ_U	1.843	0.896	0.666	0.509	0.961
	(n)	(16)	(23)	(51)	(24)	(114)
Poor	μ_U	1.000	0.700	0.879	0.111	0.778
	σ_U	1.291	0.979	1.453	0.333	1.235
	(n)	(19)	(20)	(33)	(9)	(81)
None	μ_U	1.733	1.400	0.644	0.353	1.214
	σ_U	2.658	2.356	1.283	0.702	2.182
	(n)	(75)	(50)	(59)	(17)	(201)
Total	μ_U	1.509	1.011	0.608	0.240	0.907
	σ_U	2.376	1.879	1.157	0.555	1.759
	(n)	(110)	(93)	(143)	(50)	(396)

[a] n indicates cell size. These figures are in parentheses.
[b] For definition see text.

The demographic literature has emphasized a distinction between "wanted" and "unwanted" fertility, and it is tempting to try to partition actual fertility into these two components for separate analysis.[41] The difficulty, of course, is in obtaining an estimate of wanted births distinct from the household's actual fertility. The problem is not simply one of estimation. Viewed in the context of the stochastic model described above, it is not possible, even in principle, to designate each pregnancy as "desired" or "undesired." Also, we have emphasized that the household's optimal number of children is affected by fertility control costs (i.e., $\beta_i k$ in equation 16) and the relation between mean and variance of fertility (i.e., $-K/2$). So the definition of "desired" fertility depends critically upon what is assumed about fertility control costs, the variance in actual fertility, and so on.[42]

Recognizing these limitations, we nevertheless attempted to consider "unwanted" fertility since the NFS data set contains retrospective information on the couple's fertility goals prior to each pregnancy. By summing up the number of pregnancies "wanted"[43] and subtracting this number from the total number of live births, we obtained an estimate of the number of births "unwanted" in each household. Table 7 indicates the mean number of "unwanted" births by marriage dura-

---

[41] In addition to Ryder and Westoff (1971), see Bumpass and Westoff (1970), Ryder (1973) and Part IV "Unwanted Fertility" of Volume 1 of the Commission on Population Growth (1972), particularly the essay by Ryder and Westoff (1972).

[42] That is, in the terminology of equation 16 one might define unwanted fertility as $\mu_N - N^*$ or $\mu_N - \mu_N^*$. However, since $\sigma_N > 0$, actual fertility N differs in general from μ_N, so "unwanted" fertility presumably includes not only the discrepancy between some fixed target fertility and optimal mean fertility μ_N but also the variation in actual fertility around μ_N.

[43] The NFS data contain retrospective information about the contraceptive behavior and the husband's and wife's attitudes about another pregnancy prior to each of the wife's pregnancies. Following Ryder and Westoff (1971) we considered each live birth as "wanted" or "unwanted" on the basis of the behavioral and attitudinal circumstances prior to that pregnancy. The birth was considered "wanted" if any of the following three conditions was met: (1) The birth was "wanted" if the couple had used no contraception in the interval prior to that pregnancy and responded "yes" to the question "Was the only reason you did not use any method then because you wanted to have a baby as soon as possible?" (2) The birth was "wanted" if the couple had used a contraceptive method in the interval prior to that pregnancy and had "stopped using a method in order to have a child." (3) If the couple was not using contraception but responded "no" to the question quoted above, or if the couple had conceived while using a method or while having stopped using a method but "did not want to become pregnant at that time," then the couple was asked two additional questions. If the response was "yes" to either of these additional questions the birth was considered wanted. The two questions were "Before you became pregnant this time did you want to have a (another) child sometime?" and "Did your husband want to have a (another) child sometime?" Our definition of "wanted" differs slightly from the definition used by Ryder and Westoff.

tion, wife's education, and contraceptive method used in the first pregnancy interval. There appears to be a relatively strong negative relation between the number of "unwanted" births and the wife's education level,[44] and a somewhat systematic relationship between the number of "unwanted" births and the use of good contraception.

We want to stress that the results pertaining to unwanted births are subject to many qualifications and are included here primarily as some evidence that this one measure of the intuitively appealing notion of an unwanted pregnancy seems to be related to contraception use as one would expect. The arbitrariness of the precise definition of an unwanted pregnancy helps convince us that it is more useful in studying the uncertainty related to fertility behavior to focus on the distribution of actual births than to concentrate on partitioning observed fertility into "desired" and "unwanted" fertility. We have shown in this section that across broadly defined groups of households there appears to be a systematic relationship between contraception strategies and the mean and variance of observed fertility. Couples characterized by the use of more effective contraception appear to have somewhat lower mean fertility, lower variance of fertility, a weaker relationship between their mean and variance of fertility, and perhaps a lower level of "unwanted" fertility.

V. DIFFUSION OF THE PILL

The 1965 National Fertility Study and its sequel, the 1970 National Fertility Study, provide a unique opportunity to follow, at the household level, the diffusion of a major technical innovation—the oral contraceptive—from its introduction for sale in the United States in 1960. In addition to the intrinsic interest of studying the diffusion of new technology, the observed pattern of adoption of the pill provides an important test of hypotheses derived from our theory of contraceptive choice (see Section II).

There are two main reasons why the study of pill adoption provides a more powerful test of our model of contraceptive choice than would be afforded by studying differential choices among techniques existing

[44] This finding is consistent with Ryder and Westoff's conclusion that "there is a strong negative association of education and unwanted fertility" (see Ryder and Westoff 1972, p. 483). Their conclusion is also based on the 1965 NFS data and its sequel, the 1970 NFS, which is not yet available to us. It must be stressed however that Ryder and Westoff's definition of "unwanted" pregnancies and their criteria for selection of the subsample studied differ from ours, and one should not make inferences about fertility behavior from comparisons between their tables and ours.

before 1960. First, the introduction of the pill was an exogenous event from the standpoint of potential adopters. Second, the pill is a truly new kind of contraception in comparison with alternative methods available prior to 1960: it is significantly more effective and less coitus-related than alternative methods. This second consideration suggests that the pill has a significantly lower marginal cost of fertility control than other methods, at least in terms of the psychic costs associated with forgone sexual pleasure. Thus, couples were confronted, after 1960, with a significantly different set of potential contraceptive methods to choose from, and we investigate in this section the differential rates of adoption of the pill among women with different initial conditions in 1960 (e.g., marital status, age, parity, and prior contraceptive practices).

We first present a few hypotheses about the expected pattern of diffusion, assuming that contraceptive choice is governed by factors considered in our theoretical model. Next, we utilize data from the 1965 NFS to test these hypotheses and to estimate the probability of pill use as a logistic function of the household's economic characteristics, parity in 1960, and prior use of contraception.

The main behavioral hypothesis underlying our theory of choice of contraceptive technique is that couples choose the least costly technique to achieve a given fertility goal (e.g., a given value of the mean and variance of fertility outcomes). It was shown in Section II (C) that the same technique will not be least costly for all possible goals unless the technique with the smallest marginal cost is also the technique with the lowest fixed cost. This proposition led to the derivation of the contraception cost curve for a "typical" couple in Figure 3 as the envelope of least costly segments of the curve associated with particular contraceptive techniques. According to this analysis, the more births a couple expects to avert, the more likely it is to choose a technique with relatively low marginal cost and high fixed cost.[45]

To derive hypotheses about the adoption of the pill from this theory, we shall assume that for most couples the pill has a lower marginal cost than other contraceptive techniques available in 1960–65. Since it is easy to provide examples of components of marginal cost which are higher for the pill than for alternative techniques (e.g., money cost, side effects on health, and so on), the plausibility of this assumption depends on the further assumption that the major component of

---

[45] For the time being, we shall ignore risk considerations and argue in terms of variations in expected fertility within an essentially deterministic framework.

the marginal cost of contraception for most people stems from the conflict between effective use of a method and sexual pleasure.[46] The fixed cost of the pill includes the cost of acquiring information about its existence, characteristics, and method of distribution in addition to the money cost of visiting a doctor to obtain a prescription and various psychic costs (e.g., religious principles) which are not related to information acquisition.

We can use Figure 3 (page 47) to illustrate the hypothetical fertility control costs faced by a typical couple. Recall that the line $0F_2$ represents a zero-fixed-cost, high-marginal-cost technique such as withdrawal, and line $\alpha_3 F_3$ represents another technique such as the condom. Suppose that the high-fixed-cost, lower-marginal-cost technique depicted by $\alpha_4 F_4$ represents the costs of the pill at the time of its introduction on the market in 1960.[47]

If Figure 3 depicts the cost conditions faced by a typical couple newly married in 1960, the couple will adopt the pill only if it wishes to avert all of its potential births (i.e., if it wishes to have zero children). If the couple wishes to avert between seven and eleven births (i.e., if it wishes to have one to five children) it will use the condom as its contraceptive method. As the figure is drawn, if the couple wishes to avert fewer than seven births (i.e., if it wishes to have more than five children) withdrawal will be used as its contraceptive method.

The probability P that a couple will adopt the pill is equal to the probability that the total contraception cost of using the pill is less than the total cost of using the least costly alternative technique. This statement may be expressed as:

$$P = Pr[F_p < \min (F_i)]$$
$$= Pr\{[\alpha_p + \beta_p(\mu_{\hat{N}} - \mu_N)] < \min [\alpha_i + \beta_i(\mu_{\hat{N}} - \mu_N)]\}$$

(17)

where $F_p = \alpha_p + \beta_p(\mu_{\hat{N}} - \mu_N)$ is the total cost of the pill and $F_i = \alpha_i + \beta_i(\mu_{\hat{N}} - \mu_N)$ is the total cost of the ith alternative method ($i = 1, 2, \ldots$). If all the α's, β's, $\mu_{\hat{N}}$, and μ_N were identical constants for all

[46] The IUD, a close rival of the pill in terms of effectiveness and coitus-related costs, was not widely available until after 1965.

[47] While the line $\alpha_4 F_4$ in the figure has a slope, or marginal cost β_4, of approximately zero, the cost curve for the pill could have been drawn with a positive although relatively low marginal cost.

Also, for simplicity of exposition, we will assume here that these three techniques, withdrawal, condom, and pill, represent the entire envelope cost curve. In our empirical analysis all available techniques are included.

members of the population, P would be either zero or one for everyone, and the pill would be used either universally or not at all.

In fact, of course, these variables will be distributed according to some joint probability distribution across the population so that we should expect to find some fraction, $0 \leq P \leq 1$, for whom the pill is least costly. Moreover, our theory suggests that each of these variables is a function of exogenous variables as well as purely random factors. For example, μ_N is a function of husband's lifetime income and wife's price of time, two variables which help determine the couple's demand for children. Likewise, $\mu_{\hat{N}}$ is a function of the couple's natural fecundability and the wife's age at marriage, and the α's and β's are functions of variables such as religion and education which determine the fixed and variable costs of each contraceptive technique.

These considerations suggest that we may express the aggregate proportion of households using the pill as

$$P = \int_{-\infty}^{\infty} \cdots \int_{-\infty}^{\infty} Pr\left[(F_p - \min{(F_i)}\,|x_1, \ldots, x_n) < u\right]$$
$$h(x_1, \ldots, x_n, u)\, dx_1, \ldots, dx_n du \quad (18)$$

where $Pr(\cdot)$ is the probability of using the pill conditional on the values of the exogenous variables $x_1, \ldots, x_n$, which determine natural fertility, the demand for children, and the costs of contraception, and where u is a random variable and $h(x_1, \ldots, x_n, u)$ is a joint density function of the x's and u.

If we assume that u is distributed logistically and is independent of the x's, the conditional probability of using the pill may be expressed as a logistic function of the form

$$P = \{1 + \exp\left[-(a + b_1 x_1 + \cdots + b_n x_n + u)\right]\}^{-1} \quad (19)$$

or, alternatively, the natural log of the odds of using the pill becomes a linear function of the form

$$\ln\left(\frac{P}{1 - P}\right) = a + b_1 x_1 + \cdots + b_n x_n + u \quad (20)$$

which can be estimated using standard maximum likelihood procedures. After discussing several hypotheses about the set of variables $x_1, x_2, \ldots, x_n$, we estimate the parameters of logistic functions of the form suggested in equation 20.

We shall first consider the pattern of pill use in a static setting in which the distributions of natural fertility $\mu_{\hat{N}}$, the demand for children, μ_N, and the costs of contraception, the α's and β's, are stable in the population. Subsequently, we consider the question of diffusion of the pill over time. For convenience, assume for the moment that all couples in the population face identical cost functions for the three techniques depicted in Figure 3, but differ in their natural fertility or in their demand for children. If couples are then distributed by the number of births they wish to avert, Figure 3 implies that the proportion of couples in the population which adopts the pill will be equal to the proportion wishing to avert 11.5 or more births; the proportion which uses the condom will be equal to the proportion wishing to avert between 7 and 11.5 births, and the proportion using withdrawal will equal the proportion wishing to avert fewer than 7 births. In short, given a distribution of couples by the births they wish to avert, the switching points on the envelope total cost curve determine the proportion of couples using the various available techniques.

We have suggested three sets of factors determining the proportion of couples which might be expected to adopt the pill. We will consider each in turn. Holding constant factors affecting the fertility control total cost curve (the α's and β's) and the demand for children (the μ_N), any factor which increases natural fertility $\mu_{\hat{N}}$ will increase expected births averted ($B = \mu_{\hat{N}} - \mu_N$). Thus for a group of households, an increase in $\mu_{\hat{N}}$ will, ceteris paribus, increase the proportion of households using the pill (and decrease the proportion using withdrawal).[48] The major observable variable related to $\mu_{\hat{N}}$ is the wife's age when the pill became available. So our hypothesis is that, ceteris paribus, the older the wife was in 1960 the less likely she is to adopt the pill.[49]

[48] In the simple three-technique case the effect on condom usage is uncertain, since some who previously used the condom are expected to switch to the pill, while some who previously used withdrawal are expected to switch to the condom. In the more general case of several techniques, an increase in B is expected to increase the proportion using the high-fixed-cost, low-marginal-cost technique, ceteris paribus.

[49] That is, the older she is, the shorter the remaining reproductive time span, so the smaller her remaining natural fertility and thus the smaller her remaining expected averted births. Since she wishes to avert fewer births, ceteris paribus, her incentive to adopt the high-fixed-cost pill is relatively slight.

This hypothesis should be qualified in two respects. First, there may be an advantage to postponing the investment in the fixed cost associated with pill adoption until the benefits of the reduced variable costs associated with pill use are close at hand. If these benefits are greatest when the couple wishes to contracept with high efficiency in order to prevent any additional pregnancy, the adoption of the pill might be postponed until desired fertility is reached. Second, age at marriage is likely to be inversely correlated with the couple's demand for children. So the younger the woman is at a given parity, the more likely she wants to have a large family, which would tend to offset the effect of age on expected births averted, unless desired fertility is explicitly held constant. Thus our inability to hold desired fertility precisely fixed may introduce biases on the other variables.

Alternatively, if we hold constant natural fertility $\mu_{\hat{N}}$ and the fertility control total cost curve, factors which increase the demand for children μ_N reduce the expected averted births B and, therefore reduce the probability of adopting the pill. In studies of completed fertility, the husband's lifetime income, H, and the wife's education, W (as a proxy for her potential lifetime wage or price of time), have been found to be the most important economic variables. Sanderson and Willis (1971) and Willis (1973) argued on theoretical grounds for a positive interaction effect between H and W.[50] Estimating an equation of the form

$$\mu_N = \gamma_0 + \gamma_1 H + \gamma_2 W + \gamma_3 HW \qquad (21)$$

in a number of samples of United States women, they found that γ_1 and γ_2 are negative and γ_3 is positive, as expected. If we include these three variables in the equation for P, since we hypothesize a negative relationship between μ_N and P, we expect to observe positive coefficients on H and W and a negative coefficient for HW.[51]

Estimating the effects on pill use of variation in the fixed and marginal costs of the pill and alternative methods of contraception presents a number of difficult problems. These costs are likely to be dominated by psychic or nonmarket components which may vary widely across households but which cannot be measured directly. Certain variables such as Catholicism are known to influence the costs of certain forms of contraception, and it is frequently argued that education reduces the cost of acquiring birth control information (see Michael 1973). Unfortunately, both of these variables also help determine the demand for children and it is not easy to see how this influence can be disentangled from their influence on the cost of contraception.

[50] Briefly, the argument is this. When the wife is not supplying labor to the market, the shadow price of her time is higher than her potential market wage and is an increasing function of her husband's income. When she supplies labor to the market, her price of time is equal to her market wage and is independent of her husband's income. Since children are assumed to be time intensive, the positive income effect of H on the demand for children is offset by a substitution effect against children in families with nonworking wives, while there is no offset in families with working wives. Since the wife's labor force participation is negatively related to H and positively related to W, Willis (1973) shows that the effects of H and W on number of children will be nonlinear with a positive coefficient on the interaction variable, HW. See, however, Ben-Porath (1973) for alternative interpretations of nonlinearity in the demand function for children.

[51] The husband's lifetime income and the wife's education are not, of course, the only variables relevant for the demand curve for children. The demand curve used in the previous section, for example, included several additional variables (see footnote 38) and also pertained to white non-Catholics only. For the analysis of pill adoption in this section, we again restrict ourselves to white non-Catholics.

One advantage of studying the adoption of the pill is the fact that we may study the response to the introduction of the pill by women whose initial conditions differed in 1960. This procedure enables us to study the effect of prior use of other forms of contraception before 1960 on the probability of adopting the pill after 1960. The theory suggests that couples which have incurred the fixed costs associated with some other technique will, ceteris paribus, be less likely to adopt the pill. Hence, we expect prior use of the diaphragm and condom, for example, to be negatively associated with pill adoption.[52] A second aspect of prior use which may influence the probability of adopting the pill is the success the couple has with the previous method. If the couple's previous method has had high marginal costs, our theory suggests that it would be used relatively inefficiently. The couple would have, therefore, a higher risk of an "accidental" pregnancy while using that method. Since the pill has a relatively low marginal cost, the higher the marginal cost of the alternative method, the more likely that the pill will be adopted. Consequently, we expect prior "contraceptive failure" to be positively related to the probability of adopting the pill. This expectation is strengthened by the likelihood that couples which have experienced contraceptive failure confront the prospect of larger losses of expected utility from additional "unwanted" births than do couples who have successfully contracepted in the past.

While we have discussed three separate sets of factors influencing the probability of pill adoption in a static framework, we have not as yet considered the diffusion of the pill over time. A major driving force in any process of diffusion of new technology is the reduction over time of the cost of acquiring information about the new innovation. By the simple act of adopting and using the new technique, early adopters convey information to later adopters about the existence of the technique, how it is distributed, and so on. Since the pill is a prescription

---

[52] That is, after the fixed costs are borne, the fertility control costs fall from $\alpha_i + \beta_i B$ to simply $\beta_i B$. There are difficulties in this test of the "sunk-cost" hypothesis, however. A woman's prior contraception history is not independent of residual variance caused by variation in the couple's demand for children, fecundability, or costs of contraception which we are unable to hold constant with the other variables in the model. Several potential biases tend to work against the "sunk-cost" hypothesis. For example, subfecundity or sterility, which may be one of the reasons that a woman has not contracepted in the past, would also tend to reduce her probability of adopting the pill. If this bias dominated, we might find that prior users of contraception have a higher rather than a lower probability of using the pill compared with prior nonusers.

drug, its adoption is affected by the diffusion of information among doctors as well as among potential adopters. The dynamics surrounding the cost of information about the pill and the speed and pattern of its diffusion will also be related to socioeconomic differentials in rates of adoption, since this information is spread by word of mouth.[53]

To consider the effect of decreasing information costs of pill adoption, we again make use of Figure 3 (page 47). With the passage of time the fixed cost (which includes the information cost) of the pill for the average household may fall from $0\alpha_4$ to $0\alpha_4'$. Thus the switching point —the number of averted births at which pill adoption is warranted— falls from about 11.5 births averted to about 6 births averted, as the figure is drawn. Obviously, in the aggregate, the reduction in the fixed cost increases the proportion of couples using the pill. Notice that the model implies that the users of the next-best technique will be those who most readily adopt the new technique as its costs of information fall over time. The new low-marginal-cost technique first displaces the existing technique with the lowest marginal cost.[54]

To test the hypotheses advanced above, from the 1965 National Fertility Study we have selected three samples of white non-Catholic women who began their first, second, or third pregnancy interval in the period 1960–64 (see Table 8 for a description of these samples). In each sample we estimate the probability that a woman uses the pill in the specified interval as a function of three sets of variables that determine, respectively, (1) the woman's potential (i.e., natural) fertility from the beginning of the interval until menopause; (2) the couple's demand for children; and (3) the couple's costs of contraception.

[53] Although they are not information costs, a similar mechanism may operate to reduce the costs associated with deviation from group norms as individuals in the group witness increased nonconformity with these norms. In the case of the pill, the interaction between the teachings of the Catholic church and the behavior of individual Catholics might be interpreted along these lines (see Ryder and Westoff 1971, Chapter 8).

[54] Hence, should a new contraceptive technique be introduced which further lowers the marginal cost of contraception, our theory implies that the pill could be the first technique to be displaced. Ryder (1972) shows that by 1970 pill use differentials by education, race, and religion had converged. Much of the convergence, however, was caused by an absolute decline in the use of the pill after 1967 by highly educated white non-Catholics, the group which has the highest rate of pill use. It is interesting to speculate whether new techniques such as the IUD and the increased popularity of the vasectomy and tubal ligation had begun to displace the pill in this group. Ryder emphasizes the effects of fears about long-term adverse health effects of the pill, but these alleged effects were not widely publicized until the U.S. Senate Hearings in 1969, well after the 1967 peak in pill usage in the high-use group.

TABLE 8

Means and Variances of Variables Used in Logistic Estimates of Probability of Pill Use [a]

Variable	First Interval (N = 495) [b]		Second Interval (N = 502) [b]		Third Interval (N = 472) [b]	
	Mean	Variance	Mean	Variance	Mean	Variance
% contracepted in interval	.471	.249	.775	.174	.828	.142
% used pill in interval	.083	.076	.183	.148	.242	.183
% used diaphragm in previous interval	–	–	.080	.073	.153	.129
% used condom in previous interval	–	–	.267	.196	.324	.219
% used pill in previous interval	–	–	.046	.044	.028	.027
% used other method in previous interval	–	–	.173	.143	.269	.197
% had contraceptive failure in previous interval	–	–	.129	.112	.229	.176
Date of beginning of interval (century months)	748.2	297.2	750.1	272.5	750.8	320.8
Wife's age at marriage	20.4	15.5	20.1	9.8	19.9	9.6
Wife's age in 1965	23.6	17.3	25.1	19.4	27.0	23.6
Education of wife	12.1	4.1	12.1	4.3	11.9	4.2
Husband's predicted income at age 40 ($000's)	8.58	2.2	8.56	2.6	8.44	2.7
Interaction (husband's predicted income × wife's education ($000's)	105.9	1,041	106.2	1,196	102.7	1,186

[a] The samples consist of white non-Catholic women married once whose pregnancy interval began in 1960–64. The beginning of the interval is defined as the date of marriage for the first interval, the date of birth of the first child for the second interval, and the date of birth of the second child for the third interval. These dates are stated in "century months." To find the year in which the interval began divide by 12 and add 1900 (e.g., 750 century months equals 1962.5).

[b] N indicates sample size.

These variables, which are listed in Table 8, may be grouped as follows:

Variable	(Expected Effect on P)
I. Potential fertility	
Wife's age in 1965	$(-)$
II. Demand for children	
Wife's education	$(+)$
Husband's income at age 40	$(+)$
Income-education interaction	$(-)$
III. Cost of contraception	
(A) Date interval began	$(+)$
(B) Used diaphragm in previous interval	$(-)$
Used condom in previous interval	$(-)$
Used pill in previous interval	$(+)$
Used other method in previous interval	$(-)$
(C) Contraceptive failure in previous interval	$(+)$
IV. Age at marriage	$(+)$

The sign accompanying each variable indicates the hypothesized direction of effect of that variable on the probability of using the pill in a particular pregnancy interval. These hypotheses stem from the discussion on the preceding few pages, and most seem to require no further discussion. Note that the "date the interval began" operates as a time trend in this analysis, so it is assumed to be negatively related to the information cost of pill adoption. The prior use of other specific contraceptive techniques is compared with prior nonuse of contraception, hence the fixed costs associated with each technique are expected to deter adoption of the pill.[55]

We have estimated the probability of adopting the pill P as a logistic function of the form in equation 20 by a maximum likelihood method.[56]

---

[55] One might in fact offer hypotheses about the relative magnitudes of these negative effects based on the assumed ranking of the fixed cost components (the α_i) of each. But there may be persistent or serially correlated error terms across intervals, so we have refrained from emphasizing this hypothesis. For example, couples which chose the condom in the previous interval presumably did so for reasons only some of which we have accounted for. Also, each technique has its own set of characteristics which may be related to pill adoption (e.g., the diaphragm is a prescription method, so some of its fixed costs which are related to a medical examination may in fact lower the fixed cost of pill adoption).

[56] The computer program was written by Kenneth Maurer of the Rand Corporation. The advantage of the maximum likelihood estimation procedure is that the data need

The results are indicated in Tables 9 and 10. Two different versions of the pill adoption model are investigated. First, we considered the choice of pill versus all other techniques including no contraception. These results are labeled as pertaining to the "total sample." Second, we considered the conditional choice of pill versus all other techniques, given that some contraceptive technique was used. These results pertain to the sample of "contraceptors." This latter dichotomy is the appropriate one if pill adoption is characterized by the two-stage decision: (1) contracept or not contracept and (2) select a contraceptive technique.

Table 9 indicates the estimates on the total sample for each of the first three pregnancy intervals, excluding the variables which indicate prior contraception use.[57] The time trend (the date interval began) is positive and statistically significant. This conforms with our hypothesis regarding the effects of a decline in information costs over time. The age of the wife has the expected negative sign in only the second interval, while the age at marriage has an unexpected negative effect on the probability of pill adoption.[58]

The effects of the variables related to the demand for children were computed both with and without the income-education interaction term. In all cases, the variables exhibited the expected signs. The relatively stronger effect of husband's income than wife's education, however, is quite surprising. In several studies estimating the effects of these variables on fertility demand, the wife's education has the stronger effect. The introduction of the interaction effect does strengthen the effect of the wife's education in the first and third intervals.[59] In general, the signs and magnitudes of the effects of these three variables tend to support the hypothesis that these variables affect fertility demand and have an effect of opposite sign on the probability of using

not be grouped. Thus, the effects of a relatively large number of independent variables may be estimated from relatively small samples.

[57] The estimates were computed on both the total sample (for the unconditional P) and the sample of contraceptors (for the conditional P). The results were quite similar in the two cases, so only the former are reported here.

[58] We have no explanation for the consistently negative effect of age at marriage. Holding wife's age and current parity constant, a higher age at marriage implies a shorter duration of time from marriage to current parity. Thus, we think age at marriage in these estimates may be positively related to relatively high fecundity, relatively high rates of coital frequency, or relatively low demand for children, but each of these factors implies a positive effect of age at marriage on the probability of pill adoption, ceteris paribus.

[59] The effect of the wife's education W on the probability of pill adoption in, say, the third interval, is $\partial P/\delta W = .084 - .013H$, which is positive at lower values of husband's income and negative at high values of husband's income.

TABLE 9

Estimates of Probability of Pill Use by White Non-Catholic Women in Pregnancy Intervals Beginning in 1960–1964 [a] (total sample; asymptotic t ratio in parentheses)

	First Interval ($\bar{p} = .08$)		Second Interval ($\bar{p} = .15$)		Third Interval ($\bar{p} = .24$)	
	(1)	(2)	(1)	(2)	(1)	(2)
Age at marriage	-0.003	-0.005	-0.004	-0.004	-0.028	-0.028
	(-0.77)	(-0.99)	(-0.29)	(-0.29)	(-2.30)	(-2.29)
Age of wife	-	-	-0.023	-0.023	0.001	0.001
			(-2.05)	(-2.04)	(0.13)	(0.21)
Education of wife	0.008	0.090	0.019	0.022	0.015	0.084
	(1.01)	(1.64)	(1.36)	(0.36)	(0.98)	(2.17)
Husband's predicted income ($000's)	0.03	0.14	0.06	0.06	0.03	0.19
	(2.30)	(1.85)	(3.05)	(0.76)	(1.71)	(2.32)
Income-education interaction ($000's)	-	-0.009	-	-0.000	-	-0.013
		(-1.52)		(-0.05)		(-2.01)
Date interval began	0.002	0.002	0.009	0.009	0.007	0.007
	(3.22)	(2.86)	(5.63)	(5.62)	(4.72)	(4.77)

[a] The coefficients reported above the t ratios are analogous to coefficients that would be estimated in a linear probability model of the form $p = a + b_1x_1 + \ldots + b_nx_n$. These are obtained from the β's estimated by maximum likelihood in the logistic function $p = 1/[1 + \exp(\alpha + \beta_1x_1 + \ldots + \beta_nx_n)]$ by the relation $b_j = \frac{\partial p}{\partial x_j} = \bar{p}(1 - \bar{p})\beta_j$ where $\bar{p}$ is the mean proportion using the pill. The asymptotic t ratios, of course, pertain to the β's.

TABLE 10

Estimates of Probability of Pill Use by White Non-Catholic
Women in Pregnancy Intervals Beginning in 1960–1964 for
Total Sample and for Subsample of Women Who
Contracepted during the Interval [a]
(asymptotic *t* ratios in parentheses)

	Second Interval		Third Interval	
	Total Sample (1) [b]	Contra-ceptors (2)	Total Sample (3)	Contra-ceptors (4)
Age of marriage	−.014	−.017	−.024	−.029
	(−0.95)	(−0.86)	(−1.92)	(−2.00)
Age of wife	−.015	−.014	.004	.004
	(−1.27)	(−0.89)	(0.55)	(0.49)
Education of wife	.017	.027	.137	.154
	(1.15)	(1.29)	(2.07)	(2.07)
Predicted income of husband ($000's)	.050	.041	.190	.206
	(2.6)	(1.66)	(2.23)	(2.14)
Income-education interaction ($000's)	–	–	−.013	−.015
			(−1.94)	(−1.90)
Date interval began	.009	.011	.006	.007
	(5.33)	(5.19)	(4.51)	(4.25)
Used diaphragm in previous interval	−.024	−.077	.076	−.117
	(−0.29)	(−0.75)	(0.94)	(−1.17)
Used condom in previous interval	−.089	−.195	.118	−.082
	(−1.56)	(−2.71)	(1.74)	(−0.96)
Used pill in previous interval	.286	.419	.370	.228
	(3.24)	(2.80)	(2.84)	(1.41)
Used other method in previous interval	−.119	−.223	.102	−.095
	(1.85)	(−2.70)	(1.39)	(−1.04)
Contraceptive failure in previous interval	.142	.198	.138	.153
	(2.27)	(2.54)	(2.69)	(2.62)
$\bar{p}$	.15	.23	.24	.29

[a] See note at bottom of Table 9.
[b] Minimization technique did not coverge after 11 interations.

the pill, given the wife's age, parity, and the time sequence of the pregnancy interval.

Turning to Table 10 the effect of prior use of contraception is added to the estimating equations. The table includes the results for the total sample and for the subsample of contraceptors. The effects of the fertility demand variables, the information cost variable, and the age of the wife and age at marriage variables are only slightly affected by the introduction of the set of prior-use variables, so they will not be discussed again here. The effect of failure in the preceding interval is positive as hypothesized. The effects of prior use of the diaphragm, condom, or other contraception are negative as hypothesized in the subsample of contraceptors, but are seldom statistically significant; the signs are not as hypothesized in the third interval for the total sample. The expected positive effect of prior pill use is quite strong in most cases.

While it is tempting to discuss in detail several of these estimated coefficients, we will not do so here. We think the qualitative results of our study of pill use offer rather strong support for the hypotheses we developed earlier in this section. In addition, the model can help us interpret the observed trend and differential use of the pill since 1960. In the preceding section we showed that the implications about the relationship between distributions of fertility outcomes and contraception behavior are also supported by the observed behavior from the 1965 National Fertility Survey.

APPENDIX

[Appendix tables appear on following pages.]

TABLE A.1
Frequency Distribution of Number of Live Births by Wife's Age, Wife's Education, for White Non-Catholic Women
(per cent)

Wife's Age and Education	Cell Size	Number of Live Births												
		0	1	2	3	4	5	6	7	8	9	10	11	12
Age 35–39:														
≤ 8	66	10.6	9.1	16.7	18.2	16.7	6.1	7.6	4.5	6.1	1.5	0.0	3.0	0.0
9–11	104	2.9	8.7	25.0	21.2	17.3	13.5	6.7	2.9	1.9	0.0	0.0	0.0	0.0
12	249	8.4	11.2	28.9	25.7	14.1	4.8	4.0	2.4	0.4	0.0	0.0	0.0	0.0
≥13	112	8.0	10.7	28.6	22.3	18.8	8.9	0.9	0.9	0.9	0.0	0.0	0.0	0.0
Total	531	7.5	10.4	26.6	23.2	16.0	7.5	4.3	2.4	1.5	0.2	0.0	0.4	0.0
Age 40–44:														
≤ 8	89	2.2	16.9	25.8	18.0	5.6	9.0	6.7	3.4	6.7	1.1	3.4	0.0	1.1
9–11	128	5.5	13.3	21.1	27.3	12.5	4.7	3.1	7.8	3.1	1.6	0.0	0.0	0.0
12	254	5.1	11.8	31.9	25.6	11.8	7.1	5.1	1.6	0.0	0.0	0.0	0.0	0.0
≥13	118	11.9	8.5	31.4	28.8	13.6	4.2	0.8	0.8	0.0	0.0	0.0	0.0	0.0
Total	589	6.1	12.2	28.5	25.5	11.4	6.3	4.1	3.1	1.7	0.5	0.5	0.0	0.2
Age 45–49:														
≤ 8	60	8.3	13.3	10.0	15.0	21.7	8.3	11.7	3.3	5.0	0.0	1.7	1.7	0.0
9–11	53	9.4	22.6	28.3	20.8	7.5	5.7	3.8	1.9	0.0	0.0	0.0	0.0	0.0
12	126	7.9	19.8	34.9	16.7	13.5	2.4	1.6	1.6	0.8	0.8	0.0	0.0	0.0
≥13	61	8.2	11.5	29.5	31.1	18.0	0.0	1.6	0.0	0.0	0.0	0.0	0.0	0.0
Total	300	8.3	17.3	27.7	20.0	15.0	3.7	4.0	1.7	1.3	0.3	0.3	0.3	0.0
Age 50–54:														
≤8	61	11.5	14.8	8.2	16.4	16.4	13.1	4.9	8.2	4.9	0.0	1.6	0.0	0.0
9–11	46	6.5	17.4	30.4	21.7	6.5	4.3	8.7	0.0	0.0	0.0	2.2	0.0	2.2
12	80	27.5	15.0	32.5	15.0	3.8	5.0	1.3	0.0	0.0	0.0	0.0	0.0	0.0
≥13	45	20.0	31.1	22.2	8.9	11.1	4.4	2.2	0.0	0.0	0.0	0.0	0.0	0.0
Total	232	17.7	18.5	23.7	15.5	9.1	6.9	3.9	2.2	1.3	0.9	0.9	0.0	0.4

TABLE A.2

Frequency Distribution of Best Contraceptive Method Ever
Used by Education for White Non-Catholic Women
(per cent)

Method	≤8	9–11	12	≥13	Total
			Education of Wife		
			Wife Aged 35–44		
Pill	3.2	12.1	10.9	13.0	10.5
IUD	0.6	0.4	0.8	1.7	0.9
Condom	31.0	35.8	37.4	37.4	36.2
Diaphragm	2.6	14.6	18.3	27.8	17.3
Withdrawal	8.4	4.7	4.4	1.7	4.5
Jelly	3.2	0.9	1.8	2.2	1.9
Foam	0.0	0.9	0.4	0.9	0.5
Suppository	1.3	0.4	2.0	0.4	1.2
Rhythm	3.9	3.9	5.6	2.6	4.4
Douche	3.9	7.3	4.0	1.3	4.1
Other	0.0	0.0	0.0	0.0	0.0
None	41.9	19.0	14.5	10.9	18.5
(*n*) [a]	(155)	(232)	(503)	(230)	(1,120)
			Wife Aged 45–54		
Pill	0.0	0.0	2.4	6.6	2.2
IUD	0.0	0.0	0.5	0.9	0.4
Condom	24.0	32.3	32.0	35.8	31.0
Diaphragm	5.9	13.1	22.3	24.5	17.3
Withdrawal	9.9	9.1	5.3	5.7	7.1
Jelly	0.8	2.0	4.8	1.9	2.8
Foam	0.0	0.0	0.0	0.0	0.0
Suppository	2.5	2.0	0.5	0.0	1.1
Rhythm	3.3	3.0	3.4	2.8	3.2
Douche	8.3	11.1	1.9	4.7	5.6
Other	0.8	0.0	0.0	0.0	0.2
None	44.6	27.3	26.7	17.0	28.9
(*n*) [a]	(121)	(99)	(206)	(106)	(532)

[a] *n* indicates cell size. These figures are in parentheses.

TABLE A.3

Frequency Distribution of Best Contraceptive Method Ever Used
by Education for Nonwhite, Non-Catholic Women
(per cent)

Method	Education of Wife				
	≤8	9–11	12	≥13	Total
Wife Aged 35–44					
Pill	2.4	10.9	3.0	9.4	6.1
IUD	0.0	0.0	0.0	0.0	0.0
Condom	18.5	18.5	25.4	21.9	20.2
Diaphragm	0.8	5.9	13.4	15.6	6.4
Withdrawal	4.0	3.4	6.0	3.1	4.1
Jelly	4.0	4.2	7.5	6.3	5.0
Foam	0.0	1.7	1.5	3.1	1.2
Suppository	1.6	3.4	4.5	0.0	2.6
Rhythm	0.8	0.8	1.5	6.3	1.5
Douche	12.1	8.4	9.0	12.5	10.2
Other	0.0	0.0	0.0	0.0	0.0
None	39.9	42.9	28.4	21.9	42.7
(n) [a]	(124)	(119)	(67)	(32)	(342)
Wife Aged 45–54					
Pill	0.0	3.0	0.0	0.0	0.6
IUD	1.0	0.0	0.0	0.0	0.6
Condom	8.2	15.2	10.0	35.3	12.6
Diaphragm	2.1	3.0	15.0	0.0	3.6
Withdrawal	1.0	0.0	0.0	0.0	0.6
Jelly	3.1	3.0	10.0	0.0	3.6
Foam	0.0	3.0	0.0	0.0	0.6
Suppository	0.0	0.0	5.0	0.0	0.6
Rhythm	0.0	3.0	0.0	0.0	0.6
Douche	19.6	21.2	5.0	11.8	17.4
Other	0.0	0.0	0.0	0.0	0.0
None	64.9	48.5	55.0	52.9	59.3
(n) [a]	(97)	(33)	(20)	(17)	(167)

[a] *n* indicates cell size. These figures are in parentheses.

TABLE A.4

Frequency Distribution of Best Contraceptive Method Ever Used by Education for White Catholic Women

Method	≤8	9–11	12	≥13	Total
			Education of Wife		
Wife Aged 35–44					
Pill	6.6	10.4	5.5	5.0	6.7
IUD	0.0	0.0	0.5	1.7	0.4
Condom	9.8	25.5	17.4	18.3	18.4
Diaphragm	1.6	5.7	8.3	3.3	6.1
Withdrawal	21.3	11.3	6.9	5.0	9.7
Jelly	3.3	1.9	0.0	3.3	1.3
Foam	0.0	0.9	0.0	1.7	0.4
Suppository	0.0	1.9	1.4	0.0	1.1
Rhythm	13.1	16.0	35.8	38.3	28.3
Douche	6.6	0.9	2.3	1.7	2.5
Other	0.0	0.0	0.0	0.0	0.0
None	37.7	25.5	22.0	21.7	24.9
(n) [a]	(61)	(106)	(218)	(60)	(445)
Wife Aged 45–54					
Pill	0.0	0.0	1.6	0.0	0.6
IUD	0.0	0.0	0.0	0.0	0.0
Condom	14.6	17.9	27.9	26.7	21.5
Diaphragm	6.3	5.1	9.8	0.0	6.7
Withdrawal	6.3	15.4	6.6	13.3	9.2
Jelly	2.1	0.0	0.0	6.7	1.2
Foam	0.0	0.0	0.0	0.0	0.0
Suppository	0.0	0.0	0.0	0.0	0.0
Rhythm	10.4	15.4	19.7	13.3	15.3
Douche	10.4	5.1	3.3	0.0	5.5
Other	0.0	0.0	1.6	0.0	0.6
None	50.0	41.0	29.5	40.0	39.3
(n) [a]	(48)	(39)	(61)	(15)	(163)

[a] n indicates cell size. These figures are in parentheses.

REFERENCES

Becker, Gary S. "A Theory of the Allocation of Time." *Economic Journal* 75 (September 1965): 493–517.

———. "A Theory of Marriage: Part I." *Journal of Political Economy* 81 (July/August 1973): 813–846.

Ben-Porath, Yoram. "Economic Analysis of Fertility in Israel: Point and Counterpoint." *Journal of Political Economy* 81, supplement (March/April 1973): 202–233.

Bumpass, Larry, and Westoff, Charles F. "The 'Perfect Contraceptive' Population." *Science* 169 (September 18, 1970): 1177–1182.

Cain, Glen G. "Issues in the Economics of a Population Policy for the United States." *American Economic Review* 61 (May 1971): 408–417.

Heckman, James, and Willis, Robert J. "Estimation of a Stochastic Model of Reproduction: An Econometric Approach." This volume.

Henry, Louis. "La Fécondité Naturelle, Observation, Théorie, Resultats." *Population* 16 (October/December 1961): 625–636.

Jain, A. K. "Predicting Duration-Specific Averages and Variances of Live Births: Application of a Stochastic Model of Human Reproduction." *1968 Social Statistics Section, Proceedings of the American Statistical Association*, pp. 248–255.

Keeley, Michael C. "A Model of Marital Formation: The Determinants of the Optimal Age at First Marriage." University of Chicago, August 27, 1973, processed.

Kelly, Allen C. "Demographic Changes and American Economic Development: Past, Present and Future." U.S. Commission of Population Growth and the American Future, *Economic Aspects of Population Growth*, (ed.) Morss and Reed. Vol. II. Washington, D.C., 1972, pp. 9–43.

Keyfitz, Nathan. "How Birth Control Affects Births." *Social Biology* 18 (June 1971): 109–121.

Kramer, Marcia. Ph.D. thesis in progress on the demand for legal abortion in New York City. National Bureau of Economic Research, 1973.

Kuznets, Simon. "Population Change and Aggregate Output." *Demographic and Economic Change in Developed Countries*. Princeton: Princeton University Press for NBER, 1960, pp. 324–351.

Lancaster, Kelvin J. "A New Approach to Consumer Theory." *Journal of Political Economy* 74 (April 1966): 132–157.

Lindert, Peter H. "The Relative Cost of American Children." *Discussion Paper Series Economic History*, EH 73–18. Madison, Wis.: The University of Wisconsin, March 1973.

Michael, Robert T. "Education and the Derived Demand for Children." *Journal of Political Economy* 81, supplement (March/April 1973): 128–164.

Michael, Robert T., and Becker, Gary S. "On the New Theory of Consumer Behavior." *Swedish Journal of Economics* 75 (December 1973): 378–396.

Michael, Robert T., and Lazear, Edward P. "On the Shadow Price of Children." Paper presented at the 1971 meetings of the Econometric Society, New Orleans, Louisiana, December 1971.

Mincer, Jacob. "Market Prices, Opportunity Costs, and Income Effects." In *Measurement in Economics: Studies in Mathematical Economics and Econometrics in Memory of Yehuda Grunfeld*. Stanford, Calif.: Stanford University Press, 1963.

Mincer, Jacob, and Polachek, Solomon. "Family Investments in Human Capital: Earnings of Women." *Journal of Political Economy* 82, supplement (March/April 1974): S96–S108.

Perrin, Edward, and Sheps, Mindel C. "Human Reproduction: A Stochastic Process." *Biometrics* 20 (March 1964): 28–45.

Potter, R. G. "Births Averted by Contraception: An Approach Through Renewal Theory." *Theoretical Population Biology* 3 (1970): 251–272.

––––––. "Births Averted by Induced Abortion: An Application of Renewal Theory." *Theoretical Population Biology* 3 (March 1972): 69–86.

Potter, R. G., and Sakoda, J. M. "Family Planning and Fecundity." *Population Studies* 20 (March 1967): 311–328.

Reed, Ritchie H., and McIntosh, Susan. "Cost of Children." U.S. Commission on Population Growth and the American Future, *Economic Aspects of Population Growth.* Vol. II. Washington, D.C., 1972, pp. 333–350.

Ryder, Norman B. "Contraceptive Failure in the United States." *Family Planning Persepectives* 5 (Summer 1973): 133–144.

––––––. "Time Series of Pill and IUD Use: United States, 1961–1970." *Studies in Family Planning* 3 (October 1972): 233–240.

Ryder, Norman B., and Westoff, Charles F. *Reproduction in the United States, 1965.* Princeton: Princeton University Press, 1971.

––––––. "Wanted and Unwanted Fertility in the United States: 1965 and 1970." U.S. Commission on Population Growth and the American Future, *Demographic and Social Aspects of Population Growth.* Vol. I. Washington, D.C., 1972.

Sanderson, Warren, and Willis, Robert J. "Economic Models of Fertility: Some Examples and Implications," In *New Directions in Economic Research* (National Bureau of Economic Research 51st Annual Report). New York: NBER, 1971.

Schultz, Theodore W., ed. *New Economic Approaches to Fertility,* NBER, Conference Volume OC #6, printed as *Journal of Political Economy* 81, supplement (March/April 1973).

––––––. *Marriage, Family Human Capital and Fertility.* NBER, Conference Volume OC#7, printed as *Journal of Political Economy* 82, supplement (March/April 1974).

Sheps, Mindel C. "On the Time Required for Conception." *Population Studies* 18 (July 1964): 85–97.

Sheps, Mindel C., and Perrin, Edward B. "Further Results from a Human Fertility Model with a Variety of Pregnancy Outcomes." *Human Biology* 38 (September 1966): 180–193.

Taeuber, Irene B. "Growth of the Population of the United States in the Twentieth Century." U.S. Commission on Population Growth and the American Future, *Demographic and Social Aspects of Population Growth.* Vol. I. Washington, D.C., 1972, pp. 17–84.

Tietze, Christopher. "The Clinical Effectiveness of Contraceptive Methods." *American Journal of Obstetrics and Gynecology* 78 (September 1959): 650–656.

––––––. "Probability of Pregnancy Resulting from a Single Unprotected Coitus." *Fertility and Sterility* 11 (September/October 1960): 485–488.

––––––. "The Use-Effectiveness of Contraceptive Methods." In Clyde V. Kiser, ed., *Research in Family Planning.* Princeton: Princeton University Press. 1962.

Westoff, Charles F., and Parke, Robert, Jr., eds. U.S. Commission on Population Growth and the American Future, *Demographic and Social Aspects of Population Growth.* Volume I of Commission Research Reports. Washington, D.C., 1972.

Willis, Robert J. "The Economic Determinants of Fertility Behavior." Ph.D. dissertation, University of Washington, 1971.

––––––. "A New Approach to the Economic Theory of Fertility Behavior." *Journal of Political Economy* 81 (March/April 1973): S14–S64.

Comments on "Contraception and Fertility: Household Production under Uncertainty"

SIMON ROTTENBERG

UNIVERSITY OF MASSACHUSETTS

MICHAEL and Willis have written a careful, and sometimes ingenious, paper developing the economic theory of behavior regarding the choice of contraceptive technique, deriving implications from the theory, and putting these implications to the test of consistency with observed experience.

The paper examines intensively one decision among the array of decisions made in households, which are perceived to be engaged in production activity. It is written in a context which has now come to be conventional, and which involves an extension of the theory of the firm to household behavior. According to this convention, households are viewed as being engaged in the production of utility, and this utility is postulated to be maximized subject to some cost constraint. In the abstract form most commonly employed, households produce a basket of two commodities: some quantity of the consumption services of children (which is, itself, a combination of some number of children and some distribution of what has come to be called "quality" embedded in them) and some quantity of the services of goods (which is also a combination of numbers of units of goods and embedded quality). Again, in the commonly employed abstract form, households produce this basket of commodities by employing two inputs in combination: time and goods. From here, familiar principles of equality at the margin and least-costing are applied to define optimizing rules.

Of course, no actual household is presumed to have explicitly run through the optimizing calculus. It is merely that when it is postulated that households do apply those rules, predictive statements can be made about the behavior of aggregates of individuals. Empirical work has revealed that these statements are fruitful in the sense that they are frequently upheld by experience.

Since the application of the theory of the household permits the derivation of implications about the number of children desired, Michael and Willis begin there and develop a theory of fertility control which defines optimizing rules for choosing among alternative contraceptive strategies.

Before explicitly discussing various aspects of their work, I should like to suggest two variants on the conventional literature of the theory of the household which are antecedent to their work.

In the conventional literature, households are assumed to solve the output-combination problem (some quantity of children's services and some quantity of the services of other goods) as though children's services can be produced only by own children. This is, of course, not true. If utility is derived from the presence of children, or from observing them, or from their being the object of one's tenderness, or love, or care, or from forming them physically or morally, then utility can be procured from the children of others as well as from one's own. The instruments for achieving this are myriad. Adoption and foster parenthood are obvious substitutes for own children. But one might also be a schoolteacher, a playground supervisor, a Little League coach, a worker in a day-care center, a pediatrician, a Cub Scout den mother or a scoutmaster, and so on. There are numerous forms of association with children, both in markets and nonmarkets, and, therefore, numerous forms of consumption of children's services. All of these forms of consumption appear, in principle, in the "other goods" category in the conventional "children's services–other goods" dichotomy. However, since these forms of consumption are more perfect substitutes for the children's services of own children than for other kinds of "other goods," it might pay to consider them explicitly in this context.

This is especially true, because, in some respects, the consumption of children's services through the medium of others' children is to be preferred to the consumption of children's services through own children.

Own children are usually kept by their parents, whatever their quality. Criteria for admission can be applied to the children of others. If the child is autistic or hyperactive, too quiet or too noisy, too smart or too dumb, he can be turned away. The preference set of the consumer can govern. It may also govern for the consumer of children's services from own children, but the differences in cost are enormous. Parents will work for years to fashion the child into the form that will give them most pleasure; a scout den mother, shopping among dens, will know in hours whether she has what is, for her, the right set of boys.

In addition, the consumer of the children's services of the children of others has many more degrees of freedom in the allocation of time to this consumption activity than has the consumer of the children's services of own children. To illustrate, consumption may take place during the day but not at night; in winter but not summer; during later years of life but not earlier.

This introduces the second of the two variants previously mentioned. By and large, the conventional literature has treated time — an input in household production — as though it is a homogeneous commodity. Gronau's paper (*Journal of Political Economy,* March/ April 1973) discusses the different prices of time for different subsets of the population. What I suggest is that time is nonhomogeneous in another respect: that, for a given population subset (indeed for given individuals and households), different units of time in the daily, yearly, and lifetime cycles have different prices, which are determined by the values of alternative activities in which units of time may be employed.

If different time units do have different values, desired spacing of desired births will be affected.

Thus, the explicit introduction of the two variants will affect desired number of births and the desired time-distribution of births over the whole span of life; it will, therefore, affect the definition of the maximand which strategic fertility control behavior will seek to achieve.

All of this is logically antecedent to the Michael-Willis paper, because while explaining the calculus of optimization which finally yields some desired number of children in an ancillary way, the authors take that number as a datum and proceed from there.

They have written a sensible paper of quite considerable power. Households are confronted by a set of contraceptive strategies among which they may choose. Strategies and households employing them are more or less contraceptively efficient. No strategy and no household is contraceptively certain (except where complete abstention occurs). Each strategy has associated with it a distribution of failures; each has associated with it, therefore, a mean expected number of conceptions and a variance around the mean. Households employing a contraceptive strategy choose among different probability sets of outcomes. Every strategy is costly. Costs have fixed and variable components. The magnitudes of components of cost vary among population subsets. Households choose least-cost strategies for given probable outcomes.

The theory generates behavioral implications which are spelled out, the implications are tested and, generally, the tests do not discredit the implications.

Since, in treating their topic, Michael and Willis have done what I think only a fraction of all economists would do—but what I think any good, bright, well-trained economist should do—my comments may appear to be quibbling.

1. There is some ambiguity in the notion of a "pure strategy." It is formally defined as "the adoption of some form of fertility control which sets [the monthly probability of conception] at some fixed level (during fertile periods) for the entire reproductive span," but it is sometimes used to mean an inflexibly unchanged contraceptive strategy for the entire reproductive span. These are not necessarily the same thing and will not be the same, if, for example, the fecundity of the woman changes over time.

2. People do not talk very much about what they do in bed, so information is defective. Nonetheless, if inferences can properly be drawn from a small sample, the use of a pure strategy in either of these two meanings is not common. This is not to say, given the power of abstraction and the fruitfulness of unreal postulates, that pure strategies should not be assumed to characterize behavior. Indeed, the authors say, where they assume pure strategies, that they do so for analytical convenience. Unfortunately, implications derived from pure strategy models might not be applicable in mixed strategy worlds. Or indeed they might be applicable. Only empirical tests will tell, and thus, the apologia appearing in the text may be superfluous.

3. The notion that the length of the reproductive period at risk is altered by decisions about the age at marriage clouds one's perception of the behavior of the unwed.

4. The paper assumes that the quality of a child is positively related to the quantity of time and market goods devoted to him. Beyond some point, at least, the relationship may be inverse.

5. The existence of fixed costs in adopting a fertility control strategy turns out to have considerable influence upon strategic choice outcomes. Since, at least for some strategies, the fixed cost consists of reading the label on the box, it may be that this cost component is overweighted in the paper.

6. The pill is said to have a low marginal cost associated with its use. This would not be true if women perceive (whether correctly

or not) that adverse side effects will be generated by its ingestion, and that the magnitudes of those effects will be a function of the quantity of pills ingested. Nor is it clear, on the face of it, why the pill is said to be a high-fixed-cost control strategy.

7. Some evidence that the authors believe supports the statement that technique switching does not commonly occur in the United States really seems to suggest something else. They say (p. 54): "90 per cent of women who used some contraceptive technique in the first pregnancy interval (from marriage to first pregnancy) used a contraceptive in the second interval, while only 36 per cent of nonusers in the first interval used a contraceptive in the second interval." This seems only to say that the first set of women, having applied optimizing rules the first time around, having sought to avoid conception and having failed, now, in the second interval, applying the same rules and coming to the same strategic outcome, still seek to avoid conception. The second set of women, applying the same optimizing rules and given the parameters of their experience, seek to conceive in the first interval and, having succeeded, seek to conceive in the second interval as well. The evidence does not seem to support a conclusion of no switching.

8. It is not clear whether a household will choose the pill as its contraceptive strategy if it is very important to it that its uncertainty be diminished, or whether it will do so if it is very important to it that the number of conceptions be diminished.

9. The authors explain differences in adoption rates of the pill by women of different age classes at the time the pill first became available (lower rates by older women and higher rates by younger women) by differences among them in payoff periods for investment in the fixed costs of adopting the technique. It would be useful here to take account of different strengths of preferences for avoiding conception among women of different ages.

Estimation of a Stochastic Model

of Reproduction: An

Econometric Approach *

JAMES J. HECKMAN

UNIVERSITY OF CHICAGO AND
NATIONAL BUREAU OF ECONOMIC
RESEARCH

AND

ROBERT J. WILLIS

CITY UNIVERSITY OF
NEW YORK–GRADUATE CENTER AND
NATIONAL BUREAU OF ECONOMIC
RESEARCH

INTRODUCTION

IN the past few years, there has been substantial progress in the application of the economic theory of household decision making to human fertility behavior.[1] However, as yet, the theoretical and empirical scope of the economic theory of fertility has been quite limited.

* Research for this paper was supported by grants to the National Bureau of Economic Research in population economics from the National Institute of Child Health and Human Development, Public Health Service, Department of Health Education, and Welfare and from the Ford Foundation. We want to thank C. Ates Dagli and Ralph Shnelvar for exceptionally capable computer programming. We also wish to thank participants in seminars at the NBER, the University of Chicago, and Yale University for helpful comments on an earlier draft of this paper. The final draft benefited from suggestions by Lee Lillard and Robert Michael.

[1] For a recent collection of papers on the economic analysis of fertility, and citations to earlier work, see T. W. Schultz, ed. (1973).

Observed fertility behavior is regarded as the outcome of utility maximizing choices by couples, in which the costs and satisfactions associated with the number and "quality" of children are balanced against the costs and satisfactions of other activities unrelated to children. Theoretical emphasis has been given to the effects of the costs of parental time and money resources devoted to rearing children on the demand for the total number of children in a static framework under conditions of certainty. Empirical work has focused on explaining variation in the number of children ever born to women who have completed their childbearing as a function of measures of the household's total resources and the opportunity cost of time, especially the value of the wife's time. Empirical results have been of mixed quality. The value of the wife's time, as measured by her potential market wage or her education, is almost always found to have a significantly negative impact on completed fertility, but measures of husband's lifetime income are not always significant or consistent in sign.[2]

One important objection to static theories of fertility is their failure to deal with the implications of the simple fact that reproduction is a stochastic biological process in which the number and timing of births and the traits of children (e.g., sex, intelligence, health, and so forth) are uncertain and not subject to direct control. To control fertility, a couple can only attempt to influence the monthly probability of conception and, given conception, the probability that pregnancy will terminate in live birth, by altering sexual behavior, employing contraceptives, or resorting to abortion. As recent work by Ben-Porath and Welch (1972) stresses, this implies that family fertility decisions are inherently sequential and that decisions about further children are made in light of experience with previous children. Moreover, a modest extension of this argument suggests that uncertainty may surround the valuation process itself: until a family has had one child it does not know what the costs and rewards of having a second one would be. Finally, it is evident that uncertainty concerning fertility decisions and realizations adds to and interacts with uncertainty surrounding other jointly determined household decisions about marriage and divorce, consumption and saving, labor supply, and investment in human capital.

[2] A number of explanations for the puzzling inconsistency of the "income effect" on fertility have been advanced, but it is probably accurate to say that none has been universally accepted. See Becker (1960), Becker and Lewis (1973), Ben-Porath (1973), Sanderson and Willis (1971), Simon (1973), and Willis (1973).

In this paper, we report some initial results of a study in progress whose goal is to develop an integrated theoretical and econometric model of fertility behavior within a sequential stochastic framework. The principal contribution of the paper is to the development of an appropriate econometric methodology for dealing with some new econometric problems that arise in such models. However, we also present, in more tentative form, the rudiments of a theoretical model of sequential fertility choice and some empirical estimates of the determinants of the monthly probability of conception in the first birth interval which utilize our econometric methodology.

Recognizing the sequential and stochastic nature of family decisions, Ben-Porath suggests that "the proper framework for dealing with all the theoretical considerations [involved in the economic analysis of fertility] is a dynamic programming utility maximizing model with the various risks explicitly included" (Ben-Porath 1973, p. 187). In Section I, we formulate a very simple model of this type to characterize the way in which a couple's contraception strategy evolves over its life cycle as a function of the cost of contraception, age, parity, the time paths of income, and the cost of children. In each month of the childbearing period (excluding sterile periods following pregnancy), a couple's contraception decision is assumed to reflect (expected) utility maximizing choices in which the costs of contraception are balanced against the utility associated with each possible fertility outcome weighted by the probability of that outcome. Unfortunately, analytic results are difficult to achieve in such models, even with drastic simplification of the underlying structure of family decision-making. At its present stage of development, our theoretical model serves mainly to illustrate the stochastic structure in which fertility decisions are made and their consequences realized.

Even without a fully rigorous theory, it is possible to utilize the conceptual framework of a stochastic theory of reproduction in order to determine empirically at what stages of the family-building process, and through which channels, economic variables affect realized fertility outcomes. The full reproductive history of a woman (i.e., the timing of each birth and contraceptive choices in each birth interval) can be used together with the associated economic history of her family in order to investigate the impact of economic variables and accumulated experience on the sequence of contraception decisions beginning with marriage which determine the monthly probability of conception and, hence, the probability distribution of the timing, spacing and total number of births.

In Section II, we present methods to obtain consistent parameter estimates of the effect of economic variables in modifying the monthly probability of conception in the stochastic process. In order to obtain consistent parameter estimates, a number of new econometric problems must be confronted. In particular, we demonstrate that it is important to account explicitly for sources of sample variation, including variation among individuals due to measured and unmeasured components. To avoid bias, it is especially important to take into account persistent variations in the monthly probability of conception among individuals caused by unmeasured differences in fecundity (i.e., the physiological capacity to reproduce), frequency of coition, or efficiency of contraception, which, in turn, are related to omitted economic variables and family characteristics which determine health, the cost of contraception, and the demand for children.

Bias arises when persistent variation is ignored because of a selection mechanism which confounds changes in the behavior of an "average" couple in a sample caused by a change in an economic variable—the relationship we seek—with changes in the composition of the sample caused by differential probabilities of conception. For example, the group of women who begin a given birth interval may have an average monthly probability of conception of 0.2. If all women had identical probabilities, the conditional probability of conception in the second month of women who did not become pregnant in the first month would be 0.2. If they are not identical, however, women who survive the first month without conceiving are, on the average, those with the lowest probabilities. Hence, the conditional probability of conception would tend to decline over time because of a change in sample composition, not a change in behavior. Further, we show that the mean probability of conception in the initial group of women is biased downward if persistent variation is ignored. Our econometric method enables us to estimate the fraction of persistent variance in total variance at the same time that we obtain consistent estimates of the parameters of exogenous economic and demographic variables.

In Section III, we present parameter estimates of the model from data on the interval between marriage and first pregnancy from the 1965 Princeton National Fertility Study (NFS). Our empirical results suggest that the econometric problems discussed in Section III are of considerable practical importance.

I. CONTRACEPTION STRATEGIES AND REALIZED FERTILITY IN STOCHASTIC MODELS OF REPRODUCTION

Beginning with the seminal work of Perrin and Sheps (1964), mathematical demographers have developed stochastic models of reproduction in order to study the effects of variations in fecundity (i.e., the biological capacity to reproduce) and contraceptive practice on the number and timing of births over a woman's reproductive life cycle. In this section, we first describe the stochastic structure of these demographic models and then show how choice-theoretic economic models of fertility behavior can be embedded in it.

During any month a woman is in one of five possible states:

S_0—nonpregnant and fecundable;

S_1—pregnant;

S_2—temporary sterile period due to anovulation following an abortion or miscarriage;

S_3—temporary sterile period following a stillbirth; or

S_4—temporary sterile period following a live birth.

The woman's family-building history (i.e., the number and timing of pregnancies and births) is completely described by the sequence of visits she makes to these reproductive states and by the length of time spent in each state at each visit. For instance, the total number of pregnancies she has is equal to the number of transitions from S_0 to S_1 and the total number of births to the number of transitions from S_1 to S_4. Similarly, the timing of the first conception for a woman who begins marriage in a nonpregnant fecund state is equal to the length of her first stay in S_0 while the length of her first birth interval is equal to the time from marriage until the first transition from S_1 to S_4.

If it is assumed that the length of stay in each state and the outcome of each pregnancy are random variables, reproduction may be viewed as a stochastic process such as that represented in Figure 1. Assume that a woman begins marriage in a fecund nonpregnant state (S_0). Each month (the approximate length of the ovulatory cycle) she has some probability of conception. This probability is called fecundability by demographers. After a random length of time, she becomes pregnant, passing from S_0 to S_1. The length of time she stays in S_1 is a random variable whose mean and variance depend on the pregnancy outcome. For example, pregnancy lasts an average of perhaps less than three months when terminated by abortion or miscarriage and, of

FIGURE 1

States of the Stochastic Model of Reproduction

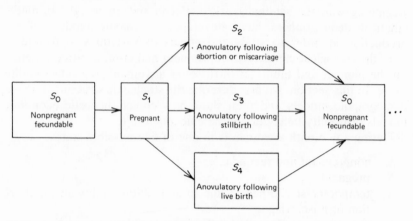

NOTE: Adapted from Perrin and Sheps, 1964, p. 33.

course, about nine months when terminated by a live birth. Finally, each type of pregnancy outcome has a given probability, which governs the likelihood that the woman involved will pass from S_1 to S_i ($i = 2, 3, 4$). After spending some random length of time in the post-partum sterile period, she reverts back to her initial nonpregnant fecund state S_0. Thus, the family-building process may be viewed as a sequence of reproductive cycles such as the one represented in Figure 1, each of which is of random length and outcome.

It is clear in this model that a couple confronts considerable uncertainty about the number and timing of births. It is also clear that if fertility outcomes are subject to choice, this choice must be exercised (excluding abortion) through control of the monthly probability of conception, p, by means of contraception or by variations in the frequency and timing of coition over the menstrual cycle. The effect of contraception on the couple's chance of conception in any month may be expressed as

$$p^* = p(1 - e)$$

where p is the couple's "natural fecundability" (i.e., the monthly probability of conception in the absence of any deliberate attempt to control fertility) and $(1 - e)$ is the proportional reduction in fecunda-

FIGURE 2

States of Contraception Decisions and Pregnancy Outcomes
within One Pregnancy Interval

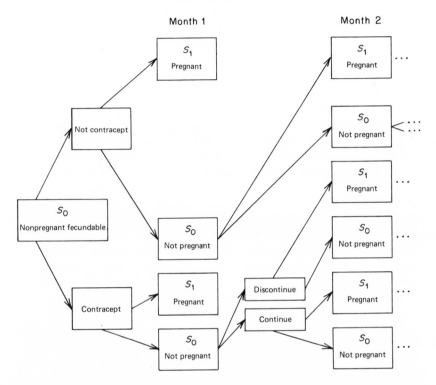

bility achieved by contracepting with efficiency e.[3] The value of e
depends on both the technical characteristics of the method chosen and
the care with which it is used.

The nature of contraception decisions and pregnancy outcomes for

---

[3] Natural fecundability is a somewhat misleading term, because it depends not only
on the physiological characteristics of a woman and her spouse but also on their "natural" pattern of sexual activity. Variations in sexual behavior may arise from differences
in sexual preferences of a given couple at different times in their marriage, from variations in preferences among couples, or from deliberate attempts to increase or decrease
the chance of conception for couples with given preferences. In the latter case, of course,
the frequency and pattern of coition should be considered as variation in contraceptive
efficiency rather than natural fecundability. Apart from reported use of "rhythm" as a
contraceptive method, however, it is difficult to distinguish empirically between these
two sources of variation.

a "typical individual" may be examined in more detail with the aid of the elementary branching process depicted in Figure 2. The process is assumed to begin in month 1, when the woman has first entered the nonpregnant fecund state (S_0) at marriage or after a previous pregnancy, and ends with her passage into the pregnant state (S_1) in month t or at the end of the period of observation. Three types of contraception decisions are made within each pregnancy interval. (1) The couple is assumed to decide whether or not to contracept when the woman first enters S_0.[4] (2) If the decision is to contracept, the couple selects a given level of contraceptive efficiency, e_t, which determines the woman's monthly probability of conception, $p_t^* = p(1 - e_t)$, $(t = 0,$ $1, \ldots)$. (3) If, at the end of month t, the woman remains nonpregnant, the couple decides whether to discontinue contraception.

Observed fertility outcomes follow as a probabilistic consequence of the contraception strategy adopted by a couple. The length of each pregnancy interval is a random variable whose mean and variance are determined by contraception decisions made within the interval. The sequence of these decisions across intervals determines the probability distribution of the total number of pregnancies and births over a woman's reproductive span. The contraception strategy chosen by a couple is assumed to reflect the interaction of the couple's demand for children (including both number and timing dimensions and embodying their attitude toward risk), the costs of contraception, and their past childbearing experience.

The effect of costly contraception on strategy choices and realized fertility can be made clearer with the aid of a simple economic model. Let us assume that a couple receives a flow of c units of child services per child per year for as long as the child remains in the household, and that it also receives a flow of s units of other satisfactions unrelated to children. The couple's lifetime utility function is assumed to be: (1) intertemporally additive, (2) of identical form in each year, and (3) characterized by a constant rate of time preference. It is written as

$$U = \sum_{t=0}^{T} d^t[u(cN_t, s_t) - f_t] \tag{1}$$

---

[4] In Figure 2, we assume that a woman who initially decides not to contracept will never decide to contracept later in this pregnancy interval. The main reason for this assumption is that our data record whether a woman contracepted in a given interval and when (and if) she discontinued contraception but do not record when she began contracepting. Since the purpose of contraception is to delay or prevent pregnancy, it seems most plausible, given our data, to assume that she begins contraception as soon as she is at risk (i.e., enters S_0).

where T is the family's time horizon in months from the date of marriage at $t = 0$, d is the rate of time preference, $u(\cdot)$ is the flow of utility per month from its consumption of c and s, N_t is the number of children in the household in month t, and f_t is the cost of contraception in month t measured in utils.[5] We assume that the monthly contraception cost function takes the form

$$f = f(e) \qquad (2)$$

where e is the efficiency of contraception, noncontraception is costless [i.e., $f(0) = 0$], and increases in efficiency are achieved at increasing cost (i.e., $df/de = f' > 0$).

The couple is assumed to maximize expected lifetime utility subject to its lifetime resource constraint. For simplicity, we make the following additional assumptions: (4) that the household's full income is an exogenous flow of I_t per month; (5) that π_{ct} and π_{st}, the full resource (i.e., time and money) costs per unit of c and s in period t, are exogenous; and (6) that no borrowing or lending is possible, so that full monthly income is equal to monthly expenditure on c and s. Thus, the flow budget constraint is

$$I_t = \pi_{ct} c N_t + \pi_{st} s_t \qquad (3)$$

Let us first examine the implications of the model under deterministic conditions by assuming that contraception is costless (i.e., $f_t \equiv 0$), and that there is no biological constraint on fertility (i.e., the couple may choose with certainty to have a birth any time it wishes). At the beginning of marriage, the couple's constrained lifetime utility maximization problem is

$$\max L = \sum_{t=1}^{T} d^t [u(c N_t, s_t) + \lambda_t(-I_t + \pi_{ct} c N_t + \pi_{st} s_t)] \qquad (4)$$

where the λ_t's are Lagrangian multipliers. It is convenient to rewrite this as an unconstrained maximization problem by substituting the flow budget constraint for s_t in the flow utility functions to obtain the problem

$$\max L = \sum_{t=1}^{T} d^t v_t(N_t) \qquad (5)$$

[5] In principle, the costs of contraception may include both resource costs (i.e., time and money) and psychic (i.e., util) costs. For simplicity, we have assumed that all costs are psychic. One implication of this is that variations in contraception costs shift the utility function, not the budget constraint. Consequently, variations in these costs cause no income effects.

where

$$v_t(N_t) = v(cN_t, I_t, \pi_{ct}, \pi_{st}) = u[cN_t, 1/\pi_{st}(I_t - \pi_{ct}cN_t)]$$

$$= u(cN_t, s_t)$$

is the couple's indirect flow utility function in period t, and where the number of units of child services per month c received from each child is set equal to one. Once born, a child is assumed to remain in the household permanently so that the stock of children can never be decreased (i.e., $N_0 \leqslant N_1 \leqslant \cdots \leqslant N_t$).

The couple's utility flow in any month $t = 1, \ldots, T$ is determined by the number of children N_t present in the household during that month, according to the indirect-flow utility function $v_t(N_t)$, which is a concave function of the form illustrated in Figure 3. Let N_t^* be the integer value of N_t that maximizes v_t. Given assumptions (1) through (6) above, the time path of N_t^* depends on the time paths of full income I_t and the relative resource costs of child services π_{ct}/π_{st}. In the simplest case, for example, N_t^* would be a constant over the life cycle if I_t and π_{ct}/π_{st} were constant, because the v_t functions would be identical over time, and, therefore, each would be maximized by the same number of children. If I_t grew during the life cycle, and child

FIGURE 3

Utility Flow as a Function of the Stock of Children

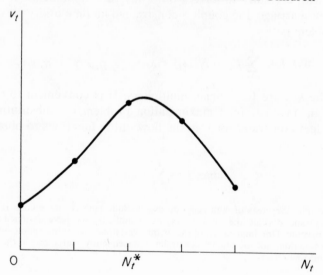

services have a positive income elasticity, the time path of N_t^* would tend to be an increasing step function.[6] Similarly, holding I_t constant, an increasing time path of π_{ct}/π_{st} would generate a time path of N_t^*, which is a decreasing step function.

In the absence of any biological constraint on acquiring children, a couple's optimal stock of children at any time t_0 is equal to $N_{t_0}^*$, provided that the future time path of N_t^* is constant or increasing; if it is decreasing, the optimal value of N_{t_0} is less than (or equal to) $N_{t_0}^*$, because the family cannot decrease its stock of children when that stock becomes "too large." In the case of constant or decreasing N_t^*, the couple would optimally have all of its children simultaneously at the beginning of marriage, and, in the case of rising N_t^*, births would be spaced. These implications suggest that births are more likely to be widely spaced, the more rapidly rising is the life-cycle profile of full income; and are more likely to be closely spaced, the more rapidly rising the time path of relative resource cost of child services.[7]

We now relax the assumption that a couple may costlessly choose any number and timing pattern of births it wishes with certainty. Instead, we assume that the couple chooses in any month of the woman's childbearing period (excluding sterile periods due to pregnancy or postpartum anovulation) a monthly probability of conception, $p_t^* = p(1 - e_t)$ by using contraception with efficiency e_t at a cost in utils of $f_t = f(e_t)$, so as to maximize expected lifetime utility in the remaining $T - t$ months of life.

The nature of the decision-making problem may be illustrated by considering the couple's decision of whether to contracept in the first month after marriage, on the assumption that the woman is initially childless, nonpregnant, and fecund. At the beginning of the month, the couple selects a value of contraceptive efficiency, e_1, ($0 \leq e_1 \leq 1$), at a cost of $f(e_1)$, where, of course, the choice of $e_1 = 0$ corresponds to a decision not to contracept, and noncontraception is costless (i.e.,

[6] Since N_t can take only integer values, income must grow by a finite amount in order to increase the utility flow maximizing number of children by one. It should be noted that the time path of N_t^* would be unrelated to the time path of I_t in a perfect capital market, because monthly resource expenditures would be constrained by wealth rather than current income. This argument also abstracts from any functional relationship between I_t and π_{ct}/π_{st} operating through the value of time (see Willis, 1973).

[7] It should be stressed again that the present model is a very simple one which should be elaborated before hypotheses derived from it are taken too seriously. As obvious examples, allowance might be made for (1) variations in child "quality" (e.g., by letting the number of units of child services per child be a choice variable), (2) variation in the scale and time intensity of resources devoted to children as a function of their age (e.g., plausibly, children become less time intensive as they age), or (3) investment in human capital by the husband and wife and its interactions with the cost of children.

$f(e_1) = f(0) = 0$. The woman's chance of conception during the month is $p_1^* = p(1 - e_1)$ and her chance of remaining nonpregnant is $1 - p_1^*$, where p is her natural fecundability (i.e., chance of conception in the absence of contraception). For simplicity, assume that all conceptions result in live births, and that all children survive to the end of the couple's time horizon T.

. The couple's expected lifetime utility at the beginning of the second month of marriage is conditional on which event, conception or nonconception, occurs in the first month. If the woman conceives in the month 1, let $V_2(b_1)$ be the couple's expected lifetime utility at the beginning of month 2, on the assumption that the couple follows an optimal, expected-utility-maximizing contraception strategy in all subsequent time periods, conditional on beginning month 2 in a pregnant state. Similarly, let $V_2(\sim b_1)$ be expected lifetime utility at the beginning of month 2, conditional on entering that month in a nonpregnant state.[8] The couple's expected lifetime utility at the beginning of marriage may then be written as

$$V_{01} = p_1^*[V_2(b_1) - f(e_1)] + (1 - p_1^*)[V_2(\sim b_1) - f(e_1)] \quad [9] \qquad (6)$$

where, recall, $p_1^* = p(1 - e_1)$.

We may now examine the conditions under which a couple will contracept in month 1 and, if so, how efficiently. If the couple chooses not to contracept (i.e., it selects $e_1 = 0$ and, since $f(0) = 0$, it incurs no costs of contraception), its expected lifetime utility is

$$V_{01} = pV_2(b_1) + (1 - p)V_2(\sim b_1) = V_2(\sim b_1) - p\Delta V_2(\sim b_1)$$

The term $\Delta V_2(\sim b_1) = V_2(\sim b_1) - V_2(b_1)$ is the expected lifetime utility of preventing a conception in month 1. If $\Delta V_2(\sim b_1)$ is positive, the couple will choose to contracept (assuming that the marginal cost of contraception $f' = df/de$ is zero in the neighborhood of $e = 0$) and, if it is negative, the couple will choose not to contracept.

Assuming that $\Delta V_2(\sim b_1)$ is positive, the couple selects the value

---

[8] More generally, we may use the notation $V_t(b_n)$ to denote the expected utility in the remaining portion of life of a couple that conceives in month t and whose parity (i.e., number of previous births) is $n - 1$ at the beginning of month $t - 1$, and $V_t(\sim b_n)$ for the corresponding case of nonconception. Later, we shall illustrate the meaning of these terms more concretely.

[9] The general notation for expected utility over the remaining portion of life for a couple with a stock of n children at the beginning of month t is V_{nt}. For expositional simplicity, the flow utility from zero children during month 1, $v_1(0)$, is omitted from equation 6, since it does not depend on whether the woman conceives and, therefore, does not affect the couple's decisions. Similarly, the term $v_t(n)$ is omitted in the more general expression for V_{nt} in equation 9 below.

of contraceptive efficiency that maximizes V_{01} in equation 6. The first-order condition for a maximum is

$$\frac{dV_{01}}{de_1} = p[V_2(\sim b_1) - V_2(b_1)] - f' = p\Delta V_2(\sim b_1) - f' = 0 \qquad (7)$$

and the second-order condition is

$$\frac{d^2V_{01}}{de_1^2} = -f'' < 0 \qquad (8)$$

In words, the first-order condition states that the optimal value of e_1 is such that the marginal cost of efficiency f' is equal to the expected marginal benefit of efficiency $p\Delta V_2(\sim b_1)$, where $p = -dp_1^*/de_1$ is the rate of decrease in the chance of conception with respect to contraceptive efficiency and, as before, $\Delta V_2(\sim b_1)$ is the expected utility of preventing a conception. The second-order condition implies that the marginal cost of efficiency must be rising if values of e_1 strictly greater than zero or less than one can be optimal.

This analysis is illustrated diagrammatically in Figure 4, where the horizontal curves MB_a, MB_b, and MB_c correspond to three possible

FIGURE 4

Marginal Benefit and Marginal Cost of Contraception

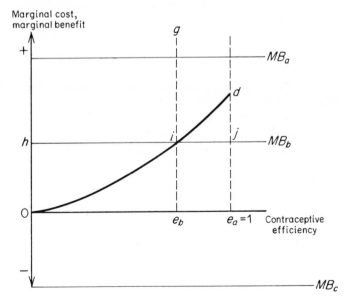

values of the expected marginal benefit of preventing a conception (i.e., $MB = p\Delta V_2(\sim b_1)$) and the curve $0d$ is the marginal cost curve of contraceptive efficiency which reaches its upper limit of one at point d. If the value of preventing a birth is sufficiently high (e.g., MB_a), the couple will contracept perfectly ($e_a = 1$), perhaps by practicing abstinence. Given a lower marginal benefit such as MB_b, the couple will practice contraception imperfectly and confront the risk $p_1^* = p(1 - e_b)$ of having an "accidental" conception in the first month of marriage. Finally, if the expected utility of preventing a conception is negative (e.g., MB_c), the couple will not contracept and will have a probability p of having a "desired" conception in month 1.

The preceding analysis is easily extended to the contraception decisions of a couple with n children at the beginning of month t.[10] Generalizing equation 6, the couple's expected utility over the remaining portion of life is

$$V_{nt} = p_t^*[V_{t+1}(b_{n+1}) - f(e_t)] + (1 - p_t^*)[V_{t+1}(\sim b_{n+1}) - f(e_t)]$$

$$= V_{t+1}(\sim b_{n+1}) - p_t^*\Delta V_{t+1}(b_{n+1}) - f(e_t) \qquad (9)$$

where $\Delta V_{t+1}(\sim b_{n+1}) = V_{t+1}(\sim b_{n+1}) - V_{t+1}(b_{n+1})$ is the expected utility of preventing the conception of the $n + 1$ child in month t. As before, the couple's optimal decision is not to contracept if $\Delta V_{t+1}(\sim b_{n+1})$ is negative and, if it is positive, to select e_t such that $f' = p\Delta V_{t+1}(\sim b_{n+1})$. The sequence of contraception decisions made by a couple depends on how the sign and magnitude of $\Delta V_{t+1}(\sim b_{n+1})$ varies with time and parity, and with the probabilistic outcome of these decisions in terms of the actual timing and number of pregnancies and births the couple experiences.

In the first birth interval (i.e., the interval between marriage and first pregnancy), parity remains constant at zero, but time varies. As is indicated schematically in Figure 2, a number of alternative sequences of decisions within this interval are possible. If $\Delta V_t(\sim b_1)$ is initially negative and remains so over time, the couple will not contracept during the interval and, therefore, faces a constant monthly probability of conception p. The length of time it takes the woman to conceive is a random variable, distributed geometrically with mean $1/p$ and variance $(1 - p)/p^2$.[11] If $\Delta V_t(\sim b_1)$ is positive and remains roughly constant over time, the couple will contracept at some given level of efficiency such as e_b in Figure 4 until an "accidental" pregnancy occurs.

---

[10] It is assumed, of course, that the woman is in a nonpregnant fecund state at this time.

[11] See, e.g., Sheps (1964).

In this case, the monthly probability of conception is the constant $p^* = p(1 - e_b)$ and the mean and variance of waiting time to conception are increased to $1/p^*$ and $(1 - p^*)/p^{*2}$, respectively.

Another possibility is that $\Delta V_t(\sim b_1)$ is initially positive, but decreases over time until it becomes negative, as would be indicated in Figure 3 by a progressive decrease in the marginal benefit of contraceptive efficiency from MB_b to MB_c. In this case, according to Figure 4, the couple initially contracepts with efficiency e_b and, assuming the woman remains nonpregnant, continues to contracept, but with decreasing efficiency, until MB becomes negative at which time the couple discontinues contraception. It follows that p_t^* continuously increases until it equals p at the time of discontinuation.[12]

To the extent that decreasing contraceptive efficiency involves a switching of contraceptive techniques rather than using a given technique with less care, the decline in efficiency may be substantially less than would be indicated by following the marginal cost curve $0d$ in Figure 3 as MB_t decreases. As an extreme example, suppose that a couple initially chooses a technique such as the IUD which has a "technologically" fixed level of efficiency equal to e_b. Further, suppose that the monthly cost of wearing an IUD is zero once it has been inserted.[13] The "supply" of contraceptive efficiency, given the choice of an IUD, is then the dotted vertical line $e_b g$ in Figure 4. As long as $\Delta V_t(\sim b_1)$ is positive, the couple contracepts with efficiency e_b and faces the constant probability of conception $p^* = p(1 - e_b)$; when $\Delta V_t(\sim b_1)$ becomes negative, the woman has the IUD removed.

The theory can easily be extended to deal with the choice of contraceptive techniques such as the IUD, which involve fixed costs as well as variable monthly "user" costs. To take the simplest example, suppose the couple must choose either the IUD or not contracept at all during the first birth interval. The maximum price (in utils) that the couple would be willing to pay to have an IUD inserted at the beginning of marriage is equal to the discounted sum of expected utility gains from wearing an IUD. This "demand price" is $\sum_{t=0}^{t_0} d^t(1 - p^*)^t M_{L_t}e_b$, where $MB_t e_b$ is the total expected utility gain from contra-

---

[12] Another less plausible possibility is that $\Delta V_t(\sim b_1)$ is initially negative and increases over time until it becomes positive. In this case, of course, the couple would begin contracepting once $\Delta V_t(\sim b_1)$ became positive, provided that the woman did not become pregnant in the initial period of noncontraception.

[13] This assumption abstracts from the possibility that the IUD produces unpleasant and "costly" side effects, such as cramping. We also abstract from the possibility that the device may be expelled involuntarily.

cepting with efficiency e_b in month t, t_0 is the duration of contraception before voluntary discontinuation, d is the rate of time discount, $p^* = p(1 - e_b)$ and $(1 - p^*)^t$ is the probability that the woman goes t months without conceiving. If the demand price exceeds the cost (in utils) of inserting an IUD, the couple will contracept. It is easy to see that the probability of choosing the IUD is greater the more effective is the IUD, the higher the marginal benefit of preventing a conception in each month, the lower the rate of discount, and the longer the desired duration of use.[14]

So far, we have discussed how the marginal (and fixed) costs of contraception interact with various possible time paths of the marginal benefit of contraception within the first birth interval to generate the sequence of decisions to contracept or not contracept, to select optimal levels of contraceptive efficiency, and to discontinue contraception which are depicted schematically in Figure 2. Clearly, a similar analysis of contraception decisions in subsequent birth intervals is possible. For example, a decision to contracept in the first month — say $t = t_2$ — that a woman enters the nonpregnant fecund state S_0 after the birth of her first child would be optimal if the marginal benefit of contraception, $p\Delta V_{t_2}(\sim b_2)$, is positive. The sign and magnitude of $\Delta V_{t_2}(\sim b_2)$ depends both on the woman's parity — she now has one child — and on the timing of her first birth, which is the probabilistic outcome of contraception decisions in the first birth interval.

In general, our model suggests that the reproductive history of a woman (i.e., the number and timing of pregnancies and births) may be regarded as the realization of a stochastic process whose parameters are determined by the biological capacity of a couple to reproduce, and by the sequence of contraception decisions the couple makes. These decisions, in turn, depend on the costs of contraception and the sign and magnitude of the marginal benefits of contraception $(p\Delta V_t(\sim b_n))$ as it varies with time and parity.

It is apparent that any hypotheses that may emerge from our model about the effect of economic variables on contraception decisions and realized fertility depend crucially on our capacity to derive the relationship between these variables and the $\Delta V_t(\sim b_n)$. Formally, the model of optimal decision making that we have specified requires a couple to solve a stochastic dynamic programming problem at the beginning of each month from marriage to menopause — a problem

---

[14] The extension of this analysis to choice among many alternative forms of contraception which have different fixed and variable costs is straightforward but beyond the scope of this paper. For an analysis of the choice of contraceptive technique in a static framework, see Michael and Willis, this volume.

whose answer is summarized by the sign and magnitude of $\Delta V_t(\sim b_n)$. Unfortunately, the rigorous analysis of these dynamic programming problems remains on our agenda of future research.[15]

It is possible, however, to use a simple two-period dynamic programming model to illustrate the meaning of $\Delta V_t(\sim b_n)$ more concretely than we have done so far, and to show how current contraception decisions are influenced by a positive probability of "accidental" pregnancies in the future, under conditions of costly and imperfect contraception. Paradoxically, we can show, for example, that a couple might find it optimal to contracept when contraception is costly in situations in which it would not contracept if contraception were perfect and costless. This implies that, under certain conditions, a decrease in the marginal cost of contraception may decrease the probability that a couple contracepts. A motivation for such behavior is suggested by the demographer Nathan Keyfitz (1971), who argues that the increase in the efficiency of modern birth control techniques has allowed couples to concentrate their childbearing in the early years of marriage instead of spacing them widely to avoid the chance of ending up with "excess" fertility.

To examine the plausibility of Keyfitz's argument for "precautionary contraception," consider the following two-period model. Let us suppose that a couple has $N^* - 1$ children at the beginning of period 1, and that the per period flow of utility from children is such that $v(N^* - 1) < v(N^*) > v(N^* + 1)$, so that we may say that N^* is the desired stock of children.[16] The couple's decision problem is to decide whether or not to contracept during period 1.

---

[15] Two issues that may occur to the reader at this point deserve brief comment. First, it is known that stochastic dynamic programming problems are difficult to solve and often do not yield many predictions. We are encouraged on this issue by the recent work of McCabe and Sibley (1973), who have obtained comparative static results using dynamic programming techniques in a model of sequential fertility behavior which assumes perfect fertility control but allows for uncertainty about future income and wage rates. Second, it may strain the credibility of the reader to suppose that behavior is in fact governed by the complex calculations implied by our model. Without attempting to add to or resolve the ancient controversy concerning the realism or relevance of deriving hypotheses by assuming optimizing behavior, we shall simply assert that it is plausible to imagine that "rules of thumb" or "behavioral norms" which emerge to guide decision-making in complex situations tend to be perpetuated to the extent that they approximate optimal decisions. If this is the case, optimizing models can be a fruitful source of empirical hypotheses about behavior.

[16] For expositional simplicity, we assume that children are conceived at the beginning of a period and born at the end of the period, after which they provide utility to their parents; that the rate of time preference is zero; and that there is no sterile period following birth. Under conditions of certainty, the couple's maximum lifetime utility at the beginning of period 1 would be $v(N^*) + v(N^*)$.

The couple begins period 2 with either N^* or $N^* - 1$ children, depending on whether or not it conceived in period 1. If it begins period 2 with $N^* - 1$ children, it maximizes expected utility in the final period by not contracepting. In this case, using the notation we defined for the general T-period model, its expected utility at the beginning of period 2 is

$$V_2(\sim b_n^*) = v(N^* - 1) + pv(N^*) + (1 - p)v(N^* - 1)$$

If the couple begins period 2 with N^* children, it is optimal to contracept in order to reduce the chance of "excess fertility." Its expected utility is

$$V_2(b_n^*) = v(N^*) + p_2^* v(N^* + 1) + (1 - p_2^*)v(N^*) - f(e_2)$$

where $p_2^* = p(1 - e_2)$ is the probability of having the $N^* + 1$ child, $f(e_2)$ is the cost of contraception in period 2, and e_2, the optimal level of contraceptive efficiency, is chosen such that the marginal benefit (i.e., $p[v(N^*) - v(N^* + 1)]$) and marginal cost (i.e., f') of contraception are equated.

The couple's decision about whether or not to contracept at the beginning of period 1 depends on the sign of $\Delta V_2(\sim b_n^*) = V_2(\sim b_n^*) - V_2(b_n^*)$, which, as before, is interpreted as the expected utility of preventing a conception in period 1 on the assumption that the couple pursues optimal (expected-utility-maximizing) decisions in future period(s). Using the expressions derived above, we see that

$$\Delta V_2(\sim b_n^*) = (2 - p)[v(N^* - 1) - v(N^*)]$$
$$+ p_2^*[v(N^*) - v(N^* + 1)] + f(e_2)$$

If contraception is perfect (i.e., $p_2^* = 0$) and costless (i.e., $f(e_) = 0$), $\Delta V_2(\sim b_n^*)$ is negative since $v(N^* - 1) < v(N^*)$. In this case, the couple will not contracept in period 1 in order to maximize its chance of having the N^* child. If, however, contraception is costly and imperfect, the positive terms, $p_2^*[v(N^*) - v(N^* + 1)] + f(e_2)$, may be of sufficient magnitude to make $\Delta V_2(\sim b_n^*)$ positive and, as Keyfitz conjectured, lead the couple to contracept before reaching its "desired" number of children.

These positive terms have a simple economic interpretation as the total opportunity cost of imperfect contraception. This may be illustrated in Figure 4 (page 111 above) on the assumption that $e_2 = e_b$ and $p[v(N^*) - v(N^* + 1)] = f' = MB_b$. The total opportunity cost of imperfect contraception is equal to the area $0ije_a$, which, in turn, is equal to the sum of the direct cost of contraception, $f(e_b)$, given by the area $0ie_b$ under the marginal cost curve, and the expected loss of potential utility from "excess" fertility, $p_2^*[v(N^*) - v(N^* + 1)] = MB_b$ $(1 - e_b)$, which is equal to the area of rectangle e_bije_a. The upper limit of the opportunity cost of imperfect contraception is equal to the direct cost of perfect contraception (i.e., $f(e_2) = f(1)$) given by area $0de_a$ in Figure 4.

In our two-period example, it is evident that a necessary condition for a couple to engage in precautionary contraception is that the loss of potential utility from one child too many $v(N^*) - v(N^* + 1)$ is substantially greater than the loss from one child too few $v(N^*) - v(N^* - 1)$. While this might be true, it need not be. Indeed, on grounds of symmetry it might be argued that, on the average, the losses from one too few children and one too many children are about equal, so that precautionary contraception would occur in only a minority of cases. Possibly, the incentive to engage in precautionary contraception is greater in the general multi-period case because of the chance of higher levels of excess fertility (i.e., the chance of having births $N^* + 2$, $N^* + 3$, and so on). Unfortunately, examination of this possibility must await rigorous analysis of the more general model.

We shall conclude this section by considering the effects of variations in economic variables on the optimal path of contraception decisions a couple would follow under the simplifying assumption that it may contracept perfectly at zero cost. In this way, we eliminate consideration of the effect on current decisions of the risk of future contraception costs and risks of "accidental" pregnancies while contracepting, since $f(e_t) = 0$ and $p_t^* = 0$ in every month in which $\Delta V_t(\sim b_n)$ is positive. The analysis is nearly identical to our earlier discussion of fertility behavior in the absence of a biological constraint on fertility, except that now the couple cannot obtain children as rapidly as it wishes.

Recall, for example, that we showed that if the flow of full income I_t and the relative cost of child services π_{ct}/π_{st} are constant over the life cycle, the optimal stock of children N_t^* is also a constant — say N^* — in every month. In this case, the couple will not contracept until a parity of N^* is reached and will contracept perfectly thereafter. Although sufficient changes in the levels of income or cost of child services may change the optimal stock of children, they will have no effect on behavior (e.g., the monthly probability of conception) until N^* is reached. For instance, if N^* is always greater than one child, variations in income and the cost of children will not influence contraception decisions in the first birth interval.

If the cost of child services follows a rising time path (e.g., because of an increasing wage profile of the wife) and I_t is constant, our earlier discussion implies that the optimal stock of children will tend to decrease at discrete time intervals during the life cycle. Provided that the optimal stock at the beginning of marriage exceeds one child, the couple will not contracept during the first birth interval. Since the timing of the first birth is a random variable, the optimal stock of children at the beginning of the second birth interval will vary across individual households which initially had identical "fertility goals." Those couples who had their first child quickly would have larger optimal stocks of children at the beginning of the second interval than those who took longer to conceive the first child. Consequently, the probability that a couple will go on to have a second child is negatively related to the length of the first birth interval. Extending the argument to subsequent birth intervals, the probability that a couple terminates childbearing with the nth child is positively related to the length of time it has taken the couple to achieve parity n. Thus, in the case of an exogenously rising time path of the cost of child services, the completed fertility of a group of initially identical households is dependent on the realized timing of births.[17]

A different pattern of behavior is implied by the assumption of a rising time path of full income assuming constant π_{ct}/π_{st}, since, as we showed earlier, the optimal stock of children N_t^* will tend to increase at discrete times during the life cycle. If $N_t^* = 0$ for a period of time, the couple will contracept at the beginning of marriage, then discontinue contraception when income has risen sufficiently to make $N_t^* = 1$.[18] If the first child is born before N_t^* increases to two, the couple will again practice contraception in the second interval, discontinue

[17] An interesting extension of this analysis would be to consider the interaction between contraception strategy and the wife's accumulation of human capital via labor force experience. See Mincer and Polachek (1974) for evidence that female wage rates are quite responsive to labor force experience which, in turn, is strongly related to the wife's reproductive history.

[18] Assuming that a major purpose of marriage is to have children, a (potential) couple may delay marriage until $N^* = 1$. Another possibility, of course, is that marriage may be delayed until an actual parity of one is imminent. Despite these considerations, we treat the date of marriage as an exogenous event in this paper.

when $N_t^* = 2$, and so on, until the highest value of N_t^* is reached at the peak of the income profile (assuming that I_t remains constant thereafter). Once actual parity reaches this level (there is, of course, some probability that it will not), the couple will contracept permanently. This analysis suggests that the more steeply rising the income profile, the more likely it is that couples will contracept in order to space their births.[19] It also implies that the probability that a couple will contracept for spacing purposes in the second or higher intervals is greater, the faster its earlier births occurred. Finally, an upward shift in the level of the income profile (or decrease in the cost of child services) will tend to increase N_t^* for all $t = 1, \ldots, T$, thus reducing the probability that a couple will contracept at any given time and increasing the maximum value of N_t^*.

In this section, we have shown how a choice-theoretic economic model of fertility behavior can be embedded in the stochastic structure of demographic models of reproduction depicted in Figures 1 and 2. Our model implies that the sequence of decisions to contracept, the choice of contraceptive efficiency, and decisions to discontinue contraception that are made as a couple proceeds through its reproductive life cycle may be interpreted as a contraception strategy in which decisions at each time and parity level are based on current and future values of income, costs of child services, and costs of contraception. It also implies that a woman's actual reproductive history can be interpreted as the probabilistic consequence of this strategy.

It is clear that much remains to be done before a complete economic model of fertility behavior within a sequential stochastic framework is achieved. The rather simple model specified in this paper has not yet been fully analyzed in the general T-period case under conditions of imperfect contraception. Consequently, we are not yet certain what implications the model has for effects of variation in the levels and time paths of income and the cost of children on optimal contraception decisions when there are risks of future "accidental" pregnancies.

It is also evident that the specification of the model abstracts from a number of aspects of family decision making and the environment in which these decisions are made, which probably have a substantial impact on contraception strategy. For example, we have assumed that

---

[19] As we noted earlier, in a perfect capital market, the value of N_t^* depends only on the present value of the income profile and is independent of its shape. In this case, the slope of the time path of N_t^* is rising, constant, or falling, according to whether the rate of interest is greater than, equal to, or less than the rate of time preference.

the flow of child services from a given child and the costs of producing these services are independent of the child's age, sex, or other traits, and the presence and characteristics of other children. We have also assumed that the flow of services from a child cannot be increased by the expenditure of resources on child "quality." Obviously, specification of a household production function for child services which incorporated these factors might considerably alter the implications of the model for desired spacing patterns under perfect contraception and considerably alter attitudes toward the risk of unwanted pregnancies under imperfect contraception. Other factors that deserve consideration include the effect on fertility decisions of uncertainty about future income and wage rates; decisions concerning investments in human capital and life-cycle labor supply by husbands and wives; and decisions about the timing of marriage and choice of spouse's characteristics.

While further theoretical progress is highly desirable, it is of equal importance to design and implement empirical methods by which we may determine the effect of economic variables on realized fertility as these effects are channeled through the sequence of decisions we have called a couple's contraception strategy. Our ultimate empirical objective is to use data on the full reproductive histories of women to estimate the effect of economic variables and prior experience with the fertility process on contraception decisions in successive birth intervals. By directly estimating the constituent probabilities of the fertility process (i.e., the probability of contracepting, the monthly probability of conception conditioned on contraception, and the probability of discontinuing contraception) as it evolves over the reproductive life cycle, we can explain completed fertility as well as the timing, spacing, and contraception decisions which lead to completed fertility. We can then use the estimated probabilities to simulate the effects of economic variables on the aggregate birthrate, and can determine at what stages and in what decisions economic variables contribute to the explanation of observed fertility outcomes.

It is obvious, however, that many additional, usually unmeasured, and frequently persistent factors influence contraception decisions and fertility outcomes. Among these are variations among couples in natural fecundability, due to differences in health or taste for sexual activity, and variations in contraceptive efficiency caused by differences in the taste for children or distaste for using contraceptives. As we demonstrate theoretically in the next section and empirically in the final section, these unmeasured components of persistent variation in

p and e raise a serious statistical problem in obtaining unbiased estimates of the effect of economic variables on the monthly probability of conception of the representative, or average, couple in a sample. We now turn to an examination of this problem and present a method for resolving it as one step toward our longer-run objective of estimating the stochastic structure of an economic model of reproduction.

II. SERIAL CORRELATION PROBLEMS

In the previous section, we presented an economic model of fertility behavior within a sequential stochastic framework. It is important to note that this structure, as represented by the schema in Figures 1 and 2 of the previous section, has been presented only for a typical individual. Unless very strong statistical assumptions are made, the simple semi-Markov structure does not lead to a sample likelihood function in which estimated parameterized probabilities can be said to predict accurately the probabilities of observed events for individuals. To see that this is so, it is important to distinguish three sources of variation in observed birth intervals among individuals: (1) purely random factors that arise independently in each time period and are independent of random factors in other time periods; (2) random factors, including unobservable variables, that are correlated across time periods; (3) deterministic variables, such as income and education, that can be measured and which are assumed to affect the probabilities.

To clarify ideas, suppose we are concerned solely with estimating the probability process determining whether a woman has a first pregnancy. Inherent in the model is the notion of a time series of events. A woman has a first pregnancy in month j only if she has not had a first pregnancy in months $1, \ldots, j - 1$. The most general way to model this probability is to imagine a set of continuous random variables $S_1, S_2, \ldots$, which may be thought of as index functions. The S_i, $i = 1, \ldots, \infty$, are assumed to be intercorrelated. The event of a woman becoming pregnant in the first interval depends on what value the "wheel of chance" throws up for S_1. Suppose that her education E is the only economic variable of interest. We may then define $\alpha_0 + \alpha_1 E$ so that if $S_1 < \alpha_0 + \alpha_1 E$, a woman becomes pregnant in the first interval and leaves the sample, while if the inequality is reversed, the woman is not pregnant and stays in the sample. The probability of a woman becoming pregnant in the jth interval is thus

$$Pr(S_1 > \alpha_0 + \alpha_1 E, \ldots, S_{-1} > \alpha_0 + \alpha_1 E_1, S_j < \alpha_0 + \alpha_1 E) \quad (10)$$

If we assume that the S_i are independently and identically distributed, this probability may be written as

$$\prod_{i=1}^{j-1} Pr(S_1 > \alpha_0 + \alpha_1 E) \, Pr(S_j < \alpha_0 + \alpha_1 E) \qquad (11)$$

If each S_i is assumed to be distributed normally with mean zero, and variance σ_s^2, the probability statement may be written using the probit function

$$\left[\int_{\frac{\alpha_0 + \alpha_1 E}{\sigma_s}}^{\infty} \frac{1}{\sqrt{2\pi}} e^{-t^2/2} dt \right]^{j-1} \int_{-\infty}^{\frac{\alpha_0 + \alpha_1 E}{\sigma_s}} \frac{1}{\sqrt{2\pi}} e^{-t^2/2} dt \qquad (12)$$

If the S_i were assumed to be logistically distributed, a similar probability statement using cumulative logistics could easily be written.

If the S_i for all women are generated by the same random process, we may use the principle of maximum likelihood to estimate α_0/σ_s and α_1/σ_s by taking a sample of women with different birth intervals, and choosing parameter values which maximize the probability of observing the sample distribution of birth intervals.

Note, however, a crucial step in the argument. We assumed that over time, the S_i were independently distributed. This assumption rules out serial correlation in the S sequence. Such serial correlation may naturally arise if there are unmeasured random variables which remain at, or near, the same level over time for a given individual, but which are randomly distributed among individuals. For example, unmeasured components of fecundability (e.g., semen counts of husbands, tastes for coital activity, and variations in contraceptive efficiency) plausibly have a persistent component for the same individual across time periods although these components may vary widely among individuals.[20] Similarly, important economic variables may be missing in a given body of data.[21]

Following a convention in the analysis of covariance, we may decompose S_i into two components

$$S_i = U_i + \epsilon \qquad (13)$$

where U_i is a random variable with mean zero and variance σ_u^2, and

[20] The problem of heterogeneity is considered in a demographic context by Sheps (1964), Potter and Parker (1964), Sheps and Menken (1972), and Sheps and Menken (1973).

[21] In this paper, we abstract from the further problem that the unobserved components may be correlated with the included variables.

ϵ is a random variable with mean zero, and variance σ_ϵ^2. We further assume that

$$E(U_i U_j) = 0, \, i \neq j$$
$$E(U_i \epsilon) \; = 0, \, i = 1, \ldots, \infty \tag{14}$$

Then S_i is a random variable with mean

$$E(S_i) = 0 \tag{15}$$

and

$$E(S_i S_j) = \sigma_\epsilon^2, \, i \neq j$$
$$= \sigma_\epsilon^2 + \sigma_j^2, \, i = j \tag{16}$$

Thus, the correlation coefficient between S_i in any two periods ρ may be defined as

$$\rho = \frac{\sigma_\epsilon^2}{\sigma_\epsilon^2 + \sigma_u^2} \tag{17}$$

Clearly, it is possible to imagine more general intercorrelation relationships such as a first-order Markov process. These generalizations are straightforward and, since they are not of direct interest in this paper, are not pursued here.

If intercorrelation applies because there are persistent omitted variables, the probability of a woman becoming pregnant in interval j can no longer be written in the simple form of equation 10 (or if S is assumed normal, as in equation 12). To see what the appropriate probability statement becomes, note that, in general, we may write the probability of the event conditional on a given value of ϵ as

$$Pr(S_1 > \alpha_0 + \alpha_1 E, \ldots, S_{j-1} > \alpha_0 + \alpha_1 E, S_j < \alpha_0 + \alpha_1 E | \epsilon) \tag{18}$$

But note that if ϵ is held fixed, the distribution of S_1 conditional on $\epsilon = \tilde{\epsilon}$ must satisfy the following properties:

$$E(S_i | \tilde{\epsilon}) = \tilde{\epsilon},$$

$$E(S_i S_j | \tilde{\epsilon}) = \begin{cases} \tilde{\epsilon}^2, \, i \neq j \\ \\ \sigma_u^2 + \tilde{\epsilon}^2, \, i = j \end{cases} \tag{19}$$

and, since the U_i are independent, the conditional values of S_i are also independent. Then we see that

$$Pr(S_1 > \alpha_0 + \alpha_1 E, \ldots, S_{j-1} > \alpha_0 + \alpha_1 E, S_j < \alpha_0 + \alpha_1 E | \bar{\epsilon})$$

$$= Pr(S_1 > \alpha_0 + \alpha_1 E | \bar{\epsilon}) Pr(S_2 > \alpha_0 + \alpha_1 E | \bar{\epsilon}), \ldots,$$

$$Pr(S_j < \alpha_0 + \alpha_1 E | \bar{\epsilon}) \quad (20)$$

so that conditional on $\epsilon = \bar{\epsilon}$, we reach precisely the same functional form as in equation 11, where persistent omitted variables are ignored. However, to solve back to the probability statement of interest, where ϵ is permitted to vary between plus and minus infinity, we note that the *unconditional* probability may be written as

$$\int_{-\infty}^{\infty} Pr(S_1 > \alpha_0 + \alpha_1 E | \epsilon) Pr(S_2 > \alpha_0 + \alpha_1 E | \epsilon), \ldots,$$

$$Pr(S_j < \alpha_0 + \alpha_1 E | \epsilon) h(\epsilon) d\epsilon \quad (21)$$

where $h(\epsilon)$ is the marginal density function of ϵ, and ϵ is permitted to vary over all possible values, as before.

In the special case with S normally distributed with zero mean and variance $\sigma_\epsilon^2 + \sigma_u^2$, equation 21 becomes

$$\int_{-\infty}^{\infty} \left[\left[\int_{(\alpha_0 + \alpha_1 E)}^{\infty} \frac{1}{\sqrt{2\pi\sigma_u^2}} e^{-\frac{1}{2}\frac{(U-\epsilon)^2}{2\sigma_u^2}} \right]^{j-1} \left[\int_{-\infty}^{(\alpha_0 + \alpha_1 E)} \frac{1}{\sqrt{2\pi\sigma_u^2}} e^{-\frac{1}{2}\frac{(U-\epsilon)^2}{2\sigma_u^2}} du \right] \right.$$

$$\frac{1}{\sqrt{2\pi\sigma_\epsilon^2}} e^{-\epsilon^2/2\sigma_\epsilon^2} d\epsilon$$

Letting $t = \dfrac{U}{\sigma_u}$, and $q = \dfrac{\epsilon}{\sigma_\epsilon}$, and using the definition of ρ in equation 17, this integral may be written as

$$\int_{-\infty}^{\infty} \left[\left[\int_{\frac{\alpha_0^* + \alpha_1^* E + \rho^{1/2} q}{(1-\rho)^{1/2}}}^{\infty} \frac{1}{\sqrt{2\pi}} e^{-t^2/2} dt \right]^{j-1} \left[\int_{-\infty}^{\frac{\alpha_0^* + \alpha_1^* E + \rho^{1/2} q}{(1-\rho)^{1/2}}} \frac{1}{\sqrt{2\pi}} e^{-t^2/2} dt \right] \right.$$

$$\frac{1}{\sqrt{2\pi}} e^{-q^2/2} dq \quad (22)$$

where $\alpha_0^* = \dfrac{\alpha_0}{(\sigma_u^2 + \sigma_\epsilon^2)^{1/2}}$ and $\alpha_1^* = \dfrac{\alpha_1}{(\sigma_u^2 + \sigma_\epsilon^2)^{1/2}}$.

If no serial correlation is present ($\rho = 0$), this expression reduces to equation 12. In the more general case, ρ allows us to measure the proportion of total variance in the index explained by systematic correlated components.

Notice that there is an alternative "incidental parameters" argument that leads directly to equation 22. Suppose it is argued that in an ordinary probit model a disturbance "ϵ" appears. This may be viewed as an incidental parameter with density function $h(\epsilon)$. Following a suggestion of Kiefer and Wolfowitz (1956), the problem of incidental parameters has precisely the solution written in equation 21, and for the normal case this solution becomes equation 22. In a simple one-period probit model, such as one designed to explain the purchase of refrigerators in a cross section, the "incidental parameters" problem becomes irrelevant as long as the incidental parameter is normally distributed. Thus, if $j = 1$, equation 22 may be written as

$$\int_{-\infty}^{\alpha_0{}^*+\alpha_1{}^*E} \frac{1}{\sqrt{2\pi}}\, e^{-t^2/2}\, dt$$

so that correlated and temporally random components cannot have separate effects, as is intuitively obvious.

Yet another interpretation of these results is possible. An individual may be imagined as having a geometric probability process characterizing the probabilities of pregnancy at each interval for a given value of ϵ; "ϵ" is, in fact, a random variable governed by a density function $h(\epsilon)$. Then the true probability of pregnancy at month j is a continuous mixture of geometric processes and is given by equation 21.[22]

The Implications of Serial Correlation

In this section we demonstrate that estimates of the coefficients α_0^* and α_1^*, defined in the previous section, that are based on techniques which ignore serial correlation will, in general, be biased although it is not possible to know the sign of the bias. To see this, we first consider the case of no serial correlation.

In this case, the conditional probability of a woman of education level E becoming pregnant in interval j, given that she was not pregnant in the $j - 1$ previous intervals is

$$m_j = \frac{[Pr(S > \alpha_0 + \alpha_1 E)]^{j-1} Pr(S < \alpha_0 + \alpha_1 E)}{[Pr(S > \alpha_0 + \alpha_1 E)]^{j-1}} = Pr(S < \alpha_0 + \alpha_1 E) \tag{23}$$

and is clearly the same for all intervals $j = 1, 2, \ldots$. However, in the case of serial correlation, this conditional probability becomes

[22] For a discussion of mixtures, see Kendall and Stuart, Vol. I (1969), Pearson (1894), Quandt (1972), and Zellner (1973).

$$\tilde{m}_j = \frac{\int_{-\infty}^{\infty} [Pr(S > \alpha_0 + \alpha_1 E|\epsilon)]^{j-1} Pr(S < \alpha_0 + \alpha_1 E|\epsilon) h(\epsilon) d\epsilon}{\int_{-\infty}^{\infty} [Pr(S > \alpha_0 + \alpha_1 E|\epsilon)]^{j-1} h(\epsilon) d\epsilon} \tag{24}$$

Using the fact that $Pr(S < \alpha_0 + \alpha_1 E|\epsilon) = 1 - Pr(S > \alpha_0 + \alpha_1 E|\epsilon)$, the conditional probability $\tilde{m}_j$ becomes

$$\tilde{m}_j = 1 - \frac{\int_{-\infty}^{\infty} Pr(S > \alpha_0 + \alpha_1 E|\epsilon)^j h(\epsilon) d\epsilon}{\int_{-\infty}^{\infty} Pr(S > \alpha_0 + \alpha_1 E|\epsilon)^{j-1} h(\epsilon) d\epsilon} \tag{25}$$

It can be proved that the conditional monthly probability of conception declines for successive months. Using the fact that

$$\ln \int_{-\infty}^{\infty} [Pr(S > \alpha_0 + \alpha_1 E|\epsilon)]^j h(\epsilon) d\epsilon$$

is a convex function of j (Hardy, Polya, and Littlewood (1952)) the difference between two successive conditional probabilities of becoming pregnant is

$$\tilde{m}_{j+1} - \tilde{m}_j = \frac{\int_{-\infty}^{\infty} [Pr(S > \alpha_0 + \alpha_1 E|\epsilon)]^{j+1} h(\epsilon) d\epsilon}{\int_{-\infty}^{\infty} [Pr(S > \alpha_0 + \alpha_1 E|\epsilon)]^{j} h(\epsilon) d\epsilon}$$

$$- \frac{\int_{-\infty}^{\infty} [Pr(S > \alpha_1 + \alpha_1 E|\epsilon)]^{j} h(\epsilon) d\epsilon}{\int_{-\infty}^{\infty} [Pr(S > \alpha_0 + \alpha_1 E|\epsilon)]^{j-1} h(\epsilon) d\epsilon}$$

$$= \frac{\left\{ -\left[\int_{-\infty}^{\infty} [Pr(S > \alpha_0 + \alpha_1 E|\epsilon)]^j h(\epsilon) d\epsilon \right]^2 + \int_{-\infty}^{\infty} [Pr(S > \alpha_0 + \alpha_1 E|\epsilon)]^{j+1} h(\epsilon) d\epsilon \int_{-\infty}^{\infty} [Pr(S > \alpha_0 + \alpha_1 E|\epsilon)]^{j-1} h(\epsilon) d\epsilon \right\}}{\int_{-\infty}^{\infty} [Pr(S > \alpha_0 + \alpha_1 E|\epsilon)]^j h(\epsilon) d\epsilon \int_{-\infty}^{\infty} Pr[S > \alpha_0 + \alpha_1 E|\epsilon]^{j-1} h(\epsilon) d\epsilon} \tag{26}$$

The cited convexity result implies that

$$\ln \int_{-\infty}^{\infty} [Pr(S > \alpha_0 + \alpha_1 E|\epsilon)]^j h(\epsilon) d\epsilon \leq$$

$$\frac{1}{2} \ln \int_{-\infty}^{\infty} [Pr(S > \alpha_0 + \alpha_1 E|\epsilon)]^{j+1} h(\epsilon) d\epsilon$$

$$+ \frac{1}{2} \ln \int_{-\infty}^{\infty} [Pr(S > \alpha_0 + \alpha_1 E|\epsilon)]^{j-1} h(\epsilon) d\epsilon$$

Multiplying both sides by 2 and exponentiating, the numerator of expression 26 is seen to be negative, thus proving that successive conditional probabilities decline.

This phenomenon is depicted in Figure 5. The slope of the curve for the case of serial correlation is negative as shown, but the precise shape of the curve is only suggestive. A simple estimation method, such as logit or probit, applied to data on fertility outcomes imposes the constraint of constancy on conditional probabilities. It is intuitively obvious, and formally correct, that if persistence is important, but neglected in forming parameter estimates, a time trend that does not belong in the model might nonetheless prove statistically significant.

FIGURE 5

Monthly Probability of Conception as a Function of Duration
of Birth Interval

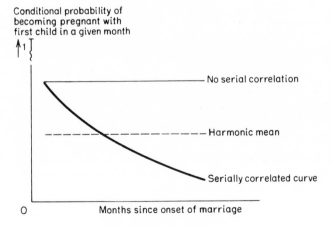

Conditional probability of becoming pregnant with first child in a given month

— No serial correlation

— Harmonic mean

— Serially correlated curve

0   Months since onset of marriage

Since serial correlation in ordinary regression models does not lead to bias in coefficient estimates, it is important to motivate why it leads to bias in our case. To show what is involved, consider specializing the simple model further so that there are only two education classes. Suppose, in particular, that E assumes the value of 0 or 1 corresponding to low or high levels of education. For each education class, we may estimate a monthly probability of becoming pregnant $P(i)$, where $i = 0$ for low-education women and $i = 1$ for high-education women. Given a functional form for the distribution of the S_t, $t = 1, \ldots, \infty$, we may solve $P(i)$ uniquely for α_0^* and α_1^*, so that a comparison of direct estimates of the $P(i)$ for the two education groups will give direct information on α_0^* and α_1^*.

Suppose estimates of $P(i)$ are formed neglecting serial correlation. This may be done in several ways, all of which lead to the same estimate. One way is to partition the data on length of time to first pregnancy by educational level, and estimate the average interval for each education class. The inverse of these two averages leads to estimates of the monthly probability of pregnancy assuming that serial correlation is absent. A second, and equivalent approach, is to maximize the sample likelihood for each education class.[23]

Note that these estimators are the correct maximum likelihood estimators, assuming no serial correlation. The procedure yields consistent estimators of mean lengths of duration to first pregnancy even in samples with serial correlation, since the population mean is the same for all observations and Khinchine's theorem readily applies.[24]

---

[23] Thus, in constructing this function, if a highly educated woman goes $l - 1$ months without pregnancy and becomes pregnant in the lth month, the probability of this event is

$$(1 - P(1))^{l-1}P(1)$$

Similarly, if the sample period is T months, a highly educated woman never gets pregnant with probability $(1 - P(1))^T$. Producting these probabilities associated with observed events, we reach the probability of the sample outcomes. Choosing a value of $P(1)$ which maximizes this probability yields maximum likelihood estimates of $P(1)$. Defining N_l as the number of women who become pregnant in month l,

$$\mathcal{L}(1) = [P(1)]^{N_1}[(1 - P(1)P(1))]^{N_2}[(1 - P(1))\,P(1)]^{N_3}, \ldots ,[(1 - P(1))]^{N_T}$$

where N_T is the number of women who do not become pregnant in the sample observation period. Thus maximizing $\mathcal{L}(1)$, or equivalently in $\mathcal{L}(1)$, the estimator for $P(1)$ is clearly

$$\hat{P}(1) = 1/\left(\sum_{i=1}^{T} \frac{N_i l}{N}\right), \text{ where } N = \sum_{i=1}^{T} N_i$$

i.e., the inverse of the average interval.

[24] For a statement and proof of Khinchine's theorem, see C. R. Rao (1965), p. 92.

However, in the presence of serial correlation, the mean length of duration is not simply related to any measure of direct interest. In fact, the inverse of the mean duration estimates the *harmonic* mean of the probabilities

$$Pr(S < \alpha_0 + \alpha_1 E | \epsilon)$$

over all values of ϵ. To see this, note that the mean duration to first pregnancy is simply

$$\int_{-\infty}^{\infty} \frac{1}{Pr(S < \alpha_0 + \alpha_1 E | \epsilon)} h(\epsilon) d\epsilon$$

so that the inverse of this is the harmonic mean

$$\left[\int_{-\infty}^{\infty} [Pr(S < \alpha_0 + \alpha_1 E | \epsilon)]^{-1} h(\epsilon) d\epsilon \right]^{-1}$$

We seek estimates of the arithmetic mean

$$\int_{-\infty}^{\infty} Pr(S < \alpha_0 + \alpha_1 E | \epsilon) h(\epsilon) d\epsilon$$

for each group ($E = 1$ or 0) to estimate the effect of education on the probabilities of birth. Since, in general, the difference in arithmetic means is different from the difference in harmonic means, estimators based on the harmonic means will be biased although it is not possible, in general, to sign the bias. The same argument applies if other explanatory variables apart from education are included as well.

In addition to solving problems of bias, direct estimation of the probabilities allows us to solve the problem of open intervals. If a given sample covers only a portion of a woman's reproductive history, it is likely that some portion of the sample will not conceive. For such women, the probability of this event is easily derived, and such data may be pooled in sample likelihood fashion with data from women who conceive. Thus no arbitrary assignment of interval length to nonconceiving women is necessary, as would be needed in an ad hoc regression study using interval length between marriage and first birth as the dependent variable.[25]

III. EMPIRICAL RESULTS

This section presents estimates of the monthly probability of conception in the first pregnancy interval following conception, using the

---

[25] Besides avoiding this ad hoc methodology, the procedure suggested in the paper provides an explicit approach to a derivation of theoretically appropriate test statistics, something lacking in the regression approximation approach.

econometric model developed in the preceding section. The data consist of a sample of white non-Catholic women, married once with husband present for 15 to 19 years, from the 1965 Princeton National Fertility Study.[26] The sample of all such women was reduced by eliminating women who reported premarital conceptions or who had missing values for relevant variables. The sample was then divided into two groups, contraceptors and noncontraceptors, on the basis of the woman's response to a question concerning the contraceptive methods she used before her first pregnancy (or in her current interval if she had not had a pregnancy). Summary statistics on the two groups are presented in Table 1, including the means and variances of the three independent variables (wife's education [W], wife's age [A], and husband's predicted income at age 40 [H]) whose influence on the monthly probability of conception is estimated.

Women in each subsample were "followed" for a maximum of 120 months, beginning with their first month of marriage. Among the noncontraceptors, we estimate the monthly probability of conception in the first pregnancy interval by estimating the parameters of an equation of the form of equation 22 in Section II by maximum likelihood methods.[27] That is, using the functional form of the likelihood function implied by equation 22, we estimate parameters which maximize the likelihood of observing the events that occurred in this subsample. These events are (1) that a given woman conceived in month $j(j = 1, \ldots, 120)$ or (2) that she went 120 months without conceiving. Among the contraceptors, we estimate in similar fashion the monthly probability of conception, given that the woman is contracepting. In this case, the events we observe are (1) that a woman conceives in month j while using a contraceptive; (2) that the woman uses a contraceptive for k months without conceiving, at which time she discontinues con-

---

[26] The 1965 National Fertility Study, conducted by Norman B. Ryder and Charles F. Westoff, is a cross-section national probability sample of 5,617 U.S. married women which is described in detail in Ryder and Westoff (1971). For our purposes, its most important characteristics are that it records (retrospectively) the date of marriage of the woman, the dates of each pregnancy termination, the use of contraception in each pregnancy interval, and the time of discontinuation of contraception prior to pregnancy, in addition to a number of household characteristics such as income and education.

[27] The methods used are described in Goldfeld and Quandt (1972, Ch. 1). Two algorithms, Powell and GRADX, were used in tandem to ensure that the estimates are stable. That is, in the first stage, the parameters of the likelihood function were estimated by the Powell method. These parameters were then given as initial values in a GRADX optimization procedure whose final parameter values are reported in this paper. The computer program, written by C. Ates Dagli and Ralph Shnelvar, is available from the authors on request.

TABLE 1

Mean and Variance of Independent Variables for Contraceptors
and Noncontraceptors in First Pregnancy Interval after Marriage [a]
(variance in parentheses)

	Noncontraceptors (N^{b} = 177)	Contraceptors (N^{b} = 246)
A: wife's age at marriage	257.1	252.3
(in months)	(2,746)	(1,687)
W: wife's education	11.2	12.2
	(6.3)	(4.6)
H: husband's predicted	7.58	8.17
income at age 40	(2.5)	(2.12)
($000's) [c]		

[a] Sample: White, non-Catholic women, married once for 15 to 19 years, no premarital conceptions and no missing values.

[b] N = number.

[c] Husband's predicted income is based on an estimated regression relationship between husband's income and his education and experience (i.e., age minus years of schooling minus 6) from data on all white non-Catholic men in the 1965 National Fertility Study sample for husbands. The variable H is then imputed for men in the current sample on the basis of the man's education, with age set arbitrarily at 40. Thus, H may be interpreted as a transformation of husband's education or as his permanent income, depending on the reader's preference.

traception (this decision is treated as an exogenous event); or (3) she continues using contraception for 120 months and does not conceive.[28]

Parameter estimates for the noncontraceptors are presented in Table 2, part A, and for contraceptors in Table 2, part B. In each group, we estimated six models which differ in the number of parameters estimated in order to determine the statistical significance of individual parameters or sets of parameters using likelihood ratio tests.[29]

Among these parameters, we have a particular interest in the magnitude of the serial correlation coefficient ρ, its statistical significance,

[28] As we noted in footnote 4, p. 106 our data only record whether a woman contracepted in a given pregnancy interval and when and if she discontinued contraception. They do not record when she began contracepting or any other interruptions in contraception other than the final decision to discontinue.

[29] A property of maximum likelihood estimation is that twice the difference in log likelihood between two equations (within set A or set B) is distributed as chi-squared with n degrees of freedom, where n is the difference in the number of parameters in the two equations.

TABLE 2

Estimates of Parameters of Model for Contraceptors and
Noncontraceptors in First Pregnancy Interval after Marriage

	Constant (α_0)	ρ	Wife's Age at Marriage (α_1)	Wife's Education (α_2)	Husband's Predicted Income (α_3)	Log_e Likelihood
A. Noncontraceptors						
(1)	2.016					−692.71
(1')	1.214	0.450				−619.50
(2)	1.154		0.0033			−680.42
(2')	0.172	0.426	0.0042			−613.36
(3)	1.022		0.0031	0.017	−0.0033	−679.80
(3')	0.132	0.426	0.0041	−0.004	0.0125	−613.33
B. Contraceptors						
(4)	2.264					−336.92
(4')	1.780	0.549				−319.43
(5)	1.307		0.0038			−332.42
(5')	0.646	0.531	0.0046			−316.32
(6)	1.072		0.0036	−0.0016	0.0387	−331.82
(6')	0.943	0.526	0.0042	−0.0068	0.0903	−314.89

and the influence of its inclusion or exclusion from the econometric model on the other parameters of the model (i.e., the constant term α_0 and the coefficients of A, W, and H, which are, respectively, α_1, α_2 and α_3). Accordingly, we present two estimates of each set of α's in Table 2, one in which ρ is constrained to be zero and one in which ρ is free to assume a nonzero value.

It is easy to see in Table 2 that ρ is positive and statistically significant in every instance.[30] Among the noncontraceptors, $\rho = 0.450$ when only the constant term is entered and falls to 0.426 when the wife's age at marriage is held constant. However, it does not fall any further when wife's education and husband's predicted income are added to the model. Similarly, the estimate of ρ in the contracepting subsample falls from 0.549 to 0.531 when A is held constant, and to 0.526 when W and H are also held constant. If we recall that the definition of ρ is

[30] Comparing lines (1) and (1') in Table 2, for example, we find that log likelihood rose from −692.71 to −619.50, a difference of 73.21. Twice the difference in log likelihood is 146.4, while the critical value of chi-squared with one degree of freedom at the .95 level is 4.6

the fraction of persistent variance (σ_ϵ^2) in total variance ($\sigma_\epsilon^2 + \sigma_u^2$), the decrease in ρ is easily understood as showing that the exogenous variable A in the noncontracepting subsample, and the variables A, H, and W in the contracepting subsample, contribute to the persistent component of variation in conception probabilities among women in the two subsamples. The small size of the decrease in ρ, however, also shows that the contribution of other factors which we have not held constant constitutes the major fraction of persistent variation. This suggests that it is unlikely that the heterogeneity problem can be overcome simply by holding constant a number of observable "control" variables.

The size of the decrease in ρ caused by the addition of exogenous variables is, of course, related to the statistical significance of these variables. The wife's age at marriage is the only variable to pass a test of statistical significance at conventional levels in either subsample.[31] Wife's education and husband's predicted income are utterly without effect on log likelihood in the noncontracepting subsample (e.g., the change in log likelihood from line (2′) to line (3′) is 0.03). This is not entirely surprising, because the channels through which education and income may affect the monthly probability of conception among noncontraceptors are essentially limited to correlations of these variables with health or coital frequency.

Our theory suggests that we should expect to find a larger impact of income and education on the monthly probability of conception among contraceptors. In this group, variation in conception probabilities is caused by variation in contraceptive efficiency due to differences in the techniques chosen and the care with which a given technique is used, as well as by variation in natural fecundability. Comparing lines (5′) and (6′), we find that the change in log likelihood is not completely trivial (twice the difference in log likelihood is 2.9), but it falls well below conventional levels of significance.[32]

Estimates of the monthly probability of conception and the effects of changes in exogenous variables on that probability differ substantially depending on whether or not serial correlation is taken into account. In Table 3, we present examples of estimates of levels and

[31] Twice the change in log likelihood from line (1′) to line (2′) for noncontraceptors is 12.1, and the corresponding change from line (4′) to line (5′) for contraceptors is 6.2, both of which exceed the 0.95 confidence level. Wife's age is also significant in the equations in which ρ is constrained to equal zero.

[32] The critical value of chi-squared with two added parameters is 6.0 at the 0.95 level. Since the critical value with one added parameter is 4.6, it is clear that neither H nor W would be significant if entered alone into the equation.

changes in the monthly probability of conception among noncontra-ceptors and contraceptors with and without ρ constrained to equal zero. These estimates are derived from the parameter estimates in Table 2. Before turning to Table 3, it will be helpful to show how the estimates in Table 3 are derived from those in Table 2 and how they are to be interpreted in light of our statistical discussion in Section II.

When ρ is constrained to equal zero, we proved in Section II that the resulting estimate of the monthly probability of conception is an unbiased estimate of the harmonic means of the conception probabil-ities of the individual women in the sample. Let the harmonic mean be $\bar{p}$ for noncontraceptors and $\bar{p}^*$ for contraceptors. If ρ were truly equal to zero (i.e., if all women in a sample had identical conception probabilities), then the harmonic means would equal the arithmetic means of the two groups, $\tilde{p}$ and $\tilde{p}^*$. If we are interested in measuring the arithmetic means, the difference between $\tilde{p}$ and $\bar{p}$ (or between $\tilde{p}^*$ and $\bar{p}^*$) measures the bias caused by ignoring serial correlation.

In order to make this comparison, it is necessary to evaluate $\tilde{p}$ and $\tilde{p}^*$ at the beginning of the first month of marriage. The reason for this is that when serial correlation is present, the conditional probability of conception in month j of the subsample of women who have gone $j - 1$ months without conceiving is smaller the larger is j, because the most fecund women tend to be selected out of the original sample by conceiving in the early months of the interval.

The derivation of estimates of $\tilde{p}$ and $\tilde{p}^*$ evaluated at the outset of marriage from the parameter estimates in Table 2 is straightforward. We need only read off the appropriate values from a table of the standard normal integral. If we consider line (1′) in Table 2, for ex-ample, then $(1 - \bar{p})$, the monthly probability of not conceiving among noncontraceptors in the first month of marriage is

$$1 - \bar{p} = \int_{-\infty}^{\alpha_0 = 1.214} \frac{1}{\sqrt{2\pi}} e^{-t_2/2} dt = .887$$

so that $\bar{p} = .113$, the value which is entered in line 1(b) in Table 3, part A. When serial correlation is not allowed, the value of α_0 in the upper limit of the integral is 2.016 (see line (1) in Table 2) so that $\tilde{p} = .022$, the value which is entered in line 1(a) of Table 3, part A. Thus, we see that bias from not considering serial correlation is quite large. Similarly, in lines 2(b) and 2(a) of Table 3 we see that the arith-metic mean monthly probability of conception among contraceptors is $\tilde{p}^* = .038$ and the harmonic mean is $\bar{p}^* = .012$.

TABLE 3

Estimates of Monthly Probability of Conception Derived from
Parameter Estimates in Table 2

	Harmonic Mean ($\bar{p}$ or $\bar{p}^*$) with Serial Correlation Ignored ($\rho = 0$) (a)	Arithmetic Mean ($\bar{p}$ or $\bar{p}^*$) with Serial Correlation Allowed ($\rho > 0$) (b)
A. Model with constant term only (α_0)		
1. Noncontraceptors	.022	.113
2. Contraceptors	.012	.038
B. Effect of wife's age at marriage (model with α_0, α_1)		
Noncontraceptors		
3. Age 20	.026	.122
4. Age 21	.023	.111
5. Age 30	.010	.048
Contraceptors		
6. Age 20	.013	.040
7. Age 21	.012	.035
8. Age 30	.004	.010
C. Effect of wife's education [a] (contraceptors only)		
9. $W = 8$	.014	.046
10. $W = 12$	.015	.048
11. $W = 16$	.015	.052
D. Effect of husband's predicted [b] income (contraceptors only)		
12. $H = 3$	.023	.097
13. $H = 7$	.015	.052
14. $H = 10$	.011	.027

[a] These estimates are obtained from parameter estimates of models with α_0, α_1, α_2, α_3 by setting $A = 20$ and $H = 7$.

[b] These estimates are obtained from parameter estimates of models with α_0, α_1, α_2, α_3 by setting $A = 20$ and $W = 12$.

In Table 3, part B we evaluate the monthly probability of conception for several values of wife's age at marriage for noncontraceptors and contraceptors with and without ρ constrained to be zero from parameter estimates in lines (2), (2'), (5) and (5') in Table 2. Here, we notice that the effect of increased wife's age is to reduce the probability of conception in both groups, and that this negative effect is markedly greater when serial correlation is taken into account. There is some evidence from these estimates that failure to account for serial correlation results in downward biased estimates of contraceptive efficiency, e. Recall from Section I, that we defined the monthly probability of conception while contracepting as $p^* = p(1 - e)$, from which it follows that $e = 1 - p^*/p$. Using the estimates for 20-year-old women in lines 3(a) and 6(a) in Table 3, we may compute contraceptive efficiency as $e = 1 - \bar{p}^*/\bar{p} = .5$, when ρ is constrained equal to zero, while, from estimates in lines 3(b) and 6(b), we compute $e = 1 - \bar{p}^*/\bar{p} = .67$, when ρ is unconstrained.[33]

In parts C and D of Table 3, we evaluate the ceteris paribus effects of variations in wife's education and husband's predicted income on the probability of conception among contraceptors, using the parameter estimates contained in lines (6) and (6') of Table 2.[34] The most notable features of these estimates are that husband's predicted income appears to have a large negative impact on $\bar{p}^*$, suggesting that higher husband's income is associated with improved contraceptive efficiency, while wife's education has, if anything, a slight positive effect on $\bar{p}^*$.

This finding, if it is not simply a result of imprecision in our parameter estimates, is rather surprising because it is wife's education that has been found repeatedly to have a substantial negative impact on completed fertility, while husband's predicted income has a weaker, nonmonotonic effect (see, for example, Willis, 1973). However, it should also be noted that Michael and Willis, in their paper in this volume, have found that husband's predicted income has a significantly positive effect on the probability that couples used the highly effective oral contraceptive pill in the period 1960–64, while wife's education had a weaker, nonmonotonic effect on this probability.

[33] The absolute values of e should not be taken too seriously, because it is quite likely that the natural fecundability, p, of noncontraceptors is lower than that of contraceptors, since one of the reasons for not contracepting is subfecundity or sterility. A more complete econometric model would allow for the decision to contracept to be determined simultaneously with the monthly probability of conception in order to reduce or eliminate this selection bias.

[34] It should be emphasized that neither W nor H was statistically significant and, therefore, that little confidence may be placed in the magnitude or signs of their effects.

While both our finding and the Michael-Willis finding are based on data from the 1965 National Fertility Study, their samples and ours are independent.[35] Moreover, estimates of completed fertility equations from 1965 NFS data yield very similar results to those estimated by Willis (1973) from 1960 Census data. These apparently contradictory effects of husband's income and wife's education on completed fertility and contraceptive efficiency present a puzzle. Hopefully, future research will determine whether the apparent contradiction is genuine and, if so, how to resolve it.

REFERENCES

Becker, Gary S. "An Economic Analysis of Fertility." In *Demographic and Economic Change in Developed Countries*. New York: NBER, 1960.

———. "A Theory of the Allocation of Time." *Economic Journal* 75 (September 1965): 493–517.

Becker, Gary S., and Lewis, H. Gregg. "On the Interaction Between the Quantity and Quality of Children." *The Journal of Political Economy* 81 (March/April 1973): 279–288.

Ben-Porath, Yoram. "Short Term Fluctuations in Fertility and Economic Activity in Israel." *Demography* 10 (May 1973): 185–204.

Ben-Porath, Yoram, and Welch, Finis. *Chance, Child Traits, and Choice of Family Size*. R-1117-NIH/RF. Santa Monica, Calif.: RAND Corporation, December, 1972.

Goldfeld, Stephen, and Quandt, Richard. *Nonlinear Methods in Econometrics*. Amsterdam-London: North-Holland, 1972.

Hardy, G. H.; Polya, G.; and Littlewood, J. E. *Inequalities*. 2nd ed. Cambridge: Cambridge University Press, 1952.

Kendall, Maurice, and Stuart, Alan. *The Advanced Theory of Statistics*. Vol. I. New York: Hafner Publishing, 1969.

Keyfitz, Nathan. "How Birth Control Affects Births." *Social Biology* 18 (June 1971): 109–121.

Kiefer, J., and Wolfowitz, J. "Consistency of the Maximum Likelihood Estimator in the Presence of Infinitely Many Incidental Parameters." *Annals of Mathematical Statistics* 27 (December 1956): 887–906.

McCabe, James, and Sibley, David. "Economic Determinants of Life Cycle Fertility." Yale Economic Growth Center, October 1973, processed.

Michael, Robert T., and Willis, Robert. "Contraception and Fertility: Household Production Under Uncertainty." NBER Working Paper No. 21, December 1973. This volume.

Mincer, Jacob, and Polachek, Solomon. "Family Investments in Human Capital: Earnings of Women." *Journal of Political Economy* 82, supplement (March/April 1974): S96–S108.

Pearson, K. "Contributions to the Mathematical Theory of Evolution: Dissection of Frequency Curves." *Philosophical Transactions of the Royal Society*, Series A, Vol. 185, 1894.

Perrin, Edward, and Sheps, Mindel C. "Human Reproduction: A Stochastic Process." *Biometrics* 20 (March 1964): 28–45.

[35] Our sample consists of women whose first birth interval began in 1946–1950, while their sample consists of women who were married, had their first birth, or had their second birth, in the period 1960–1964.

Potter, R. G., and Parker, M.P. "Predicting the Time Required to Conceive." *Population Studies* 18 (1964): 99–116.

Quandt, Richard. "New Methods for Estimating Switching Regressions," *Journal of the American Statistical Association,* June 1972.

Rao, C. R. *Linear Statistical Inference and its Applications.* New York: John Wiley & Sons, 1965.

Ryder, Norman B., and Westoff, Charles F. *Reproduction in the United States 1965.* Princeton: Princeton University Press, 1971.

Sanderson, Warren, and Willis, Robert J. "Economic Models of Fertility: Some Examples and Implications." In *New Directions in Economic Research.* 51st Annual Report of the National Bureau of Economic Research. New York, NBER, 1971, pp. 32–42.

Schultz, Theodore W., ed. "New Economic Approaches to Fertility." NBER, Conference volume OC #6, printed as *Journal of Political Economy* 81, Supplement (March/April 1973).

Sheps, Mindel C. "On the Time Required for Contraception." *Population Studies* 18 (July 1964): 85–97.

Sheps, Mindel C., and Menken, Jane A. "On Estimating the Risk of Conception from Censored Data." In T. N. E. Greville, ed., *Population Dynamics.* New York: Academic Press, 1972, pp. 167–200.

———. *Mathematical Models of Conception and Birth.* Chicago: University of Chicago Press, 1973.

Simon, Julian L. "The Effect of Income and Education Upon Successive Births." University of Illinois, 1973, processed.

Willis, Robert J. "A New Approach to the Economic Theory of Fertility Behavior." *Journal of Political Economy* 81 supplement (March/April 1973): pp. S14–S64.

Zellner, A., "Bayesian and Non-Baysesian Analysis of the Regression Model with Multivariate Student-t Error Terms." May 1973, unpublished.

Comments on "Estimation of a Stochastic Model of Reproduction: An Econometric Approach" *

DANIEL McFADDEN

UNIVERSITY OF CALIFORNIA, BERKELEY

JAMES HECKMAN and Robert Willis have embarked on a program of research that extends economic rationality to the bedroom and promises to make them the Masters and Johnson of economics. Their paper contains some ingenious ideas for modeling and estimation; ideas that are potentially useful in other areas of economics where discrete choices or outcomes occur. On the other hand, the authors' empirical results are not an unmixed success, and fail to establish that the technology of childbearing is a fertile area for application of the theory of rational behavior. The lack of significance of economic factors in explaining fecundability suggests that this paper may be approaching the outer limits of the universe of the new home economics.

My discussion will be divided into three parts. First, I shall comment on the modeling of the childbearing technology. Second, I shall make a few observations on the statistical methods developed in the paper. Third, I shall comment on the empirical results.

A. MODELING FECUNDABILITY

The authors stress the sequential, uncertain nature of contraception and childbearing decisions and suggest that a realistic model of the reproductive history of the household must take into account the stream of incoming information on child quality, income, and occupational opportunities. Second, the authors emphasize the imperfection of contraceptive techniques and their cost, which suggests that particular stress must be placed empirically on contraceptive method and regularity of use. Third, the authors recognize the importance of

---

* This comment was prepared after extensive discussions with Donald Sant of the University of California, Berkeley, who is responsible for the empirical results reported here.

variation across the population in "natural" fertility and the role such variability plays in determining the way to model behavior and what statistical methods to adopt.

It is only with respect to the last point that the authors have fully succeeded in achieving the theoretical desiderata in their empirical analysis. Neither the consumer's optimization model written down by the authors to motivate the estimated equations nor the choice of independent variables in the empirical analysis conforms well to a model of sequential information gathering. For example, predicted income at age 40 is used as an independent variable in the empirical analysis; the possibility is precluded that information on income evolves over the first ten years of marriage. Second, the authors make no use of the choice-of-technique data in the National Fertility Study, distinguishing only contraceptors and noncontraceptors. The decision to contracept and, if so, what technique to use should be thought of as behavior jointly determined with the monthly probability of conception. There are no conceptual problems, although there may be statistical ones, involved in looking at monthly probabilities of conception conditioned on the decision to contracept, as the authors do now. One could, in fact, go further and look at these probabilities conditioned on choice of technique. However, this analysis leaves the decision to contracept unexplained.

One can formulate a model of the joint events of choice of contraceptive technique j (with no contraception being one alternative, $j = 0$) and conception, with the schematic form

$$(1) \quad \begin{bmatrix} \text{Probability} \\ \text{of choosing} \\ \text{contraceptive} \\ \text{technique } j \end{bmatrix} = f \left(\begin{bmatrix} \text{Socio-} \\ \text{economic} \\ \text{variables} \end{bmatrix}, \begin{bmatrix} \text{Costs of each} \\ \text{contraceptive} \\ \text{technique} \end{bmatrix}, \begin{bmatrix} \text{Natural} \\ \text{fecund-} \\ \text{ability} \end{bmatrix}, \right.$$

$$\left. \begin{bmatrix} \text{Reliability} \\ \text{of each} \\ \text{contraceptive} \\ \text{technique} \end{bmatrix}, \begin{bmatrix} \text{Safety of each} \\ \text{contraceptive} \\ \text{technique} \end{bmatrix}, \begin{bmatrix} \text{Nuisance} \\ \text{cost of each} \\ \text{contraceptive} \\ \text{technique} \end{bmatrix}, \ldots \right)$$

$$(2) \quad \begin{bmatrix} \text{Monthly} \\ \text{probability} \\ \text{of conception} \\ \text{conditioned on} \\ \text{contraceptive} \\ \text{technique} \end{bmatrix} = g \left(\begin{bmatrix} \text{Socio-} \\ \text{economic} \\ \text{variables} \end{bmatrix}, \begin{bmatrix} \text{Choice of} \\ \text{contra-} \\ \text{ceptive} \\ \text{technique} \end{bmatrix}, \begin{bmatrix} \text{Natural} \\ \text{fecund-} \\ \text{ability} \end{bmatrix}, \ldots \right)$$

Equation 1 gives the frequencies of choosing alternative contraceptive techniques in the subpopulation facing specified values of the right-hand-side variables. Equation 2, the one considered by the authors, gives the monthly probability of conception for the subpopulation with a specified natural fecundability who choose specific contraceptive techniques. Natural fecundability is unobserved. One can think of generating a sample by first specifying the observed socioeconomic variables and characteristics of contraceptive techniques; second, drawing a natural fecundability level from the distribution of this variable in the subpopulation with the observed independent variables; third, drawing a contraceptive technique from the multinomial distribution with probabilities given by equation 1, and fourth, drawing sequentially from the negative binomial distribution with probabilities given by equation 2 until pregnancy occurs, or the experiment period ends. This description could be formalized to yield a likelihood function from which maximum likelihood estimators of the parameters of the functions in equations 1 and 2 could be obtained. It should be noted that consideration of equation 2 above may lead to statistical difficulties unless the event of the choice of contraceptive technique is independent of natural fecundability.

B. STATISTICAL METHODS

The authors' treatment of variation of natural fertility in the population and their development of statistical methods to fit this structure deserve special commendation. There has been a tendency in the new home economics to emulate the traditional practice in consumer theory: treating the choices of a population as if they were generated by a single "representative" consumer. Thus, for example, a model of choice of number of children is postulated with a representative consumer demanding, say, 2.2 children, with price and income elasticities determined by the usual marginal calculations. In fact, the population is made up of some families with two children and some with three, depending on tastes, and the effect of price and income changes is at the *extensive* margin, where families switch from two to three. Heckman and Willis do a great service by abandoning this tradition of the representative consumer and modeling explicitly the binary nature of the observed outcome.

An important aspect of this work is the recognition of variability of natural fecundability across women and (to a lesser extent) across time for the same woman. The authors introduce a "components of variance" structure to account for this unobservable effect; one of the most interesting of the empirical findings is the confirmation of the existence of these differences. It should be pointed out that this topic is one of considerable current interest. Recent related papers have been circulated by Gary Chamberlain and Zvi Griliches [2], Arthur Goldberger [3], and Robert Hall [4].

The normally distributed error components assumed by the authors lead to their forbidding equation 22, giving the monthly probability of conception. Alternative distributional assumptions are equally plausible and lead to forms which are easier to analyze and utilize in iterative statistical procedures. Let $P(\alpha, \epsilon)$ denote the monthly probability of *not* conceiving, where α is a term summarizing the observed socioeconomic factors and ϵ is unobserved natural fecundability. Let $h(\epsilon)$ denote the frequency distribution of ϵ in the population. Then, the probability of *not* conceiving for j months is given by

$$Q_j = \int_0^\infty P(\alpha, \epsilon)^j h(\epsilon) d\epsilon$$

Now suppose that $P(\alpha, \epsilon) = e^{-\alpha - \epsilon}$, where $\alpha > 0$, $\epsilon > 0$, and suppose that ϵ has a gamma distribution with mean one and variance v,

$$h(\epsilon) = \frac{v^{-1/v} \epsilon^{(1/v)-1} e^{-\epsilon/v}}{\Gamma(1/v)}$$

Then,

$$Q_j = \frac{\int_0^\infty e^{-j\alpha - j\epsilon} v^{-1/v} \epsilon^{(1/v)-1} e^{-\epsilon/v} d\epsilon}{\Gamma(1/v)} = \frac{e^{-j\alpha}}{(1+jv)^{1/v}}$$

The monthly probability of conception is then

$$P_j = Q_j - Q_{j+1} = \frac{e^{-j\alpha}}{(1+jv)^{1/v}} - \frac{e^{-(j+1)\alpha}}{(1+(j+1)v)^{1/v}}$$

While this expression is quite nonlinear in v and α, it avoids the difficulties of manipulating integrals and performing numerical integration. For example, one easily sees that the conditional probability of *not* becoming pregnant in period j,

$$Q_{j+1}/Q_j = \frac{e^{-\alpha}}{\left(1 + \dfrac{v}{1+jv}\right)^{1/v}}$$

increases as j increases if, and only if, $v > 0$.

C. EMPIRICAL RESULTS

In the joint determination of the technique of contraception and the occurrence of pregnancy outlined earlier in these comments, it is clear that economic choice, conditioned on costs and socioeconomic characteristics, will influence primarily the choice of contraceptive technique. Except for socioeconomic influences on coital frequency, one would expect the monthly probability of conception to be biologically determined, and to display the "serial correlation" effect associated by the authors with variations in natural fecundability across the population. The authors' empirical results tend to confirm these expectations. Only age of wife is significant among socioeconomic variables, probably because it influences the distribution of natural fecundability. The "serial correlation" effect is highly significant.

The family choice of contraceptive technique, not investigated by the authors, promises to be a much more fruitful ground for investigating economic influences on fertility. If this relation failed to exhibit a dependence on socioeconomic factors, expected and completed family sizes would also be independent of these factors. But there is considerable evidence that socioeconomic factors *are* important in determining fertility (see T. Schultz [6]). I conclude these comments by reporting on some further estimates of the relation between socioeconomic factors and expected family size obtained by Donald Sant of the University of California. These estimates confirm the importance of education and income in influencing the expectation of having additional children, and provide indirect evidence that families form expectations on conception probabilities that depend on socioeconomic factors via the choice of contraceptive technique.

The sample consists of families drawn from the Survey of Economic Opportunity according to the following criteria: residence in twelve identifiable SMSA's, intact family, age of mother between 18 and 35, and family income $4,000 or more. Binary logit models were fitted to individual observations by the maximum likelihood method for the subsamples of families having two, three, or four children, with the dependent variable being a response from the mother that she expected to have one or more additional children. The results are given in Table 1. All independent variables are dichotomized, and standard errors are given in parentheses. The coefficients of each type of socioeconomic variable (sex ratio, education of wife, family income) are constrained to sum to zero. With respect to family income, the results show a consistent drop in the probability of expecting additional children at high incomes. presumably because of the opportunity cost

TABLE 1

Dependent Variable: Expect to Have an Additional Child; Model:
Maximum Likelihood Estimation of Binary Logit Model

Independent Variable	Current Number of Children		
	2	3	4
Constant	−.761	−1.364	−1.131
	(.233)	(.327)	(.488)
Sex ratio of current family			
0 boys	.032	.438	.946
	(.191)	(.316)	(.716)
1 boy	−.214	−.213	.068
	−	−	−
2 boys	.182	−.630	−.899
	(.192)	(.282)	(.413)
3 boys	−	.405	.038
		(.352)	(.437)
4 boys	−	−	−.017
			(.767)
Education of wife			
Less than 12 years	−.469	−.748	.050
	(.257)	(.340)	(.386)
12 years	−.204	.086	.448
	−	−	−
13–15 years	.338	.056	−.498
	(.268)	(.440)	(.517)
More than 15 years	.335	.606	−
	(.352)	(.480)	
Family Income			
$4,000 to $8,000	.205	.393	−.672
	(.227)	(.353)	(.491)
$8,000 to $12,000	.288	.219	1.016
	−	−	−
Over $12,000	−.493	−.612	−.344
	(.369)	(.569)	(.783)
Race			
Black	−.165	−.290	.400
	(.147)	(.185)	(.275)
Sample size	324	247	163

NOTE: Standard errors are in parentheses.

of having children and the income effect on the demand for expensive effective contraceptive techniques. A clear economic disincentive to large lower-income families also appears. Wife's education shows little consistent relation to the expectation of more children, although the results for families with two or three children suggest that the expectation may rise with education, contrary to the usual conclusion that opportunity cost of children rises with education. It would be interesting to isolate the employment opportunities of the wife from wife's education in assessing this effect. Sex ratio appears to be an important determinant of the expectation to have more children in a large family, with an imbalance of either sex tending to increase the expectation. In a family with three children, having at least one child of each sex is a significant disincentive to additional children. There is some proboy bias in three-child families, in that the sum of the coefficients in predominantly (two or three) boy families is negative. Similar conclusions hold for families with four children; there is a significant incentive to expect additional children in a no-boy family.

These empirical results tend to support the conclusion that fertility decisions are sequential, depending on cumulative information such as sex ratio; and are significantly influenced by income, and to a lesser degree, by education. Since contraceptive technique is the instrument by which families can control family size, these results suggest that the authors' methods applied to the choice of technique relation should yield significant results. The theoretical and statistical tools developed by the authors offer the possibility of fruitful and revealing glimpses into the economic determinants of these aspects of sexual behavior.

REFERENCES

[1] Ben-Porath, Yoram, and Welch, Finis. "Uncertain Quality: Sex of Children and Family Size." Santa Monica, Calif.: RAND Corporation, 1972.

[2] Chamberlain, Gary, and Griliches, Zvi. "Unobservables with a Variance–Components Structure: Ability, Schooling, and the Economic Success of Brothers." *International Economic Review*, June 1975: 422–449.

[3] Goldberger, Arthur. "Unobservable Variables in Econometrics." In Paul Zarembka, ed., *Frontiers in Econometrics*. New York: Academic Press, 1973.

[4] Hall, Robert. "On the Statistical Theory of Unobserved Components." Massachusetts Institute of Technology, 1973, processed.

[5] McFadden, Daniel. "Conditional Logit Analysis of Qualitative Choice Behavior." In P. Zarembka, ed., *Frontiers in Econometrics*. New York: Academic Press, 1973.

[6] Schultz, Theodore W., ed. *New Economic Approaches to Fertility*. NBER, Conference Volume OC #6, printed as *Journal of Political Economy* 81, supplement (March/April 1973).

The Correlation between Health and Schooling*

MICHAEL GROSSMAN

GRADUATE CENTER OF THE CITY UNIVERSITY OF NEW YORK
AND NATIONAL BUREAU OF ECONOMIC RESEARCH

THE relationship between health status and socioeconomic conditions is a subject of increasing concern for both medicine and social science. Several recent studies in the United States indicate that among socioeconomic variables, years of formal schooling completed is probably the most important correlate of good health (Stockwell 1963; Fuchs 1965; Hinkle et al. 1968; Kitagawa and Hauser 1968; Auster, Leveson, and Sarachek 1969; Breslow and Klein 1971; Grossman 1972b; Silver 1972). This finding emerges whether health levels are measured by mortality rates, morbidity rates, or self-evaluation of health status, and whether the units of observation are individuals or groups. The relationship is usually statistically significant at levels of confidence of .05 or better in both simple and partial correlations.

This paper has two purposes. The first is to develop a methodological framework that can be used to introduce and discuss alternative explanations of the correlation between health and schooling. The second is to test these explanations empirically in order to select the most relevant ones and to obtain quantitative estimates of different effects. The empirical work is limited to one unique body of data and uses two measures of health that are far from ideal. The methodological framework can, however, serve as a point of departure for future research when longitudinal samples with more refined measures of current and past health and background characteristics become available.

In a broad sense, the observed positive correlation between health

* Research for this paper was supported by PHS Grant Number 5 P01 HS 00451 from the Bureau of Health Services Research and Evaluation. I owe a special debt to Victor R. Fuchs for urging me to investigate the relationship between health and schooling in detail and for interacting with me many times while I was working on the paper. I should also like to thank Gary S. Becker, Barry R. Chiswick, Reuben Gronau, F. Thomas Juster, William M. Landes, Robert T. Michael, Jacob Mincer, Melvin W. Reder, James P. Smith, Finis Welch, and Robert J. Willis for helpful comments and suggestions; and Carol Breckner, Janice Platt, and Elizabeth H. Rand for research assistance.

and schooling may be explained in one of three ways. The first argues that there is a causal relationship that runs from increases in schooling to increases in health. The second holds that the direction of causality runs from better health to more schooling. The third argues that no causal relationship is implied by the correlation. Instead, differences in one or more "third variables," such as physical and mental ability and parental characteristics, affect both health and schooling in the same direction.

It should be noted that these three explanations are not mutually exclusive and can be used to rationalize any observed correlation between two variables. But from both a public policy and a theoretical point of view, it is important to distinguish among them and to obtain quantitative estimates of their relative magnitudes. A stated goal of public policy in the United States is to improve the level of health of the population or of certain groups in the population. Given this goal and given the high correlation between health and schooling, it might appear that one method of implementing it would be to increase government outlays on schooling. In fact, Auster, Leveson, and Sarachek (1969) suggest that the rate of return on increases in health via higher schooling outlays far exceeds the rate of return on increases in health via higher medical care outlays. This argument assumes that the correlation between health and schooling reflects only the effect of schooling on health. If, however, the causality ran the other way or if the third-variable hypothesis were relevant, then increased outlays on schooling would not accomplish the goal of improved health.

From a theoretical point of view, recent new approaches to demand theory assume that consumers produce all their basic objects of choice, called commodities, with inputs of market goods and services and their own time (Becker 1965; Lancaster 1966; Muth 1966; Michael 1972; Ghez and Becker 1973; Michael and Becker 1973). Within the context of the household production function model, there are compelling reasons for treating health and schooling as jointly determined variables. It is reasonable to assume that healthier students are more efficient producers of additions to the stock of knowledge, or human capital, via formal schooling. If so, then they would tend to increase the quantity of investment in knowledge they demand as well as the number of years they attend school. Similarly, the efficiency with which individuals transform medical care and other inputs into better health might rise with schooling. This would tend to create a positive correlation between schooling and the quantity of health demanded. Moreover, genetic and early childhood environmental factors might be important determinants of both health and intelligence.[1] Since intelligence and parental characteristics are key variables in the demand curve for schooling, the estimated effect of schooling on health would, under certain conditions, be biased if relevant third variables were omitted from the demand curve for health.[2]

The plan of this paper is as follows. In Section I, I formulate a recursive system whose two fundamental equations are demand curves for health and schooling. The former equation is based on a model of the demand for health that I have developed in previous work (Grossman 1972a, 1972b). The system as a whole is similar to those that have been used by Bowles (1972); Griliches and Mason (1972); Lillard (1973); and Leibowitz (1974) to study relationships among schooling, ability, and earnings. In Section II, I describe the empirical implementation of the model to data contained in the NBER-Thorndike sample, and in Section III, I present empirical estimates. In Section IV, I expand the model by treating current health and current market wage rates as simultaneously determined variables and show the results of estimating wage and health functions by two-stage least squares. Finally, in Section V, I examine the mortality experience of the NBER-Thorndike sample between 1955 and 1969.

I. THE MODEL

A. Demand Curve for Health

Elsewhere (Grossman 1972a, 1972b), I have constructed and estimated a model of the demand for health. For the purpose of this paper, it will be useful to summarize this model and to comment on the nature of the reduced-form demand curve for health capital that it generates. As a point of departure, I assume that individuals inherit an initial stock of health which depreciates with age, and which can be increased by investment. By definition, net investment in the stock of health equals gross investment minus depreciation:

$$H_{t+1} - H_t = I_t - \delta_t H_t \qquad (1)$$

where H_t is the stock of health at age t, I_t is gross investment, and δ_t is the rate of depreciation. Direct inputs into the production of gross

---

[1] Early childhood environment is shaped, to a large extent, by parental characteristics such as schooling, family income, and socioeconomic status.

[2] The effect of schooling on the health of adults would not be biased by the omission of third variables if one had a perfect measure of their health during the years that they attended school, and if schooling were the only determinant of the efficiency of nonmarket production. For a complete discussion of this point, see Section I, part B.

investments in health include the time expenditure of the consumer, medical care, proper diet, housing facilities, and other market goods and services as well.

In the model, consumers demand health for two reasons. As a consumption commodity, it directly enters their utility functions, or put differently, illness is a source of disutility. As an investment commodity, it determines the total amount of time available for work in the market sector of the economy, where consumers produce money earnings, and for work in the nonmarket or household sector, where they produce commodities that enter their utility functions. The investment motive for demanding health is present because an increase in the stock of health lowers the amount of time lost from market and nonmarket activities in any given period, say a year, due to illness and injury. The monetary value of this reduction in lost time measures the return to an investment in health.

In much of my work, I have ignored the consumption aspects of the demand for health and have developed in detail a pure investment version of the general model.[3] The pure investment model generates powerful predictions from simple analysis and innocuous assumptions and also emphasizes the difference between health capital and other forms of human capital. In particular, persons demand knowledge capital because it influences their market and nonmarket productivity. On the other hand, they demand health capital because it produces an output of healthy time that can then be allocated to the production of money earnings and commodities. Since the output of health capital has a finite upper limit of 8,760 hours in a year (365 days times 24 hours per day), the marginal product of this capital diminishes. This suggests a healthy-time production function of the form

$$h_t = 8{,}760 - BH_t^{-C} \tag{2}$$

where h_t is healthy time and B and C are positive constants. From (2), the marginal product of health capital would be

$$G_t = (\partial h_t/\partial H_t) = BCH_t^{-C-1} \tag{3}$$

In the pure investment model, given constant marginal cost of gross investment in health, the equilibrium stock of health at any age can be determined by equating the marginal monetary rate of return on health capital to the opportunity cost of this capital. If W_t is the hourly wage rate, and if π_t is the marginal cost of gross investment in health,

---

[3] In the pure investment model, the marginal utility of healthy time or the marginal disutility of sick time equals zero.

then the rate of return or the marginal efficiency of health capital can be defined as

$$\gamma_t = W_t \, G_t / \pi_t \tag{4}$$

In equilibrium,

$$\gamma_t = r - \tilde{\pi}_t + \delta_t \tag{5}$$

where r is the rate of interest and $\tilde{\pi}_t$ is the continuously compounded percentage rate of change in marginal cost with age.[4] Equations 3, 4, and 5 imply a demand curve for health capital or a marginal efficiency of capital schedule of the form [5]

$$\ln H_t = \ln BC + \epsilon \ln W_t - \epsilon \ln \tilde{\pi}_t - \epsilon \ln \delta_t \tag{6}$$

where $\epsilon = 1/(1 + C)$ is the elasticity of the schedule.

By making assumptions about the nature of the depreciation rate function and the marginal cost of gross investment function, I have used equation 6 to obtain and estimate a reduced-form demand curve for health capital. If $\tilde{\delta}$ is the constant continuously compounded rate of increase in the rate of depreciation with age, and if δ_1 is the rate of depreciation during some initial period, then

$$\ln \delta_t = \delta_1 + \tilde{\delta} t \tag{7}$$

It should be noted that δ_1 is not the rate of depreciation at the very beginning of the life cycle. Instead, it is the rate at an age, say age sixteen, when individuals rather than their parents begin to make their own decisions.

I develop an equation for marginal cost by letting the gross investment production function be a member of the Cobb-Douglas class:

$$\ln I_t = \alpha \ln M_t + (1 - \alpha) \ln T_t + \rho E \tag{8}$$

The new variables in this equation are M_t, a market good or a vector of market goods used to produce gross investments in health; T_t, an

---

[4] Equilibrium condition 5 assumes that gross investment in health is always positive. For a discussion of this point, see Grossman (1972a, pp. 233–234).

[5] From equation 3

$$\ln G_t = \ln BC - (C + 1) \ln H_t$$

Substitute $\ln \gamma_t - \ln W_t + \ln \pi_t$ for $\ln G_t$ in this equation, and solve for $\ln H_t$ to obtain

$$\ln H_t = \ln BC + \epsilon \ln W_t - \epsilon \ln \pi_t - \epsilon \ln \gamma_t$$

where $\epsilon = 1/(1 + C)$. Replacing γ_t by $r - \tilde{\pi}_t + \delta_t$ in the last equation and assuming that the real own rate of interest, $r - \tilde{\pi}_t$, is equal to zero, one obtains equation 6. For a justification of the assumption that $r - \tilde{\pi}_t$ is zero, see Grossman (1972b, p. 42).

input of the consumer's own time; and E, an index of the stock of knowledge, or human capital.[6] The new parameters are α, the output elasticity of M_t or the share of M_t in the total cost of gross investment; $(1 - \alpha)$, the output elasticity of T_t; and ρ, the percentage improvement in nonmarket productivity due to human capital. It is natural to view medical care as an important component of M_t, although studies by Auster, Leveson, and Sarachek (1969); Grossman (1972b); and Benham (in progress) reach the tentative conclusion that medical care has, at best, a minor marginal impact on health.[7]

Equations 6, 7, and 8 generate a reduced-form demand curve for health capital given by [8]

$$\ln H_t = \alpha\epsilon \ln W_t - \alpha\epsilon \ln P_t + \rho\epsilon E - \tilde{\delta}\epsilon t - \epsilon \ln \delta_1 \qquad (9)$$

where P_t is the price of M_t. It should be realized that although the subscript t refers to age, H_t will vary among individuals as well as over the life cycle of a given individual. It should also be realized that the functional form of equation 9 is one that is implied by the model rather than one that is imposed on data for "convenience." According to the equation, the quantity of health capital demanded should be positively related to the hourly wage rate and the stock of human capital and should be negatively related to the price of M_t, age, and the rate of depreciation in the initial period.

In previous empirical work (Grossman 1972b, Chapter V), I fitted equation 9 to data for individuals who had finished their formal schooling. I measured health by self-rated health status, and alternatively by sick time, and measured the stock of knowledge, or human capital, by years of schooling completed. Since I had no data on depreciation rates of persons of the same age, I assumed that $\ln \delta_1$ was not correlated with the other variables on the right-hand side of equation 9. Put differently, I treated $\ln \delta_1$ as the random disturbance term in the reduced-form demand curve.

---

[6] Note that certain inputs in the M vector, such as cigarette smoking and alcohol consumption, have negative marginal products in the gross investment function. They are purchased because they also produce other commodities, such as "smoking pleasure." Therefore, joint production occurs in the household. For an analysis of this phenomenon, see Grossman (1971). Note also that, if health were produced in a family context, then T_t might be a vector of time inputs of various family members.

[7] Grossman and Benham (1974) produce some evidence to the contrary, but this evidence should also be viewed as tentative.

[8] For a derivation of equation 9, see Grossman (1972b, Appendix D). This equation, as well as the remainder of those in this paper, does not contain an intercept, because all variables are expressed as deviations from their respective means.

In general, my empirical results were consistent with the predictions of the model. In particular, with age, the wage rate, and several other variables held constant, schooling had a positive and significant effect on health.[9] I interpreted this result as evidence in support of the hypothesis that schooling raises the efficiency with which health is produced. That is, I interpreted it in terms of a causal relationship that runs from more schooling to better health. If, however, the unobserved rate of depreciation on health capital in the initial period were correlated with schooling, or if schooling were an imperfect measure of the stock of human capital, then my finding would be subject to more than one interpretation.

B. A General Recursive System

I now show that a general model of life-cycle decision making would lead to a negative relationship between schooling and the rate of depreciation. Moreover, this model would predict positive relationships between schooling and other components of nonmarket efficiency; and between schooling and additional third variables that should, under certain conditions, enter equation 9. These relationships arise because, in the context of a life-cycle model, the amount of schooling persons acquire and their health during the time that they attend school are endogenous variables. I do not develop the model in detail but instead rely heavily on previous work dealing with the demand for preschool and school investments in human capital, and the demand for child quality.[10]

1. Demand Curve for Schooling. The optimal quantity of school investment in human capital in a given year and the number of years of formal schooling completed should be positive functions of the efficiency with which persons transform teachers' services, books, their own time, and other inputs into gross additions to the stock of knowledge. As Lillard (1973, p. 32) points out, efficiency in producing human capital via schooling is determined by factors such as physical

[9] This finding complements the negative relationships among schooling and various age-adjusted mortality rates that are reported in a number of studies. See Stockwell (1963); Fuchs (1965); Hinkle et al. (1968); Kitagawa and Hauser (1968); Auster, Leveson, and Sarachek (1969); Breslow and Klein (1971); and Silver (1972).

[10] For models of the determination of optimal investment in human capital, see, for example, Becker (1967); Ben-Porath (1967); and Lillard (1973). For models of the demand for child quality, see, for example, Leibowitz (1972); Ben-Porath (1973); DeTray (1973); and especially Willis (1973). For studies that view preschool investment in human capital as one aspect of child quality, see, for example, Lillard (1973) and Leibowitz (1974).

ability, mental ability (intelligence), and health.[11] Another reason for expecting a positive effect of health on schooling is that the returns from an investment in schooling last for many periods. Since health status is positively correlated with life expectancy, it should be positively correlated with the number of periods over which returns can be collected. In addition to efficiency and to the number of periods over which returns accrue, the opportunity to finance investments in human capital, measured by parents' income or by parents' schooling, should be a key determinant of the quantity of schooling demanded.

Let the factors that determine variations in years of formal schooling completed (S) among individuals be summarized by a demand curve of the form

$$S = a_1 \ln H_1 + a_2 X \tag{10}$$

where X is a vector of all other variables besides health that influences S. In a manner analogous to the interpretation of δ_1, H_1 may be interpreted as health capital at the age (age sixteen) when individuals begin to make their own decisions. I will assume, however, that a given person's health capital at age sixteen is highly correlated with his or her own health capital at the age (age five or six) when formal schooling begins. One justification for this assumption is that the rate of increase in the rate of depreciation might be extremely small and even zero at young ages.[12]

The demand curve for schooling given by equation 10 differs in a fundamental respect from the demand curve for health given by equation 9. Since the production function of gross investment in health exhibits constant returns to scale and since input prices are given, the marginal cost of gross investment in health is independent of the quantity of investment produced. Therefore, consumers reach their desired stock of health capital immediately, and equation 9 represents a

---

[11] A common specification of the production function of new human capital at age t, due originally to Ben-Porath (1967), is

$$\ln Q_t = \ln B + \alpha_1 \ln s_t E_t + \alpha_2 \ln D_t$$

where s_t is the proportion of the existing stock of human capital allocated to the production of more human capital, D_t is an input of market goods and services, and $\alpha_1 + \alpha_2 < 1$. Following Lillard (1973), I assume that ability and health primarily affect the Hicks-neutral technology parameter B, rather than the stock of human capital that individuals possess when they first begin to make their own decisions. Leibowitz (1974) stresses the effect of ability on the preschool stock of human capital but reaches the same conclusion with regard to the effect of ability on schooling.

[12] Indeed, at young ages, the rate of depreciation might fall rather than rise with age.

demand curve for an equilibrium stock of capital at age t. Implicit in this equation is the assumption that people never stop investing in their health.[13]

On the other hand, following Becker (1967) and Ben-Porath (1967), I allow the marginal cost of gross investment in knowledge to be a positive function of the rate of production of new knowledge.[14] Thus, consumers do not reach their equilibrium stock of knowledge immediately, and equation 10 represents a demand curve for the equilibrium length of the investment period, measured by the number of years of formal schooling completed. Since persons typically have left school by age thirty, investment in knowledge ceases after some point in the life cycle.[15]

2. Demand Curve for Children's Health. Although the health and intelligence of children depend partly on genetic inheritance, these variables are not completely exogenous in a life-cycle model. In particular, they also depend on early childhood environmental factors, which are shaped to a large extent by parents.[16] If children's health is viewed as one aspect of their quality, then one can conceive of a demand curve for H_1 whose key arguments are variables that determine the demand for child quality. Children's health should rise with their parents' income if quality has a positive income elasticity and should rise with their parents' schooling if persons with higher schooling levels are relatively more efficient producers of quality children than of other commodities. Most important for my purposes, the quantity of H_1 demanded should be negatively related to δ_1. This follows because, regardless of whether one is examining the demand for children's health capital or adults' health capital, an increase in the rate of depreciation raises the price of such capital.

---

[13] One justification for this assumption is that it is observed empirically that most individuals make positive outlays on medical care throughout their life cycles.

[14] This assumption is required because, from the point of view of any one person, the marginal product of the stock of knowledge is independent of the stock. For a complete discussion of this point, see Becker (1967) and Ben-Porath (1967). Grossman (1972a, pp. 234–235) compares and contrasts in detail the alternative assumptions made about the marginal products of health and knowledge capital and about the marginal costs of producing gross additions to these two stocks.

[15] After leaving school, persons can continue to acquire human capital via investments in on-the-job training. I assume that human capital obtained in this manner is a much less relevant determinant of efficiency in the production of health than human capital obtained via formal schooling. For analyses of the forces that cause the quantity of investment in human capital to decline with age, see Becker (1967); Ben-Porath (1967); and Mincer (1970, 1972).

[16] This point is emphasized by Lillard (1973) and especially by Leibowitz (1974).

Let the demand curve for children's health be given by

$$\ln H_1 = b_1 Y - \epsilon' \ln \delta_1 \tag{11}$$

In equation 11, Y is a vector of all other variables in addition to δ_1 that affects H_1, and ϵ' is the price elasticity of H_1.[17] This elasticity will not, in general, equal the price elasticity of H_t (ϵ). Surely, in a developed economy such as the United States, a healthy child is primarily a consumption commodity. Since my model treats adult health as primarily an investment commodity, the substitution effect associated with a change in the price of H_t will differ in nature from the substitution effect associated with a change in the price of H_1.

It should be realized that the stock of health capital inherited at birth does not enter equation 11 directly. Given constant marginal cost of gross investment in health, any discrepancy between the inherited stock of children's health and the stock that their parents demand in the period immediately following birth would be eliminated instantaneously. This does *not* mean that H_1 is independent of genetic inheritance and birth defects. Variations in these factors explain part of the variation in δ_1 among children of the same age. According to this interpretation, children with inferior genetic characteristics or birth defects would have above-average rates of depreciation, and their parents would demand a smaller optimal quantity of H_1.[18] Of course, one could introduce a direct relationship between current and lagged stock by dropping the assumption of constant marginal cost. Such a framework would, however, greatly complicate the interpretation and empirical estimation of demand curves for children's health and adults' health. Consequently, I will not pursue it in this paper.

3. Human Capital Equation. To complete the analytical framework, it is necessary to specify an equation for the stock of knowledge, or human capital, after the completion of formal schooling. Recall that it is this stock that determines the efficiency with which adult health is produced. Assume that the stock (E) depends on years of formal schooling completed (S) and a vector of other variables (Z) as in [19]

---

[17] Along similar lines, one could specify a demand curve for children's intelligence. For one specification and some empirical estimates, see Leibowitz (1974).

[18] The same conclusion would be reached if an inferior genetic endowment or a birth defect lowered the amount of gross investment in health obtained from given amounts of medical care and other inputs.

[19] The variable E does not have an age subscript, because it is the stock of knowledge after schooling ends. If the rate of depreciation on knowledge capital were positive, E would fall with age. I assume that this effect is small enough to be ignored, at least at most stages of the life cycle.

$$E = c_1 S + c_2 Z \qquad (12)$$

The variables in Z include the initial or inherited stock of human capital and determinants of the "average" quantity of new knowledge produced per year of school attendance, such as ability, health, quality of schooling, and parental characteristics. In one important respect, equation 12 is misspecified, for the function that relates E to S and Z is almost certainly nonlinear.[20] In this paper, I use equation 12 as a first approximation in assessing the biases that arise when determinants of human capital other than schooling are omitted from the demand curve for health. In future work, I plan to modify the assumption of linearity.

4. Comments and Interpretation of Health-Schooling Relationships. The system of equations that I have just developed provides a coherent framework for analyzing and interpreting health-schooling relationships and for obtaining unbiased estimates of the "pure" effect of schooling on health. Before I turn to these matters, it will be useful to make a few comments about the general nature of this system. The stock of knowledge is a theoretical concept and is difficult to quantify empirically. Because it will not, in general, be possible to estimate the human capital function given by 12, substitute it into the demand curve for adults' health given by 9. This reduces the system to three basic equations, which are demand curves for children's health, schooling, and adults' health: [21]

$$\ln H_1 = b_1 Y - \epsilon' \ln \delta_1 \qquad (11)$$

$$S = a_1 \ln H_1 + a_2 X \qquad (10)$$

and

$$\ln H_t = \alpha\epsilon \ln W - \alpha\epsilon \ln P + c_1\rho\epsilon S + c_2\rho\epsilon Z - \tilde{\delta}\epsilon t - \epsilon \ln \delta_1 \qquad (9')$$

Since the endogenous variables are determined at various stages in the life cycle, these three equations constitute a recursive system rather than a full simultaneous-equations model. For example, although children's health is the endogenous variable in equation 11, it is predetermined when students select their optimal quantity of schooling at age sixteen. Similarly, schooling is predetermined when adults select

[20] Employing Ben-Porath's model of investment in human capital, Lillard (1973) obtains a specific solution for the stock of human capital as a function of schooling, ability, and age. His equation is highly nonlinear.

[21] From now on, age subscripts are deleted from all variables on the right-hand side of the demand curve for adults' health except the rate of depreciation in the initial period.

their optimal quantity of health capital at age t. It is well known that estimation of each equation in a recursive system by ordinary least squares is equivalent to estimation of the entire system by the method of full-information maximum likelihood.[22]

I have specified demand curves for adults' health and for children's health, but I have not specified a demand curve for health at an age when persons are still in school but are making their own decisions. Formally, if the decision-making process begins at age sixteen, and if schooling ends at age t^*, then I ignore demand at age j, where $16 < j \leqslant t^*$. It might appear that I have done this to avoid a problem of instability in the system. Specifically, variations in H_1 would cause the quantity of human capital produced in period 1 (Q_1) to vary. An increase in Q_1 would raise the stock of human capital (E_2) in period 2, which should raise efficiency in the production of health and the quantity of H_2 demanded. In turn, the increase in H_2 would raise Q_2, and so on. Although this process is potentially unstable, it is observed empirically that persons do not attend school throughout their life cycles. Rather, the equilibrium quantities of S and the stock of human capital ($E = E_t^*$) are reached at fairly young ages, and the system would retain its recursive nature even if a demand curve for H_j were introduced.

The simultaneous determination of health and knowledge in the age interval $16 \leqslant j < t^*$ does suggest that E_t^* should depend either on all quantities of H, or on an average quantity of H, in this interval. But such an average undoubtedly is highly correlated with the stock of health at age sixteen. This simultaneous determination also blurs to some extent the sharp distinction that I have drawn between knowledge capital as a determinant of productivity and health capital as a determinant of total time. Note, however, that E_t^* depends on H_1 rather than on the contemporaneous stock of health. Therefore, the distinction between health and knowledge capital remains valid as long as it is applied to contemporaneous stocks of the two types of capital at ages greater than t^*.

The wage rate and the stock of human capital obviously are positively correlated, yet I treat the wage rate as an exogenous variable in the recursive system. The wage rate enters the demand curve for adults' health in order to assess the pure effect of schooling on non-market productivity, with market productivity held constant. The wage

---

[22] See, for example, Johnston (1963). This proposition is valid only if the unspecified disturbance terms in the equations are mutually independent.

should have an independent and positive impact on the quantity of health demanded, because it raises the monetary value of a reduction in sick time by a greater percentage than it raises the cost of producing such a reduction. If market and nonmarket productivity were highly correlated, it would be difficult to isolate the pure nonmarket productivity effect, but this is an empirical issue that can ultimately be decided by the data. As long as the current stock of health is not a determinant of the current stock of human capital, nothing would be gained by specifying an equation for the wage rate. Until Section IV, I assume that, at ages greater than t^*, E_t and, therefore, W_t do not depend on H_t.

In the remainder of this section, I discuss the interpretation and estimation of health-schooling relationships within the context of the recursive system. Given an appropriate measure of the rate of depreciation in the initial period, an ordinary least squares fit of equation 9' would yield an unbiased estimate of the pure effect of schooling on health. Now suppose that no measure of δ_1 is available. From equation 11, H_1 is negatively related to δ_1, and from equation 10, S is positively related to H_1. Therefore, S is negatively related to δ_1. Since an increase in δ_1 causes H_t to fall, the expected value of the regression coefficient of S in equation 9' would be an upward-biased estimate of the relevant population parameter. This is the essence of the reverse causality interpretation of an observed positive relationship between schooling and health. Due to the prediction of the recursive system that healthier students should attend school for longer periods of time, the effect of schooling on health would be *overstated* if δ_1 were not held constant in computing equation 9'.

In general, it should be easier to measure the stock of health in the initial period empirically than to measure the rate of depreciation in this period. Therefore, the easiest way to obtain unbiased estimates of the parameters of equation 9' would be to solve equation 11 for ln δ_1 and substitute the resulting expression into 9':

$$\ln H_t = \alpha \epsilon \ln W - \alpha \epsilon \ln P + c_1 \rho \epsilon S + c_2 \rho \epsilon Z - \tilde{\delta} \epsilon t$$
$$+ (\epsilon/\epsilon') \ln H_1 - (b_1 \epsilon/\epsilon')Y \quad (9'')$$

A second justification for this substitution is that H_1 is one of the variables in the Z vector, because it is a determinant of the average quantity of new knowledge produced per year of school attendance. Consequently, ln H_1 should enter the regression whether or not ln

δ_1 can be measured, and the elimination of $\ln \delta_1$ from 9' makes it simpler to interpret variations in key variables within the recursive system.[23]

Formally, if $Z = Z' + c_3 \ln H'_1$, then the regression coefficient of $\ln H_1$ in equation 9'' would be $c_3 c_2 \rho \epsilon + (\epsilon/\epsilon')$. Although it would not be possible to isolate the two components of this coefficient, both should be positive. Therefore, one can make the firm prediction that H_1 should have a positive effect on H_t. This relationship arises not because of any direct relationship between current and lagged stock but because H_1 is negatively correlated with the depreciation rate in the initial period and is positively correlated with the equilibrium stock of human capital.

The "third variable" explanation of the observed positive correlation between health and schooling asserts that no causal relationship is implied by this correlation. Instead, differences in one or more third variables cause health and schooling to vary in the same direction. The most logical way to introduce this hypothesis and to examine its relevance within the context of the recursive system is to associate third variables with the Y vector in the demand curve for children's health and with the X vector in the demand curve for schooling. Many of the variables in these two vectors represent factors, such as parents' schooling and parents' income, that shape early childhood environment. If years of formal schooling completed were the only determinant of the stock of human capital, and if one had a perfect measure of δ_1 or H_1, then the third-variable effect would operate solely via the relationship between H_1 and H_t. That is, provided H_1 were held constant, the estimated schooling parameter in equation 9'' would not be biased by the omission of environmental variables that induce similar changes in schooling and children's health.[24]

The situation would be somewhat different if one had no measure of δ_1 or H_1. Then a variable in the Y vector might have a positive effect on H_t if it were negatively correlated with δ_1.[25] The assumption of a

---

[23] If $\ln H_1$ varied with S and $\ln \delta_1$ held constant, then one would be imposing a negative correlation between Y and X. Since the variables in these two vectors primarily reflect childhood environment, such a correlation is not plausible.

[24] Indeed, according to equation 9'', an increase in Y, with $\ln H_1$ constant, would cause $\ln H_t$ to fall. Note, however, that, if $\ln \delta_1$ and Y were independent, then Y should be omitted from (9'').

[25] If equation 9'' were fitted with $\ln H_1$ omitted, the expected value of the regression coefficient of Y would be $(\epsilon/\epsilon')(\hat{b} - b_1)$, where $\hat{b}$ is the partial regression coefficient of $\ln H_1$ on Y, with other variables in the demand curve for adults' health held constant. If $\hat{b}$ were positive, the expected value of the regression coefficient of $\ln H_t$ on Y would be positive provided $\hat{b} > b_1$.

negative correlation between Y and δ_1 is not as arbitrary as it may seem, for δ_1 is not entirely an exogenous variable. To the extent that variations in δ_1 reflect variations in birth defects, these defects should depend in part on the quantity and quality of prenatal care, which in turn may be related to the characteristics of parents. For instance, at an empirical level, birth weight is positively correlated with mothers' schooling.[26] Moreover, there is evidence that physical health is influenced by mental well-being.[27] Some of the differences in δ_1 among individuals may be associated with differences in mental well-being that are created by early-childhood environmental factors.

In an intermediate situation, one may have some data on past health, but it may be subject to errors of observation. Then it would make sense to include Y in a regression estimate of equation 9″ in order to improve the precision with which past health is estimated. In general, Y would have a larger effect on current health, the greater is the error variance in H_1 relative to the total variance.

If efficiency in the production of adults' health were not determined solely by years of formal schooling completed, then third variables could have effects on current health independent of their effects on past health. These effects are represented by the coefficients of the variables in the Z vector in equation 9″. Since some of these variables also enter the X vector in the demand curve for schooling, the estimated impact of schooling on current health would be biased if the Z variables were excluded from the demand curve for adults' health. I have interpreted the variables in this vector primarily as measures of a person's capacity to assimilate new knowledge in a given year of school attendance and have associated them with physical and mental ability, health, parental characteristics, and school quality. In general, it will not be possible to distinguish the effects of Y variables from those of Z variables in the demand curve for health. For example, given an imperfect measure of past health, parents' schooling may have a positive impact on current health because it is positively correlated with past health or because it is one determinant of the stock of human capital.

The overlap between elements in the Z vector and those in the X and Y vectors suggests that certain third variables must operate in an indirect manner only in the demand curve for adults' health. Clearly, it would not be feasible to vary schooling, with past health and all of

---

[26] See, for example, Masland (1968).
[27] See, for example, Palmore (1969a, 1969b).

the other variables in the X vector held constant. That is, one could not use schooling and all of its systematic determinants as independent variables in a regression with current health as the dependent variable. Specifically, intelligence, like children's health, is one aspect of the quality of children that depends on genetic inheritance and early childhood environment. Therefore, these factors may affect the current stock of health solely through their influence on intelligence.[28]

At this point, two caveats with regard to the third variable effect are in order. First, I have assumed that efficiency in health production is a function of a homogeneous stock of knowledge, or human capital. Efficiency may, however, depend on "general" human capital (knowledge) and on "specific" (health-related) human capital. It is plausible to associate schooling and mental intelligence with general capital and to associate physical characteristics with specific capital. Suppose that genetic inheritance affects physical and mental ability and suppose that an inferior genetic endowment is not reflected in poor health until later stages of the life cycle. Then, there is a rationale for including physical ability in the demand curve for health, even if this dimension of ability is not directly related to the quantity of schooling demanded. Indeed, given the health-specific nature of physical ability, it should have a larger effect on current health than mental ability. On the other hand, given the schooling-specific nature of mental ability, it should have a larger impact on schooling than physical ability.

Second, if one considers the production of health in a family context, then years of formal schooling completed by one's spouse becomes a relevant third variable. To anticipate the empirical work in the following sections of this paper, consider the process by which the health of married men is produced. Typically, such men devote most of their time to market production, while their wives devote most of their time to nonmarket production. This suggests that wives' time should be an important input in the production of husbands' health. If an increase in wives' schooling raises their nonmarket productivity, then it would tend to raise the quantity of husbands' health demanded. To be sure, an increase in schooling should raise the value of time, measured by the potential market wage rate, as well as nonmarket productivity.[29] Suppose that wives' schooling but not their potential market wage

[28] For a similar discussion with regard to the effects of parental characteristics and intelligence on earnings, see Leibowitz (1974).

[29] I do not consider here the difficult problem of measuring the value of time of persons not in the labor force. For discussions of this issue, see Gronau (1973) and Heckman (1974).

were included in a demand curve for husbands' health. Then the wives' schooling parameter would be $\epsilon(\rho_f - \alpha_f \hat{W}_f)$, where ρ_f is the percentage increase in wives' nonmarket productivity due to a one year increase in schooling, $\hat{W}_f$ is the percentage change in market productivity, and α_f is the share of wives' time in the total cost of gross investment in husbands' health. This parameter would be positive provided ρ_f exceeded $\alpha_f \hat{W}_f$. Thus, it would definitely be positive if schooling raised market and nonmarket productivity by the same percentage.[30]

To summarize, given data on current health, past health, and third variables for persons who had completed formal schooling, one could estimate the demand curves for adults' health and schooling given by equations 9″ and 10. The coefficient of schooling in equation 9″ would indicate the contribution of this variable to current health, with past health and third variables held constant. That is, it would measure the degree to which more schooling causes better health. The coefficient of past health in equation 10 would measure the extent to which good health at young ages induces people to attend school for longer periods of time. Since the two equations constitute a recursive system rather than a full simultaneous-equations model, consistent estimates of each may be obtained by ordinary least squares.

III. EMPIRICAL IMPLEMENTATION OF THE MODEL

A. The Sample

I have used data contained in the NBER-Thorndike sample to estimate health and schooling functions. This is a sample drawn from a population of 75,000 white males who volunteered for, and were accepted as candidates for, Aviation Cadet status as pilots, navigators, or bombardiers in the Army Air Force in the last half of 1943.[31] To be accepted as a candidate, a man had to pass a physical examination and the Aviation Cadet Qualifying Examination, which measured scholastic aptitude and achievement. According to Thorndike and Hagen, the minimum passing score on the Qualifying Examination was "one that could be achieved by about half of high-school graduates (1959, p. 53)." Thus, the candidates were selected almost entirely from the upper half of the scholastic ability (IQ) distribution of all draft-eligible white males in the United States in 1943. After passing the Qualifying Examination, candidates were given seventeen specific

---

[30] Since $\alpha_f < 1$, $\rho_f > \alpha_f \hat{W}_f$ if $\rho_f = \hat{W}_f$.

[31] For complete descriptions of the sample, see Thorndike and Hagen (1959) and Taubman and Wales (1974).

tests that measured five basic types of ability: general intelligence, numerical ability, visual perception, psychomotor control, and mechanical ability.[32] A candidate's scores on these tests determined whether he was accepted as an Aviation Cadet for training in one of the programs, and his subsequent performance in training school determined whether he actually served in the Air Force.

In 1955, Robert L. Thorndike and Elizabeth Hagen collected information on earnings, schooling, and occupation for a civilian sample of 9,700 of these 75,000 men. In 1969, the National Bureau of Economic Research mailed a questionnaire to the members of the Thorndike-Hagen sample and received 5,085 responses. In 1971, the NBER sent a supplementary questionnaire to the persons who answered its initial questionnaire and received 4,417 responses. In Section V, I examine the mortality experience of the NBER-Thorndike sample between 1955 and 1969. Until then, my empirical analysis is limited to men who responded to both NBER questionnaires, were married in 1969, were members of the labor force in that year, and did not have unknown values for certain key variables.[33] The sample size of this group is 3,534.

The NBER resurveys greatly increased the amount of information available in the data set. In particular, Thorndike and Hagen did not obtain any measures of health, parental characteristics, or spouses' characteristics. The NBER surveys included questions on all these variables and also updated the information on earnings, schooling, and work history since 1955. Most of this information was gathered in the 1969 survey. The 1971 survey collected several background characteristics that were omitted from the 1969 survey and also expanded the measures of health to include an index of past health as well as an index of current health. Since the measure of past health is available only for persons who responded to both the 1969 and 1971 surveys, I limit my analysis to such persons.

It should be emphasized that, for several reasons, the white males in the NBER-Thorndike sample by no means constitute a representative sample of all white males in the United States. First, everyone in the sample is around the same age. The mean age in 1969 was forty-seven years, and the age range was from forty-one years to fifty-five years. Second, these men are drawn mainly from the upper tails of the schooling, earnings, and scholastic ability distributions. All of them

---

[32] The identification of these five basic types of ability is due to Thorndike and Hagen (1959). It is discussed in more detail in part C of this section.

[33] The specific sample that I utilize is described in more detail in the appendix.

graduated from high school, and their mean full-time salary was approximately $18,000 in 1969. As I have already indicated, in order to pass the Aviation Cadet Qualifying Examination in 1943, one had to have a level of scholastic ability at least as high as half of all high-school graduates. Third, since the men passed a physical examination in 1943, they were at least fairly healthy in that year. As I will show presently, their current health tends to exceed that of a random sample of white males.

It is plausible to postulate that the effect of past health on schooling and the effect of schooling on current health decline as the levels of these variables increase. Therefore, it may be more difficult to uncover significant health-schooling relationships in the NBER-Thorndike sample than in other samples. In particular, with past health held constant, any impact of schooling on current health represents the effect of college attendance versus completion of formal schooling after graduation from high school. As a corollary, if significant health-schooling relationships exist in the NBER-Thorndike sample, even more significant relationships may exist in the general population. The main advantage in using the sample to study these relationships is that data on past health and a fairly wide set of potential third variables are available.

B. Measurement of Health

The stock of health, like the stock of knowledge, is a theoretical concept that is difficult to define and quantify empirically. A proxy for it is, however, available in the 1969 NBER-Thorndike survey. The men in the sample were asked whether the state of their general health was excellent, good, fair, or poor. I use their response to this question as an index of the amount of health capital they possessed in 1969. This measure of health capital suffers from the defect that it depends on an individual's subjective evaluation of the state of his health: what one person considers to be excellent health may be viewed as good or only fair health by another. Moreover, it is not immediately obvious how to quantify the four possible responses. That is, one must determine exactly how much more health capital a man in, say, excellent health has compared to a man in poor health.

Table 1 contains a frequency distribution of health status in 1969 for married men in the NBER-Thorndike sample. For comparative purposes, the table also contains a frequency distribution of this variable for white married men in a 1963 health interview survey conducted by the National Opinion Research Center (NORC) and the

TABLE 1

Frequency Distributions of Health Status, Married Men

	Percentage Distribution	
Class	NBER-Thorndike Sample [a]	NORC Sample [b]
Excellent	59.51	48.54
Good	37.29	37.45
Fair	2.80	11.87
Poor	0.40	2.14

[a] Sample size is 3,534. Until Section V, all subsequent tables based on the NBER-Thorndike sample pertain to this sample size.

[b] Sample size is 1,028.

Center for Health Administration Studies of the University of Chicago. The NORC sample is an area probability sample of the entire civilian noninstitutionalized population of the United States.[34] Therefore, its white male members are much more representative of the population at large than the members of the NBER-Thorndike sample.

In the table, I show that most of the men in the NBER-Thorndike sample are in either good or excellent health. I also show that the level of health of these men is higher than that of men in the NORC sample. Approximately 97 per cent of the former sample report that their health is at least good. The corresponding figure in the latter sample is approximately 86 per cent.

In Table 2, I present relationships between self-rated health status and more objective measures of health for both samples. These relationships take the form of regressions of number of work-loss weeks due to illness, medical expenditures, or number of symptoms reported from a checklist of twenty common symptoms[35] on three health status dummy variables ($HS1$, $HS2$, and $HS3$). The dummy variables are coded as follows: $HS1 = 1$ if health status is good, fair, or poor;

[34] Data were obtained from 2,367 families containing 7,803 persons. For a complete description of the NORC sample, see Andersen and Anderson (1967). I do not employ it to study health-schooling relationships in this paper, because it has no data on past health and very limited data on third variables.

[35] Examples of these symptoms include persistent cough, swelling in joints, frequent backaches, unexplained loss of weight, and repeated pains in or near the heart.

TABLE 2

Regressions of Work-Loss Weeks Due to Illness,
Medical Expenditures, and Symptoms on Health
Status Dummy Variables [a]

Dependent Variable	Intercept	Regression Coefficient of:			R^2
		$HS1$	$HS2$	$HS3$	
Work-loss weeks [b]	.103	.235	.571	8.019	.102
		(3.94)	(3.23)	(16.55)	
Work-loss weeks [c]	.524	.584	1.749	4.929	.106
		(2.43)	(4.75)	(6.00)	
Medical expenditures [c]	55.854	61.235	75.231	49.089	.067
		(4.85)	(3.89)	(1.14)	
Symptoms [c]	.940	.741	1.401	3.463	.224
		(5.87)	(7.25)	(8.04)	

[a] t ratios in parentheses. R^2 is the unadjusted coefficient of multiple determination.
[b] Regression based on the NBER-Thorndike sample.
[c] Regression based on the NORC sample.

$HS2 = 1$ if health status is fair or poor; and $HS3 = 1$ if health status is poor. All three dependent variables pertain to the year preceding the survey.

Since there are no data on medical expenditures or symptoms in the NBER-Thorndike sample, only the first regression in Table 2 is relevant for this sample. It shows that the number of work-loss weeks in 1968 rises as health status declines. The intercept of the regression indicates that the mean number of work-loss weeks for men in excellent health equals .1. The regression coefficient of $HS1$ indicates that men in good health have .2 more work-loss weeks on the average than men in excellent health. Similarly, men in fair health have .6 more work-loss weeks than men in good health, and men in poor health have 8.0 more work-loss weeks than men in fair health. These differences in work-loss by health status are statistically significant at all conventional levels of confidence.

The second regression in Table 2 demonstrates a similar inverse relationship between work-loss and health status in the NORC sample. The third and fourth regressions show that medical expenditures and symptoms rise as health status falls. The negative relationship between medical expenditures, an input into the production of health, and health can be traced to a positive correlation between medical care and the rate of depreciation on health capital. An increase in the rate of depreciation would cause the quantity of health capital demanded to fall. At the same time, the quantity of medical care demanded would rise if the price elasticity of demand for health capital were less than one.[36]

Taken together, the regression results in Table 2 give evidence that variations in self-rated health status reflect true variations in more objective measures of health. Additional considerations support the use of this variable as an index of health. Palmore (1969a, 1969b) reports that work satisfaction, itself an important correlate of self-rated health, and health status are key determinants of survival in a longitudinal sample of older persons. Rahe and Holmes (1965); Holmes and Masuda (1970); and Rahe (1972) find that physical illness is often associated with changes in life events that cause changes in mental well-being. Variations in mental well-being may cause current health status to vary but may affect work-loss and other measures of disability only with a long lag.

The first regression in Table 2 and the production function of healthy time given by equation 2 can be employed to select a set of scales for health status. The scaling scheme is based on the proposition that health capital, like knowledge capital, is a units-free measure of an existing stock. Setting this index equal to one for men in poor health, one could then express the amount of health capital of men in one of the other three categories relative to that of men in poor health. To be specific, if time is measured in weeks, then the production function of healthy time given by equation 2 implies

$$52 - h = WLW = BH^{-C} \tag{13}$$

where WLW denotes the number of work-loss weeks due to illness. Solve equation 13 for H to obtain

$$H = B^{1/C} \, WLW^{-1/C} \tag{14}$$

and let WLW_P, WLW_F, WLW_G, and WLW_E be mean work-loss of men in poor, fair, good, and excellent health. Then, to express the stock of health in an index number form with $H_P = 1$, write $H_F/H_P = (WLW_P/WLW_F)^{1/C}$, et cetera.

According to regression 1 in Table 2, $WLW_P/WLW_F = 9.82$, $WLW_P/$

---

[36] For a proof, see Grossman (1972b, pp. 16–19). Given the production function of healthy time specified in equation 2, the price elasticity of demand for health capital is $\epsilon = 1/(1 + C)$. This elasticity is smaller than one since C exceeds zero.

$WLW_G = 26.41$, and $WLW_P/WLW_E = 86.68$. Thus, the health capital series, termed $H69$ in subsequent analysis, is 1.00, 9.82, 26.41, and 86.68. The dependent variable in the demand curve for adults' health should be $\ln H_J/H_P$ ($J = P, F, G, E$). Therefore, the use of $\ln WLW_P/WLW_J$ as the dependent variable would generate regression coefficients that would exceed, equal, or fall short of the true coefficients as C exceeds, equals, or falls short of one. However, because C is a constant, the t ratios associated with these coefficients would be unaffected.

In most of my empirical analysis in the next two sections, I emphasize the qualitative effects of independent variables on $H69$. To examine the sensitivity of results to the scaling scheme, I estimate some equations with a dichotomous dependent variable (*EXCELL*) that is equal to one if a man is in excellent health and is equal to zero otherwise. In a few instances, I discuss quantitative effects in conjunction with $H69$, and in these instances, I assume that C is equal to one. Of course, the quantitative analysis is based on the specification of the production function of healthy time given by equation 13. This specification is not the only one that is consistent with diminishing marginal productivity to health capital and an upper asymptote of 52 healthy weeks in a year, but it is the most simple one. I have investigated the behavior of the health capital series with more complicated functional forms such as the logistic function. Provided that the mean number of work-loss weeks for the entire sample and the mean for men in poor health are relatively small, this series is almost unaffected.[37] The existence of other functional forms and the somewhat arbitrary assumption about the value of C does suggest, however, that quantitative results should be interpreted with caution.

I could have employed the actual number of work-loss weeks reported by an individual as a negative measure of health, but only 9 per cent of the NBER-Thorndike sample reported positive work-loss in 1968.[38] Undoubtedly, there is a large random component in work-loss in a given year. Therefore, it is reasonable to associate variations

[37] These two means are small in the NBER-Thorndike sample: .3 weeks for the entire sample and 9.8 weeks for men in poor health.

[38] The corresponding figure in the NORC sample is 33 per cent. Although part of this difference reflects the higher level of health in the NBER-Thorndike sample, part of it is due to the manner in which the work-loss data were collected. The members of the NORC sample were asked for work-loss *days,* while the members of the NBER-Thorndike sample were asked for work-loss *weeks.* The mean number of work-loss days in the NORC sample is 5, and many persons reported 1 to 4 days. Therefore, at least some of the zero values in the NBER-Thorndike sample may represent positive amounts of work-loss days. This is another reason why I do not use work-loss itself as a measure of health.

in work-loss due to variations in health status with "permanent" differences in health. On the other hand, variations in work-loss not accounted for by variations in health status may be viewed as more "transitory" in nature.

The 1971 NBER-Thorndike resurvey contains a proxy variable for past health. The men in the sample were asked whether the state of their health during the years they were attending high school was excellent, good, fair, or poor. The frequency distribution of responses is as follows: excellent, 87.29 per cent; good, 11.72 per cent; fair, 0.88 per cent; and poor, 0.11 per cent. The men were also asked how many weeks per year they lost from high school, on the average, due to illness. I analyze the relationship between self-rated high-school health status and average school-loss weeks due to illness (SLW) in the same manner as I analyzed the relationship between current health status and work-loss weeks. Specifically, I estimate a regression of SLW on three dummy variables for high-school health status: $HSHS1$ = 1 if high-school health status is good, fair, or poor; $HSHS2 = 1$ if high-school health status is fair or poor; and $HSHS3 = 1$ if high-school health status is poor. The regression is as follows (t ratios in parentheses):

$$SLW = .403 + .384 \ HSHS1 + .907 \ HSHS2 + 1.306 \ HSHS3$$
$$\quad\quad\quad\quad (15.04) \quad\quad\quad (10.00) \quad\quad\quad\quad (5.05)$$

$$R^2 = .132$$

Based on this regression, I create a series for health capital in high school the same way that I created a series for health capital in 1969. Let SLW_P, SLW_F, SLW_G, and SLW_E be mean school-loss of students in poor, fair, good, and excellent health. According to the regression, $SLW_P/SLW_F = 1.77$, $SLW_P/SLW_G = 3.81$, and $SLW_P/SLW_E = 7.44$. Thus, the past or high-school health capital series, termed HHS in subsequent analysis, is 1.00, 1.77, 3.81, and 7.44. This measure of past health suffers from the defect that it was obtained in a retrospective fashion. Note, however, that the information on current health was requested in 1969, while the information on past health was requested in 1971. Since the two variables were obtained at different points in time, the possibility of a spurious positive correlation between them is greatly mitigated. That is, respondents could not have used their answer to a question on current health status as the basis for an answer to a question on past health status.

C. Regression Specification

The most general versions of the health and schooling regressions that I estimate with the NBER-Thorndike sample are given by

$$\ln H69 = b_1 A + b_2 S + b_3 SFAT + b_4 SMOT + b_5 V + b_6 P$$
$$+ b_7 MECH + b_8 NUM + b_9 GEN + b_{10} \ln HHS + b_{11} SWIFE$$
$$+ b_{12} JSAT + b_{13} WTDIF + b_{14} \ln W + b_{15} OTINC \quad (15)$$

$$S = a_1 A + a_2 SFAT + a_3 SMOT + a_4 V + a_5 P + a_6 MECH$$
$$+ a_7 NUM + a_8 GEN + a_9 \ln HHS \quad (16)$$

Table 3 contains definitions of the variables in these two regressions, Table A.1 in the appendix contains their means and standard devia-

TABLE 3

Definition of Variables, NBER-Thorndike Sample

Variable	Definition
ln $H69$	Natural logarithm of stock of health in 1969 [a]
A	Age in 1969
S	Years of formal schooling completed
$SFAT$	Years of formal schooling completed by father
$SMOT$	Years of formal schooling completed by mother
V	Visual perception [a]
P	Psychomotor control [a]
$MECH$	Mechanical ability [a]
GEN	General intelligence [a]
NUM	Numerical ability [a]
ln HHS	Natural logarithm of stock of health while attending high school [a]
$SWIFE$	Years of formal schooling completed by wife
$JSAT$	Job satisfaction: 1 = lowest; 5 = highest [a]
$WTDIF$	Weight difference: absolute value of difference between actual weight and ideal weight for a given height [a]
ln W	Natural logarithm of hourly wage rate on current job [a]
$OTINC$	Nonearnings income of the family in 1968
$EXCELL$	Excellent health in 1969 = 1 [b]

[a] See text for a more complete definition.
[b] See Section III for a discussion of the use of this variable.

tions, and Table A.2 contains a matrix of simple correlation coefficients. All variables except past health, mothers' schooling, and the test scores are taken from the 1969 survey. Mothers' schooling and past health are taken from the 1971 survey, and the 1943 test scores are taken from military records. I formulated specific hypotheses concerning the roles of most of the right-hand side variables in equations 15 and 16 in Section I. Therefore, in the remainder of this section, I clarify a few of the definitions in Table 3 and comment on the predicted effects of several variables that I did not discuss in Section I.

The hourly wage rate equals a man's full-time salary on his current job divided by the product of fifty weeks and the average number of hours per week he worked on his main job in 1968. The five ability variables (V, P, $MECH$, GEN, NUM) are derived from Thorndike and Hagan's factor analysis (1959, p. 19) of scores on the seventeen specific tests that candidates for Aviation Cadet status were given in 1943. Based on their analysis, Thorndike and Hagan identified the five basic types of ability given in Table 3. The tests included in each of these categories are listed in Table 4.

I generate an aggregate index of visual perception, for example, by computing the first principal component of its three test scores, where each score is normalized to have a zero mean and a unitary standard deviation. Specifically, if X_i ($i = 1, 2, 3$) denotes the normalized value of the ith test score included in visual perception, then $V = \sum_{i=1}^{3} a_i X_i$, where the a_i are selected to maximize the variance in V subject to the constraint that $\sum_{i=1}^{3} a_i^2 = 1$.[39] I follow a similar procedure to aggregate the scores in the other four categories. One justification for my procedure is that the units in which ability is measured are arbitrary. It should be noted that health functions estimated with, for example, visual perception defined as a simple average of its three test scores (not shown) do not differ in a qualitative sense from those estimated with the principal components measures in the next section.

When the men in the NBER-Thorndike sample took the seventeen tests in 1943, practically all of them had graduated from high school but had little additional schooling. Most of those who went on to college did so after World War II. Thus, in this data set, one largely avoids the problem that a person's performance on a general intelli-

---

[39] The a_i coincide with the elements of the characteristic vector associated with the largest characteristic root of the correlation matrix of the X_i.

TABLE 4
Categories of Ability

Category	Tests Included [a]
Visual Perception	Speed of Identification
	Spatial Orientation I
	Spatial Orientation II
Psychomotor Control	Complex Coordination
	Rotary Pursuit
	Finger Dexterity
	Aiming Stress
Mechanical Ability	Mechanical Principles
	Two-Hand Coordination
	Biographical Data-Pilot [b]
General Intelligence	Reading Comprehension
	General Information-Navigator [c]
	Arithmetic Reasoning
	Mathematics
Numerical Ability	Numerical Operations I
	Numerical Operations II
	Dial and Table Reading

[a] For a description of each test, see Thorndike and Hagen (1959, pp. 55–76).

[b] Items on a biographical data form that proved to be important predictors of performance in pilot training school of candidates who were accepted as Pilot Aviation Cadets.

[c] A vocabulary test that dealt with terminology in astronomy, trigonometry, and science.

gence test will depend on the amount of schooling he has had. A small percentage of the men, chiefly the older ones, did attend college prior to World War II. Moreover, high-school graduates who participated in the labor force for several years before the war might have scored lower on the general intelligence tests than recent high-school graduates. To eliminate a potential reverse causality relationship running from schooling to general intelligence, I include age in the schooling function. Due to the upward secular trend in years of formal schooling completed, age and schooling are negatively correlated in random samples of the population of the United States. This negative correlation is also present in the NBER-Thorndike sample ($r = -.172$) despite the narrow age range of the sample. Therefore, by including age in the schooling function, I control for the trend factor and avoid biasing the estimated effect of intelligence on schooling.

There are two reasons for employing a measure of job satisfaction as an independent variable in the health function. First, someone who is satisfied with his job and with his life style in general may also be more satisfied with the state of his health than someone who is dissatisfied with his job and life style. Thus, the first person may be more likely to report that his health status is good or excellent, even though the two persons may have the same level of physical health measured in an objective fashion. Consequently, by holding job satisfaction constant, I purge self-rated health status of some of its subjective elements. Second, the studies that I have already cited by Rahe and Holmes (1965); Palmore (1969a, 1969b); Holmes and Masuda (1970); and Rahe (1972) indicate that dissatisfaction with life style creates tensions that cause mental and ultimately physical health to deteriorate. In this context, Palmore's finding that job satisfaction is the most important correlate of longevity in a longitudinal sample of older persons is particularly striking. Along these lines, one can view job satisfaction as an input into the production of health and estimate the sensitivity of health output to variations in this input.

The men in the NBER-Thorndike sample were asked whether they enjoy their work, whether their work provides a challenge, and whether their work is interesting. Each question has five possible numerical responses that constitute a scale ranging from five (the highest) to one (the lowest). The job-satisfaction index that I use is simply an average of a man's responses to these three questions.

Obesity and malnutrition, like job satisfaction, may be treated as inputs into the production of health. By computing the absolute value of the difference between actual weight and ideal weight for a given height, I create one variable to measure these mutually exclusive states. The 1969 questionnaire included items on actual height and actual weight. I calculate ideal weight for a given height from estimates made by the Metropolitan Life Insurance Company.[40] These estimates take the form of ideal weights for men by height and body frame (small, medium, or large). Since there is no information on body frames of men in the NBER-Thorndike sample, I define ideal weight for a given height as an average of the weight given for each body frame.

[40] These estimates are reported by Netzer (1969, p. 129).

The inclusion of two input variables, job satisfaction and weight difference, in the health function makes this function a mixture of a demand curve and a production function. If most of the variation in job satisfaction and weight difference were due to variation in the "prices" of these inputs, the estimated equation would be primarily a demand curve for health.[41] Under this interpretation, nonearnings income would enter the health function to take account of the pure consumption aspects of the demand for health. Alternatively, the wage rate and nonearnings income can be viewed as proxies for inputs besides job satisfaction and weight difference that affect health. Under this interpretation, the estimated equation would be primarily a production function of health. I do not emphasize one of these two extreme interpretations of the health function in the next section. I do, however, examine the extent to which the productivity effect of schooling on health operates via the impact of schooling on contemporaneous variables such as job satisfaction and weight difference.

III. EMPIRICAL RESULTS

A. Estimates of Recursive Health-Schooling System

Table 5 contains ordinary least squares estimates of health functions, and Table 6 contains corresponding estimates of schooling functions. The empirical analysis reflected by the regressions in these two tables represents a compromise between rigorous hypothesis testing of the effects of given variables and attempts to come to grips with somewhat more broad issues. These issues include the answers to such questions as: Which components of ability are the major determinants of health or schooling? By how much is the estimated effect of schooling on current health biased when past health and third variables are omitted from the health function? Do contemporaneous variables such as wives' schooling, job satisfaction, weight difference, the hourly wage rate, and nonearnings income play a more important role in the health function than lagged variables such as parents' schooling, ability in 1943, and past health? Does the inclusion of the set of lagged variables have a greater impact on the coefficient of own schooling than the in-

---

[41] Admittedly, it would be difficult to define these input prices, although elsewhere (Grossman 1971) I have shown that the concept and theory of joint production would aid in accomplishing this task. The price of job satisfaction might be defined as the reduction in the wage rate required to increase this variable by one unit, with schooling held constant. But the partial correlation between job satisfaction and the wage is positive in the NBER-Thorndike sample possibly because the "income effect" dominates the "substitution effect."

TABLE 5

Ordinary Least Squares Estimates of Health Functions [a]

Variable	Eq. 1 Regr. Coef.	Eq. 2 Regr. Coef.	Eq. 3 Regr. Coef.	Eq. 4 Regr. Coef.	Eq. 5 Regr. Coef.	Eq. 6 Regr. Coef.	Eq. 7 Regr. Coef.
A	−.017	−.012	−.011	−.011	−.010	−.010	−.011
	(−3.31)	(−2.33)	(−2.07)	(−2.14)	(−1.92)	(−2.00)	(−2.17)
S	.035	.028	.028	.019	.019	.012	.012
	(7.41)	(5.51)	(5.94)	(3.76)	(3.92)	(2.26)	(2.26)
$SFAT$		.005	.006	.004	.004	.003	.002
		(1.51)	(1.58)	(1.00)	(1.23)	(0.72)	(0.65)
$SMOT$		.006	.007	.005	.006	.004	.003
		(1.57)	(1.87)	(1.30)	(1.73)	(1.21)	(0.94)
V		.027	.036	.035	.033	.033	.027
		(2.81)	(4.19)	(4.19)	(3.87)	(3.91)	(2.86)
P		.010					.008
		(1.02)					(0.83)
$MECH$		.012					.013
		(1.16)					(1.26)
NUM		.004					−.001
		(0.42)					(−0.12)
GEN		.005					.002
		(0.60)					(0.27)
ln HHS		.479	.481	.461	.459	.445	.445
		(11.05)	(11.12)	(10.74)	(10.66)	(10.39)	(10.37)
$SWIFE$				.019		.018	.018
				(3.25)		(3.16)	(3.16)
$JSAT$				.094		.082	.082
				(6.67)		(5.76)	(5.72)
$WTDIF$				−.002		−.002	−.002
				(−3.57)		(−3.52)	(−3.41)
ln W					.167	.146	.147
					(7.00)	(6.10)	(6.05)
$OTINC$					−.001	−.0005	−.001
					(−0.29)	(−0.28)	(−0.30)
R^2	.021	.064	.063	.080	.076	.090	.091

[a] Intercepts not shown. t ratios in parentheses. See Table 3 for definitions of all variables.

TABLE 6

Ordinary Least Squares Estimates of Schooling Functions [a]

Variable	Equation 1 Regression Coefficient	Equation 2 Regression Coefficient	Equation 3 Regression Coefficient
A	−.146 (−8.40)	−.124 (−7.08)	−.131 (−7.58)
SFAT	.067 (5.47)	.066 (5.52)	.067 (5.61)
SMOT	.032 (2.56)	.050 (4.03)	.050 (4.05)
V		.052 (1.65)	.030 (1.00)
P		.004 (0.11)	
MECH		−.339 (−9.98)	−.318 (−10.30)
NUM		−.082 (−2.62)	
GEN	.446 (18.40)	.534 (18.85)	.499 (19.94)
ln HHS	.419 (2.86)	.416 (2.87)	.396 (2.74)
R^2	.146	.173	.171

[a] *t* ratios in parentheses.

clusion of the set of current variables? Which of the contemporaneous variables have the most significant effects on health and on the estimated coefficient of schooling? Which of the lagged variables influence health only indirectly, via their effects on schooling?

To examine these issues, in Tables 5 and 6, I show alternative versions of health and schooling equations. In addition, in Table 7, I show the percentage reduction in the coefficient of schooling when specific sets of variables are held constant.[42] My discussion of the regression results is organized as follows. First, I comment on variations in the

[42] The computations in Table 7 are based on the regressions in Table 5, as well as on some additional regressions not shown in the table. These computations do not depend on the value of the parameter *C* in the production function of healthy time given by equation 2 or equation 13.

TABLE 7

Estimated Bias in Schooling Coefficients

Initial Variables	Variables Added	Initial Schooling Coefficient	Final Schooling Coefficient	Percentage Reduction[a]
A	SFAT, SMOT, V, ln HHS	.035	.028	20.00
A	SWIFE, JSAT, WTDIF	.035	.023	34.28
A	ln W, OTINC	.035	.021	40.00
A	SWIFE, JSAT, WTDIF, ln W, OTINC	.035	.014	60.00
A	SFAT, SMOT, V, ln HHS, SWIFE, JSAT, WTDIF, ln W, OTINC	.035	.012	65.71
A, SFAT, SMOT, V, ln HHS	SWIFE, JSAT, WTDIF	.028	.019	32.14
A, SFAT, SMOT, V, ln HHS	ln W, OTINC	.028	.019	32.14
A, SFAT, SMOT, V, ln HHS	SWIFE, JSAT, WTDIF, ln W, OTINC	.028	.012	57.14
A, SWIFE, JSAT, WTDIF	SFAT, SMOT, V, ln HHS	.023	.019	17.39
A, ln W, OTINC	SFAT, SMOT, V, ln HHS	.021	.019	9.52
A, SWIFE, JSAT, WTDIF, ln W, OTINC	SFAT, SMOT, V, ln HHS	.014	.012	14.28

[a] Defined as one minus the ratio of the final schooling coefficient to the initial schooling coefficient.

estimated schooling parameter in the health function as the set of independent variables varies. Then, I examine some specific health effects of current variables other than schooling. Finally, I discuss health effects of past variables and the roles of these variables in the schooling equation.[43]

Regardless of the other variables held constant, schooling has a positive effect on current health that is statistically significant at the .025 level of confidence on a one-tail test. Since past health is included in each equation in Table 5 except the first, this finding may be interpreted as evidence in favor of a causal relationship that runs from schooling to current health. The actual regression coefficients indicate the continuously compounded percentage rate of increase in health capital associated with a one-year increase in schooling. These coefficients range from 3.5 per cent, when only age is held constant, to 1.2 per cent, when all relevant variables are held constant.

Suppose that the health functions were viewed primarily as demand curves, and suppose that the price elasticity of demand for health were equal to one-half. Then the schooling parameter estimates would imply that schooling raises health productivity by 2.4 per cent at a minimum.[44] This may be compared to the approximately 5.5 per cent increase in the *hourly* wage rate due to an additional year of formal schooling in the NBER-Thorndike sample.[45] Although the nonmarket productivity effect of schooling may appear to be small in an absolute sense, it is approximately 40 per cent as large as the market productivity effect. Moreover, in assessing the magnitude of the effect, it should be realized that all of the men in the sample are high-school graduates. If the nonmarket productivity improvement falls as schooling rises, then my estimate would understate the effect that would be observed in a sample of men at all schooling levels.

In Table 7, I reveal that the estimated bias in schooling coefficients is larger when current variables are excluded from the health function

[43] My empirical analysis in parts A and B of this section is similar to Griliches and Mason's (1972) analysis of interrelationships among schooling, ability, and earnings.

[44] The price elasticity of health would equal one-half if C in the production function of healthy time given by equation 2 or 13 were equal to one. According to the reduced form demand curve for health given by equation 9″, the schooling parameter should be $c_1 \rho \epsilon$, where c_1 gives the effect of schooling on the stock of human capital. My estimate of ρ assumes that c_1 equals one, but this assumption would not affect the comparison of market and nonmarket productivity effects.

[45] This figure is based on a regression of the natural logarithm of the hourly wage rate on schooling, years of experience in the labor force, general intelligence, and several other variables.

than when past variables are excluded. For example, the estimated bias due to the omission of parents' schooling, visual perception, and past health is 20 per cent (line 1 of Table 7).[46] The corresponding bias due to the omission of wives' schooling, weight difference, job satisfaction, the wage rate, and nonearnings income is 60 per cent (line 4). When past variables are held constant initially but current variables are not, the bias is 57 per cent (line 8). When this procedure is reversed, the bias is only 14 per cent (line 11). These results arise because the set of current variables is more highly correlated with schooling than the set of past variables.

In Table 7, I also reveal that the bias from omitting the subset of contemporaneous variables consisting of wives' schooling, job satis-faction, and weight difference is approximately the same as the bias that arises from omitting the subset consisting of the wage rate and nonearnings income. In particular, when past variables are included in the regressions, the bias due to the exclusion of each subset is 32 per cent (lines 6 and 7). This is an important finding if one is seeking to uncover channels via which the pure effect of schooling on non-market productivity operates. If one does not control for any of the con-temporaneous variables, then schooling may increase health simply because it raises market productivity and therefore command over market resources. If one takes account of this factor by holding the wage rate and nonearnings income constant, then part of the remain-ing effect of schooling on health may operate via the effect of this variable on spouses' characteristics, satisfaction with life style, and diet.

According to equation 6 or 7 in Table 5, with the wage rate and non-earnings income held constant, an increase in wives' schooling, an increase in job satisfaction, or a reduction in the absolute value of the difference between actual and ideal weight causes health to rise. The regression coefficients of these three variables are statistically sig-nificant at all conventional levels of confidence. The effect of wives' schooling is striking, because the coefficient of this variable exceeds the coefficient of own schooling. The difference between these two coefficients is not, however, statistically significant ($t = .68$ in both equations).

Even if the coefficients of husbands' and wives' schooling were the same, provided that the estimated health functions primarily reflected

[46] The other test scores are omitted from the computations in Table 7, because they have statistically insignificant effects on health. This procedure is justified in more detail when the effects of third variables are discussed below.

demand forces, one could conclude that wives' schooling has a larger impact on the efficiency with which husbands' health is produced than husbands' schooling. Since there is no specific measure of the value of wives' time, the demand parameter of their schooling would equal $\epsilon(\rho_f - \alpha_f \hat{W}_f)$, where ϵ is the price elasticity of health, ρ_f is the percentage increase in wives' nonmarket productivity for a one-year increase in schooling, α_f is the share of wives' time in the total cost of gross investment in husbands' health, and $\hat{W}_f$ is the percentage increase in the "shadow price" of time due to schooling. On the other hand, since husbands' wage rates are held constant, the demand parameter of their schooling should equal $\epsilon\rho$, where ρ is the percentage increase in their nonmarket productivity due to schooling. If these two demand parameters are identical, then

$$\rho_f = \rho + \alpha_f \hat{W}_f$$

Heckman in "Shadow Prices, Market Wages, and Labor Supply," [47] estimates that a one-year increase in wives' schooling raises the shadow price of time by 5.3 per cent, and I have already estimated that ρ equals 2.4 per cent. Therefore, ρ_f would equal 3.7 per cent if α_f were one-quarter, and would equal 5.0 per cent if α_f were one-half.

An alternative explanation of the effect of wives' schooling is that it reflects selective mating in the marriage market.[48] According to this interpretation, healthier men marry women with more schooling. Yet I control for important correlates of selective mating, such as general intelligence, parents' schooling, and past health.[49] Therefore, it is very unlikely that a significant part of the relationship between wives' schooling and husbands' health can be traced to selective mating.

With regard to the other contemporaneous variables, age is negatively related to health, which reflects the positive impact of this variable on the rate of depreciation on health capital. The hourly wage rate has a positive and very significant effect on health, while nonearnings income has an insignificant negative effect. These two findings support the predictions of my pure investment model of the demand for health. In a production function sense, the weak negative coefficient of nonearnings income may represent a compromise

[47] *Econometrica* 42 (July 1974):679–694.

[48] See Becker (1973) for a general discussion of the economics underlying this phenomenon and Fuchs (1974) for a discussion of health differentials among married men in terms of selective mating and other factors.

[49] Welch (1974) criticizes Benham (1974) for measuring the effect of wives' schooling on husbands' market productivity without controlling for husbands' ability and background characteristics.

between the consumption of beneficial and detrimental health inputs as income rises, with the wage rate held constant. Clearly this interpretation should not be pushed too far because the coefficient of non-earnings income is not statistically significant. But it may appeal to those who are surprised to learn that the pure income elasticity of health ranges from −.01 to −.02 at an income of $20,000.[50]

As shown by the *t* ratios associated with the regression coefficients of past health in Table 5, the partial correlation between this variable and current health exceeds the partial correlation between current health and any of the other independent variables in the regressions. The elasticity of current health with respect to past health varies from .44 to .48. In a demand-curve sense, this elasticity should estimate the ratio of the price elasticity of adults' health to the price elasticity of children's health.[51] Since the coefficient of ln *HHS* is smaller than one, the demand curve for children's health is more elastic than the demand curve for adults' health. If, as I have assumed in other computations, the price elasticity of adults' health equals one-half, then the price elasticity of children's health would approximately equal one.

The equations in Table 6 demonstrate that although past health is certainly not the most important determinant of schooling, it does have a statistically significant positive effect on years of formal schooling completed. Despite this, and despite the important role of past health in the current health function, the parameter estimate of schooling is not greatly affected by the inclusion of past health. This follows because schooling and past health are not nearly as highly correlated as schooling and the set of current variables. If the past health parameter estimate in the schooling function and the schooling parameter estimate in the health function are both converted into elasticities, then the elasticity of schooling with respect to past health would equal .03 and the elasticity of current health with respect to schooling would equal .18. It is clear that the latter elasticity dominates the former.

According to equation 7 in Table 5, among the past variables other than health in high school, only visual perception has a statistically significant effect on current health when all relevant factors are held constant. According to equation 2, this is true even if the set of predictor variables is limited to age, schooling, parents' schooling, the

[50] The pure income elasticity is computed as the product of the regression coefficient of nonearnings income (∂ ln $H69/\partial OTINC$) and total income in thousands of dollars.
[51] See equation 9″.

test scores, and past health.[52] As the equations in Table 6 reveal, parents' schooling and general intelligence are important determinants of schooling. Therefore, my results suggest that the effects of these variables on current health operate indirectly, via their effects on schooling. Once schooling is held constant, they have almost no direct impact on health.

In Section I, I argued that given the health-specific nature of physical ability, it should have a larger impact on current health than does mental ability. On the other hand, given the schooling-specific nature of mental ability, it should have a larger impact on schooling than does physical ability. Tables 5 and 6 contain some evidence in support of this hypothesis, provided visual perception is interpreted as a measure of health-specific ability and general intelligence is interpreted as a measure of schooling-specific ability. In interpreting the positive effect of visual perception on current health in this manner, I do not necessarily assume that this variable per se has a direct impact on current health. Rather, I assume that it is the best available proxy for genetic or biological characteristics that do influence the efficiency with which health is produced.[53]

Based on the above argument, and given that visual perception is the only component of ability that has a positive effect on health, I prefer a regression specification of the health function that omits the four other ability variables. Another reason for preferring such a specification is that, with general intelligence and parental characteristics held constant, it is not obvious what causes schooling to vary.[54] Since general intelligence plays a very important role in the estimated schooling function and plays an unimportant role in the estimated health function, it is logical to exclude it from the latter function. In theory, the appropriate way to take account of the insignificant effects of the four ability variables would be to reestimate the health function with another

[52] The simple correlation coefficient between fathers' schooling and mothers' schooling is .467. If either of these two variables is excluded from the set of independent variables, the remaining one is statistically significant in equation 2, borders on significance in several other equations in Table 5, but is not significant in equation 7. For this reason, I include both variables in the estimates of biases in schooling coefficients in Table 7.

[53] In this context, note that two of the scores in the mechanical ability component measure knowledge of mechanical principles rather than mechanical ability in a physical sense. Since persons may have acquired this knowledge in the labor force prior to 1943, the large negative effect of mechanical ability on schooling may be spurious.

[54] One source of variation may be traced to complementarity between number of years of schooling completed and the quality of schooling.

sample. Since this is not a feasible course of action at the present time, I omit these variables from the empirical analysis in the rest of this section and in Section IV.

B. *Decomposition Analysis*

It is well established that schooling raises market productivity, and my results in part A of this section suggest that it raises health productivity as well. Indeed, the recent work on the household production function approach to demand theory emphasizes the pervasive impact of schooling on many aspects of consumer behavior, including fertility, contraceptive knowlege, efficiency in producing quality children, and consumption patterns.[55] If schooling enhances productivity and knowledge in many areas, then it should increase a person's knowledge about an appropriate diet and raise his or her ability to select a productive mate and to produce a "high quality life style." Therefore, with market productivity, measured by the wage rate, and past variables held constant, the effect of schooling on health may be decomposed into direct and indirect components. The direct component represents the ability of those with additional schooling to obtain a larger health output from given amounts of all relevant inputs. The indirect component represents the ability of those with extra schooling to select a better input mix.[56]

In Table 8, I decompose an estimate of a total nonmarket productivity effect of schooling on health of 1.9 per cent into a direct component of 1.2 per cent and an indirect component of 0.7 per cent. The total effect equals the regression coefficient of schooling in an equation that includes age, parents' schooling, visual perception, past health, the wage rate, and nonearnings income as independent variables. The direct component equals the regression coefficient of schooling in an equation that adds wives' schooling, weight difference, and job satisfaction to the set of independent variables. The three positive indirect components are present because an increase in husbands' schooling is associated with an increase in wives' schooling, an increase in job satisfaction, and a reduction in the absolute value of the difference between actual and ideal weight. In turn, each of these three factors causes current health to rise.

---

[55] See, for example, the references cited in the introductory section of this paper.

[56] This decomposition is due to Welch (1970), who terms the direct component the "worker effect" and the indirect component the "allocative effect."

TABLE 8

Estimates of Direct and First-Order Indirect
Effects of Schooling on Health

Source of Effect	Magnitude	Percentage of Total Effect
Direct [a]	.012	63.16
First-order indirect:		
Wives' schooling	.005	26.32
Job satisfaction	.001	5.26
Weight difference	.001	5.26
Total [b]	.019	100.00

[a] Regression coefficient of schooling from equation 6 in Table 5.
[b] Regression coefficient of schooling from equation 5 in Table 5.

The statistical model that underlies this decomposition is a recursive system of the form:

$$SWIFE = a_1 S + a_2 Z$$
$$JSAT = c_1 S + c_2 Z + c_3 SWIFE$$
$$WTDIF = d_1 S + d_2 Z + d_3 SWIFE + d_4 JSAT$$
$$\ln H69 = b_1 S + b_2 Z + b_3 SWIFE + b_4 JSAT + b_5 WTDIF$$

where Z is a vector of predetermined variables. By substituting the first three equations into the fourth, one obtains an estimate of the total or reduced-form parameter of schooling. The direct component of this parameter estimate is given by b_1, the first-order indirect component due to wives' schooling by $a_1 b_3$, the first-order indirect component due to job satisfaction by $c_1 b_4$, and the first-order indirect component due to weight difference by $d_1 b_5$.[57]

In Table 8, I show that of the three indirect channels, the one due to wives' schooling is by far the most important. This channel accounts for 26.32 per cent of the total effect of husbands' schooling and 71.43 per cent of the combined indirect effect. Table 9 contains modified

[57] There are also second- and higher-order indirect effects that arise, for example, because wives' schooling influences job satisfaction. But these are *extremely* small and are not shown in Table 8. It may seem arbitrary to assume that the determination of *JSAT* precedes the determination of *WTDIF*. Since, however, the higher-order effects are very small, this assumption does not affect the computations in Table 8.

TABLE 9

Ordinary Least Squares Estimates of Wives' Schooling,
Weight Differences, and Job Satisfaction Functions [a]

	SWIFE Function	*WTDIF* Function	*JSAT* Function
Variable	Regression Coefficient	Regression Coefficient	Regression Coefficient
A	.018	.032	.001
	(1.21)	(0.24)	(0.23)
S	.302	−.282	.014
	(21.50)	(−2.15)	(2.23)
SFAT	.077	−.157	−.0001
	(7.51)	(−1.73)	(−0.02)
SMOT	.055	−.164	.006
	(5.20)	(−1.78)	(1.37)
V	−.002	−.172	−.006
	(−0.06)	(−0.80)	(−0.56)
ln *HHS*	.173	1.643	.177
	(1.39)	(1.51)	(3.50)
ln W	.046	−.279	.240
	(0.67)	(−0.46)	(8.54)
OTINC	.015	.014	−.003
	(2.80)	(0.29)	(−1.52)
SWIFE		−.114	.006
		(−0.77)	(0.85)
R^2	.189	.008	.036

[a] t ratios in parentheses.

estimates of the first three equations in the recursive system.[58] These equations may be viewed as demand curves for three inputs into the production of health although wives' schooling, weight difference, and job satisfaction also enter the production functions of other household commodities.

According to Table 9, schooling is the only predictor variable that has a significant effect on all three inputs. For example, while the hourly wage rate is the best predictor of job satisfaction, it is not related to wives' schooling or weight difference. These results reveal

[58] Since the sequence in which job satisfaction and weight difference are determined is somewhat arbitrary, job satisfaction is omitted from the weight difference equation.

TABLE 10

Ordinary Least Squares Estimate of Dichotomous
Excellent Health Function [a]

Variable	Regression Coefficient	Variable	Regression Coefficient
A	−.009	*SWIFE*	.011
	(−2.53)		(2.75)
S	.010	*JSAT*	.053
	(2.82)		(5.18)
SFAT	.001	*WTDIF*	−.002
	(0.39)		(−3.97)
SMOT	.005	ln W	.101
	(1.76)		(5.88)
V	.022	*OTINC*	−.001
	(3.71)		(−0.55)
ln *HHS*	.314	R^2	.089
	(10.21)		

[a] t ratios in parentheses.

the important role of schooling in many aspects of consumer behavior. Clearly, a more careful examination of the process by which schooling influences behavior and the mechanisms by which it operates should be given high priority on an agenda for future research.[59]

C. Estimates of Excellent Health Functions

To examine the sensitivity of the results in part A of this section to the manner in which I scaled health status, I created a dichotomous variable (*EXCELL*) that is equal to one if a man is in excellent health and is equal to zero otherwise. This variable has a mean of .5951, which indicates that approximately 60 per cent of the sample are in excellent health. Table 10 contains an ordinary least squares regression of the dichotomous excellent health variable on the same set of independent variables that enter equation 6 in Table 5. For given values of the independent variables, the predicted value of the dependent variable can be interpreted as the conditional probability that a man is in excellent health. Similarly, the regression coefficient of a

[59] I have probably "contaminated" the NBER-Thorndike sample for research along these lines, but other data sets can be utilized.

given independent variable shows the change in the conditional probability of being in excellent health for a one-unit (1 per cent in the case of ln *HHS* or ln *W*) change in this variable.

The magnitudes of the regression coefficients in Table 10 should and do differ from the magnitudes of the corresponding coefficients in Table 5. The signs of these two sets of regression coefficients are, however, identical, and the same patterns of statistical significance emerge from the two equations. These findings should strengthen confidence in the results obtained with ln *H*69 as the dependent variable in the current health function. This variable, like the theoretical index of health capital, is free of units. Moreover, there is some theoretical justification for the scales used to create it, and for the magnitudes of its regression coefficients.

It is well known that certain statistical problems arise when the dependent variable in an ordinary least squares regression is dichotomous.[60] In particular, the regression in Table 10 does not take account of the restriction that the conditional probability of being in excellent health should lie between zero and one. To take account of this restriction, I have estimated a dichotomous logit excellent health function by the method of maximum likelihood. This technique assumes that the probability that the ith individual is in excellent health (p_i) is given by the logistic function

$$p_i = 1/(1 + e^{-a}e^{-bx_i})$$

where x_i is an independent variable (or a vector of variables) and a and b are parameters to be estimated. With the logistic function, the predicted value of p_i must fall between zero and one. By solving for the logarithm of the odds of being in excellent health, one transforms the logistic function into a linear equation:

$$\ln[p_i/(1 - p_i)] = a + bx_i$$

which is called the logit function.[61] The logit coefficient b shows the percentage change in the odds for a one-unit change in x_i. The marginal effect of x_i on p_i (the change in p_i due to a one-unit change in x_i) is given by

$$(\partial p_i/\partial x_i) = bp_i(1 - p_i)$$

[60] For an extensive discussion of these problems and a complete description of alternative estimation techniques, see Nerlove and Press (1973).
[61] See Berkson (1944, 1955) for detailed analyses of the properties of the logit function.

TABLE 11

Maximum Likelihood Estimate of Dichotomous
Logit Excellent Health Function [a]

Variable	Logit Coefficient	Marginal Effect	Variable	Logit Coefficient	Marginal Effect
A	−.041	−.010	$SWIFE$	.053	.013
	(−2.49)			(2.76)	
S	.046	.011	$JSAT$	.237	.057
	(2.74)			(5.12)	
$SFAT$	.004	.001	$WTDIF$	−.008	−.002
	(0.36)			(−3.91)	
$SMOT$	.020	.005	ln W	.466	.112
	(1.73)			(5.79)	
V	.101	.024	$OTINC$	−.003	−.001
	(3.66)			(−0.54)	
ln HHS	1.427	.344			
	(9.56)				

[a] Asymptotic t ratios in parentheses.

Table 11 contains an estimate of a dichotomous logit excellent health function.[62] The marginal effects in the table are computed at the mean value of p for the sample of .5951. A comparison of the results in Tables 10 and 11 reveals that all variables have the same signs in the ordinary least squares excellent health function as they have in the logit function. Tests of statistical significance yield identical conclusions when applied to either function. Moreover, the marginal effects in Table 11 are approximately equal to the corresponding regression coefficients in Table 10. It should be noted that problems similar to

---

[62] To see how this function is obtained, consider a sample in which, for simplicity, the first m men are in excellent health and the next $n - m$ are not. The natural logarithm of the likelihood function associated with this sample is

$$\ln L = \sum_{i=1}^{m} \ln p_i + \sum_{i=m+1}^{n} \ln (1 - p_i)$$

Assuming that the relationship between p_i and x_i is given by the logistic function and maximizing ln L with respect to a and b, one obtains the estimates in Table 11. The ratios of logit coefficients to their standard errors do not have Student's t distribution. These ratios do, however, approach the normal distribution as the sample size becomes large. Therefore, the t test is an asymptotic one, which can be applied to the logit function I estimate, since there are over 3,500 observations.

those that are encountered when a dependent variable is dichotomous are also encountered when it is polytomous.[63] Since my health capital series has only four possible values, it generates a polytomous variable. Yet an extrapolation of the comparison between ordinary least squares and logit excellent health functions would suggest that one would gain little by using estimation techniques other than ordinary least squares simply because ln $H69$ is polytomous.

IV. ESTIMATES OF A SIMULTANEOUS-EQUATIONS HEALTH-WAGE MODEL

A. Introduction

In previous sections of this paper, I assumed that the current stock of health is not a determinant of the current stock of human capital. I now relax this assumption and examine the possibility that health capital, as one component of human capital, raises market productivity and the hourly wage rate. Empirically, I estimate a simultaneous-equations model by the method of two-stage least squares, in which current health and the hourly wage rate are endogenous variables.

There are both theoretical and empirical reasons for proceeding along these lines. At a theoretical level, the distinction that I have drawn between adults' health capital as a determinant of their total available time and their human capital as a determinant of their productivity may be too extreme. If, as I have postulated, students' health influences their productivity in school, then should not adults' health influence their productivity in the labor market? Moreover, Malkiel and Malkiel (1973) hypothesize that employers may lower the wage offered to employees who work fewer hours in a year due to illness and other reasons. Finally, Mincer (1970, 1974) stresses that investment in on-the-job training, measured by the total amount of time spent in such activity, plays a major role in the wage function. This variable is imperfectly measured in most data sets. The best available proxy is years of experience in the labor market, which itself is subject to measurement error. To the extent that poor health reduces the amount of time spent in the labor market, current health may affect the current wage via its impact on past investment in on-the-job training.

At an empirical level, studies by Boskin (1971); Hall (1973); and Luft (1972) suggest that health, treated as an exogenous variable, does have a positive effect on the wage rate. Benham and I (Grossman and Benham 1974) also find a positive impact of health on the wage

[63] See Nerlove and Press (1973).

when both variables are treated as endogenous in the NORC sample. Therefore, part of the positive relationship between these two variables in the regressions in Section III may reflect causality from health to market productivity. The health-wage model that I estimate in this section may be viewed as an extension of the Grossman-Benham model, although the measure of health and the set of exogenous variables are somewhat different.

I want to emphasize that there are costs to be paid as well as benefits to be gained as a result of simultaneous-equations estimation. In particular, I have found in previous work that when this method is applied to microdata, results tend to be fairly sensitive to the manner in which equations are "identified." Although it might be clear in theory that a certain subset of exogenous variables should be included in one equation and excluded from another, key members of this subset might not be available in the data. Another problem in applying two-stage least squares, for example, to microdata is that coefficients of determination in the first stage rarely exceed 30 or 40 per cent. Therefore, in selecting between two-stage least squares and ordinary least squares estimates, one is forced to make a tradeoff between consistency and efficiency.[64] Given these factors, and given the far from ideal way in which health is measured in the NBER-Thorndike sample, I view the model that is formulated and fitted in this section as an *illustration* of the kind of model that could be fitted with more refined data. The parameter estimates that I present are by no means definitive. For the same reasons, I also view the simultaneous-equations model as a complement to, rather than a substitute for, the ordinary least squares model.

B. Specification of Structural Equations

The structural equations for health and the hourly wage rate are as follows:

$$\ln H69 = b_1 A + b_2 S + b_3 V + b_4 \ln HHS + b_5 SWIFE$$
$$+ b_6 JSAT + b_7 WTDIF + b_8 \ln W^* + b_9 OTINC \quad (17)$$

$$\ln W = a_1 \ln H69^* + a_2 S + a_3 EXP + a_4 GEN + a_5 SOUTH + a_6 CS1$$
$$+ a_7 CS2 + a_8 CS3 + a_9 CS4 + a_{10} CS5 \quad (18)$$

An asterisk next to a variable in equation 17 or 18 means it is endogenous. Variables in the wage function that were not included in the analy-

---

[64] Finis Welch has stressed this point to me on a number of occasions.

TABLE 12
Definition of Supplementary Variables

Variable	Definition
EXP	Years of experience in the labor force [a]
SOUTH	Reside in South = 1
CS1 [b]	Reside in a small town (2,500–10,000 people) = 1
CS2 [b]	Reside in a town (10,000–50,000 people) = 1
CS3 [b]	Reside in a moderate-sized city (50,000–250,000 people) = 1
CS4 [b]	Reside in a large city (250,000–1 million people) = 1
CS5 [b]	Reside in a major metropolitan area (over 1 million people) = 1

[a] See text for a more complete definition.
[b] Omitted class is reside in a rural area (under 2,500 people).

sis in Section III are defined in Table 12. The specification of the health function was fully discussed in previous sections. Here, I would simply point out that I omit mothers' schooling and fathers' schooling from this function. That is, I assume that any gross effects of these two variables on health operate solely via their effects on own schooling or past health.[65]

The wage function is based on work on wage determination by Becker and Chiswick (1966); Mincer (1970, 1974); and Lillard (1973). These authors emphasize that wage rates should be positively related to correlates of the stock of human capital, such as years of formal schooling completed, years of experience in the labor force, general intelligence, and current health. Obviously, years of formal schooling completed is a partial measure of the quantity of investment in knowledge via schooling, while years of experience in the labor market, defined as the number of years since a man was last in school, is a partial measure of the quantity of investment in on-the-job training. General intelligence and health may influence the quantities of both types of investment. Note that, if the dependent variable in equation 18 were annual earnings or weekly earnings, a positive health effect might simply mean that health raises weeks worked per year or hours worked per week but has no effect on market productivity. Since, however, the dependent variable in the equation is the natural logarithm of the *hourly* wage rate, one cannot interpret a positive health coefficient along these lines.[66]

[65] Two-stage least squares estimates obtained with these two variables in the health function (not shown) are almost identical to those presented in part C of this section.
[66] I exclude the square of years of experience from equation 18, because the dependent variable is the hourly wage rate. Although theory and previous empirical research sug-

I add dummy variables for region and city size to the basic set of human capital variables in the wage function. I assume that these variables mainly capture shifts in the demand curve for labor around a fairly stable supply curve among labor markets in the United States. Undoubtedly, part of the variation in wages by region and city size is due to differences in the cost of living. Since the health function should relate health to the wage rate, with the prices of medical care and other market goods used to produce health held constant, region and city size might also be entered in the health function. However, in that function, they might reflect other factors as well, such as variation in the availability of medical care, not associated with the price of care and climate. Some of these factors might offset differences in the cost of living. Moreover, the health components of an aggregate price index might not vary in the same manner as the index itself among regions and cities of various sizes. Since I have not emphasized region and city-size health differentials, and since predictions concerning these differentials are ambiguous, I do not include these variables in the health function. To the extent that the money wage rate is positively correlated with the prices of health inputs, the estimated wage elasticity of health would be biased *downward*.[67]

C. Results

Table 13 contains two-stage least squares estimates of health functions, and Table 14 contains two-stage least squares estimates of wage functions.[68] The results in the latter table reveal that the endogenous current health variable has a positive and very significant effect on the hourly wage rate. As shown by its regression coefficient in equation 1,

gest that experience-earnings profiles or experience–weekly-wage profiles should be concave to the origin (Becker 1967; Ben-Porath 1967; Mincer 1970, 1974; Lillard 1973), I find no empirical evidence that experience–hourly-wage profiles are concave. This may be due in part to the limited age range in the NBER-Thorndike sample.

[67] If the health demand curve given by equation 9″ is differentiated with respect to the wage rate, and if the composite price of medical care and other inputs (P) varies with the wage, then

$$(d \ln H/d \ln W) = \alpha\epsilon[1 - (d \ln P/d \ln W)]$$

[68] When two-stage least squares estimation is employed, the ratios of regression coefficients to their standard errors do not have Student's t distribution but do have an asymptotic normal distribution. Therefore, the t test is an asymptotic one. The unadjusted coefficients of multiple determination (R^2) in Tables 13 and 14 should be interpreted with caution. I forced the R^2 to fall between zero and one, for example, by using the variance in the logarithm of the predicted wage rather than the variance in the logarithm of the actual wage in computing the ones in Table 13. I used this procedure to get a rough approximation of "explanatory power." Since age, schooling, and experience are almost perfectly collinear, I omitted experience from the first-stage health equation. Similarly, I omitted age from the first-stage wage equation.

TABLE 13

Two-Stage Squares Estimates of Health Functions [a]

Variable	Equation 1 Regression Coefficient	Equation 2 Regression Coefficient	Equation 3 Regression Coefficient
A	−.013	−.014	−.014
	(−2.56)	(−2.63)	(−2.63)
S	.004	.012	.013
	(0.58)	(1.66)	(1.82)
V	.031	.032	.032
	(3.62)	(3.67)	(3.71)
ln HHS	.427	.438	.440
	(9.63)	(9.72)	(9.78)
SWIFE	.020		
	(3.42)		
JSAT	.070		
	(4.25)		
WTDIF	−.002		
	(−3.49)		
ln W^*	.297	.325	.310
	(3.03)	(3.31)	(3.39)
OTINC	−.003	−.003	
	(−1.18)	(−1.18)	
R^2	.082	.063	.063

[a] An asterisk next to a variable means that it is endogenous. Asymptotic t ratios in parentheses. See Tables 3 and 12 for definitions of variables.

a 10 per cent increase in the stock of current health causes the hourly wage rate to rise by approximately 4 per cent. The signs of the regression coefficients of the other variables in the wage equation are consistent with a priori expectations.

In Table 13, I demonstrate that when the wage is treated as an endogenous variable, a striking change occurs in the health function coefficient of this variable. In equation 6 in Table 5, the wage elasticity of health equals .15. In equation 1 in Table 13, this elasticity equals .30. This doubling in the wage elasticity occurs despite the presumed upward bias in the ordinary least squares estimate because it reflects causality from health to the wage as well as causality from the wage to

TABLE 14

Two-Stage Least Squares Estimates of Wage Functions [a]

Variable	Equation 1 Regression Coefficient	Equation 2 [b] Regression Coefficient	Equation 3 [c] Regression Coefficient
ln $H69$*	.403	.314	.254
	(7.83)	(5.23)	(4.31)
S	.043	.046	.048
	(9.10)	(10.15)	(10.80)
EXP	.007	.007	.007
	(4.35)	(4.90)	(4.98)
GEN	.031	.033	.034
	(5.46)	(5.98)	(6.35)
$SOUTH$	−.013	−.014	−.015
	(−0.63)	(−0.73)	(−0.79)
$CS1$	.157	.155	.154
	(4.56)	(4.73)	(4.81)
$CS2$	.182	.190	.195
	(5.75)	(6.25)	(6.58)
$CS3$	.207	.213	.217
	(6.24)	(6.71)	(7.00)
$CS4$	.224	.236	.243
	(6.23)	(6.80)	(7.18)
$CS5$	.348	.358	.365
	(9.86)	(10.56)	(11.03)
R^2	.166	.156	.153

[a] An asterisk next to a variable means it is endogenous. Asymptotic t ratios in parentheses.

[b] $SWIFE$, $JSAT$, and $WTDIF$ excluded from the set of instrumental variables.

[c] $SWIFE$, $JSAT$, $WTDIF$, and $OTINC$ excluded from the set of instrumental variables.

health.[69] A possible explanation of this finding is that there might be measurement error in the computed hourly wage variable, which would bias the ordinary least squares parameter estimate downward. This

[69] Suppose that the wage elasticity of health (b_8) and the health elasticity of the wage (a_1) are positive. Then the simultaneous-equations system given by equations 17 and 18 would have a stable solution if, and only if, the product of b_8 and a_1 were smaller than one. This follows because the reduced-form health parameter of ln HHS, for example, is $b_4/(1 - b_8 a_1)$. Since b_8 equals .30 and a_1 equals .40, the stability condition is satisfied at an empirical level.

bias should be reduced by the use of a set of instrumental variables via the method of two-stage least squares.

In the health-wage model that Benham and I (Grossman and Benham 1974) fit to the NORC sample, the endogenous wage rate has a *negative* effect on health rather than a positive effect. We argue that this might reflect a greater tendency to select occupations that are hazardous or otherwise detrimental to health as the wage rate rises, with schooling and experience held constant. It should be noted that Benham and I include proxy variables for preventive medical care in our health function. This is one source of the discrepancy between the signs of the wage elasticities in the NORC and NBER-Thorndike samples. Another source is that the NORC health function is estimated for all white men, while the NBER-Thorndike health function is estimated for a high-earnings, high-schooling, and high-ability sample. Variations in wages associated with harmful health characteristics of occupations might be much more important at low levels of earnings and schooling than at high levels.

In general, there are two theoretical reasons for an increase in the wage elasticity of health as the wage rate rises. First, if the elasticity of substitution between own time and market goods in the health production function exceeded one, then the share of market goods in the total cost of producing health (α) would rise with the wage. This would increase the wage parameter ($\alpha\epsilon$) in the health demand curve. Second, the positive relationship between the wage rate and what I have termed "the inconvenience costs of illness" (Grossman 1972b, p. 69) might become stronger as the wage grows. This relationship arises because the complexity of a particular job and the amount of responsibility it entails certainly are positively correlated with the wage. Thus, when an individual with a high wage becomes ill, tasks that only he can perform accumulate. These increase the intensity of his work load and give him an incentive to avoid illness by demanding more health capital. I suspect that the importance of inconvenience costs in the NBER-Thorndike sample is the major source of the large wage elasticity of health that is observed in this sample. By using a set of instrumental variables for the wage rate, I probably create a variable that more accurately reflects these costs than the measured wage.

With two exceptions, the health coefficients of variables other than the wage are not altered much when the wage is treated as endogenous. The two exceptions are that the coefficient of nonearnings income increases in absolute value and the coefficient of own schooling falls dramatically (compare equation 1 in Table 13 to equation 6 in Table

5). The pure income elasticity of health rises in absolute value from −.01 to −.06 at an income of $20,000 when the health function is estimated by two-stage least squares rather than by ordinary least squares. Although the pure income elasticity is still not statistically significant, its sign suggests that, at high income levels, the consumption of detrimental health inputs grows at least as rapidly as the consumption of beneficial inputs as income grows. In a statistical sense, the reduction in the coefficient of own schooling is due to multicollinearity between schooling and the predicted wage rate. These two variables are much more highly correlated than schooling and the actual wage rate ($r = .642$ versus $r = .289$). In a literal sense, according to equation 1 in Table 13, schooling has no direct effect on health, with the wage rate and other variables held constant.

Even if the literal interpretation of the schooling coefficient in equation 1 is correct, this does *not* mean that schooling has no impact on health independent of its impact on the wage rate. In part B of Section II, I showed that schooling influences health in part because of its effects on wives' schooling, weight difference, and job satisfaction. Equation 2 in Table 13 allows the schooling coefficient to reflect these channels by omitting wives' schooling, job satisfaction, and weight difference from the model. The omission of these three variables causes the schooling coefficient to triple in magnitude and to achieve statistical significance at the .05 level of confidence on a one-tail test. Greenberg (1972) and Smith (1973) argue that it is not entirely appropriate to treat nonearnings income as an exogenous variable in the context of a model of life-cycle decision making. Therefore, equation 3 excludes this variable as well as the three excluded in equation 2. This results in a slightly larger and a slightly more significant schooling coefficient.[70]

[70] Clearly, within the context of a life-cycle model, wives' schooling, job satisfaction, weight difference, and nonearnings income are endogenous variables. If these variables are determined prior to the determination of current health and the current wage, it would be appropriate to use them as instruments in two-stage least squares. If, however, they are determined simultaneously with current health and the current wage, they should not be used as instruments. I have not tried to estimate equation 1 in Table 13 by specifying separate equations for *SWIFE, JSAT, WTDIF,* and *OTINC.* I have estimated equation 1 with these variables entered in the second-stage health function but excluded from the first-stage. Coefficients obtained in this manner are almost identical to those shown in equation 1.

Equation 2 in Table 14 gives the wage function that is obtained when *SWIFE, JSAT,* and *WTDIF* are excluded from the health function, and equation 3 gives the wage function that is obtained when these three variables and *OTINC* are excluded. The main impact of these exclusions is to reduce the elasticity of the wage with respect to health from approximately .4 to approximately .3. The smaller elasticity is still significant at all conventional levels of confidence.

TABLE 15

Estimates of Direct, Indirect, and Total Effects of
Schooling on Health and the Wage Rate

	Health Effects	Wage Effects
Direct effect	.014	.052
Indirect effect	.016	.003
Total effect (reduced-form parameter)	.030	.055

Due to the importance of schooling as a policy variable from the point of view of both the individual and society, it is useful to examine the reduced-form health and schooling parameters of this variable. In Table 15, I show estimates of these parameters based on a specification of the health function that omits wives' schooling, job satisfaction, weight difference, and nonearnings income. I also decompose each parameter into a direct component and an indirect component.[71] The reduced-form health parameter of schooling indicates that a one-year increase in this variable raises health by 3.0 per cent. The indirect component, which is present because schooling raises the wage rate and the wage rate raises health, is slightly larger than the direct component. The reduced-form wage parameter of schooling suggests a rate of return to investment in schooling via an expansion in market productivity of 5.5 per cent. A small percentage of this increase (approximately 5.45 per cent) can be attributed to the increase in health caused by an increase in schooling.

In a sense, the direct component of the reduced-form health parameter is itself an indirect component, because it measures the effects of schooling on health that operate via wives' schooling, job satisfaction, and weight difference. Regardless of the manner in which the direct component is interpreted, its magnitude suggests that schooling influences health by channels other than the wage rate. Given the high degree of multicollinearity between schooling and the predicted wage, this is an impressive finding. Future research is necessary in order to ascertain whether the direct nonmarket productivity component of the

[71] Given the simultaneous-equations system specified by equations 17 and 18, the reduced-form health parameter of schooling equals $(b_2 + a_2 b_8)/(1 - b_8 a_1)$. The term $b_2/(1 - b_8 a_1)$ gives the direct component, and the term $a_2 b_8/(1 - b_8 a_1)$ gives the indirect component. Similarly, the reduced-form wage parameter of schooling equals $(a_2 + b_2 a_1)/(1 - b_8 a_1)$, where $a_2/(1 - b_8 a_1)$ is the direct component and $b_2 a_1/(1 - b_8 a_1)$ is the indirect component.

schooling coefficient in the health function is really as small as the simultaneous-equations model indicates, and whether the indirect non-market component is as large.

V. MORTALITY EXPERIENCE OF THE THORNDIKE SAMPLE BETWEEN 1955 AND 1969

A. Nature of the Analysis

Death is the most objective, although the most extreme, measure of ill health. Therefore, in this section I examine the mortality experience of the Thorndike sample between the year of the initial survey by Thorndike and Hagen (1955) and the year of the first resurvey by the NBER (1969). In particular, I want to see whether relationships that are observed when health is measured by self-rated health status are also observed when health is measured by mortality or survival.

Of the 9,700 men in the original Thorndike sample, 275 had died by 1969.[72] This gives a mortality rate of 2.84 per cent over a period that extends roughly from 1956 through 1968. In 1955, the mean age of the sample was thirty-three years, and the age-specific death rate in the United States of white males ages thirty-five to forty-four was 0.34 per cent (National Center for Health Statistics 1961). Since this age-specific death rate was practically constant between 1956 and 1968, 4.32 per cent of the Thorndike sample would have died by 1968 if the sample had the same mortality experience as the population at large.[73] Thus, the survival rate in a sample drawn from the upper tails of the schooling, earnings, and scholastic-ability distributions exceeds the survival rate in the general population. This complements my finding that the levels of self-rated health status and healthy time in the NBER-Thorndike sample exceed the levels of these health indexes in the NORC sample.

To examine the partial effects of various factors on survival in the Thorndike sample, I have estimated a dichotomous logit survival function by the method of maximum likelihood.[74] If p_i is the probability that the ith individual survives, then this function is given by

---

[72] Although the response rate to the 1969 questionnaire was only slightly higher than 50 per cent, it is known with certainty that exactly 275 men died. This information was supplied by the Veterans Administration.

[73] If the age-specific death rate of a cohort (d) is constant over time, then the fraction who die in a t-year period would equal $1 - (1 - d)^t$.

[74] I have also estimated dichotomous survival functions by ordinary least squares. The results (not shown) are almost identical to those obtained with the logit functions in part B of this section.

$$\ln [p_i/(1 - p_i)] = b_1S + b_2V + b_3P + b_4MECH + b_5GEN$$
$$+ b_6NUM + b_7JSAT55 + b_8 \ln SAL55$$

where S is years of formal schooling completed in 1955, $JSAT55$ is an index of job satisfaction in 1955, ln $SAL55$ is the natural logarithm of full-time salary in 1955, and the other variables are defined in Section II. The logit function contains only eight independent variables, because no information is available on people who died between 1955 and 1969 other than that collected by Thorndike and Hagen in 1955. Full-time salary rather than the hourly wage rate measures the value of time, because there are no data on hours worked per week in 1955. Job satisfaction in 1955 is simply the answer to the question: How well do you like the type of work you are doing now? The four possible numerical responses constitute a scale ranging from four (the highest) to one (the lowest).

I could have used all 9,700 men in the original sample as a base for estimating the logit function, but, for two reasons, I have limited observations on survivors to men who responded to the 1969 NBER questionnaire. First, a significant fraction of the sample completed their formal schooling after 1955.[75] Therefore, a positive relationship between schooling in 1955 and survival might reflect the incentive of persons with a longer life expectancy and a higher level of general health to invest more in schooling. By using the 1969 survey as a base, I can restrict the survivors to men who had completed their formal schooling by 1955.

Second, Thorndike and Hagen did not obtain age as a variable in 1955. Since age and schooling are negatively correlated and age and survival are presumably negatively correlated, the effect of schooling on survival is biased upward by the omission of age from the survival function. By selecting survivors who had completed their formal schooling by 1955, I select a set whose mean age is somewhat greater than the mean age of all survivors. At the same time, I reduce the size of the correlation between age and schooling. This procedure mitigates, although it does not entirely eliminate, the bias caused by omitting age from the survival function.[76]

[75] Of the 5,085 respondents to the 1969 questionnaire, 11 per cent completed schooling after 1955.

[76] My procedure assumes that men who completed schooling by 1955 and responded to the 1969 questionnaire have the same characteristics as all men who survived and completed schooling by 1955. Taubman and Wales (1974) indicate that men who responded to the 1969 questionnaire reported slightly higher schooling levels in 1955 than the entire 1955 sample. But their comparison is *not* restricted to men who finished schooling by 1955.

TABLE 16

Characteristics of Samples in Survival Analysis

Sample	Size	Deaths	Adjusted Mortality Rate (Per Cent)
Positive salary in 1955	4,386	248	2.83
Salary exceeds one-half the median salary	4,277	238	2.78
Salary exceeds the median salary	2,013	107	2.66

Note that men with zero or unknown full-time salaries in 1955 are excluded from the analysis. Therefore, persons who died shortly after 1955 and were not able to work at all in that year are eliminated from the survival function. To further reduce the magnitude of a possible relationship from survival to full-time salary, I estimate survival functions for men whose 1955 full-time salary exceeds one-half the median full-time salary of $6,000 and for men whose salary exceeds the median salary. This procedure alleviates problems that arise because I do not know whether decedents completed their formal schooling by 1955. It is unlikely that a decedent whose salary exceeded the median salary had not finished his schooling.

The sample size, number of deaths, and "adjusted mortality rate" in each of the three logit functions that I fit are shown in Table 16. Since the response rate to the 1969 questionnaire was approximately 50 per cent, the decedents in each sample represent 100 per cent of all decedents, but the survivors represent 50 per cent of all survivors. Therefore, in computing the adjusted mortality rate, I give double weight to survivors. In calculating logistic functions, I do not give double weight to survivors, but I do estimate marginal effects at the adjusted mean probability of survival (one minus the adjusted death rate).[77]

B. Results

Table 17 contains maximum likelihood estimates of dichotomous logit survival functions. The three equations in the table reveal that

[77] In regression analysis, weighting is employed to produce efficient estimates rather than to produce consistent estimates. Consequently, it is by no means obvious that logistics survival functions should be weighted.

TABLE 17

Maximum Likelihood Estimates of Dichotomous
Logit Survival Functions [a]

Variable	Equation 1 [b]		Equation 2 [c]		Equation 3 [d]	
	Logit Coeffi- cient	Marginal Effect	Logit Coeffi- cient	Marginal Effect	Logit Coeffi- cient	Marginal Effect
S	.135 (4.06)	.004	.142 (4.15)	.004	.147 (3.04)	.004
V	.037 (0.68)	.001	.037 (0.67)	.001	.058 (0.71)	.002
P	−.038 (−0.67)	−.001	−.034 (−0.59)	−.001	−.085 (−0.97)	−.002
MECH	.013 (0.22)	.0004	.015 (0.25)	.0004	.012 (0.13)	.0003
GEN	.056 (1.05)	.002	.070 (1.28)	.002	.032 (0.42)	.001
NUM	−.013 (−0.24)	−.0004	−.009 (−0.17)	−.0003	.014 (0.17)	.0004
JSAT55	.084 (0.84)	.002	.116 (1.14)	.003	.027 (0.17)	.001
ln SAL55	.037 (0.21)	.001	−.087 (−0.46)	−.002	.129 (0.39)	.003

[a] Asymptotic t ratios in parentheses.
[b] Includes all men who completed schooling by 1955 and who had a positive salary in that year. Sample size is 4,386.
[c] Includes men whose salary exceeded one-half the median salary. Sample size is 4,277.
[d] Includes men whose salary exceeded the median salary. Sample size is 2,013.

schooling has a positive and statistically significant effect on the probability of survival. Indeed, schooling is the only variable whose logit coefficient differs from zero in a statistical sense. The schooling effect is independent of the level of median salary in 1955 and suggests that in the vicinity of the adjusted death rate a one-year increase in schooling lowers the probability of death by .4 percentage points. The important role of schooling in the survival function is a further justification for the emphasis that I have given to this variable as a determinant of health throughout this paper.

Although none of the other variables has a statistically significant effect on survival, the signs of job satisfaction and visual perception are consistent with the signs of these variables in the self-rated health status functions. When the lower tail of the salary distribution is included in the analysis, general intelligence is a better predictor of survival than visual perception. This is not, however, the case when the sample is limited to the upper tail of the salary distribution. In general, the estimated schooling parameter and the estimated parameter of a given test score are not sensitive to the other test scores that are included in the survival function.

Two difficulties with the mortality analysis are that the men in the Thorndike sample were only in their thirties in 1955, and that relatively few variables are available for that year. The sample has now reached a point in the life cycle at which death rates in future years should be much higher than in the past. Consequently, one promising area for future research would be to trace the mortality experience of the sample for the next five or ten years. Mortality could then be related to a wide variety of factors that can be measured with the large set of variables that was collected by the NBER in 1969 and 1971.

VI. SUMMARY AND CONCLUSION

In this paper, I have used the household production function approach to consumer behavior to develop recursive and simultaneous models of decision making that can be used to formulate and estimate health-schooling relationships. In the theoretical section, I have shown how a recursive system whose principal equations are demand curves for children's health, schooling, and adults' health generates causal relationships from schooling to health and from health to schooling. In addition, this system generates relationships from third variables to both health and schooling. In the main empirical section, I have estimated a recursive health-schooling model by ordinary least squares, using data contained in the NBER-Thorndike sample. In this model, I have measured health capital by self-rated health status. In other empirical sections, I have conducted "sensitivity analyses" that show how the ordinary least squares results are affected (1) when the health equation is specified as a dichotomous logit function and estimated by the method of maximum likelihood, and (2) when the health function is fitted in the context of a simultaneous-equations health-wage model. Finally, I have examined the mortality experience of the Thorndike sample between 1955 and 1969.

The major empirical results of the recursive health-schooling model can be summarized as follows. With past health and third variables held constant, schooling has a positive and statistically significant effect on current health. This is evidence in favor of a causal relationship that runs from schooling to current health. The estimated bias in schooling coefficients is larger when current variables are omitted from the health function than when past variables are omitted. Current variables include the hourly wage rate, wives' schooling, weight difference, and job satisfaction; while past variables include past health, parents' schooling, and visual perception. Past health has an extremely significant positive effect on current health and also has a positive and significant effect on years of formal schooling completed. Yet the parameter estimate of schooling in the current health function is not greatly altered by the inclusion of past health. Current health is positively related to physical ability, measured by visual perception, but it is not related to mental ability, measured by general intelligence. A decomposition analysis of the effect of schooling on health, with the wage rate held constant, reveals that a substantial fraction of this effect operates via the impact of schooling on wives' schooling, job satisfaction, and weight difference. Indeed, these three channels of influence account for nearly 40 per cent of the total nonmarket productivity effect of schooling on health.

The sensitivity analysis reveals that the qualitative results of the recursive model are not altered when the health equation is specified as a dichotomous logit function and estimated by the technique of maximum likelihood. In the context of the simultaneous-equations health-wage model, schooling has a somewhat smaller impact on health than it does in the pure recursive system. In fact, the simultaneous-equations model shows that, with the wage rate held constant, the entire effect of schooling on health operates via the channels of wives' schooling, job satisfaction, and weight difference. This model also shows that health is an important determinant of market productivity and the hourly wage rate. The mortality experience of the Thorndike sample between 1955 and 1969 confirms the important role of schooling in the health function.

I view the empirical work in this paper as preliminary or ongoing rather than definitive or final. Given the uniqueness of the Thorndike sample and the less than ideal measures of health, the models that I have formulated and estimated should be treated as examples of the kinds of models that could be fitted with longitudinal samples that contain more refined measures of current and past health and background characteristics. Due to the preliminary nature of my work,

I have not hesitated to suggest alternative explanations of certain findings, to speculate and to be provocative in discussing results, and to propose a partial agenda for future research.

One topic on such an agenda would be a careful study of the process by which schooling influences health and other aspects of consumer behavior. In such a study, one would delineate in detail all channels through which the nonmarket productivity effect of schooling on health operates. A second topic would be an examination of the mortality experience of the NBER-Thorndike sample after 1969. A third topic, not previously mentioned, would be a study that takes full account of my notion that children's health is one aspect of their quality. In this research, one would formulate and estimate a demand curve for children's health. One would also use this demand curve to derive and estimate a demand curve for children's medical care along the same lines that I have used in the past to derive and fit a demand curve for adults' medical care (Grossman 1972b). At a somewhat deeper level, my empirical results suggest that what some persons might call "attitudinal variables," such as self-rated health status and job satisfaction, are amenable to economic analysis. Consequently, practitioners of the "new economics of the household" should not relegate the analysis of these variables to sociologists and psychologists, just as they do not relegate the analysis of fertility and contraception to demographers.

APPENDIX

The empirical analysis in Sections III and IV in this paper is limited to men who responded to both the 1969 and the 1971 NBER questionnaires, were married in 1969, and were members of the labor force in that year. In addition to these restrictions, men were excluded from the analysis if there was no information on their current health status, age, height, actual weight, full-time salary, family income, wives' schooling, health status in high school, and school-loss weeks. In cases where there were unknown values of variables other than the ones just listed, the mean value of the relevant variable was substituted.

Table A.1 contains means and standard deviations of all variables that are used in Sections III and IV for the sample of 3,534 men. Table A.2 contains a matrix of simple correlation coefficients. Note that the principal components analysis of the test scores was performed on the entire sample of men who responded to the 1969 questionnaire. Therefore, the five ability variables do not necessarily have zero means.

TABLE A.1

Means and Standard Deviations, Married Men
in NBER-Thorndike Sample [a]

Variable	Mean	Standard Deviation
ln $H69$	3.938	.684
A	46.733	2.196
S	15.054	2.431
$SFAT$	9.812	3.528
$SMOT$	9.977	3.464
V	.035	1.330
P	.012	1.304
$MECH$	.019	1.301
NUM	.072	1.454
GEN	.072	1.595
ln HHS	1.917	.258
$SWIFE$	13.320	2.100
$JSAT$	4.415	.786
$WTDIF$	23.102	16.641
ln W	1.963	.498
$OTINC$ [b]	1.508	5.896
$EXCELL$ [c]	.595	
EXP	21.387	6.807
$SOUTH$ [c]	.229	
$CS1$ [c]	.153	
$CS2$ [c]	.265	
$CS3$ [c]	.195	
$CS4$ [c]	.134	
$CS5$ [c]	.148	

[a] Sample size is 3,534.
[b] Thousands of dollars.
[c] Standard deviations of dummy variables not shown.

Matrix of Simple Correlation Coefficients, Married Men in NBER-Thorndike Sample

	ln H69	A	S	SFAT	SMOT	V	P	MECH	NUM	GEN	ln HHS	SWIFE
ln H69	1.000											
A	−.078	1.000										
S	.135	−.172	1.000									
SFAT	.079	−.093	.176	1.000								
SMOT	.081	−.130	.163	.467	1.000							
V	.095	−.114	.094	.120	.125	1.000						
P	.047	.088	−.022	.039	.019	.294	1.000					
MECH	.048	.034	−.061	.114	.196	.276	.387	1.000				
NUM	.055	.061	.130	.030	.036	.306	.197	−.031	1.000			
GEN	.089	−.077	.327	.155	.186	.273	.145	.255	.468	1.000		
ln HHS	.193	−.059	.063	.022	.018	.022	.027	−.008	.054	.026	1.000	
SWIFE	.118	−.067	.389	.235	.209	.058	−.009	.013	.060	.172	.048	1.000
JSAT	.134	−.023	.098	.040	.049	.012	−.002	.020	−.00002	−.012	.075	.060
WTDIF	−.064	.021	−.061	−.062	−.062	−.027	−.066	−.036	−.048	−.065	.020	−.046
ln W	.170	−.085	.289	.122	.104	.084	.027	.025	.163	.220	.088	.147
OTINC	.028	−.008	.020	.032	.059	.009	−.0005	.013	.037	.067	.013	.062
EXCELL	.927	−.087	.142	.077	.089	.093	.039	.050	.046	.100	.189	.114
EXP	−.067	.305	−.550	−.071	−.070	−.068	.020	.006	−.017	−.146	−.022	−.182
SOUTH	.004	−.037	.080	.0005	.085	−.017	−.007	.019	−.049	−.008	−.005	.048
CS1	−.056	.017	−.029	−.033	−.017	−.049	−.011	.017	−.029	−.016	−.037	.002
CS2	.019	.010	.004	.021	.008	.028	.052	−.008	.021	.008	.025	.006
CS3	.004	−.006	.039	−.004	.002	.013	−.005	−.014	.005	−.007	.003	.038
CS4	.036	.008	.035	.033	.028	.010	−.018	.016	.012	.004	.006	.005
CS5	.038	−.040	.053	.015	−.004	.026	.012	−.056	.039	.064	.035	.018

TABLE A.2 (concluded)

	JSAT	WTDIF	ln W	OTINC	EX-CELL	EXP	SOUTH	CS1	CS2	CS3	CS4	CS5
SWIFE												
JSAT	1.000											
WTDIF	.024	1.000										
ln W	.168	−.028	1.000									
OTINC	.010	−.001	.210	1.000								
EXCELL	.124	−.072	.166	.023	1.000							
EXP	.007	.013	−.096	−.005	−.069	1.000						
SOUTH	.040	−.029	.012	.024	.001	−.045	1.000					
CS1	−.005	−.012	−.068	−.021	−.054	.021	−.051	1.000				
CS2	−.038	.016	−.002	−.012	.017	.001	.075	.255	1.000			
CS3	.018	−.022	.021	−.008	.007	.006	.070	−.210	−.296	1.000		
CS4	.018	−.022	.047	−.002	.038	−.044	.053	−.167	−.236	−.194	1.000	
CS5	.023	.006	.162	.077	.034	−.044	.029	−.177	−.250	−.206	−.164	1.000

REFERENCES

Andersen, Ronald, and Anderson, Odin W. *A Decade of Health Services: Social Survey Trends in Use and Expenditure*. Chicago: University of Chicago Press, 1967.

Auster, Richard D.; Leveson, Irving; and Sarachek, Deborah. "The Production of Health: An Exploratory Study." *Journal of Human Resources* 4 (Fall 1969): 411–436. Reprinted in Victor R. Fuchs, ed., *Essays in the Economics of Health and Medical Care*. NBER, 1972.

Becker, Gary S. *Human Capital and the Personal Distribution of Income: An Analytical Approach*. W. S. Woytinsky Lecture No. 1. Ann Arbor: University of Michigan, 1967.

———. "A Theory of the Allocation of Time." *Economic Journal* 75 (September 1965): 493–517.

———. "A Theory of Marriage: Part I." *Journal of Political Economy* 81 (July/August 1973): 813–846.

Becker, Gary S., and Chiswick, Barry R. "Education and the Distribution of Earnings." *American Economic Review, Papers and Proceedings* 56 (May 1966): 358–369.

Benham, Lee. "Benefits of Women's Education within Marriage." In T. W. Schultz, ed., *Marriage, Family Human Capital, and Fertility*. Proceedings of a conference sponsored by the National Bureau of Economic Research and the Population Council. *Journal of Political Economy* 82, No. 2, Part II (March/April 1974).

———. "Resource Allocation and Health Status." In progress.

Ben-Porath, Yoram. "Economic Analysis of Fertility in Israel: Point and Counterpoint." In W. T. Schultz, ed., *New Economic Approaches to Fertility*. Proceedings of a conference sponsored by the National Bureau of Economic Research and the Population Council. *Journal of Political Economy* 81, No. 2, Part II (March/April 1973).

———. "The Production of Human Capital and the Life Cycle of Earnings." *Journal of Political Economy* 75 (August 1967): 353–367.

Berkson, Joseph. "Application of the Logistic Function to Bio-Assay." *Journal of the American Statistical Association* 39 (September 1944): 357–365.

———. "Maximum Likelihood and Minimum χ^2 Estimates of the Logistic Function." *Journal of the American Statistical Association* 50 (March 1955): 130–162.

Boskin, Michael J. "The Economics of the Labor Supply." In Glen G. Cain and Harold W. Watts, eds., *Income Maintenance and Labor Supply*. New York, Academic Press, 1973.

Bowles, Samuel. "Schooling and Inequality from Generation to Generation." In T. W. Schultz, ed., *Investment in Education: The Equity-Efficiency Quandary*. Proceedings of a conference sponsored by the Committee on Basic Research in Education of the National Research Council. *Journal of Political Economy* 80, No. 3, Part II (May/June 1972).

Breslow, Lester, and Klein, Bonnie. "Health and Race in California." *American Journal of Public Health* 61 (April 1971): 763–775.

De Tray, Dennis N. "Child Quality and the Demand for Children." In T. W. Schultz, ed., *New Economic Approaches to Fertility*. Proceedings of a conference sponsored by the National Bureau of Economic Research and the Population Council. *Journal of Political Economy* 81, No. 2, Part II (March/April 1973).

Fuchs, Victor R. "Some Economic Aspects of Mortality in Developed Countries." In Mark Perlman, ed., *The Economics of Health and Medical Care*. London: Macmillan, 1974.

———. "Some Economic Aspects of Mortality in the United States." New York: National Bureau of Economic Research, 1965. Processed.

Ghez, Gilbert R., and Becker, Gary S. "The Allocation of Time and Goods Over the Life Cycle." New York: National Bureau of Economic Research, 1975.

Greenberg, David H. "Problems of Model Specification and Measurement: The Labor Supply Function." Santa Monica: The RAND Corporation, 1972. Processed.

210   *Demographic Behavior of the Household*

Griliches, Zvi, and Mason, William M. "Education, Income, and Ability." In T. W. Schultz, ed., *Investment in Education: The Equity-Efficiency Quandary.* Proceedings of a conference sponsored by the Committee on Basic Research in Education of the National Research Council. *Journal of Political Economy* 80, No. 3, Part II (May/June 1972).

Gronau, Reuben. "The Effect of Children on the Housewife's Value of Time." In T. W. Schultz, ed., *New Economic Approaches to Fertility.* Proceedings of a conference sponsored by the National Bureau of Economic Research and the Population Council. *Journal of Political Economy* 81, No. 2, Part II (March/April 1973).

Grossman, Michael. "On the Concept of Health Capital and the Demand for Health." *Journal of Political Economy* 80 (March/April 1972a): 223–255.

———. *The Demand for Health: A Theoretical and Empirical Investigation.* New York: NBER, 1972b.

———. "The Economics of Joint Production in the Household." Center for Mathematical Studies in Business and Economics, University of Chicago, 1971. Processed.

Grossman, Michael, and Benham, Lee. "Health, Hours, and Wages." In Mark Perlman, ed., *The Economics of Health and Medical Care.* London: Macmillan, 1974.

Hall, Robert E. "Wages, Income, and Hours of Work in the U.S. Labor Force." In Glen G. Cain and Harold W. Watts, eds., *Income Maintenance and Labor Supply.* New York: Academic Press, 1973.

Heckman, James J. "Estimating Indifference Curves to Determine the Effect of Child Care Programs on Women's Work Effort." In T. W. Schultz, ed., *Marriage, Family Human Capital, and Fertility.* Proceedings of a conference sponsored by the National Bureau of Economic Research and the Population Council. *Journal of Political Economy* 82, No. 2, Part II (March/April 1974).

———. "Shadow Prices, Market Wages, and Labor Supply." *Econometrica* 42 (July 1974): 679–694.

Hinkle, Lawrence E., Jr., et al. "Occupation, Education, and Coronary Heart Disease." *Science* 161 (July 19, 1968): 238–246.

Holmes, Thomas H., and Masuda, Minoru. "Life Change and Illness Susceptibility." Paper presented at a symposium on "Separation and Depression: Clinical and Research Aspects." American Association for the Advancement of Science, December 1970.

Johnston, J. *Econometric Methods.* New York: McGraw-Hill, 1963.

Kitagawa, Evelyn M., and Hauser, Philip M. "Education Differences in Mortality by Cause of Death: United States, 1960." *Demography* 5, no. 1 (1968): 318–353.

Lancaster, Kelvin J. "A New Approach to Consumer Theory." *Journal of Political Economy* 75 (April 1966): 132–157.

Leibowitz, Arleen S. "Home Investments in Children." In T. W. Schultz, ed., *Marriage, Family Human Capital, and Fertility.* Proceedings of a conference sponsored by the National Bureau of Economic Research and the Population Council. *Journal of Political Economy* 82, No. 2, Part II (March/April 1974).

———. "Women's Allocation of Time to Market and Nonmarket Activities: Differences by Education." Ph.D. dissertation, Columbia University, 1972.

Lillard, Lee A. "Human Capital Life Cycle of Earnings Models: A Specific Solution and Estimation." New York: National Bureau of Economic Research Working Paper No. 4, July 1973.

Luft, Harold S. "Poverty and Health: An Empirical Investigation of the Economic Interactions." Ph.D. dissertation, Harvard University, 1972.

Malkiel, Burton G., and Malkiel, Judith A. "Male-Female Pay Differentials in Professional Employment." *American Economic Review* 63 (September 1973): 693–705.

Masland, Richard L. Tables presented at Twelfth International Congress of Pediatrics, Mexico City, December 1968.

Michael, Robert T. *The Effect of Education on Efficiency in Consumption.* New York: NBER, 1972.

Michael, Robert T., and Becker, Gary S. "On the New Theory of Consumer Behavior." *Swedish Journal of Economics* 4 (1973): 378–396.

Mincer, Jacob. "The Distribution of Labor Incomes: A Survey with Special Reference to the Human Capital Approach." *Journal of Economic Literature* 8 (March 1970): 1–26.

———. *Schooling, Experience and Earnings.* New York: NBER, 1974.

Muth, Richard. "Household Production and Consumer Demand Functions." *Econometrica* 34 (July 1966): 699–708.

Nerlove, Marc, and Press, S. James. "Notes on the Log-Linear or Logistic Model for the Analysis of Qualitative Socioeconomic Data." Santa Monica: The RAND Corporation, 1973. Processed.

Netzer, Corinne T. *The Brand-Name Calorie Counter.* New York: Dell, 1969.

Palmore, Erdman B. "Physical, Mental, and Social Factors in Predicting Longevity." *The Gerontologist* 9 (Summer 1969a): 103–108.

———. "Predicting Longevity: A Follow-up Controlling for Age." *The Gerontologist* 9 (Winter 1969b): 247–250.

Rahe, Richard H. "Subjects' Recent Life Changes and Their Near-Future Illness Reports." *Annals of Clinical Research* 4 (1972): 250–265.

Rahe, Richard H., and Holmes, Thomas H. "Social, Psychologic, and Psychophysiologic Aspects of Inguinal Hernia." *Journal of Psychosomatic Research* 8 (1965): 487–491.

Silver, Morris. "An Econometric Analysis of Spatial Variations in Mortality by Race and Sex." In Victor R. Fuchs, ed., *Essays in the Economics of Health and Medical Care.* New York: NBER, 1972.

Smith, James P. "Family Decisionmaking over the Life Cycle: Some Implications for Estimating Labor Supply." Santa Monica: The RAND Corporation, 1973. Processed.

Stockwell, Edward G. "A Critical Examination of the Relationship Between Socioeconomic Status and Mortality." *American Journal of Public Health* 53 (June 1963): 956–964.

Taubman, Paul J., and Wales, Terence J. "Higher Education and Earnings: College as an Investment and a Screening Device." New York and Berkeley: National Bureau of Economic Research and Carnegie Commission of Higher Education, 1974.

Thorndike, Robert L., and Hagen, Elizabeth. *Ten Thousand Careers.* New York: John Wiley and Sons, 1959.

U.S., Department of Health, Education, and Welfare, Public Health Service, National Center for Health Statistics. *Vital Statistics of the United States.* Volume II: *Mortality,* Part A, 1961.

Welch, Finis. "Comment: Benefits of Women's Education within Marriage, by Lee Benham." In T. W. Schultz, ed., *Marriage, Family Human Capital, and Fertility.* Proceedings of a conference sponsored by the National Bureau of Economic Research and the Population Council. *Journal of Political Economy* 82, No. 2, Part II (March/April 1974).

———. "Education in Production." *Journal of Political Economy* 78 (January/February 1970): 35–59.

Willis, Robert, "A New Approach to the Economic Theory of Fertility Behavior." In T. W. Schultz, ed., *New Economic Approaches to Fertility.* Proceedings of a conference sponsored by the National Bureau of Economic Research and the Population Council. *Journal of Political Economy* 81, No. 2, Part II (March/April 1973).

Comments on

"The Correlation between

Health and Schooling"

DAN USHER

QUEEN'S UNIVERSITY, ONTARIO

MICHAEL GROSSMAN'S paper is an extension of the analysis in his pioneering book *The Demand for Health*. In that work, he develops an inter-temporal model to explain how a person decides on the amount of medical care to purchase today and in every year until the end of his life. The new element in this paper is a critical examination of a two-fold interaction between education and health, in which human capital augments the productivity of medical care, and good health augments the rate of return to education.

My comments pertain to the model which is common to this paper and to the book. The model represents what is to the best of my knowledge the first attempt at a complete inter-temporal analysis of the consumer's decision to purchase medical care; and even if, as I think is the case, it is inadequate in certain respects, it is at a minimum a starting point from which economic analysis can proceed. I shall try to assess the reasonableness of some of the assumptions in Grossman's model, to draw out certain unintended implications of the model, and to consider whether the model constitutes an adequate foundation for Grossman's empirical work.

I think it worthwhile to commence by presenting Grossman's model in its entirety. It is set out formally in Table 1. The model is fairly large and difficult to manipulate, but it seems to be internally consistent, and one can see how the parts fit together. The terminology in the table is exactly Grossman's, except that I have used superscripts to refer to years, subscripts to refer to commodities, and the symbol ˆ to designate a vector.

TABLE 1

Grossman's Model of Health as it appears in
The Demand for Health [a]

Choose:

$M^0, \ldots, M^n$	medical expenditure each year t, $i = 0, \ldots, n$;
$TH^0, \ldots, TH^n$	time devoted to health care each year t;
$\hat{X}^0, \ldots, \hat{X}^n$	vector of goods consumed each year t; and
$\hat{T}^0, \ldots, \hat{T}^n$	vector of amounts of time devoted to consumption of each good in each year t to maximize $U(h^0, \ldots, h^n; \hat{Z}^0, \ldots, \hat{Z}^n)$, where h^t is the number of illness-free days in the year t and where $\hat{Z}^t$ is a vector of activities in the year t.

The constraints are as follows:

i) $H^{t+1} = H^t + I^t - \delta^t H^t$ \quad (health accounting identity), where H is one's stock of health from which illness-free days flow, and I is investment in health, and δ^t is the rate of depreciation of health capital in the year t.

ii) $H^0 = \bar{H}$ \quad (endowment of health today).

iii) $I^t = \begin{cases} f(M^t, TH^t; E^t) \\ 0 \text{ if } H^t < \bar{\bar{H}} \end{cases}$ \quad (production function of investment in health in the year t),

where E is one's stock of human capital, and $\bar{\bar{H}}$ is the minimum stock of health required to be alive.

iv) $Z_j = g_j(X_j, T_j; E_j)$ \quad (production function of activity j),

where T_j is time spent in consuming the good X_j.

v) $TW^t + TH^t + T^t = \begin{cases} h^t \\ 0 \text{ if } H^t < \bar{\bar{H}} \end{cases}$ \quad (usage of time),

where TW^t is time spent working in the year t.

vi) $T^t = \Sigma_j T_j^t$

vii) $h^t = \begin{cases} h(H^t) \\ 0 \text{ if } H^t \leq \bar{\bar{H}} \end{cases}$ \quad (production of illness-free days by means of health).

viii) $\sum_{tj} \dfrac{X_j^t P_j^t}{(1 + r)^t} = \sum_t \dfrac{W^t T W^t}{(1 + r)^t} - \sum_t \dfrac{M^t P^t}{(1 + r)^t}$,

where W is the wage, P_j is the price of the good j, P^t is the price of medical care in the year t, and r is the externally given rate of interest.

[a] Michael Grossman, *The Demand for Health: A Theoretical and Empirical Investigation* (New York: NBER, 1972).

In the model, utility is a function of activities $\hat{Z}^t$ and illness-free days h^t in every year of one's life from today, the year 0, until the year n, which is far enough ahead so that no one can expect to live that long. If the consumer dies in the year t^*, then $\hat{Z}^t = 0$ and $h^t = 0$ for every $t \geqslant t^*$. The consumer's quota of illness-free days in the year t depends upon his state of health H^t, which is a variable with the dimension of a stock. Each year the consumer chooses an investment in health I^t. The rate of depreciation of health capital increases as a man grows older ($\delta^t > \delta^{t-1}$), and he chooses a length of life such that utility over his lifetime is maximized. The rest of the model shows the allocation of the available time each year among competing uses (equation v),[1] the identity between the present value of earnings and the present value of expenditures (equation viii), the household production functions of activities with goods and time in the manner of Lancaster (equation vi), and the household production function of investment in health with medicine and time (equation iv).

The first issue I should like to raise may be put in the form of a question: "Why, according to Grossman's model, do I go to the doctor?" The answer is not what one would expect. I do not go to the doctor because I am sick today. I do not go to the doctor because I have a broken arm that must be healed or a flu that must be treated or an appendix that must be removed if I am to live normally from now on. I go to the doctor to invest in health. Medical expenditure buys an increment to health capital which yields a flow of illness-free days each year for the rest of my life. Except for the effect of depreciation of health capital, there is no special connection between medical expenditure today and illness-free days today, for health capital yields its flow of services steadily over time. If the model were strictly true, we would expect to find a negative correlation among people between current medical expenditure related to heart disease and the incidence of heart disease tomorrow, or between current medical expenditure related to cancer and the incidence of cancer tomorrow. I hope this is not the basis for Grossman's remark on page 152 that researchers have reached "the tentative conclusion that medical care has, at best, a minor impact on health." The model may well be a reasonable representation of the effects of public expenditure on epidemiology.

There is, of course, a sense in which any medical expenditure is an investment in health, for the effects of an untreated illness will linger

---

[1] Equations designated by arabic numerals are from Grossman's paper. Equations designated by roman numerals are from Table 1 above. Equations designated by letters are introduced in this comment.

over time. Nonetheless, medical expenditure differs from ordinary investment in two important respects. First, most medical expenditure is not a profitable investment unless I happen to be ill. I cannot obtain a positive rate of return from having a cast put on my arm unless my arm is broken; I cannot obtain a positive rate of return from radiation treatment unless I have cancer. In Grossman's model, one can purchase health capital at any time at all. Second, there is something special about the timing of the benefits of medical expenditure. Some medical expenditure, such as having a case of flu treated, yields me illness-free days in the current year only. Other medical expenditure, such as having an appendix out, is necessary for the preservation of my life. It is not true that all benefits from medical expenditure flow uniformly over time as postulated in Grossman's model.

An alternative way of modeling the decision to purchase medical care is to suppose that health is a disposition not to be sick too often, that falling ill is a random process dependent on the state of one's health, and that medical expenditure can be either a cost of being sick today or an investment in health tomorrow. According to the alternative model, a positive correlation between medical expenditure today and illness tomorrow need not signify that medical expenditure causes illness because today's illness and tomorrow's illness may both be manifestations of a propensity to fall ill and because the benefit of medical expenditure consists in limiting the extent of the discomfort and damage to one's future health when one falls ill.

A second comment may also be introduced by a question, namely, "In what units is health to be measured?" In the model, health is nothing other than the propensity to enjoy illness-free days, for health, H^t and illness-free days h^t are linked in a one-to-one relation which appears in general form in Table 1 above as equation viii and in constant elasticity form in the paper under review as equation 2

$$h^t = 8,760 - B(H^t)^{-c} \qquad (2)$$

This equation is something of an exception among postulated stock-flow relations because it is nonlinear. It is the practice in accounting and in economics to postulate that stocks and flows are directly proportional. So, for instance, we say that ten workers do ten times the work of one worker, and eight cars yield eight times the service of one car, and n houses yield n units of service, not n^2 or $\sqrt{n}$ or $h(n)$ where h is an arbitrary function. We measure the size of the stock according to the size of the flow of services it yields, for there is normally no way of distinguishing the size of the stock and the size of the flow independently. To adopt this practice, one would measure the stock of health on a scale from 0 to 365, and the proper form of equation 2 would be

$$h^t = H^t \qquad\qquad (A)$$

The issue is confused by the fact that there is a distinction in common speech between health and illness-free days. I may say without contradiction that I was sick for the greater part of last year, but that I do not expect to be sick much from now on, because I am a basically healthy person. However, the distinction in common speech between health and illness-free days is not really a way out of the difficulty, because the source of that difference — the fact that health is a propensity to illness-free days, and that one may be healthy but nonetheless sick, or unhealthy but well, for most of the year — is explicitly assumed away by equation 2 in Grossman's model.

Grossman does try to obtain an independent measure of the stock of health. He makes use of sample surveys in which people are asked, in effect, to specify whether they are (a) very healthy; (b) moderately healthy; (c) moderately unhealthy; or (d) very unhealthy — and H is given values proportional to the average rate of illness of people identifying themselves in each category. There are two main problems with this procedure. The first is that the questionnaire scales health ordinally, so that health can be measured equally well by any four monotonically decreasing numbers. One could have used the numbers 4, 3, 2, 1 or 4000, 300, 20, 1 or any decreasing set, and Grossman's way of getting four decreasing numbers seems no better than any other. This matters, because the parameter c in equation 2 could take on any positive value, depending on which set of numbers is chosen. Second, a man who is asked to state how healthy he is can respond by telling us something other than the number of illness-free days he has enjoyed in the last year, because he has a concept of health which is different from that employed in Grossman's model, and not because he makes some mental transformation between H^t and h^t as implied in equation 2. To postulate that the flow of illness-free days is a curved function of the stock of health, where the stock of health is alleged to be a medical or biological variable, is to put into one's model a term H, which is unmeasurable, and to render ambiguous every function in which the term appears.

One might try to avoid these problems by measuring health in financial rather than medical terms. Just as real capital in the automotive industry may be measured as the accumulated and discounted value of investment, so health capital may be measured as accumulated and discounted medical expenditure. Indeed, a measure of this kind is implied in the model. Look at equations 1 and 8 together, [2] and make the special assumption that $\alpha = 1$, so that the marginal cost of investment in health is constant. It follows from these equations that health is to be measured in dollars worth, and equation 2 becomes a relation between dollars worth of accumulated investment in health and the number of illness-free days per year.

The difficulty with measuring health in financial terms is that the model acquires an implication that most of us would find unacceptable. Since the cost of health is constant by definition, and since the number of illness-free days is an invariant function of the stock of health, equations 1 and 8 together imply that a man can obtain full health at any age if he is prepared to make the appropriate medical expenditure, that health should be highly correlated with income and wealth as long as longevity is of value in itself, and that if a man is wealthy enough, he can arrange matters so that he lives forever. The observed negative correlation in Grossman's Table 5 between unearned income and health is not implied by the model, except under the special assumption that longevity itself is of no value.

Finally, I should like to make a technical point concerning the derivation of the demand curve for health. Though there is a fairly elaborate model of health set out in Table 1, Grossman makes very little use of it in determining the consumer's behavior. Instead, he employs a relation which is true of any investment whatsoever, as long as the investor makes himself better off by raising the present value of his income stream, and either the capital good can be sold at the end of the current period, or some of the capital good will be bought next year, too. It is an equilibrium condition for such an investment that

$$M.V.P. = M.C.[r + \delta - \frac{1}{M.C.} \frac{d}{dt}(M.C.)] \qquad \text{(B)}$$

where $M.V.P.$ is marginal value product in the current year; $M.C.$ is marginal cost of the capital good; r is the current rate of interest; and δ is the current rate of depreciation.

All of the terms in equation B can be translated into the language of Grossman's model. From equations 2 and 3, we see that

$$M.V.P. = W^t G^t = W^t BC(H^t)^{-c-1} \qquad \text{(C)}$$

because it is assumed in the investment version of the model that the

---

[2] Equations 1 and 8 appear in a slightly altered form as equations i and iii in Table 1.

value of a marginal illness-free day G^t is given by the wage rate W^t. From equation 8, it follows that the marginal cost of a unit of health capital is invariant so that

$$M.C. \equiv P^t \qquad (D)$$

From B, C, and D one can immediately derive that

$$\ln H^t = \epsilon\ln BC + \epsilon\ln W^t - \epsilon\ln P^t - \epsilon\ln \left(r^t + \delta^t - \frac{\dot{P}^t}{P^t}\right) \qquad (E)$$

which is essentially Grossman's demand for health schedule of equation 9, where $1/(1 + c)$ is replaced by the variable ϵ.

The demand for health schedule in equation 9 is illustrated in Figure 1. The figure shows the negative relation between H and $r + \delta$ when W, δ, and P are held constant.

The derivation of the demand schedule in equation 9 and Figure 1 is satisfactory as far as it goes, but it is essential to assume that the marginal cost of health capital is constant if H is to be expressed as a unique function of W, P, r, $\dot{P}$ and δ in the current year. A more likely possibility is that the marginal cost of a given increment to health is an increasing function of investment in health in the current year as represented by the schedule in Figure 2. In that case, the market price P in equation E would have to be replaced by $M.C.$, which is a function of the flow of health in the current year and the term $\frac{1}{P}\frac{d}{dt}(P)$ would have to be replaced by the term $\frac{1}{M.C.}\frac{d}{dt}(M.C.)$, which is dependent on the rates of depreciation of health in every future year until the end of a man's life. We are confronted with Hobson's choice. Either

FIGURE 1

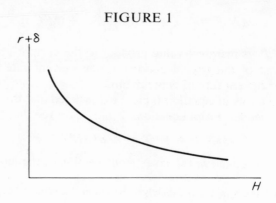

FIGURE 2

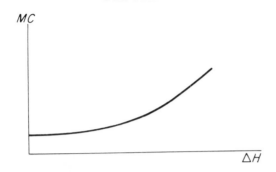

we assume that P^t is independent of the amount of investment in health, in which case, as mentioned above, a wealthy enough man can choose to live forever, or we restrict the options for investing in health by postulating a schedule such as is shown in Figure 1, in which case the optimal quantity of health today depends on all the parameters in the model, all wages, all depreciation rates, and all prices of health capital from now until the end of one's life.

Consider Grossman's full model once again. Although the mathematics required to derive time series of endogenous variables such as $\hat{Z}^t$, h^t, H^t is very complex, it seems reasonable to assume that some solution exists, and, in particular, that H^t has some determinate history from time 0 to time t^*, when our consumer chooses to die. One such history, in which health declines from $\bar{H}$ at time 0 to $\bar{\bar{H}}$ at time t^*, is illustrated in Figure 3. Furthermore, though I cannot work it out explicitly, there must be some comparative dynamic solution to

FIGURE 3

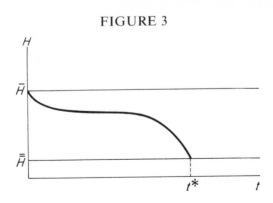

the problem in which H^t in any year t is a function of all of the exogenous variables

$$H^t = H^t(\hat{r}, \hat{W}, P, \hat{\delta}, E; f, \hat{g}_j, h),$$

where $\hat{r}$, $\hat{W}$, and $\hat{\delta}$ are vectors of the rate of interest, the wage rate, and the rate of depreciation of health capital in all future years; where P and E represent all prices and environmental conditions; and where f, $\hat{g}_j$, and h are the functional forms of the constraints. It seems reasonable to suppose that the partial derivative of H^t with respect to r^t is negative, though Grossman does not prove it, and I cannot.

In the final analysis, my dissatisfaction with Grossman's derivation of the demand curve for capital lies in the fact that he uses the methods of comparative statics in circumstances in which comparative dynamics would seem to be appropriate.[3] The demand curve for capital in which the desired stock depends on its price or on the rate of interest, independently of time or history, is a construct that is valid only in a world where there is no history. It does not exist in a world where life is finite and the benefits that flow from a given stock of health capital depend on the rates of depreciation throughout one's life.

On the empirical work, I would like to make three points: First, nothing in the model suggests that education ought to lead to good health. The proposition is not inconsistent with the model, and it can be made very plausible on other grounds, but it is not implied. Second, the model does suggest that there should be a strong positive correlation between income and health because health can be purchased at constant marginal cost. Third, I suspect that much, if not all, of the empirical work can stand regardless of the model.

---

[3] Some investigation of the subject of comparative dynamics has been undertaken by my colleague Hajimi Oniki. Perhaps the methods employed in the Heckman and Willis paper in this volume can be of use.

Reply to Dan Usher

MICHAEL GROSSMAN

IN general, Usher ignores most of the work that I have done in this paper. Instead, he criticizes my theoretical model of the demand for health and medical care (Grossman 1972a, 1972b) that I use as a point of departure for my present paper. In what follows, I reply to his major points.

Usher claims that my model cannot account for an observed negative relationship between medical care and health. That is, it cannot explain why sicker people are likely to report higher outlays on medical care than healthy people. I do not agree. An increase in the rate of depreciation on health capital would raise the shadow price of health and would cause the quantity of health capital demanded to fall. At the same time, the quantity of medical care demanded would rise, provided the price elasticity of demand for health were smaller than one. With the depreciation rate held constant, health and medical care should be positively related. But since it is not possible to control completely for these variations empirically, the gross correlation is negative. (For a detailed discussion, see Grossman 1972b, pp. 43–44 and p. 48.)

My statement that researchers have reached the tentative conclusion that medical care has, at best, a minor marginal impact on health is based on sophisticated studies that take account of the two-way relationship between these variables. These studies estimate the effect of medical care on health either by using two-stage least squares or by employing proxy measures of preventive medical care. This conclusion is not, as Usher implies, based on ordinary least squares regressions of health on medical care outlays.

I agree with Usher that my model does not explicitly deal with uncertainty (random illness). Indeed, I, myself, have pointed out that the model should be extended along these lines by assuming that a given consumer faces a probability distribution of depreciation rates at any age (Grossman 1972a, pp. 247–248). Using my basic framework, Phelps (1973) has shown that the introduction of uncertainty does not alter the basic properties of the demand curve for medical care that I derive. Moreover, Rand and I (Grossman and Rand 1974) have demonstrated that my model can be used as the basis for constructing separate demand curves for preventive and remedial medical care.

Usher criticizes my assumption that the relationship between the stock of health and the flow of healthy days is nonlinear. I make this assumption because the output produced by health capital has a finite upper limit of 365 healthy days in a year. Therefore, I assume that the marginal product of health capital diminishes. This, together with the assumption that the marginal cost of investment in health is constant, means that the demand curve for health capital depends only on current values of the exogenous variables.

I agree with Usher that, given constant cost and constant marginal product, the optimal stock of health would essentially be infinite. I also agree that, given rising marginal cost, the demand curve would depend on future values. Nonetheless, I see no reason to complicate what is an already complicated model by introducing rising marginal cost. The basic nature of health capital suggests that its marginal product should fall. I admit that if one took account of the quality of the output of health capital as well as the quantity, diminishing marginal productivity would be somewhat less plausible. Since, however, the stock of health is specific to an individual and is used in the household as well as in the market, the marginal product of this capital should diminish after some point.

The assumption of linear stock-flow relationships is not as universal as Usher would have us believe. Rosen (1969) assumes that labor input depends on employment and hours per man but that this input is not simply the product of employment and hours per man. Jorgenson (1967), Arrow (1968), and Sandmo (1971) construct models of the demand for capital stock by firms in which the marginal cost of gross investment is constant. In these models, capital services are proportional to capital stock. The firm's production function, however, exhibits diminishing returns *to scale* in all inputs, so that output and demand for inputs are finite. Provided gross investment is positive, these models generate myopic demand curves for physical capital that are very similar to my demand curve for health capital.

Usher claims that if healthy time is a curved function of the stock of health, then the latter variable cannot be measured, and all functions containing it become ambiguous. As I imply in Section II.B of my paper, given the functional form specified in equation 12, my health capital series is unique up to a linear transformation. That is, it is essentially cardinal in nature, rather than ordinal. In my discussion of this series, I also indicate that it does not change very much when a more complicated functional form is selected.

I agree with Usher that the parameter C in equation 12 could take on any value. But in the context of regression analysis, tests of significance are not affected by the value of C. In the few instances in which I discuss quantitative rather than qualitative effects, I do assume that C is equal to one. One rationale for this assumption is that it generates a reasonable value for the price elasticity of demand for medical care. Suppose, for example, that substitution between medical care and own time in the production of health were difficult, and that medical care accounted for one-half of the total cost of producing health. Then if C were equal to one, the price elasticity of medical care would approximately equal one-quarter. This figure is within the range of existing estimates. (See, for example, Phelps and Newhouse 1973.)

REFERENCES

Arrow, Kenneth J. "Optimal Capital Policy with Irreversible Investment." In J. N. Wolfe, ed., *Value, Capital and Growth.* Edinburgh: Edinburgh University Press, 1968.

Grossman, Michael. "On the Concept of Health Capital and the Demand for Health." *Journal of Political Economy* 80 (March/April 1972a): 223–255.

———. *The Demand for Health: A Theoretical and Empirical Investigation.* New York: NBER, 1972b.

Grossman, Michael, and Rand, Elizabeth H. "Consumer Incentives for Health Services in Chronic Illness." In Selma J. Mushkin, ed., *Consumer Incentives for Health Care.* New York: Prodist for the Milbank Memorial Fund, 1974.

Jorgenson, Dale W. "The Theory of Investment Behavior." In Robert Ferber, ed., *Determinants of Investment Behavior.* New York: NBER, 1967.

Phelps, Charles E. "Demand for Health Insurance: A Theoretical and Empirical Investigation." Santa Monica: The RAND Corporation, 1973.

Phelps, Charles E., and Newhouse, Joseph P. "Coinsurance and the Demand for Medical Services." Santa Monica: The RAND Corporation, 1973.

Rosen, Sherwin. "On the Interindustry Wage and Hours Structure." *Journal of Political Economy* 77 (March/April 1969): 249–273.

Sandmo, Agnar. "Investment and the Rate of Interest." *Journal of Political Economy* 79 (November/December 1971): 1335–1345.

Part II
Market and Nonmarket Aspects
of Real Earnings

Estimates of a Human Capital Production Function Embedded in a Life-Cycle Model of Labor Supply *

JAMES J. HECKMAN

NATIONAL BUREAU OF ECONOMIC RESEARCH
AND THE UNIVERSITY OF CHICAGO

IN this paper, I present estimates of the structural parameters of a human capital production function embedded in a life-cycle model of labor supply. Several recent papers (e.g., Becker and Ghez 1972, Heckman 1971 and Stafford and Stephan 1972) attempt to merge the classical theory of labor supply with models of human capital accumulation. In joining these topics, traditional labor supply theory has been expanded to an inter-temporal framework in which current and future wages and prices determine current labor supply. Human capital theory has been expanded to explicitly incorporate a three-way division of human time among work, investment, and leisure.

Although the marriage of these topics leads to a more complete theory of labor supply behavior and a more "realistic" description of the process of investment in human capital, it has not been empirically fruitful. There are two principal reasons for this: one, mathematical, and the other, statistical in nature. The mathematical problem is that dynamic models are difficult to solve explicitly. The difficulties encountered in the literature on optimal growth are compounded by the particular features that characterize investment in human beings.

* This research was sponsored by National Science Foundation and National Institute of Health grants to the National Bureau. I have benefited from comments by Emmett Keeler, Zvi Griliches, Jacob Mincer, James Smith, Finis Welch, and Robert Willis, as well as from the remarks by Paul Schultz printed in this volume. However, I retain full responsibility for all errors. Ralph Shnelvar performed the computations.

Life is finite, human capital is not resalable, and the presence of both budget constraints and death leads to optimal solutions that are not steady state. Accordingly, the luxury of the long-run path afforded economists dealing with infinite horizon problems is simply not available to economists attempting to characterize the full life-cycle behavior of human beings. Consequently, even the simplest specifications for inter-temporal preferences and human capital production functions lead to mathematically intractable functions and to theories which yield few predictions.

There is also a statistical problem which must be faced even if explicit solutions to the dynamic problem are obtained. The union of labor supply theory and human capital theory introduces an unobservable variable into the analysis: time spent investing. In considering schooling decisions, it seems acceptable to assume that a year in school is a year of complete specialization of nonconsumption time in investment. Even this assumption is open to debate. However, there is no ready way to estimate the proportion of time spent investing in on-the-job training. Since it seems likely that postschool investment occurs on the job (Stafford and Stephan 1972 assume otherwise), measured hours of work are a mixture of pure work time and investment time. Assuming that workers forgo productive work, and the associated earnings, to invest in themselves, *measured* wage rates obtained by dividing weekly income by weekly reported hours on the job systematically *understate* the true wage rate. The understatement is greatest at those ages at which the proportion of work time spent in investing is greatest.

This age-related understatement of wage rates poses a serious problem in testing life-cycle models of labor supply and consumption joined with human capital models. I demonstrate below in one model that the "true" wage rate, even though it is endogenous to the model, retains its role as the price of time in consumption, leisure, and time-investment decisions. However, in the absence of any data on the correct wage rate, tests of the life-cycle model are impossible unless the theory is recast in terms of observable variables.

While it is a relatively straightforward matter to develop testable implications of life-cycle models for consumption and leisure given the wage rate, predictions for investment time are far more difficult to obtain. Since the proportion of work time spent investing is directly related to the amount of time spent investing, the theoretically more appealing route of stating the theory solely in terms of observable phenomena is not available.

An alternative to this procedure, and the approach followed in this paper, is to devise methods for estimating the proportion of time spent investing. Once these estimates are produced, it is possible to measure the true wage rate over the life cycle and, therefore, to test life-cycle models of consumption, saving, and labor supply.

Apart from providing estimates of a corrected wage series, the methodology affords estimates of the time expended in investment over the life cycle, and its dollar value. En route to the final wage series, I estimate the parameters of a human capital production function.

In the first part of the paper, a general model of life-cycle consumption, investment, and labor supply is developed. Specific investment models are considered in an attempt to develop theoretical predictions about the life-cycle variations in the proportion of time spent investing. In the second section, a method for estimating the proportion of time spent investing is proposed and implemented, and the empirical results are discussed. The principal empirical findings are: (1) the neutrality hypothesis of Ben-Porath (1967) is rejected; (2) human capital appears to have negative productivity in its own production; (3) the estimated profile of investment over the life cycle does not follow the simple profile assumed by Mincer (1973) or the profile proposed by Haley (1973).

I

In this section, I present a simple model of human capital accumulation in a life-cycle model of labor supply. Some of the results in this section have been presented elsewhere in the literature (Becker and Ghez 1972, Heckman 1971, Stafford and Stephan 1972).

A. The Utility Function

Assume a one-person consumer unit with an instantaneous, strictly concave twice continuously differentiable utility function

$$U[X(t), L(t)]$$

defined for the rate of consumption of goods ($X(t)$) and leisure ($L(t)$). The first partials are assumed to be positive. The assumption of an identical utility function at each point in time is conventional. Assuming an exponential rate of time discount ρ, the aggregate of utility over the planning horizon T may be written as

$$\int_0^T e^{-\rho t} U[X(t), L(t)]dt \qquad (1)$$

As is well known (Strotz 1956), this utility specification has the convenient property that, in a world of certainty, a consumer's initial decision on his course of action is precisely that yielded by any subsequent maximization of his remaining lifetime utility, subject to the constraints resulting from previous decisions.

B. The Budget Constraint

Assuming a perfect credit market with constant and equal marginal costs of borrowing and lending at rate r, total financial assets at time t may be written as

$$A(t) = \int_0^t e^{r(t-\tau)}[w(\tau)H(\tau) - P(\tau)X(\tau)]d\tau + A(0),$$

where $H(\tau)$ is hours of work at time τ, at wage rate $w(\tau)$, and where $P(\tau)$ is the price of goods at age t. Since in a perfect credit market all loans are repaid, it must be the case that $A(T) \geq 0$ (i.e., discounted discrepancies between earnings ($w(t)H(t)$) and consumption ($P(t)X(t)$) must not exceed initial net worth). Note that saving (or dissaving) in financial assets is simply the rate of change of assets at time t

$$\dot{A}(t) = w(t)H(t) - P(t)X(t) + rA(t) \qquad (2)$$

C. Human Capital Production

Very little is known about specific mechanisms for acquiring knowledge. The most widely used model in the human capital literature follows the suggestion of Ben-Porath (1967). Work time ($H(t)$) is distinguished from training time ($I(t)$) although the two may be intermingled in any proportion on a given job. Assuming that a continuum of training opportunities exists in firms and occupations, individuals select optimal quantities of investment time. In this framework, schools are viewed as firms specializing exclusively in training.

Since human capital is assumed to be homogeneous, firms do not pay for any of the costs of training received by their employees. An hour spent investing is an hour not spent working; and for a working individual, its cost is the wage rate $w(t)$. These training costs may be broken into direct costs (e.g., books and tuition) and indirect costs (the value of time not spent at work or consumption). Note that jointness is excluded. If work per se raises future wages, the cost of an hour of leisure is the market wage forgone plus the increment to future earnings of the last unit of work. In the Ben-Porath specification, work time and training time can be varied and are, in principle, distinguishable. Even if training and work come in fixed proportions in one job, these proportions can be varied by selecting alternative jobs (Rosen 1972).

Throughout this paper, I follow the Ben-Porath convention. Within its scope, further hypotheses have become conventional. Without much justification, it has been argued that human capital is self-productive, and that higher stocks of human capital raise the marginal product of time in producing human capital. Letting $\dot{w}$ be the time rate of change in wage rates, and ignoring direct costs, wage growth is assumed to be governed by

$$\dot{w} = F[w(t), I(t)] - \sigma w(t), \quad w(0) = w_o \tag{3}$$

where σ is an exponential depreciation factor, w_o is the initial value of wage rates, F is a concave twice continuously differentiable production function with positive own partial derivatives, and a *positive* cross partial derivative. An even more extreme view of the role of human capital in self-production has been proposed under the name of the "neutrality hypothesis." This hypothesis restricts F so that the wage function may be written as a strictly concave function of the time cost of investment:

$$\dot{w} = k(Iw) - \sigma w \tag{4}$$

Little justification, other than that of mathematical simplicity, supports the neutrality hypothesis. Empirical work by Ben-Porath (1970) has shown that earnings data are inconsistent with this hypothesis. Nonetheless, its continued popularity makes it an important benchmark case which will be considered in this paper.

D. Equilibrium Conditions

The optimality conditions for a consumer maximizing utility function (1) subject to wage constraint (2) and $A(T) \geq 0$ are presented below. Letting D be total time available at t, and noting that $H(t) = D - L(t) - I(t)$, the Hamiltonian function becomes

$$e^{-\rho t}U[X(t), L(t)] + \lambda\{w(t)[D - L(t) - I(t)] - P(t)X(t) + rA(t)\}$$
$$+ \mu\{F[w(t), I(t)] - \sigma w(t)\} \tag{5}$$

where λ and μ are dynamic multipliers to be interpreted below. For an interior solution, the optimality conditions are

(a) $e^{-\rho t}U_X(t) - \lambda P(t) = 0$

(b) $e^{-\rho t}U_L(t) - \lambda w(t) = 0$

(c) $\dot{\lambda} + r\lambda = 0$

(d) $\lambda(T)A(T) = 0$

(e) $\mu F_I - \lambda w(t) = 0$

(f) $\dot{\mu} = (\sigma - F_w)\mu - \lambda[D - L(t) - I(t)]$

(g) $\mu(T)w(T) = 0$ $\qquad\qquad$ (6)

and equations 2 and 3.

Investment ($I(t)$), leisure ($L(t)$) and goods ($X(t)$) will be nonzero if Inada-type conditions are assumed

$$\lim_{I \to 0} F_I \to \infty \qquad \lim_{X \to 0} U_X \to \infty \qquad \lim_{L \to 0} U_L \to \infty$$

For convenience, these conditions are maintained throughout the paper. These conditions also ensure the existence of an optimal program and concavity ensures its uniqueness. The only possibility of a corner solution is that the sum of leisure plus investment may exhaust the instantaneous time budget D.

In this case, during intervals when $L + I = D$, equations 6(b) and 6(e) reduce to

$$e^{-\rho t}U_L = \mu F_I \qquad\qquad \text{6(b)}'$$

so that the marginal cost of investment time is the (discounted) marginal utility of leisure. Further, equation 6(f) becomes

$$\dot{\mu} = (\sigma - F_w)\mu \qquad\qquad \text{6(f)}'$$

At the boundary points for these intervals, $\mu(t)$ is a continuous function of time, but $\dot{\mu}$ is not, nor in general are the control variables $X(t)$, $L(t)$, $I(t)$.[1]

Equations 6(a)–6(d) are the familiar consumer equilibrium conditions. Since $U(\cdot)$ is assumed unbounded, $A(T) = 0$, and the marginal utility of income received at $t(\lambda(t))$ is seen to be an exponentially declining function of time

$$\lambda(t) = \lambda(0)e^{-rt}$$

Note that for a given consumer held at his optimal level of utility, $\lambda(0)$ is fixed, and the investment system (equations 6(c)–6(g)) is detachable from the consumer equilibrium system once $L(t)$ is specified.

---

[1] See, e.g., Hestenes, Theorem 2.1, p. 234.

I now turn to a more detailed examination of the optimality conditions.

E. Demand for Leisure and Goods

From the strict concavity of U, we solve for the differentiable demand relations

$$\text{(a)} \quad X(t) = X[\lambda(0)e^{(\rho-r)t}P(t), \lambda(0)e^{(\rho-r)t}w(t)]$$

$$\text{(b)} \quad L(t) = L[\lambda(0)e^{(\rho-r)t}P(t), \lambda(0)e^{(\rho-r)t}w(t)] \tag{7}$$

Since strict concavity of U implies

$$U_{11} < 0, \; U_{22} < 0$$

$$\begin{vmatrix} U_{11} & U_{12} \\ U_{21} & U_{22} \end{vmatrix} > 0$$

a logical consequence of the assumed concavity is $X_1 < 0$, $L_2 < 0$. From the twice continuous differentiability of U

$$X_2(t) = L_1(t)$$

In the Ramsey (1928) case of independence in the utility function, $U_{12} = 0$, which implies $X_2(t) = 0 = L_1(t)$.

Several propositions are immediately obvious with respect to the timing of the consumption of goods ($X(t)$) and leisure ($L(t)$). Differentiate 7(a) and (b) to obtain

$$\text{(a)} \quad \dot{X}(t) = \lambda(0)e^{(\rho-r)t}\{(\rho - r)[X_1P(t) + X_2w(t)] + X_1\dot{P}(t) + X_2\dot{w}(t)\}$$

$$\text{(b)} \quad \dot{L}(t) = \lambda(0)e^{(\rho-r)t}\{(\rho - r)[L_1P(t) + L_2w(t)] + L_1\dot{P}(t) + L_2\dot{w}(t)\} \tag{8}$$

If leisure and goods are normal in each time period the terms $X_1P(t) + X_2w(t)$ and $L_1P(t) + L_2w(t)$ are negative.[2]

---

[2] Normality is used in the following sense. Disregard human capital accumulation and insist that the consumer live within his means for each instant of time, but give him allotment $Y(t)$ to supplement his earnings. Then he maximizes $U[X(t), L(t)] + \lambda(t)\{Y(t) + W(t)[D - L(t)] - P(t)X(t)\}$ and assuming interior solutions, the Hessian for displacement analysis, which yields income and substitution effects, is

$$\begin{bmatrix} U_{11} & U_{12} & -P(t) \\ U_{21} & U_{22} & -w(t) \\ -P(t) & -w(t) & 0 \end{bmatrix}$$

For a maximum, the Hessian must have a positive determinant K. Then the income effect for goods is

$$\frac{U_{12}w(t) - U_{22}P(t)}{K} = -[X_1P(t) + X_2w(t)]$$

[Concluded on p. 234]

To interpret these equations, suppose, for the moment, that independence in preferences is assumed so that $X_2 = 0$ and $L_1 = 0$, and that the rate of interest (r) equals the rate of time preference (ρ) so that

$$\dot{X}(t) = \lambda(0)X_1\dot{P}(t)$$

$$\dot{L}(t) = \lambda(0)L_2\dot{w}(t)$$

If wages are assumed to be smooth functions of time, at that age $(\hat{t})$ with peak wages $(\dot{w}(\hat{t}) = 0)$, leisure is at a minimum, $(\dot{L}(\hat{t}) = 0)$ and as wage rates increase $(\dot{w}(t) > 0)$ leisure declines $(\dot{L}(t) < 0)$ since $L_2 < 0$. Similar conditions apply to $\dot{X}(t)$ with respect to $\dot{P}(t)$.

Suppose that we retain independence in utility $(X_2 = L_1 = 0)$, but allow for $\rho \neq r$. Then

$$\dot{X}(t) = \lambda(0)e^{(\rho - r)t}\{(\rho - r)[X_1 P(t)] + X_1\dot{P}(t)\}$$

Then, if $\rho > r$, the peak in consumption, if it occurs, arises after the peak in prices, since $X_1 < 0$. If prices are stable, goods consumption decreases with age t. If $\rho < r$, the trough in goods consumption occurs before the peak in the price. Similar conditions apply to the demand for leisure and its price $w(t)$.

In the more general case of nonindependence in utility, the life-cycle profile of consumption of goods and leisure depends on the pattern of wage rates and prices. In contrast to previous work on life-cycle consumption by Modigliani and Brumberg (1954), and Yaari (1964), the trajectories of earnings and consumption expenditure are linked through life-cycle variations in the price of time, $w(t)$. Given data on the life cycle of a representative individual, it is possible to test hypotheses about the signs of the derivatives of $X(t)$ and $L(t)$, and to estimate $\rho - r$.

F. Investment Relationships

In contrast to the analysis of life-cycle consumption of goods and leisure, the analysis of investment time leads to few predictions about life-cycle behavior. This ambiguity reduces our ability to test the predictions of the previous section, since the measured price of time is

while the income effect for leisure is

$$\frac{U_{12}w(t) - U_{12}P(t)}{K} = -[L_1 P(t) + L_2 w(t)]$$

If augmenting income allotment $Y(t)$ raises the consumption of $X(t)$ and $L(t)$, both goods are normal in the sense used in the text, and the proposition in the text follows immediately.

systematically related to the proportion of working time spent investing.

To establish this ambiguity, consider equations 6(e)–6(g). These are more easily understood if $\mu(t)/\lambda(t)$ is replaced by $g(t)$. This substitution is permissible since $\lambda(t)$ is nonzero. The investment equilibrium conditions become

$$w(t) = g(t)F_I(t) \qquad\qquad\qquad 6(e)'$$

$$\dot{g}(t) = [\sigma + r - F_w(t)]g(t) - [D - L(t) - I(t)] \qquad 6(f)'$$

$$g(t)W(T) = 0 \qquad\qquad\qquad 6(g)'$$

Since $w(t)$ is nonzero, the expression for $g(t)$ may be written as

$$g(t) = \int_t^T e^{-\int_t^\tau [\sigma + r - F_w(l)]\,dl}\, H(\tau)\,d\tau$$

so that $g(t)$ is a discounted stock of future working hours. Note that capital productivity F_w tends to offset the depreciation and interest rates in calculating the present value of future hours of work. Equation 6(e)' is the familiar condition that at an optimum, the marginal cost of investment time ($w(t)$) equals the marginal contribution of investment time to the present value of future earnings.

From these conditions, it is possible to conclude little about optimal investment patterns except the obvious point that at the end of life ($t = T$) no investment will be undertaken. To gain further insight into the nature of optimal investment policies, more structure has to be imposed on the problem. The Ben-Porath neutrality model serves as a convenient benchmark. In the Ben-Porath case, the human capital production function becomes

$$\dot{w} = k(Iw) - \sigma w$$

where $k' > 0$, $k'' < 0$. Letting $\tilde{g}$ be the value of $g(t)$ for the Ben-Porath model, conditions 6(e)'–6(g)' become

$$1 = \tilde{g}(t)k'[I(t)w(t)] \qquad\qquad\qquad 6(e)''$$

$$\dot{\tilde{g}} = (\sigma + r)\tilde{g} - [D - L(t)] \qquad\qquad 6(f)''$$

$$\tilde{g}(T)w(T) = 0 \qquad\qquad\qquad 6(g)''$$

In the original Ben-Porath model, leisure is assumed to be fixed at the same value at each point in the consumer's life cycle. Letting $\bar{L}$ be that value, $\tilde{g}(t)$ becomes

$$\tilde{g}(t) = (D - \bar{L}) \int_t^T e^{-(\sigma + r)(\tau - t)} d\tau$$

so that $\dot{\tilde{g}} < 0$. From equation 6(e)″, the dollar cost of time investment, $(I(t)w(t))$, is inversely related to $\tilde{g}(t)$, and hence for ages beyond the period of specialization, gross investment declines with age.[3] If depreciation is zero, the amount of time invested must also decline over the life cycle, so that the understatement of true wage rates by measured wage rates continuously declines with age.

If the path of leisure were to decrease continuously so that total hours spent in the market increase with age, $\tilde{g}$ need not be negative at all post-specialization-period ages of the life cycle, and gross investment, and the proportion of market time spent investing may increase for a while. Of course, the approach of the retirement period eventually causes both gross investment and the proportion of working time alloted to investment to decrease to zero.

To apply the Ben-Porath model to a life-cycle model of labor supply, the assumption of a fixed amount of leisure must be relaxed. Of course, it is possible that leisure is fixed as a result of utility maximizing decisions. An alternative argument, suggested by the work of Michael (1973) shows how leisure time may be neutralized from the analysis of investment decisions in precisely the same way that investment time is neutralized in the Ben-Porath model.

If human capital effectively expands the amount of leisure time available, and does it in such a way that a 10 per cent increase in human capital leads to a 10 per cent increase in the quantity of effective leisure time, the instantaneous utility function may be written as

$$G = G[X(t), w(t)L(t)]$$

so that utility is a function of market goods and the dollar cost of time consumption. Condition 6(f)′ becomes

$$\dot{\tilde{g}} = (\sigma + r)\tilde{g} - D$$

so that $\dot{\tilde{g}} < 0$ and all of the implications of the Ben-Porath model concerning the life-cycle profile of investment remain intact. If the rate of depreciation (σ) is zero, and the rate of time preference is less than the rate of interest $(\rho < r)$, work time increases over the life cycle, and the proportion of work time spent investing decreases monotonically.

If Michael neutrality is ignored, it is clear from inspection of the general expression for $\tilde{g}(t)$

[3] During a period of specialization, gross investment must increase, since wages increase and the amount of time spent in investment remains constant.

$$\tilde{g}(t) = \int_t^T e^{-(\sigma + r)(\tau - t)} [D - L(\tau)]d\tau$$

that if hours of time supplied to the market for both work and investment time (i.e., $D - L(t)$) remain constant (Ben-Porath) or decline beyond age t, $\dot{\tilde{g}} < 0$, the Ben-Porath implications for investment time remain valid. Only if future hours of market activity increase will gross investment increase with age, and the rate of increase in hours must be "suitably large." Intuitively, $\tilde{g}(t)$ may increase with time if the loss in the total stock of market time due to aging $(D - L(t))$ is more than offset by the reduction in the discount factor applied to the remaining stock of future hours.

However, it is not possible, a priori, to rule out the increase in future hours of work, so that even within a very simple model, no prediction about the behavior of the proportion of working time spent investing is possible. Without greater specificity about the structure of preferences and the human capital production function, little can be said about the structure of optimal investment policies. In the next section, a very specific model is analyzed in an attempt to derive refutable propositions about investment behavior.

G. A Specific Model

In the last section, an inconclusive discussion of investment behavior was presented. In this section, much stronger structure is imposed on the problem in an attempt to derive testable implications. Depreciation and time preference are ignored. Human capital is excluded from its own production. These assumptions simplify the analysis and help pinpoint the sources of ambiguity, but as we shall see, they do not yield an unambiguous theory of life-cycle investment.

The instantaneous utility function is specialized to an additive form to ignore complications about substitution between time and goods. Thus, using the same notation for the variables as utilized in the previous section, the instantaneous utility function is

$$U(t) = aX^\alpha + fL^\phi, \ 0 < \alpha < 1, \ 0 < \phi < 1, \ a > 0, f > 0 \quad \text{(G-1)}$$

Saving is as before

$$A = w(D - L - I) - PX + rA, \ A(0) = A_0 \quad \text{(G-2)}$$

Wage growth is governed by

$$\dot{w} = cI^\gamma, \ 0 < \gamma < 1, \ w(0) = w_o \quad \text{(G-3)}$$

where depreciation is ignored and human capital is excluded from its own production. Using the notation of the previous section, Pontryagin necessary conditions for a maximum for lifetime utility are

$$\alpha a X^{\alpha-1} = \lambda P \qquad \text{(G-4a)}$$

$$\phi f L^{\phi-1} = \lambda w \qquad \text{(G-4b)}$$

$$c\gamma \mu I^{\gamma-1} = \lambda w \qquad \text{(G-4c)}$$

$$\mu(T)w(T) = 0 \qquad \text{(G-4d)}$$

$$\lambda(T)A(T) = 0 \qquad \text{(G-4e)}$$

$$\dot{\lambda} = -r\lambda \qquad \text{(G-4f)}$$

$$\dot{\mu} = -\lambda(D - L - I) \qquad \text{(G-4g)}$$

Since

$$\lim_{X \to 0} X^{\alpha-1} \to \infty, \qquad \lim_{L \to 0} L^{\phi-1} \to \infty, \qquad \lim_{I \to 0} I^{\gamma-1} \to \infty,$$

the only possibility of a corner solution comes from the constraint $D \geq L + I$. If this is binding, equations G-4b and G-4c condense to

$$\beta b L^{\beta-1} = c\gamma \mu I^{\gamma-1} \qquad \text{(G-4b)}'$$

and equation G-4g' becomes

$$\dot{\mu} = 0 \qquad \text{(G-4g)}'$$

Existence of optimal controls is assured by a theorem of Cesari (1965) since the Hamiltonian is concave in the control variables.

From equation G-4f, since $A(T) = 0$ (because $U(t)$ is unbounded),

$$\lambda(t) = \lambda(0)e^{-rt}$$

Since $w(T) = 0$

$$\mu(t) = \int_t^T e^{-r\tau}[D - L(\tau) - I(\tau)]d\tau$$

From equations G-4a, G-4b, and G-4c, if $L + I < D$

$$X = \left(\frac{\lambda(0)e^{-rt}P}{a\alpha}\right)^{\frac{1}{\alpha-1}} \qquad \text{(G-5a)}$$

$$L = \left(\frac{\lambda(0)e^{-rt}w}{\phi f}\right)^{\frac{1}{\phi-1}} \qquad \text{(G-5b)}$$

$$I = \left(\frac{\lambda(0)e^{-rt}w}{c\gamma\mu}\right)^{\frac{1}{\gamma-1}} \tag{G-5c}$$

During periods of specialization, $L + I = D$. From equation G-4b', since $\dot\mu = 0$, L and I are constant during a period of specialization, and the rate of growth of wages must decrease throughout such a period. During such a period

$$c\gamma\mu(t)I(t)^{\gamma-1} > \lambda(0)e^{-rt}w(t)$$

while at the end of the period, this inequality becomes a strict equality. Since $\mu(t)$ is a continuous function of time, and since $w(t)$ is also continuous, no jump occurs in I at the end of a period of specialization. For the interval to terminate, the *average* rate of growth of wages must exceed the interest rate. Otherwise, a strict equality would never hold, and there would be no end to the period of specialization. But it is clearly never optimal to invest without ever working. Thus, if investment is never sufficiently productive, no period of specialization need arise.[4]

Suppose that time is sufficiently productive so that a period of specialization occurs. Will there be more than one period of specialization? If not, when does it occur? I will show that, at most, one period of specialization occurs, and that if it occurs, it comes at the earliest stage of the life cycle.

Before demonstrating these propositions, assume they are correct, and consider the behavior of the variables at the end of the period of specialization. Since $\mu(t)$ is continuous and $w(t)$ is continuous, $I(t)$ and $L(t)$ are also continuous functions of time. If, coming out of the period of specialization, wages grow at a rate exceeding the interest rate r, leisure decreases as does investment time. Thus, time in the market increases, and hours of productive work must increase. Some care must be taken in interpreting this result. If time at school is not counted as work or investment time, the period following the period of specialization will appear to have a sharp jump in working hours. In fact, a large portion of initial market time is, in reality, a continuation of investment time to an alternative institutional arrangement.

To establish these propositions, logarithmically differentiate equations G-5b and G-5c with respect to time to reach

---

[4] For example, if $cD^\gamma < rw(0)$ (i.e., if all available time were devoted to investment and the rate of growth of wages is less than the rate of interest), no specialization would ever occur.

$$\left(\frac{\dot{L}}{L}\right) = \frac{1}{1-\beta}\left(r - \frac{\dot{w}}{w}\right)$$

$$\left(\frac{\dot{I}}{I}\right) = \frac{1}{1-\gamma}\left(r - \frac{\dot{w}}{w} + \frac{\dot{\mu}}{\mu}\right)^5$$

Since $1 > \phi > 0$, and $1 > \gamma > 0$, if $\dot{w}/w > r$, leisure declines and, a fortiori, investment declines ($I < 0$) since $\dot{\mu} < 0$. Accordingly, the proportion of market time spent investing declines monotonically and earnings rise. Wage growth rates decelerate, since investment is decreasing and the base of the rate is expanding. Sometime before, or at the end of life, $\dot{w}/w < r$, and leisure begins to increase.

As investment decreases, the growth rate in wages falls below the rate of interest, so that the consumption of leisure begins to increase while investment hours and hours of work both decrease. As investment continues to decrease, the wage rate grows at an ever slower rate, so that it is possible (but by no means necessary) that investment time will begin to increase, and total hours of productive work will fall if wage growth is low enough so that

$$\frac{\dot{w}}{w} < r + \frac{\dot{\mu}}{\mu}$$

Intuitively, at this stage in the life cycle, the discounted marginal cost of investment is low. Eventually, investment time must decrease again, since at the end of the horizon, investment terminates $I(T) = 0$, and I is a continuous function of time. (Equivalently, $\dot{\mu}/\mu$ becomes increasingly more negative near the end of the horizon.)

Note that the "position" of wage growth rates defined by

$$\frac{\dot{w}}{w} = r + \frac{\dot{\mu}}{\mu}$$

has a stability property. If the rate of wage growth falls below $r + (\dot{\mu}/\mu)$, investment begins to increase, tending to raise $\dot{w}/w$, and to shut off the growth in investment time. If the wage growth exceeds $r + (\dot{\mu}/\mu)$, investment decreases, and wage growth is slowed.

To gain further insight into this case, it is of some interest to interpret $\dot{\mu}/\mu$. From equation G-4g, it is seen that

---

[5] Note that although $w(t)$ and $\dot{w}(t)$ are continuous functions of time, $\dot{\mu}$ need not be continuous. Accordingly, right derivatives are used where appropriate.

$$\frac{\dot{\mu}}{\mu} = -\frac{e^{-rt}H(t)}{\int_t^T e^{-r\tau}H(\tau)d\tau}$$

The term in the denominator is that portion of the discounted (from $t = 0$) stock of lifetime hours of work from t to the end of life. Accordingly, $\dot{\mu}/\mu$ is the percentage decline of discounted remaining lifetime hours of work. Near the end of life, this is large in absolute value. Moreover, if hours of work are constant from t on

$$\frac{\dot{\mu}}{\mu} = -\frac{r}{1 - e^{-r(T-t)}} < -r$$

so that if future hours of work are constant or decreasing, $r + (\dot{\mu}/\mu) < 0$. Since $\dot{w} \geq 0$, investment can never increase if future hours of work at each instant are less than, or equal to, current hours of work.

Note that the increase in investment time must come at an age after the total amount of time spent in the market has peaked ($\dot{L} = 0$), and at a time when total productive hours of work are decreasing. Moreover, for investment to increase, subsequent hours of work must increase to a level greater than the level of hours worked at the age at which investment time begins to increase. "Greater" is the appropriate term since the paths of all variables are continuous, and in the initial phase of increasing investment, hours of work must decrease. Note, too, that once the rate of growth of wages falls below the rate of interest, it never again exceeds that rate. This follows from the previously stated stability property that $\dot{I} \gtrless 0$ as $\dot{w}/w \lessgtr r + (\dot{\mu}/\mu)$ since $\dot{\mu} < 0$. Accordingly, the lifetime peak in market hours supplied is never reattained, and no further period of specialization arises. Moreover, the period of specialization, if one occurs, must be in the first part of life. For, if investment were to increase until a time when specialization arises, $(\dot{w}/w) < r + (\dot{\mu}/\mu) = > (\dot{w}/w) < r$, at the beginning of the specialization interval, and so the specialization interval would never terminate, and hence it is nonoptimal. If investment were to *decrease* or remain constant up to the beginning of the specialization interval level of investment, it must be the case that leisure is increasing, and $(\dot{w}/w) < r$, and hence, the previous argument applies. Thus, investment time is specialized in one period in the first part of life if, indeed, specialization of time ever arises.

Thus far, I have pursued the case of wage growth greater than the rate of interest immediately after the period of specialization. Suppose that wage growth is less than the rate of interest at the end of the specialization period. Leisure increases (i.e., total time spent in the market is at lifetime peak just after the period of specialization is over), investment decreases and hours of work increase. Precisely the same analysis as before holds for this case of $(\dot{w}/w) < r$. Again, investment may fluctuate around the "stability point" for wage growth

$$\frac{\dot{w}}{w} = r + \frac{\dot{\mu}}{\mu}$$

This second case appears to be empirically uninteresting, since it has the very strong, and empirically unacceptable, prediction that the peak in market activity arises just after the completion of schooling.

To summarize this discussion, consider Figure 1, in which the time derivative of investment is plotted against the time derivative of leisure. At any point in time, the graph is broken into three shaded regions. The lower left region (A) is the case of wage growth greater than the rate of interest. In this region, both leisure and investment time decrease. If the rate of growth of wages is less than r, but greater than $r + (\dot{\mu}/\mu)$, leisure increases, the total amount of time spent in the market contracts, and investment time decreases (region B). Only if the rate of growth of wages falls below $r + (\dot{\mu}/\mu)$ will investment time increase (region C), but the growth in wages will choke off this investment increase, and eventually the path returns to region B. However, the fact that investment is declining (and wage growth falls) keeps the trajectory in region B or region C. It can never reenter region A. One possible path is sketched for a case in which immediately after the period of specialization, the proportional rate of growth in wage rates exceeds the rate of interest.[6]

II. ESTIMATING A HUMAN CAPITAL
PRODUCTION FUNCTION
A. Choice of Functional Form and Methodology

No simple profile characterizes human capital accumulation programs. Depending on initial conditions, preferences, and the nature of the production function, almost any accumulation pattern may be generated. If more information is available about the form of the production function, it might be possible to narrow the band of ignorance about capital accumulation profiles, and through simulations with

---

[6] Remember that the vertical boundary between B and C will shift with time.

FIGURE 1

The Three Phases of the Investment-Leisure Relationship

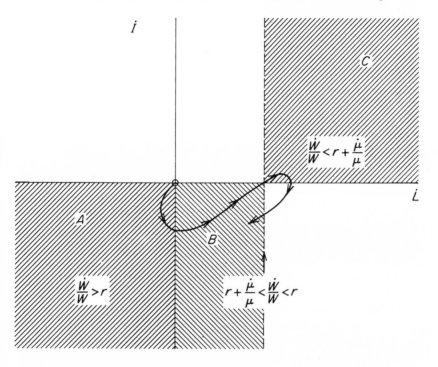

different initial wage rates and asset levels, to determine typical profiles.

In this section, a Cobb-Douglas production function for human capital is estimated. En route to the production parameter estimates, provisional estimates of the proportion of market time spent investing at each age are generated. The methodology is quite general, and the approach is applicable to human capital models with exogenous or endogenous labor supply.

The human capital production function is specialized to

$$\dot{w} = cI^{\gamma}w^{\beta} - \sigma w, \ 0 < \gamma < 1 \tag{9}$$

If $\gamma = \beta$, the production function satisfies the neutrality hypothesis. If $\beta = 0$, and $\sigma = 0$, the production function is precisely that analyzed in Section I(G). If $\gamma = \beta = 1/2$, the production function is equivalent to the production functions in the models of Haley (1973) and Rosen (1973).

For postspecialization investment periods, the optimality conditions equivalent to equations 6(e)' and 6(f)' become

$$\dot{g}(t) = (\sigma + r)g(t) - \left[D - L(t) - I(t)\left(1 - \frac{\beta}{\gamma}\right) \right] \qquad (10)$$

and

$$w(t) = g(t)c\gamma I^{\gamma-1}w^{\beta} \qquad (11)$$

Equation 10 dramatically underscores the very special nature of the "neutrality" hypothesis. Only if $\gamma = \beta$ will the shadow price of investment $g(t)$ be independent of the pattern of future investment. Note further that unless leisure is fixed, as in conventional income maximizing models, or as in models in which Michael neutrality is invoked, the shadow price of investment depends on the profile of future time supplied to the market $D - L(t)$. For both reasons, Becker's (1967) conjecture that market bias ($\beta < \gamma$) leads to an accelerated decline in investment compared to the neutrality case ($\gamma = \beta$) is seen to apply only to the cost schedule. When neutrality is relaxed, and labor supply is endogenous, the demand price of human capital need not monotonically decline with age, and so investment may increase with age, at least for some age ranges.[7]

The wage rate plays two distinct roles. Looking backward, the current wage rate is a result of previous investment. Integrating equation 9, the current wage rate is the accounting identity [8]

$$w(t) = e^{-\sigma t}[(1 - \beta) \int_0^t cI^{\gamma}(\tau)e^{(1-\beta)\sigma\tau}d\tau + (1 - \beta)w(0)^{1-\beta}]^{\frac{1}{1-\beta}} \qquad (12)$$

Looking forward, the wage rate is also the marginal cost of current investment time. Integrating equation 10 and substituting into equation 11,

$$w(t) = c\gamma I^{\gamma-1}w(t)^{\beta} \int_t^T e^{-(\sigma+r)(\tau-t)}\left[D - L(\tau) - I(\tau)\left(1 - \frac{\beta}{\gamma}\right) \right] d\tau \qquad (13)$$

Suppose that there are data on a typical consumer's profile of time supplied to the market ($M(t) = D - L(t) = H(t) + I(t)$). but that it is

---

[7] Even if labor supply is set exogenously, and it increases with time, investment may increase for a period in the life cycle.

[8] This equation is analogous to Becker's income identity equation (Becker 1964, eq. 28, and Mincer 1973, eq. 3.1).

not possible to distinguish work time from investment time. Although the true wage rate is unknown, the consumer's earnings $(w(t)H(t))$ are known. Denote the proportion of market time devoted to investment by $S(t)$. Measured wage rates $(w^*(t))$ obtained by dividing earnings by reported hours in the market may be written as

$$w^*(t) = w(t)[1 - S(t)]$$

since only $1 - S(t)$ of the reported working hours have no investment content.

Conditional on a profile of $S(t)$, equations 12 and 13 may be written in terms of observable variables, and upon taking natural logarithms, the following optimality conditions for postschool investment are obtained:

$$\ln w^*(t) = \frac{\ln c\gamma}{1 - \beta} + \frac{\gamma - 1}{1 - \beta} \ln S(t)M(t) + \ln [1 - S(t)]$$

$$+ \frac{1}{1 - \beta} \ln \left\{ \int_t^T e^{-(\sigma+r)(\tau-t)}M(\tau)[1 + (1 - \beta/\gamma)S(\tau)]d\tau \right\} \quad (14)$$

and

$$\ln w^*(t) = \ln [1 - S(t)] - \sigma t$$

$$+ \frac{1}{1 - \beta} \ln \left\{ \int_0^t c[S(\tau)M(\tau)]^\gamma e^{(1-\beta)\sigma\tau}d\tau + w(0)^{1-\beta} \right\} \quad (15)$$

Since actual data come in discrete time intervals, it is necessary to make a discrete approximation to the continuous equations to estimate the parameters.[9]

The consumer is assumed to have T years in his postspecialization working life so that there are T observations for $M(t)$ and $w^*(t)$, and $2T$ approximate equations generated by $S(t)$, σ, β, γ, c, and r. If $S(t)$ is a judiciously parameterized function of time,[10] it is possible to estimate the parameters determining the $S(t)$, as well as β, σ, γ, c, and r. In this paper, r is assumed to be 10 per cent.[11]

A measure of concordance of the parameters with the data may be defined as the squared deviation of each equation at each age from a

[9] The discrete approximations are discussed more fully in Section II (B), footnote 14.

[10] In particular, if $S(t)$ is a polynomial in time, it is necessary that the degree of the polynomial be less than $T - 4$ so that degrees of freedom are left to determine the remaining parameters β, σ, γ, and c, assuming r is fixed. To determine these parameters with any precision, the degree of the polynomial should be much less than $T - 4$.

[11] Given data on consumption expenditure, earnings, and initial assets, an r can be determined which sets $A(t)$ on page 230 to zero. This approach was not pursued in this paper.

perfect fit. Thus, introducing disturbances in the discrete approximation, and letting $V(i)$ be the disturbance for the first equation at age i, and letting $U(i)$ be the disturbance for the second equation, parameters may be chosen to minimize

$$\begin{vmatrix} \Sigma V_i^2 & \Sigma U_i V_i \\ \Sigma U_i V_i & \Sigma V_i^2 \end{vmatrix} \tag{16}$$

or its logarithm. Note that this criterion allows for inter-equation correlation in disturbances. If there are errors of measurement in the wage series, it is plausible that there is such inter-equation residual correlation. Minimizing this function conditional on a set of realized values for market time $(M(t))$ is equivalent to maximizing the likelihood function if equation errors are normally distributed, and independent of measurement error in the hours of market-time series.[12]

In such a complicated statistical model, identification of parameters is difficult to determine analytically. Recent work by Smallwood (1970) in estimating a somewhat similar model suggests that even when formal identification is secured, the likelihood function may be virtually indeterminate, and a wide variety of parameter estimates may lead to practically the same value for sample likelihood. Moreover, recent work by Rosen (1973) in estimating models of human capital accumulation suggests that determination of even a limited number of parameters may be a difficult task.

With these considerations in mind, the discrete $S(t)$ series is parameterized in a general logistic form to

$$S(t) = \left(1 + e^{\sum_{i=0}^{R} \chi_i t^i}\right)^{-1} \tag{17}$$

where R, and the χ_i, $i = 0, \ldots, R$ are estimable parameters. One advantage of this parameterization is that it constrains the estimated proportions of market time spent investing to lie inside the interval 0 to 1. The procedure followed in this paper is to begin with a simple model, adding successive polynomial time terms until their contribution to sample likelihood is negligible.[13]

B. The Data

In actual practice, no complete life-cycle data on any "representative consumer" exist, and resort to a synthetic cohort is necessary.

[12] Note, however, that the normality assumption is not crucial for establishing desirable asymptotic properties for nonlinear least squares. See Jennrich (1969).

[13] The actual test is a multiple equation heuristic F which asymptotically becomes a likelihood ratio test. For details, see Goldfeld and Quandt, Chapter 2. Each *parameter* was assumed to remove one degree of freedom from the data series.

Following the suggestion of Becker and Ghez (1972) and Rosen (1973), data from a cross section of individuals may be used to approximate the time series for a typical individual. This procedure ignores vintage effects and a variety of historical conditions that might influence the optimal paths of human capital accumulation for individuals of different birth cohorts.[14]

The data used in this study are from the 1970 One in a Hundred Census Tape for white college-educated employed males who are not enrolled in school, and who have not undertaken postgraduate education. These data are plotted in Figures 2A and 2B. The postschool work life is assumed to run from age 23 to age 65. A synthetic representative profile is constructed from computing geometric means of estimated annual hours worked, and geometric means of hourly wage rates. A major defect of these data is that the hourly wage data are generated by dividing reported earnings by estimated annual hours worked. Accordingly, the assumption that measurement error in the wage series is uncorrelated with measurement error in the hours-of-work series may be untenable if there is measurement error in constructing the hours-of-work variable. Since the current study is largely exploratory in nature, a more sophisticated analysis was felt to be inappropriate until some experience with simpler techniques was available.[15]

C. Empirical Results

Since identification is a touchy issue, a cautious approach is adopted in forming parameter estimates. The first model estimated is one with the production function of Section I(G), in which human capital is excluded from its own production ($\beta = 0$) and the rate of deprecia-

---

[14] In fairness to Becker and Ghez (1972) and Rosen (1973), it should be stated that both studies propose methods for eliminating "smooth" vintage effects although only the first study actually implements such methods.

[15] In order to facilitate duplication of the reported results, it is necessary to describe the nature of the discrete approximations. Data on a given age group, e.g., 25 year olds, refers to information on people who just turned 25 as well as to information on people almost 26. Since the relevant census data refer to events in the previous calendar year, and since the census is taken one-quarter of a year away from the previous year, the census 25 year old is actually, on average, 24 ¾ years old, so far as the relevant data are concerned. In order to generate discrete approximations, this age was used for 25 year olds, as is a similar displaced age for other age groups.

An initial wage rate is needed in equation 12. Age 23 was selected as the initial date. This age is felt to be sufficiently far removed from college graduation and is used only as an initial value. The residuals for the likelihood function were generated from age 24 to the end of life. Note that inclusion of age 65 implies that the retirement age is actually assumed to be 65 ¾ on average. The integrals are approximated by finite sums with one year increments in each step, and midpoint values for $S(t)$ assigned.

FIGURE 2A

Hourly Wage Rates by Age, Derived from 1970 U.S. Census Data
to Construct a Synthetic Cohort Used in the Empirical Analysis
Data are for White College-Educated Employed Males
Not Currently Enrolled in School

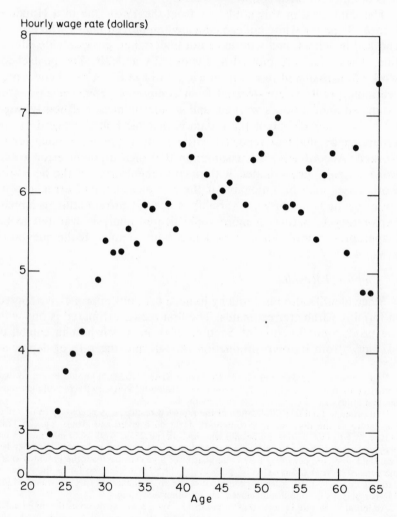

FIGURE 2B

Annual Hours Worked by Age, Derived from 1970 U.S. Census
Data to Construct a Synthetic Cohort Used in the Empirical
Analysis. Data are for White College-Educated Employed Males
Not Currently Enrolled in School

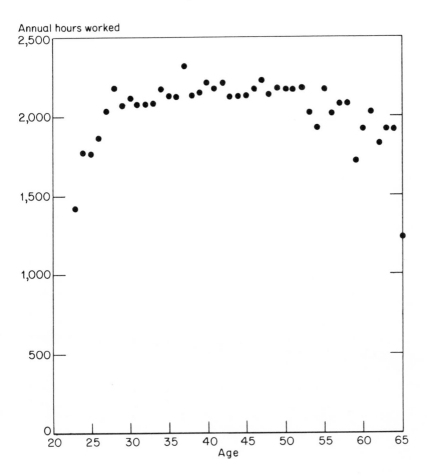

TABLE 1

(asymptotic standard errors in parentheses)

	Model I (G)		General Model [a,b]	
c	$.14 \times 10^{-2}$	$(.04 \times 10^{-2})$	45.49	(3.034)
γ	.67	(.052)	.99	(.003)
β	–		−6.69	(.043)
σ	–		.0016	(.00025)
χ_0	.99	(.16)	.6073	(.065)
χ_1	.035	(.010)	.0906	(.0081)
χ_2	$.39 \times 10^{-2}$	$(.12 \times 10^{-2})$	−.00537	(.0005)
χ_3	–	–	.00240	(.0007)
Value of log likelihood	−12.89		4.69	

[a] Test for $\gamma = 1$ rejects that hypothesis. $\left(\dfrac{\gamma - 1}{.0031}\right) = 3.33$.

[b] Test for neutrality hypothesis $\gamma - \beta = 0$, $\dfrac{\gamma - \beta}{[\text{Var}(\gamma - \beta)]^{1/2}} = \dfrac{7.68}{.229} = 33$.

tion (σ) is set at zero.[16] The interest rate is fixed at 10 per cent. The error sum of squares function (16) was minimized using both the Powell conjugate gradient method and Grad X.[17] Experimentation with polynomial time-trend terms beyond the second power failed to produce any significant improvement in likelihood. The results with this model are reported in the first column of Table 1. The estimated proportion of time spent investing is plotted in Figure 3. The initial proportion of time spent investing is quite high but, by age 47, becomes negligible.

Figure 4 graphs the amount of time invested against age. Note that the *initial* increase in investment time is in apparent contradiction with the pattern predicted in Section I(G). The dollar costs of investment plotted in Figure 5 show a similar initial increase followed by a decline. With the precision afforded by these data, the logically possible

[16] Note that no special assumption is made about preferences. The effect of preferences is embodied in the observed hours-of-work series. However, given an assumption about preferences such as that made in Section I(G), it is possible to make some refutable statements about the time profile of investments.

[17] For a discussion of these techniques, see Goldfeld and Quandt (1972), Chapter 1. Both sets of optima reported in this paper were tested by using "substantial" displacements from the reported optimum parameter estimates. Both optima were stable. Of course, these experiments do not prove that a truly global optimum has been located.

FIGURE 3

Estimate of the Age Profile of the Proportion of Measured Working
Hours Devoted to Learning and Investment Activities, Derived
from a Model That Assumes Human Capital Is Not Self-Productive

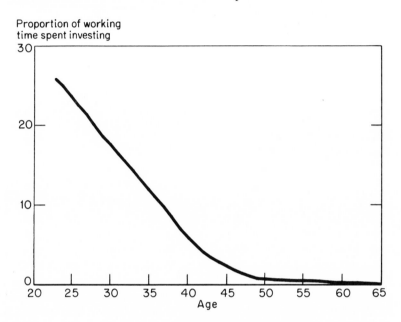

phenomenon of rising investment time following an initial decline in
postschool investment appears to be empirically irrelevant.

The increase in postschool investment time immediately after the
completion of schooling may be interpreted as a refutation of one of
the predictions of model I(G). Either the assumption about preferences
or the assumption about technology may be incorrect. With this result in mind, a more general model is also estimated. In this model,
both β and σ are estimated, rather than assumed to be zero. Thus, it
becomes possible to make a direct parametric test of the neutrality hypothesis ($\gamma = \beta$).

Empirical results with the revised model are reported in the right-
hand column of Table 1. The heuristic F test indicates that a cubic
time-trend term should be included. The most dramatic result with the
more general model is that the returns-to-scale parameter (γ) is near

FIGURE 4

Estimate of the Age Profile of the Number of Hours Devoted to
On-the-Job Learning and Investment Activities, Derived from
a Model That Assumes Human Capital Is Not Self-Productive

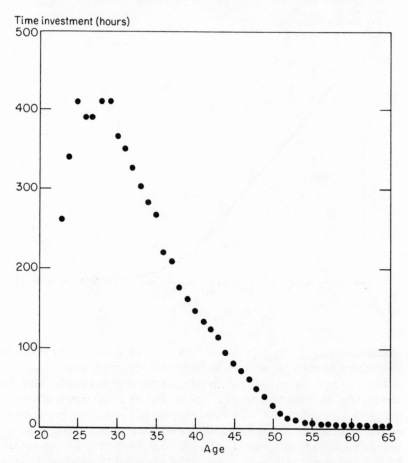

unity, although as noted in the first footnote of the table, it is statistically significantly different from unity. If γ were unity, the model would
collapse into a "bang-bang" control problem, and a continuous postschool investment profile would not exist. Although there are few
empirical results with which this finding can be compared, estimates
produced in two other papers suggest that γ may in fact be near unity.

FIGURE 5

Estimate of the Age Profile of the Dollar Value of the Time
Devoted to On-the-Job Learning and Investment Activities,
Derived from a Model That Assumes Human Capital Is Not
Self-Productive

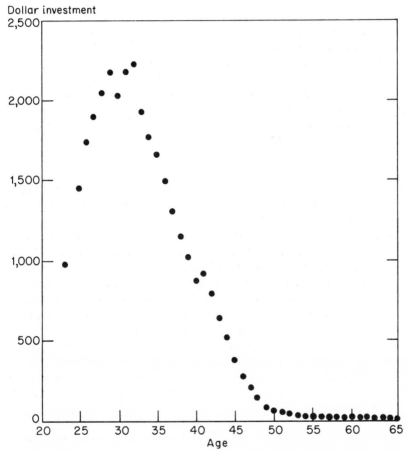

In his commentary on a paper by Ben-Porath, Mincer (1970) estimates the inverse of γ as approximately 1.01. No confidence interval
is stated. A recent paper by Brown (1973) estimates the inverse of γ
as 1.15. Again, no confidence interval is available. The comparison
between the results in these studies and the results reported here must
be qualified since both authors assume neutrality (i.e., $\gamma = \beta$).

The rate of depreciation is estimated to be quite small (one-sixth of 1 per cent or so). Human capital is seen to have *negative* self-productivity. The estimate of β is large and negative, and the test in the footnote to the table suggests that the neutrality hypothesis is resoundingly rejected. However, the value of β is too negative to be accepted without some skepticism.[18]

The analogues of Figures 3, 4, and 5 are presented in Figures 6, 7, and 8 respectively. Not surprisingly, in view of the large market bias implicit in the estimate of β, investment time falls off more sharply than in the previous case and, by age 37, becomes negligible.

It is noteworthy that in both models, the profile of the proportion of time spent investing at each age falls off more steeply than the linearly declining profile assumed by Mincer (1972). Moreover, in both models, the curvature of this profile has convexity properties directly opposite to those proposed by Haley (1973).

CONCLUSION

In this paper, I have discussed life-cycle models of labor supply and human capital accumulation. Methods for estimating the parameters of the human capital production function have been proposed and implemented. By assuming a functional form for the human capital production function, it is possible to utilize both the accounting identity that wage growth is the result of investment, and the optimality condition that the wage rate should equal the marginal benefit of time investment, to estimate the parameters of the underlying production function and to determine the proportion of time spent investing at each age and the empirical relevance of the neutrality hypothesis. The estimates presented in this paper confirm Ben-Porath's (1970) finding that the neutrality hypothesis is not consistent with data on life-cycle profiles, and suggest that the simple time profiles assumed by Mincer (1970) and deduced by Haley (1973) are not empirically relevant for white college-educated males.

---

[18] One possible reason for the large negative value of β may be that market inputs into postschool investment are omitted, tending to overstate the value of β (in absolute value) if investment time is negatively correlated with the level of the wage rate. A negative correlation is plausible if β is, in fact, negative. For the same reasons, γ will be overstated. Another source of bias may be spurious correlation between the disturbances and the hours of work series. However, preliminary results with the Survey of Economic Opportunity data, in which wage and hours data are independently derived, suggest that estimates of β remain large and negative.

FIGURE 6

Estimate of the Age Profile of the Proportion of Measured Working
Hours Devoted to Learning and Investment Activities from a
Model That Allows Human Capital to Enter Its Own Production

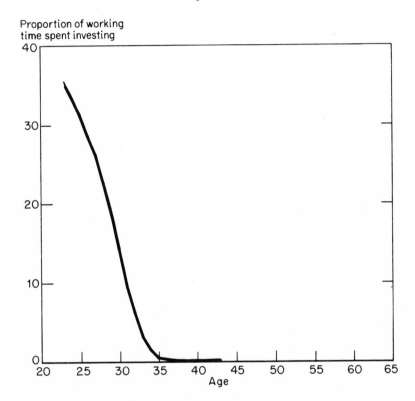

FIGURE 7

Estimate of the Age Profile of the Number of Hours Devoted to
On-the-Job Learning and Investment Activities, Derived from a
Model That Allows Human Capital to Enter Its Own Production

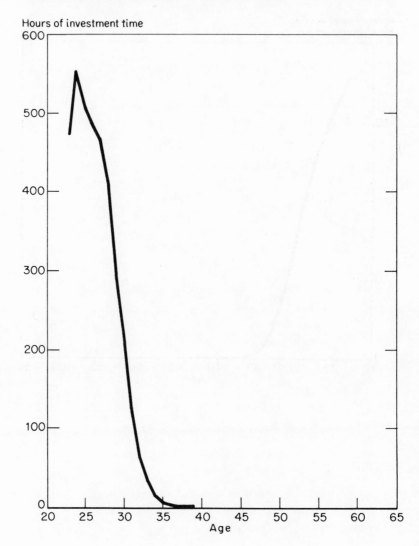

FIGURE 8

Age Profile of the Dollar Value of Time Devoted to On-the-Job
Learning, Derived from a Model in Which Human Capital Enters
Its Own Production

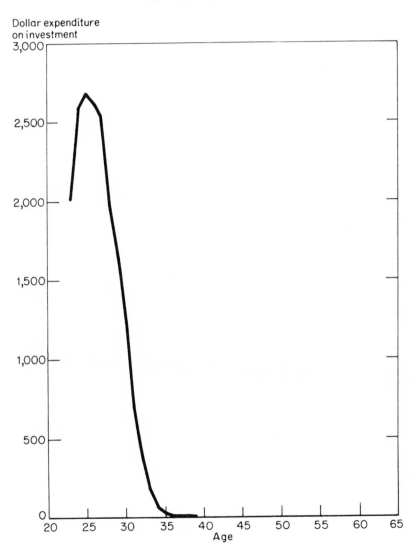

REFERENCES

Becker, Gary. *Human Capital: A Theoretical and Empirical Analysis, with Special Reference to Education.* New York: NBER, 1964.

———. "Human Capital and the Personal Distribution of Income." W. S. Woytinsky Lecture Number 1, University of Michigan, 1967.

Becker, Gary, and Ghez, Gilbert. "The Allocation of Time and Goods Over the Life Cycle." Unpublished NBER Paper, 1972.

Ben-Porath, Yoram. "The Production of Human Capital and the Life Cycle of Earnings." *Journal of Political Economy 75* (August 1967), Part I: 352–365.

———. "The Production of Human Capital over Time." In W. Lee Hansen, ed., *Education, Income and Human Capital.* New York: NBER, 1970.

Brown, C. "Optimal Self Investment and the Earnings of Young Workers." Unpublished paper, Harvard University, December 1973.

Cesari, Luigi. "Existence Theorems for Optimal Solutions in LaGrange and Pontryagin Problems." *Journal of the Society for Industrial and Applied Mathematics, Series A: Control 3* (March 1965): 475–498.

Goldfeld, Stephen, and Quandt, Richard. *Nonlinear Methods in Econometrics.* London and Amsterdam: North-Holland, 1972.

Haley, William. "Human Capital: The Choice Between Investment and Income." *American Economic Review 63* (December 1973): 929–944.

Heckman, James. "Three Essays on the Supply of Labor and the Demand for Goods, Essay 1: Life Cycle Saving, Consumption and Labor Supply." Ph.D. dissertation, Princeton University, May 1971.

Hestenes, Magnus. *Calculus of Variations and Optimal Control Theory.* New York: John Wiley & Sons, 1966.

Jennrich, Richard. "Asymptotic Properties of Nonlinear Least Squares Estimators." *The Annals of Mathematical Statistics 40* (April 1969): 633–643.

Michael, Robert. *The Effect of Education on Efficiency in Consumption.* New York: NBER, 1973.

Mincer, Jacob. *Schooling, Experience, and Earnings.* New York: NBER, 1974.

Modigliani, Franco, and Brumberg, R. "Utility Analysis and the Consumption Function: An Interpretation of Cross Section Data." In K. K. Kurihara, ed., *Post Keynesian Economics.* New Brunswick, New Jersey: Rutgers University Press, 1954.

Rosen, Sherwin. "Learning and Experience in the Labor Market." *Journal of Human Resources 7* (1972).

———. "Income Generating Functions and Capital Accumulation," Harvard Institute of Economic Research, Discussion Paper No. 306, June 1973.

Smallwood, Dennis E. "Problems of Indeterminacy with the Fixed Coefficients, Vintage Model," *Yale Economic Essays 10* (Fall 1970): 45–75.

Stafford, Frank, and Stephan, Paula. "Labor, Leisure and Training Over the Life Cycle." Paper presented to the Econometric Society, December 1972.

Strotz, Robert. "Myopia and Inconsistency in Dynamic Utility Maximization." *Review of Economic Studies 33* (June 1956): 165–180.

Yaari, Menahem E. "On the Existence of An Optimal Plan in a Continuous Time Allocation Process." *Econometrica 32* (October 1964): 576–590.

———. "On the Consumer's Lifetime Allocation Process." *International Economic Review 5* (October 1964): 304–317.

Comments on "Estimates of a Human Capital Production Function Embedded in a Life-Cycle Model of Labor Supply"

T. PAUL SCHULTZ

UNIVERSITY OF MINNESOTA

JAMES HECKMAN'S paper presents a dynamic framework for analyzing the life-cycle allocation of time among three ends: activities that augment the individual's market wage (i.e., human capital), market production, and leisure. The process producing human capital is specified such that the optimal path of investment determines the current wage by past investments and equates this wage to the marginal value of future investments of time. The future pattern of investment is relevant because the Ben-Porath neutrality of human capital assumption is relaxed and the labor supply decision is made endogenous. The exposition of the model is clear and thoughtful, and in my view, it represents a unified generalization and extension of the Ben-Porath (1967, 1970) formulation. First, I will restate the problem of under-identification that appears to limit what we can learn about the human capital production function, and describe how Heckman has approached this problem. Then I shall indicate why the econometric techniques and data used by Heckman may not be the most appropriate for estimating the parameters to his formulation of the model.

To understand why market wage rates vary over an individual's life cycle, the human capital framework postulates that investments occur that augment the productive capacity of the human agent, while other processes, such as depreciation and obsolescence, may work to diminish that capacity over time. In the postschooling period of the life cycle, there is, regrettably, no obvious way to measure directly the proportion of time an individual allocates only to increase his future market productivity. Consequently, the general form of the human-capital production function must be restricted if a single time series on market wage rates is to shed much light on the time profile of postschooling investment and the many parameters that can be used to characterize the processes that produce and depreciate the stock of human capital.

Ben-Porath's approach to this problem was to assume that non-working time or leisure was fixed, or alternatively that leisure did not enter the utility function. Heckman relaxes this unappealing assumption, making labor supply decisions endogenous and permitting $\lambda(t)$, the shadow value of time in leisure, to vary independently of $\mu(t)$, the shadow cost of time in human capital investments. The "neutrality" assumption of Ben-Porath, that human capital increases equally the productivity of time in the marketplace and in the production of further human capital, is another restriction that Heckman relaxes, that is, γ need not equal β. Finally, Heckman explores in some detail the effects of depreciation σ, the market rate of interest r, and individual time preference ρ on the optimal regime of life-cycle investment.

From this dynamic allocative model, the demands for leisure and goods can be obtained, with predictions on the signs of the time derivatives of the marginal value of goods and leisure, and on the difference between the individual time preference and the market rate of interest. The parameters to these derived demand equations have already been estimated by Heckman (1971) from individual (synthetic) life-cycle information on the consumption of goods and leisure (or labor supply) and the pattern of wages. With great clarity (and candor), Heckman states why the general model leads to regrettably few predictions about *investment behavior* over the life cycle. The critical question is, therefore, How should the generality of the model be restricted to yield new insights and possible empirical applications for the framework?

In his specific model, Heckman assumes that time preference and depreciation can be eliminated altogether (ρ, $\sigma = 0$), and the polar case from that proposed by Ben-Porath is adopted, the assumption being that human capital has *no effect* on the efficiency with which subsequent human capital is produced. Also, an additive utility function is posited that implies strong restrictions. Even with these specific assumptions, testable implications for investment behavior are scarce. Several interesting interrelationships are, nonetheless, explored and diagramed. It is not clear in my mind, however, that this exercise in generalization has not collapsed to a less realistic model than that used by Ben-Porath, and in neither instance are the empirical implications of the restricted model particularly powerful in accounting for anomalous empirical evidence.

In his empirical estimation of the human capital production function, Heckman has set the interest rate to 10 per cent, and initially assumed that depreciation is zero ($\sigma = 0$), and human capital is excluded from its own production ($\beta = 0$). Average information on single age groups of white college-educated males for "hours worked" and "hourly wage rates" from the 1970 Census cross section are used to estimate the model's remaining five parameters: the market productivity of human capital c, the returns to scale in human capital investment γ, an intercept parameter and a quadratic function in age: χ_0, χ_1, χ_2.

The initial restrictions, namely that β and σ are zero, are then relaxed, and a second set of estimates reported for the general model. These unrestricted estimates might provide one with a better basis for choosing between Ben-Porath's "neutrality" hypothesis and Heckman's strong "market-bias" hypothesis. Getting a better sense of the confidence ellipses obtained around these two parameters, γ and β, might provide a further opportunity to explore the sensitivity (or lack thereof) of the model to these analytically convenient restrictions.

Heckman's approach is conceptually attractive because he incorporates into the human capital investment model additional relevant information about life-cycle labor supply decisions to facilitate identification of his parameterization of the human capital production function. Unfortunately, the expected value of labor supply for United States college-educated white males does not vary much from age 27 to age 52 (see Figure 2). And as Sherwin Rosen pointed out, the variation in labor supply from age 22 to age 26 among this group may be in large part a reflection of frictional lags in labor force entry or part-time and part-year employment by persons still in school. Thus, this critical source of variability in the labor supply series that helps to identify the model may be largely spurious from the point of view of the behavioral process Heckman is trying to study. Reestimating the model without these few younger observations would therefore seem reasonable.

There is also the question of how empirical materials can best be used to discriminate among hypotheses and to estimate more confidently the several interesting parameters to the human capital production function. In my judgment, cross-sectional information from age-specific groups is no longer a satisfactory data base for estimating dynamic models of life-cycle behavior. The synthetic cohort was a tolerable first approximation when the questions asked of earnings data were relatively simple. This is no longer true. Meanwhile, longitudinal data for individuals are becoming publicly available. Interpolating wage rate and labor supply series for all ages from the several jobs reported in the Parnes Longitudinal Labor Force Survey (which Heckman [1972] has already used to great advantage) might permit one to estimate Heckman's general model or more restricted variants thereof. Coleman's life-history survey might also be a useful data base. New problems would also arise, of course, by the nature of these time-series data sources. If such longitudinal data are still unable to identify confidently the parameters to the underlying human capital production function, it may be possible to incorporate information on variation in both cross sections and cohort series, specifying with care the stochastic structure of the resulting composite disturbances. Error-component models can also be formulated to derive information about unobserved variables from common effects across related behavioral equations (Griliches). A variety of such new approaches applied to more appropriate longitudinal individual data may clarify the relevant dimensions of the human capital production function.

Two aspects of the maximum likelihood estimation procedure employed by Heckman deserve note. First, in defining the criterion for estimating the parameters to equations 14 and 15, equal weight is attached to the mean square error of both the past and future investment-wage relationships, plus inter-equation residual correlations. As Zvi Griliches suggested at the Conference, there may be reason to think that people do somewhat better optimizing their current behavior as a function of past outcomes than they do in adjusting their behavior to their (uncertain) knowledge of future outcomes. Perhaps past consistency should be weighted more heavily than future consistency in obtaining the "best" parameter estimates. At least some sensitivity analysis might be warranted, given the arbitrary nature of this criterion.

Second, and much more important, the estimates to equations 14 and 15 are obtained conditional on the realized values of market time $(M(t))$. For this labor supply series to be independent of the disturbances in the investment equations, the investment decision-making process must *not* be jointly and simultaneously determined with life-cycle labor supply. Admittedly, Heckman's assumption of independence from stochastic simultaneity and joint errors of measurement [1]

---

[1] As is widely recognized in the labor supply literature, the Census wage-rate series is obtained by dividing annual earnings by annual hours worked. Hence there is a negative spurious correlation introduced into the wage and hours series by definition if there are errors in measurement of labor supply. The importance of this bias, of course, is much reduced through aggregation by age, but it must still be present to some degree in Heckman's data.

eases the job of estimation. But, in my view, it also contradicts the essential analytical advance proposed in the paper. I have difficulty imagining how the "Human Capital Production Function" can be "Embedded in a Life-Cycle Model of Labor Supply" and yet permit one to maintain the assumption that these two behavioral processes are not part of a jointly and simultaneously determined system of equations. If the life-cycle labor supply decision has an important bearing on human capital investment behavior, the analytical approach of this paper is interesting. But, in that case, the empirical estimates obtained by taking labor supply as predetermined in estimating the parameters to the human capital production function are subject to simultaneous-equations bias. Can one have it both ways? In my opinion, the analytical approach makes sense but the estimation procedure does not.

What is one to conclude from the empirical estimates? Investment rates decline over the life cycle according to the estimated polynomial time trend, in much the same manner as estimated by Mincer's simpler procedures. Diminishing returns to scale in the production of human capital, i.e., $\gamma < 1$, is implied by the restricted model, whereas constant returns to scale is implied for the generalized model, $\gamma = 1$. The large negative value of β, in the latter model, suggests that the accumulation of human capital *decreases* substantially the efficiency with which human capital can be subsequently produced. Despite the relatively small asymptotic standard errors, I cannot be confident that the parameter values of the generalized model are precise or even plausible.

One unusual empirical finding is the implied *increase* in the dollar and time costs of investment for the first several years after college, followed by the anticipated monotonic decline. Although dismissed as "empirically irrelevant," this anomaly may deserve further attention, for it is also noted in an empirical investigation of a population of engineering college graduates in Sweden (Klevmarken and Quigley 1973).

One interpretation of these results is that trying to estimate the general parameters of a human capital production function is not now a promising avenue for empirical research. Without additional sources of information that can aid discrimination among the several relevant parameters, the presumption that postschooling investment causes life-cycle variation in wage rates is plausible but also virtually tautological. As a heuristic device for discounting lifetime wage streams, the on-the-job investment hypothesis is a useful accounting mechanism that has not yet been rejected by any empirical tests.[2] What seems clear to me is that we are seeking a great deal of information about several complex processes from very little observable data. Have we any alternative research strategies? How are we more likely to improve our understanding of the related processes of individual time allocation, investment, and savings, which would seem to be responsible for both differences in individual wage rates at one point in time, and differences in wage rates for specific individuals over time?

REFERENCES

Ben-Porath, Yoram. "The Production of Human Capital and the Life Cycle of Earnings." *Journal of Political Economy* 75 (August 1967) Part 1: 352–365.

————. "The Production of Human Capital Over Time." In W. Lee Hansen, ed., *Education, Income and Human Capital.* New York: NBER, 1970.

Griliches, Zvi. "Errors in Variables and Other Unobservables." Harvard Discussion Paper No. 333, December 1973.

Heckman, James J. "Three Essays on the Supply of Labor and the Demand for Goods." Ph.D. dissertation, Princeton University, 1971.

————. "Shadow Prices, Market Wages and Labor Supply." Paper presented at the December 1972 meetings of the Econometrics Society, Toronto.

Klevmarken, Anders, and Quigley, John M. "Age, Experience, Earnings and Investment in Human Capital." Working paper of the Center for the Study of the City and Its Environment, Yale University, March 1973.

[2] Approximately the view expressed in a moment of perverseness by colleague John Hause.

The Value of Saving a Life:
Evidence from the Labor Market *

RICHARD THALER

UNIVERSITY OF ROCHESTER

AND

SHERWIN ROSEN

UNIVERSITY OF ROCHESTER

INTRODUCTION

LIVELY controversy has centered in recent years on the methodology for evaluating life-saving on government projects and in public policy. It is now well understood that valuation should be carried out in terms of a proper set of compensating variations, on a par with benefit measures used in other areas of project evaluation. To put it plainly, the value of a life is the amount members of society are willing to pay to save one. It is clear that most previously devised measures relate in a very imperfect way, if at all, to the conceptually appropriate measure.[1] However, in view of recent and prospective legislation on product and industrial safety standards, some new estimates are sorely needed.

This paper presents a range of rather conservative estimates for one important component of life value: the demand price for a person's own safety. Estimates are obtained by answering the question, "How much will a person pay to reduce the probability of his own death by a 'small' amount?" Another component of life value is the amount other people (family and friends) are willing to pay to save the life

* This research was partially funded by a grant from the National Institute of Education. Martin J. Bailey, Victor Fuchs, Jack Hirshleifer, and Paul Taubman provided helpful comments on an initial draft.
[1] See Schelling (1968), Usher (1972) and especially Mishan (1971) and the references therein.

of a particular individual. This second component is ignored. As a matter of course, a new conceptual framework for analyzing this problem is offered. We believe our model will be valuable for other investigations in this and related areas.

The usual methodology of preference revelation from observed behavior in demand theory is the most natural way of approaching the problem. Two types of behavior are relevant in this connection. First, individuals voluntarily undertake many risks of death and injury that are not inherent in their everyday situation, and which could be avoided through expenditure of their own resources.[2] Suppose a person is observed taking a known incremental risk that could be removed by spending one dollar. Then the implicit value of avoiding the additional risk must be something less than one dollar or else it would not have been observed. For example, many people would not purchase automobile seat belts if they were not mandatory. Further, when installation was required, many individuals did not use them, or at least that was so prior to the tied installation of ignition locks and warning buzzers. Some people make a point of crossing streets in the middle of the block rather than at corners, most do not completely fireproof their homes, and so forth. While these and other examples provide scattered evidence on death and injury risk evaluation, it appears doubtful whether they can be systematized enough to yield very convincing evidence on the matter. The second kind of behavior is observed in the labor market in conjunction with risky jobs. Analysis of those data is pursued here.

Our method follows up Adam Smith's ancient suggestion that individuals must be induced to take risky jobs through a set of compensating differences in wage rates. Here the evidence is highly systematic and the data are good. Different work situations exhibit vastly different work-related probabilities of death and injury. Moreover, lots of data are available on wages in these jobs, on the personal characteristics of people who work at them, and on the industrial and technical characteristics of firms who offer them. Further, parties who voluntarily face such risks daily and as a major part of their lives, or production processes, have a special interest in obtaining reliable and objective information about the nature of the risks involved. This is especially true of very risky jobs. Finally, we have uncovered a new source of genuine actuarial data on death rates in risky occupations that is superior to other existing data sources and that until now has not been used for estimation.

[2] Such an approach is suggested by Bailey (1968) and Fromm (1968).

Smith's theory has been familiar to economists for almost two hundred years and, in fact, forms the basis for the best recent inquiries into the economics of safety.[3] Yet very little effort has gone into empirical implementation of the idea. Some people have been hostile to it, asserting—without proof—that forces producing observed wage variation are so varied and complex as to preclude isolating the effect of risk. As will be demonstrated below, Smith's logic suggests that the labor market can be viewed as providing a mechanism for implicit trading in risk (and in other aspects of on-the-job consumption) with the degree of risk (and other job attributes) varying from one job to another. It certainly is not clear why price determination in such markets should be more complex than in any other markets where tied sales occur, such as the housing market. Indeed, the hedonic reconstruction of demand theory suggests that tied sales and package deals of product "characteristics" are the rule and not the exception in virtually all market exchange. Moreover, estimates presented below belie the assertion that partial effects of job risk on wage rates cannot be observed.

Given that risk-wage differentials can be estimated, How are the estimates to be interpreted, and How do they relate to the demand price for safety? Existence of a systematic, observable relationship between job risk and wage rates means that it is possible to impute a set of implicit marginal prices for various levels of risk. Like other prices, the imputations result from intersections of demand and supply functions. In the present case, there are supplies of people willing to work at risky jobs and demands for people to fill them. Alternatively, workers can be viewed as demanding on-the-job safety and firms can be regarded as supplying it.

Difficulties of interpretation arise from two sources. Individuals have different attitudes toward risk bearing and/or different physical capacities to cope with risky situations. In addition, it is not necessarily true that observed risks are completely and technologically fixed in various occupations and production processes. For example, changing TV tower light bulbs on top of the World Trade Building in New York is inherently more risky than changing light bulbs inside the offices of that building. However, it is conceivable to think of ways in which the first job could be made safer, though at some real cost. Whether, in general, firms find it in their interest to make safety-enhancing expenditures, and in what amounts, depends on weighing the costs of providing additional safety to workers against prospective

[3] For example, see Calabresi (1972).

returns. Costs are incurred from installing and maintaining safety devices and returns come in the form of lower wage payments and a smaller wage bill. How can it be known whether observed risk-wage relationships reflect mainly marginal costs of producing safety — the supply of job safety — rather than the demand for it?

This question raises fundamental and familiar issues of identification. Its resolution in terms of job attributes (or in terms of goods attributes in the hedonic view of demand, for that matter) requires a framework of analysis slightly altered from the usual one. The identification problem is resolved on a conceptual level in the following sections, where the nature of equilibrium in the implicit market for job risk is examined in some detail.[4] We show how the observations relate to underlying distributions of worker attitudes toward risk and to the structure of safety technology and particular production processes. The extent to which inferences about the demand for safety can be unscrambled from wage and risk observations quite naturally follows from this exercise. Data, estimates and interpretation of the results are presented subsequently.

THE MARKET FOR JOB SAFETY

As noted above, the theory of equalizing differences suggests labor market transactions can be treated as tied sales. Workers sell their labor, but at the same time purchase nonmonetary and psychic aspects of their jobs. Firms purchase labor, but also sell nonmonetary aspects of work. Thus, firms are joint producers: some output is sold on products markets and other output is sold to workers in conjunction with labor-service rentals. For purposes of exposition, we concentrate on one nonmonetary aspect of jobs, namely the risks of injury and death to which they give rise. The model can easily be extended to several attributes such as free lunches, good labor relations, prospects for on-the-job learning and the like, but the resulting complexity would detract from the main point.

For purposes of analyzing demand for job safety, it is sufficient to consider a market for productively and personally homogeneous workers. Assume worker attitudes toward death and injury risk are independent of their exogenously acquired skills. Workers in this market all have the same skill and personal characteristics, though tastes for job risk bearing generally differ among them. Workers are productively homogeneous, and the only distinguishing characteristic of jobs is the amount of death and injury risk associated with

---

[4] In fact, the model is an empirical application of a general model suggested by Rosen (1974).

each of them.[5] Jobs exhibiting the same risks are identical, and, by assumption, the personal identity of particular employers and employees is irrelevant to the problem. Job risk itself is a multidimensional concept and requires, at least, a distinction between deaths and injury probabilities, on one hand, and various levels of injury severity, on the other. Again, in line with our aim at simplification, represent job risk by a univariate index p. Further, let p denote the probability of a "standard accident." Then, each job is perfectly described by a particular value of p on the unit interval.

Equilibrium in the job market is characterized by a *function* $W(p)$, yielding the wage rate associated with each value of p. In fact $W(p)$ is a functional generalization of Smith's equalizing differences concept. Given an equilibrium function $W(p)$, each worker chooses an optimal value of p by comparing psychic costs of increased risk with monetary returns in the form of higher wages. This assumes, of course, that workers are risk averse and $W(p)$ is increasing in p. Operationally, optimal choice is achieved through each worker applying for a job offering the desired degree of risk (p). Firms decide what risks their jobs contain by comparing costs of providing additional safety with returns in the form of lower wage payments, and are constrained by their basic underlying technologies. $W(p)$ is an equilibrium function when the number of workers applying for jobs at each value of risk equals the number of jobs offered at each risk. Therefore, $W(p)$ serves as an equilibrating device for matching or marrying off workers and firms, the same role that prices play in standard markets.

Analysis of optimal choices of workers and firms gives an intuitive picture of the mechanism generating the observations on risk and prices (the function $W(p)$). Both decisions are considred in turn. We have sometimes found it convenient to think in terms of supply of workers to risky jobs and firms' demands for job risk, rather than the obverse concepts of workers' demand for job safety and firms' supply of it: safety is the negative of risk.

---

[5] The reader should note that analysis of worker job choice is confined to people with identical personal characteristics. The point is tricky and will be considered again below. For now, the following example will have to do. Suppose clumsy and careless persons have large negative externalities in risky settings involving groups of workers. Then a set of equalizing differences must arise on worker characteristics (one of which is "carelessness") that are not independent of risk. Costs of employing a careless worker exceed the costs of employing a careful one, and the latter must be paid less than the former. Employers attempt to internalize these externalities by choosing employees with the optimal packages of personal characteristics. It is as if there are separate risk markets for workers with each bundle of personal characteristics, and the present analysis of worker choice is confined to only one of those markets.

AN EXAMPLE

A good starting point for our analysis is the essay by Walter Oi (1973). Some fundamental aspects of the problem and our basic methodology are well illustrated by proving a variant of Oi's main result in very simple fashion and going on from there.

Again, suppose all job risk involves standard injuries and can be represented by work time lost and, consequently, by earnings lost. Deaths and "pain and suffering" due to injuries are ignored for the time being. Adopting this simplification, injuries can be measured in monetary equivalents: a proportion of the wage permanently lost, say, kW, where k is an exogenously determined constant and $0 < k < 1$. Workers choose jobs offering injury probability p, basing decisions on maximization of expected utility. Let $U(Y)$ represent some worker's utility function, where Y is the prospect of certain income. Assume risk aversion: $U' > 0$ and $U'' < 0$. Assume a perfect insurance market: the cost of insurance equals its actuarial value, with no additional load factor, and workers choosing jobs offering injury probability p can purchase insurance at price $p/(1 - p)$ per dollar coverage. Both workers and insurance companies know the true probabilities and there is no moral hazard. Let I denote the amount of insurance purchased. Expected utility is given by

$$E = (1 - p)U[W(p) - \frac{p}{1 - p} I] + pU[(1 - k)W(p) + I] \qquad (1)$$

where $W - [p/(1 - p)]I$ is net income if an accident does not occur, and $W(1 - k) + I$ is income if it does. The worker chooses p and I to maximize E.

Consider optimal amounts of insurance coverage first, conditional on an arbitrary value of p. Differentiate E with respect to I, set the result equal to zero and simplify to obtain

$$U'(W - \frac{p}{1 - p} I) = U'[W(1 - k) + I] \qquad (2)$$

or equalization of marginal utility in both states of the world. In that losses are converted into monetary equivalents and U is strictly increasing in its argument, condition (2) can be realized only if incomes in both states of the world are equated. That is, (2) implies $I = (1 - p)$ kW. Substituting this result into equation 1 and simplifying gives

$$E = U[(I - pk)W(p)] \qquad (3)$$

The problem has been converted to optimal choice of p, conditional on prior optimization of insurance coverage.

Define an *acceptance wage* θ as the payment necessary to make the worker indifferent to jobs offering alternative risks, again conditioned on purchasing optimal insurance coverage for each risk. The acceptance wage is defined for a constant expected utility index E, and with recourse to (3) implicitly is defined by

$$E = U[\theta(p, E; k)(1 - pk)] \tag{4}$$

Invert equation (4)

$$\theta(p, E; k) = U^{-1}(E)/(1 - pk) \equiv f(E)/(1 - pk) \tag{5}$$

Equation 5 defines a family of indifference curves in the earnings/risk (θ, p) plane such that the compensated (utility held constant) acceptance wage is increasing in risk at an increasing rate: The marginal rate of substitution between job risk and money is positive and increasing. Differentiating the log of (5) with respect to p shows that the relative marginal acceptance wage, $\dfrac{1}{\theta}\dfrac{\partial\theta}{\partial p} = k/(1 - pk)$, depends only on risk, and k is independent of E. In other words, relative marginal acceptance wages are the same for all workers, independently of workers' degrees of risk aversion. This is due to the presence of perfect insurance so that full coverage is rational.

The fact that the function $\dfrac{1}{\theta}\dfrac{\partial\theta}{\partial p}$ is equal for all workers yields some arbitrage restrictions on observable wage/risk relationships in the market. Arbitrage mandates the restriction $W'(p)/W(p) = \dfrac{1}{\theta(p,E)} \cdot \dfrac{\partial\theta(p,E)}{\partial p}$ for every possible value of p. For proof, assume to the contrary that at some value of p, say p^*, $W'(p^*)/W(p^*) > \dfrac{1}{\theta(p^*,E)} \cdot \dfrac{\partial\theta(p^*,E)}{\partial p}$. Then, everybody currently working at a job with risk p^* could improve themselves by applying for jobs involving slightly higher risk. Additional wages on higher-risk jobs exceed relative marginal valuations of them and expected utility must rise from taking slightly larger risks. Jobs such as p^* are unfilled, and relative wages have to change in an obvious way to induce people to apply for them. Exactly the opposite logic applies when the inequality goes in the other direction. In that case, it is also not rational for anyone to apply for any job offering risk p^*. Jobs offering smaller risks yield larger expected utility and $W'(p^*)/W(p^*)$ must increase if p^* type jobs are to be filled. Therefore $W'(p)/W(p) = \dfrac{1}{\theta} \dfrac{\partial \theta}{\partial p}$ must hold for all p, and the observed market wage-risk function must satisfy $W'(p)/W(p) = k/(1 - pk)$. This market equilibrium condition can be integrated to yield

$$W(p) = C/(1 - pk) \tag{6}$$

In (6), C is a constant of integration, determined by the side condition that total quantity of labor supplied to the market equals total demand for it. Only if market observations lie along an approximately semi-log function such as (6) can the labor market be in equilibrium in this simple example.

The problem considered above reveals the basic essentials of Smith's theory. In this case, wage differentials are exactly equalizing everywhere, at both the margin and on the average, and wage differences only reflect actuarial differences in risk between jobs. To see this, note that expected earning is $(1 - p)W(p) + p(1 - k)W(p)$, which, from (6), equals C: Expected earning is constant across all jobs, independent of job risk and the distribution of risk aversion in the labor force. Following the general "free lunch theorem," such a distinct and strong result comes from strong assumptions. Perfect insurance implies all risk-averse workers act as expected income maximizers and induces them to act alike, independently of their degree of risk aversion. The result would not have been true had we allowed for pain and suffering, imperfect insurance (nonzero load and hence incomplete coverage), or interpersonal differences in physical capacities to cope with job risk.[6] Equalizing wage-risk relationships depends on the demand for workers, as well as on the supply of them, in those cases, as will be spelled out below.

It is important to note differences between compensation and earnings before turning to a more general formulation of the problem. The

---

[6] Suppose realized risks in a given situation differ from person to person for exogenous reasons and that personal characteristics (e.g., sense of balance) involve no externalities. Also, in line with footnote 5, assume equalizing difference functions for job risk $W(p)$ and personal characteristics are independent of each other in the relevant sense. Differences in real risks can be handled in the example by specifying a distribution on k across workers. Then the arbitrage-everywhere argument breaks down because all workers cannot be indifferent to all jobs. Even in the presence of perfect insurance, relative marginal acceptance wages depend on k and are not equal for everyone. Obviously those individuals for whom k is small apply for the riskier jobs.

two are related by an identity: Compensation $\equiv$ earnings + fringe benefits. Fringe benefits were ignored above. Had they been included (employers "pay" insurance premiums), no systematic relationship between earnings and risk would have occurred. However, the relationship between compensation and risk would have been described by (6). Insurance fringes act like a tax that is completely "backward shifted" and nominal earnings fall by the amount of the benefit. Workers always pay these costs, whether or not they nominally do so. Therefore, since earnings before fringe benefits and insurance premiums stand in a fixed relationship to each other (the insurance premium is pkW), differences in compensation serve to equalize the market, not differences in net earnings. For example, workmen's compensation is a force making for uniformity in net wage rates across jobs with alternative risks, so long as benefit schedules reflect true monetary (and psychic) losses and the amount of insurance is no more than workers would buy voluntarily. Henceforth the words wage and compensation will be used interchangeably.

SUPPLY PRICE OF JOB RISK

Now the assumptions of perfect insurance and the absence of pain and suffering are relaxed. Only two states of the world were distinguished in the example above, accident-no accident. Taking account of alternative levels of injury severity requires introducing N possible states. For example, N might be 4, a value of 1 indexing no accident, 2 indexing "minor" accidents, 3 "nonminor," nondeath accidents, and 4 indexing death. Demarcation between states 2 and 3 or any other boundaries along the injury-severity continuum are achieved through the use of dummy variable splits on an index such as work days lost. For instance days lost greater than zero but less than some number D_1 correspond to state 2, days lost between D_1 and D_2 correspond to state 3, and so forth. Finer distinctions (and more states) can be made by combining work-days-lost severity indexes and the physical nature of accidents, such as loss of limb, impairment of hearing, and so on.

Conceptually, pain and suffering are represented by different-state utility functions depending on the states themselves. For example, suppose losses for states n through $n + m$ can be converted into monetary equivalents. Then the n through $n + m$ state utility functions are of the same functional form as utility associated with the no-accident state. All other states have utility functions specific to themselves measured in such a way as to be conformable with expected utility axioms.[7]

In general, each possible job is described by an $N - 1$ component vector of probabilities $(p_2, p_3, \ldots, p_N)$ with p_i indexing the probability of state i. [The no-accident probability is ignored because it can be inferred from all the other probabilities: $p_1 = 1 - \prod_{j=2}^{N} p_j$, assuming independence.] In other words, each job is perfectly described by a bundle of different accident probabilities, with the package varying from one job to another. Jobs are associated with a multivariate function, $W(p_2, \ldots, p_N)$, giving the market wage for alternative bundles of job risk. Workers maximize expected utility over all states subject to the equalizing difference function $W(p_2, \ldots, p_N)$. Each worker chooses an optimal p-vector and applies for the job offering those probabilities.

We shall not attempt to present a completely general treatment of the problem. Discussion is specialized to two states for purposes of illustration. State 1 represents no-accident; and state 2, accidents resulting in death. Workers either survive their jobs or they don't, certainly two mutually exclusive events! Each job is associated with a number p, now indexing the probability of death. The market reveals an equalizing difference function $W(p)$ giving compensation as a function of death risk. $W'(p)$ is positive, and other restrictions will be put on it later. Insurance is available at market price $\lambda p/(1 - p)$ per dollar of coverage, with $\lambda \geq 1$. The load factor is $(\lambda - 1)$.

Assume a concave utility function $U(Y)$ for the life state as before, choosing the origin so that $U(0) = 0$. The utility (bequest) function for the death state is $\psi(Y)$, also concave with $\psi(0) = 0$. For obvious reasons, U and ψ are restricted to obey the inequality $U(Y) > \psi(Y)$ for all common values of Y. The worker chooses p and I to maximize

$$E = (1 - p)U[W(p) + y - \frac{\lambda p}{1 - p} I] + p\psi(y + I) \qquad (7)$$

where y is nonlabor income. $W + y - [\lambda p/(1 - p)]I$ is income if the worker lives and $y + I$ is beneficiaries' income if he dies. Assuming E is strictly concave in p and I, necessary and sufficient conditions for a maximum are

$$E_I = -p(\lambda U' - \psi') = 0$$

$$E_p = -U + \psi + (1 - p)U'[W' - \lambda I/(1 - p)^2] = 0 \qquad (8)$$

[7] See Hirshleifer (1965).

Equations (8) jointly determine optimal values of p and I. Notice that it is no longer true that marginal utilities in both states are equal. Even if they were (i.e., if $\lambda = 1$), equality would not imply equal incomes in both states, because U' and ψ' are not identical functions. Hence the arbitrage argument used in the example above no longer applies because people with alternative utility functions behave differently.

Conditions (8) are not very informative in and of themselves unless functional forms are specified for U and ψ. In the absence of that, a very general picture of equilibrium is obtained by going the route described in the section above. Again define an acceptance wage θ as the amount of money the worker would willingly accept to work on jobs of different risks at a constant utility index, conditioned on optimal purchase of insurance. Then $\theta(p, E; y, \lambda)$ is defined implicitly by solving for θ and I in terms of E, y and λ from

$$E = (1 - p)U[\theta + y - \frac{\lambda p}{1 - p} I] + p\psi(y + 1)$$

$$0 = \lambda U'\{\theta + y - [\lambda p/(1 - p)]I\} - \psi'(y + I) \qquad (9)$$

The following properties of θ can be derived from the implicit function theorem [8]

$$\theta_p > 0, \theta_{pp} > 0 \qquad (i)$$

The marginal acceptance wage is positive and increasing in risk. θ_p is the expected-utility compensated supply price to risky jobs and is rising because of risk aversion, imperfect insurance, and pain and suffering (U is not the same as ψ). Property (i) is crucial to what follows.[9]

$$\theta_E > 0, \theta_y < -1 \qquad (ii)$$

The acceptance wage is increasing in expected utility and decreasing in nonlabor income at any given risk. Moreover, an additional dollar of nonlabor income lowers the acceptance wage (utility held constant) by more than a dollar. The reason for the latter is that additional dollars of nonlabor income increase utility in both states, thereby reducing

[8] These results can easily be checked by the reader. Take care always to treat θ *and* I as dependent variables and p, E, y, and λ as independent variables in the differentiation.

[9] It is conceivable that no insurance is purchased if strict concavity in (7) is not assumed. Suppose marginal utility of bequests rapidly approach zero after some dollar value. A husband might want to leave his wife with at least $100,000 if he dies, but bequest dollars in excess of 100,000 do not yield much additional utility. It may be rational for him not to purchase insurance if his nonlabor wealth is in the neighborhood of $100,000. Even in such cases, the fundamental convexity property of indifference curves in Figure 1 still applies.

optimal amounts of insurance and payments of insurance premiums in the life state.

$$\theta_{pE} > 0, \, \theta_{py} < 0, \, \theta_{p\lambda} > 0 \tag{iii}$$

The marginal acceptance wage increases at higher levels of welfare: the better off a person is, the larger the monetary inducement necessary to coax him into a higher risk job. On the other hand, marginal acceptance wages decrease as nonlabor income rises (utility "held constant") for reasons stated under property (ii). Finally, increasing λ renders risk bearing more expensive and increases its reservation price.

Risk/earnings indifference curves $\theta(p; E, y)$ for a worker with some fixed amount of nonlabor income are shown in Figure 1. Labels E_1, $E_2, \ldots$, are in ascending order of expected utility, from property (ii). Convexity follows from property (i). Notice that the slopes of the indifference curves rise along a vertical line, a result of property (iii).

The heavy line labeled $W(p)$ represents risk/earnings opportunities or the market equalizing-difference wage function.[10] As usual, optimum choice of p (represented by p^* in the figure) occurs where the budget line and an adjoining indifference curve have a common tangent. Clearly, the curvature of $\theta(p)$ and $W(p)$ must stand in a proper relationship to each other if the solution is to be unique and interior, as is true in the assumption of strict concavity of (7).

Three empirically meaningful propositions emerge from properties (i)–(iii) and the equilibrium condition in Figure 1.[11]

Proposition 1: Job safety is a normal good.

This statement needs careful interpretation and qualification. Consider the following parameterization of the budget: $W(p) = A + BV(p)$, where $V(p)$ is an increasing function of p and A and B are parameters. The statement holds true for changes in A. For example, let A increase. The budget line rises parallel to its initial position and expected utility also rises. But property (iiia) implies marginal acceptance wages rise too. Hence risk falls and the worker chooses a safer job.[12] Changes in A are analogous to pure income effects in demand

[10] As shown by example in the preceding section, there is no reason for $W(p)$ to be linear in p. The budget constraint can be distinctly nonlinear.

[11] These statements are easy to prove analytically. Differentiate equations (8) and exploit second-order conditions for a maximum, as usual.

[12] Some casual evidence is relevant here. Secularly increasing job safety in the U.S. has been accompanied by a trend of rising real wages. No doubt improvements in safety technology have decreased the price of safety as well.

FIGURE 1

Worker Equilibrium

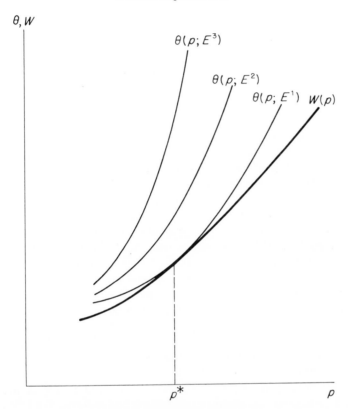

theory. The statement does not hold for changes in B. An increase in B results in a negative income effect (on risk), but a positive substitution effect (on risk) in that increasing marginal earnings on riskier jobs makes risk bearing more attractive. The net outcome is unpredictable without further specification.

Proposition II: Job safety is positively related to the price of insurance.

This is an immediate consequence of (iiic). Decreasing the insurance load factor makes risk bearing cheaper, everywhere decreasing marginal rates of substitution between money and risk. More risk necessarily is purchased.

Proposition III: Job safety is not necessarily normal with respect to property income.

This nonintuitive result can be motivated in part as follows: Increasing nonlabor income provides a kind of self-insurance against the death state, since nonlabor income (willed to one's heirs) is not at risk in the labor market. This reduces needs for market insurance and makes risk bearing less expensive, a kind of substitution effect. However, increasing y also increases expected utility and has the effect of increasing the marginal acceptance wage for any incremental risk, a kind of income effect. The two effects work against each other. Mechanically, the result comes from properties (iib), (iiia) and (iiib). An additional dollar of nonlabor income shifts the entire indifference map downward by more than a dollar (iib) and also reduces marginal rates of substitution for given expected utility measures (iiib). However, marginal valuation of risk is increasing in expected utility (iiia) and marginal rates of substitution still increase along any vertical line in Figure 1. The first effect is a force making for increased risk, while the second works in the opposite direction. Curiously, it can be shown analytically that risk is necessarily inferior in nonlabor income when the insurance load is zero (i.e., $\lambda = 1$). Evidently, when the price of insurance exceeds its actuarial value there is a possibility for the kind of substitution effect described above to dominate the real income effect, tantamount to a type of risk preference.

EQUALIZING DIFFERENCES AND SUPPLY PRICES

The discussion above shows that worker choice is characterized by two equilibrium conditions: $W(p) = \theta(p, E)$ and $W'(p) = \partial\theta/\partial p$, two equations in two unknowns, p and E. Workers differ in their attitudes toward risk, bequest motives, and nonlabor income. Consequently there is a distribution of acceptance wage functions in the market. Those with less risk aversion have smaller marginal acceptance wages (i.e., smaller values of $\partial\theta/\partial p$) and lower reservation prices to risky jobs. The opposite might be true of people with many dependents or with high degrees of risk aversion in the accident state. Whatever the source of interpersonal differences, workers with lower marginal acceptance wages work on riskier jobs.

A picture of market equilibrium on the supply side of the market is shown in Figure 2. Ignore the curves labeled ϕ^j for the moment. $W(p)$ is the equalizing difference function as in Figure 1. Two workers are shown in Figure 2, one with acceptance wage θ^1 and the other with θ^2. $(\partial\theta^1/\partial p) > (\partial\theta^2/\partial p)$ and worker 2 is employed on a riskier job, since

FIGURE 2

Market Equilibrium

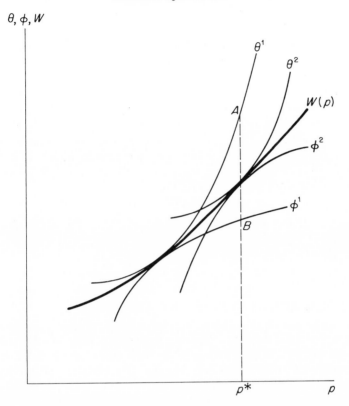

safety is not as valuable to him. The picture may be generalized. Add more workers and fill in all points on the $W(p)$ line. It is apparent that $W(p)$ is the lower envelope of a family of acceptance wage functions depending on the joint distribution of y, U and ψ across workers. $W(p)$ is observed, while the functions θ^i are not. However, evaluate the derivative of the equalizing wage difference function at some value of p, say p^*. Then, from the equilibrium conditions, $W'(p^*) = \partial \theta^i(p^*, E^*)/\partial p$ for workers finding p^* optimal, and $W'(p^*)$ identifies the marginal acceptance wage for such workers. Therefore, $W'(p^*)$ identifies $\partial \theta^i/\partial p$. $W'(p^*)$ estimates how much money is necessary to induce a person into accepting a small incremental risk. Alternatively, it estimates how much the person will pay to reduce risk by a small amount, exactly the number we seek.

The empirical work reported below uses data from very risky jobs, on the average perhaps as much as five times more risky than most jobs in the U.S. economy. It must be true that individuals working on such jobs have lower reservation supply prices and consequently smaller demand prices for safety than the average worker. The point is illustrated in Figure 2. Evaluating W' at p^* provides the correct estimate for person 2, but is an underestimate for person 1. The price the latter is willing to pay for safety at p^* is given by the slope of his acceptance wage function evaluated at p^*, the slope of θ^1 at the point marked A in Figure 2. It follows from the fact that compensated supply functions to risky jobs are rising (i.e., acceptance wage functions are convex) that $\partial \theta^1(p^*, E^*)/\partial p$ exceeds $W'(p^*)$. Most people in the labor force do not work on risky jobs. Therefore, use of data on very risky jobs understates average demand prices for safety at the observed risk levels in our sample. This justifies our initial assertion that the estimates below are conservative and probably biased downward when extrapolated to the population as a whole.

DEMAND PRICE FOR JOB RISK

It was demonstrated above that $W'(p)$ identifies supply price of risk at the relevant margin. That conclusion was reached independently of demand considerations. We now consider a very simple model of demand prices and firm decisions in order to complete the model. It will hardly be shocking to discover that $W'(p)$ also identifies demand price for risk at some margin.

Accidents are an unpleasant, though in part avoidable, by-product of production. This fact of life (or of death!) can be represented analytically by a joint production function $F(x, p, L) = 0$ for some firm, where x is marketable output, p is the accident rate, and L is labor input. Inputs other than labor are ignored. p can be a vector of state accident probabilities as mentioned above. However, to simplify, collapse it into a univariate index denoting the probability of death. Invert F and assume the following properties for $x = g(p, L)$: (i) $g_L > 0$ and $g_{LL} < 0$. Labor has positive and diminishing marginal product. (ii) $g_{Lp} < 0$. Safety increases the marginal product of labor. (iii) $g_p > 0$ for $0 \leqslant p < \bar{p}$, $g_p \gtrless 0$ for $p \geqslant \bar{p}$, where $\bar{p}$ is some "large," technically determined constant, and $g_{pp} < 0$. The assumptions on

g_p are best explained by noting that they imply that the transformation locus between output (x) and safety ($1 - p$) is negatively inclined, except possibly at very low levels of safety. Accidents are "productive," at least up to a certain point, and can be avoided only by changing the organization of production within the firm away from marketable output and toward accident prevention. The assumption on g_{pp} means the transformation function is concave.

The production function $g(p, L)$ has been written so that safety is, in effect, produced internally by the firm. Safety devices (such as guard rails and hard hats) can also be purchased and installed externally. Let $G(1 - p)$ represent the cost of externally provided safety (converted to an annual flow), with G' and $G'' > 0$. The latter means installation activities are subject to increasing costs, though that is not strictly necessary to what follows.

The firm maximizes profit Π with respect to L and p

$$\Pi = g(p, L) - W(p)L - G(1 - p) \tag{10}$$

where the price of x has been normalized at unity. Again $W(p)$ represents the competitive wage that must be paid for alternative levels of risk. Necessary conditions for a maximum are

$$g_p + G' = W'(p)L$$

$$g_L = W(p) \tag{11}$$

Labor is hired up to the point where its wage and marginal product are equal. Marginal costs of risk are the additional market wage payments necessary to attract workers to riskier jobs. Marginal benefits come in the form of additional market output and cost savings from installing fewer safety devices. Second-order conditions require certain curvature restrictions on $W(p)$ as will be shown.

Symmetrically with the treatment above, define an *offer* function ϕ as the amount the firm willingly pays the optimal number of workers at alternative levels of risk and constant profit. With recourse to the definition of profit and the marginal condition on labor, $\phi(p, \Pi)$ is defined implicitly by

$$\phi = [g(p, L) - G(1 - p) - \Pi]/L$$

$$\phi = g_L(p, L) \tag{12}$$

Clearly $\partial\phi/\partial p$ is the compensated demand price for risk. Differentiating (12) [again, always treat ϕ and L as dependent variables, and Π and p as independent variables]

$$\partial\phi/\partial\Pi = -1/L$$

$$\partial\phi/\partial p = (g_p + G')/L$$

$$\frac{\partial^2\phi}{\partial p^2} = [(g_{pp} - G'')g_{LL} - (\phi_p - g_{Lp})^2]/Lg_{LL} \lessgtr 0$$

The marginal demand price for risk is positive. However, even the common assumption of concavity of the production function does not guarantee that the compensated demand schedule is negatively inclined: $\partial^2\phi/\partial p^2$ can be positive.

The offer function $\phi(p, \Pi)$ defines a family of indifference curves in money and risk, one member of which is shown in Figure 2. ϕ^1 refers to one firm and ϕ^2 refers to another firm, possibly in a different industry and in any case, with a different technology than firm 1. The diagram assumes $\partial^2\phi/\partial p^2 < 0$, which is not necessarily true. Equilibrium of each firm is characterized by tangency between the market availabilities function $W(p)$ and the lowest possible constant-profit indifference curve (profit increases as ϕ decreases at any level of risk, since $\partial\phi/\partial\Pi < 0$). W'' must exceed $\partial^2\phi/\partial p^2$ at the point of tangency for an interior maximum.

Similarly to the case of worker choice, $W'(p) = \partial\phi/\partial p$ at equilibrium, and $W(p)$ represents an upper envelope of the distribution of offer functions in the market. The family of offer functions depends on the nature of production functions in various firms and industries and on corresponding distributions of industrial safety technology. In any event $W'(p^*)$ also identifies $\partial\phi^i(p^*, \Pi^*)/\partial p$, where firm i is one that has chosen p^* optimally. Using the same logic as above, $W'(p^*)$ overestimates the average supply price of safety (again, at p^*) if p^* is a very risky job. This is easily seen in Figure 2, since the slope of $\partial\phi^1/\partial p$ at point B necessarily is smaller than the slope of $\partial\phi^2/\partial p$ evaluated at the same level of job risk.[13]

MARKET EQUILIBRIUM: SUMMARY

It will be useful to summarize results of the model so far.

(a) The observable wage-risk relation represents a double envelope

---

[13] Suppose L is exogenous. Then, the offer function is defined by the first equation in (12), and it is easy to show that increased values of L reduce demand price for risk ($\phi_{pL} < 0$), providing incentives to offer safer jobs. Increasing incentives toward job safety vary directly with establishment size because of larger cost savings from lower wage rates. It is well known that accident rates decline with establishment size, at least after some minimum size. Accident rates also tend to be low in very small establishments as well, so this cannot be the entire story.

function: It is the lower boundary of a set of acceptance wage functions and the upper boundary of a set of offer wage functions. Marriages between jobs and applicants at each level of risk are represented by common tangents of appropriate acceptance wage and offer wage functions.

(b) The envelope property in (a) implies that the derivatives of observed risk-wage differentials (evaluated at each level of risk) identify *marginal* supply and demand prices of workers and firms choosing those particular job risks.

(c) Supply price of risk (equivalently, demand price for safety) identified in (b) from very risky jobs underestimates the average supply price in the labor force for those risks, since people choosing risky jobs have a comparative advantage at job risk bearing. Similarly, demand price for risk (supply price of safety) identified from very risky jobs overestimates the average demand price for most firms in the economy, since firms offering risky jobs have a comparative disadvantage at producing safety.

(d) The numbers identified in (b) represent single points on compensated supply and demand functions, not the functions themselves. Use of such numbers for evaluation overestimates consumer surplus of finite increases in safety because workers' compensated demand schedules for safety are negatively inclined.

EQUILIBRIUM AND WORKER CHARACTERISTICS

A very simple demand model has been specified above, and it may be too simple. Recall the production function has been written $x = g(p, L)$, where L is labor and p is risk. But what is labor? [14] Our data contain indicators of personal productivity such as education and work experience. Suppose there are m such indicators, denoted by a vector $c = (c_1, \ldots, c_m)$. Of course, sample wages vary with worker characteristics as well as with job risk. Let $W(p, c)$ represent the market wage-risk–characteristics equalizing difference function. Writing the production function for a firm as we did implies that firms act as if there exists a single index of labor input, $L = f(c_1, \ldots, c_m)$ defined independently of job risk. If so, the production function must be separable in c and p. This is also a sufficient condition for separability of $W(p, c)$ as well. Suppose $W(p, c)$ is additive in p and c: $W(p, c) = V(p) + T(c)$. Hence, firms care only about total amounts of "skill" they employ (i.e., L) independently of how skills come packaged in

[14] The reader may be thinking, "What is risk?" The two questions are very much related. See below.

people and also independently of job risks to which their employees are subjected. In effect, it means that packages of worker characteristics can be untied. For example, firms might be indifferent between a worker with 8 years of schooling and 10 years of experience and another with 12 years of school and 3 years of experience, or between workers with other combinations of these characteristics.

The real issue under discussion here involves how many interactions to allow in the risk and characteristics wage-explaining regression. At one extreme is the possibility for a universal implicit market for risk, independent of worker personal productivities (no interactions). At the other extreme are separate implicit markets for all possible combinations of personal characteristics (complete interactions). The former case corresponds to the firm choice model sketched above. Yet there is a distinct possibility that risk affects productivity in a nonhomogeneous manner with respect to various productivity indicators. Then some interactions are required. In general, the market reveals implicit prices for both risk and worker characteristics. All prices are determined simultaneously and cannot be separated,[15] and the firm choice model sketched above must refer to a single type of worker (c held constant).

If there is no interaction in production between worker characteristics and safety, only one risk premium for each value of risk appears in the market. Furthermore, the risk-wage function is independent of any further interaction between worker characteristics and attitudes toward risk. Differences in worker characteristics (age, marital status, and so on) that result in different acceptance wage functions simply help identify which workers accept riskier jobs. On the other hand, if there are interactions in production, differential risk premiums according to personal characteristics generally appear, so long as the preferred characteristics are in sufficiently scarce supply. If these characteristics are not in short supply, only those workers with preferred attributes work on risky jobs and no differential risk premium need arise in the market. Finally, if differential risk premiums exist, $W(p)$ in Figures 1 and 2 becomes a family of curves $W(p, c)$, one for each value of c, as was noted above (see footnote 5).

[15] In part, firm decisions can be handled formally as follows. The production function is $x = h(p, c_1, \ldots, c_m) = h(p, c)$. Profit is $h(p, c) - W(p, c)$, maximized over p and c. The firm organizes production taking account of factor supplies (i.e., $W(p, c)$), designing jobs and their risks and determining a set of worker-characteristics requirements. Workers not meeting requirements are not hired by the firm. Now define a joint offer-requirements function $\zeta(p, c, \Pi)$, indicating offer prices for alternative risk-characteristics requirements at constant profit, and compare the resulting indifference surfaces in (money, p, c) space with market availabilities $W(p, c)$.

The issue is rather thorny, but an example will clarify it. Consider the regression model

$$W = a_0 + a_1p + a_2(pz) + \text{random error} \qquad (13)$$

where W is observed wages, p is risk, z is worker age, and the a's are regression coefficients. The pure effect of age, higher order terms in p, and all other explanatory variables are impounded in the constant term a_0 for purposes of this discussion.

Age presumably affects worker's acceptance wages. Young workers risk entire lifetimes of future consumption in taking high risk jobs and have far more to lose than their older counterparts. Supply price to risky jobs should fall with age on that account. Further, a typical individual may become more or less risk averse over his lifetime, inducing shifts in acceptance wage functions over the life cycle. Job risk should be systematically related to age for both reasons. However, variations of this variety are completely captured by movements along the observed risk-wage function (taking account of possible effects of age on a_0) and there is no role here for extra marginal effects of age on risk premiums per se. Look at Figure 1. The changes under consideration are represented by systematic variations in money-risk preferences, resulting in moving points of tangency between a life-cycle shifting acceptance wage function and a fixed risk, market opportunities function. Movements along $W(p)$ should not be confused with shifts in it, and all such changes are already counted in the pure risk coefficient a_1.

Age can affect market risk premiums only insofar as it reflects unmeasured characteristics whose productivities are affected by differential risk. Exposure to risky situations makes some people far less effective agents of production than others. They not only accomplish less work of their own, but also impose extra costs on others. Both effects have to reduce wage rates of these persons if they are observed working at risky jobs. Such wage differentials serve as compensation for additional costs firms incur in employing them. For example, "nerves of steel" is a scarce factor, but steely nerves capture rents only in risky situations. Good balance is valuable to iron workers on building sites but not to desk clerks, and so forth. In the present case, young workers on the average have speedier reflexes than older ones and have faster reactions to potential accidents. But older workers have had more exposure and experience with job risk, and experience and quick reflexes probably are substitutes. Hence the effect of age on productivity in the presence of risk is uncertain, though we might expect the reflex effect to dominate, by and large, for workers past some age that varies across occupations.

Whatever the interactions between risk differentials and personal characteristics, the analysis underlying Figure 1 still applies. The marginal effect of risk on wages evaluated at the person's exogenously determined characteristics estimates supply price for risk or demand price for safety. It also estimates firms' supply price of safety to workers with those characteristics. It is certainly possible, however, that observed risk differentials vary with worker attributes.

THE DATA

Empirical implementation of the model requires information on earnings of individuals, job risks they face, and their personal and job-related characteristics. It involves augmenting standard wage equations with job-risk measures. Many cross-sectional sources of earnings data are available and we have chosen one of them, the 1967 Survey of Economic Opportunity (SEO). The SEO survey was designed to heavily represent low-income populations and our sample is restricted to an extract of the data, consisting of a random sample of 9,488 representative households in the U.S. population. Of these observations, the sample was further reduced to adult male heads of households. The SEO data provides information on personal and industrial characteristics and labor force activities of individuals. It also lists individuals' industry of employment and occupation.

The standard source of data on industrial hazards is published by the Bureau of Labor Statistics (BLS) in conjunction with compliance and experience surveys under the Workmen's Compensation Act. These data give accidental death and injury rates for 4-digit SIC industry codes on an annual basis. Unfortunately, the BLS death and injury data cannot be adequately matched to individuals and is unsuitable for the purposes of this study. For example, it is possible to assign the BLS average death and injury indexes (by industry) to individuals in the SEO tape because the individual's industrial attachment is known. However, using the death and injury statistics in that manner implies introducing a huge component of measurement error for individuals, because job risks in each industry are not uniform across occupations. Hence, any estimates of the risk premium obtained in this way will probably be biased.

Luckily, another data source was discovered which does not suffer from the aggregation problems inherent in published BLS sources. The data used here come from the 1967 Occupation Study of the

Society of Actuaries. The purpose of the 1967 study was to measure *extra* risks associated with some very hazardous occupations and the study was based on a sample of insurance company records covering 3,252,262 policy years of workers' experience over the period 1955–1964. The data were tabulated on a combined industry and occupational basis, and can be matched directly to individuals on the SEO sample, using Census categories contained in the latter. The matching procedure yielded 37 occupations on about 900 individuals. The occupations and their sample actuarial risks are listed in Table 1. Of course, it would be quite rash to assert that the actuarial data overcome all matching difficulties, because Table 1 shows that the actuarial classifications are rather broad. However, they are far more narrowly defined than the BLS data. We are extremely confident that the degree of measurement error in attributing risks to SEO individuals using the actuarial data is perhaps as much as an order of magnitude smaller than would be true had we matched with BLS risk data — especially for individuals working on very risky jobs, such as most of those in Table 1. In other words, the actuarial study simply provides the best data that are available for estimating risk premiums in the labor market.[16]

The actuarial data have one other very good feature. An expected number of deaths was estimated in each occupation, based on the age distribution of persons in the sample records and standard life tables. Expected deaths were then subtracted from actual deaths and the result normalized to yield an *extra* deaths per thousand policy years statistic (those numbers are multiplied by 100 in Table 1). Hence the numbers in Table 1 are net of normal age-specific death experience and measure extra death risk associated with occupations. These statistics reflect genuine occupational hazards that may cumulate with time spent in the profession. To see how risky these jobs are, note that the mean value in Table 1 is approximately 100. In probability terms, this amounts to an extra 1 in 1,000 probability of death. The probability of death from the 1967 life table for white males 35 years of age was 2 in 1,000. Thus, though the probabilities are small in absolute terms, they are very large relative to the risks most people incur in the ordinary course of their lives.

[16] After this study was completed, we discovered a paper by R. Smith (1973), who used the BLS hazard data. At an earlier stage of our research, and before discovering the Actuaries Study, we too experimented with BLS data. Our results were very similar to Smith's. However, in view of the measurement error, we believe that Smith's very strong conclusions about the workings of the labor market are totally unwarranted and that his estimates must surely be seriously biased.

TABLE 1

Sample Occupations and Risks

Occupation	Risk [a]	Occupation	Risk [a]
Fishermen	19	Truck drivers	98
Foresters	22	Bartenders	176
Teamsters	114	Cooks	132
Lumbermen	256	Firemen	44
Mine operatives	176	Guards, watchmen, and	
Metal filers, grinders and		doorkeepers	267
polishers	41	Marshals, constables,	
Boilermakers	230	sheriffs and bailiffs	181
Cranemen and derrickmen	147	Police and detectives	78
Factory painters	81	Longshoremen and steve-	
Other painters	46	dores	101
Electricians	93	Actors	73
Railroad brakemen	88	Railroad conductors	203
Structural iron workers	204	Ships' officers	156
Locomotive firemen	186	Hucksters and peddlers	76
Power plant operatives	6	Linemen and servicemen	2
Sailors and deckhands	163	Road machine operators	103
Sawyers	133	Elevator operators	188
Switchmen	152	Laundry operatives	126
Taxicab drivers	182	Waiters	134

SOURCE: Society of Actuaries.
[a] Units of measure are extra deaths per 100,000 policy years. To convert to the probability of an extra death per year on each job multiply by 0.00001.

A less attractive feature of the actuarial risk data is that they only include death rates. Separate indexes for death and nondeath accidents would be preferable, but nondeath accident statistics comparable to those in Table 1 are not available. We must rest content with the knowledge that death rates and injury rates in the BLS industry data are highly correlated, and there is no reason for that not to be true in our data as well.

Several earnings measures are available from SEO data. We have experimented with all of them and settled on the weekly wage, because it probably is measured most accurately. We would prefer to use a measure of total compensation, but the value of fringe benefits are not available on the SEO tape or any other data set on individuals known to us. This omission must reduce the observed risk differential, again pointing toward conservative estimates. The extent of bias depends on the size of the load factor and the importance of pain and suffering, as well as on the precise differences between life (U) and bequest (ψ) utility functions. In any event, the average amount of life insurance provided in fringe benefits is not very large, and this source of bias must be rather small.

ESTIMATION

Our goal is to estimate the equalizing difference function $W(p, c)$. Four types of independent variables are used to control for factors determining wage rates other than job risk. These are the content of the c variables. The first set controls for regional and urban-nonurban wage differentials. The second set measures individuals' personal characteristics, including age, education, family size (or marital status), and race. The square of age and education can be included to allow for nonlinearities. The third set controls for other characteristics of the job, including unionization, dummy variables for manufacturing and service industries, and three major occupational dummy variables, one for operatives (OC1), another for service workers (OC2), and a third for laborers (OC3). Socioeconomic status (SES) was used at one stage instead of the occupational dummies as a crude measure of other nonpecuniary aspects of work. SES is an index number based on occupation, education, and income, and it might capture some other types of equalizing differences, though it was not constructed for that purpose.

Means and standard deviations of all variables are shown in Table 2. Note that the sample includes a much higher proportion of union members than obtains in the labor force generally. Sample mean earnings on an annual basis is about \$6,600 ($= 132 \times 50$), which is a bit less than average earnings among male manufacturing workers during this period.

Regression planes have been fitted by least squares, using arithmetic values of earnings as the dependent variable; and alternatively, using the log of earnings as the dependent variable. The arithmetic results are shown in Table 3. Results using the log of earnings are reported in Table 4 and are very similar to the arithmetic results when evaluated at sample means.

The first two columns in Table 3 give alternative estimates of $W(p, c)$ on the strong assumption of no interactions. All the nonrisk variables are assumed to simply shift the wage-risk relationship, leaving its slope intact. Regression coefficients of almost all characteristics

TABLE 2

Summary Statistics

Variable	Mean	Standard Deviation
Dummy variables [a]		
Urban	.69	.46
Northeast	.28	.45
South	.29	.45
West	.17	.38
Family size exceeds 2	.76	.42
Manufacturing industry	.24	.42
Service industry	.58	.49
Worker is white	.90	.30
Worker is employed full time	.98	.10
Worker belongs to union	.45	.49
Worker is married	.92	.26
Occupation is operative	.27	.44
Occupation is service	.45	.49
Occupation is laborer	.22	.42
Continuous variables		
Age (years)	41.8	11.3
Education (years)	10.11	2.73
Weeks worked in 1966	49.4	5.4
Hours worked last week	44.9	11.6
Risk (probability $\times 10^5$)	109.8	67.6
Weekly wage (week prior to survey)	\$132.65	50.80

[a] Mean is proportion in sample with designated characteristic. The number of observations is 907.

variables have the expected signs found in most other studies, and most are statistically significant. Further discussion is unwarranted here.

The theory requires the wage-risk function to be positively inclined, and that is certainly the case on the appropriate one-tailed test of significance (see equations 1 and 2 in Table 3). [It is interesting to note that the simple correlation between risk and wage (not shown) is negative in these data.] (Risk)^2 was also entered in the regression but was not significant. We are not trying to argue here that $W(p, c)$ is linear in p, since most of the results using log W as dependent variable in Table 4 are at least as good as those in Table 3. The data simply do

TABLE 3

Regression Estimates of $W(p, c)$ — Linear Form

Independent Variable	Equation 1	Equation 2	Equation 3	Equation 4
Risk	.0352	.0520	.100	.0410
	(.0210)	(.0219)	(.108)	(.102)
Risk × age	–	–	−.0019	−.0030
			(.0018)	(.0019)
Risk × married	–	–	.0791	.0701
			(.0380)	(.0412)
Risk × union	–	–	.0808	.0869
			(.040)	(.042)
Risk × white	–	–	−.118	–
			(.072)	
Urban	13.80	15.71	17.0	17.0
	(4.2)	(2.95)	(3.0)	(3.2)
Northeast	−3.71	−4.29	−4.27	−4.92
	(3.65)	(3.67)	(3.63)	(3.83)
South	−8.86	−8.90	−10.5	−8.18
	(3.70)	(3.74)	(3.72)	(3.97)
West	9.13	10.30	9.57	9.50
	(4.13)	(4.18)	(4.12)	(4.37)
Age	3.89	3.81	3.83	3.78
	(0.80)	(0.83)	(0.82)	(0.87)
$(\text{Age})^2$	−.0479	−.0468	−.0442	−.0415
	(.0092)	(.0097)	(.010)	(.011)
Education	3.40	3.27	4.13	4.81
	(0.55)	(2.40)	(2.39)	(2.80)
$(\text{Education})^2$	–	−.021	−.0237	−.042
		(.128)	(.128)	(.148)
Manufacturing industry	–	–	−13.0	−14.7
			(4.3)	(4.62)
Service industry	–	–	−9.45	−10.9
			(3.95)	(4.24)
White	22.92	22.93	37.7	–
	(4.53)	(4.50)	(9.6)	
Family size > 2	–	–	.400	2.10
			(3.57)	(3.89)
Union	25.5	27.16	15.9	15.39
	(3.25)	(3.23)	(5.4)	(5.72)
Full-time	−1.63	−.86	−1.16	.45
	(12.9)	(12.6)	(12.6)	(15.0)
Hours worked	1.50	1.41	1.47	1.44
	(.12)	(.12)	(.123)	(.129)
Occupation 1: operative	−18.7	–	−13.9	−13.5
	(9.2)		(3.24)	(3.51)

TABLE 3 (concluded)

Independent Variable	Equation 1	Equation 2	Equation 3	Equation 4
Occupation 2: service worker	−24.6 (9.5)	–	−18.1 (4.66)	−19.9 (5.05)
Occupation 3: laborer	−25.0 (13.4)	–	–	–
SES 1	–	4.68 (5.17)	–	–
SES 2	–	−17.17 (3.34)	–	–
SES 3	–	−20.69 (5.53)	–	–
R^2	.41	.41	.42	.39
Number of observations	907	907	907	813
Sample	All	All	All	White only

NOTE: The dependent variable is the weekly wage rate. The SES index has been converted to dummy variables. Standard errors are in parentheses.

not provide enough resolution on functional form to make a choice. The implied t statistic on risk is larger when SES is used in place of occupation (equation 2, Table 3), though the point estimates are not very different. First, consider the point estimate 0.0352 obtained from equation 1 of Table 3. The risk variable has been scaled by 10^5 for computational purposes and the estimate 0.0352 implies that jobs with extra risks of 0.001 (a value near the sample' mean) pay $3.52 per week more than jobs with no risk. This amounts to about $176 per year, and the slope of the regression on a yearly basis is $176,000 (= .0352 × 50 × 10^5). Recall that the slope of the wage-risk relation $W'(p)$ estimates the implicit supply and demand price to risky jobs. To interpret the result, think in terms of the following conceptual experiment. Suppose 1,000 men are employed on a job entailing an extra death risk of .001 per year. Then, on average, one man out of the 1,000 will die during the year. The regression indicates that each man would be willing to work for $176 per year less if the extra death probability were reduced from .001 to .0. Hence, they would together pay $176,000 to eliminate that death: the value of the life saved must be $176,000. Furthermore, it must also be true that those firms actually offering jobs involving .001 extra death probabilities must have to spend more than $176,000 to reduce the death probability to zero, be-

TABLE 4

Regression Estimates of $W(p, c)$ — Semilog Linear Form

Independent Variable	Equation 1	Equation 2	Equation 3	Equation 4
Risk	.000206	.000286	.000943	.000108
	(.000167)	(.000174)	(.000856)	(.000782)
Age × risk	–	–	−.000022	−.000032
			(.000014)	(.000015)
Married × risk	–	–	.000969	.000907
			(.000301)	(.000316)
Union × risk	–	–	.000823	.000895
			(.000315)	(.000320)
Race × risk	–	–	−.001312	–
			(.000572)	
Urban	.114	.132	.144	.135
	(.033)	(.024)	(.023)	(.024)
Northeast	−.00357	−.00573	−.00904	−.0131
	(.00289)	(.0291)	(.0288)	(.0293)
South	−.0632	−.0568	−.0729	−.0459
	(.0293)	(.0298)	(.0295)	(.0304)
West	.0857	.0974	.0933	.0855
	(.0327)	(.0332)	(.0327)	(.0334)
Age	.0381	.0385	.0390	.0380
	(.0063)	(.0065)	(.0065)	(.0067)
$(Age)^2$	−.000469	−.000475	−.000450	−.000419
	(.000073)	(.000077)	(.000078)	(.000081)
Manufacturing industry	–	–	−.0790	−.0888
			(.0340)	(.0353)
Service industry	–	–	−.0758	−.0922
			(.0314)	(.0324)
Education	.0332	.0531	.0623	.0613
	(.00436)	(.0190)	(.0189)	(.0215)
$(Education)^2$	–	−.00129	−.00147	−.00133
		(.00101)	(.00102)	(.00113)
White	.228	.228	.389	–
	(.036)	(.036)	(.076)	
Family size > 2	–	−.00204	−.0194	−.00220
		(.0274)	(.0283)	(.0297)
Union	.203	.214	.108	.0997
	(.026)	(.025)	(.043)	(.0437)
Full-time	.275	.303	.284	.340
	(.103)	(.101)	(.100)	(.115)
Hours worked	.0113	.0105	.0109	.0101
	(.00096)	(.00095)	(.00098)	(.00099)
Occupation 1: operative	−.0885	–	−.105	−.101
	(.0728)		(.026)	(.027)

TABLE 4 (concluded)

Independent Variable	Equation 1	Equation 2	Equation 3	Equation 4
Occupation 2: service worker	−.126 (.075)	–	−.110 (.037)	−.124 (.039)
Occupation 3: laborer	−.218 (.106)	–	–	–
SES 1	–	.0152 (.0411)	–	–
SES 2	–	−.128 (.026)	–	–
SES 3	–	−.194 (.042)	–	–
R^2	.47	.46	.48	.43
Number of observations	907	907	907	813

NOTE: The dependent variable is the log of the weekly wage rate. The SES index has been converted to dummy variables. Standard errors are in parentheses.

cause there is a clear-cut gain from risk reduction if costs were less than that amount.

Use of SES dummies instead of occupational dummies increases the point estimate of the risk variable to .0520, with virtually no change in its standard error. Going through the same argument as above implies a value of life of $260,000. Though the t statistic is larger in equation 2 than in equation 1 of Table 3, we are not prepared to accept equation 2 as a necessarily better specification because of some reservations on the meaning of the SES variable. Corresponding estimates in Table 4 evaluated at the sample mean wage range somewhat smaller than those in Table 3. Equation 1 of Table 4 implies a point estimate of $136,000 (= .000206 × 132 × 50 × 10⁵), while equation 2 implies an estimate of $189,000 (= .000286 × 50 × 132 × 10⁵). Further, standard errors of risk coefficients are slightly larger in Table 4. Nevertheless, the estimates lie in a reasonably narrow range of about $200,000 ± $60,000.

Equation 3 in Tables 3 and 4 shows the results of limited interactions between risk and some of the other characteristics. Limitations on sample size forced a simple cross-product specification, rather than separate regressions on corresponding data cells. Risk is crossed with age, union membership, marital status and race in equation 3. As explained earlier, cross-product terms do not reflect differences in individual's utility functions. Instead, they represent differences in the locus of opportunities available to them, due to differential ability to work in risky situations.

A. Age

To reiterate our example above, age is likely to cut two ways on risky jobs. Young workers lack caution and experience, but have superior reflexes and recuperative ability. Our hypothesis was that physical deterioration of skills would eventually dominate and the results seem to be consistent with it. The age-risk cross-product term is negative though not significant, and firms offer older workers smaller risk premiums than younger workers. Evidently younger workers are more productive in risky situations. However, the estimate may also reflect measurement error.[17]

B. Marital Status

There is also some evidence that marital status affects risk premiums. Of course, we expect married workers to have a higher supply price to risky jobs than nonmarried workers, because they have more dependents. Again, this should induce married workers to apply for less risky jobs, other things being equal, and not change the observed risk premium. The fact that marital status increases the risk premium must mean that when married workers do in fact take risky jobs they are more productive at working on them. Exactly how such differential productivity arises is difficult to say, though we conjecture that married workers might on the average be more careful and cautious than the nonmarried.

C. Unionism

Unionism also increases the risk premium. Here the market is restricted, and unions might collect their rents through higher risk premiums rather than by other means. It is possible that lack of free entry into these markets renders the typical union member more risk averse than would be true in free markets, forcing firms to pay higher risk premiums in order to entice unwilling union members to work on

---

[17] There is a possibility that the negative regression coefficient reflects measurement error. Older workers may be heavily weighted in the low risk end of each occupation and our risk measures may overstate the real risks they face. If $W(p)$ is truly increasing, earnings are lower for older workers appearing to work on riskier jobs in our data than they really do. We know age-specific extra-risk data must be available on the work sheets of the actuarial study because the published statistics have been age adjusted in the manner described above. Unfortunately, we were unable to obtain the raw data.

the riskier jobs. Again, we cannot rule out the hypothesis that unionism and its resulting "industrial discipline" make workers more productive on risky jobs.

D. Race

The relationship between race and risk premiums is very complex. The white-risk cross-product term is negative (and not significant at conventional levels), but the results are not easy to interpret. For one thing, we know from other studies that nonwhites tend to be loaded in the low wage end of occupational job classifications. Notice again that the occupations in Table 1 may be too broadly defined for detecting racial differences. If nonwhites tend to be highly represented in the riskier subcategories of each classification, our risk index is measured erroneously for them. This in itself would tend to produce the result found in Tables 3 and 4 and cross-terms would reflect measurement error in the data. The coefficient suggests that nonwhites receive higher risk premiums than whites, but it may simply be the case that they work at even more risky jobs than our data say they do (again, assuming $W'(p) > 0$). Alternative hypotheses are also available. (1) Nonwhites may be better workers in risky situations than whites. For example, we know that a large fraction of structural iron workers are nonwhite, and it is said that these individuals have an unusual sense of balance compared to most people in the population. (2) There may be less discrimination against nonwhites in risky jobs than in less risky ones.

To get around possible measurement errors, we reran the regression excluding nonwhites from the sample. The result is shown by equation 4 in Table 3, and previous conclusions regarding other variables are hardly affected.[18]

CONCLUSION

We have estimated marginal valuations of safety for a select group of individuals in 1967. All qualifications surrounding our estimates have

---

[18] Computation of the marginal risk premium under the cross-product specification must be made at specific values of the interactive variables (age, race, and so on) because $W'(p)$ is then a function of those variables. A little experimentation with equations (3) and (4) of Tables 3 and 4 shows that the imputations vary a great deal, depending on the point in the sample at which they are made. Indeed, some of these imputations are actually negative (e.g., older white nonunion, nonmarried individuals), which may indicate an undesirable restriction of the functional form or measurement error and not necessarily a model defect. We have not imposed any nonnegative restrictions on the estimates. Further, the possibilities of measurement error extensively pointed out at several points in the text preclude too much massaging of the data. Hence, we regard the cross-product results as suggestive only.

been given in the text and there is no need to repeat them here.[19] Certainly this study indicates feasibility of the method, the usual caveats about data quality notwithstanding. Are the estimates reasonable? We are unaware of similar studies with which to compare our results. However an example suggested by Bailey (1968) may be informative in this regard, and also illustrates how the estimates can be used.

The National Safety Council estimates that highway deaths would be reduced by about 10,000 per year if all automobile users wore lap safety belts. Assuming that the estimate is correct, seat belts reduce the probability of dying in an automobile accident from about 25 per hundred thousand (25×10^{-5}) per year to about 20 per hundred thousand per year (20×10^{-5}). Using the risk coefficient in equation 1 of Table 3 we estimate that the *average person in our sample* would be willing to pay *at least* $8.80 per year (in 1967 dollars) for a seat belt for himself. The cost of seat belts includes not only the purchase price and installation costs, but also costs associated with use, including bother and time spent buckling and unbuckling, so that it is easily within the realm of possibility that decisions not to purchase seat belts prior to the law were rational. We can make some more back-of-the-envelope calculations. How much would the time and bother costs (of individuals in our sample) have to be to justify not using seat belts even after they are mandatory? The sample mean hourly wage was about $3.50. Using that as an estimate of the value of time, time spent buckling and unbuckling would have to be about 2.5 hours per year to cost as much as $8.80. Assuming 500 trips per year, this amounts to about 18 seconds per trip in time-equivalent costs of using seat belts, a much smaller number than Bailey assumed. We leave it to the reader to experiment with other possibilities.

REFERENCES

Bailey, M. J. "Comment on T. C. Schelling's Paper." In S. B. Chase, ed., *Problems in Public Expenditure*. Washington, D.C.: Brookings Institution, 1968.

Calabresi, G. *The Costs of Accidents: A Legal and Economic Analysis*. New Haven: Yale University Press, 1970.

Fromm, G. "Civil Aviation Expenditures." In R. Dorfman, ed., *Measuring Benefits of Government Investments*. Washington, D.C.: Brookings Institution, 1965.

Hirshleifer, J. "Investment Decision Under Uncertainty: Choice Theoretic Approaches." *Quarterly Journal of Economics* 79 (November 1965): 509–536.

Mishan, E. "Evaluation of Life and Limb: A Theoretical Approach." *Journal of Political Economy* 79 (July/August 1970): 687–705.

Oi, W. "An Essay on Workmen's Compensation and Industrial Safety." In *Supplemental Studies for the National Commission on State Workmen's Compensation Laws*, Vol. I, pp. 41–106, 1973.

[19] These issues are discussed in greater depth in Chapter 1 of Thaler (1974).

Rosen, S. "Hedonic Prices and Implicit Markets: Product Differentiation in Pure Competition." *Journal of Political Economy* 82 (January/February 1974): 34–55.

Schelling, T. C. "The Life You Save May Be Your Own." In S. B. Chase, ed., *Problems in Public Expenditure*. Washington, D.C.: Brookings Institution, 1968.

Smith, R. S. "Compensating Wage Differentials and Hazardous Work," Technical Analysis Paper No. 5, Office of Evaluation, Department of Labor, August, 1973.

Thaler, R. "The Value of Saving a Life: A Market Estimate." Ph.D. dissertation, University of Rochester, 1974.

Usher, D. "An Imputation to the Measure of Economic Growth for Changes in Life Expectancy." In Milton Moss, ed., *The Measurement of Economic and Social Performance*. New York: NBER, 1973.

Comments on "The Value of Saving a Life:
Evidence from the Labor Market"

MARVIN KOSTERS

AMERICAN ENTERPRISE INSTITUTE

IN their everyday conversations and discussions, people are often reluctant to espouse the view that a monetary value can or should be placed on life. Yet, as Thaler and Rosen point out, in the normal course of their working and leisure activities, people are constantly making choices involving risks and rewards. Through these choices, they are implicitly placing some valuation on life or on the risk of death. In addition, public policy decisions very often involve choices concerning public expenditure of funds or the cost of applying regulations compared to their impact on the risk of accident, injury, or death.

In making public policy choices, it would be extremely useful to have information on the value society places on risk reduction in terms of the choices of its members, even though determining how much *ought* to be spent may remain elusive. The conceptual framework developed by Thaler and Rosen in this paper is extremely valuable in gaining insight into what might be meant by questions like: How much are people willing to pay (or forgo) to reduce the risk of serious injury or death? How does what they are willing to pay relate to the resource costs of restructuring jobs or altering equipment to reduce these risks? What interpretation can be placed on data and analyses dealing with alternative risk/reward situations? In addition, the propositions that emerge from the analysis are of considerable interest on their own right, since they are not all easily derived through intuition.

The empirical section presents estimates of the implicit price that is paid through wage differentials in the job market for variation in exposure to risk of death. The results are of particular interest because they were generated by using a set of data providing risk measures for quite detailed occupational categories, and the data provide relatively clean measures of net risk. The conceptual framework developed in the paper enables the authors to make careful distinctions between the price concept for which they were able to obtain estimates and concepts involving demand curves for safety or cost curves for risk reduction.

The price estimates obtained, while difficult to judge in terms of plausibility, are not so high or so low that they can be easily dismissed as irrelevant for application in a real-world policy-problem situation. The experiments with interaction terms are also extremely interesting, but unfortunately the data cannot provide sufficient resolution to explore them in any great detail. These relations are also likely to be extraordinarily complex because it is easily conceivable that there are differences in the direction of the effects between occupations. For example, age may reduce the price of risk bearing in some instances, while in other instances, increased age may be more than compensated for by work experience. The interpretation of these interaction effects is quite subtle, and the conceptual framework developed in the paper is valuable for distinguishing between movements along the wage risk function and differences in its slope represented by these interaction effects. As indicated in the paper, these interactions must reflect differences in productivity, market power, discrimination, and the like.

The higher risk premium estimated for unionism, however, suggests the possibility that better occupational risk information could play a role. It seems likely that unions are better equipped to assemble good information on risk and utilize it more effectively in bargaining than might be the case for nonunion workers. If poor information on differences in risk between occupations leads to a relatively greater emphasis placed by workers on wage premiums when they make their wage/risk choices, differences in the quality of risk information could influence the observed wage/risk tradeoff. If workers make their wage risk decisions as if they were applying a Bayesian decision framework, with more emphasis placed on the risk side of the bargain as the quality of information on real risk improves, a bias would be introduced into the estimated price of risk that operates in the opposite direction of the bias from analyzing occupations at the riskier end of the occupational spectrum. The role of information is not addressed in the paper, but a glance at the occupational risk data makes it hard to avoid the feeling that information quality may be important. For example, I would not have thought that it is more risky to be an elevator operator than a marshal, constable, sheriff, or bailiff, or that risk of death is nearly twice as high for waiters as it is for police and detectives! It is worth noting, however, that although it would be plausible to assume that nonwhites might have poorer information on risk than whites, the evidence suggests that nonwhites obtain higher risk premiums than whites.

The estimates developed in the paper are based on data drawn from the "demand for safety" side of the conceptual framework. It would be interesting to know how private firms treat the analysis of the supply side in making decisions on altering job content, working conditions, or equipment in order to devote optimal resources to provision of safety. If engineering studies of such alternatives were available, they could provide information from an independent source on the implicit price attributed by firms to variations in risks. It would also be interesting to explore decisions by the military concerning death risks to see if the implicit price of risk is significantly higher in what must be an occupation with significantly higher risk than those considered in this paper.

The qualifications on the meaning and interpretation of the estimate of the increase in wage premiums accompanying higher risk are so carefully spelled out in the paper that cautious analysts might be reluctant to place much reliance on the estimate for policy purposes. For small policy changes, however, the conceptual basis of the estimate is probably adequate for policy purposes. Most policy changes that might be analyzed using estimates of this sort in an effort to quantify their impact and desirability are likely to be small compared to the entire package of risk-reward choices that confronts the average person. Of course, policies that influence risk in a person's working environment may have the largest single impact on the typical person's overall risk portfolio, since such a large fraction of most peoples' lives is spent at work. The significance of work in the typical person's life makes the case for approaching the question of the price people are willing to pay for reduction in risk through analysis of wage-risk relations in the marketplace very persuasive.

Comments on "The Value of Saving a Life: Evidence from the Labor Market"

ROBERT E. LIPSEY

NATIONAL BUREAU OF ECONOMIC RESEARCH
AND QUEENS COLLEGE

THALER and Rosen wish to find a measure of the risk an individual incurs by working in a given hazardous occupation rather than in the average occupation. They wish to associate this risk with the additional wage that is required to induce an individual to accept the hazardous occupation, in order to calculate individuals' valuations of safety. However, as we might infer from some of the surprises in their list of hazardous occupations, the data on risk that they use measure something else: the extra risk to an insurance company of insuring those who are in a particular occupation. That insurance company risk includes both the true occupational risk and something we might call personal-characteristics risk—the risk that arises from the fact that people who go into bartending, for example, may have habits or characteristics aside from a lesser aversion for risk, which Thaler and Rosen mention, that would produce high mortality rates no matter what occupation they entered. Since these personal characteristics are attached to the individuals, rather than to the occupations they enter, the associated mortality risks will not be compensated for by higher wages. The only case in which the personal-characteristics risk might enter the wage rate for an occupation is that of interaction between the effects of the two types of risks (a person who leans toward heavy drinking may lean further in that direction if he becomes a bartender). Thus, the independent variable for risk in the Thaler-Rosen equations is not entirely the risk measure they want, and it is not clear whether the irrelevant personal-characteristics part of the insurance risk is systematically related to the relevant part. One might guess that the presence of this personal-characteristics element in the risk measure produces a downward bias in the estimate of the price of occupational risk, additional to the bias from self-selection of less risk-averse workers.

Part III
Level of Aggregation
in Consumer Analysis

Consumer Demand and Characteristics of Consumption Goods *

JACK E. TRIPLETT

U.S. DEPARTMENT OF LABOR, BUREAU OF LABOR STATISTICS

RECENT extensions of the theory of consumer behavior have led us to consider, on the one hand, production processes that occur in what has traditionally been regarded as the location of consumption activity (the household production literature), and on the other, to analyze consumption activity in the production place (consumption on the job). In the present session, we remain in territory with a longer history of habitation: we are considering consumption in the consumption place.

The three papers of this session have in common their concern with consumer behavior toward the kinds of market-purchased goods (food, housing, and automobiles) that have traditionally been thought of under the rubric "consumption." In this respect, they are in contrast to the papers of the previous two sessions, which have dwelt on extensions of the concepts of consumption and household behavior to encompass relatively new subject matter. But though the ground may seem familiar, the three papers of this session lead us down some paths hitherto unexplored, and expose new vistas along some old ones.

One paper (Christensen and Manser) is a demand analysis on goods, as goods have traditionally been defined. It shows us that despite an already extensive body of empirical estimates of systems of demand relations,[1] there is a great deal yet to be said about the traditional

* This paper comprises an introduction to the session on "The Level of Aggregation in Consumer Analysis," together with a discussion of some problems associated with estimating characteristics of consumption goods and conducting empirical analyses of behavior toward characteristics.

I wish to thank Richard J. McDonald, Robert A. Pollak, and Nestor Terleckyj for comments on an earlier draft; Robert F. Gillingham for valuable discussion of closely related points; and Dale W. Jorgenson for first setting me, a number of years ago, to thinking about the problems discussed in this paper. The views expressed are those of the author and do not represent an official position of the Bureau of Labor Statistics.

[1] A recent survey of this literature is Brown and Deaton (1972).

economic world of consumer behavior—that is, a world in which consumers purchase market-provided goods and services, and these goods and services are entered directly into utility functions (without first feeding the goods into some intermediate transformation function, and without taking explicit account of nonmarket inputs to the consumption process).

With all the emphasis in the past several years on new approaches to consumption theory, and the attention captured by novel applications of the theory of consumer behavior, it is easy to overlook the fact that the implications of traditional theory have never really been thoroughly tested. In the past, empirical implementation has been hindered by the fact that devising sets of demand equations which could be estimated required severe restrictions on the utility functions from which they were derived. The price of producing estimable relations has been the a priori exclusion of a good part of the economic behavior that traditional theory admits. The translog function employed by Christensen and Manser promises—as do some other functional forms for demand analysis that have recently appeared—to permit more adventuresome exploration of the standard theory of consumer behavior, so that we may, with some confidence, determine responses to price and income changes, allowing for the full range of interaction effects between related goods.

Another paper (Ohta and Griliches) may be interpreted as an exercise in specifying and measuring *characteristics* of goods, in the sense that the term "characteristics" has been used in the "New Theory of Demand" associated with Lancaster (1966, 1971). The Ohta-Griliches mechanism for doing this is a hedonic quality function.

Finally, we have the paper by King, which investigates consumer behavior toward sets of characteristics—characteristics which have been measured, and their respective prices estimated, by means of a hedonic function.

I shall have little to say directly about the Christensen-Manser paper, largely because I think it is an excellent piece of work that stands on its own within the context of previous literature on estimating sets of consumer demand functions, and partly because both authors were colleagues during the period when most of the research for the paper was carried out. Any slight input I am capable of making to that paper has long since been imparted to the authors.

The papers of Ohta and Griliches and of King, however, raise once again the specter of the relation between hedonic quality functions and consumer demand functions or consumer preference systems. On this matter, there has already been a not inconsiderable volume of speculation or criticism (much of which has remained in an oral tradition, rather than appearing in print). Certain comments on the conceptual framework of hedonic studies, and on the relation between hedonic estimates and consumer preferences or consumer demand functions, seem to me an appropriate accompaniment to the Ohta-Griliches and King papers—a judgment which is reinforced by the lively discussion which took place during the session. I am, however, making no attempt to summarize any of the discussion. Rather, the present paper represents my own views, distilled from the experience of having perpetrated one or two of the hedonic recipes on the profession, and having from time to time wrestled with trying to improve the flavor of the dish. Moreover, it is not intended that this introduction should be taken as implying disagreement with any of the papers in the session, or with the remarks of any of the discussants, except where explicitly indicated. Finally, the reader should not infer that Ohta, Griliches, or King necessarily agree that my view of the conceptual setting within which they are working corresponds to their own.[2]

By "hedonic function," or "hedonic quality function" or "hedonic price function" (all three designations are used interchangeably in the literature), I mean a regression of the form

$$P = f(\chi) \tag{1}$$

The dependent variable P is a vector of prices of different varieties of some product (for Ohta-Griliches, prices refer to different makes and models of automobiles of equivalent vintage; in King's study, product varieties are particular houses offered for sale within a specified geographical area); χ is a matrix, the columns of which designate a set of specifications, attributes, or "characteristics," and there is, of course, one row of values on the characteristics for each variety of the product. The statistical analysis is designed to determine which of the specifications are relevant to explaining the value of the transaction, and to estimate values—or implicit prices—for the specifications variables which are revealed as important ones. These implicit prices are

---

[2] Though in the following I discuss only aspects of hedonic measures that have a bearing on consumer demand studies, this does not imply that I think the hedonic results are without relationships on the supply side. For some purposes, one might wish to treat disaggregation through hedonic methods as supplying a set of joint outputs, which could, for example, replace a single output measure in a production function study. However, because the topic of this session is aggregation in *consumption,* supply or production relationships are more appropriately discussed elsewhere.

estimated in the form of the regression coefficients (i.e., $\partial P/\partial \chi$), or else are derived from them.

A partially developed relationship between consumer theory and empirical hedonic functions may, it is well known, be provided through the medium of Lancaster's (1966, 1971) "New Theory of Demand." I would emphasize the partially developed state of the relationship. Hedonic studies and the "New Theory" both embrace the concept of disaggregation of the units ("goods") in which transactions are conducted into some less aggregative (and presumably more basic) quantities that New Demand theorists and hedonicists alike call "characteristics." But after agreeing that it is desirable, or even imperative, to shift the analysis away from goods in the direction of characteristics (after their opening pages, that is) the hedonicists and the New Demand theorists more or less go their separate ways.[3]

Theoretical and conceptual clarification of the nature of hedonic estimates, and of the implications of their employment in various contexts, deserves high priority. If we do not know, to use the words of Ohta and Griliches, "what meaning, if any, is to be given to the [hedonic] constructions," and if we do not have at least some idea "what [hedonic] indexes measure and under what conditions . . . they measure it unambiguously,"[4] we have little basis for asserting that employment of hedonic estimates would really lead to improvement in existing price or quantity measures. Because of the nature of the measurement provided by hedonic estimates, we are very much in need of establishing a firm understanding of the conceptual underpinnings of the hedonic technique, from which to develop a theoretical rationale for the appropriate employment of hedonic results. Thus, the set of questions raised by Ohta and Griliches at the beginning of their paper is an exceedingly important (though by no means exhaustive) agenda for research. Finding at least provisional answers to such questions is crucial for using hedonic results to improve economic measurement of various sorts, and even more crucial if one hopes to employ hedonic results in studies of behavior toward characteristics, on the lines of the "New Theory of Demand."

Having said this, and I trust making clear my support for additional theoretical analysis in this area, I must at the same time strongly demur

---

[3] That separate roads are taken seems to me as much the fault of the degree of operational content — or lack of same — provided by the theorists as the excessively empiricist orientation of some of the contributors to the hedonic literature. I have elaborated on this view elsewhere (Triplett, 1973).

[4] The quotations are from Ohta and Griliches, pages 325–326.

from the general tenor of some of the proposals that have been made for theoretical work on the hedonic technique. My reservations stem from the formulation of the problem or problems on which it has sometimes been alleged that theoretical work is required.[5] In short, I think that some of the proposals for a "theory" of hedonic functions suffer from misconception of the setting in which hedonic estimates are made, and from consequent mis-specification of the theoretical problem to be attacked.

It was perhaps inevitable that work on the theoretical structure of the hedonic technique should become enmeshed in a discussion on defining what the problem is or is not. A large part of the literature on the "Quality Problem" (the problem of producing economic measurements of quality differences) is similarly introspective and concerned with the attempt to formulate, define, or understand the nature of the quality phenomenon.[6] At worst, such discussions descend to metaphysical speculation, and one cannot claim that the quality literature is entirely free from a taint of this. Nevertheless, it should be recognized that the quality problem has been formidably elusive, and that formulating approaches to elusive problems often requires a largely verbal setting.

One way to formulate the theoretical problems that need attention is to make use of analogs to other problems in economic analysis whose parameters are more familiar to us. Not surprisingly, the analytical framework we seek is thus likely to contain elements borrowed from other applications. The trick is to select the most useful analogies, and to identify aspects of the problem wherein the analogy is not exact.

The most useful analogies for this problem, it seems to me, are a set which involve the concept of characteristics (the same concept that is central to the ideas of the "New Theory of Demand"). The notion of characteristics, however, is abstract and unfamiliar. In order to free ourselves from the task of trying to reason exclusively in terms of characteristics of products, I offer the following parable or simile. In it, product characteristics, and the results of hedonic investigations, may be discussed in language which is usually employed in conventional consumer theory, so that correspondences may readily be arrayed between analyses in characteristics space and in commodity space.

[5] As already noted, part of the reference here is to a strand of reasoning that emerges frequently whenever hedonic research is discussed within the profession, and which cannot be associated with the work of any particular economist or group of economists. A flavor of this thought is contained in some of the items cited at the beginning of the Ohta-Griliches article. Some of the points in the following pages are particularly relevant to the last half of the Muellbauer (1974) article.

[6] See the bibliography in Griliches, ed. (1971).

Suppose that grocers, rather than placing their wares on shelves with unit prices marked on them, instead loaded various assortments of items into grocery carts or baskets, attaching prices to each of the pre-loaded baskets. Buyers in this marketing system would select a pre-loaded basket, and pay the specified price for the collection of groceries that it contains.

It is instructive to examine the hedonic methodology in the context of this simile, and to consider the nature of Lancastrian characteristics and the questions of economic behavior that arise in this same context. First, applying the hedonic technique to the simile would yield the usual hedonic regression, $P = f(\chi)$. The dependent variable (which in hedonic regressions is normally the price of some product, such as a group of automobiles) in this regression consists of the prices charged for the various preloaded baskets of groceries. The independent variables (the matrix χ), which are, in the usual hedonic study, measures of attributes or specifications, are here the quantities of various groceries in the available preloaded baskets. Thus, in the context of the simile, groceries found in the carts may be regarded as characteristics of the grocery bundle. The estimated regression coefficients are usually interpreted as implicit prices for characteristics – which are, in this case, groceries. We can therefore think of the hedonic investigation as an attempt to find out what prices of individual grocery items would have been, had the groceries been stocked on the shelves in the customary way.

Notice that what is written as a price in the hedonic regression (the dependent variable, P) is readily interpretable as expenditure on groceries when a cartload is purchased.[7] Similarly, when in normal hedonic studies we move from the level of the good to that of characteristics, the quantity we normally think of as *the* price (the price of the good) has no further interpretation as a price. It becomes, instead, the expenditure on characteristics implied by the act of purchasing the variety in which the characteristics are embedded.

Two questions – both of which seem to me unproductive lines of inquiry – have repeatedly emerged in discussion of the hedonic technique. Within the context of the simile, the first can be put thus: Are implicit prices derived from the hedonic function estimates of consumer valuations or of the grocer's costs?

---

[7] This quantity does not necessarily correspond to the usual concept of total expenditure for an individual consumer over any time period, because he may well purchase more than one cartload. It is simply total expenditure on the groceries included in one transaction.

Posing this question of hedonic prices has exactly the same import as posing the same query regarding the prices we do, in fact, observe on grocery store shelves – no more and no less.[8] The standard welfare implications of those prices which are observed in the usual way tell us that if consumers are competitive, then relative prices can be taken as measures of marginal rates of substitution; and if producers are competitive, they also measure transformation rates. Furthermore, if competition does not prevail on, say, the seller side of the market, then prices do not necessarily reflect marginal costs, though the interpretation of them as measures of marginal consumer evaluations remains valid.[9] All this is well known. That so much argument has been carried on over a question of so little real difficulty probably indicates that the framework within which hedonic estimates are obtained has not been adequately comprehended.

The second question commonly posed of the hedonic results concerns the *form* of the hedonic estimating function. Specifically, the question is usually framed as: Which possible estimating forms are derivable from behavioral relations (preference functions, or production or cost functions), and which functional forms are theoretically inappropriate? Although the functional form question can encompass some interesting problems, trying to derive information about functional form from behavioral postulates is not likely to yield dividends. Basically, the problem here is that the hedonic function has often been confused with some sort of demand or cost function, when in fact it corresponds to an opportunity locus, or a portion of one.

Recall that in the grocery cart simile, the price or ticket on the preloaded cart was interpretable as the expenditure on the groceries contained in it. The form of the hedonic function establishes the nature of characteristics prices (Are they straight dollar values, as is customary for true shelf prices, or are they determined as percentages of the total, or by some other procedure?); and the function also tells us how expenditures on each of the groceries are to be combined to reach the total (the ticket on the cart).

Because the ticket on the preloaded grocery cart is interpreted as an expenditure, it is tempting to infer that the hedonic function is akin to a consumer demand function, perhaps one expressed in expenditure

---

[8] That is, provided that the implicit prices derived from the hedonic function can be used as if they were estimates of shelf prices (an important question, which is considered below).

[9] One still hears repeated the canard that imperfect competition among sellers destroys the consumer-valuation interpretation of hedonic prices, when just the opposite is plainly the case.

form. That is, the hedonic function $P = f(\chi)$ is to be interpreted as an equation that says

$$\text{Expenditure} = f(\chi) \tag{2}$$

We then proceed to estimate regression coefficients which are interpreted as implicit prices, so that equation 2 looks deceptively like the consumer demand function

$$\text{Expenditure} = g(\Pi, y) \tag{3}$$

where Π is the vector of prices of all related goods, and y is a measure of income.

This is, however, not the correct correspondence. We can indeed find an analog to the demand or expenditure function of equation 3 in the grocery cart simile. The direct characteristics analog to equation 3 would be a relation that explained how the consumer determined *what quantitites of the various groceries he wanted to consume.* This relation would, as is true of familiar consumer demand functions, be derived from the utility function via the usual constrained maximization process; but in the context of the simile, it would explain *which cart,* given a set of grocery prices and the consumer's income, the consumer selects.

The distinction between equations 2 and 3 is that equation 3 is a behavioral relation that pertains to an individual consumer, who is assumed to carry out a specified maximization process under prescribed constraints. Equation 3 tells us his response to values of variables over which the maximization process is defined. The analog to equation 3, in a characteristics world, is a demand function for characteristics.

The hedonic function tells us something entirely different. With respect to the theory of consumer behavior, a hedonic function on consumer goods assumes the role of an empirical estimate of the constraint (or, in the general case, part of it) to which the consumer is subject.

Consider equation 2 in the context of the grocery cart simile. Hold total expenditure on groceries (the ticket on the cart) constant, but vary the quantities in χ (that is, let one or more χ_i increase, but decrease one or more χ_j just sufficiently so that the total outlay for groceries in the basket remains unchanged). The resulting locus is an iso-expenditure line for groceries. This iso-expenditure line resembles the familiar budget constraint from conventional consumer theory. And this is precisely where the analogy lies. The hedonic function corresponds, not to a demand or expenditure function, but rather to a function from which we can derive the budget constraint.

To conduct analysis on consumer behavior toward characteristics, we replace the quantity of a good with a vector of quantities of characteristics derived from it. The hedonic function can be used to determine what those characteristics are, and to establish prices for them; moreover, from the hedonic function, a budget constraint may be derived which can be employed in a study of the demand for characteristics.

Therefore, any theoretical questions we can ask of the form of the hedonic function have nothing to do with deriving it from the consumer's preference function — that is impossible, for the same reason that one cannot derive the budget constraint in the conventional consumption problem from the consumer's preference function. Neither will the form of the hedonic function be determined directly by the form of any "household production function" which may combine characteristics, time, and other elements. Rather, we may ask whether the functional form chosen for the hedonic study gives rise to budget constraints with appropriate properties for conducting demand analyses. I return to this matter later in the paper.

One point with respect to supply deserves to be made. It has sometimes been said that hedonic studies have been technically deficient because investigators have failed to consider supply conditions when estimating hedonic functions, or because they have overlooked identification problems of the type that have become familiar in the usual demand or supply studies. The argument, of course, is simple transference to hedonic studies of problems associated with demand studies. The reply is largely a reiteration of points made earlier: the hedonic function is not a demand function, and conditions which must be satisfied in order to identify empirical demand estimates are not necessarily requirements for carrying out hedonic studies. If one is interested in carrying out a *demand* study on characteristics, of course, then it is essential to consider these matters: King's study of the demand for housing characteristics, for example, requires the assumption that buyers are adjusting their requirements for space and other characteristics to characteristics prices, but sellers are not varying the amount of the characteristic space they sell in response to these same prices. However, the validity of estimated implicit prices for housing characteristics does not depend on equivalent assumptions.

Yoram Barzel, during the discussion, noted that there must be some reason why grocers stock shelves instead of behaving as in the simile. Quite so. Some characteristics are sold prepackaged, rather than separately, for economic or technical reasons, and one can think of many of them.[10]

The implication of this observation, however, is that even though we want to employ hedonic prices for purposes similar to the ways in which we use directly observed prices, implicit prices derived from a hedonic function are nevertheless not the same thing as prices directly observed. There are quite a number of differences, which should be considered carefully when using the hedonic prices for purposes such as demand analysis, or for constructing price or cost-of-living indexes. Moreover, if one believes (as many economists apparently do) that a better understanding of the hedonic estimates is required in order to justify their employment in various applications, then the analytical work that will give us the understanding we need must focus on the differences between hedonic prices and directly observed ones.

In the remaining portion of this paper, I intend to discuss a few of these differences (and also some similarities). The list I present is not an exhaustive one nor is it meant to be. Rather, it should be viewed as providing a few illustrative examples.

I. TRANSLATING HEDONIC ISO-EXPENDITURE LINES INTO BUDGET CONSTRAINTS ON CHARACTERISTICS

The usual hedonic function is estimated using an array of prices — that is, the data for a hedonic investigation almost always include a number of different levels of expenditure on characteristics of the product under investigation. This means that the data, in combination with hedonic estimates of characteristics prices, generate a family of iso-

---

[10] There is nothing very obscure or arcane about these reasons. In a few cases, it may be technically impossible to break up characteristics. In most cases, however, the usual bundle of characteristics incorporated into a good are by no means technically immutable; rather, they are tied together mainly for convenience or cost advantages. For example, it is clearly technically feasible to sell cars without engines (so performance characteristics could be sold as a package separate from the rest of the car). At one time, cars could be purchased without bodies, and sent to a firm which specialized in construction of the body and finishing the completed car (and this practice was by no means uncommon, among expensive cars especially). The reason cars are now sold complete with engines and bodies is mainly that it is much cheaper to put the whole package of characteristics together at the factory than to buy the packages separately and have them assembled. On the other hand, there seems to be no production-economy reason why refrigerators and other appliances have come to be included in the package of characteristics we call "housing," rather than purchased separately. Here, the reason seems to be related primarily to inefficiencies in the distribution system for appliances, and partly to institutional mortgage practices.

expenditure lines, not just one. All the commonly used functional forms for hedonic studies yield families of iso-expenditure lines that are radial displacements of each other.

Moreover, data on characteristics for automobiles, or housing, or groceries must be combined with information on other goods consumed — or on characteristics of those goods — in order to define the full budget constraint. This means that, in the general case, one may derive from a hedonic function for *one* product a family of segments of budget constraints. If there are many different products, and each product has many characteristics, the number of budget segments, or characteristics, that must be considered in a demand study may easily become unmanageable.

The data size problem is not, however, unknown in conventional demand studies on goods. Specifying all possible cross-effects quickly results in a very large matrix of parameter estimates. The solution has been to find recourse to the notions of separability and "branches" of utility functions,[11] which impose restrictions on some of the cross-price terms. Obviously, a similar approach will be appealing for use in demand studies on characteristics. If it can be assumed that the utility function is separable with respect to the characteristics derived from the product for which the hedonic study was carried out, then the hedonic estimates can be taken as defining a "branch" budget constraint, or a family of them (this is precisely the use King has made of the housing hedonic function in his paper).

Thus, this question is not really so different in characteristics and in goods worlds. Very probably, however, appropriate separable branches will be more difficult to find in a characteristics world, and the characteristics in the branch frequently will not coincide with the characteristics that happen to come prepackaged in the product being investigated. King notes that some of his housing characteristics are undoubtedly made up using goods not included in the home-purchase transaction; and a demand study for automotive characteristics could hardly neglect the price of gasoline.

Another problem is the treatment of services of durable goods. Most hedonic studies are concerned with durables, but there have been few attempts to define characteristics as service flows. Moreover, although this precedent is well established for single-equation demand studies, it has not so far been extended to the estimation of sets of simultaneous demand equations.

---

[11] The reference is to the "utility tree" concept proposed by Strotz (1957).

II. "MARGINAL" CHARACTERISTICS PRICES

One of the most striking differences between hedonic and directly observed prices is the fact that in the hedonic world, the summation of price times quantity seldom yields total expenditure. For one thing, a significant, positive intercept term has been reported in almost all existing hedonic studies. A nonzero intercept means that multiplying estimated prices of characteristics by the quantities of characteristics included in the package falls short of total expenditure on the package. This is true even with a linear hedonic function (such as the one used by King), which yields estimated prices for characteristics in terms of dollars, unless some economic interpretation is forthcoming for the expenditures accounted for by the intercept.[12] More crucially, with other forms (such as the semilog and double-log functions) the price of incremental units does not remain constant as larger packages are purchased.

In other words, all three functional forms yield a "marginal price" (the price paid for incremental units of characteristics when purchased as part of the same bundle) which differs from the average price; moreover, in the semilog and double-log cases, this marginal price is an increasing function of the quantities of characteristics purchased in the bundle. Our conventional theory of consumer behavior does not encounter such phenomena, and so, not surprisingly, existing empirical consumer demand systems cannot deal with them.[13] Nor does any of our conventional upward-sloping supply price notions seem adequate to characterize these situations.[14]

There is, however, more than one marginal price concept that may plague attempts to explore behavior toward characteristics using hedonic prices. The preceding marginal price concept corresponds to an increment in expenditures on characteristics. Call this, for convenience, the "marginal Engel price of characteristics."

Demand studies are typically concerned with consumption effects of relative price changes. In demand studies carried out on goods, one assumes that the relative prices consumers face are not affected by

---

[12] A good example of such an interpretation is provided by Stone (1956), who interpreted the positive intercept in a hedonic regression of transportation fares and distances as the charge for loading and unloading. In other instances, the intercept may measure the value of characteristics which were omitted from the investigation.

[13] King evades the problem by throwing the intercept into the "price" of two of his characteristics.

[14] There is, however, a crude analog to the Phelps-Winter (1970) result that pushing more purchases into a fixed time dimension will only be possible by increasing the price paid. In the present case, increasing unit price (of characteristics) is paid when more units of characteristics are forced into a single physical package.

individual decisions on proportions in the consumption basket — that is, budget constraints are straight lines, with constant slopes.

In the hedonic, or characteristics, world relative prices may have altogether different properties. Lancaster (1971) explicitly introduces the possibility that in a world of characteristics, budget opportunity sets may be convex, such as Figure 1 (the segmented linearity of Lancaster's locus stems from assuming that only a limited number of characteristics proportions are available).

With hedonic estimates of a characteristics world, whether branch budget constraints have constant slopes depends on the form of the hedonic function. Two of the three most commonly employed functional forms for hedonic studies (the linear and the semilog forms) yield budget constraints with constant slopes.[15] The double-log form, however, yields the awkward budget constraint of Figure 2, which would pose analytical problems for studies of consumer behavior unless indifference curves on characteristics χ_1 and χ_2 were sharply bent.

Thus, functional forms that have been used for hedonic studies admit price phenomena that are not present under the assumptions employed in working out the conventional theory of consumer behavior toward goods. What can economic theory say about the admissibility of these various functional forms?

Basically, theory can say very little. The characteristics world, or the hedonic world, contains a consumer optimization problem that is in many ways analogous to the standard textbook problem. However, they are not identical problems. The nature of the budget constraint facing the consumer in the standard problem stems from the assumption that he can buy all he wants at the prevailing price, without influencing that price.[16] In the Lancastrian, or hedonic, world, charac-

---

[15] Contrary to assertions that have been made, the semilog form, though producing nonconstant marginal Engel prices, exhibits *constancy* of relative prices with respect to changes in *proportions* of characteristics. Recall that the price of product variety i (call it P_i) is interpreted as total expenditures on characteristics when variety i is purchased. Then, with the semilog hedonic function

$$\ln P = a_0 + a_1\chi_1 + a_2\chi_2$$

the budget constraint is the slope $d\chi_1/d\chi_2$ ($\ln P_i$ constant), which is: $-a_2/a_1$ — clearly a constant. I presume that the notion that the semilog function yields nonlinear budget constraints has arisen because of confusion over the concept of expenditures in a world of characteristics.

[16] Actually, there are such things as one cent sales, special prices for limited quantities, tied sales, and so forth, even when we are considering markets for goods; if the standard theory were modified to take account of these details, budget constraints on goods would become more complex than the usual textbook case (see also the closing sentence in Barzel's comment).

FIGURE 1

A Lancastrian Budget Constraint

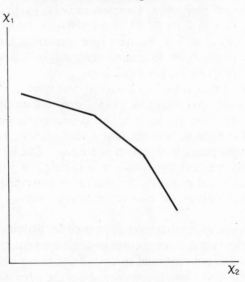

FIGURE 2

A Budget Constraint Implied by a Double-Log Hedonic Function

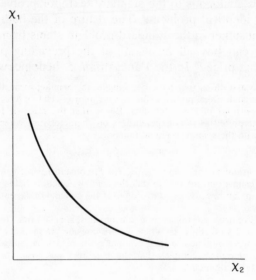

teristics must be packaged into goods before they are sold. The consumer may indeed buy as many *goods* as he wishes without affecting the prices of goods; but he may not be able to insist that larger quantities of characteristics be built into a particular variety of good without changing the terms on which he acquires characteristics, and he may find that proportions of characteristics contained in a single characteristics bundle are not infinitely variable at constant characteristics prices. Just because the standard theory of consumer behavior defined on goods is set in a world where relative prices are insensitive to individual budget allocations does not mean that we can assume (or insist!) that the world of characteristics must exhibit like properties. Therefore, if the double-log form (or any other form that yields concave iso-expenditure segments) does indeed describe the situations encountered empirically, then this is simply a fact that must be dealt with.

III. VARIANCE IN THE COMPOSITION OF CONSUMER'S BUDGET ALLOCATIONS

In performing demand analyses on goods, it is conventional to treat aggregative data as appropriate for estimating behavior of a "representative consumer." Whether time series or cross-section data are employed, the investigator typically attempts to determine how the average budget allocation changes in response to price or income variations.

Normally, variance among budget allocations of different individuals is treated as an annoying aggregation problem. Suppose we observe two individuals (I and II) whose preferences for apples and oranges are depicted in Figure 3. It is a formidable step to propose aggregating these two observations into a point midway between, and to use the resulting mean quantities of apples and oranges as observations applicable to studies of economic behavior. This is a well-known point (see Brown and Deaton, 1972, pp. 1167–1170, for a discussion of some proposals for dealing with it).

In the characteristics world, we encounter similar budget variance, though we usually give it a different name. If we substitute, for the apples and oranges of Figure 3, characteristics *r* and *s*, we may find that individuals I and II choose them in different proportions; if this occurs in characteristics space, then when the event is transferred back into goods space, we say that individual I chose variety A (a variety which combines characteristics *r* and *s* in the proportions indicated by point *A* in Figure 3), and individual II chose variety B.

FIGURE 3

Budget Allocation in a Goods World and in a Characteristics World

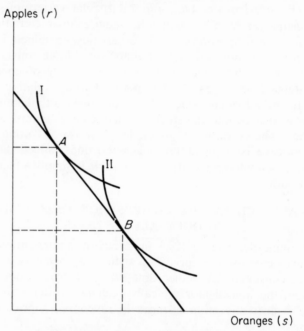

Therefore, the "taste difference" problem (or at least this aspect of it) has much the same force in empirical work on goods or on characteristics. Interpreting Figure 3 as applying to the characteristics world signals the death of the "representative consumer" to exactly the same degree that that embattled individual's existence is threatened by Figure 3 as it depicts budget allocations in the goods world.

But there is a difference. In the goods world, budget variance is merely a hindrance to performing demand analysis on aggregative data. If there were no variance (for given prices and income), we should be pleased. In the characteristics world, budget variance is still an annoyance, if the objective is to perform demand studies. But to obtain characteristics prices from hedonic studies, we need the variance. If everyone had identical tastes, then the number of varieties of a good on the market could not exceed the number of characteristics it contains, and it would not be possible to estimate the hedonic function.

Conventional demand studies usually assume that budget variance does not exist (through the assumption of the representative consumer). Though empirically incorrect, this assumption does no violence to the logic of the investigation. With respect to studies on demands for characteristics, assuming no budget variance is equally inaccurate empirically; but in addition, this necessary assumption for the demand study contradicts the framework required to develop prices for characteristics.

IV. PACKAGING

Characteristics come as a tied sale, in packages. This fact results in a number of problems which are not usually considered in consumer demand studies. Lumpiness, corner solutions, and discontinuities are the most obvious points, but packaging may also account for nonconstant marginal characteristics prices (discussed in point II above). As Rosen (1974) has pointed out, if characteristics were not packaged into a limited number of varieties of goods, arbitrage could enforce linearity on the hedonic function.

Unfortunately, it is a fact that the number of packages is usually limited. Since this fact is so fundamental a part of the quality phenomenon, and of the analysis of the implications of characteristics of consumption goods, one cannot really expect to get very far without taking it into explicit consideration. In particular, assuming packaging discontinuities away in order to be able to employ traditional calculus methods (as does Rosen, 1974) seems a dubious methodology, particularly in view of Lancaster's (1971) demonstration of alternative programming models which can encompass these problems.[17]

V. ECONOMIC REALITY OR STATISTICAL ARTIFACT?

One may interpret hedonic results as measures of characteristics and characteristics prices. That does not make them so. Can we be sure that estimated hedonic prices represent something real, and that they are valid measurements for use in studies on consumer behavior?

The problem of determining whether a pricing concept or measure is an appropriate one is not a problem unknown in economic research in the realm of goods. One can cite, for example, the distinction between a true cost-of-living index (or constant-utility price index) and a fixed-weight index, or the choice between the price of a durable good

---

[17] As noted in the preceding footnote (and also in Barzel's comment), traditional consumer theory defined on goods assumes away discontinuities and corner solutions, but greater empirical applicability requires that they be taken into account in the goods domain, as well as in that of characteristics.

and the price of its service flow; in both cases, the statistic readily available may not be the one appropriate for the problem at hand.

But if in this respect the difference between goods and characteristics worlds is one of degree, rather than of kind, nevertheless the degree is sufficient to be troubling. We are relatively inexperienced in research on characteristics, and only recently have hedonic studies emerged from the state where the investigator is both pleased and content if he can find some set of variables which seem to be associated with the price of the product. Now that we have evidence that such variables are around, the more difficult question of the validity of hedonic measures requires serious attention.

If hedonic results prove successful in dealing with other research problems, this would provide perhaps the most convincing evidence that hedonic estimates represent economic reality and not just some statistical accident. King's study is one persuasive test. Studies by Cowling and Cubbin (1971, 1972) apply an entirely different test, one first suggested by Griliches (in his now classic 1961 article, reprinted in his 1971 book). Cowling and Cubbin find that residuals from hedonic functions (which may be measures of over- or underpricing for packages of characteristics) are associated with changes in market shares among different sellers.[18] And although Barzel raises supply and demand factors for characteristics as an estimating problem, if hedonic prices are valid then one should expect that changes in them would be explainable by supply and demand factors—which suggests another form of test (partly applied in the Cowling and Cubbin papers).

One step that investigators can take to assure that hedonic measures are valid for research on consumer behavior is to require that, wherever possible, variables chosen for explanatory variables in hedonic functions should be in fact characteristics, and not some other variables which stand in proxy relations of some sort to what consumers want. For this reason, I would prefer measures of automotive characteristics somewhat along the lines of Ohta-Griliches' set of *Consumer Reports* data, in place of specifications such as weight and length, which stand as the roughest sort of proxies for attributes that are useful.[19] If, as Ohta-Griliches show, one gets about the same "fit" and results with one set as with the other, the possible use of hedonic

---

[18] However, a similar test applied to data on the U.S. automobile market (Triplett and Cowling, 1971) found no association between hedonic residuals and changes in market shares.

[19] Though there may well be a "two-state" relation between engineering variables and the performance characteristics buyers want, I am not convinced that Ohta-Griliches' specification variables can be regarded as engineering variables either.

measures in other economic studies swings the balance toward working with measures that can be regarded as characteristics.

REFERENCES

Brown, Alan, and Deaton, Angus. "Surveys in Applied Economics: Models of Consumer Behavior." *Economic Journal* 82 (December 1972): 1145–1236.

Cowling, Keith, and Cubbin, John. "Price, Quality and Advertising Competition: An Econometric Investigation of the United Kingdom Car Market." *Economica* 30 (November 1971): 378–394.

———. "Hedonic Price Indexes for United Kingdom Cars." *Economic Journal* 82 (September 1972): 963–978.

Griliches, Zvi, ed. *Price Indexes and Quality Change: Studies in New Methods of Measurement.* Cambridge: Harvard University Press, 1971.

Lancaster, Kelvin. "A New Approach to Consumer Theory." *Journal of Political Economy* 74 (April 1966): 132–157.

———. *Consumer Demand: A New Approach.* Columbia Studies in Economics, No. 5. New York and London: Columbia University Press, 1971.

Muellbauer, John. "Household Production Theory, Quality, and the 'Hedonic Technique,'" *American Economic Review* 64 (December 1974): 977–994.

Phelps, Edmund S., and Winter, Sidney G. "Optimal Price Policy under Atomistic Competition." In Edmund S. Phelps et al. *Microeconomic Foundations of Employment and Inflation Theory.* New York: W. W. Norton & Co., 1970.

Rosen, Sherwin. "Hedonic Prices and Implicit Markets: Product Differentiation in Pure Competition." *Journal of Political Economy* 82 (January/February 1974): 34–55.

Stone, Richard. *Quantity and Price Indexes in National Accounts.* Paris: Organization for European Economic Cooperation, 1956.

Strotz, R. H. "The Empirical Implications of a Utility Tree." *Econometrica* 25 (April 1957): 269–280.

Triplett, Jack E. "Review of *Consumer Demand: A New Approach,* by Kelvin Lancaster." *Journal of Economic Literature* 11 (March 1973): 77–81.

Triplett, Jack E., and Cowling, Keith. "A Quality-Adjustment Model for Determining Market Shares in Oligopoly." BLS Working Paper Number 4, U.S. Bureau of Labor Statistics, Washington, D.C., 1971.

Automobile Prices Revisited: Extensions of the Hedonic Hypothesis *

MAKOTO OHTA

TOHOKU UNIVERSITY

AND

ZVI GRILICHES

HARVARD UNIVERSITY

I. INTRODUCTION

THE "hedonic" approach to price indexes has been reviewed recently in a number of places (Gordon 1973, Griliches 1971, Muellbauer 1972, Ohta 1973, and Rosen 1973, among others) and we will not go over the same ground again except for a few brief remarks. The hedonic hypothesis assumes that a commodity can be viewed as a bundle of characteristics or attributes for which implicit prices can be derived from prices of different versions of the same commodity containing differing levels of specific characteristics. The ability so to disaggregate a commodity and price its components facilitates the construction of price indexes and the measurement of price change across differing versions of the same commodity. Several issues arise in trying to implement such a program: (1) What are the relevant characteristics of a commodity bundle? (2) How are the implicit prices to be estimated from the available data? (3) How are the resulting estimates to be used to construct price or quality indexes for a particular commodity? (4) What meaning, if any, is to be given to the

* We are indebted to R. J. Gordon and J. Triplett for comments on an earlier draft and to National Science Foundation grant No. G.X. 2762X for financial support. This is a much abbreviated version of a longer manuscript, Ohta and Griliches (1972), containing a detailed literature review and additional discussion, tables, and documentation.

resulting constructs? What do such indexes measure and under what conditions do they measure it unambiguously?

Much of the recent critical literature on the hedonic approach has dealt with the last two questions, pointing out the restrictive nature of the assumptions required to establish the "existence" and meaning of such indexes. While instructive, we feel that this literature has misunderstood the original purpose of the hedonic suggestion. It is easy to show that except for unique circumstances and under very stringent assumptions, it is not possible to devise a perfect price index for *any* commodity classification. With finite amounts of data, different procedures will yield (hopefully not very) different answers, and even "good" formulae, such as Divisia-type indexes, cannot be given a satisfactory theoretical interpretation except in very limiting and unrealistic circumstances. Most of the objections to attempts to construct a price index of automobiles from the consideration of their various attributes apply with the same force to the construction of a motor-vehicles price index out of the prices of cars, trucks, and motor-cycles.

Despite the theoretical proofs to the contrary, the Consumer Price Index (CPI) "exists" and is even of some use. It is thus of some value to attempt to improve it even if perfection is unattainable. What the hedonic approach attempted was to provide a tool for estimating "missing" prices, prices of particular bundles not observed in the original or later periods. It did not pretend to dispose of the question of whether various observed differentials are demand or supply determined, how the observed variety of models in the market is generated, and whether the resulting indexes have an unambiguous welfare interpretation. Its goals were modest. It offered the tool of econometrics, with all of its attendant problems, as a help to the solution of the first two issues, the detection of the relevant characteristics of a commodity and the estimation of their marginal market valuation.

Because of its focus on price explanation and its purpose of "predicting" the price of unobserved variants of a commodity in particular periods, the hedonic hypothesis can be viewed as asserting the existence of a reduced-form relationship between prices and the various characteristics of the commodity. That relationship need not be "stable" over time, but changes that occur should have some rhyme and reason to them, otherwise one would suspect that the observed results are a fluke and cannot be used in the extrapolation necessary for the derivation of missing prices. All this has an air of "measurement without theory" about it, but one should remember the limited aspirations of the hedonic approach and not confuse it with attempts to provide a complete structural explanation of the events in a particular market.

To accomplish even such limited goals, one requires much prior information on the commodity in question (econometrics is not a very good tool when wielded blindly), lots of good data, and a detailed analysis of the robustness of one's conclusions relative to the many possible alternative specifications of the model. In what follows, we take up a few limited topics in the analysis of automobile prices, focusing on the role of "makes" or "brands" in explaining price differentials among different models of automobiles, the additional information to be derived from analyses of used car prices, and the gains to be had, if any, from using performance instead of physical (specification) characteristics in defining the relevant attributes of a commodity.

II. QUESTIONS, MODELS, AND RESEARCH STRATEGY

A. Preliminaries

We distinguish between the physical characteristics of a car (x_1, x_2, ..., x_m) and its performance variables (y_1, y_2, ..., y_n). Physical characteristics (specifications) are such things as horsepower, weight and length, while acceleration, handling, steering, accommodation, and fuel economy are performance variables. In our general setting, physical characteristics of a car enter the cost function of producing it but do not affect the utility function of the consumer directly.[1] We postulate a "two-stage hypothesis" which asserts that the physical characteristics of a car produce its performance.[2]

Note that the mapping from physical characteristics to performance variables need not be one to one. Some performance levels, such as engine performance and accommodation indexes, are produced by the physical characteristics and are costly. These are closely connected with the physical characteristics of power and size. But other performance variables, such as prestige or design differences, cost little and may not be related to measured physical characteristics. They may be produced by demonstration effects, advertising, and good service and quality-control policies. The mapping may also be stochastic

---

[1] Tautologically, we consider those attributes of a car that enter the cost function as its physical characteristics and those that enter the consumers' utility function as performance variables. There may be some attributes which enter both functions. These are performance variables as well as physical characteristics.

[2] Our "two-stage hypothesis" is similar to the idea of "consumption activity" in Lancaster (1966).

rather than deterministic and it may change over time. Experienced and inexperienced drivers may get different performances from a car with the same physical characteristics. Users may get accustomed to a car over time by learning to deal with its idiosyncrasies. And, most important for our purposes, unmeasured physical characteristics may change the relationship between measured physical characteristics and performance levels over time.

We consider performance variables as well as physical characteristics because, ideally, quality adjustments should be based on performance variables, which presumably enter the utility function directly, rather than on physical characteristics. If the transformation function from physical characteristics to performance levels shifts systematically over time, then hedonic price indexes based on physical characteristics alone will be biased.[3]

So far, we have discussed our model only in general terms. One cannot, however, solve all problems immediately and simultaneously. The most general model is rarely operational. We have chosen, therefore, to concentrate on finding an appropriate strategy for each specific problem. Because the number of observations available on performance variables is very limited, we postpone the discussion of tests of the two-stage hypothesis to the last section of this paper, concentrating first on narrowing down the range of possible alternative models, using the much larger physical characteristics sample.

The typical regression model which we shall use throughout the empirical sections of the study is based on the following semilogarithmic form

$$P_{kits} = Const. \cdot M_i \cdot \bar{P}_t \cdot D_s \cdot e^{\sum\limits_j a_{tj} x_{kivj}}$$

where

   P_{kits}: price of model k of make i and age s at time t
   M_i: effect of the ith make (the effect of make 1 is set at 1)
   $\bar{P}_t$: pure (hedonic) price index at time t
   D_s: effect of age s (depreciation)
   a_{tj}: parameter reflecting the imputed price of physical characteristic j at time t
   x_{kivj}: the level of the physical characteristic j embodied in model k of make i and vintage v ($v = t - s$)

We chose the semilogarithmic form as our basic regression equation

---

[3] See, for example, Triplett (1966).

for the same reasons as those reported by Griliches (1961); it provided a good fit to the data. In the following chapters we shall also, occasionally, allow D_s to depend on make (i) and time (t), and a_i to depend on age (s), make (i), time (t), and on whether the car is new or used. That is, generally, we can write

$$D_s = D_s(i, t)$$

$$a_{tj} = a_j(s, j, t, \text{new or used})$$

In some of the empirical sections, we shall restrict D_s to an exponential function of s, and when we study performance variables y, we shall substitute them for the physical characteristics x in this type of model.

B. Make-Effects [4]

Because hedonic studies try to infer the marginal market valuation of different characteristics from observed market data, they require observations on models or variants of the commodity that differ significantly in the combination and range of characteristics contained in them. To accomplish that, and to increase sample size, authors are tempted to define the commodity broadly and to assume that there is enough substitution and competition across various boundaries to lead to relatively stable equalizing price differentials. One of the major boundaries that such studies cross are those connected with makes or brands. The essence of the hedonic approach is the assumption that one can find a metric for crossing such boundaries, that specifying the underlying characteristics creates adequate conmensurability. However, since the list of measurable characteristics is never complete, there may be systematic differences across makes in the levels of the "left-out" variables, real (physical) or putative. This will not create too serious a problem provided that these left-out variables are "separable" from the measured characteristics and constant over time. Given several observations per make or brand and repeated

[4] Griliches (1967) first pointed to model effects as a possible source of the observed fluctuations in the estimated hedonic price indexes and warned that without further analysis of the size of the model effect, we should not interpret the time dummy estimates of hedonic regression equations as unbiased estimates of pure price change, unless the size and composition of samples are kept constant over time. He thought of it primarily as the effect of left-out physical characteristics making it a special case of the omitted variables problem. He did not consider the role of market structure and related brand loyalty considerations as potentially important sources of such effects. We shall pursue this lead but use the "make" rather than the model as our unit of classification and object of study. We do this because various market structure hypotheses appear to be more relevant at the make or even manufacturer level and because the classification at the model level is much too fine for empirical study.

observations over time, some of these hypotheses are testable. Since "make effects" are also of intrinsic interest, we devote a major part of our effort in this study to their identification and analysis.

Imagine a new car market dominated by markup pricing. Let r_i be the markup ratio for make i, W the input price index, z_{ki} the output of model k of make i, and $c = C(.)$ the unit cost function connecting these variables.[5] Suppose that physical characteristics $x_{ki1}, \ldots, x_{kih}$ are measurable, while $x_{kih+1}, \ldots, x_m$ are not measurable. To simplify exposition, suppose that

$$c = C(x) = C_1(x_{ki1}, \ldots, x_{kih}) \cdot C_2(x_{kih+1}, \ldots, x_m)$$

i.e., it is separable in the unobserved characteristics. Then, we can write equation 1 as follows

$$P_{ki} = \underbrace{(1 + r_i)} \cdot \underbrace{C(x_{ki1}, \ldots, x_{kih},} \ \underbrace{x_{kih+1}, \ldots, x_{kim};} \ \underbrace{\Sigma Z_{ki}, W)}$$

reflects dif-	measured	unmeasured	not in-
ferential	characteristics	characteristics	cluded
market		↓	in the
power		omitted	hedonic
across		variables	regression
makes			equation [6]

$$= \underbrace{(1 + r_i) \cdot C_2(x_{kih+1}, \ldots, x_{kim} \colon \Sigma z_{ki}, W)} \cdot \underbrace{C_1(x_{ki1}, \ldots, x_{kih} \colon \Sigma z_{ki}, W)}$$

make-effect M_i hedonic part

There are thus two paths through which the make effect M_i comes into a hedonic equation: the markup ratio r_i and the cost function C_2, whose arguments are the left-out physical characteristics. Accordingly, we can differentiate between two kinds of make-effects: "real" and "putative."

A "real" make-effect is the consequence of unmeasured, left-out

---

[5] In the used car market, sellers as well as buyers are users of the automobile, not its producers. Hence, the cost function does not appear explicitly in this market. But the interpretation of the model effect in the new car market applies also to the used car market.

[6] Total output level $\sum_k z_{ki}$ and the input price index W are usually not included in hedonic regression equations. This is partly because the orthodox hedonic hypothesis tried to explain price solely by the physical characteristics of goods and partly because it did not pay much attention to the economic rationale underlying the hedonic regression equation. Ohta (1971) is an exception.

physical characteristics which enter the cost function, such as durability and body strength, and costly performance variables which are highly related to left-out physical characteristics, such as reliability (repair record), fuel economy, and so forth.[7] Since real model effects are based on physical characteristics, they will persist in the used car market and hence can be thought of as "permanent."

A "putative" make-effect is not based on physical characteristics and hence does not enter the per unit cost function of producing the good, though it may enter the utility function and the cost function (profit function) of sales. This effect does not come through the cost function C_2, whose arguments are left-out physical characteristics, but is reflected in the markup ratio r_i. Examples of this are prestige, reputation, and services availability. They are not "costless," but their cost does not depend closely on the current volume of output. Such effects may also persist in the used car market, though their durability may be lower than that of effects based on unmeasured physical characteristics.

The firm's pricing policy is based on the make-effect. If it is positive and large, then the price listed by the firm will be high relative to the level of the included physical characteristics. If the make-effect is negative, the price will be low relative to the level of the included physical characteristics. The firm will, however, sometimes overprice or underprice relative to its permanent make-effect. The overpricing or underpricing (i.e., the pricing error) will decrease or increase its market share in the new car market,[8] and will disappear (i.e., will not persist) in the used car market. This will also affect the observed depreciation rates in the used car market. A large transitory effect will result in a larger rate of depreciation. Hence the study of depreciation patterns is interrelated with the study of make-effects.

C. Major Questions

It is clear from our earlier discussion that our main interests center on (1) the study of make-effects, including a reexamination of

---

[7] As will be shown later, fuel economy is relatively well explained by the standard set of physical characteristics (horsepower, weight, length, V-8 or not, hardtop or not). But Gordon (1971) showed that the gas mileage of closely similar low-priced models increased from 14.2 in 1959 to 15.9 in 1970. This improvement in the gas mileage implies that fuel economy depends not only on the standard set of physical characteristics but also on unknown, left-out design characteristics.

[8] See Cowling and Raynor (1970), Cowling and Cubbin (1970) and Triplett and Cowling (1971) for work along these lines. The idea was suggested by Griliches (1961), p. 177.

Dhrymes's (1967) test of equality of imputed prices of physical characteristics across manufacturers and makes, (2) depreciation patterns, and (3) the role of performance variables. More specifically, we are interested in the following questions:

(1) Can we observe make-effects in the new car market and in the used car market? Do the effects observed in the new car market persist in the used car market?

(2) Do make-effects affect the depreciation pattern so that different makes depreciate differently? Or, do they depreciate at the same rate as physical characteristics?

(3) Do performance variables explain enough of the variation in prices to allow us to substitute them successfully for physical characteristics in a hedonic regression?

(4) Does the recognition of make-effects affect hedonic price index computations seriously? Are indexes based on performance variables very different from those based on physical characteristics?

(5) Are the imputed prices of physical characteristics constant across different makes and manufacturers? If this were not true, at least approximately, it would seriously undermine the hedonic hypothesis. Are the imputed prices of the characteristics the same in the used and new car markets? Differences could be caused by the differing tastes of consumers in the new and used car markets, by pricing errors in the new market, and/or by differential depreciation patterns of the various characteristics. Do the imputed prices of the characteristics shift over time? If they do, it would indicate either changing supply conditions or shifts in consumer tastes.

(6) Are depreciation rates of different physical characteristics the same? This is equivalent to the question of whether imputed prices of physical characteristics are the same across age at a given point in time and is similar to the question of whether technical progress is neutral.[9] Is depreciation exponential? Are the rates stable over time?

D. The Relationship among the Various Hypotheses

We have already mentioned some of the hypotheses that have to be assumed explicitly or implicitly to allow one to use the standard single-equation hedonic approach. This section tries to lay out and to organize the relationship among the various hypotheses, starting from the most general hedonic equation and then narrowing it down by imposing additional restrictions in as nested a form as possible. A

---

[9] This question was first raised by Griliches (1971) in commenting on Hall (1971).

pictorial representation in the form of a nested tree of hypotheses is given in Figure 1. Starting at the top, we have:

(1) The most general form of the hedonic hypothesis is the "two-stage hypothesis in general functional form and without any unmeasured performance variables and physical characteristics." Let P_{ts} be a price of a good of age s at time t. Let $s = 0$ mean that the good is new. Let $y = (y_1, y_2, \ldots, y_n)$ be its performance variables, and $x = (x_1, x_2, \ldots, x_m)$ be its physical characteristics when new. Then, the two-stage hypothesis can be written as follows, in general.

$$P_{ts} = h(y_1, \ldots, y_l, y_{l+1}, \ldots, y_n, s, t)$$

$$\left.\begin{cases} y_1 = f_1(x_1, \ldots, x_m, t) \\ \quad | \\ \quad | \\ \quad | \\ y_l = f_l(x_1, \ldots, x_m, t) \end{cases}\right\} \text{costly performance variables}$$

$y_{l+1}, \ldots, y_n$ no-cost performance variables

(2) The two-stage hypothesis can be reduced to a "one-stage hypothesis, using only physical characteristics without any unmeasured characteristics in a general functional form," if there are no no-cost performance variables. The one-stage hypothesis can be written as follows:

$$P_{ts} = g(x_1, \ldots, x_m, s, t)$$

The one-stage hedonic approach based on physical characteristics may result, however, in a biased hedonic price index if the transformation function f from x to y depends on time t.

(3) In order to reduce the general hedonic functional form g to the familiar semilogarithmic form and interpret it as something more than just a convenient approximation, one has to assume some hypotheses about utility and cost functions, such as the input-output separability of the production technology and the nonjointness of the physical characteristics as outputs in the cost function and in the utility function. In general, the functional form g of the hedonic hypothesis is determined simultaneously by the functional forms of the demand and the supply curves of the various characteristics.[10] The semilogarithmic

---

[10] Ohta (1971) studies the problem of specification of the functional forms for the hedonic hypothesis in some detail.

FIGURE 1

Nested Tree of the Hypotheses in the Hedonic Study

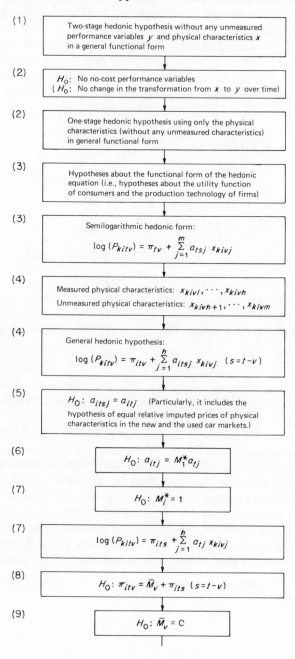

(1) Two-stage hedonic hypothesis without any unmeasured performance variables y and physical characteristics x in a general functional form

(2) H_0: No no-cost performance variables
(H_0: No change in the transformation from x to y over time)

(2) One-stage hedonic hypothesis using only the physical characteristics (without any unmeasured characteristics) in general functional form

(3) Hypotheses about the functional form of the hedonic equation (i.e., hypotheses about the utility function of consumers and the production technology of firms)

(3) Semilogarithmic hedonic form:
$$\log (P_{kitv}) = \pi_{tv} + \sum_{j=1}^{m} a_{tsj} \, x_{kivj}$$

(4) Measured physical characteristics: $x_{kivl}, \cdots, x_{kivh}$
Unmeasured physical characteristics: $x_{kivh+1}, \cdots, x_{kivm}$

(4) General hedonic hypothesis:
$$\log (P_{kitv}) = \pi_{itv} + \sum_{j=1}^{h} a_{itsj} \, x_{kivj} \quad (s=t-v)$$

(5) H_0: $a_{itsj} = a_{itj}$ (Particularly, it includes the hypothesis of equal relative imputed prices of physical characteristics in the new and the used car markets.)

(6) H_0: $a_{itj} = M_i^* a_{tj}$

(7) H_0: $M_i^* = 1$

(7) $$\log (P_{kitv}) = \pi_{its} + \sum_{j=1}^{h} a_{tj} \, x_{kivj}$$

(8) H_0: $\pi_{itv} = \bar{M}_v + \pi_{its} \quad (s=t-v)$

(9) H_0: $\bar{M}_v = C$

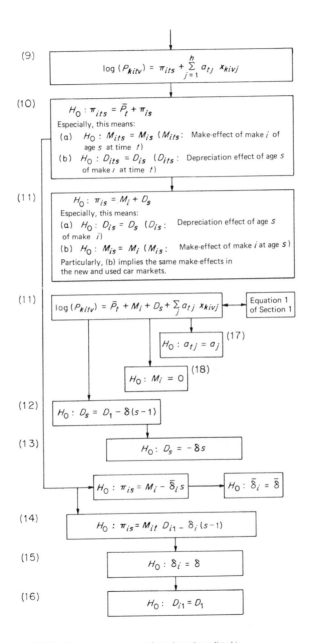

(9)

$$\log (P_{kitv}) = \pi_{its} + \sum_{j=1}^{h} a_{tj}\, x_{kivj}$$

(10)

$H_O : \pi_{its} = \bar{P}_t + \pi_{is}$

Especially, this means:

(a) $H_O : M_{its} = M_{is}$ (M_{its}: Make-effect of make i of age s at time t)

(b) $H_O : D_{its} = D_{is}$ (D_{its}: Depreciation effect of age s of make i at time t)

(11)

$H_O : \pi_{is} = M_i + D_s$

Especially, this means:

(a) $H_O : D_{is} = D_s$ (D_{is}: Depreciation effect of age s of make i)

(b) $H_O : M_{is} = M_i$ (M_{is}: Make-effect of make i at age s)

Particularly, (b) implies the same make-effects in the new and used car markets.

(11)

$$\log (P_{kitv}) = \bar{P}_t + M_i + D_s + \sum_{j} a_{tj}\, x_{kivj}$$

Equation 1 of Section 1

(17)

$H_O : a_{tj} = a_j$

(18)

$H_O : M_i = 0$

(12)

$H_O : D_s = D_1 - \delta (s-1)$

(13)

$H_O : D_s = -\delta s$

$H_O : \pi_{is} = M_i - \bar{\delta}_i s$

$H_O : \bar{\delta}_i = \bar{\delta}$

(14)

$H_O : \pi_{is} = M_{it}\, D_{i1} - \delta_i (s-1)$

(15)

$H_O : \delta_i = \delta$

(16)

$H_O : D_{i1} = D_1$

NOTE: The attached numbers refer to hypotheses listed in the text. Symbols also are defined in the text.

form can be written as follows, taking the automobile as an example

$$\log (P_{kitv}) = \pi_{tv} + \sum_{j=1}^{m} a_{tsj}x_{kivj} \qquad (s = t - v)$$

where P_{kitv} is the price of a car of model k of make i and vintage v at time t, and x_{kivj} is the jth physical characteristic of model k of make i and vintage v.

(4) When there are unmeasured physical characteristics (x_{kivh+1}, ..., x_{kivm}), the above semilogarithmic form can be rewritten as follows, using the earlier discussion of make-effects

$$\log (P_{kitv}) = \pi_{itv} + \sum_{j=1}^{h} a_{itsj}x_{kivj} \qquad (s = t - v)$$

where π_{itv} now also incorporates make effects.

(5) If the hypothesis of equal depreciation across the physical characteristics or, equivalently, the hypothesis of equal relative imputed prices of the physical characteristics (H_0: $a_{itsj} = a_{itj}$ for any s) holds, the semilogarithmic form simplifies to

$$\log (P_{kitv}) = \pi_{itv} + \sum_{j=1}^{h} a_{itj}x_{kivj}$$

This hypothesis includes as a particular case the hypothesis of equal relative imputed prices of physical characteristics in both the new and the used car markets.

(6) If the hypothesis of equal relative imputed prices of the physical characteristics across makes (H_0: $a_{itj} = M_i^* a_{tj}$) is satisfied, the equation simplifies further to

$$\log (P_{kitv}) = \pi_{itv} + M_i^* \sum_{j=1}^{h} a_{tj}x_{kivj}$$

(7) If the hypothesis of no multiplicative make-effects (H_0: $M_i^* = 1$) is satisfied, the equation reduces to:

$$\log (P_{kitv}) = \pi_{itv} + \sum_{j=1}^{h} a_{tj}x_{kivj}$$

(8) If the hypothesis of the separation of vintage-specific effects from make-time-age effects (H_0: $\pi_{itv} = \bar{M}_v + \pi_{its}$ where $s = t - v$) is satisfied, we have

$$\log (P_{kitv}) = \bar{M}_v + \pi_{its} + \sum_{j=1}^{h} a_{tj}x_{kivj}$$

(9) If the hypothesis of no vintage-specific effect (H_0: $\bar{M}_v = 0$) is satisfied, we can write the hedonic equation as follows

$$\log (P_{kitv}) = \pi_{its} + \sum_{j=1}^{h} a_{tj}x_{kivj}$$

(10) If the hypothesis of the separability of the pure (hedonic) price index $\bar{P}_t$ from the make-age effects π_{is} (H_0: $\pi_{its} = \bar{P}_t + \pi_{is}$) is satisfied, we can write it as

$$\log (P_{kitv}) = \bar{P}_t + \pi_{is} + \sum_{j=1}^{h} a_{tj}x_{kivj}$$

This hypothesis can be restated as the hypothesis of constancy of the make-age effects over time. It implies the following two specific hypotheses:

(a) The constancy of make effects over time (H_0: $M_{its} = M_{is}$ for any t, where M_{its} is the make-effect of make i at time t and age s).

(b) The constancy of age effects (depreciation pattern) over time (H_0: $D_{its} = D_{is}$ for any t, where D_{its} is the age effect of make i of age s at time t).

(11) If the hypothesis of the separability of make-effects from age effects (depreciation pattern) (H_0: $\pi_{is} = M_i + D_s$) is satisfied, the hedonic equation reduces to

$$\log (P_{kitv}) = \bar{P}_t + M_i + D_s + \sum_{j=1}^{h} a_{tj}x_{kivj}$$

which is the typical regression equation to be used in the empirical sections below. This hypothesis (H_0: $\pi_{is} = M_i + D_s$) implies the following two subcases:

(a) The depreciation pattern is equal across makes (H_0: $D_{is} = D_s$ for any i, where D_{is} is the age effect of age s of make i).

(b) Make-effects are constant across all ages (H_0: $M_{is} = M_i$ for any s, where M_{is} is the make-effect of make i at age s). It asserts, in particular, the same structure of make-effects in the new and the used car markets.

(12) If the hypothesis of geometric depreciation in the used car market (H_0: $D_s = D_1 - \delta(s - 1)$, where s denotes age) is satisfied, then the hedonic equation can be written as follows

$$\log (P_{kitv}) = \bar{P}_t + M_i + D_1 - \delta(s - 1) + \sum_{j=1}^{h} a_{tj}x_{kivj}$$

This hypothesis still allows the transition between "new" and "used" car status to occur at a rate different from the common geometric depreciation rate in the used car market.

(13) If the hypothesis of geometric depreciation is satisfied for all ages including the transition from "new" to "used" of age 1 (H_0: $D_s = -\delta s$), we have

$$\log (P_{kitv}) = \bar{P}_t + M_i - \delta s + \sum_{j=1}^{h} a_{tj} x_{kivj}$$

Now, returning to hypothesis (10):

(14) If the hypothesis of geometric depreciation holds separately for each make in the used car market (H_0: $\pi_{is} = M_i + D_{i1} - \delta_i(s - 1)$ for $s \geq 1$, where $M_i \equiv \pi_{i0}$), then the hedonic equation can be written as follows [11]

$$\log (P_{kitv}) = \bar{P}_t + M_i + D_{i1} - \delta_i(s - 1) + \sum_{j=1}^{h} a_{tj} x_{kivj}$$

(15) If the hypothesis of equal geometric depreciation rates for all makes in the used car market (H_0: $\delta_i = \delta$ for any i) is satisfied, the equation is

$$\log (P_{kitv}) = \bar{P}_t + M_i + D_{i1} - \delta(s - 1) + \sum_{j=1}^{h} a_{tj} x_{kivj}$$

(16) If the hypothesis of equal depreciation rate from "new" to the "used status of age 1" holds for all makes (H_0: $D_{i1} = D_1$ for any i), then the equation can be written as follows

$$\log (P_{kitv}) = \bar{P}_t + M_i + D_1 + \delta(s - 1) + \sum_{j=1}^{h} a_{tj} x_{hivj}$$

Now, returning to hypothesis (11):

(17) If the hypothesis of no change over time in the imputed prices of physical characteristics (H_0: $a_{tj} = a_j$ for any t) holds, then the hedonic equation is

$$\log (P_{kitv}) = \bar{P}_t + M_i + D_s + \sum_{j=1}^{h} a_j x_{kivj}$$

This would occur if there were no changes in supply conditions and in tastes, or if such changes cancel each other out.

---

[11] For the used car data, M_i and D_{i1} are perfectly collinear. M_i can be estimated, however, using the data on new car prices alone.

Return again to hypothesis (11):

(18) If the hypothesis of no make effects (H_0: $M_i = 0$ for all i) is satisfied, then the hedonic equation simplifies to

$$\log (P_{kitv}) = \bar{P}_t + D_s + \sum_{j=1}^{h} a_{tj} x_{kivj}$$

E. Criteria for Hypothesis Testing

Most of our hypotheses, such as the equality of imputed prices of physical characteristics across firms or years, can be tested using the standard F-test methodology. But such hypotheses are not the "truth." They are, at best, potentially useful approximations to it. The real world is, of course, much more complex. Having large samples and using standard tests, we are likely to reject most such simplifying hypotheses on purely statistical grounds, even though they may still serve as adequate approximations for our purposes.

The rejection or acceptance of a hypothesis should depend on the researcher's interests and his loss function.[12] If the researcher is interested in predicting price differentials, then he should be interested in the difference in fit between the unconstrained and constrained regressions. He should compare the standard errors of both regressions instead of following formal F tests and not reject the simpler hypothesis unless they are very different.

Since our hedonic regressions are semilogarithmic, the standard errors of the regressions measure the unexplained variation in prices in, roughly, percentage units. It is reasonable, therefore, to use the difference in the standard errors of the unconstrained and constrained regressions as a relevant measure of the price-explanatory power of a particular model. The standard errors of our regressions are about 0.1. Consider a difference in the standard errors of the constrained and unconstrained regressions of 0.01. It implies that: (i) the lack of fit of the constrained regression is increased by 10 per cent compared with that of the unconstrained regression ($0.01/0.1 = 0.1$). (ii) The fit to actual price data is smaller by 1 per cent in the constrained regression than in the unconstrained regression. This seems to us to be a just noticeable difference in our own measure of economic significance. We shall, therefore, not reject null hypotheses if differences between the standard errors of the unconstrained and the constrained regressions are less than or equal to 0.01. We will, however, list also the results of the formal F tests for the benefit of interested readers.

[12] See Arrow (1960) for an exposition of the difference between statistical (classical Neyman-Pearson) and economic significance (decision theoretic) tests, and Lindley (1963) and Leamer (1973) for a more recent exposition of this viewpoint from a Bayesian perspective.

III. SAMPLE, SOURCES, AND DEFINITIONS

Our sample consists of U.S. domestic four-door sedans and four-door hardtops of thirteen makes from the model years 1955 through 1971.[13] The thirteen makes are (1) American Motors, (2) Buick, (3) Cadillac, (4) Chevrolet, (5) Chrysler, (6) Dodge, (7) Ford, (8) Imperial, (9) Lincoln, (10) Mercury, (11) Oldsmobile, (12) Plymouth, and (13) Pontiac.[14]

We did not attempt to collect as many models as possible in each year as had been done in previous studies. Instead, we tried to keep the size and composition of the sample across makes representative and constant over time. We tried to keep the number of models in each make constant over time to avoid introducing shifts into our hedonic price indexes due to changes in the sample distribution across makes. Also, repeated observations on models with very similar physical characteristics increase computational costs without providing much additional information. We tried to get about 4 models per make on average (thus, about 52 models in each year), choosing models with high sales and as variable physical characteristics as possible. We chose high-sales models because they represent the automobile market better and also because these same models are included in our sample of used cars, and high sales provide some assurance of quality of data in the secondhand market. We tried to choose models whose production was above 10,000 units per year on the average.[15] Makes that have high sales and many models are represented by many models in our sample. The distribution of our sample across makes and the total sales of all included models are given in Table 1. Because of the proliferation of models, our sample increases slightly over time. It was difficult to obtain 4 models per make with significant variation in characteristics in the earlier years (especially 1955).

A major problem in such studies is the treatment of optional equip-

[13] We shall concentrate below on analyzing the 1961–1971 period. However, because 1955 to 1960 models appear in our used car prices analyses for 1961 and subsequent years, we also collected new price data for those years and included them in some of our analyses of new car prices.

[14] These are the major domestic makes. They are produced by the following four companies: American Motors Corporation (American Motors), Chrysler Corporation (Chrysler, Imperial, Dodge, and Plymouth), Ford Motor Company (Ford, Lincoln, and Mercury), and General Motors Corporation (Buick, Cadillac, Chevrolet, Oldsmobile, and Pontiac).

[15] *Ward's* provides detailed production data. In deciding on the particular model to include, we also paid attention to relative sales by engine type (6 cylinder or V-8). For example, Fury III had a large production for the V-8 model, but only a few 6-cylinder units were sold.

TABLE 1

Part 1: The Distribution and Average Sales per Sample Model

Vintage Year	1955	1956	1957	1958	1959	1960	1961	1962	1963
Number of observations	30	45	47	48	47	50	51	52	52
Number of observations for:									
$M1$	1	2	4	4	4	4	4	4	4
$M2$	6	5	6	6	6	6	6	6	6
$M3$	2	2	2	2	2	2	2	2	2
$M4$	2	4	4	4	4	5	5	6	6
$M5$	2	4	4	4	4	4	4	4	4
$M6$	3	5	5	5	5	5	5	5	5
$M7$	2	5	5	5	4	6	6	6	6
$M8$	1	1	1	1	1	1	1	1	1
$M9$	1	1	1	1	1	1	1	1	1
$M10$	2	3	3	3	3	3	3	3	3
$M11$	4	5	4	5	5	5	5	5	5
$M12$	2	4	4	4	4	4	4	4	4
$M13$	2	4	4	4	4	4	5	5	4
Average sales per sample model	212,320	123,629	117,601	83,191	82,011	93,019	83,966	102,070	110,343

(continued)

341

TABLE 1 (concluded)

Vintage Year	1964	1965	1966	1967	1968	1969	1970	1971	1955–1971
Number of observations	52	56	56	56	56	56	56	55	865
Number of observations for:									
M1	3	4	4	4	4	4	4	4	62
M2	6	6	6	6	6	6	6	6	101
M3	2	3	3	3	3	3	3	2	40
M4	6	6	6	6	6	6	6	6	88
M5	4	4	4	4	4	4	4	4	66
M6	6	6	6	6	6	6	6	6	91
M7	6	6	6	6	6	6	6	6	93
M8	1	1	1	1	1	1	1	1	17
M9	1	1	1	1	1	1	1	1	17
M10	3	3	3	3	3	3	3	3	50
M11	5	5	5	5	5	5	5	5	83
M12	4	5	5	5	5	5	5	5	73
M13	5	6	6	6	6	6	6	6	84
Average sales per sample model	105,164	110,517	104,808	94,400	105,497	105,690	86,706	96,625	–

Part 2: The Distribution of the Used Car Sample over Years and Makes

Year	1961	1962	1963	1964	1965	1966	1967	1968	1969	1970	1971	1961–1971
Number of observations	267	288	295	300	304	313	319	324	328	332	336	3,406
Number of observations for:												
$M1$	19	22	24	24	23	23	23	23	23	23	24	251
$M2$	35	35	36	36	36	36	36	36	36	36	36	394
$M3$	12	12	12	12	12	13	14	15	16	17	18	153
$M4$	23	26	28	30	32	34	35	36	36	36	36	352
$M5$	22	24	24	24	24	24	24	24	24	24	24	262
$M6$	28	30	30	30	31	32	33	34	35	36	36	355
$M7$	27	31	32	33	34	36	36	36	36	36	36	373
$M8$	6	6	6	6	6	6	6	6	6	6	6	66
$M9$	6	6	6	6	6	6	6	6	6	6	6	66
$M10$	17	18	18	18	18	18	18	18	18	18	18	197
$M11$	28	29	29	30	30	30	30	30	30	30	30	326
$M12$	22	24	24	24	24	25	26	27	28	29	30	283
$M13$	22	25	26	27	28	30	32	33	34	35	36	328
Vintage	1955–1960	1956–1961	1957–1962	1958–1963	1959–1964	1960–1965	1961–1966	1962–1967	1963–1968	1964–1969	1965–1970	1955–1970

NOTE: See the "Notes to Tables" at the end of this paper for the definition of M.

343

ment such as power steering, air conditioning, and other attachments. While the main "body" of the car is well specified, much less information is available on such options, their prices, and the changes in their use.[16] We experimented at length with various treatments of optional equipment but there was no clear outcome. On the whole, the results were not very sensitive to the particular choice. Since they are described in detail in our larger manuscript, we shall not go into it here. In what follows, we shall use two price concepts interchangeably, though there is a clear conceptual difference between them. The first (PAA) includes the price of automatic transmission and power steering on all cars, while the second (PA) treats power steering as a "cost of weight and size" and includes it only on those cars where such equipment is "standard" and hence deemed to be required for adequate performance. Power brakes are treated as a cost of weight and included only on those models where they are standard equipment (this is true for both PA and PAA). Air conditioning is not included, heaters are included where the price information was available, and radios are included in used car prices and in new car prices when the latter are compared to used car prices.

List prices of new cars and used car prices are taken from the National Automobile Dealers Association (NADA) *Used Car Guide* (Central Edition), April issues (May in 1961), and were checked against the new car prices listed in the *Automotive News Almanac*. For the used cars part of our study, we did not use the data on cars that were less than a year old or more than 6 years old. Seven year old and older cars are not commonly traded in the organized part of the used car market and hence the quality of the data listed in the *Used Car Guide* for these cars is quite poor. Similarly, the market in cars less than a year old is also quite thin and the information base is not as firm as we would like it to be. Thus, for example, our sample in 1967 contains the list prices for the 1967 models and the used prices in April 1967 of the 1966, 1965, 1964, 1963, 1962, and 1961 vintage models.

We use the following standard set of physical characteristics which have been used with some success in previous hedonic studies:

(1) Shipping weight of the car in pounds (W)
(2) Overall length of the car in inches (L)
(3) Maximum brake horsepower in horsepower units (H)

---

[16] See Griliches (1961), Triplett (1966), and Dewees (1971). The issue is discussed at great length in Ohta and Griliches (1972).

(4) Dummy for body type (*HT*)

$$HT = \begin{cases} 1 \text{ for the hardtop} \\ 0 \text{ for the sedan} \end{cases}$$

(5) Dummy for the number of cylinders (*V*)

$$V = \begin{cases} 1 \text{ for V-8} \\ 0 \text{ for the 6-cylinder engine} \end{cases}$$

The data on these physical characteristics are taken from the *Used Car Guide*.[17] They were checked against data listed in *Ward's* and *Automotive Industries* (March issue). The source and choice of performance characteristics will be discussed later, in Section V.

Several notes of warning should be sounded at this point. The treatment of optional equipment is somewhat arbitrary, but that doesn't seem to affect the results significantly. New car prices are "list" prices, not transaction prices. There may be differential discounting practices by makes which need not be stable over time. Used car prices are closer to the "transaction" concept, but the provenance and quality of these data are clouded by a lack of clear description of the methods used in collecting and editing them. Toward the end of the period, prices are affected by changes in excise taxes and new requirements for safety and antipollution equipment. All of this makes comparisons with published official price indexes difficult, a topic which we shall come back to below.

IV. RESULTS BASED ON PHYSICAL CHARACTERISTICS

A. New Cars

We shall skip over several important side issues and concentrate our analysis on make-effects and depreciation patterns. We did also experiment, however, with different functional forms, different definitions of the dependent variable, and different weighting schemes. As to functional form, we quickly settled on the semilogarithmic form for reasons of ease of comparison with earlier studies and somewhat better fit. Also, the choice of functional form was not the main focus of our inquiry. We did experiment at length with different treatments of optional equipment and, hence, different concepts of price but found little empirical evidence for preferring one treatment to another. Because of our careful choice of sample models to represent their dis-

---

[17] The specific months of the *Guide* are the same as for the list price of the car stated before.

tribution in the total car market as closely as possible, it turned out that weighting by the square root of model sales leads to essentially the same results as the analysis of the unweighted but self-weighting samples. Hence, we report here only the latter results.[18]

Table 2 lists the results of adjacent year regressions for selected pairs of years between 1955 and 1971 and provides a representative sample of the results of our more extensive analysis of new car prices. They are similar to the Griliches (1961, 1964), Triplett (1966), and Dewees (1970) results for earlier years, except that including make-effects reduces somewhat the size of the weight coefficient, while at the same time increasing the size and statistical significance of both horsepower and length in such regressions. Make-effects are statistically and economically significant, their inclusion reducing the standard errors of the regressions from about .08 to .04. While there is quite a bit of instability in the coefficients of the primary physical characteristics (H, W, and L), there is no clear trend in these coefficients and the instability appears to be the result of multicollinearity between H and W and sampling fluctuation.

A formal statistical test of the constancy of the coefficients of the physical characteristics over time, utilizing pair-wise comparisons of 1962 and 1967 and 1961 and 1971, does not reject the null hypothesis at the 5 per cent significance levels (the computed F statistics are each approximately 2.3) and the standard errors of the constrained regressions are not increased by more than .004. We can, therefore, maintain the hypothesis that the coefficients (implicit price schedules) of physical characteristics did not change significantly between 1961 and 1971. It implies largely neutral shifts in supply conditions of these characteristics and the cancelling out of changes in consumer tastes, if any.

Dhrymes (1967) claimed that imputed prices of physical characteristics are significantly different among companies and concluded from his evidence that the valuation of physical characteristics is not based on consumers' preferences but rather on different markup pricing policies of different firms. We can introduce firm dummies (both in additive and in multiplicative form) to test the null hypothesis that relative imputed prices of physical characteristics are the same among companies.[19] Weighted regression should be used to reflect

---

[18] See Ohta and Griliches (1972) for more details on these and other issues.

[19] Given our emphasis on make-effects, we should also have tested the null hypotheses that imputed prices are the same across makes rather than just across companies. We did not do it because of the limitation of the computer program RAPFE, which was used for the analysis of the new car market.

the valuation of these characteristics by consumers in the new car market. The firms are American Motors, Chrysler, Ford, and General Motors. The value of the F statistic for the null hypothesis that imputed prices are the same across companies is 1.81 for 1955–1958 and 1.82 for 1959–1962.[20] Both values are only slightly larger than the critical $F_{.05}$ of about 1.75 but smaller than the critical $F_{.01}$ of about 2.20. Allowing also for multiplicative firm effects would only reduce the values of these test statistics further, because it would allow more degrees of freedom to the constrained regression. Moreover, the difference in the standard errors between the constrained and the unconstrained regressions does not exceed .003. It is reasonable, therefore, to consider the null hypothesis as not rejected.

Table 2 also lists the estimated make-effects with American Motors as the base. It appears that from about 1960 on, the estimated make-effects are reasonably constant, but that is not true for the pre-1960 period. This could be due to the smaller and poorer sample in those years and to the changing position of American Motors (which was used as a base) during those years. To get around the latter problem, we present in Table 3 rescaled make coefficients for selected years, with the major make, Chevrolet, as the base of comparison. These coefficients do not tell a very different story, indicating stability in the post-1960 period. Pair-wise tests of equality of make coefficients in 1962 and 1967, and in 1961 and 1971, do not reject the null hypothesis even at the .05 level, the standard error of the constrained regressions rising by less than .002. In discussing make effects we will, therefore, treat the whole 1961–1971 period as one unit.

Significant positive make-effects (compared to Chevrolet) are indicated in Table 3 for Cadillac, Imperial, and Lincoln in the post-1960 period. The make-effect of Plymouth appears to be negative throughout. The other make-effects were not consistent and/or significantly different from the Chevrolet level.

The Cadillac, Lincoln, and Imperial effects are roughly of comparable size (with Imperial having the smallest of the three effects), indicating an "overpricing" of about 35 per cent relative to Chevrolet (and other makes).[21] This is surprisingly large (about $1,500 in a $6,000 car). It appears that the hedonic approach, using the standard set of

---

[20] The results of tests allowing the imputed prices of the physical characteristics to vary over the different companies is reported only for 1955–1958 and 1959–1962. For other periods, the unconstrained regressions suffered from almost perfect multicollinearity.

[21] The median effect of these makes appears to be on the order of .3. Exp $(.3) - 1 = .35$ and $1/1.35 = .74$.

TABLE 2

Adjacent-Year Regression with Make Dummies: Selected Years
(*PAA* as the price variable)

	1955–57	1958–59	1960–61	1962–63	1964–65	1966–67	1968–69	1970–71
H^*	0.023	0.049	0.138	0.111	0.116	0.069	0.085	0.072
	(0.96)	(1.89)	(7.12)	(6.23)	(5.95)	(4.34)	(5.99)	(3.96)
W^*	0.437	0.345	0.034	0.006	0.102	0.172	0.142	0.217
	(10.25)	(4.51)	(0.78)	(0.16)	(2.88)	(3.86)	(3.14)	(5.74)
L^*	0.050	0.072	0.040	0.049	0.021	0.007	0.022	0.015
	(3.51)	(2.71)	(2.27)	(3.85)	(1.64)	(0.50)	(1.55)	(1.19)
V	0.020	−0.006	−0.004	0.026	−0.010	0.002	−0.001	−0.014
	(1.15)	(−0.25)	(−0.25)	(1.86)	(−0.63)	(0.15)	(−0.09)	(−0.77)
HT	0.045	0.031	0.033	0.050	0.022	0.028	0.033	0.027
	(5.16)	(2.86)	(3.10)	(5.06)	(2.11)	(2.78)	(3.77)	(2.33)
$M2$	−0.309	−0.288	0.029	0.038	0.019	0.069	0.035	0.023
	(−8.53)	(−5.49)	(1.14)	(1.69)	(0.78)	(3.08)	(1.88)	(1.02)
$M3$	−0.158	−0.050	0.424	0.451	0.345	0.381	0.320	0.261
	(−3.00)	(−0.66)	(12.54)	(15.97)	(11.27)	(12.96)	(11.79)	(7.50)
$M4$	−0.124	−0.133	0.051	0.000	0.004	0.045	0.006	−0.032
	(−5.62)	(−3.38)	(1.81)	(0.01)	(0.18)	(2.24)	(0.35)	(−1.54)
$M5$	−0.230	−0.099	0.061	−0.003	−0.012	0.086	0.065	−0.005
	(−5.67)	(−2.14)	(1.76)	(−0.12)	(−0.46)	(3.34)	(2.76)	(−0.17)
$M6$	−0.184	−0.127	−0.005	−0.063	−0.054	0.011	0.026	−0.031
	(−5.93)	(−2.78)	(−0.16)	(−2.33)	(−2.39)	(0.51)	(1.20)	(−1.45)

348

M7	-0.167	-0.117	0.015	-0.024	-0.002	0.049	0.027	-0.029
	(-7.27)	(-3.58)	(0.56)	(-1.02)	(-0.09)	(2.44)	(1.53)	(-1.40)
M8	-0.077	-0.075	0.324	0.303	0.250	0.305	0.286	0.189
	(-1.19)	(-1.00)	(7.79)	(8.65)	(6.26)	(7.36)	(8.72)	(4.56)
M9	-0.117	-0.038	0.567	0.554	0.411	0.306	0.290	0.242
	(-2.31)	(-0.45)	(12.19)	(13.73)	(8.87)	(5.84)	(6.69)	(5.27)
M10	-0.188	-0.275	0.004	-0.027	-0.022	0.028	0.013	-0.029
	(-5.97)	(-5.79)	(0.12)	(-0.98)	(-0.82)	(1.06)	(0.56)	(-1.12)
M11	-0.243	-0.218	0.055	0.026	-0.028	0.040	0.029	0.005
	(-7.01)	(-4.74)	(2.11)	(1.10)	(-1.11)	(1.77)	(1.49)	(0.21)
M12	-0.170	-0.090	-0.014	-0.082	-0.040	0.014	0.024	-0.034
	(-6.78)	(-2.53)	(-0.50)	(-3.12)	(-1.77)	(0.69)	(1.24)	(-1.61)
M13	-0.179	-0.180	0.050	0.012	-0.021	-0.006	-0.028	-0.043
	(-5.77)	(-4.14)	(1.77)	(0.49)	(-0.84)	(-0.26)	(-1.51)	(-1.92)
T_1	5.436	5.253	6.727	6.748	7.013	7.072	6.902	6.884
	(26.27)	(13.99)	(29.80)	(43.16)	(41.96)	(37.61)	(41.93)	(40.20)
T_2	5.453	5.246	6.744	6.737	6.988	7.089	6.913	6.942
	(26.20)	(13.77)	(30.02)	(42.66)	(41.73)	(37.46)	(41.85)	(40.80)
T_3	5.459	—	—	—	—	—	—	—
	(26.04)							
SSR	0.1676	0.1794	0.1652	0.1182	0.1357	0.1499	0.1064	0.1748
SEE	0.041	0.049	0.045	0.037	0.039	0.040	0.034	0.044
R^2	0.978	0.964	0.975	0.983	0.978	0.976	0.982	0.974

NOTE: In the above table, T_1, T_2, and T_3 stand for the year dummies in the order of time lapse. That is, T_1 is earlier than T_2. See the text and the "Notes to Tables" given at the end of this paper for definitions of the various symbols. Figures in parentheses are estimated t ratios.

TABLE 3

Make-Effects in the New Car Market with Respect to Chevrolet:
Selected Years

Make	1955–57	1960–61	1965–66	1970–71
American Motors	.124	−.051	−.024	.032
	(5.62)	(−1.81)	(−1.10)	(1.54)
Buick	−.185	−.022	.026	.055
	(−6.45)	(−.87)	(1.22)	(2.87)
Cadillac	−.035	.373	.325	.293
	(−.77)	(10.30)	(11.09)	(9.50)
Chrysler	−.107	.010	.004	.028
	(−3.28)	(.34)	(.16)	(1.18)
Dodge	−.060	−.055	−.049	.001
	(−2.47)	(−2.38)	(−2.68)	(.07)
Ford	−.043	−.035	−.000	.004
	(−2.39)	(−1.82)	(−.01)	(.19)
Imperial	.046	.273	.242	.222
	(.81)	(6.53)	(5.58)	(5.88)
Lincoln	.007	.517	.307	.274
	(.15)	(9.88)	(5.55)	(6.43)
Mercury	−.064	−.047	−.021	.003
	(−2.59)	(−1.90)	(−.84)	(.12)
Oldsmobile	−.119	.005	−.017	.037
	(−4.39)	(.19)	(−.69)	(1.91)
Plymouth	−.046	−.065	−.032	−.002
	(−2.34)	(−2.84)	(−1.73)	(−.08)
Pontiac	−.055	−.001	−0.29	−.010
	(−2.25)	(−.04)	(−1.36)	(−.54)

NOTE: PAA as the price; unweighted regression. The values in parentheses are t statistics.

physical characteristics, fails to explain about a quarter of the price of high-priced cars. This conclusion is robust with respect to the different treatments of optional equipment and the use or nonuse of weights in the estimation procedure.

Since only Cadillac, Imperial, and Lincoln have very significant and consistently large make-effects, and since these three makes are at the upper range of the physical characteristics, the observed make-effects may merely reflect additional nonlinearity in the effect of physical characteristics on price. To check on this, we included the squares of horsepower and weight in a regression for the combined 1967–1971 period. Although the estimated coefficient of the square of weight was significantly positive at the 1 per cent level, the make-effects of Cadillac, Imperial, and Lincoln changed only slightly and were still statistically significant and large (.27, .21, and .21 respectively). They do not appear, thus, to be caused solely by additional nonlinearities in the effect of physical characteristics on price.

Since the thirteen makes are produced by only four firms (American Motors, Chrysler, Ford, and General Motors), make-effects could be merely a reflection of firm effects at a more disaggregated level. Because firm dummies are sums of make dummies, we can easily test the null hypothesis that make dummies can be aggregated into firm dummies. To reduce the number of observations so that the null hypothesis is not rejected solely because of a large sample, we used the 1957–1958 and 1961–1962 regressions. The values of the test statistics for this hypothesis was 10 for 1957–1958 and 31 for 1961–1962. Since $F_{.01}(9, 76) = 2.7$, the null hypothesis is strongly rejected.

Makes which had large, positive, and significant effects (Cadillac, Imperial, Lincoln) did not lose their market position over time. Neither did Buick, Chrysler, and Oldsmobile, which had slightly positive make-effects during the same period. These effects are not pricing errors. They have lasted in the new car market, and we expect them also to persist in the used car market. Such make-effects should be subtracted from hedonic regression residuals before they are used to explain changes in market shares and should be allowed for in the construction of hedonic price indexes.

B. Used Car Prices

A major additional source of data on prices is the used car market. If we extend the hedonic hypothesis across the new and used markets, we gain a great deal of additional information. In particular, we can observe, in effect, today's and yesterday's models being sold concurrently. "Except" for aging effects, much of the problem of measuring quality change over time disappears when we have repeated observations on the price of a particular vintage. To measure quality change we have to assume that aging effects (depreciation patterns) are separable from the characteristics levels and are stable over time and make. These are testable hypotheses. Because depreciation patterns are also of some intrinsic interest, they form the second major focus of our study.

TABLE 4

Used Car Prices (log PAA): Pooled Regression with Constant
Imputed Prices of Physical Characteristics and Constant
Coefficients of Age and Make Dummies over 1961–1971

Variable		Estimated Coefficient	t Statistic
Constant		6.9662	232.01
1962		0.0235	1.80
1963		0.1430	10.95
1964		0.1449	11.13
1965		0.1465	11.27
1966		0.0959	7.40
1967		0.1087	8.38
1968		0.1153	8.88
1969		0.1436	11.07
1970		0.1244	9.58
1971		0.2511	19.37
Age 2		−0.2369	−26.37
Age 3		−0.5004	−55.47
Age 4		−0.7758	−85.55
Age 5		−1.0857	−118.71
Age 6		−1.4417	−154.72
Buick	($M2$)	0.1933	13.78
Cadillac	($M3$)	0.6449	32.27
Chevrolet	($M4$)	0.1885	13.96
Chrysler	($M5$)	0.1490	9.74
Dodge	($M6$)	0.0231	1.77
Ford	($M7$)	0.0457	3.44
Imperial	($M8$)	0.3625	14.47
Lincoln	($M9$)	0.4776	18.24
Mercury	($M10$)	0.0142	0.91
Oldsmobile	($M11$)	0.1815	12.67
Plymouth	($M12$)	−0.0092	−0.68
Pontiac	($M13$)	0.1619	11.65
H^*		0.0510	5.19
W^*		0.0838	7.27
L^*		0.0	0.0
V		0.1155	11.59
HT		0.0831	13.15
SSR		80.0625	
SEE		0.160	
R^2		0.9259	
Number of observations		3,406	
Number of parameters		33	

NOTE: See "Notes to Tables" at the end of this paper for definitions of the various symbols.

352

Our analysis of the used car market is based on unweighted, semi-logarithmic regression equations. Table 4 provides an overview of the results, constraining all of the coefficients, except the time dummies, to be constant during the 1961–1971 period. Weight, horsepower, and the dummy variables for hardtop (*HT*) and V-8 (*V*) engine have nonnegative and statistically significant estimated coefficients. The estimated coefficient of length is practically zero. Table 5 presents more detailed adjacent-years regression results, allowing all of the coefficients to change over time. There is quite a bit of instability in the estimated coefficients, primarily in the rise of the horsepower coefficient relative to the weight and length coefficients, and in the decline, in recent years, in the age coefficients for the older cars in the sample. Relative to the new car price results, tabulated in Table 2, the main differences are in the lower estimate of the effect of weight and in the higher estimated effect of having a V-8 engine on prices in the used car market. The fit is significantly improved by letting some of the coefficients change over time (the SEE falls from about .16 to .10), but the improvement comes largely from allowing the age coefficients to change over time. The fluctuations in the coefficients of the physical characteristics appear to be due largely to multicollinearity, and constraining them alone to be constant over time is not very costly in terms of the overall fit of the estimated relation. Pair-wise tests of the hypothesis of constancy of the physical characteristics coefficients over time for the years 1962 and 1967, and for 1961 and 1971, yielded conflicting results. The hypothesis is not rejected for the first comparison [F = 0.95, critical $F_{.05}(5, 590) \simeq 2.2$] but is rejected for the second (estimated F = 2.4) comparison (1961 and 1971). The latter results may be due to too large a sample (N = 603), the standard error in the constrained regression rising only by .004. It appears that the imputed prices of physical characteristics did not on the whole change much or consistently over time.

The hedonic hypothesis assumes the existence of markets for "imaginary" physical characteristics, with physical characteristics of various models of different ages having the same relative prices. We test the null hypothesis that relative imputed price schedules of physical characteristics are the same across all ages and that the effect of aging is incorporated only in the age dummies. This hypothesis of independence of imputed prices from age is equivalent to the null hypothesis of equal depreciation patterns for the different physical characteristics. We test it separately for 1965 and 1971. The unconstrained regression is

TABLE 5

Used Car Prices (log PAA): Adjacent-Year Regressions with Make Dummies

	1961-63	1963-64	1964-65	1965-66	1966-67	1967-68	1968-69	1969-70	1970-71
H^*	0.062	0.077	0.076	0.029	0.030	0.061	0.093	0.131	0.140
	(4.93)	(4.59)	(4.30)	(1.79)	(1.95)	(5.01)	(5.21)	(6.81)	(9.51)
W^*	0.052	-0.028	0.028	0.153	0.123	0.065	0.060	0.001	-0.013
	(1.90)	(-0.81)	(0.82)	(5.01)	(4.39)	(2.73)	(1.60)	(0.03)	(-0.37)
L^*	0.024	0.050	0.046	0.017	0.027	0.029	-0.006	-0.021	-0.026
	(2.26)	(3.63)	(3.37)	(1.44)	(2.54)	(3.19)	(-0.40)	(-1.40)	(-2.18)
V	0.075	0.089	0.089	0.109	0.123	0.115	0.112	0.119	0.098
	(5.74)	(5.27)	(5.25)	(7.30)	(9.13)	(10.39)	(6.74)	(6.59)	(6.85)
HT	0.091	0.100	0.106	0.099	0.086	0.073	0.061	0.057	0.061
	(12.73)	(10.45)	(10.38)	(10.31)	(9.32)	(9.49)	(5.35)	(4.71)	(6.46)
$Age\ 2$	-0.2625	-0.2629	-0.2528	-0.2432	-0.2254	-0.2206	-0.2314	-0.2398	-0.2426
	(-23.69)	(-18.24)	(-17.07)	(-18.35)	(-18.57)	(-22.03)	(-15.54)	(-15.10)	(-19.38)
$Age\ 3$	-0.5392	-0.5145	-0.5202	-0.5047	-0.4802	-0.4713	-0.4830	-0.4972	-0.5001
	(-47.70)	(-34.91)	(-34.52)	(-37.49)	(-38.93)	(-46.46)	(-32.22)	(-31.18)	(-39.89)
$Age\ 4$	-0.8304	-0.7650	-0.8057	-0.8063	-0.7625	-0.7414	-0.7419	-0.7427	-0.7566
	(-73.27)	(-50.26)	(-52.52)	(-58.67)	(-60.65)	(-71.64)	(-48.73)	(-46.16)	(-60.12)
$Age\ 5$	-1.1911	-1.1237	-1.0928	-1.1463	-1.1049	-1.0321	-1.0329	-1.0194	-1.0159
	(-105.59)	(-73.28)	(-70.10)	(-82.35)	(-85.93)	(-97.21)	(-66.25)	(-62.29)	(-80.17)
$Age\ 6$	-1.5195	-1.5581	-1.5887	-1.5211	-1.4711	-1.3747	-1.3460	-1.3423	-1.3245
	(-127.48)	(-102.04)	(-101.32)	(-108.73)	(-113.08)	(-126.00)	(-83.67)	(-79.89)	(-102.75)
$M2$	0.012	0.100	0.202	0.263	0.181	0.113	0.160	0.225	0.241
	(0.60)	(4.26)	(8.31)	(11.65)	(8.62)	(6.47)	(6.12)	(8.16)	(11.43)
$M3$	0.578	0.632	0.640	0.650	0.599	0.545	0.577	0.633	0.603
	(21.47)	(19.25)	(19.25)	(21.90)	(22.15)	(24.53)	(17.40)	(17.69)	(21.39)

354

M4	0.129	0.143	0.206	0.205	0.150	0.088	0.193	0.204	0.193
	(6.87)	(5.69)	(7.96)	(9.02)	(6.35)	(5.32)	(5.75)	(8.12)	(10.04)
M5	0.047	0.042	0.080	0.155	0.111	0.057	0.102	0.136	0.135
	(2.07)	(1.42)	(2.63)	(5.67)	(4.49)	(2.83)	(3.48)	(4.36)	(5.59)
M6	−0.080	−0.133	−0.086	0.005	−0.018	−0.037	−0.001	0.051	0.084
	(−3.83)	(−4.91)	(−3.04)	(0.20)	(−0.81)	(−2.12)	(−0.05)	(1.89)	(4.08)
M7	−0.018	−0.042	0.014	0.042	−0.004	−0.027	0.014	0.051	0.057
	(−0.97)	(−1.70)	(−.56)	(1.82)	(−0.18)	(−1.62)	(0.59)	(2.01)	(2.98)
M8	0.331	0.304	0.331	0.334	0.277	0.266	0.292	0.309	0.280
	(10.36)	(7.72)	(8.22)	(9.14)	(8.13)	(9.33)	(6.77)	(6.56)	(7.57)
M9	0.351	0.498	0.552	0.537	0.522	0.472	0.399	0.417	0.403
	(10.93)	(11.96)	(12.63)	(13.33)	(13.66)	(14.48)	(7.93)	(7.51)	(9.33)
M10	−0.091	−0.097	−0.043	0.032	−0.001	−0.055	−0.031	0.022	0.050
	(−4.41)	(−3.53)	(−1.49)	(1.22)	(−0.03)	(−2.71)	(−1.04)	(0.70)	(2.01)
M11	0.093	0.108	0.175	0.243	0.155	0.076	0.090	0.119	0.155
	(4.83)	(4.46)	(6.86)	(10.34)	(7.08)	(4.22)	(3.37)	(4.22)	(7.20)
M12	−0.126	−0.150	−0.100	−0.016	−0.026	−0.050	−0.014	0.031	0.043
	(−6.50)	(−5.86)	(−3.71)	(−0.65)	(−1.20)	(−2.86)	(−0.55)	(1.18)	(2.17)
M13	0.102	0.098	0.161	0.225	0.134	0.064	0.111	0.138	0.097
	(5.08)	(3.77)	(5.98)	(9.26)	(6.02)	(3.52)	(4.16)	(4.92)	(4.52)
Constant	6.737	6.548	6.364	6.557	6.422	6.571	7.205	7.638	7.753
	(46.84)	(36.19)	(35.11)	(41.35)	(44.60)	(54.90)	(39.76)	(38.66)	(50.26)
YD_1	0.003	−0.001	0.002	−0.046	0.015	0.004	0.027	−0.019	0.127
	(0.42)	(−0.08)	(0.22)	(−5.90)	(2.10)	(0.70)	(3.11)	(−2.10)	(17.57)
YD_2	0.122	—	—	—	—	—	—	—	—
	(14.96)								
SSR	7.460	6.074	6.523	5.481	4.912	3.452	7.768	8.966	5.637
SEE	0.095	0.103	0.106	0.096	0.090	0.075	0.111	0.119	0.094
R^2	0.973	0.968	0.968	0.974	0.978	0.983	0.960	0.952	0.969

NOTE: See "Notes to Tables" at the end of this paper for definitions of the various symbols. Figures in parentheses are estimated t ratios.

355

$$\log (\text{Price}) = \text{Const.} + \sum_{i=2}^{6} d_i A_i + \sum_{i=1}^{6} \sum_{j=1}^{5} a_{ij} x_{ij} + u$$

where $x_{ij} = x_j$ if the sample model is of age i and 0 otherwise (see above for the rest of the notation). The constrained regression is:

$$\log (\text{Price}) = \text{Const.} + \sum_{i=2}^{6} d_i A_i + \sum_{j=1}^{5} a_j x_j + u$$

The value of the test statistic is 0.5 for 1965 and 1.2 for 1971, while the critical value of $F_{.05}(25, 300)$ is approximately 1.5. The null hypothesis is not rejected in either year, allowing us to consider imputed prices of physical characteristics as equal across age and the depreciation patterns as equal across physical characteristics.

Buyers of new cars and buyers of used cars may be different, however, and used and new cars may not be perfect substitutes. One way to see if they are good substitutes is to test if the relative imputed prices of physical characteristics are the same for used and new cars at the same point in time. This allows us also to test whether the price-setting firms in the new market evaluate physical characteristics of cars in the same way as do the consumers in the used market. Because our used car prices are for cars with radios in them, we also included radio prices in the new car prices for this comparison. We use cars of *Age* 2 and make the number of used cars comparable to the number of new cars. We choose *Age* 2, because it takes some time for consumers to evaluate these cars and because the data on older cars are less reliable. The null hypothesis of no difference in imputed prices in the two markets is tested separately for 1962, 1965, 1967, and 1971. The unconstrained regression is as follows.

$$\log (\text{Price}) = \text{Const.} + d_2 A_2 + \sum_{j=1}^{5} a_{0j} x_{0j} + \sum_{j=1}^{5} a_{2j} x_{2j} + u$$

where x_{0j} is x_j if the sample model is a new car and 0 if it is a used car of *Age* 2. The constrained regression is given by

$$\log (\text{Price}) = \text{Const.} + d_2 A_2 + \sum_{j=1}^{5} a_j x_j + u$$

The values of the test statistic for 1962, 1965, 1967, and 1971 are .5, 1.6, .8, and 2.7, respectively. Since the critical value of $F_{.05}(5, 100)$ is approximately 2.3, the null hypothesis is not rejected on statistical grounds for 1962, 1965, and 1967. It is rejected at the 5 per cent but not at the 1 per cent level for 1971. But even in 1971, the SEE in the

constrained regression increases only by .004. We may conclude, therefore, that by and large, firms evaluate physical characteristics correctly
in the sense that they do so in the same way as consumers, and that
new and used cars are the same goods (perfect substitutes), differing
only in the "quantity" of the good contained per market unit.

Table 6 presents estimated make-effects with respect to Chevrolet
for the whole period (1961–1971) and for selected subperiods. They
appear to be related, perhaps unsurprisingly, to the "price class" of a

TABLE 6

Make-Effects in the Used Car Market (Chevrolet as Base)

	1961–62	1966–67	1970–71	1961–71
American Motors	−.143	−.130	−.193	−.106
	(−6.09)	(−6.35)	(−10.04)	(−2.55)
Buick	−.126	.051	.048	.029
	(−5.24)	(2.89)	(2.70)	(.78)
Cadillac	.457	.468	.411	.504
	(13.42)	(17.97)	(15.42)	(9.17)
Chevrolet	0	0	0	0
Chrysler	−.057	−.019	−.057	−.041
	(−2.21)	(−.91)	(−2.74)	(−.93)
Dodge	−.181	−.148	−.109	−.171
	(−8.12)	(−8.76)	(−6.59)	(−4.71)
Ford	−.127	−.134	−.135	−.131
	(−6.72)	(−8.81)	(−8.63)	(−3.94)
Imperial	.257	.147	.087	.215
	(6.41)	(4.51)	(2.47)	(3.11)
Lincoln	.213	.391	.210	.390
	(5.31)	(9.63)	(4.83)	(5.02)
Mercury	−.208	−.131	−.143	−.171
	(−8.85)	(−6.83)	(−6.78)	(−4.11)
Oldsmobile	−.032	.025	−.038	.013
	(−1.38)	(1.29)	(−2.02)	(.34)
Plymouth	−.250	−.156	−.150	−.190
	(−12.19)	(−9.02)	(−8.92)	(−5.20)
Pontiac	−.028	.004	−.096	−.023
	(−1.28)	(.22)	(−5.38)	(−.64)
Average	−.015	.028	−.006	.024

NOTE: The figure in parentheses are *t* statistics.

particular make. High-priced makes (Cadillac, Imperial, and Lincoln) have the largest make-effects, while "low priced" makes (American Motors, Ford, Plymouth, Dodge, and Mercury) have negative make-effects (relative to Chevrolet). Cadillac and Plymouth have the largest (.5) and the smallest effects (−.27), respectively.

Since the estimated make-effects are based on price data, they measure the degree of "overpricing" compared to the "hedonically" estimated quality. But since our list of physical characteristics is unlikely to be complete, we interpret *systematic* pricing deviations as reflecting unmeasured aspects of quality rather than just pricing errors. Can we say something about the total quality level (measured plus unmeasured) of makes? One way to do so is to use stock data, i.e., registration data on each vintage of each make over the years and to calculate its average life expectancy from such data. A make with a longer life can be thought of as having a higher quality and/or a lower deterioration rate of this quality, scrapping occurring when quality (performance) falls below a certain minimum level. Table 7 lists estimated median lives for each make based on the 1953, 1954, and 1955 vintages and their registration rates over the next fifteen years. The median life for all makes was 10.5 years. Only Cadillac and Chevrolet had median lives one year longer than the average. The life of American Motors cars appeared to be 2 years shorter and the lives of Lincoln and Mercury models were a year shorter than the median. Except for Lincoln, this is consistent with our estimated make-effects.

Comparing the estimated make-effects in the new and used car markets we find that they are not too different in relative position and

TABLE 7

Median Life of Cars: Average for 1953–1955 Model Years

Make	Median Life (Years)	Make	Median Life (Years)
American Motors	8.5	Lincoln	9.5
Buick	10.5	Mercury	9.5
Cadillac	11.5	Oldsmobile	10.5
Chevrolet	11.5	Plymouth	10.5
Chrysler	10.5	Pontiac	10.5
Dodge	10.5		
Ford	10.5	Average	10.5

size. (Compare Tables 3 and 6.) The main difference is that the estimated make-effects are much more widely spread out in the used market than in the new market.

We test the rather stringent hypothesis that make-effects are the same in the new and used markets. We computed such tests for the 1962, 1965, 1967, and 1971 cross sections. The values of the test statistics are shown in Table 8. Since $F_{.01}(12, 300) \simeq 2.25$, the null hypothesis is rejected at the 1 per cent level for all the years. But the F values are not large for such sample sizes (about 350). Moreover, the standard errors of the constrained regressions do not rise by more than .0065. From a practical point of view, there is little reason to reject the null hypothesis. It appears that, on the whole, make-effects observed in the new car market persist in the used car market at roughly similar orders of magnitude.

We look next at changes in make-effects with age, within the used car market. We test the null hypothesis that make-effects are the same at *Age* 1 and *Age* 6, with American Motors as the base at both ages. This hypothesis is tested for 1964 and 1971. The values of the test statistics for 1964 and 1971 are 6.8 and 2.9 respectively. Since the critical $F_{.01}(12, 80)$ is about 2.4, the null hypothesis is rejected at the 1 per cent level in both years. Also, the standard errors of the constrained regressions rise by .0203 and .0103 in 1964 and 1971, respectively. The null hypothesis is thus also rejected by our "economic sig-

TABLE 8

Test of Equality of Make-Effects in the New
and Used Car Markets (All Ages)

	(1)	(2)	(3)	(4)	(5)	(6)
1962	3.36	.0831	.0868	340	36	24
1965	5.05	.0933	.0998	360	36	24
1967	3.23	.0723	.0750	375	36	24
1971	2.86	.0864	.0889	391	36	24

NOTE:
(1): value of the test statistic (F value).
(2): standard error of the unconstrained regression.
(3): standard error of the constrained regression.
(4): number of observations.
(5): number of parameters in the unconstrained regression.
(6): number of parameters in the constrained regression.

TABLE 9

Estimated Coefficients of the Age Dummies; 1961–1971
Pooled, Differing Imputed Prices for Different Years

	Dependent Variable			
	PA [a]	*PAA* [a]	*PAD* [a]	*PAA* [b]
Age 2	−0.2516	−0.2501	−0.2536	−0.2544
Age 3	−0.4916	−0.4886	−0.4956	−0.4980
Age 4	−0.7529	−0.7478	−0.7600	−0.7626
Age 5	−1.0756	−1.0683	−1.0857	−1.0877
Age 6	−1.4395	−1.4273	−1.4505	−1.4522

NOTE: See "Notes to Tables" at the end of this paper for definitions of the various price concepts.
[a] With make dummies.
[b] Without make dummies.

nificance" criterion. It appears that depreciation patterns are not constant over makes. Nor, as we shall see below, are they constant over time.

Table 9 lists our estimated age coefficients using various price concepts and including and excluding make dummies. All the different versions produce roughly the same results. They are very similar to Ramm's (1971) earlier estimates. Returning to Table 5 we note that the age coefficients are smaller in the more recent years. A formal test of the statistical significance of the difference in the age coefficients in 1962 and 1967, and in 1961 and 1971, rejects the null hypothesis at the 1 per cent level (estimated F levels are 11 and 6.3 respectively, while the critical $F_{.01}(5, 600)$ is about 3). The change in the standard errors is not very large, however, only .006 and .003 for the 1962–1967 and 1961–1971 comparisons respectively.

We noted earlier that make-effects do not appear to be constant over ages. Table 10 gives more detail on the deviations of the age coefficients by makes from their average (for the pooled 1961–1971 regression). The only really significant deviations are the lower than average depreciation of Chevrolets and higher than average depreciation of Lincolns. This is not too different from the conclusions reached earlier by Cagan (1965) and Wykoff (1970).

Geometric (declining balance or exponential) depreciation is often

TABLE 10

Deviations from the Average Age
Coefficients: 1961–1971 Period

Make	Age 2	Age 3	Age 4	Age 5	Age 6
American	.0000	−.0232	−.0099	−.0817	.0231
Motors	(.00)	(−.35)	(−.13)	(−.28)	(.33)
Buick	.0104	.0387	.0354	.0346	.0481
	(.19)	(.72)	(.66)	(.64)	(.89)
Cadillac	.0048	−.0006	−.0011	.0082	.0414
	(.06)	(.01)	(−.01)	(.09)	(.48)
Chevrolet	.0949	.1366	.1926	.2378	.3250
	(1.73)	(2.44)	(3.44)	(4.17)	(5.60)
Chrysler	−.0030	.0002	−.0080	−.0069	−.0491
	(−.05)	(.00)	(−.12)	(−.10)	(−.73)
Dodge	−.0157	−.0197	−.0320	−.0386	−.0621
	(−.28)	(−.35)	(−.57)	(−.69)	(−1.09)
Ford	−.0150	−.0114	.0061	.0276	.0288
	(−.28)	(−.21)	(.11)	(.50)	(.51)
Imperial	−.0594	−.0743	−.1120	−.1071	−.1069
	(−.90)	(−1.12)	(−1.76)	(−1.62)	(−1.64)
Lincoln	−.0338	−.0702	−.1134	−.1720	−.2243
	(−.51)	(−1.07)	(−1.72)	(−2.15)	(−3.40)
Mercury	−.0075	−.0277	−.0278	−.0457	−.0539
	(−.01)	(−.36)	(−.37)	(−.60)	(−.70)
Olds-	.0181	.0460	.0528	.0629	.0596
mobile	(.31)	(.78)	(.89)	(1.07)	(.99)
Plymouth	−.0241	−.0309	−.0533	−.0511	−.1009
	(−.39)	(−.50)	(−.85)	(−.81)	(−1.58)
Pontiac	.0309	.0359	.0707	.0685	.0706
	(.54)	(.63)	(1.22)	(1.16)	(1.18)
Average	−.245	−.512	−.792	−1.104	−1.461

NOTE: Figures in parentheses are *t* statistics.

assumed in capital theory. We test the null hypothesis that depreciation is geometric for 1962, 1965, 1967, and 1971. The unconstrained regression equation is

$$\log (PAA) = \text{Const.} + \sum_{s=2}^{6} d_s A_s + \sum_{j=1}^{5} a_j x_j + u$$

where A_s is a dummy variable for age s. The constrained regression equation is

$$\log (PAA_s) = \text{Const.} - \delta(s - 1) + \sum_{j=1}^{5} a_j x_j + u$$

where s denotes age in years and PAA_s is a price of a used car of age s with automatic transmission and power steering. The null hypothesis of geometric depreciation is that $d_s = -\delta s(s = 2, 3, \ldots, 6)$. This is equivalent to the following linear hypothesis: $2d_2 = d_3$, $3d_3 = 2d_4$, $4d_4 = 3d_5$, $5d_5 = 4d_6$.

The test statistics are summarized in Table 11. Since $F_{.01}(4, 300) \simeq 3.4$ and $F_{.05}(4, 325) \simeq 2.4$, the null hypothesis is rejected at the 1 per cent level for 1962, 1965, and 1967, but not even at the 5 per cent level for 1971. However, the difference between the standard errors of the unconstrained and the constrained regression is less than .01 for all the years. Geometric depreciation is thus not too bad an assumption "on the average" although it may be rejected when the sample gets very large.

To check how our data deviate from the geometric depreciation pattern rejected for 1962, 1965, and 1967, we ran the following regression, for the 1962, 1965, and 1967 samples:

$$\log (PAA_s) = \text{Const.} - \delta(s - 1) + \sum_{s=3}^{6} d_s A_s + \sum_{j=1}^{5} a_j x_j + u$$

TABLE 11

Tests of the Geometric Depreciation Hypothesis

	(1)	(2)	(3)	(4)	(5)	(6)
1962	4.00	.1566	.1600	288	11	7
1965	3.66	.1569	.1597	304	11	7
1967	10.60	.1223	.1296	319	11	7
1971	0.60	.1230	.1227	336	11	7

NOTE:
(1): value of the test statistic (F value).
(2): standard error of the unconstrained regression.
(3): standard error of the constrained regression.
(4): number of observations.
(5): number of parameters in the unconstrained regression.
(6): number of parameters in the constrained regression.

TABLE 12

Estimated Deviations of Depreciation at Age *s* from the
Exponential Depreciation Path

Parameter	1962	1965	1967
δ	0.2853	0.2570	0.2185
	(9.06)	(8.32)	(9.44)
d_3	0.0273	0.0159	−0.0318
	(0.50)	(0.30)	(−0.79)
d_4	−0.0828	−0.0885	−0.0822
	(−0.99)	(−1.09)	(−1.34)
d_5	−0.1136	−0.1417	−0.1604
	(−1.00)	(−1.27)	(−1.92)
d_6	−0.2209	−0.2681	−0.3208
	(−1.52)	(−1.89)	(−3.02)

NOTE: The values in parentheses are *t* statistics of the estimates.

where d_s measures the deviation of depreciation at age *s* from the exponential depreciation path. The relevant results are listed in Table 12. The only statistically significant deviation from the exponential path occurs at *Age* 6 in 1967. All the other deviations are not significant at the 5 per cent level. Geometric depreciation is thus not too bad a hypothesis. However, deviations from it are systematic. Actual depreciation occurs at a faster rate with age.

Table 13 lists estimated geometric depreciation rates by makes for the years 1962, 1965, 1967, and 1971. Most of the rates appear to decline over time. Chevrolet has consistently the lowest rate of depreciation, while higher priced cars (such as Cadillac, Imperial, and Lincoln) appear to have an above average depreciation rate. However, these differences are not very consistent or significant. Letting the average depreciation change over time, but constraining it to be the same across makes, raises the standard error of the constrained regression by only .006 (for the pooled 1962, 1965, and 1971 sample).

We also estimated depreciation patterns for the combined new and used car price data set with largely similar results. The first-year depreciation rate was consistently higher than the depreciation rate in the subsequent years, but the difference was not very significant, either statistically or by our change in the SEE criterion. The overall depreciation pattern that emerged is summarized in Figure 2. We can-

TABLE 13

Geometric Depreciation Rates by Make of Car

	1962	1965	1967	1971
American Motors	.3117	.3358	.2705	.2533
Buick	.3469	.2713	.2532	.2456
Cadillac	.3169	.2795	.2707	.2886
Chevrolet	.2684	.2259	.2463	.2258
Chrysler	.3149	.3177	.2854	.2717
Dodge	.3319	.3430	.2935	.2534
Ford	.2879	.2739	.2822	.2509
Imperial	.3077	.2742	.3280	.3232
Lincoln	.4342	.3051	.2684	.3306
Mercury	.3740	.3268	.2740	.2650
Oldsmobile	.3236	.2263	.2521	.2733
Plymouth	.3452	.3233	.2980	.2682
Pontiac	.3256	.2575	.2621	.2571
Average	.3299	.2893	.2757	.2694
Common rate [a]	.3280	.3086	.2786	.2561

[a] Constrained to be equal across makes.

not tell whether the larger first-year drop is real without having access to transaction prices in the new car market.

Differences across makes in the depreciation from new to used status (*Age* 1) are the result of transitory make-effects and differential price discounting in the new car market. It is interesting, therefore, to estimate new-to-used depreciation rates for the various makes separately.

To simplify our analysis, we assume that imputed prices of physical characteristics are the same in the new and used car markets and that depreciation is geometric. We want then to estimate d_{1i} ($i = 1$, $2, \ldots, 13$) in the following combined equation for the new and used car markets

$$\log (PAA_{is}) = \sum_{i=1}^{13} b_{0i}M_i - \sum_{i=1}^{13} d_{1i}A_uM_i - \sum_{i=1}^{13} \delta_i(s - 1)A_uM_i + \sum_{j=1}^{5} a_jx_j + u$$

where PAA is the price of a car of make i and age s (including the price of a radio for both new and used cars); M_i is a dummy variable for make i; A_u is 1 if the model is used ($s > 1$) and 0 if it is new ($s = 0$); s

FIGURE 2

Typical Depreciation Path

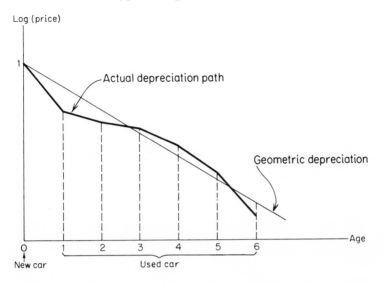

denotes age s $(s = 0, 1, \ldots, 6)$. d_{1i} is the depreciation rate to *Age* 1 of make i. δ_i is the geometric depreciation rate of make i in the used car market. This equation is equivalent to the following set of two equations.

$$\log (PAA_{is}) = \sum_{i=1}^{13} b_{0i}M_i + \sum_{j=1}^{5} a_jx_j + u \qquad \text{if } s = 0$$

$$\log (PAA_{is}) = \sum_{i=1}^{13} b_{0i}M_i - \sum_{i=1}^{13} d_{1i}M_i - \sum_{i=1}^{13} \delta_i(s-1)M_i$$

$$+ \sum_{j=1}^{5} a_jx_j + u = \sum_{i=1}^{13} b_{1i}M_i - \sum_{i=1}^{13} \delta_i(s-1)M_i$$

$$+ \sum_{j=1}^{5} a_jx_j + u \qquad \text{if } s \geq 1$$

where $b_{1i} = b_{0i} - d_{1i}$ and the imputed prices of the physical characteristics a_j are constant across the two equations.

Instead of computing the above regression with many parameters, we can estimate d_{1i} from our previous results. These estimates, shown in Table 14, indicate that low-priced makes (American Motors,

TABLE 14

Estimates of the Depreciation Rate from New to
Used Car Status (*Age* 1) for Each Make [a]

	1962	1965	1967	1971
Average rate $\hat{d}_1$ [b]	.3701	.2924	.3974	.4308
American Motors	.0317	.0731	.0240	.1707
Buick	.0002	−.0435	.0310	−.0286
Cadillac	−.1200	−.1544	−.1733	−.1849
Chevrolet	.0038	.0615	.0159	.0221
Chrysler	.0428	−.0365	.0601	−.0322
Dodge	.0838	.0006	.0640	.0277
Ford	.0363	.1359	.0770	.0705
Imperial	.0256	.0574	−.0743	−.0233
Lincoln	−.0675	−.1210	−.2557	−.0556
Mercury	.0018	.0274	.1089	.0375
Oldsmobile	−.0249	−.0533	.0530	−.0656
Plymouth	.0646	.0909	.0487	.0331
Pontiac	−.0781	−.0469	−.0255	.0290

[a] What is listed in the table are the deviations from the average depreciation rate $(\hat{d}_{1i} - \hat{d}_1)$ for each make.
[b] Constrained to be the same across makes.

Chevrolet, Ford, Plymouth) depreciate at a faster than average rate in the transition from new to used car status, as do Dodge and Mercury, while Cadillac and Lincoln depreciate at a much lower rate than the average car in the transition from new to used car status. The other makes do not show a systematic pattern over time. On the whole, high-priced makes depreciate at a lower than average rate in the first year, which may just reflect the fact that they are discounted less in the new car market.

We can combine our estimates of the first year depreciation rate and the estimates of the geometric depreciation rate for the other ages and consider the depreciation path over the whole life of a car, including the transition from the new to used, for each make separately. Looking at Tables 13 and 14 we note only a few significant deviations from the average: Cadillac appears to depreciate much less than average in the transition from new to used status but then continues to depreciate at the average geometric rate. Oldsmobile and Pontiac have a similar pattern, although their first-year depreciation is larger than that of Cadillac. Chevrolets have a slightly larger depreciation rate in the first year but then they depreciate at a much lower geometric rate in the used market. Ford has a somewhat similar pattern, although its geometric depreciation rate in the used market is larger than that of Chevrolet. American Motors, Plymouth, Dodge, and Mercury show a slightly faster depreciation than average in the transition from new to used status but then continue to depreciate at the average rate or a slightly higher rate.

V. PERFORMANCE VARIABLES IN HEDONIC REGRESSION

We discussed earlier the following "two-stage hypothesis": Physical characteristics x of a good produce its performance levels y as outputs; physical characteristics are inputs into the cost function of the firm, but they do not enter the utility function of the consumer directly, only performance variables entering the latter. Previous hedonic studies have relied exclusively on physical characteristics variables to explain the variation in prices of important durable goods, such as automobiles, tractors, houses, refrigerators, turbo-generators, and boilers. Performance variables have not been used before as explanatory variables in hedonic regressions.[22]

Previous studies did not use performance variables because there was very little data on them, compared to the relative accessibility of data on the physical characteristics (specifications) of different goods.[23] We use the information on the performance of various automobile models given in the rating tables of *Consumer Reports*. We are interested in seeing if such variables perform as well in a hedonic regression as do the physical characteristics measures.[24] We would also like

---

[22] The R^2s are lower here.

[23] The situation may be changing for automobiles, as new safety regulations generate an entirely new set of data. See U.S. Department of Transportation, *Performance Data,* 1972.

[24] In our usage, "performance variables" are variables that are measured in some sense directly after the model is put on the market and are not derived simply from listings given by the manufacturer. We use tests and evaluations performed by the Consumers Union, an independent organization financed by consumers who buy its rating publications. It is possible, however, to proceed halfway and to construct "performance" variables out of physical characteristics, postulating a known transformation function from the first to the second stage. This is the procedure followed by Hogarty (1972) and Cowling and Cubbin (1972). The first study uses a "comfort" index which is the product of the sum of headroom and legroom times seatwidth and a "performance" variable which is the ratio of horsepower to weight. The second study uses a "passenger area" variable which is the product of "legroom" times "elbowroom." These can be thought of as a priori constrained versions of more general physical-characteristics-based regressions. Our accommodation or performance variables are based on scaled evaluations or actual tests, rather than on a direct transformation of listed specifications. It remains to be seen whether there is much gain in what we do. In any case, the Hogarty and Cowling and Cubbin studies are clearly a step in the right direction.

to know which performance variables are most significant in explaining the variation in car prices. Are they connected closely to specific physical characteristics, so that the latter would be good proxies for them in the hedonic regression? Can one think of performance variables as the output of a transformation function from physical characteristics to performance variables? Are there any performance variables that are not explained well by physical characteristics? Are the price indexes, make-effects, and depreciation patterns estimated using performance variables similar to those derived from estimates based on physical characteristics? A stable mapping from physical characteristics to performance variables would imply an affirmative answer to the last question.

Our sample is based on four-door U.S. sedans of 1963–1966 vintage that were rated by *Consumer Reports*. We use these ratings together with the prices of these cars in the used car market as of *Age* 1 through *Age* 6. The observation years and sample sizes are shown for each vintage in Table 15.

Our performance variables are derived from the results of road tests, ratings, and frequency of repair records given in *Consumer Reports*. Table 16 lists the performance variables used by us. Acceleration (AL), top speed (TS) and fuel economy (EC) are measured in specific (numerical) units defined in the notes to this table. The rest of the variables, such as handling (HL) or frequency of repair records ($R56$, $R66$, etc.), are given only qualitatively in the *Reports* and require scaling (or a long list of additional dummy variables). The scaling is to some extent arbitrary. It is described in detail in our manuscript (Ohta-Griliches, 1972) and will not be expounded here. It consists essentially of converting ratings such as excellent, good, or fair, or

TABLE 15

Performance Variables: Observation Years,
Vintage, and Sample Size

Vintage	Observation Years	Ages	Number of Models in Sample
1963	1964–69	1–6	16
1964	1965–69	1–5	20
1965	1966–71	1–6	33
1966	1967–71	1–5	35

TABLE 16

Performance Variables Available for each Vintage

1963	*HL, ST, EN* & *PO, AT, RI, AC, TR, RE, R*65, *R*66, *R*67, *R*68, *R*69, *AL, TS, EC*
1964	*HL, ST, EN* & *PO, AT, RI, AC, TR, RE, R*66, *R*67, *R*68, *R*69, *AL, TS, EC*
1965	*HL, ST, EN, PO, AT, RI, AC, DE, RE, R*66, *R*67, *R*68, *R*69, *R*70, *R*71
1966	*HL, ST, EN, PO, AT, RI, AC, DE, RE, R*67, *R*68, *R*69, *R*70, *R*71, *BR*

NOTE : Notations are as follows:
HL: handling, scale 0 to 8, from "fair" to "excellent."
ST: steering, sum of separate scales for manual and power steering, 0–7.
EN: engine, 0–5, 5 "very smooth and quiet."
PO: engine power, 0–2, 2 "high."
AT: automatic transmission, 0–5.5.
RI: Ride, 0–11.
AC: accommodation, 0–4.5.
TR: probable trade-in value, 0–5.
DE: probable dollar depreciation, 0–4.
RE: frequency of repair record of past models. Number of categories with better than average record minus the number of worse than average categories. (*RE* is used as the repair record in 1964 for the 1963 vintage and is used as the one in 1965 for the 1964 vintage.)
*R*65: Frequency of repair record reported in *Consumer Reports* in 1965.
*R*66, *R*67, . . . , *R*71: similar to *R*65.
AL: acceleration (time [seconds] required to increase the speed from 30 to 40 mph on 9% grade).
TS: top speed (mph) attainable on 9% grade.
EC: fuel economy (mpg at steady speed of 30 mph).
BR: brake, 0–7.
SOURCE: All performance variables are taken from *Consumer Reports: HL, ST, EN, PO, AT, RI, AC, TR, DE, RE,* and *BR* are taken from the *Rating* table. *R*65, *R*66, . . . , *R*71 are from *Frequency-of-repair records. AL, TS,* and *EC* are from the *Road test.*

"very easy" to "heavy," to numbers running from 8, or 5, to zero, with larger numbers reflecting a more positive evaluation.

The ratings of cars in *Consumer Reports* are based on road tests and hence, strictly speaking, we should use only those particular models that were actually road tested. This was done for the 1963 and 1964 vintages. So restricted, we had only 16 and 20 models left, respectively. To enlarge the sample, we use all the models that are reported in the ratings section of *Consumer Reports* and were also included in our earlier, Section IV, sample. We get, this way, 33 and 35 models for the 1965 and 1966 vintages, respectively. Since *AL*, *TS*, and *EC* are available only for those models which were road tested, we do not have them for all of our sample models in these vintages. In place of *AL* and *TS*, we use *PO* separately from *EN* & *PO* for these (1965 and 1966) vintages.

The physical characteristics used in this section are again *H* (horsepower), *W* (weight), *L* (overall length) and *V* (dummy for V-8) and are the same as discussed in the earlier sections. So are also the new and used prices of these models.

If the cars tested and rated by *Consumer Reports* include optional equipment, then we add the price of those particular options to the price of the car. Since the ratings include automatic transmission on all cars in these vintages (1963–1966) so do our prices for the same models.

We concentrate on the analysis of used car prices in this section, because we expect *Consumer Reports* ratings to affect them much more than the list prices of new cars—if the ratings are correct and consumers are conscious of the particular qualities rated.

Since the rating criteria of *Consumer Reports* may not necessarily remain constant over time, first we analyzed each vintage separately. However, the results were not too different across vintages, and the range of models was too small to sustain an intensive investigation. We present, therefore, only the relevant test statistics from these regressions in Table 17, and list the coefficients for all the variables only for the combined 1963–1966 vintages regressions in Table 18.

From the viewpoint of fit, performance variables are quite successful in explaining car prices. They do about as well as physical characteristics or better. The standard errors are comparable to the standard errors of the regressions reported in Section IV.[25] Statistics for formal tests of the null hypotheses that the coefficients of physical characteristics are all zero in the regression containing performance variables, and that the coefficients of performance variables are all zero in the regression containing physical characteristics, are listed in Table 17. The first null hypothesis is not rejected at the 5 per cent level for 1963, but it is rejected at the 1 per cent level for 1964, 1965, and 1966. The difference between the standard error of the unconstrained regression and that of the constrained regression is more than 0.01 for the 1964 and 1966 vintages (the maximum difference is .024) but not for the 1963 and 1965 vintages. The second null hypoth-

---

[25] These R^2's are lower, between .6 and .8, but that is due to the restricted range of these samples.

TABLE 17

Test of the Hypotheses that (A) the Coefficients of Physical
Characteristics are All Zero and (B) that the Coefficients of
Performance Variables are All Zero

Vintage	(1)	(2)	(3)	(4)	(5)	(6)	(7)	(8)	(9)
1963	.111	.121	.155	96	21	17	10	1.35	8.43
1964	.060	.075	.075	100	20	16	9	13.13	5.73
1965	.099	.106	.116	198	20	16	10	7.08	7.63
1966	.075	.099	.093	175	20	16	9	26.75	8.40

NOTE:
(1): standard error of the unconstrained regression.
(2 & 3): standard error of the constrained regressions A and B, respectively.
(4): number of observations.
(5): number of parameters in the unconstrained regression.
(6 & 7): number of parameters in the constrained regressions A and B, respectively.
(8 & 9): the values of the test statistic (F value) for hypothesis A and B, respectively.

esis is rejected at the 1 per cent level for all the vintages. Moreover, the difference between the standard error of the unconstrained
regression and that of the constrained regression is more than 0.01
for all the vintages. Thus, both performance variables and physical
characteristics appear to be useful in explaining car prices, with
performance variables having a slight but inconclusive edge. Pooling
all the vintages reverses this conclusion, the regression with physical
characteristics and make dummies having a residual standard error
which is lower, but not by much (.012), than the comparable regression containing only performance variables.[26]

Let us look at the imputed prices of performance variables more
closely. Most of them are not statistically significant at conventional
significance levels. The correctly signed, significant performance
variables can be classified into two groups. The first group consists
of performance variables that are closely related to physical characteristics. AC is highly correlated with weight. PO and AL are highly
correlated with horsepower. The second group consists of performance
variables which correspond to the depreciation rate (TR and DE) and
are correctly signed and significant in the absence of make-effects.
Performance variables that are not highly correlated with measured
physical characteristics are not statistically significant and often

[26] The edge does not come from the "traditional" characteristics variables H, W, or
L, but from the significant dummy variable for V-8 engines.

TABLE 18

Pooled Regression of All the Vintages (1963–1966)
A: Performance Variables

Variable	With Make Dummies Estimated Coefficient	With Make Dummies t Statistic	Without Make Dummies Estimated Coefficient	Without Make Dummies t Statistic
HL	0.003	0.74	0.009	2.74
ST	−0.007	−1.43	−0.001	−0.29
EN & PO	0.044	12.52	0.040	12.88
AT	−0.010	−2.22	−0.024	−6.22
RI	0.003	1.09	0.002	0.59
AC	0.011	3.49	0.023	8.57
TR (or DE)	−0.007	−1.09	0.022	5.40
RE	0.001	0.42	−0.000	−0.21
A_2	−0.2603	−14.23	−0.2445	−12.76
A_3	−0.5432	−24.18	−0.5107	−22.13
A_4	−0.8301	−30.07	−0.7807	−27.99
A_5	−1.1417	−34.55	−1.0763	−32.60
A_6	−1.4812	−36.71	−1.4083	−34.74
$M2$	0.1822	5.66		
$M4$	0.1644	5.32		
$M5$	0.2193	5.85		
$M6$	0.0459	1.68		
$M7$	0.0297	1.29		
$M10$	0.0482	1.61		
$M11$	0.0867	2.85		
$M12$	0.0281	1.04		
$M13$	0.1190	4.21		
T_1	7.2778	175.98	7.2681	179.23
T_2	7.2461	197.61	7.2273	204.90
T_3	7.2187	206.09	7.1768	211.97
T_4	7.2248	194.29	7.1687	195.47
T_5	7.2636	173.08	7.1911	170.98
T_6	7.3105	157.90	7.2228	154.56
T_7	7.3353	143.09	7.2273	139.47
T_8	7.5235	133.19	7.4037	129.29
Number of observations	569		569	
SSR	7.0929		8.0777	
SEE	0.115		0.121	
R^2	0.878		0.861	

NOTE: T_i is a dummy for year i ($i = 1$ for 1964, . . . , $i = 8$ for 1971); A_i is a dummy for age i; M_i is a dummy for make i. ($M3$, $M8$, and $M9$ are not in the sample. $M1$ is taken as the base make [i.e., its make-effect is 0].) Average make-effect is 0.0924.

TABLE 18 (concluded)

B: Physical Characteristics

$$\log (P) = \sum_{j=1}^{4} a_j x_j + \sum_{i=1}^{8} t_i T_i + \sum_{i=2}^{6} d_i A_i + \sum_{i=2}^{13} m_i M_i + u$$

Variable	With Make Dummies Estimated Coefficient	With Make Dummies t Statistic	Without Make Dummies Estimated Coefficient	Without Make Dummies t Statistic
H^*	0.026	1.17	0.057	2.62
W^*	0.080	2.05	0.045	1.16
L^*	0.002	0.15	0.023	1.88
V	0.153	8.71	0.124	6.62
A_2	−0.2585	−16.20	−0.2525	−14.12
A_3	−0.5373	−28.90	−0.5249	−25.48
A_4	−0.8198	−37.66	−0.8009	−33.63
A_5	−1.1266	−44.99	−1.1015	−40.61
A_6	−1.4555	−48.92	−1.4269	−43.96
$M2$	0.1558	6.77		
$M4$	0.1139	6.19		
$M5$	0.1053	3.27		
$M6$	0.0043	0.21		
$M7$	0.0010	0.05		
$M10$	−0.0124	−0.47		
$M11$	0.0708	3.09		
$M12$	0.0064	0.33		
$M13$	0.891	3.86		
T_1	7.1289	44.25	6.8418	43.94
T_2	7.1068	44.42	6.8175	44.26
T_3	7.0840	43.49	6.7866	43.46
T_4	7.0806	43.04	6.7771	43.06
T_5	7.1158	42.62	6.8060	42.68
T_6	7.1574	42.35	6.8417	42.45
T_7	7.1804	41.67	6.8571	41.80
T_8	7.3610	42.35	7.0328	42.54
Number of observations	569		569	
SSR	5.7155		7.3809	
SEE	0.103		0.116	
R^2	0.901		0.873	

NOTE : The average make-effect is 0.0534. See Table 16 and "Notes to Tables" at the end of this paper for definitions.

have wrongly signed coefficients. This may be the result of inappropriate scaling of the qualitative information on our part. Also, consumers may not be very conscious of these particular qualities.

To test the two-stage hypothesis more explicitly, we look for two things: (1) Is there anything left that can be explained by physical characteristics in the residuals from the hedonic regression using performance variables? (2) Are performance variables explained well by physical characteristics?

The answer to the first question is already contained in Table 17, examined earlier. Adding physical characteristics to the performance variables regression does improve the fit somewhat, but not by much. The standard errors of the individual vintage regressions drop by .01, .015, .007, and .024 for the 1963, 1964, 1965, and 1966 vintages, respectively. Thus, the regressions with performance variables do not leave much to be additionally explained by physical characteristics variables. The assumed causal direction (physical characteristics produce performance variables and performance variables determine prices) of the two-stage hypothesis seems not too poor a simplification of what is clearly a more complex reality.

To answer the second question, we estimated linear transformation functions of physical characteristics into performance variables. Table 19 illustrates the results for the 1965 vintage. *PO* (power) is well explained by horsepower and the V-8 dummy variable, and *AC* (accommodation) is well explained by weight. The other performance variables are not well explained (except for *EN* which is close to *PO*), even by the combination of all the physical characteristics, but they also have little power in explaining the variation in car prices.

Table 20 compares estimated age coefficients from Table 18 to those estimated in Section IV (Table 4), based on the much larger sample of used cars and their prices. There are no systematic differences in depreciation patterns, whether we use performance variables or physical characteristics. All the differences are small. The depreciation rate increases with age, but as before, the hypothesis of geometric depreciation will be a good approximation to reality. We reestimated our equations imposing the geometric depreciation assumption but allowing the rate of depreciation to differ across makes. We shall not report these results here, both for lack of space and because they were not much different from the results reported earlier in Section IV.

Table 21 presents the estimated make-effects with Chevrolet as the base and compares them to make-effects using physical characteristics, both in the same sample, and in the larger sample of Section IV. They

TABLE 19

Performance Variables Related to Physical Characteristics: the 1965 Vintage
(number of observations = 33)

	HL	ST	EN	PO	AT	RI	AC	DE	RE
H	−0.015	−0.013	0.035	0.049	0.010	−0.022	−0.021	0.022	0.003
	(−0.72)	(−0.91)	(2.40)	(3.88)	(1.30)	(−1.19)	(−2.35)	(1.57)	(0.07)
W	0.004	0.002	−0.007	−0.002	0.000	0.005	0.008	−0.004	−0.002
	(1.13)	(0.80)	(−3.14)	(−1.18)	(0.20)	(1.71)	(5.75)	(−2.07)	(−0.31)
L	−0.035	−0.059	0.223	0.032	−0.018	−0.015	0.027	0.048	−0.021
	(−0.38)	(−0.95)	(3.47)	(0.58)	(−0.55)	(−0.19)	(0.69)	(0.77)	(−0.12)
V	0.067	0.380	0.447	4.016	−0.499	1.041	0.070	−0.776	0.188
	(0.04)	(0.36)	(0.42)	(4.33)	(−0.88)	(0.76)	(0.11)	(−0.74)	(0.06)
Constant	6.267	13.19	−22.30	−4.611	4.555	−2.498	−20.48	2.775	10.59
	(0.54)	(1.69)	(−2.78)	(−0.67)	(1.08)	(−0.24)	(−4.11)	(0.36)	(0.48)
R^2	0.092	0.101	0.551	0.922	0.148	0.358	0.913	0.265	0.047

NOTE: See Table 16 for definitions of the dependent variables. Figures in parentheses are t ratios.

TABLE 20

Estimated Age Coefficients in the Semilogarithmic
Regressions Using Performance Variables and
Physical Characteristics Respectively

	(1)	(2)	(3)
Age 2	−0.2603	−0.2585	−0.2369
Age 3	−0.5432	−0.5373	−0.5004
Age 4	−0.8301	−0.8200	−0.7758
Age 5	−1.1417	−1.1266	−1.0857
Age 6	−1.4812	−1.4555	−1.4417

NOTE:
(1): 1964–71 pooled regression with make dummies, all data,
performance variables.
(2): 1964–71 pooled regression with make dummies, all data,
physical characteristics.
(3): From Table 4. 1961–71 pooled regression with make dummies, big sample, physical characteristics.

are very similar to each other, particularly those estimated from the
same sample. The largest difference, .056, occurs for Chrysler, but it
is not statistically significant. It does not appear to be the case that
make-effects estimated using physical characteristics can be explained
away by differential performance levels relative to characteristics
levels, at least not by the set of performance variables available to us.

Finally, let us look at the rate of the price decline of a car from new to
used status (*Age* 1) using performance variables. Let $\hat{Q} = EXP$
$\left(\sum_j \hat{b}_j y_j \right)$ be the estimated quality based on performance variables (y)
in the used car market. Let P_n and P_u be the new and used price (of
Age 1) of a car, respectively. If the firm overprices new cars from the
consumer evaluation viewpoint of $\hat{Q}$, then the price decline $(1 - P_u/P_n)$
from new to used status should be large. If the firm underprices it,
then the price decline will be small. The rate of underpricing by the
firm is measured by $\hat{Q}/P_n$. We are interested, therefore, in the coefficient α in the following equation

$$\log (P_u/P_n) = \text{Const.} + \alpha \log (\hat{Q}/P_n) + T_i + u$$

where α is the elasticity of the first-year depreciation coefficient with
respect to the quality-price ratio in the new car market and the T_i's

TABLE 21

Performance Variable Regressions with Comparisons:
Make-Effects with Respect to Chevrolet (*M*4)

Make	(1)	(2)	(3)
American Motors (*M*1)	−.164	−.114	−.106
	(−5.32)	(−6.19)	(−2.55)
Buick (*M*2)	.018	.042	.029
	(.74)	(2.09)	(.78)
Chrysler (*M*5)	.055	−.009	−.041
	(1.58)	(−.28)	(−.93)
Dodge (*M*6)	−.119	−.110	−.171
	(−3.97)	(−6.35)	(−4.71)
Ford (*M*7)	−.135	−.113	−.131
	(−5.55)	(−7.32)	(−3.94)
Mercury (*M*10)	−.116	−.126	−.171
	(−3.48)	(−5.36)	(−4.11)
Oldsmobile (*M*11)	−.078	−.043	.013
	(−3.15)	(−2.08)	(.34)
Plymouth (*M*12)	−.136	−.107	−.190
	(−4.48)	(−6.43)	(−5.20)
Pontiac (*M*13)	−.045	−.025	−.023
	(−1.82)	(−1.25)	(−.64)
Arithmetic average	−.072	−.061	−.079

NOTE :
(1): make-effects estimated in the pooled regression (1964–71) using performance variables.
(2): make-effects estimated in the pooled regression (1964–71) using physical characteristics.
(3): make-effects estimated in the pooled regression (1961–71) of the big sample of Section IV, using physical characteristics as the explanatory variables and *PAA* as the dependent variable.
The figures in parentheses are *t* statistics. Note that column (3) is not strictly comparable to columns (1) and (2), because the observation period and sample size are different.

are time-vintage dummies, allowing the overall price level to shift over time. We expect α to be positive. The results of such a regression for the combined 1963–1966 vintages sample is shown in Table 22. The estimated elasticity of P_u/P_n with respect to $\hat{Q}/P_n$ is positive, statistically significant, and on the order of .3. Adding *TR* (trade-in value) and make dummies to this regression does not change the results signifi-

TABLE 22

First Year Depreciation Related to the
"Quality"–List-Price Ratio

Variable	Estimated Coefficient	t Statistic
$\log (\hat{Q}/P_n)$	0.2798	3.49
T_1	1.8215	3.00
T_2	1.8022	2.97
T_3	1.7463	2.89
T_4	1.7341	2.86
SSR	0.38262	
SEE	0.062	
R^2	0.109	

NOTE: Dependent variable $\log (P_u/P_n)$. $\hat{Q}$ is based on the coefficients of Table 18, not including make dummies.

cantly. Letting P_n have an independent coefficient (not constrained to equal $-\alpha$) raises the estimated α to 0.4 but reduces the estimate standard error by only .002. The unconstrained coefficients of $\hat{Q}$ and P_n add up to 1.14, implying a slightly lower price decline for larger and more expensive cars.

Price decline from the new to the used status of *Age* 1 may be affected more by the quality estimated in the new car market than by the quality estimated in the used market. Consumers could be using physical characteristics (x) rather than performance variables (y) to evaluate the qualities of cars. A year may be too short a time to gather adequate information about their performance. Hence we tried also $\hat{P}_n = EXP \left(\sum_j \hat{a}_j x_j \right)$ in place of $\hat{Q}$ in the above equation, where the $\hat{a}_j$'s are estimated physical characteristics coefficients in the earlier regression of new car prices. The estimated elasticity of P_u/P_n with respect to $\hat{P}_n/P_n$ is $\hat{\alpha} = .61$, larger than our estimate of this elasticity using $\hat{Q}$ as the measure of car quality. However, the fit of the two regressions is about the same, indicating no clear superiority for either $\hat{P}$ or $\hat{Q}$ in explaining P_u/P_n. This is consistent with our earlier acceptance of the two-stage hypothesis: both sets of variables tell largely the same story.

VI. HEDONIC PRICE INDEXES

This section will be relatively brief because we do not have the space, nor have we had the time, to explore the relevant issues adequately. The most interesting question, comparison with the official indexes, is hampered by lack of detailed description of the construction methods and specific adjustments made to these indexes.

We shall discuss our indexes in reverse order, starting with the small performance-variables sample, going on to the larger and most comparable used-car-prices sample, and concluding with a presentation of our new car price indexes and some comparisons.

Table 23 summarizes our comparisons for performance-variables-based versus physical-characteristics-based price indexes. The two tell largely the same story. The lack of significant discrepancies between the two (except perhaps for 1965–1966, for which period performance-variables-based indexes indicate a larger price decline) implies that there has been no significant progress in the transformation of physical characteristics into performance variables, or perhaps more correctly, that we have not been able to detect any, given the fragmentary data at hand.[27]

Table 24 summarizes the price indexes derived from our used car regressions, indicating that there is some difference, though not much, that arises from the treatment of optional equipment such as power steering. If one treats some of the increase in the use of power steering as a "cost of weight," then the constant quality price of used cars has gone up by more than is measured by indexes that link out such changes. (Compare the results for *PA* versus *PAA* or *PAD* in Table 24.) Also, allowing for make-effects results in a slower-rising index. Since the CPI does not go across makes in constructing its price index of used cars and tries to link out such changes as the increased use of power steering, the appropriate comparison for it is our *PAA* with make-effects-based index.

---

[27] Our sample is too small to be conclusive on this point. We have only 4 vintages (1963–1966) with a relatively small number of models each to derive price indexes for 8 years (1964–1971). A constrained price index, without make dummies, based on performance variables shows 6.5 percent less price increase than one based on physical characteristics for 1964–1971. This suggests that there may have been some progress in the transformation process over time. Constrained indexes without make dummies may be more accurate here, because our sample is too small to obtain reliable adjacent-year regression results (hence chain indexes). Also, because the sample composition was not kept constant, make dummies may absorb some of the price changes. More data for more models and vintages are needed to answer this important problem (i.e., the bias of hedonic price indexes based on physical characteristics, as compared with those based on performance variables).

TABLE 23

Annual Percentage Changes in Different Chain Price Indexes of
Used Passenger Cars in the U.S.: Based on Adjacent-Year
Regressions

Year	(1)	(2)	(3)	(4)	(5)	(6)
1964–65	−1.0	−4.0	−1.9	0.2	−0.2	2.5
	(2.4)	(2.6)	(1.8)	(0.9)		
1965–66	−6.1	−5.9	−2.0	−4.5	−2.7	−6.2
	(1.9)	(1.7)	(1.4)	(0.8)		
1966–67	−1.4	−0.0	−0.3	1.5	1.2	−0.4
	(1.5)	(1.3)	(1.0)	(0.7)		
1967–68	2.6	4.3	3.1	0.4	6.3	9.8
	(1.7)	(1.6)	(1.3)	(0.6)		
1968–69	4.8	6.6	4.1	2.8	3.9	−4.5
	(2.3)	(2.2)	(1.9)	(0.9)		
1969–70	−1.3	0.8	−2.0	−1.9	−7.6	−3.4
	(3.3)	(3.3)	(2.4)	(0.9)		
1970–71	20.1	16.4	14.6	13.6	10.1	8.9
	(5.3)	(5.5)	(2.6)	(0.7)		
1964–71	16.9%	17.6%	15.5%	11.7%	8.1%	8.4%

NOTE:
(1): based on performance variables, without make dummies.
(2): based on performance variables, with make dummies.
(3): based on physical characteristics, with make dummies.
(4): chain index from Section IV regressions (physical characteristics, with make dummies, PAA as the price).
(5): CPI of used cars as of April of each year.
(6): CPI of used cars, January-March average.
The figures in parentheses are standard errors.

Table 25 takes a closer look at the PAA (with make-effects) index and compares it to Ramm's (1971) estimates and the CPI index of used car prices. Note that we used April issues of the *Used Car Guide* for 1962 through 1971 and the May issue for 1961. Since the April issue is published at the beginning of April, our indexes are probably based on data collected in March and February. Hence, we have listed annual changes in the CPI for the January-March average, as well as for April. For the 1961–1962 comparison, we used the April and May indexes of the CPI, respectively. Large price increases occurred before

TABLE 24

Used Cars: Chain Hedonic Price Indexes and the
Consumer Price Index (1962 = 100.0)

	(1)	(2)	(3)	(4)	(5)	(6)
1961	99.7	99.7	99.7	99.2	89.7	88.4
1962	100.0	100.0	100.0	100.0	100.0	100.0
1963	113.1	112.6	113.2	113.4	101.8	102.5
1964	112.8	112.5	113.0	114.9	106.6	110.4
1965	112.3	112.7	112.3	116.7	106.3	113.1
1966	106.6	107.7	106.5	112.5	103.5	106.1
1967	108.5	109.3	108.1	115.0	104.8	105.7
1968	112.2	109.8	107.4	116.0	111.4	115.3
1969	115.3	112.8	110.5	119.1	115.7	113.6
1970	113.2	110.6	107.7	116.6	106.9	109.8
1971	127.8	125.7	121.2	132.0	117.7	119.6

NOTE: Chain indexes are based on *Used Car Guide;* May issue for 1961, April issue
for 1962 through 1971.
- (1): *PA* with make-effects.
- (2): *PAA* with make-effects.
- (3): *PAD* with make-effects.
- (4): *PAA* without make-effects.
- (5): *CPI* Index of Used Cars as of April of each year.
- (6): *CPI* Index of Used Cars, January-March average (except for 1968, where
  January-February average is used).

1963 and after 1970. Between 1963 and 1970 there was little overall
price change. We pooled the data for 1963 and 1970 to check the statistical significance of a time dummy coefficient for 1970. The estimated
coefficient is -0.032 ($\hat{t} = -3.4$) with make dummies, with 600-plus
degrees of freedom. The price change is statistically significant but
negative, and its absolute value quite small.

Discrepancies between our indexes and the other two occur in
1961–1962, 1962–1963, 1967–1968, and 1969–1970. In 1961–1962,
both Ramm's index and the CPI show a large price increase but ours
does not. On the other hand, our index shows a big increase in 1962–
1963 when the other two do not. This may be due to a discrepancy in
the timing of the various indexes. In 1967–1968, our indexes do not
show any significant change while the two other indexes show a somewhat large price increase. On the whole, our index is closer to the CPI
than Ramm's. Both our index and the CPI index show a large price

TABLE 25

Annual Percentage Changes in Price Indexes of U.S. Used Passenger Cars: 1961–1971

Calendar Year	Our Index (1)	Ramm (2)	CPI April (3)	CPI January-March average (4)
1961–62	0.3 (0.8)	17.2	9.4	13.1
1962–63	12.6 (0.8)	1.6	1.8	2.4
1963–64	−0.1 (0.9)	2.8	4.8	7.7
1964–65	0.2 (0.9)	0.4	−0.2	2.5
1965–66	−4.5 (0.8)	−12.1	−2.7	−6.2
1966–67	1.5 (0.7)	10.8	1.2	−0.4
1967–68	0.4 (0.6)	5.8	6.3	9.8
1968–69	2.8 (0.9)	N.A.	3.9	−4.5
1969–70	−1.9 (0.9)	N.A.	−10.0	−3.4
1970–71	13.6 (0.7)	N.A.	10.1	8.9
1961–68	14.4%	26.8%	22.1%	30.4%
1961–71	26.1	N.A.	26.4	35.2

NOTE: N.A. = not available.

(1): chain index based on adjacent-year regressions with *PAA* (with automatic transmission and power steering for all the models) as the dependent variables and with make dummies. Figures in parentheses are standard errors.

(2): chain index in column (1) of Table XIII of Ramm (1971): based on May-June issue of *Red Book National Used Car Market Reports* (Chicago: National Market Reports, Inc.).

increase from 1970 to 1971. On the other hand, we do not show as large a price decline in 1969–1970 as the CPI. Since our indexes and the CPI have been based on the same data base, we assume that discrepancies between our indexes and the CPI come from differential treatment of quality adjustments, optional equipment, and differences in the actual timing of the collected data.[28]

Our new car price indexes results are summarized in Table 26 with additional information to be gleaned from the earlier Table 2. There is little difference in results for the various versions in the post-1961 period. Weighting and the treatment of power steering make little difference to the final story. Including make-effects does, but the discrepancy is large for only the earlier part of the sample, where sample size is smaller and more variable from year to year. For the 1955 to 1960 period, our indexes, with make dummies and without, bracket Griliches' (1961) earlier estimates, which did not use make dummies but were based on a somewhat larger sample. For 1960–1965, our indexes with make dummies are significantly below, while those without are rather close to Triplett's (1969) price indexes for the same period.[29]

Comparisons with the CPI index of new car prices are hazardous because of a long list of different factors of unknown magnitude which could account for the observed discrepancies, the major ones being list versus transaction prices, differential methods of adjusting for quality change, different treatment of changes in warranties, and different treatment of safety and pollution abatement equipment. We shall concentrate on the 1961 to 1971 comparison, and our index (2) (*PA*, weighted, with make dummies) which is our best estimate of what might actually have happened. Figure 3 plots the two indexes (and the comparable used car price indexes). There is little difference between the two over the 1961–1971 period, both indexes rising rather consistently since the mid-sixties. The rate of increase since 1969 has been somewhat less for the CPI than in our estimated hedonic price index of new cars. This may be related to a substantial increase in the rate of "quality adjustment" by the Bureau of Labor Statistics (BLS), including such items as safety equipment and antipollution devices, which are costly to manufacture but are not necessarily a quality improvement from the point of view of the consumer.

[28] The −10 per cent, +10 per cent changes in 1969–1970 and 1970–1971 shown by the CPI are not very credible. The methods of constructing the used car component of the CPI are not very satisfactory (see U.S. BLS, 1967) and recently there have been some procedural changes made to improve matters.

[29] See Ohta-Griliches (1972) for more detailed comparisons.

TABLE 26

New Cars: Chain Hedonic Price Indexes and the
Consumer Price Index (1962 = 100.0)

Model Year	(1)	(2)	(3)	(4)	(5)	(6)	(7)
1955	95.6	93.5	84.0	83.2	91.3	82.3	6
1956	97.7	96.4	89.1	88.5	90.5	83.1	6
1957	98.0	97.8	92.7	92.2	95.1	93.4	6
1958	96.2	96.2	91.6	91.2	99.2	95.1	6
1959	95.1	95.1	91.8	91.2	103.3	100.9	6
1960	95.8	95.6	92.6	92.2	103.4		
1961	97.4	97.0	95.8	95.5	99.6		
1962	100.0	100.0	100.0	100.0	100.0		
1963	98.8	98.9	100.0	100.0	99.9		
1964	97.5	97.7	99.3	99.3	99.3		
1965	95.0	95.4	96.6	96.4	98.7		
1966	96.1	96.6	97.9	97.8	94.5		
1967	97.5	97.8	99.9	100.2	95.6	96.0	7
1968	100.5	100.7	102.4	102.9	97.6	100.5	7
1969	101.5	101.5	103.6	104.4	99.9	103.3	7
1970	103.9	103.4	105.1	106.0	101.1	105.3	7
1971	110.5	110.4	110.4	111.2	106.2	111.4	7

NOTE:
(1): *PA*, unweighted regression with make dummies.
(2): *PA*, weighted regression with make dummies.
(3): *PA*, unweighted regression without make dummies.
(4): *PDD*, unweighted regression without make dummies.
(5): November of previous year index of CPI.
(6): CPI adjusted for error in linking-in discounting, based on Triplett (1971), p. 28.
(7): Linked out "safety" and "exhaust emission" adjustments added back in, *approximately,* on the basis of scattered Wholesale Price Index (WPI) and CPI releases.

There is a rather large difference between the movements of the used car and new car price indexes. Used car prices rose significantly above new car prices in the early 1960s and then paralleled, very roughly, the movement in new car prices over time. On the whole, used car prices fluctuate more than new car prices, which is not surprising, and the CPI used car price index fluctuates more than the hedonic price index computed by us. There are at least two puzzles here: (1) Why did used car prices rise relative to new car prices in

FIGURE 3

Alternative Automobile Price Indexes

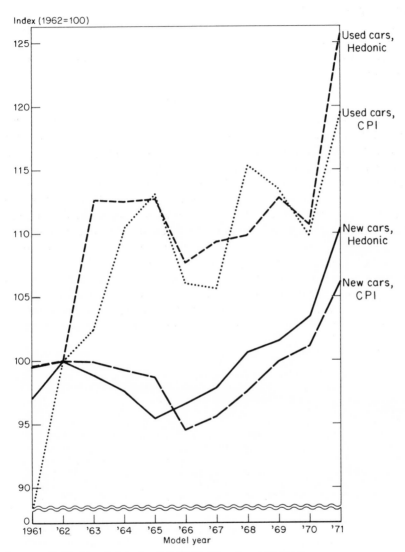

SOURCE: Table 24, columns 2 and 6; Table 26, columns 2 and 5.

the early 1960s? A possible interpretation is that the actual quality of new cars was falling in this period, the observed fall in new car prices not being "real" after all, and the used market reflecting the resulting appreciation of older cars.[30] (2) The used car component of the CPI drops sharply in 1969–1970 in the face of rising new car prices. Why? We need to know more about how the official indexes are actually constructed to be able to answer such questions and evaluate the various indexes.[31]

VII. SUMMARY

We have found some support for our "two-stage hypothesis," implying that there is little to be gained, at least given the currently available fragmentary data base, from moving away from physical characteristics to performance variables. We have also found that the declining balance (geometric) depreciation assumption is an adequate approximation for index number construction, but that depreciation rates appear not to be constant across time or makes. We found quite large make-effects, which we have not been able to explain away successfully. We also found that the new and used car markets can be analyzed jointly successfully, but that there have been shifts over time in the relative quality of new cars and the rate of depreciation of old ones, resulting in changing units of constant quality services per car between the new and used markets. These changes could use more analysis. So could the discrepancies between the price indexes

---

[30] We should have run our used car price analyses allowing for vintage effects. Not having done so, we cannot really answer this question at the moment.

[31] The construction of the CPI new car price index can be gleaned from the articles by Larsgaard and Mack (1961), Stotz (1966), and subsequent BLS releases. Differences that would have to be evaluated are: (1) coverage (we cover a broader range of cars than the CPI), (2) transaction versus list price, (3) differences in methods of adjusting for quality change and in the range of such adjustment, (4) differences in the concept of "quality," and (5) differences in the treatment of conditions of sale such as warranties. The construction of the CPI used car price index is described in some detail in BLS (1967). Until recently in constructing this index the BLS used data supplied to it by the National Automobile Dealers Association, which also form the base for the *Used Cars Guide* figures. We differ from the CPI index of used cars in (1) coverage (only Chevrolets, Fords, and Plymouths were priced by the CPI before 1962, and only Chevrolets and Fords were priced between 1962 and 1967, when the above mentioned article was written), (2) treatment of optional equipment (no allowance was made for it before 1966), (3) allowance for quality change (none in the CPI), (4) treatment of depreciation (linear interpolation of an annual rate), and (5) unknown discrepancies in the timing of the underlying data. It is our opinion, that whatever the merits of our indexes, they constitute a significant improvement on the CPI *Used Car Price Component Index.* In the case of the *New Car Price Indexes,* the discrepancies are smaller and harder to evaluate.

computed by us and the comparable official indexes. In particular, we could, and hope to do so in the future, analyze whether "quality" adjustments made by the CPI in new car prices are recognized by consumers and validated in the used car market.

Given the recent (fall 1973) worldwide developments, many of the specific findings listed above are by now obsolete. The sharp rise in fuel prices has led and will lead to a substantial revaluation of the desired characteristics of automobiles. The curse of "you should live in interesting times" having caught up with us, we should use the methodology developed above to observe and analyze the coming changes in these markets.

NOTES TO TABLES

(1) Physical characteristics

H: maximum brake horsepower.
W: shipping weight (pound).
L: overall length (inch).
V: $= 1$ if the car has a V-8 engine; $= 0$ if it has a 6-cylinder engine.
HT: $= 1$ if the car is a hardtop; $= 0$ if it is not.
x_j: level of the jth physical characteristic ($j = 1, \ldots, 5$) (x_1 for H, x_2 for W, $\ldots$, x_5 for HT).

(2) Prices and dummies for options

P: list price of a car including the prices of standard equipment (except air conditioners).
PS: list price of power steering.
AT: list price of automatic transmission if it is not standard; $= 0$ if it is standard.
D_0: $= 1$ if power steering is an option; $= 0$ if it is standard.

$$PAA = P + AT + PS \cdot D_0$$

$$PAD = P + AT - PS \cdot (1 - D_0)$$

$$PA = P + AT$$

$$PDD = P - \max_i (AT_i) \cdot \overline{AT} - PS \cdot (1 - D_0)$$

where $\max_i (AT_i)$ is the maximum price of automatic transmission in that year over all models on which it is optional; $\overline{AT}$ is 1 if AT is 0 and is 0 if it is not.

(3) Used cars

PA: average retail price of a used car (including the price of automatic transmission for all the models but the price of power steering only for the models whose prices include it in the *Used Car Guide*).
PS: $\begin{cases} \text{average retail price of power steering for the used car.} \\ \text{list price of power steering for the new car.} \end{cases}$
D: dummy for the model whose price includes power steering in the *Used Car Guide*.

$$PAA = PA + PS \cdot D$$

$$PAD = PA - PS \cdot (1 - D)$$

T_i: dummy for vintage year i($i = 1$ for 1955, $i = 2$ for 1956, . . . , $i = 17$).
Y_j: dummy for calendar year j ($j = 1$ for 1961, $j = 2$ for 1962, . . . , $i = 11$ for 1971).
A_i: dummy for age i ($i = 2, 3, . . . , 6$).

(4) Make dummies

MI: $= 1$ if the make of the car is I; $= 0$ if it is not. (Abbreviated as a dummy for make I.)

$M1$	American Motors	$M8$	Imperial
$M2$	Buick	$M9$	Lincoln
$M3$	Cadillac	$M10$	Mercury
$M4$	Chevrolet	$M11$	Oldsmobile
$M5$	Chrysler	$M12$	Plymouth
$M6$	Dodge	$M13$	Pontiac
$M7$	Ford		

(5) Notations for regressions:

u: disturbance
R^2:   multiple correlation coefficient squared
SSR: sum of squared residuals
SEE: standard error of estimate

(6) Further specifications

(a) Unless stated otherwise, the regression is unweighted.
(b) In the weighted regression, the weight is $\sqrt{\text{sales}}$ of the sample model divided by the average of $\sqrt{\text{sales}}$ over all the sample models in the year.
(c) In the table of the regression results, the figures in parentheses under the estimates are t statistics of those estimates.
(d) *denotes: divide the estimated coefficients of H, W, and L by 100, 1000, and 10, respectively.

REFERENCES

Arrow, K. J. (1960)
   "Decision Theory and the Choice of a Level of Significance for the t-Test." In Ingram Olkin et al., eds., *Contributions to Probability and Statistics*, pp. 70–78. Stanford: Stanford University Press.
Cagan, P. (1965, 1971)
   "Measuring Quality Changes and the Purchasing Power of Money: An Exploratory Study of Automobiles." *National Banking Review* 3 (December 1965): 217–236. Reprinted in Griliches (1971).
Cowling, K., and Cubbin, J. (1971)
   "Price, Quality and Advertising Competition: An Econometric Analysis of the U.K. Car Market." *Economica* 38 (November): 378–394.
Cowling, K., and Cubbin, J. (1972)
   "Hedonic Price Indexes for U.K. Cars." *Economic Journal* 82 (September 1972): 963–978.
Cowling, K., and Raynor, A. J. (1970)
   "Price, Quality and Market Share." *Journal of Political Economy* 78 (November-December): 1292–1309.

Dewees, D. N. (1970)
"Econometric Valuation of Automotive Attributes." Discussion Paper #70-4, Environmental Systems Program, Harvard University, December.

Dhrymes, P. (1967, 1971)
"On the Measurement of Price and Quality Changes in Some Consumer Capital Goods." Discussion Paper No. 67, University of Pennsylvania. A modified version is collected in Griliches (1971).

Gordon, R. J. (1971)
"Measurement Bias in Price Indexes for Capital Goods." *The Review of Income and Wealth* 17 (June 1971): 121–174.

Gordon, R. J. (1973)
Measurement of Durable Goods Prices. NBER, processed.

Griliches, Z. (1961, 1971)
"Hedonic Price Indexes for Automobiles: An Econometric Analysis of Quality Change." In *The Price Statistics of the Federal Government,* 1961. Collected in Griliches (1971).

Griliches, Z. (1964)
"Notes on the Measurement of Price and Quality Changes." In *Models of Income Determination.* Studies in Income and Wealth, Vol. 28, New York: NBER.

Griliches, Z. (1971), editor
Price Indexes and Quality Change, Cambridge: Harvard University Press.

Hall, R. E. (1969, 1971)
"The Measurement of Quality Change from Vintage Price Data," Working Paper 144, C.R.M.S. and I.B.E.R., University of California (Berkeley), 1969. Reprinted in Griliches (1971).

Hogarty, T. F. (1972)
"Hedonic Price Indexes for Automobiles: A New Approach." Virginia Polytechnic Institute, unpublished.

Lancaster, K. J. (1966)
"A New Approach to Consumer Theory." *Journal of Political Economy* 74 (April): 132–157.

Larsgaard, O. A., and Mack, L. J. (1961)
"Compact Cars in the Consumer Price Index." *Monthly Labor Review* 84 (May 1961): 519–523.

Leamer, E. E. (1973)
"Tests for Simplifying Linear Models," Harvard Institute of Economic Research Discussion Paper No. 303.

Lindley, D. V. (1968)
"The Choice of Variables in Multiple Regression," *Journal of the Royal Statistical Society,* Series B, 30(1): 31–66.

Muellbauer, J. N. J. (1971)
"Testing the 'Cagan-Hall' and the 'Hedonic' Hypotheses." Paper presented at the Econometric Society summer meetings.

Muellbauer, J. N. J. (1972)
"Characteristics, Substitution between Goods and Quality." Birkbeck College, unpublished.

National Automobile Dealers Association
Official Used Car Guide, Washington, D.C., monthly.

Ohta, M. (1971)
"Hedonic Price Index for Boiler and Turbo-Generator: A Cost Function Approach." Technical Report No. 40, Project for the Evaluation and Optimization of Economic Growth, University of California (Berkeley).

Ohta, M. (1973, 1975)
"Production Technologies in the U.S. Boiler and Turbo-generator Industries and

Hedonic Price Indexes for Their Products: A Cost Function Approach." *Journal of Political Economy* 83 (February 1975): 1-26.

Ohta, M., and Griliches, Z. (1972)
"Makes and Depreciation in the U.S. Passenger Car Market: An Application of the Hedonic Hypothesis to the Construction of Price Indexes and the Study of Market Structure." Cambridge, Mass., unpublished.

Powers and Co.
Ward's Automotive Yearbook, 1955-1971, Detroit (Abbreviated as *Ward's*).

Ramm, W. (1971)
"The Valuation and Estimations of Automobile Service 1961-1968." Ph.D. dissertation, Northwestern University.

Rosen, S. (1973, 1974)
"Hedonic Prices and Implicit Markets: Product Differentiation in Price Competition." Harvard Institute of Economic Research Discussion Paper No. 296 and *Journal of Political Economy* 82 (January/February 1974): 34-55.

Slocum Publishing Co.
Automotive News Almanac, 1955-1971. Detroit.

Stotz, M. S. (1966)
"Introductory Prices of 1966 Automobile Models." *Monthly Labor Review* 89 (February 1966): 178-184.

Triplett, J. E. (1969)
"Automobiles and Hedonic Quality Measurement." *Journal of Political Economy* 77 (May/June): 408-417.

Triplett, J. E. (1971)
"Determining the Effects of Quality Change on the CPI." *Monthly Labor Review* 94 (May 1971): 27-32.

Triplett, J. E., and Cowling, K. (1971)
"A Quality-Adjustment Model for Determining Market Shares in Oligopoly." Paper presented at the Winter 1971 meeting of the Econometric Society.

U.S. Bureau of Labor Statistics
The Consumer Price Index, 1955-1971.

U.S. Bureau of Labor Statistics (1967)
"Seasonal Demand and Used Car Prices." *Monthly Labor Review:* 12-16.

Wyckoff, F. C. (1970)
"Capital Depreciation in the Postwar Period: Automobiles." *Review of Economics and Statistics* 52 (May): 168-172.

Comments on "Automobile Prices Revisited: Extensions of the Hedonic Hypothesis"

YORAM BARZEL

UNIVERSITY OF WASHINGTON

HEDONIC price indexes are coming of age, and automobiles constitute the foremost example in the application of this technique. Griliches, of course, pioneered this wave; now Ohta is also a major contributor. The empirical work done by Ohta and Griliches (O & G) is so excellent that it seems fitting here to consider only some general methodological issues—of which Ohta and Griliches are clearly aware, but which they choose not to explore. I shall concentrate on two problems: that of unobserved characteristics, and that of discontinuities of characteristics. I shall then indicate the relevance of these problems to price indexes in general.

UNOBSERVED QUALITY CHANGES

The hedonic method of measuring a price index of a good subject to "model changes" appears on the surface almost as a miniature construction of a cost-of-living index. The good—an automobile in this particular application—is thought of as a set of attributes. In measuring the real price of the good, changes in quality have to be corrected for. In other words the levels of the attributes, equivalent to the quantity weights of a price index, have to be held constant. A major apparent difference in obtaining a price index for automobiles is that prices have to be inferred instead of directly observed. The main effort of the Ohta-Griliches paper is in determining the quantity base and in estimating the prices of the attributes.

There is another, perhaps more fundamental, difference: the process of obtaining a cost-of-living index essentially attempts a total enumeration of commodities, so that the consumer's budget is exhausted. In practice, the list approaches a complete tally at least of the market components. On the other hand, the set of variables used to construct hedonic indexes not only falls short of totality but does not even constitute enumeration. For automobiles, most of the available hedonic indexes cover such attributes as length, weight, and power. In the current study, Ohta and Griliches try also "performance" variables such as "handling" and "ride." No matter how many attributes are added to either list, neither could ever constitute an exhaustive enumeration.[1]

Whether it would be worthwhile to redefine attributes so as to make enumeration possible, and then to try to obtain such an enumeration, I do not know. However, as long as full enumeration is not attempted in practice, the hedonic index varies from the conventional one. What are the implications of that lack of correspondence?

The difficulty in obtaining a correct measure of the price of automobiles is due to change in "quality." Except that relative levels of the attributes vary substantially over time, the problem of quality change would be immaterial and there would be no point in using data on automobiles made in different years in estimating the (shadow) prices of the attributes.

The first question that comes to mind is: What forces induce the changes in quality? In the presence of stable demand functions, one source of variability is that changes in income lead to shifts in demand. The income-effected changes in the levels of each of the attributes and in their prices, then, would trace the attributes' supply curves.[2] If neither income elasticities nor supply elasticities of the different attributes — measured and unmeasured — differ much from each other, the hedonic approach is likely to produce a close approximation to the desired result, since the levels of the unmeasured components would change in approximately the same proportions as those of the measured attributes.

Changes in supply conditions of attributes, however, are much more troublesome. There is no particular reason why these would all change in the same proportion or even be correlated. In fact, many of the relative variations in the regression coefficients of attributes through time, as obtained by Ohta and Griliches, may be interpreted as just such changes. Thus, to take the very first example at hand, the ratio of the

---

[1] The above distinction between conventional and hedonic indexes points to another problem. For a conventional price index, the quantity base can be obtained by directly observing what commodities the consumer purchases and in what quantities. The set of attributes to be used in an hedonic index have to be guessed by the economist.

[2] Competitive conditions are implicitly assumed here.

coefficient of weight to that of horsepower, which in this context is a measure of their relative prices, fell from 19 in 1955–1957 to 7 in 1958–1959 and to 0.25 in 1960–1961 (see O & G, Table 2). In general, it is unlikely that a change in the price of steel will be accompanied by a similar change in the price of such other inputs as upholstery materials, rubber, or labor. More important, there is no reason why the supply conditions of attributes the investigator chooses and is able to observe will change in the same proportion as those of the unobserved ones. If the change in the regression coefficients of weight relative to horsepower is an indication of the potential changes in supply conditions of observed relative to unobserved attributes, the consequence of leaving out some of the attributes may be rather serious.[3]

To simplify the analysis of the relation between observed and unobserved attributes, let us now assume that the entire set of attributes of a commodity such as an automobile can be collapsed into just two — the (composite) attribute accounted for and the (composite) one left out. Suppose that the marginal cost of producing the observed attribute has increased, while that of the unobserved attribute has remained unchanged. The supply curve of the observed attribute shifts along its demand curve; the price of the observed attribute will increase and its equilibrium quantity decline. As a result of the higher price, the demand for substitutes will increase and that for complements will decline. Without a priori knowledge of whether the observed and unobserved attributes are substitutes or complements, one cannot say what will happen to the quantity of the unobserved attribute.[4]

The question we are concerned with, however, is more specific. How, and in what direction, will the quantity of the unobserved attribute change *per unit* of the observed one? Under rather (but not quite) general conditions, the law of demand dictates that the higher price of the observed attribute will cause an upward shift in the *relative* quantity of the unobserved attribute.[5]

When the relative level of the unobserved attribute is increased, the measured change in quality will be biased downward. Moreover, the increased demand for the unobserved attribute will be accompanied by

---

[3] It seems ironic that a charge of not exploring the consequences of a "left-out variable" is thus brought against a paper in which Griliches collaborates.

[4] Though, given that these attributes are sold as a single package, complementarity seems more plausible.

[5] Interactions with other commodities, as well as income distribution considerations, could conceivably reverse the conclusion. Fixed proportions in consumption could also change the result, but given the observed variability in the empirical studies, it seems safe to reject that notion.

increased expenditures on it and, thus, also by higher expenditure per unit of the measured attribute. If the supply of the unobserved attribute is perfectly elastic, the changes in quantity and in expenditures will be proportional.[6] This change in expenditures is induced by, and consequently is correlated with, the change in price of the observed attribute [7] and will lead to an upward bias in the estimate of its coefficient.[8]

If the supply of the unobserved attribute is not perfectly elastic the basic argument still holds, but the results become less useful. The expenditure on the unobserved attribute may increase more or less than proportionately to its quantity, depending on whether the two are substitutes or complements. If complementarity prevails, the absolute amount of the attribute is less and the move down the supply curve will lead to a lower unit price of the unobserved attribute. It is even possible, then, that the increase in the *relative* quantity of the unobserved attribute will be exactly matched by a decline in its price so that total expenses on it per unit of the observed attribute remain constant – or the fall in price may so dominate that expenditure on the unobserved attribute will actually decline per observed unit.

A combination of strong forces of complementarity on the demand side and of highly inelastic supply, then, makes it difficult to detect what quality change may result from an increase in the relative level of the unobserved attribute. Since, however, both these forces tend to lose impact as adjustments are made to the initial change, the effects on quality can be more readily ascertained for long-run relationships.

A similar analysis carried out for the case of changing supply conditions of the unobserved attribute yields even more unwieldy results; in a sense that is of no great relevance, because while we can test for the implications of changes in the observed component, we cannot even detect changes in the unobserved one directly, let alone test for their implications.

---

[6] The unobserved attribute might be the retail services supplied by automobile dealers as compared with the observed "wholesale" commodity. The notion of perfectly elastic supply does not seem unreasonable in that case.

[7] Note that the correlation between the coefficients of horsepower and of weight (O & G, Table 2) is close to −1. Failure to account for one of them obviously could have resulted in seriously biased estimates.

[8] As an illustration, consider the removal of the automobile excise tax. The lowering of the tax constitutes a reduction in the wholesale cost but not in that of the attribute "retail services." Since the relative cost of retail services has increased, their quantity per wholesale unit should fall. It should not be surprising then to observe that the retail price of a car of given technical specifications had fallen by more than the tax.

DISCONTINUITY IN ATTRIBUTES

The regression coefficients of horsepower center around 0.1 (O & G, Table 2). In constructing the hedonic index such a coefficient is interpreted as a function of price. Given the semilogarithmic form employed, the price depends on the levels of the other variables and will also change with the level of horsepower itself. We will now proceed by assuming for simplicity that price is constant and is equal to $1 per horsepower.

If a market existed where consumers could purchase as much horsepower as they wanted at the going price, the use of that price to construct the index would pose no new problems. However, since no such market is at hand, the price of horsepower can be derived only by indirect methods. The normal justification for using prices in the construction of indexes is that since consumers adjust their behavior to the prices (or, more properly, to the price-ratio) underlying the index, these properly constitute a measure of *marginal* rates of substitution in consumption. That justification is invalid when marginal adjustments at the going price are not available.

The actual choice facing consumers is between, say, a 200- and a 250-horsepower engine at a price differential of $50. At a price of $1 per horsepower, one consumer might have chosen 190 units; a second, 220 units; and a third, 260. Each now has, however, to settle on one of the two actually available.[9] At a single point in time, the market offers a variety of all-or-nothing propositions, with no provision for continuous marginal adjustments.

Suppose now that a new model in introduced with engine sizes increased to 220 and 270 horsepower, the implicit price per horsepower remaining at $1. The hedonic index will then stay constant, but the true cost of living will not. The second consumer, whose demand at $P = 1 is 220, can now get exactly what he wants and is obviously better off.[10] The third consumer still cannot get his desired quantity; 250 horsepower was too small for him but the new 270 horsepower is too big, and the change leaves him about as well off as before. The first consumer is now worse off since the available engine sizes are farther from the size he prefers.[11] The hedonic index, then, gives a correct result only by accident, as in the case of the third consumer.

[9] It may be possible to modify the engine to change its power, but the price of $1 per horsepower does not apply to such modifications.
[10] If the slope of his demand curve is −0.01, he is now better off by $2, to *him* the real cost of the engine fell by about 1 per cent.
[11] If the slope of his demand curve is also −0.01, he is now worse off by $5.

The new engine sizes are presumably introduced due to some change in market conditions; for instance, the new and larger engine sizes may be in response to an increase in average income. However, it is important to recognize that some individuals, particularly those on the low end of the scale whose incomes did not increase, are actually hurt even though the price index did not record any change.

In the previous illustration, it was assumed that exactly two engine sizes are offered. It is clear that if one of them is withdrawn, and the price of the other is held constant, some consumers will be worse off and none better off. If a single new intermediate-size engine replaces the other two and is still priced at $1 per horsepower, one may presume that the sum of the dollar losses of the losers will exceed the corresponding gain to those better off. If a third engine size is added, some consumers will be better off and none worse off. The hedonic approach, however, by failing to incorporate discreteness in the offering of attributes, rather implicitly adopts a model that assumes perfect divisibility. Thus, if over time the number of engine sizes is increasing, the hedonic method is biased upwards.[12]

The limited number of engine sizes offered seems to reflect economies of scale in their production. May there not also be economies of scale with respect to the size of the engine? [13] If there are, the regression coefficient which measures the *average* price per horsepower will differ from the marginal price, which would decline with engine size.[14] Construction of a meaningful hedonic index under such conditions might present insurmountable problems.

UNOBSERVED ATTRIBUTES, INDIVISIBILITIES, AND CONVENTIONAL PRICE INDEXES

Although the foregoing comments have been explicitly directed to the hedonic approach, they actually apply, though probably somewhat less acutely, to other price indexes. How is a commodity defined and measured for purposes of, say, the Consumer Price Index? Most likely, the units adopted to construct the index are the same as those actually

---

[12] While Ohta and Griliches do not explicitly give the number of engines available in the market, they make it clear that the number of automobile models has increased substantially in recent years.

[13] The semilogarithmic form employed by Ohta and Griliches implies *diseconomies.* They report that experimentation with the squares of the hedonic variables proved significant, but signs of coefficients are not provided.

[14] The diseconomies implicit in the form Ohta and Griliches are using means that average price is higher than price on the margin. Consumers presumably will use the latter in their calculus.

used in the market. It is costly to measure and to explicitly price all dimensions of a commodity. Consequently, the market is likely to select a limited number of attributes by which a commodity is measured while others remain implicit. A change in the price of the explicit attributes relative to the implicit ones will lead to substitution and produce results of the type just discussed with respect to the unobserved hedonic attributes.

For instance, the Consumer Price Index often controls the physical features of a commodity but not the conditions of purchase — whether the service in a store is speedy, whether air conditioning is provided, whether it is well stocked, and so on. We would predict that as the wholesale cost of a commodity rises while the supply conditions of retail services remain constant, the quantity of retail services per unit of the good will increase. This will result in an increase in the retail price as normally measured exceeding that in the wholesale price. The increase in the quantity of retail services is a quality improvement, but since it is not accounted for, the consumer price index becomes biased upwards.

Most commodities are subject to significant indivisibilities and most commodities command substantial quantity discounts. There are, for example, economies of scale to headaches: the per-tablet price of aspirin is about three times higher by the dozen than by the hundred, and the cheapest way to get exactly thirty-five tablets is by buying a bottle of fifty and throwing away fifteen. The simplification adopted for purposes of constructing the index — assuming a single price (Which one?) and continuity of quantity — seems rather costly, and it obscures a wide range of economic behavior.

The problematic nature of enumerating attributes and of divisibility as brought to the fore by the hedonic method may help economists in realizing that all market transactions are more complex than virtually any text in economics, elementary or advanced, may lead us to believe. It also may help us realize that equalizing on *all* economic margins is not a common market phenomenon.

The previous discussion points to difficulties associated with the hedonic as well as with conventional price indexes, without suggesting how the difficulties may be resolved. If our only purpose is to obtain more accurate price indexes, the criticism is indeed unconstructive.

However, if we are interested in understanding the economic process, I believe that the preceding comments can serve some useful ends. The problem of the unobserved attributes offers a tool for testing the law of demand. The explicit recognition of discontinuities points to the need of constructing a testable model to indicate how choices are made with respect to the spacing and number of discrete offerings. These two issues, I feel, are ubiquitous and important and call for a major effort toward providing satisfactory explanations.

Reply to Yoram Barzel

MAKOTO OHTA AND ZVI GRILICHES

IT is not clear to us that the CPI and similar indexes are much better at "complete" enumeration. The hedonic indexes never aimed at "completeness," concentrating instead on a few, hopefully major, variable dimensions, letting the rest be impounded in the constant term. In any case, there is no cure against "left-out" characteristics without specifying more explicitly what has actually been left out. Otherwise, it is no different from a general allegation of "unmeasured quality change" against any kind of index.

Discontinuity and nonlinearity of the price schedule is a serious problem not treated adequately anywhere, as far as we know. To discuss it here will take us too far afield. We shall therefore only note, for whatever cold comfort this may bring us, that the same problem plagues also the CPI and all other similar indexes.

Cost-of-Living Indexes and Price Indexes for U.S. Meat and Produce, 1947–1971 *

LAURITS R. CHRISTENSEN

UNIVERSITY OF WISCONSIN

AND

MARILYN E. MANSER

STATE UNIVERSITY OF NEW YORK AT BUFFALO

I. INTRODUCTION

CONSUMER price indexes are usually computed as Laspeyres indexes of the components of the consumer budget. For example, the official Consumer Price Index for the U.S. is basically a Laspeyres index, although various ad hoc adjustments are included. A Laspeyres price index provides a comparison of the cost of a fixed bundle of goods relative to the cost in some base period. Such an index is not a "cost-of-living" index because it does not reflect the possibilities of substituting away from goods that become relatively more expensive. A cost-of-living index would provide a comparison of the cost of maintaining a particular level of well-being relative to the cost in the base period. It is well known that a Laspeyres index must be greater than, or equal to, a cost-of-living index, i.e., use of a Laspeyres index as an estimator for a cost-of-living index will result in an upward bias.

* The authors were both employed at the U.S. Bureau of Labor Statistics, Price Research Division, when the bulk of the analysis for this paper was performed. The authors are grateful to Leo de Bever, Brenda Erickson, and Brian Hedges for assistance with the research, to Ernst Berndt for invaluable advice on computational methods, and to Dianne Cummings, W. Erwin Diewert, Robert Pollak, and Jack Triplett for helpful comments.

The principal reason that Laspeyres indexes have not been replaced in use by cost-of-living indexes is that construction of the latter requires a knowledge of the utility function representing consumer preferences. In practice, the best that could be done would be to assume a particular utility function, estimate its unknown parameters, and construct a cost-of-living index using the estimated consumer preferences. This has been done by various researchers, for example, Tran Van Hoa (1969), Goldberger and Gamaletsos (1970), and Thangiah (1973).

The utility functions which have been specified for estimating consumer preferences have invariably maintained restrictions of additivity or homotheticity on consumer behavior. If additivity or homotheticity is not consistent with the set of data under consideration, the implied cost-of-living indexes may not be reliable. It would be desirable to specify a utility function which does not maintain additivity or homotheticity. The corresponding estimated cost-of-living indexes could then be compared with cost-of-living indexes from restricted utility functions and with price indexes such as the Laspeyres.

Christensen, Jorgenson, and Lau (1972) have proposed the translog utility function for estimating consumer preferences. The translog function is attractive because it does not maintain additivity or homotheticity. Additivity and homotheticity, however, can be achieved by imposing linear restrictions on the parameters of the translog function, thus permitting statistical tests of their validity. The translog function can be used to represent consumer preferences via a direct utility function or an indirect utility function. The indirect utility function leads more conveniently to a cost-of-living index, thus we use the indirect translog utility function as our most general representation of consumer behavior. For comparison, we also specify that consumer preferences can be represented by the following utility functions: the linear logarithmic utility function; the constant elasticity of substitution (CES) utility function; the Klein-Rubin (1947) utility function; a generalization of the Klein-Rubin utility function; Houthakker's (1960) indirect addilog utility function; the additive indirect translog utility function; and the homothetic indirect translog utility function. We compute the cost-of-living indexes implied by all of these utility functions.

It would be desirable to include many commodities in this study. This is precluded by considerations both of cost and of the availability of computer software. The software we have available would allow for the estimation of a translog utility function with six commodities. The cost of estimation increases much more than in proportion to the number of commodities. Rather than attempting to analyze a single set of six commodities, we decided to analyze two sets of data—each including four commodities. The two data sets are for U.S. consumption of meat and produce, 1947–1971.

We estimate the parameters of eight distinct utility functions for both U.S. meat consumption and U.S. produce consumption. For the functions which do not maintain additivity or homotheticity, we decisively reject the hypotheses that these restrictions hold. The indirect translog function dominates all the other functions in the ability to explain the observed budget shares for meat and produce. Thus, we argue that the translog function provides the most reliable cost-of-living indexes for meat and produce. Using the translog indexes as yardsticks, we compare cost-of-living indexes estimated from restrictive models of consumer behavior. We also compare the estimated cost-of-living indexes with the Laspeyres and other price indexes.

II. NEOCLASSICAL UTILITY FUNCTIONS WITH RESTRICTIONS OF HOMOTHETICITY AND ADDITIVITY

A direct utility function relates the level of consumer utility to the levels of consumption of commodities available. We find it convenient to express the direct utility function in the logarithmic form

$$\ln U = F(\ln X_1, \ldots, \ln X_n) \tag{1}$$

Classical utility theory requires the U be monotonic ($\partial U/\partial X_i > 0$) and strictly quasi-concave (have strictly convex indifference curves). A direct utility function will be strictly quasi-concave if the bordered Hessian matrix for U has all its principal minors of order greater than or equal to three alternating in sign, beginning with a plus.[1] Necessary conditions for the maximization of utility are $\partial U/\partial X_i = \lambda p_i$, where λ is the marginal utility of total expenditure.

A direct utility function, together with the necessary conditions for utility maximization, imply the existence of an indirect utility function, defined on total expenditure and the prices of all commodities.[2] The indirect utility function is homogeneous of degree zero and can be expressed as a function of the ratios of prices of all commodities to total expenditure. For convenience, we express the indirect utility function in the logarithmic form

---

[1] See Katzner (1970, pp. 210–211) for a clear statement of necessary and sufficient conditions for strict convexity of indifference curves.

[2] The concept of an indirect utility function is due to Hotelling (1932). See Lau (1969ab) and Diewert (1974) for many useful theorems relating the properties of direct and indirect utility functions.

$$\ln V = G(\ln p_1^*, \ldots, \ln p_n^*) \tag{2}$$

where $p_i^* = p_i/M$ are the normalized prices, and M is total expenditure on all commodities $\Sigma p_i X_i$. The indirect utility function has monotonicity and convexity conditions which correspond to those for the direct utility function. The monotonicity conditions are $\partial V/\partial p_i^* < 0$. The indirect utility function will correspond to strictly convex indifference curves if it is strictly quasi-convex. The indirect utility function will be strictly quasi-convex if the bordered Hessian for V has all negative principal minors of order greater than two.

A direct utility function U is said to be homothetic if it can be written as a monotonic transformation of a function which is homogeneous of degree one in the X_i. Similarly, an indirect utility function V is said to be homothetic if it can be written as a monotonic transformation of a function which is homogeneous of degree one in the p_i^*. An indirect utility function is homothetic if, and only if, the corresponding direct utility function is also homothetic.

A direct utility function is said to be additive if it can be written

$$\ln U = \sum_{i=1}^{n} \ln U^i(X_i) \tag{3}$$

where each of the functions U^i depends only on one of the commodities consumed, X_i. Similarly, an indirect utility function is said to be additive if it can be written

$$\ln V = \sum_{i=1}^{n} \ln V^i(p_i^*) \tag{4}$$

In general an additive indirect utility function does not correspond to an additive direct utility function.

The behavioral implications of particular utility functions can be illuminated conveniently by examining the corresponding price and expenditure elasticities of demand. For any utility function there are restrictions among these elasticities as shown by the Slutsky (1915) equations

$$\eta_{ij} = w_j \sigma_{ij} - w_j \eta_{iM} \qquad (i, j = 1, \ldots, n) \tag{5}$$

where $\eta_{ij} = \partial \ln X_i/\partial \ln p_j$ gives the uncompensated response to a price change with other prices and total expenditure held fixed; $w_j \sigma_{ij} = (\partial \ln X_i/\partial \ln p_j)_{\bar{U}}$ gives the compensated response to a price change with other prices held fixed but allowing total expenditure to adjust to maintain the initial utility level; and $\eta_{iM} = \partial \ln X_i/\partial \ln M$ gives the response to a change in total expenditure with prices held fixed. The σ_{ij} are the Allen (1938) Elasticities of Substitution (AES). We summarize here well-known restrictions on the elasticities: [3]

$$\sum_{i=1}^{n} w_i \eta_{ij} = -w_j \qquad (j = 1, \ldots, n) \tag{6}$$

$$\sum_{i=1}^{n} w_i w_j \sigma_{ij} = 0 \qquad (j = 1, \ldots, n) \tag{7}$$

$$\sum_{i=1}^{n} w_i \eta_{iM} = 1 \tag{8}$$

$$\sum_{j=1}^{n} w_j \sigma_{ij} = 0 \qquad (i = 1, \ldots, n) \tag{9}$$

$$\sum_{j=1}^{n} \eta_{ij} = -\eta_{iM} \qquad (i = 1, \ldots, n) \tag{10}$$

Homotheticity and additivity restrictions on utility functions imply additional restrictions on price and expenditure elasticities. Homotheticity of a direct or indirect utility function implies that $\eta_{iM} = 1$ for all commodities, but does not impose any explicit restrictions on the price elasticities.

Direct additivity has several implications for the demand elasticities: Theil (1967) has shown that

$$\eta_{iM} > 0 \qquad (i = 1, \ldots, n) \tag{11}$$

and Goldberger (1967) has shown that

$$w_j \sigma_{ij} > 0 \qquad (i \neq j; i, j = 1, \ldots, n) \tag{12}$$

Thus, direct additivity rules out inferior goods and complementary goods. In addition Houthakker (1960) has shown that for direct utility functions

$$\eta_{ik}/\eta_{jk} = \eta_{iM}/\eta_{jM} = \sigma_{ik}/\sigma_{jk} \qquad (i \neq k, j \neq k; i, j, k = 1, \ldots, n) \tag{13}$$

Thus, direct additivity implies that the relative percentage response of any two commodities to a price change must be the same as the relative response to a change in total expenditure.

The restriction of additivity on the direct utility function is neither necessary nor sufficient for additivity of the corresponding indirect

[3] This summary is taken from Henderson and Quandt (1971). For derivation and discussion, see, for example, Goldberger (1967).

utility function. Houthakker has shown that indirect additivity implies that all commodities have equal percentage responses to the change in any single commodity price.

$$\eta_{ik} = \eta_{jk} \qquad (i \neq k, j \neq k; i, j, k = 1, \ldots, n) \qquad (14)$$

III. ALTERNATIVE UTILITY FUNCTIONS FOR MODELING CONSUMER BEHAVIOR

In this section, we present eight different utility functions which can be used to represent consumer behavior. From each utility function, we derive a set of budget share equations which are functions only of the normalized prices.

Christensen, Jorgenson, and Lau (1972) have proposed the translog function to represent consumer preferences with no a priori restrictions of homotheticity or additivity. The translog function can be used as a direct utility function or an indirect utility function. Since indirect utility functions are convenient for estimating true cost-of-living indexes, we deal only with the indirect translog utility function in this paper.[4] The indirect translog utility function V is conveniently written in the logarithmic form

$$-\ln V = \sum_{i=1}^{n} \alpha_i \ln p_i^* + \frac{1}{2} \sum_{i=1}^{n} \sum_{j=1}^{n} \beta_{ij} \ln p_i^* \ln p_j^* \qquad (15)$$

where $p_i^* = p_i/M$ are the normalized prices, M is total expenditure, $\sum_{i=1}^{n} p_i X_i$, and $\beta_{ij} = \beta_{ji}$

Making use of Roy's (1943) identity

$$\frac{p_i X_i}{M} = -\frac{\partial \ln V}{\partial \ln p_i} \bigg/ \frac{\partial \ln V}{\partial \ln M} \qquad (i = 1, \ldots, n)$$

we obtain a set of budget share equations corresponding to the indirect translog utility function

$$w_i = \frac{\alpha_i + \sum_j \beta_{ij} \ln p_j^*}{\sum_j \alpha_j + \sum_j \sum_i \beta_{ij} \ln p_j^*} \qquad (i = 1, \ldots, n) \qquad (16)$$

where $w_i = p_i X_i/M$.

[4] See Christensen, Jorgenson, and Lau (1972) and Christensen and Manser (1974) for estimates of direct, as well as indirect, translog utility functions.

Homotheticity can be imposed on the indirect translog function by restricting sums of second-order parameters to be equal to zero[5]

$$\sum_i \beta_{ij} = 0 \qquad (j = 1, \ldots, n) \tag{17}$$

Imposition of the homotheticity restrictions reduces (16) to

$$w_i = \left(\alpha_i + \sum_j \beta_{ij} \ln p_j^*\right) \bigg/ \sum_j \alpha_j \qquad (i = 1, \ldots, n) \tag{18}$$

Additivity can be imposed on the indirect translog function by eliminating all interactions between normalized prices.

$$\beta_{ij} = 0 \qquad (i \neq j; \ i,j = 1, \ldots, n) \tag{19}$$

With these restrictions imposed, (15) becomes

$$-\ln V = \sum_i \alpha_i \ln p_i^* + \sum_i \beta_{ii}(\ln p_i^*)^2 \tag{20}$$

and the budget share equations (16) become

$$w_i = \frac{\alpha_i + \beta_{ii} \ln p_i^*}{\sum_j \alpha_j + \sum_j \beta_{jj} \ln p_j^*} \qquad (i = 1, \ldots, n) \tag{21}$$

The simultaneous imposition of homotheticity and additivity reduces the indirect translog form to the indirect linear logarithmic utility function

$$-\ln V = \sum_i \alpha_i \ln p_i^* \tag{22}$$

and the budget share equations (16) to

$$w_i = \alpha_i \bigg/ \sum_j \alpha_j \qquad (i = 1, \ldots, n) \tag{23}$$

The budget share equations (23) implied by the indirect linear logarithmic utility function are identical to those obtained by maximizing the direct linear logarithmic function

$$\ln U = \sum_i \alpha_i \ln X_i \tag{24}$$

subject to a budget constraint.

[5] See Christensen, Jorgenson, and Lau (1972) for detailed discussion of the points in this paragraph.

Several utility functions have been proposed, which are generalizations of the direct linear logarithmic function. The Klein-Rubin (1947) function, which adds n nonhomogeneity parameters, can be written [6]

$$\ln U = \sum_i \alpha_i \ln (X_i - \gamma_i) \tag{25}$$

Budget share equations for the Klein-Rubin function can be written

$$w_i = \gamma_i p_i^* + \frac{\alpha_i}{\sum \alpha_j} (1 - \sum_j \gamma_j p_j^*) \qquad (i = 1, \ldots, n) \tag{26}$$

The linear logarithmic function (24) entails that all elasticities of substitution are equal to unity. The function can be generalized to the CES function, which has elasticities of substitution which are equal, but not necessarily equal to unity. The CES function, which is homothetic and additive, can be used to represent either the direct or indirect utility function. We write the direct CES function

$$\ln U = \frac{\sigma}{\sigma - 1} \ln \sum_i \delta_i X_i^{\frac{\sigma-1}{\sigma}} \tag{27}$$

Budget share equations for the direct CES form can be written

$$w_i = \frac{\alpha_i (p_i^*)^{1-\sigma}}{\sum_j \alpha_j (p_j^*)^{1-\sigma}} \qquad (i = 1, \ldots, n) \tag{28}$$

where $\alpha_i = \delta_i^\sigma$. Several authors have noted that the generalizations to the linear logarithmic form provided by the Klein-Rubin function and the CES function can be made simultaneously.[7] This results in what we shall call the generalized Klein-Rubin function, which can be written

$$\ln U = \frac{\sigma}{\sigma - 1} \ln \sum_i \delta_i (X_i - \gamma_i)^{\frac{\sigma-1}{\sigma}} \tag{29}$$

Budget share equations for the generalized Klein-Rubin function can be written

$$w_i = \gamma_i p_i^* + \frac{\alpha_i (p_i^*)^{1-\sigma}}{\sum_j \alpha_j (p_j^*)^{1-\sigma}} \left[1 - \sum_j \gamma_j p_j^* \right] \qquad (i = 1, \ldots, n) \tag{30}$$

[6] The expenditure system corresponding to the Klein-Rubin utility function is often referred to as the Stone-Geary linear expenditure system; see Stone (1954) and Geary (1949).

[7] See, for example, Christensen (1968), Johansen (1969), Pollak (1971a), Wales (1971), Gamaletsos (1972), and Brown and Heien (1972).

where $\alpha_i = \delta_i^\sigma$ and σ is the elasticity of substitution. If $\sigma =$
reduces to (26); while if $\gamma_i = 0$, $i = 1, \ldots, n$, (30) reduces t
Similarly if $\sigma = 1$, (28) reduces to (23); while if $\gamma_i = 0$, $i = 1, \ldots$
(26) reduces to (23).

The Klein-Rubin, CES, and generalized Klein-Rubin functions
all additive; the CES is homothetic, while the Klein-Rubin and g
eralized Klein-Rubin functions are marginally homothetic. Houthakke
(1960) proposed another additive but nonhomothetic function, whic
has proved to be popular for empirical work. The indirect addilo
utility function can be written

$$-\ln V = \ln \sum_i \delta_i (p_i^*)^{1-\sigma_i} \tag{31}$$

Budget share equations for the indirect addilog function can be written

$$w_i = \frac{\alpha_i (p_i^*)^{1-\sigma_i}}{\sum_j \alpha_j (p_j^*)^{1-\sigma_j}} \tag{32}$$

where $\alpha_i = \delta_i (1 - \sigma_i)$. If all the σ_i are equal, (32) is equivalent to (28),
the budget shares for the CES form which is homothetic.

All the budget share systems we have described are homogeneous of
degree zero in the α_i's. Thus, only $n - 1$ of the α_i's can be estimated
subject to some normalization restriction. It is convenient to use the
normalization $\sum_i \alpha_i = 1$ for all budget share systems.[8]

IV. ALTERNATIVE ESTIMATES OF U.S. CONSUMER PREFERENCES FOR MEAT AND PRODUCE, 1947–1971

In the previous section, we derived eight distinct sets of budget share
equations, which can be used to represent consumer preferences. In
this section we implement the various sets of budget share equations
for two sets of time series for United States food consumption.

---

[8] We impose a second normalization restriction, $\sum\sum_{i \neq j} \beta_{ij} = 0$, on the indirect translog
form, which is not required for identification or adding up. The original motivation for
this restriction in Christensen, Jorgenson, and Lau (1972) was to assure that a translog
approximation to an additive function was itself additive. This restriction is not necessary if the translog function is being used as a utility function in its own right. Christensen
and Manser (1974) obtained slightly preferable empirical results by maintaining this
second normalization restriction. We maintain the restriction here to avoid presenting
results which differ from our earlier paper.

In substantially revising their 1972 paper, Christensen, Jorgenson, and Lau (1975)
dropped the second normalization. The publication deadline did not permit us to reflect
the new developments in CJL (1975). However, the empirical results of this paper would
be only slightly affected by recognition of these developments.

A. Data for U.S. Meat and Produce Consumption 1947–1971

There are no official time series available for United States consumption of major types of food. We have constructed price and quantity indexes for four categories of meat and four categories of produce from data given in U.S. Department of Agriculture (USDA) (1968, 1971). Quantity data are given for numerous commodities in terms of pounds per capita. We convert these data to constant dollar expenditures by multiplying them by the U.S. Bureau of Labor Statistics (BLS) average retail price for 1957–1959. We aggregate subcomponents of meat and produce by summing constant dollar values.

The four meat series are computed as follows: [9] (1) Fish—fresh and frozen plus canned plus cured (Table 9); (2) Beef—beef plus veal (Table 8); (3) Poultry—chicken plus turkey (Table 10); (4) Pork (Table 8). We use the BLS price indexes given in Table 97 of USDA (1968) corresponding to our four types of meat. The price and quantity indexes for meat are presented in Tables 1 and 2. The budget shares constructed from the price and quantity indexes are presented in Table 3. Our data are similar to the meat data analyzed by Brown and Heien (1972).[10]

The four constant dollar series for produce are computed from the 78 subcomponents of fruit and vegetables in Tables 13 through 23 of USDA (1968). The fresh fruit category includes oranges, tangerines and tangelos, grapefruit, lemons and limes, apples, bananas, grapes, peaches, pears, strawberries, cantaloups, watermelons, and other fresh fruit. The processed fruit category includes canned fruit (apples and applesauce, apricots, cherries, citrus segments, cranberries, fruit cocktail, peaches, pineapple, and other), canned fruit juice (orange, grapefruit, blended citrus, pineapple, and other), chilled fruit and juice, frozen fruit and juice (orange juice, other citrus juice, strawberries, peaches, raspberries, and other) and dried fruit (prunes, raisins, and other). The fresh vegetables category includes potatoes, asparagus, snap beans, broccoli, cabbage, carrots, cauliflower, celery, corn, lettuce, onions and shallots, spinach, tomatoes, and other fresh vegetables. The processed vegetables category includes canned vegetables (potatoes, asparagus,

---

[9] The table numbers given are from *USDA* (1968).

[10] Originally, we used the 1946–1968 meat data constructed by Brown and Heien. In attempting to update their data, we discovered several details which we found unappealing. The most important was that they included edible offals with beef. It seemed to us inappropriate to lump a relatively inexpensive commodity (which is probably not very income elastic) with beef (which is highly income elastic). Thus, we reworked the entire data set, which we present in Tables 1, 2, and 3.

TABLE 1

Price Indexes for Meat, U.S., 1947–1971
(1957–1959 = 1.000)

Year	Fish p_1	Beef p_2	Poultry p_3	Pork p_4
1947	.783	.780	1.260	.932
1948	.903	.944	1.397	.961
1949	.907	.881	1.317	.890
1950	.890	.970	1.261	.878
1951	1.016	1.133	1.321	.931
1952	.990	1.124	1.326	.921
1953	.953	.886	1.293	1.025
1954	.958	.853	1.167	1.057
1955	.939	.844	1.215	.910
1956	.938	.831	1.065	.864
1957	.950	.892	1.038	.995
1958	1.016	1.038	1.026	1.061
1959	1.034	1.069	.935	.944
1960	1.035	1.042	.950	.938
1961	1.058	1.025	.858	.982
1962	1.102	1.062	.907	.991
1963	1.100	1.050	.893	.966
1964	1.074	1.019	.873	.961
1965	1.106	1.068	.900	1.094
1966	1.178	1.124	.949	1.251
1967	1.218	1.131	.889	1.148
1968	1.238	1.177	.917	1.150
1969	1.306	1.295	.969	1.252
1970	1.437	1.352	.964	1.331
1971	1.586	1.413	.969	1.205

green beans, lima beans, corn, peas, pickles, spinach, whole tomatoes, tomato catsup, tomato paste, vegetable juices, and other), frozen vegetables (potatoes, asparagus, green beans, lima beans, broccoli, brussels sprouts, cauliflower, corn, peas, spinach, and other) and other processed potatoes.

The price series corresponding to each of these four categories is constructed from component BLS price indexes. The procedure used is as close as possible to that used by BLS in constructing the con-

TABLE 2

Per Capita Constant Dollar (1957–1959) Expenditures
on Meat, U.S., 1947–1971

Year	Fish X_1	Beef X_2	Poultry X_3	Pork X_4
1947	6.734	45.522	10.068	36.879
1948	7.288	41.016	9.893	35.967
1949	7.172	41.134	10.585	35.910
1950	7.766	40.264	11.460	36.708
1951	7.333	35.267	12.114	38.076
1952	7.338	39.051	12.453	38.418
1953	7.460	49.020	12.416	33.687
1954	7.338	50.429	13.087	31.806
1955	6.867	50.752	12.251	35.397
1956	6.817	52.283	13.755	35.625
1957	6.696	51.000	14.622	32.376
1958	6.968	47.160	15.794	31.920
1959	7.162	46.704	16.367	35.796
1960	6.751	48.596	15.900	34.428
1961	7.023	49.270	17.445	32.889
1962	6.963	49.475	17.233	33.687
1963	7.035	51.680	17.443	34.656
1964	6.879	54.612	17.941	34.656
1965	7.156	54.403	19.031	31.122
1966	7.145	56.470	20.407	30.837
1967	6.963	57.210	21.327	33.972
1968	7.206	58.732	21.092	35.055
1969	7.312	59.067	22.025	34.428
1970	7.711	60.307	23.009	35.226
1971	7.323	59.881	23.258	38.646

TABLE 3

Budget Shares and Per Capita Expenditures
for Meat, U.S., 1947–1971

| Year | Budget Shares | | | | Total Meat Expenditures, Dollars Per Capita |
	Fish	Beef	Poultry	Pork	
1947	.060	.404	.144	.391	87.84
1948	.070	.413	.148	.369	93.69
1949	.073	.409	.157	.361	88.65
1950	.075	.422	.156	.348	92.65
1951	.075	.404	.162	.359	98.86
1952	.070	.426	.160	.343	103.05
1953	.070	.429	.159	.341	101.12
1954	.071	.435	.154	.340	98.94
1955	.067	.444	.154	.334	96.38
1956	.067	.456	.154	.323	95.27
1957	.064	.458	.153	.325	99.24
1958	.067	.461	.153	.319	106.10
1959	.070	.469	.144	.318	106.43
1960	.067	.482	.144	.307	105.02
1961	.071	.480	.142	.307	105.20
1962	.070	.481	.143	.306	109.23
1963	.070	.489	.140	.301	111.06
1964	.066	.497	.140	.297	112.00
1965	.068	.496	.146	.291	117.19
1966	.065	.489	.149	.297	129.83
1967	.065	.493	.145	.297	131.14
1968	.065	.502	.140	.293	137.70
1969	.063	.508	.142	.286	150.49
1970	.069	.504	.137	.290	161.68
1971	.070	.512	.136	.282	165.33

sumer price index in order to make the data series for produce comparable with the data series for meat. The price index for each of the four categories in 1947 includes only the few price indexes given for that year; as BLS increased coverage, the new price index was brought into the series using a forward linking procedure. The price and quantity indexes for produce are presented in Tables 4 and 5. The budget shares constructed from the price and quantity indexes are presented in Table 6.

B. Estimation of U.S. Consumer Preferences for Meat and Produce

For convenience of comparison, we draw together the budget share equations derived in Section III and present them in Table 7. We illustrate the relationships among the budget share equations in Figures 1 and 2. The indirect translog form and its special cases are illustrated schematically in Figure 1. The generalized Klein-Rubin form and its special cases are illustrated schematically in Figure 2. The indirect addilog form specializes to the indirect CES form. The budget share equations for the indirect CES have the same form as for the direct CES; thus the direct CES budget share equations can be viewed as a special case of the indirect addilog equations.

We specify classical additive disturbance terms for all the budget share equations in Table 7. To estimate the unknown parameters of the budget share equations, we use the iterative-Zellner (1962, 1963) estimation procedure (IZEF). This procedure has been used by Berndt and Christensen (1973 a, b, c) for the homothetic version of the translog model, which is linear in the parameters. We have followed the same procedures generalized to our nonlinear functional forms. It is well known that IZEF is equivalent to maximum likelihood estimation (assuming a joint normal error structure) for linear models. We have confirmed that this also holds for our nonlinear models. We used a maximum likelihood computer program (by Yonathan Bard, IBM) on our models and obtained results identical to our IZEF results. Our IZEF computations were carried out on the CDC 6600, using program TSP. The nonlinear estimation routine in TSP uses a combination of the Gauss-Newton method and the method of steepest descent.

For convenience in estimation, the price indexes p_1, p_2, p_3, p_4 and per capita total expenditure M were all scaled to equal 1.0 in 1959, for both sets of data. The parameter estimates reported above are not invariant to the scaling of the data, but the fitted budget shares are invariant. It can also be shown that the monotonicity and convexity conditions are invariant to scaling, as are all the implied price and in-

TABLE 4

Price Indexes for Produce, U S., 1947–1971
(1957–1959 = 1.000)

Year	Fresh Fruit p_1	Processed Fruit p_2	Fresh Vegetables p_3	Processed Vegetables p_4
1947	.798	.952	.812	.989
1948	.807	.936	.893	.962
1949	.867	.922	.872	.933
1950	.835	.855	.754	.898
1951	.814	1.006	.875	1.017
1952	.896	.846	1.100	1.005
1953	.929	.869	.890	1.002
1954	.925	.833	.855	.983
1955	.920	.835	.917	.983
1956	.947	.882	.994	1.010
1957	.982	.841	.965	.982
1958	1.025	1.092	1.022	1.008
1959	.994	1.067	1.013	1.010
1960	1.039	.964	1.050	1.018
1961	1.067	1.020	.990	1.072
1962	1.076	.916	1.052	1.062
1963	1.165	1.169	1.070	1.047
1964	1.178	1.203	1.179	1.040
1965	1.129	1.018	1.302	1.065
1966	1.184	.980	1.253	1.096
1967	1.197	.873	1.250	1.142
1968	1.346	.971	1.328	1.177
1969	1.317	1.029	1.401	1.178
1970	1.341	1.008	1.482	1.217
1971	1.422	1.055	1.525	1.261

come elasticities, Allen elasticities of substitution (AES), and test results reported in this paper.[11]

We first estimate by IZEF the translog budget share equations with only the two normalization restrictions imposed. The IZEF estimated covariance matrix is then used to fit the homothetic translog, the additive translog, and linear logarithmic budget share equations. As dis-

[11] See Christensen and Manser (1974) for proof for the translog function. Proofs for the other functions are similar.

TABLE 5

Per Capita Constant Dollar (1957–1959) Expenditures
on Produce, U.S., 1947–1971

Year	Fresh Fruit X_1	Processed Fruit X_2	Fresh Vegetables X_3	Processed Vegetables X_4
1947	25.000	9.667	24.375	10.144
1948	23.064	9.994	23.334	9.802
1949	21.934	10.248	22.807	9.989
1950	19.640	11.045	22.296	10.740
1951	21.073	10.802	22.172	11.175
1952	20.081	12.148	21.287	11.718
1953	19.319	12.323	21.309	12.252
1954	18.711	12.564	20.972	12.233
1955	17.791	13.734	20.960	12.994
1956	17.766	13.964	20.716	13.909
1957	17.252	14.326	21.300	14.247
1958	16.946	13.563	20.554	14.976
1959	17.176	13.681	20.475	15.784
1960	16.818	14.242	21.141	16.487
1961	16.317	13.838	21.010	16.783
1962	15.522	14.349	20.400	17.860
1963	14.318	13.164	20.385	18.355
1964	14.928	12.755	19.710	19.446
1965	15.270	13.534	19.266	20.861
1966	15.167	13.593	19.015	21.370
1967	15.216	15.053	18.715	23.714
1968	15.024	14.498	18.990	23.861
1969	15.106	15.411	18.127	25.016
1970	15.471	15.604	18.565	25.778
1971	15.221	15.990	18.222	26.201

TABLE 6

Budget Shares and Per Capita Expenditures
for Produce, U.S., 1947–1971

| Year | Budget Shares | | | | Total Produce Expenditures, Dollars Per Capita |
	Fresh Fruit	Processed Fruit	Fresh Vegetables	Processed Vegetables	
1947	.338	.156	.336	.160	58.96
1948	.320	.161	.358	.162	58.23
1949	.330	.164	.345	.162	57.67
1950	.314	.181	.321	.184	52.30
1951	.292	.185	.330	.193	58.79
1952	.283	.162	.369	.186	63.46
1953	.300	.179	.317	.205	59.91
1954	.300	.181	.310	.208	57.74
1955	.274	.192	.321	.213	59.82
1956	.264	.193	.323	.220	63.78
1957	.267	.190	.324	.220	63.54
1958	.254	.217	.308	.221	68.28
1959	.250	.214	.303	.233	68.34
1960	.249	.195	.316	.239	70.20
1961	.248	.201	.296	.256	70.31
1962	.238	.187	.305	.270	70.28
1963	.228	.211	.298	.263	73.09
1964	.230	.201	.304	.265	76.39
1965	.220	.176	.320	.284	78.32
1966	.229	.170	.303	.298	78.53
1967	.223	.161	.286	.331	81.84
1968	.231	.161	.288	.321	87.60
1969	.220	.175	.280	.325	90.61
1970	.217	.165	.289	.329	95.38
1971	.218	.170	.280	.333	99.35

TABLE 7

Budget Share Equations for Estimating Consumer Preferences

Utility Function	Budget Share Equations	Number of Parameters General	Four Commodities	Restrictions Used In Estimation	Number of Free Parameters General	Four Commodities
Indirect Translog	$w_i = \dfrac{\alpha_i + \sum \beta_{ij} \ln p_j^*}{\sum \alpha_j + \sum \sum \beta_{ij} \ln p_j^*}$ $\beta_{ij} = \beta_{ji}$	$n(n+3)/2$	14	$\sum \alpha_i = 1$ $\sum_i \sum_{i \neq j} \beta_{ij} = 0$	$[n(n+3) - 4]/2$	12
Homothetic Indirect Translog	$w_i = \left(\alpha_i + \sum \beta_{ij} \ln p_j^*\right) \Big/ \sum \alpha_j$ $\beta_{ij} = \beta_{ji}$	$n(n+3)/2$	14	$\sum \alpha_i = 1$ $\sum_i \sum_{i \neq j} \beta_{ij} = 0$ $\sum_j \beta_{ij} = 0$	$[n(n+3) - 8]/2$	8
Additive Indirect Translog	$w_i = \dfrac{\alpha_i + \beta_{ii} \ln p_i^*}{\sum \alpha_j + \sum \beta_{jj} \ln p_j^*}$	$2n$	8	$\sum \alpha_i = 1$	$2n - 1$	7
Indirect Addilog	$w_i = \dfrac{\alpha_i (p_i^*)^{1-\sigma_i}}{\sum \alpha_j (p_j^*)^{1-\sigma_j}}$	$2n$	8	$\sum \alpha_i = 1$	$2n - 1$	7

416

Generalized Klein-Rubin	$w_i = \gamma_i p_i^* + \dfrac{\alpha_i (p_i^*)^{1-\sigma}}{\sum_j \alpha_j (p_j^*)^{1-\sigma}}$ $\times [1 - \sum_j \gamma_j p_j^*]$	$2n+1$	9	$\sum \alpha_i = 1$	$2n$	8
Klein-Rubin	$w_i = \gamma_i p_i^* + \dfrac{\alpha_i}{\sum_j \alpha_j}\left(1 - \sum_j \gamma_j p_j^*\right)$	$2n$	8	$\sum \alpha_i = 1$	$2n-1$	7
CES	$w_i = \dfrac{\alpha_i (p_i^*)^{1-\sigma}}{\sum_j \alpha_j (p_j^*)^{1-\sigma}}$	$n+1$	5	$\sum \alpha_i = 1$	n	4
Linear Logarithmic	$w_i = \alpha_i \Big/ \sum_j \alpha_j$	n	4	$\sum \alpha_i = 1$	$n-1$	3

417

FIGURE 1

Schematic Representation of Budget Shares for
the Translog Form and Its Special Cases

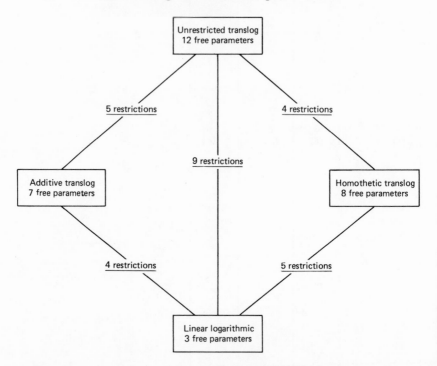

cussed in Christensen and Manser (1974), we test the validity of the
homotheticity and additivity restrictions. The test results reported in
Table 8 indicate that homotheticity and additivity are decisively rejected. The rejection of additivity does not preclude groupwise additivity. As reported in Christensen and Manser (1974) the hypothesis
that (fish) and (beef, poultry, and pork) comprise additive groups cannot be rejected. All other types of groupwise additivity are rejected
for both the meat and produce data.

Since the imposition of fish additivity does not result in a significant
loss of fit, we adopt this form as our preferred translog specification for
the meat data. The preferred specification for the produce data, however, does not have any additivity restrictions imposed. In Table 9 we
present parameter estimates for the translog and its special cases for

FIGURE 2

Schematic Representation of Budget Shares for the
Generalized Stone-Geary Form, the Indirect Addilog
Form, and Their Special Cases

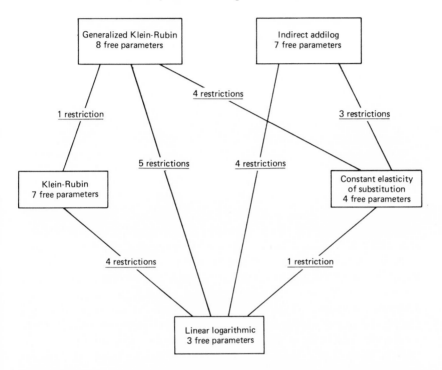

the meat data; in Table 10 we present the corresponding estimates for the produce data. For the meat data, the parameters β_{12}, β_{13}, and β_{14} are equal to zero, since fish additivity is imposed. The monotonicity and convexity conditions for the translog forms are satisfied in all years for the meat data. For the produce data, the montonicity and convexity conditions for the translog forms are also satisfied in all years — with the exception that the convexity conditions are not satisfied for the homothetic translog form for any year.

In Table 11, we present parameter estimates for the indirect addilog function, the generalized Klein-Rubin function and their special cases (except the linear logarithmic function for the meat data). In Table 12 we present the corresponding estimates for the produce data. For the

TABLE 8

Tests of Homotheticity and Additivity Restrictions
on the Translog Utility Function

Hypothesis	Number of Restrictions	F Statistic		Residual Degrees of Freedom	Critical Value (.01 Level)
		Meat Data	Produce Data		
Homotheticity	4	20.86	11.76	63	3.63
Additivity	5	10.15	13.48	63	3.32
Homotheticity and Additivity	9	31.45	37.61	63	2.71
Homotheticity, Conditional on Additivity	4	34.71	35.34	68	3.61
Additivity, Conditional on Homotheticity	5	18.27	35.48	67	3.61

meat data, we present IZEF estimates for the generalized Klein-Rubin and indirect addilog models. The IZEF estimated covariance matrix from the generalized Klein-Rubin model is used to obtain the Klein-Rubin parameter estimates; similarly, the IZEF estimated covariance matrix from the indirect addilog model is used to obtain the CES parameter estimates. For the produce data, the IZEF estimation procedure did not converge for the generalized Klein-Rubin model. Thus, we report IZEF estimates for the Klein-Rubin and indirect addilog models. The IZEF estimated covariance matrix from the indirect addilog model is used to obtain the CES parameter estimates. The monotonicity and convexity conditions for the generalized Klein-Rubin and indirect addilog utility functions and their special cases are satisfied for all years in both the meat and produce data.

We perform tests of homotheticity on the Klein-Rubin, generalized Klein-Rubin, and indirect addilog functions. The imposition of homotheticity on either the generalized Klein-Rubin or the indirect addilog function results in the CES function; similarly the imposition of homotheticity on the Klein-Rubin function results in the linear logarithmic function. The test results reported in Table 13 indicate that homotheticity is decisively rejected for both the meat and produce data. This implies the rejection of the CES and linear logarithmic functional forms.

TABLE 9

Parameter Estimates for the Indirect Translog
Function and Special Cases:
(1) Fish, (2) Beef, (3) Poultry, and (4) Pork
(standard errors in parentheses)

Parameter	Translog	Homothetic Translog	Additive Translog	Linear Logarithmic
α_1	.0710	.0690	.0711	.0683
	(.0006)	(.0012)	(.0008)	(.0016)
α_2	.4621	.4681	.4612	.4626
	(.0033)	(.0043)	(.0042)	(.0055)
α_3	.1449	.1392	.1494	.1481
	(.0016)	(.0019)	(.0016)	(.0022)
α_4	.3220	.3237	.3183	.3210
	(.0037)	(.0039)	(.0038)	(.0043)
β_{11}	.0440	.0207	.0635	0
	(.0130)	(.0147)	(.0158)	
β_{12}	0	−.0018	0	0
		(.0114)		
β_{13}	0	.0042	0	0
		(.0037)		
β_{14}	0	−.0231	0	0
		(.0198)		
β_{22}	−.2606	.0225	−.1923	0
	(.0501)	(.0161)	(.0630)	
β_{23}	−.0582	−.0710	0	0
	(.0128)	(.0151)		
β_{24}	.0103	.0502	0	0
	(.0208)	(.0289)		
β_{33}	.0209	.0253	.0358	0
	(.0053)	(.0063)	(.0048)	
β_{34}	.0479	.0414	0	0
	(.0309)	(.0233)		
β_{44}	.1464	−.0685	.3086	0
	(.0535)	(.0310)	(.0505)	

TABLE 10

Parameter Estimates for the Translog Function and Special Cases:
(1) Fresh Fruit, (2) Processed Fruit, (3) Fresh Vegetables,
and (4) Processed Vegetables
(standard errors in parentheses)

Parameter	Translog	Homothetic Translog	Additive Translog	Linear Logarithmic
α_1	.2693	.2593	.2581	.2614
	(.0055)	(.0058)	(.0053)	(.0114)
α_2	.1879	.2029	.1867	.1818
	(.0048)	(.0049)	(.0048)	(.0170)
α_3	.3166	.3179	.3037	.3132
	(.0030)	(.0034)	(.0030)	(.0166)
α_4	.2262	.2227	.2515	.2436
	(.0056)	(.0063)	(.0054)	(.0086)
β_{11}	−.1228	−.0281	.0943	0
	(.1277)	(.0262)	(.0622)	
β_{12}	.0911	−.0296	0	0
	(.0314)	(.0230)		
β_{13}	−.1250	−.2140	0	0
	(.0924)	(.0229)		
β_{14}	.1087	.2717	0	0
	(.0443)	(.0274)		
β_{22}	.1072	.1539	.0608	0
	(.0275)	(.0213)	(.0257)	
β_{23}	.1167	.0291	0	0
	(.0313)	(.0159)		
β_{24}	−.1486	−.1534	0	0
	(.0344)	(.0304)		
β_{33}	.2692	.0887	.3197	0
	(.0795)	(.0167)	(.0559)	
β_{34}	−.0430	.0962	0	0
	(.0427)	(.0192)		
β_{44}	−.4289	−.2145	−.5086	0
	(.0581)	(.0311)	(.0616)	

TABLE 11

Parameter Estimates for the Indirect Addilog,
Generalized Klein-Rubin Function, and Special Cases:
(1) Fish, (2) Beef, (3) Poultry, and (4) Pork

Parameter	Generalized Klein-Rubin	Klein-Rubin	CES	Parameter	Indirect Addilog
γ_1	.0508	.0566	0	σ_1	.1176
γ_2	−1.0211	−.1229	0	σ_2	1.1918
γ_3	−.1542	.0334	0	σ_3	.7070
γ_4	.2190	.2698	0	σ_4	.2435
α_1	.0097	.0170	.0684	α_1	.0705
α_2	.7841	.7808	.4726	α_2	.4651
α_3	.1588	.1490	.1432	α_3	.1472
α_4	.0474	.0532	.3157	α_4	.3172
σ	.3267	1	.6634		

TABLE 12

Parameter Estimates for the Indirect Addilog,
Klein-Rubin, and CES Functions: [a]
(1) Fresh Fruit, (2) Processed Fruit, (3) Fresh Vegetables, and
(4) Processed Vegetables

Parameter	Klein-Rubin	CES	Parameter	Indirect Addilog
γ_1	.0269	0	σ_1	.4758
γ_2	.1418	0	σ_2	.7033
γ_3	.2026	0	σ_3	.0156
γ_4	−2.5859	0	σ_4	3.3297
α_1	.0717	.2586	α_1	.2589
α_2	.0164	.1923	α_2	.1868
α_4	.0324	.3093	α_3	.3057
α_4	.8795	.2398	α_4	.2486
σ	1	.5093		

[a] The generalized Klein-Rubin did not provide a statistically significant generalization of the Klein-Rubin function for the produce data.

TABLE 13

Tests of Homotheticity Restrictions on the Klein-Rubin,
Generalized Klein-Rubin, and Indirect
Addilog Utility Functions

	Number of Re- strictions	F Statistic		Residual Degrees of Freedom	Critical Value (0.1 Level)
		Meat Data	Produce Data		
Generalized Klein-Rubin	4	18.76	a	67	3.61
Klein-Rubin	4	69.64	72.93	68	3.61
Indirect Addilog	3	12.10	46.89	68	3.61

a We did not succeed in obtaining IZEF estimates for the produce data.

To indicate the explanatory power for each of the models, R^2's are presented in Table 14.[12] The R^2's for the indirect translog dominate those for any of the other functional forms for both meat and produce. For the meat data either the Klein-Rubin or generalized Klein-Rubin dominates all forms except the translog; there is no clear dominance among the remaining forms. For the produce data, the homothetic translog dominates the nontranslog forms for fruit, but the pattern is mixed for vegetables.

C. Expenditure, Price, and Substitution Elasticities for Meat and Produce

The implications for consumer behavior of the various estimated budget share equations can be illuminated by computing the expenditure and price elasticities and the AES. The expenditure and price elasticities can be calculated directly from the budget share equations by using the following general formulas

$$\eta_{iM} = 1 + \frac{\partial \ln w_i}{\partial \ln M} \qquad (i = 1, \ldots, n);$$

$$\eta_{ii} = -1 + \frac{\partial \ln w_i}{\partial \ln p_i} \qquad (i = 1, \ldots, n);$$

$$\eta_{ij} = \frac{\partial \ln w_i}{\partial \ln p_j} \qquad (i \neq j; i, j = 1, \ldots, n)$$

[12] The R^2's are computed as one minus the ratio of the sum of squared errors to the total sum of squares for the budget shares.

TABLE 14

R^2's for the Estimated Budget Share Equations

A. Meat Data	Number of Free Parameters	Fish	Beef	Poultry	Pork
Indirect translog [a]	9	.4789	.8828	.5803	.7971
Homothetic indirect translog	8	.2855	.6952	−.1785	.4716
Additive indirect translog	7	.2442	.7023	.3954	.5104
Indirect addilog	7	.2192	.6543	.3194	.3631
Generalized Klein-Rubin	8	.4787	.7619	.5190	.5513
Klein-Rubin	7	.4784	.7924	.3431	.5632
CES	4	−.4267	.2849	.1032	−.1792
Linear logarithmic [b]	3	.0000	.0000	.0000	.0000

B. Produce Data	Number of Free Parameters	Fresh Fruit	Processed Fruit	Fresh Vegetables	Processed Vegetables
Indirect translog	12	.7884	.3994	.8344	.9073
Homothetic indirect translog	8	.7267	.1965	.6783	.8159
Additive indirect translog	7	.4486	−.4751	.6431	.7811
Indirect addilog	7	.4644	−.4947	.7285	.8158
Klein-Rubin	7	.6046	−.5658	.4797	.8544
CES	4	−.2827	.1922	−.5246	−.2235
Linear logarithmic [b]	3	.0000	.0000	.0000	.0000

[a] Fish additivity is imposed, resulting in 9 rather than 12 free parameters.
[b] R^2's are identically zero, since only an "intercept" is estimated.

In Table 15 we present the expenditure and price elasticity formulas for each of our eight utility functions. The AES can be computed from the Slutsky equation (5). In general, the elasticities are functions of the p_i^*, but for our data the variation over the sample period is not great. Thus, in Tables 16 through 18 we present the elasticities only for the midyear of our sample, 1959. The elasticities for 1947, 1959, and 1971 are presented in Manser (1974).

TABLE 15

Elasticity Formulas for Models of Consumer Preferences [a]

Utility Function	Expenditure Elasticities	Own-Price Elasticities	Cross-Price Elasticities
Indirect translog	$\eta_{iM} = 1 + \dfrac{-\sum_j \beta_{ji}\big/ w_i + \sum_i\sum_j \beta_{ji}}{1 + \sum_i\sum_j \beta_{ij}\ln p_j^*}$	$\eta_{ii} = -1 + \dfrac{\beta_{ii}\big/ w_i - \sum_j \beta_{ji}}{1 + \sum_i\sum_j \beta_{ij}\ln p_j^*}$	$\eta_{ij} = \dfrac{\beta_{ij}\big/ w_i - \sum_i \beta_{ij}}{1 + \sum_i\sum_j \beta_{ij}\ln p_j^*}$
Homothetic indirect translog	$\eta_{iM} = 1$	$\eta_{ii} = -1 + \beta_{ii}\big/ w_i$	$\eta_{ij} = \beta_{ij}\big/ w_i$
Additive indirect translog	$\eta_{iM} = 1 + \dfrac{-\beta_{ii}\big/ w_i + \sum_i \beta_{ii}}{1 + \sum_j \beta_{jj}\ln p_j^*}$	$\eta_{ii} = -1 + \dfrac{\beta_{ii}\big/ w_i - \beta_{ii}}{1 + \sum_j \beta_{jj}\ln p_j^*}$	$\eta_{ij} = \dfrac{-\beta_{jj}}{1 + \sum_j \beta_{jj}\ln p_j^*}$

	η_{iM}	η_{ii}	η_{ij}
Indirect addilog	$\eta_{iM} = \sigma_i + \sum_j (1 - \sigma_j) w_j$	$\eta_{ii} = -1 + (1 - \sigma_i)(1 - w_i)$	$\eta_{ij} = -(1 - \sigma_j) w_j$
Generalized Klein-Rubin	$\eta_{iM} = \dfrac{\alpha_i (p_i^*)^{1-\sigma}}{w_i \sum_j \alpha_j (p_j^*)^{1-\sigma}}$	$\eta_{ii} = -w_i \eta_{iM} - \sigma \left(1 - \dfrac{p_i^* \gamma_i}{w_i}\right)$ $\times (1 - w_i \eta_{iM})$	$\eta_{ij} = -p_j^* \gamma_j \eta_{iM} - (1 - \sigma) \eta_{iM} \eta_{jM} w_j$
Klein-Rubin	$\eta_{iM} = \dfrac{\alpha_i}{w_i}$	$\eta_{ii} = -1 + \dfrac{(1 - \alpha_i) p_i^* \gamma_i}{w_i}$	$\eta_{ij} = \dfrac{-\alpha_i p_j^* \gamma_j}{w_i}$
CES	$\eta_{iM} = 1$	$\eta_{ii} = -1 + (1 - \sigma)(1 - w_i)$	$\eta_{ij} = -(1 - \sigma) w_j$
Linear logarithmic	$\eta_{iM} = 1$	$\eta_{ii} = -1$	$\eta_{ij} = 0$

[a] The w_i's refer to fitted budget shares. The normalization $\Sigma \alpha_i = 1$ has been imposed to simplify the formulas in this table.

TABLE 16

Estimated Expenditure Elasticities (η_{iM}) for 1959

A. Budget Share Equations	Fish	Beef	Poultry	Pork
Indirect translog	.331	1.619	.877	.315
Homothetic indirect translog	1.000	1.000	1.000	1.000
Additive indirect translog	.322	1.633	.976	.246
Indirect addilog	.374	1.448	.963	.500
Generalized Klein-Rubin	.140	1.658	1.070	.153
Klein-Rubin	.344	1.651	1.013	.171
CES	1.000	1.000	1.000	1.000
Linear logarithmic	1.000	1.000	1.000	1.000

B. Budget Share Equations	Fresh Fruit	Processed Fruit	Fresh Vegetables	Processed Vegetables
Indirect translog	1.003	−.062	.136	3.086
Homothetic indirect translog	1.000	1.000	1.000	1.000
Additive indirect translog	.601	.641	−.087	2.988
Indirect addilog	.389	.616	−.071	3.243
Klein-Rubin	.279	.084	.106	3.646
CES	1.000	1.000	1.000	1.000
Linear logarithmic	1.000	1.000	1.000	1.000

In Table 16, we present estimated expenditure elasticities. As expected, all the homothetic forms exhibit unitary expenditure elasticities. For the meat data, the rest of the forms show remarkable agreement: the demand for beef is highly expenditure elastic; the other types of meat are expenditure inelastic, but poultry is more elastic than fish or pork. For the produce data, the agreement is almost as good: processed vegetables are highly expenditure elastic, while fresh vegetables and processed fruits are very inelastic; the translog indicates that fresh fruit is expenditure elastic—an implication not shared by the other models.

In Table 17, we present estimated price elasticities. Beef, fresh fruit, and processed vegetables are found to be own-price elastic; the rest of the commodities are own-price inelastic. The imposition of additivity results in lower own-price elasticities for meat; while those for produce are not strongly affected—with the exception of fresh fruit. Although some of the own-price elasticities are quite large, the cross-price elasticities are, with minor exceptions, all quite moderate. The imposition of homotheticity or additivity severely alters the price elasticities. The cross-price elasticities are arranged in Table 17 so that the restrictions from indirect additivity ($\eta_{ij} = \eta_{jk}$) are clearly displayed.

TABLE 17

Estimated Price Elasticities (η_{ij}) for 1959

IA. Meat: (1) Fish, (2) Beef, (3) Poultry, (4) Pork						
Budget Share Equations	η_{11}	η_{22}	η_{33}	η_{44}	η_{21}	η_{31}	η_{41}
(a) Indirect translog	−.425	−1.255	−.866	−.750	−.044	−.044	−.044
(b) Homothetic indirect translog	−.700	−.952	−.818	−1.212	−.004	−.030	−.071
(c) Additive indirect translog	−.170	−1.225	−.796	−.339	−.064	−.064	−.064
(d) Indirect addilog	−.180	−1.103	−.750	−.483	−.062	−.062	−.062
(e) Generalized Klein-Rubin	−.096	−1.007	−.719	−.318	−.105	−.068	−.010
(f) Klein-Rubin	−.200	−1.057	−.807	−.177	−.093	−.057	−.010
(g) CES	−.686	−.823	−.712	−.770	−.023	−.023	−.023
(h) Linear logarithmic	−1.000	−1.000	−1.000	−1.000	.000	.000	.000

IB. Produce: (1) Fresh Fruit, (2) Processed Fruit, (3) Fresh Vegetables, (4) Processed Vegetables						
Budget Share Equations	η_{11}	η_{22}	η_{33}	η_{44}	η_{21}	η_{31}	η_{41}
(a) Indirect translog	−1.408	−.596	−.368	−2.383	.533	−.347	.528
(b) Homothetic indirect translog	−1.109	−.242	−.721	−1.975	−.146	−.673	1.236
(c) Additive indirect translog	−.729	−.735	−.267	−2.513	−.094	−.094	−.094
(d) Indirect addilog	−.612	−.759	−.317	−2.751	−.136	−.136	−.136
(e) Klein-Rubin	−.903	−.283	−.361	−2.292	−.002	−.003	−.098
(f) CES	−.636	−.604	−.661	−.627	−.127	−.127	−.127
(g) Linear logarithmic	−1.000	−1.000	−1.000	−1.000	.000	.000	.000

(continued)

TABLE 17 (concluded)

IIA.

	η_{12}	η_{32}	η_{42}	η_{13}	η_{23}	η_{43}	η_{14}	η_{24}	η_{34}
(a)	.309	−.093	.341	−.011	−.137	.138	−.205	−.182	.126
(b)	−.026	−.510	.155	.061	−.152	.128	−.335	.107	.298
(c)	.192	.192	.192	−.036	−.036	−.036	−.309	−.309	−.309
(d)	.089	.089	.089	−.043	−.043	−.043	−.240	−.240	−.240
(e)	.002	.016	.002	−.007	−.080	−.007	−.040	−.476	−.307
(f)	.030	.124	.021	−.008	−.055	−.006	−.066	−.445	−.273
(g)	−.159	−.159	−.159	−.048	−.048	−.048	−.106	−.106	−.106
(h)	.000	.000	.000	.000	.000	.000	.000	.000	.000

IIB.

	η_{12}	η_{32}	η_{42}	η_{13}	η_{23}	η_{43}	η_{14}	η_{24}	η_{34}
(a)	.172	.202	−.823	−.682	.404	−.408	.915	−.279	.376
(b)	−.114	.091	−.697	−.825	.143	.437	1.048	−.756	.302
(c)	−.061	−.061	−.061	−.320	−.320	−.320	.509	.509	.509
(d)	−.055	−.055	−.055	−.301	−.301	−.301	.579	.579	.579
(e)	−.039	−.015	−.517	−.056	−.017	−.739	.720	.218	.273
(f)	−.094	−.094	−.094	−.152	−.152	−.152	−.118	−.118	−.118
(g)	.000	.000	.000	.000	.000	.000	.000	.000	.000

In Table 18, we present estimated Allen Elasticities of Substitution. The AES, which are weighted price elasticities computed along an indifference curve, show most clearly the extent of the differences between consumer preferences as estimated by the translog model and the more restrictive models. The translog model indicates that beef, poultry, and pork are all reasonably good substitutes; but of these, only beef is very substitutable with fish. Pork and fish appear to be complements. The variation in the substitution relationships among the types of produce is much stronger than for meat. Fresh fruit and vegetables are complementary, as are processed fruits and vegetables. On the other hand, all four pairs of fresh and processed produce are highly substitutable—the most pronounced is between fresh fruit and processed vegetables.

TABLE 18

Estimated Allen Elasticities of Substitution (σ_{ij})

A. Meat: (1) Fish, (2) Beef, (3) Poultry, (4) Pork						
Budget Share Equations	σ_{12}	σ_{13}	σ_{14}	σ_{23}	σ_{24}	σ_{34}
Indirect translog	.999	.258	−.304	.675	1.052	1.269
Homothetic indirect translog	.945	1.437	−.035	−.089	1.332	1.920
Additive indirect translog	.739	.083	−.647	1.393	.663	.007
Indirect addilog	.565	.081	−.383	1.155	.691	.207
Generalized Klein-Rubin	.145	.094	.013	1.104	.158	.102
Klein-Rubin	.308	.189	.032	1.276	.216	.132
CES	.663	.663	.663	.663	.663	.663
Linear logarithmic	1.000	1.000	1.000	1.000	1.000	1.000

B. Produce: (1) Fresh Fruit, (2) Processed Fruit, (3) Fresh Vegetables, (4) Processed Vegetables						
Budget Share Equations	σ_{12}	σ_{13}	σ_{14}	σ_{23}	σ_{24}	σ_{34}
Indirect translog	1.919	−1.152	5.048	1.213	−1.295	1.798
Homothetic indirect translog	.438	−1.596	5.765	1.451	−2.438	2.375
Additive indirect translog	.275	−.452	2.623	−.412	2.663	1.935
Indirect addilog	.092	−.596	2.718	−.368	2.946	2.258
Klein-Rubin	.075	.095	3.264	.029	.987	1.238
CES	.509	.509	.509	.509	.509	.509
Linear logarithmic	1.000	1.000	1.000	1.000	1.000	1.000

V. COST-OF-LIVING INDEXES FOR MEAT AND PRODUCE, 1947–1971

The cost-of-living index is the minimum expenditure required to attain a given level of utility in year t relative to the minimum expenditure required to attain the same level of utility in some reference period.[13] We denote the fixed utility level to be attained as V^s; we refer to s as the base period and V^s as the base-period utility level. We denote the

---

[13] The discussion in this section follows Pollak (1971b).

minimum expenditure to attain V^s in any period t as $M_*^t(p^t, V^s)$. We denote the cost-of-living index

$$I(p^t, p^b, V^s) = \frac{M_*^t(p^t, V^s)}{M_*^b(p^b, V^s)} \tag{33}$$

where b is referred to as the reference period. If the reference period b and base period s coincide, $M_*^s(p^s, V^s) = M^s$ is simply the actual expenditure in period s. The choice of reference period simply results in a particular normalization for the cost-of-living index since the ratio of any two indexes is independent of the reference period

$$\frac{I(p^t, p^b, V^s)}{I(p^{t'}, p^b, V^s)} = \frac{M_*^t(p^t, V^s)}{M_*^{t'}(p^{t'}, V^s)}$$

Calculation of a cost-of-living index requires a functional representation of consumer preferences. The most convenient representation is the indirect utility function $V(p^t/M^t)$. When the base-period utility level is fixed, the indirect utility function can be viewed as an implicit function $V(p^t/M_*^t) - V^s = 0$ with solution M_*^t. The resulting M_*^t's can be plugged into (33) to obtain the cost-of-living index. Utility functions which are homothetic or marginally homothetic imply explicit cost-of-living indexes. We now derive the explicit indexes where possible and describe the numerical computation of the cost-of-living indexes which do not have an explicit form.

Fixing utility at V^s, the indirect translog utility function can be written as an implicit function of M_*^t

$$\frac{1}{2} \sum_i \sum_j \beta_{ij} (\ln M_*^t)^2 - \left(1 + \sum_i \left(\sum_j \beta_{ij}\right) \ln p_i^t\right) (\ln M_*^t)$$

$$+ \left(\ln V^s + \sum \alpha_i \ln p_i^t + \frac{1}{2} \sum \sum \beta_{ij} \ln p_i^t \ln p_j^t\right) = 0 \tag{34}$$

This is a quadratic in $\ln M_*^t$, which can be solved for any given set of prices.[14] We compute cost-of-living indexes for three base years, 1947, 1958, and 1967; it is convenient to use 1947 as the reference year to reveal clearly the rate of increase of the cost-of-living for the three base years. In the first three columns of Table 19, we present the translog cost-of-living indexes for meat; in Table 20, we present the cost-of-living indexes for produce.

[14] Two solutions for $\ln M_*^t$ are obtained. For all results reported below, only one of the solutions was of the proper order of magnitude to be considered. In (34) and in the remainder of the paper, we simplify expressions by using $\sum \alpha_i = 1$.

It is of interest to compute cost-of-living indexes for the models of consumer preferences which are additive or homothetic. We first discuss the models with additive preferences and then those with homothetic preferences. Cost-of-living indexes for the additive translog form can be computed from (34) using the translog estimates with additivity imposed. The results are presented in the fourth, fifth, and sixth columns of Tables 19 and 20.

Fixing utility at V^s, the indirect addilog utility function can be written

$$- \ln V^s = \ln \sum_i \delta_i (p_i/M_*)^{1-\sigma_i} \tag{35}$$

This function cannot be solved analytically for M_*; we use numerical methods to compute M_*. The cost-of-living indexes for the indirect addilog function are presented in the seventh, eighth, and ninth columns of Tables 19 and 20.

The Klein-Rubin (25) and generalized Klein-Rubin (29) functions that we have estimated are direct utility functions. We compute indirect utility functions corresponding to the direct utility functions by substituting the demand functions $X_i = X_i(p_i^t)$ into the direct utility function. The demand functions are obtained by multiplying our budget share equations by M/p_i. The indirect utility function for the generalized Klein-Rubin function can be written

$$\ln V = \ln \left(M - \sum_i \gamma_i p_i \right) - \frac{1}{1-\sigma} \ln \sum \alpha_i p_i^{1-\sigma} \tag{36}$$

Fixing the level of utility at V^s, (31) can be solved explicit for M^*

$$M_* = V^s \left[\sum \alpha_i p_i^{1-\sigma} \right]^{\frac{1}{1-\sigma}} + \sum \gamma_i p_i \tag{37}$$

Similarly the indirect utility function for the Klein-Rubin function can be written

$$\ln V = \sum \alpha_i \ln \alpha_i + \ln \left(M - \sum \gamma_i p_i \right) - \sum \alpha_i \ln p_i \tag{38}$$

which can be solved explicitly for M_*

$$M_* = V^s \prod_i \left(\frac{p_i}{\alpha_i} \right)^{\alpha_i} + \sum \gamma_i p_i \tag{39}$$

For the meat data, generalized Klein-Rubin and Klein-Rubin cost-of-living indexes are presented in columns ten through fifteen of Table 19. Since generalized Klein-Rubin estimates were not obtained for the produce data, only Klein-Rubin cost-of-living indexes are presented in Table 20.

TABLE 19

Cost of Living Indexes for Meat

	Indirect Translog			Additive Indirect Translog			Indirect Addilog		
	1947	(Base Year) 1958	1967	1947	(Base Year) 1958	1967	1947	(Base Year) 1958	1967
1947	1.000	1.000	1.000	1.000	1.000	1.000	1.000	1.000	1.000
1948	1.126	1.127	1.134	1.128	1.129	1.136	1.128	1.129	1.134
1949	1.055	1.056	1.062	1.057	1.058	1.064	1.057	1.058	1.062
1950	1.086	1.088	1.100	1.090	1.092	1.104	1.090	1.092	1.100
1951	1.205	1.209	1.226	1.211	1.214	1.233	1.212	1.214	1.227
1952	1.195	1.198	1.216	1.201	1.204	1.223	1.202	1.205	1.217
1953	1.110	1.111	1.112	1.111	1.111	1.112	1.111	1.111	1.111
1954	1.087	1.086	1.085	1.088	1.088	1.086	1.087	1.087	1.085
1955	1.033	1.034	1.036	1.034	1.034	1.037	1.034	1.034	1.036
1956	.988	.989	.993	.989	.990	.994	.989	.989	.992
1957	1.065	1.066	1.069	1.067	1.068	1.070	1.067	1.067	1.069
1958	1.167	1.169	1.177	1.170	1.171	1.178	1.169	1.170	1.176
1959	1.123	1.125	1.139	1.124	1.127	1.140	1.125	1.127	1.137
1960	1.110	1.113	1.125	1.112	1.114	1.126	1.113	1.115	1.123
1961	1.105	1.107	1.116	1.107	1.108	1.117	1.107	1.108	1.115
1962	1.138	1.141	1.151	1.140	1.142	1.152	1.141	1.142	1.150
1963	1.120	1.123	1.134	1.122	1.124	1.135	1.123	1.124	1.132
1964	1.098	1.100	1.110	1.100	1.102	1.111	1.100	1.101	1.108
1965	1.179	1.180	1.188	1.182	1.183	1.190	1.181	1.182	1.187
1966	1.277	1.278	1.283	1.283	1.283	1.286	1.281	1.282	1.285
1967	1.235	1.237	1.245	1.239	1.240	1.247	1.239	1.240	1.245
1968	1.265	1.268	1.278	1.268	1.270	1.279	1.269	1.270	1.277
1969	1.375	1.378	1.390	1.378	1.380	1.391	1.379	1.380	1.388
1970	1.440	1.442	1.454	1.444	1.446	1.456	1.445	1.446	1.453
1971	1.433	1.437	1.455	1.435	1.438	1.455	1.437	1.440	1.452

TABLE 19 (concluded)

	Generalized Klein-Rubin (Base Year)			Klein-Rubin (Base Year)			Homothetic Indirect Translog	CES	Linear Logarithmic
	1947	1958	1967	1947	1958	1967			
1947	1.000	1.000	1.000	1.000	1.000	1.000	1.000	1.000	1.000
1948	1.126	1.127	1.134	1.126	1.128	1.135	1.128	1.130	1.131
1949	1.055	1.056	1.063	1.055	1.056	1.063	1.057	1.059	1.060
1950	1.087	1.090	1.102	1.087	1.090	1.103	1.089	1.093	1.095
1951	1.209	1.213	1.230	1.209	1.214	1.233	1.209	1.216	1.218
1952	1.199	1.203	1.220	1.199	1.204	1.223	1.199	1.206	1.208
1953	1.111	1.111	1.111	1.110	1.111	1.112	1.110	1.111	1.113
1954	1.089	1.088	1.084	1.089	1.088	1.086	1.084	1.086	1.088
1955	1.032	1.033	1.036	1.032	1.033	1.037	1.034	1.035	1.036
1956	.987	.988	.991	.987	.988	.993	.989	.990	.992
1957	1.066	1.066	1.066	1.066	1.067	1.070	1.065	1.067	1.070
1958	1.167	1.168	1.173	1.168	1.170	1.177	1.169	1.171	1.175
1959	1.122	1.125	1.136	1.123	1.126	1.140	1.128	1.130	1.133
1960	1.110	1.112	1.122	1.110	1.113	1.126	1.115	1.117	1.120
1961	1.104	1.106	1.112	1.105	1.107	1.117	1.108	1.110	1.113
1962	1.138	1.140	1.147	1.138	1.141	1.152	1.142	1.145	1.147
1963	1.120	1.122	1.130	1.120	1.123	1.135	1.124	1.127	1.129
1964	1.097	1.099	1.106	1.098	1.100	1.111	1.101	1.104	1.106
1965	1.180	1.181	1.184	1.180	1.182	1.189	1.180	1.184	1.186
1966	1.281	1.281	1.280	1.282	1.283	1.286	1.276	1.282	1.283
1967	1.237	1.238	1.241	1.238	1.239	1.247	1.237	1.241	1.243
1968	1.266	1.268	1.273	1.267	1.269	1.279	1.269	1.272	1.274
1969	1.376	1.378	1.385	1.376	1.379	1.391	1.380	1.383	1.384
1970	1.442	1.443	1.449	1.443	1.445	1.455	1.444	1.449	1.449
1971	1.433	1.437	1.450	1.434	1.438	1.456	1.441	1.444	1.443

435

TABLE 20

Cost of Living Indexes for Produce

	Indirect Translog (Base Year)			Additive Indirect Translog (Base Year)			Indirect Addilog (Base Year)		
	1947	1958	1967	1947	1958	1967	1947	1958	1967
1947	1.000	1.000	1.000	1.000	1.000	1.000	1.000	1.000	1.000
1948	1.029	1.030	1.026	1.024	1.025	1.021	1.024	1.025	1.021
1949	1.033	1.034	1.031	1.028	1.027	1.021	1.026	1.028	1.022
1950	.955	.954	.956	.949	.950	.948	.949	.950	.947
1951	1.048	1.049	1.047	1.047	1.048	1.046	1.047	1.048	1.046
1952	1.124	1.128	1.117	1.117	1.119	1.109	1.118	1.120	1.110
1953	1.067	1.067	1.066	1.057	1.058	1.054	1.057	1.058	1.054
1954	1.041	1.041	1.041	1.030	1.031	1.028	1.030	1.031	1.028
1955	1.062	1.063	1.060	1.051	1.053	1.048	1.052	1.053	1.048
1956	1.115	1.117	1.111	1.105	1.107	1.100	1.106	1.108	1.100
1957	1.100	1.102	1.098	1.089	1.091	1.083	1.089	1.091	1.083
1958	1.194	1.196	1.190	1.183	1.186	1.174	1.184	1.187	1.175
1959	1.176	1.178	1.172	1.166	1.168	1.158	1.167	1.169	1.158
1960	1.184	1.186	1.180	1.173	1.176	1.165	1.174	1.177	1.165
1961	1.198	1.199	1.197	1.187	1.189	1.182	1.188	1.190	1.182
1962	1.199	1.200	1.196	1.186	1.188	1.179	1.187	1.189	1.180
1963	1.280	1.282	1.277	1.267	1.271	1.257	1.268	1.272	1.257
1964	1.325	1.329	1.319	1.312	1.316	1.298	1.312	1.317	1.297
1965	1.318	1.323	1.308	1.310	1.314	1.296	1.310	1.315	1.295
1966	1.320	1.324	1.313	1.310	1.314	1.298	1.311	1.316	1.298
1967	1.314	1.318	1.308	1.302	1.305	1.292	1.303	1.306	1.292
1968	1.415	1.418	1.408	1.403	1.407	1.390	1.404	1.409	1.390
1969	1.442	1.447	1.433	1.433	1.438	1.419	1.434	1.439	1.418
1970	1.482	1.487	1.472	1.474	1.479	1.459	1.475	1.481	1.459
1971	1.544	1.549	1.534	1.535	1.541	1.520	1.536	1.542	1.519

TABLE 20 (concluded)

	Klein-Rubin			Homothetic Indirect Translog	CES	Linear Logarithmic
	1947	(Base Year) 1958	1967			
1947	1.000	1.000	1.000	1.000	1.000	1.000
1948	1.024	1.025	1.021	1.029	1.021	1.023
1949	1.026	1.027	1.021	1.033	1.021	1.025
1950	.949	.950	.947	.954	.946	.947
1951	1.047	1.047	1.046	1.048	1.047	1.047
1952	1.116	1.118	1.111	1.120	1.112	1.114
1953	1.058	1.058	1.055	1.068	1.053	1.057
1954	1.031	1.032	1.029	1.042	1.027	1.030
1955	1.052	1.053	1.049	1.062	1.047	1.051
1956	1.105	1.107	1.101	1.114	1.100	1.105
1957	1.089	1.091	1.084	1.098	1.084	1.088
1958	1.183	1.187	1.174	1.194	1.179	1.182
1959	1.166	1.169	1.158	1.176	1.161	1.165
1960	1.173	1.176	1.165	1.181	1.168	1.173
1961	1.187	1.189	1.182	1.197	1.182	1.186
1962	1.186	1.189	1.180	1.196	1.181	1.185
1963	1.268	1.272	1.256	1.280	1.264	1.267
1964	1.314	1.319	1.299	1.327	1.312	1.315
1965	1.310	1.315	1.297	1.309	1.306	1.309
1966	1.311	1.315	1.299	1.310	1.305	1.309
1967	1.303	1.306	1.295	1.303	1.296	1.298
1968	1.403	1.408	1.392	1.400	1.398	1.401
1969	1.434	1.439	1.420	1.426	1.429	1.431
1970	1.475	1.480	1.462	1.461	1.469	1.470
1971	1.536	1.542	1.522	1.523	1.531	1.532

It is well known that cost-of-living indexes for homothetic preferences are independent of the base-period utility level. This follows because any homothetic indirect utility function can be written

$$V_{HOM} = M \cdot f(p) \tag{40}$$

and thus $I(p^t, p^b, V^s) = M_*^t/M_*^b = f(p^t)/f(p^b) = I(p^t, p^b)$. The homothetic translog form can be written

$$\ln V = \ln M - \sum_i \alpha_i \ln p_i - \frac{1}{2} \sum_i \sum_j \beta_{ij} \ln p_i \ln p_j \tag{41}$$

resulting in cost-of-living indexes

$$I(p^t,p^b) = \exp \left(\sum_i \alpha_i \ln (p_i^b/p_i^t) + \frac{1}{2} \sum_i \sum_j \beta_{ij} \ln p_i^b \ln p_j^b \right.$$
$$\left. - \frac{1}{2} \sum_i \sum_j \beta_{ij} \ln p_i^t \ln p_j^t \right)$$

The indirect CES utility function can be derived by plugging the demand equations into the direct utility function to obtain

$$\ln V = \ln M - \frac{1}{1-\sigma} \ln \sum \alpha_i (p_i)^{1-\sigma} \tag{42}$$

Thus the CES cost-of-living indexes can be written

$$I(p^t,p^b) = \left[\frac{\sum_i \alpha_i (p_i^t)^{1-\sigma}}{\sum_i \alpha_i (p_i^b)^{1-\sigma}} \right]^{\frac{1}{1-\sigma}} \tag{43}$$

Finally, the linear logarithmic indirect utility function can be written

$$\ln V = \sum \alpha_i \ln \alpha_i + \ln M - \sum \alpha_i \ln p_i \tag{44}$$

implying the cost-of-living index

$$I(p^t,p^b) = \prod_i (p_i^t/p_i^b)^{\alpha_i} \tag{45}$$

The cost-of-living indexes for these homothetic utility functions are presented in Tables 19 and 20.

Assessing the cost-of-living indexes in Tables 19 and 20, we find that the restriction of additivity has a surprisingly small impact. The indexes for the additive translog, indirect addilog, and Klein-Rubin forms deviate very little from the unrestricted translog indexes. For the meat data, changing the base year has more impact on the indexes than does the imposition of additivity. The restriction of homotheticity requires cost-of-living indexes to coincide for all base years. The homothetic translog, CES, and linear logarithmic indexes are extremely close together. Thus even conditional on homotheticity, the imposition of additivity has little impact. Furthermore, the homothetic indexes do not differ markedly from the nonhomothetic indexes for any of our three base years. We conclude that the loss of information for cost-of-living indexes from use of restrictive neoclassical utility functions is quite small, at least for our two applications.

If we accept that the translog cost-of-living indexes are reliable, we must conclude that quite good estimates of cost-of-living indexes can be obtained from using functional forms with either additivity or homotheticity imposed. The question which now arises is: Do traditional price indexes not motivated by utility functions, such as the Laspeyres, also provide good facsimiles of cost-of-living indexes? [15] We investigate this question by computing various price indexes suggested in the literature and comparing them with our translog cost-of-living indexes.

The best-known price indexes are the Laspeyres and the Paasche. The Laspeyres index can be written

$$L(p^t,p^s) = \frac{\sum x_i^s p_i^t}{\sum x_i^s p_i^s} \sum w_i^s \left(\frac{p_i^t}{p_i^s}\right) \tag{46}$$

where $w_i^s = x_i^s p_i^s \big/ \sum x_i^s p_i^s$.

The Laspeyres index is of special interest because it provides an upper bound for the cost-of-living index $I(p^t,p^s,V^s)$ defined over any preference field. The Paasche index can be written

$$P(p^t,p^s) = \frac{\sum x_i^t p_i^t}{\sum x_i^t p_i^s} = \frac{1}{\sum w_i^t \left(\frac{p_i^s}{p_i^t}\right)} = \frac{1}{L(p^s,p^t)} \tag{47}$$

A Paasche index is the inverse of a Laspeyres index for a different base period; thus, Paasche indexes do not provide any information on admissible bounds for cost-of-living indexes beyond that provided by Laspeyres indexes. We compute Laspeyres and Paasche price indexes

---

[15] The widespread use of the Laspeyres index was not motivated by considerations of consumer preferences. However, Pollak (1971b) has shown that the Laspeyres price index is the cost-of-living index corresponding to a fixed coefficients utility function. Unlike the neoclassical utility functions considered in this paper, the fixed coefficients utility function allows no substitution among commodities.

TABLE 21

Laspeyres and Paasche Price Indexes for Meat

	Laspeyres			Paasche		
	(Base Year)			(Base Year)		
	1947	1958	1967	1947	1958	1967
1947	1.000	1.013	1.031	1.000	.992	.986
1948	1.120	1.140	1.163	1.118	1.113	1.106
1949	1.049	1.068	1.090	1.047	1.046	1.041
1950	1.081	1.098	1.122	1.073	1.077	1.072
1951	1.203	1.221	1.247	1.173	1.189	1.188
1952	1.193	1.211	1.238	1.171	1.183	1.181
1953	1.111	1.119	1.136	1.110	1.106	1.102
1954	1.094	1.093	1.105	1.086	1.083	1.081
1955	1.030	1.041	1.059	1.031	1.026	1.023
1956	.986	.992	1.007	.985	.984	.983
1957	1.072	1.068	1.079	1.060	1.064	1.066
1958	1.178	1.169	1.181	1.154	1.169	1.174
1959	1.134	1.128	1.141	1.107	1.124	1.129
1960	1.120	1.115	1.128	1.100	1.113	1.117
1961	1.122	1.108	1.116	1.089	1.107	1.114
1962	1.153	1.142	1.152	1.123	1.141	1.147
1963	1.134	1.124	1.134	1.108	1.124	1.129
1964	1.112	1.101	1.110	1.088	1.101	1.107
1965	1.200	1.182	1.188	1.160	1.179	1.187
1966	1.308	1.281	1.285	1.249	1.271	1.283
1967	1.263	1.240	1.245	1.208	1.233	1.245
1968	1.292	1.271	1.277	1.244	1.266	1.277
1969	1.407	1.382	1.389	1.348	1.376	1.390
1970	1.479	1.449	1.454	1.407	1.439	1.454
1971	1.467	1.446	1.455	1.402	1.436	1.451

for our meat and produce data for the same base years as the cost-of-living indexes. The meat price indexes are presented in Table 21, and the produce price indexes are presented in Table 22. In order to facilitate comparison with the cost-of-living indexes in Tables 19 and 20, we normalize the Laspeyres and Paasche indexes to equal the translog cost-of-living indexes in the base year. Interpreting the Laspeyres and Paasche price indexes as estimates of the translog cost-of-living indexes, we find that they provide poorer estimates than the cost-of-

TABLE 22

Laspeyres and Paasche Price Indexes for Produce

	Laspeyres			Paasche		
	(Base Year)			(Base Year)		
	1947	1958	1967	1947	1958	1967
1947	1.000	1.014	1.041	1.000	.989	.959
1948	1.030	1.036	1.053	1.030	1.020	.993
1949	1.040	1.035	1.047	1.037	1.029	1.004
1950	.961	.958	.975	.953	.951	.934
1951	1.047	1.062	1.087	1.047	1.044	1.023
1952	1.146	1.126	1.131	1.124	1.126	1.112
1953	1.077	1.066	1.081	1.059	1.063	1.052
1954	1.052	1.038	1.054	1.031	1.036	1.027
1955	1.075	1.059	1.071	1.047	1.056	1.053
1956	1.131	1.113	1.123	1.099	1.111	1.109
1957	1.122	1.096	1.102	1.081	1.094	1.093
1958	1.209	1.196	1.200	1.179	1.196	1.192
1959	1.189	1.178	1.184	1.159	1.178	1.174
1960	1.208	1.183	1.185	1.161	1.182	1.180
1961	1.213	1.196	1.207	1.175	1.197	1.194
1962	1.224	1.194	1.199	1.166	1.193	1.194
1963	1.308	1.283	1.281	1.246	1.278	1.273
1964	1.363	1.333	1.323	1.289	1.325	1.317
1965	1.367	1.325	1.313	1.277	1.317	1.313
1966	1.369	1.323	1.314	1.275	1.316	1.313
1967	1.364	1.312	1.308	1.257	1.304	1.308
1968	1.481	1.417	1.404	1.352	1.403	1.404
1969	1.509	1.449	1.433	1.369	1.425	1.432
1970	1.556	1.490	1.474	1.408	1.465	1.471
1971	1.623	1.553	1.534	1.460	1.522	1.531

living indexes from the restrictive utility functions—at least over long time periods. For example, with 1947 as the base year, the Laspeyres index indicates that meat prices increased 46.7 per cent by 1971, and the Paasche index indicates a 40.2 per cent increase; the translog function indicates, however, that the cost of meat increased 43.7 per cent. The discrepancies for the produce data are greater: the Laspeyres index increased 62.3 per cent, the Paasche 46.0 per cent, and the cost-of-living index 54.4 per cent. Over shorter time periods, however, the

Laspeyres indexes appear to provide acceptable approximations to the translog cost-of-living indexes.

The Laspeyres and Paasche price indexes are examples of fixed-weight indexes; the same base period is used for the computation of the index in every year t. The disparity between cost-of-living indexes and Laspeyres and Paasche price indexes typically increases with the distance between the base year s and the comparison year t. It has often been suggested that changing base periods every few years would reduce the disparity with cost-of-living indexes. In fact, the U.S. Bureau of Labor Statistics changes base period approximately every ten years. In order to assess the impact of changing base years, we compute chain-link Laspeyres and Paasche price indexes, where each base period is used to compute the index only for the successive year. The chain-link Laspeyres price index can be written

$$L(t)/L(t-1) = \sum w_i^{t-1}(p_i^t/p_i^{t-1}) \tag{48}$$

and the chain-link Paasche can be written

$$P(t)/P(t-1) = \left[\sum w_i^t(p_i^{t-1}/p_i^t)\right]^{-1} \tag{49}$$

We present chain-link Laspeyres and Paasche indexes for meat and produce in Table 23. The linked indexes for produce are closer to the 1947 base cost-of-living index; the linked indexes for meat, however, differ from the 1947 base cost-of-living index more than the 1947 base nonlinked indexes. Thus the effect of using chain-linked Laspeyres or Paasche indexes does not seem to be predictable.

Among the many index formulas discussed by Fisher (1922) is a chain-linked index, which has subsequently been advocated by Tornqvist (1936) and Theil (1967). The index, which we refer to as the Tornqvist chain-link index, can be written

$$\ln (T(t)/T(t-1)) = \sum [(w_i^t + w_i^{t-1})/2] \ln (p_i^t/p_i^{t-1}) \tag{50}$$

The interesting thing about the Tornqvist chain-link index is that it is very closely related to a cost-of-living index for a particular functional form. Diewert (1973), Sato (1973), and Thangiah (1973) have shown that (50) corresponds to the cost-of-living index from the homothetic indirect translog utility function. The only difference is that (50) uses observed budget shares as weights, while the homothetic translog cost-of-living index uses fitted values from the budget share equations (18) as weights

$$\ln (H(t)/H(t-1)) = \sum_i ((\hat{w}_i^t + \hat{w}_i^{t-1})/2) \ln (p_i^t/p_i^{t-1}) \tag{51}$$

TABLE 23

Chain-Link Price Indexes for Meat and Produce

	Meat			Produce		
	Laspeyres	Paasche	Tornqvist	Laspeyres	Paasche	Tornqvist
1947	1.000	1.000	1.000	1.000	1.000	1.000
1948	1.120	1.118	1.119	1.030	1.030	1.030
1949	1.049	1.047	1.048	1.039	1.037	1.038
1950	1.078	1.074	1.076	.959	.957	.958
1951	1.196	1.186	1.191	1.055	1.050	1.052
1952	1.186	1.176	1.181	1.142	1.127	1.135
1953	1.121	1.085	1.102	1.078	1.064	1.071
1954	1.099	1.061	1.080	1.051	1.037	1.044
1955	1.045	1.005	1.025	1.073	1.058	1.066
1956	1.000	.961	.980	1.129	1.113	1.121
1957	1.081	1.035	1.058	1.112	1.096	1.104
1958	1.188	1.134	1.161	1.216	1.195	1.205
1959	1.146	1.090	1.118	1.197	1.177	1.187
1960	1.133	1.077	1.105	1.202	1.181	1.192
1961	1.127	1.070	1.098	1.217	1.196	1.206
1962	1.162	1.103	1.132	1.214	1.191	1.203
1963	1.144	1.085	1.114	1.303	1.273	1.288
1964	1.120	1.063	1.091	1.351	1.319	1.335
1965	1.202	1.137	1.169	1.348	1.313	1.330
1966	1.299	1.228	1.263	1.349	1.314	1.331
1967	1.261	1.190	1.225	1.343	1.308	1.325
1968	1.293	1.220	1.256	1.442	1.403	1.422
1969	1.407	1.327	1.367	1.472	1.432	1.452
1970	1.472	1.389	1.430	1.512	1.471	1.492
1971	1.474	1.387	1.430	1.574	1.532	1.553

The chain-link Tornqvist indexes are presented in Table 23. As expected, they are very similar to the homothetic translog indexes. Since we argued above that the homothetic translog indexes provided good approximations to the translog cost-of-living indexes, we conclude that Tornqvist chain-link price indexes provide good estimates for cost-of-living indexes.

VI. CONCLUDING REMARKS

We have fitted sets of budget share equations corresponding to eight different utility functions. The translog function is the only one which does not impose homotheticity or additivity on consumer preferences.

The translog budget share equations explain observed budget shares better than the other forms, and have price and expenditure elasticities which differ substantially from the other forms. Furthermore, hypotheses of homotheticity and additivity for the translog form are decisively rejected by statistical tests. In light of these results, one might expect that cost-of-living indexes implied by the various estimated budget share equations would differ substantially. This expectation is not fulfilled; the cost-of-living indexes for homothetic and additive functional forms do not differ substantially from those for the translog form. This finding is analogous to the finding of Berndt and Christensen (1973c), using a translog production function. They found that the imposition of separability restrictions on the translog form led to a substantial loss of fit for the cost share equations. On the other hand, Berndt and Christensen found a very high correlation between output predicted by the separable and nonseparable translog forms. In the present study, the "output" of the indirect utility function must not be substantially altered by the imposition of homotheticity or additivity—or else the implied cost-of-living indexes would differ substantially.

Theil (1971) argued that the necessity of estimating unknown parameters and specifying a base year made the explicit computation of cost-of-living indexes unattractive. He suggested using an approximation to the true cost-of-living index, which is based on observed rather than predicted budget shares—and also allows for substitution possibilities. Based on these and other arguments, Theil advocated the Tornqvist price index (50) as a good estimate for the "true" cost-of-living index. We have found that the Tornqvist index corresponds much better to cost-of-living indexes than do fixed-weight or chain-linked Laspeyres and Paasche indexes. This should not be surprising, since the Tornqvist index corresponds to the cost-of-living index for the homothetic indirect translog utility function.

Pending additional research, extension of our empirical conclusions should be made with caution. We have limited our attention to the meat and produce budgets, thereby excluding large portions of total consumer expenditures. It would be desirable to extend coverage to additional commodities, and to consider additional price indexes. We have not investigated the effects of the degree of commodity aggregation nor have we experimented with the length of interval between linking fixed-weight indexes.

REFERENCES

Allen, R. G. D. (1938). *Mathematical Analysis for Economists*. London: Macmillan, pp. 503–509.

Berndt, E. R., and Christensen, L. R. (1973a). "The Translog Function and the Substitution of Equipment, Structures, and Labor in U.S. Manufacturing 1929–68." *Journal of Econometrics* 1 (March 1973): 81–114.

―――― (1973b). "Testing for the Existence of a Consistent Aggregate Index of Labor Inputs." *American Economic Review* 64 (June 1974): 391–404.

―――― (1973c). "The Specification of Technology in U.S. Manufacturing." Social Systems Research Institute, Workshop Paper 7321, University of Wisconsin.

Brown, Murray, and Heien, Dale (1972). "The S-Branch Utility Tree: A Generalization of the Linear Expenditure System," *Econometrica* 40 (July 1972): 737–747.

Christensen, L. R. (1968). "Saving and the Rate of Return." Ph.D. dissertation, University of California, Berkeley.

Christensen, L. R.; Jorgenson, D. W.; and Lau, L. J. (1972). "Transcendental Logarithmic Utility Functions." Discussion Paper, Harvard Institute of Economic Research, Cambridge, Mass., August 1972.

Christensen, L. R., and Manser, M. E. (1974). "Estimating U.S. Consumer Preferences for Meat." Social Systems Research Institute, Workshop Paper 7403 (Feb. 1974), University of Wisconsin.

―――― (1975). "Transcendental Logarithmic Utility Functions." *American Economic Review* 65 (June 1975): 367–383.

Diewert, W. E. (1974). "Applications of Duality Theory." In M. D. Intrilligator and D. A. Kendrick, eds., *Frontiers of Quantitative Economics*. Vol. 2. Amsterdam: North-Holland.

―――― (1973). "Lecture Notes on Aggregation and Index Number Theory." Department of Economics, University of British Columbia, October 1973.

Fisher, I. (1972). *The Making of Index Numbers*. Boston and New York: Houghton Mifflin.

Geary, R. C. (1949). "Note on 'A Constant Utility Index of the Cost of Living,'" *Review of Economic Studies* 18, no. 45 (1949–1950): 65–66.

Goldberger, A. S. (1967). "Functional Form and Utility: A Review of Consumer Demand Theory." Social Systems Research Institute, University of Wisconsin, Workshop Paper SFM 6703.

Goldberger, Arthur S. and Gamaletsos, Theodore (1970). "A Cross-Country Comparison of Consumer Expenditure Patterns." *European Economic Review* 1 (Spring 1970): 357–400.

Henderson, J. M., and Quandt, R. E. (1971). *Microeconomic Theory,* Second Edition, New York: McGraw-Hill.

Hotelling, H. (1932). "Edgeworth's Taxation Paradox and the Nature of Demand and Supply Functions." *Journal of Political Economy* 40 (October 1932): 532–555.

Houthakker, H. S. (1960). "Additive Preferences." *Econometrica* 28 (April 1960): 244–257.

Johansen, L. (1969). "On the Relationships Between Some Systems of Demand Functions." University of Oslo: Institute of Economics Reprint Series, No. 47, 1969.

Katzner, D. W. (1970). *Static Demand Theory*. New York: Macmillan.

Klein, L. R., and Rubin, H. (1947). "A Constant Utility Index of the Cost of Living." *Review of Economic Studies*, 15, no. 38 (1947–1948): 84–87.

Lau, L. J. (1969a). "Duality and the Structure of Utility Functions." *Journal of Economic Theory* 1 (December 1969): 374–396.

―――― (1969b). "Duality and Utility Structure." Ph.D. Dissertation, University of California, Berkeley.

Manser, M. E. (1974). "Estimating Consumer Preferences and Cost of Living Indexes for U.S. Meat and Produce, 1947–1971: An Application of the Translog Utility Function." Ph.D. dissertation, University of Wisconsin.

Pollak, R. A. (1971a). "Additive Utility Functions and Linear Engel Curves." *Review of Economic Studies* 38 (October 1971): 401–414.

—————— (1971b). "The Theory of the Cost of Living Index." Research Discussion Paper No. 11, Research Division, Office of Prices and Living Conditions, U.S. Bureau of Labor Statistics, June 1971.

Roy, R. (1943). *De l'Utilité: Contribution á la Théorie des Choix,* Paris: Hermann et Cie.

Sato, K. (1973). "Generalized Ideal Cost-Of-Living Indexes and Indirect Utility Functions." Discussion Paper No. 290, Department of Economics, State University of New York at Buffalo, October 1973.

Slutsky, E. E. (1915). "On the Theory of the Budget of the Consumer." *Giornale degli Economisti* 51 (July 1915): 1–26.

Stone, R. (1954). "Linear Expenditure Systems and Demand Analysis: An Application to the Pattern of British Demand." *Economic Journal* 64 (September 1954): 511–527.

Thangiah, S. G. (1973). "True Cost of Living Indexes Under Certainty." Discussion Paper No. 284, Economics Dept., State University of New York at Buffalo, July 1973.

Theil, H. (1967). *Economics and Information Theory.* Amsterdam, North-Holland.

—————— (1971). *Introduction to Demand and Index Number Theory,* Report 7126, The University of Chicago Center for Mathematical Studies in Business and Economics, May 1971.

Tornqvist, L. (1936). "The Bank of Finland's Consumption Price Index." *Bank of Finland Monthly Bulletin,* no. 10 (1936): 1–8.

U.S., Department of Agriculture (1968). "Food Consumption, Prices, and Expenditures." Agricultural Economic Report No. 138, Washington, D.C.

—————— (1971). "Food Consumption, Prices, and Expenditures," Supplement to Agricultural Economic Report No. 138, Washington, D.C.

Van Hoa, Tran. (1969). "Additive Preferences and Cost of Living Indexes: An Empirical Study of the Australian Consumer's Welfare." *Economic Record* 45 (September 1969): 432–440.

Wales, Terence J. (1971). "A Generalized Linear Expenditure Model of the Demand for Non-Durable Goods in Canada." *Canadian Journal of Economics* 4 (November 1971): 471–484.

Zellner, A. (1962). "An Efficient Method of Estimating Seemingly Unrelated Regressions and Tests for Aggregation Bias." *Journal of the American Statistical Association* 57 (June 1962): 348–368.

—————— (1963). "Estimators for Seemingly Unrelated Regression Equations: Some Exact Finite Sample Results." *Journal of the American Statistical Association* 58 (December 1963): 977–992.

Comments on "Cost-of-Living Indexes and Price Indexes for U.S. Meat and Produce, 1947–1971"

LESTER D. TAYLOR

UNIVERSITY OF ARIZONA

IN this paper, Christensen and Manser apply the indirect translog utility function to the demand for meat and to the demand for garden produce with the purpose of using the parameters of the utility function thus estimated to construct "true" cost-of-living indexes for these two components of the consumer's budget. The results with the indirect translog function are compared with ones obtained with several other utility functions, namely, the Klein-Rubin, generalized Klein-Rubin, CES, linear logarithmic, and the indirect addilog of Houthakker. Cost-of-living indexes constructed from these preference orderings for meat and produce for the period 1947–1971 are compared with one another, with traditional Laspeyres and Paasche indexes, and also with the chain-link index proposed by Tornqvist.

Let me begin my discussion with a few remarks about the translog utility function, which has been developed by Laurits Christensen in collaboration with Dale Jorgenson and Lawrence Lau. The exploitation of this function clearly marks an important innovation in applied demand analysis. The function expresses the logarithm of utility as a quadratic function in the logarithms of its arguments – quantities in the case of the direct utility function, and ratios of prices to income in the case of the indirect utility function – and, as such, it can be interpreted as a utility function in its own right or else as an approximation, accurate to the second order, of an arbitrary utility function. Unlike most utility functions currently in use, the translog form can be estimated without imposing homotheticity or additivity restrictions, and it is this feature that makes the translog function especially appealing. In my opinion, the only defect of consequence of the translog function is that it does not appear to lend itself with any ease to dynamization. At least, my own efforts in this direction have so far not led to any success.

The present paper by Christensen and Manser represents an interesting and useful attempt to employ the translog function in the construction of cost-of-living indexes for meat and garden produce. Not unexpectedly, the technical aspects of specification and estimation are very competently executed and I have no comments to make on this front. The cost-of-living indexes that finally emerge seem, on the whole, to be quite sensible, and I think that it is of more than passing interest that their construction has utilized only the indirect utility function. The results here, together with those obtained by Christensen, Jorgenson, and Lau in their 1972 paper, confirm that the indirect utility function has not received its just due in applied work. Yet, despite these positive features, the paper presents a number of problems in my opinion, and, at the risk of appearing unappreciative, I shall address the remainder of my remarks to these.

In terms of exposition, it is not clear to me, the title of the paper notwithstanding, exactly what the central focus of the paper is. Is its purpose primarily further to illustrate the translog utility function by putting it through some demanding new hoops? Or is it the cost-of-living indexes themselves that are of primary interest? In view of the fact that the title of the paper is changed from the one listed in the preliminary program ("Testing for Existence of Distinct Components in the Food Budget"), it would appear that the authors have themselves had some uncertainty as to the central message of their exercise.

Assuming that the principal purpose of the paper is, in fact, the estimation of cost-of-living indexes for subcomponents of the consumer's market basket of goods, the authors unfortunately do not provide any justification in the framework of an overall cost-of-living index for the subindexes that they derive. In a 1971 paper ("Subindices of the Cost of Living Index), Pollak has shown that the overall cost-of-living index can be written as a weighted average of component cost-of-living indexes only in the case where the underlying preference ordering is described by a generalized Cobb-Douglas utility function. Since the translog function is not of this type, partial indexes for meat and produce calculated from it accordingly cannot be interpreted as cost-of-living subindexes.

An alternative procedure, and one which can solve the problem in principle, would be to interpret the partial indexes as conditional cost-of-living indexes in the sense of Pollak. In the case of meat, for example, the conditional cost-of-living index would be interpreted as measuring the ratio of expenditures required to attain a particular indifference curve in a comparison and reference-price situation conditional on given prices and quantities for all other goods in the consumer's market basket. As I have mentioned, viewing the partial indexes as conditional cost-of-living indexes solves the interpretation problem in principle, yet I am very dubious whether, as a practical matter, consumers approach their budgeting for meat and produce in the manner that such an interpretation implies.

One other thing that I am uneasy about, but which I don't have an answer to (and I'm not aware that anyone else has an answer either), is the calculation of cost-of-living indexes from parameters that have been estimated using other price indexes. Christensen and Manser employ Laspeyres subindexes in estimation of their budget share equations and, among other things, I wonder to what extent this may have influenced the final results. More generally, my question here deals with the type of price index that is most appropriate in applied demand analysis. Pollak addressed this question to some degree in his 1971 survey paper, but as far as I am aware, it really still awaits final resolution.

I know from much personal experience that rationalizing empirical results in exercises such as this is always hazardous and problematic. However, some of the authors' results stretch even my understanding. In particular, the results show pork and fish to be complements — well, maybe — but how about fresh fruits and *fresh* vegetables being complements, but fresh fruits and *processed* vegetables being substitutes!

The Demand for Housing: Integrating the Roles of Journey-to-Work, Neighborhood Quality, and Prices *

A. THOMAS KING

UNIVERSITY OF MARYLAND

I. INTRODUCTION

THE household must resolve a number of interrelated questions when purchasing a dwelling. Ignoring problems of financing—what down payment, what interest rate, what mortgage life, and the like—the questions directly relevant to the dwelling are of three types: first, what characteristics should the dwelling have? That is, how much space, how many rooms, and what lot size? Second, where should the dwelling be located? Clearly, location will determine neighborhood crime rates, air pollution, public school quality, and the necessary commute to work. Third, what should be spent?

There is no lack of empirical studies of the "demand for housing," [1] but oddly, with only few and partial exceptions, they are all concerned with the third of these questions only, and fail to treat either of the first two.[2] The diversity encompassed by the term housing is ignored; instead, housing is treated as though it were a homogeneous good like milk, which households buy more or less of as their incomes, family characteristics, and the prices they face change. On the assump-

* Helpful comments on earlier drafts of this paper were received from Roger Betancourt, Jack Triplett, Orley Ashenfelter, and Curtis Harris. They are, of course, not responsible for any errors still remaining. Computations were made possible by a faculty research grant from the University of Maryland Computer Science Center.

[1] Paldam (1970) lists some 50 recent studies and this is by no means exhaustive.

[2] Winger (1962) and Kain and Quigley (1975) examine some aspects of the demand for special characteristics, such as number of rooms purchased. Straszheim (1975) has studied demands for characteristics very grossly defined and some aspects of location choice. Quigley (1972) has examined locational choice and housing demand with a model somewhat similar to that proposed in this paper.

tion that expenditures equal price multiplied by quantity, it is customary to measure the quantity of housing purchased in uniform, quasi-physical units by dividing expenditures by a price index. These studies of housing as a homogeneous commodity may be justified by convenience or, more formally, by invoking separability in the utility function; nevertheless, the approach clearly precludes any examination of such questions as whether some kinds of families are especially concerned with interior space, others with exterior space, and others with quality.

The general suppression of the locational aspect of housing is much less defensible. Unlike milk which can be purchased in one place and consumed in another, the services of the housing unit must be consumed where the dwelling is located. Thus, location is an integral part of the commodity, with implications for commuting costs, neighborhood quality, and, as will be seen, for housing prices themselves.

The present study makes some progress toward ameliorating both of these long-standing deficiencies. Instead of treating housing as a single homogeneous good, I treat it as a bundle of distinct items, each having its own price, and each to be bought or not, depending as would any good, on the income, relative prices, and special family characteristics. The analysis at this level has a strong resemblance to the Lancastrian "New Demand Theory" (1966, 1971), since it assumes that households perceive dwellings as supplying specific characteristics which are desired for themselves. "Housing," in this view, refers to nothing more meaningful than the total value of the parts, and two households buying the same "housing" could purchase commodities that are quite unlike.

A more satisfactory treatment of location as an aspect of housing is important because the question: What quantity and type of housing shall I buy? is inseparable from the question: Where shall I buy it? This is evident in even the simplest theoretical models of urban structure (Alonso [1964], Muth [1969]) which have predicted the existence of housing price gradients for some years. As Muth (1969, Chapter 2) demonstrates, if the costs of commuting rise less rapidly with income and distance from the Central Business District (CBD) than do potential savings on housing, wealthy households desiring to purchase relatively much housing will locate in the edges of the urban area where housing prices are low. Similarly, if housing is treated as a bundle, it should be true that households wishing to purchase relatively much of some components will find it advantageous to locate where the items are relatively cheap. For this reason, it can be said that a satisfactory model of housing demand carries within it a model of residential location choice.

Abandoning the assumption that housing is a homogeneous good and incorporating the choice of location as a part of the bundle greatly complicates the analysis of housing demand. But in return, the approach substantially improves understanding of household behavior. The reader must be warned that this paper does not complete all that it might; much work still remains. However, I am able to provide a model of household behavior which treats the choice of location and the purchase of particular components as related decisions, and which possesses considerable intuitive appeal. Supporting evidence demonstrates that households behave as though they perceive "housing" to consist of specific items with individual prices which vary throughout the metropolitan area studied; in addition, some simple tests imply that households locate in a pattern which can be explained by considering work sites, neighborhood quality, and the variation in housing prices.

II. MODELING THE HOUSEHOLD'S DECISIONS IN THE HOUSING MARKET

I have suggested that to purchase a dwelling, the household must decide not merely how many units of a homogeneous commodity to purchase, but rather what combination of particular attributes is most satisfying. In addition, the question of location cannot be ignored. Consider the following schema as a description of how these decisions are made.

A. A General Model of Location Choice and Housing Demand

The location problem for the household is that a dwelling close to work will minimize commuting costs but may limit the household to neighborhoods with unsatisfactory sets of amenities, since there is no presumption that all varieties of neighborhoods are available at all distances from the work site. Consequently, there will usually be some tradeoff between the goals of low commuting costs and a high quality neighborhood. Moreover, a third goal exists: an optimal set of prices for the housing components. Even if all households have the same utility function and face the same prices, if they have different incomes the desired proportional composition of the housing bundle will change among, for example, interior space, exterior space, and quality if these have different income elasticities of demand. Given that prices for housing components can vary in different parts of a metropolitan region,[3] it will be advantageous for the household to locate in that sub-market where the goods it wishes to buy relatively much of will be relatively cheap. Consequently, even if all households work in the same place and all neighborhoods offer the same amenities, one would expect to find households of different incomes selecting different sub-markets in which to purchase their dwellings. More generally, since neighborhoods and work sites do differ, one would expect the house-hold to choose its location in a three-way tradeoff: commuting costs against neighborhood quality against advantageous housing prices.

The demand problem for the house-hunting household is not merely how much to spend, but also what type of dwelling to buy. Since the prices for individual characteristics vary among submarkets, what is bought should depend, as with any good, not just on preferences, but also on relative prices. However, as argued above, the set of prices will depend on the resolution of the location choice. Let me suggest the following as a reasonable description of how these interrelated decisions are made.

Suppose that the household begins its search process knowing three things: (1) the place of work for each worker, which is not necessarily or even usually the CBD, (2) the division of the metropolitian area into housing submarkets with differing sets of relative prices for housing bundle components, and (3) the division of the area into neighborhoods with different public services and natural amenities in each. Imagine the household to go now from submarket to submarket considering what dwelling it would purchase in each and what its utility would be. In each place, the commuting costs—both monetary and in terms of time—are known. This permits the calculation of an adjusted income with the wages received reduced by commuting costs. Assume now that the adjusted income is apportioned among groups of com-modities, "food," "clothing," "housing," and the like. Then, given the amount to be spent on the housing bundle and the set of prices for commodities in the bundle, the household selects that particular dwel-ling it most prefers. At this point, the household can determine its utility level were it to locate in this place.[4]

Moving on then in the search process, the household can consider

---

[3] Why this occurs is discussed in Section III.

[4] Formally, the assumption made here is that the household's utility function is weakly separable, a "tree" with housing as one "branch." It can be shown (Pollak, 1970) that demand functions derived from such a function can be written in a simplified form. Instead of

$$q_i = f_i(p_1, p_2, \ldots, p_n, Y) \qquad i = 1, n$$

locating in another submarket with another set of relative prices, neighborhood quality, and commuting costs. Each site can be assigned a utility level by this procedure,[5] and the household is predicted to choose that location where its satisfaction is greatest.

One particularly significant implication of this schema is that certain decisions are made sequentially rather than simultaneously. In particular, the choice of components within the housing bundle is dependent only on the allocation to it and the relative prices within. This permits an empirical study of demand parameters to proceed in isolation from the complete model. Later, when the characteristics of the demand functions are understood, it will be possible to examine how prices, work site, and neighborhood quality interact to determine location.[6]

one has

$$q_i = g_i(p_1^\theta, p_2^\theta, \ldots, p_m^\theta, \alpha^\theta(p_1, p_2, \ldots, p_n, Y)) \qquad i = 1, n$$

where

θ is the branch designation;
m is the number of goods in branch θ;
$p_1^\theta, p_2^\theta, p_m^\theta$ are the prices of goods in the θth branch; and
$$\alpha^\theta(p_1, p_2, \ldots, p_n, Y) = Y - \sum_{k \epsilon \theta} p_k q_k(p_1, \ldots, p_n, Y).$$

The decision process is consequently in two stages: first, income is allocated among branches; second, commodities within a branch are purchased in response to prices in that branch only and to the total allocation to the branch. This behavior is both plausible and highly desirable from the standpoint of empirical estimation, since the number of prices in each demand function is greatly reduced.

[5] Of course, it is unnecessary that all potential locations be examined in the same detail. Those offering clearly unacceptable neighborhood quality or requiring "excessive" commuting can be excluded immediately.

[6] It is useful at this point to compare the model just developed to other work. Of the previous studies of household behavior in housing markets, the work of Quigley (1972), (1973) most closely resembles the present model. There are important differences, however. Quigley does not introduce the tradeoff of commuting costs, housing prices, and neighborhood quality; instead, he defines what he calls a "gross price surface" for each type of housing, which is created by adding commuting costs to the "on site" cost of the dwelling. The hypothesis, then, is that the household buying a particular type of housing will locate where the "gross price" is lowest. One of the difficulties of this approach is the need to specify types of dwellings, e.g., a two-bedroom, single-family home, constructed between 1940 and 1950. In order to examine the tradeoffs between different types of dwellings, a very great number of different types must be specified. Since the "gross price" will differ for each income level and work site, the data base rapidly becomes exceedingly cumbersome to manipulate.

The model in this paper assumes, in contrast, that households distinguish travel costs from housing costs. The journey-to-work becomes in effect the price paid for obtaining particular locational advantages; consequently, prices for housing characteristics in a

B. *Housing as a Bundle of Characteristics: A Lancastrian View*

Up to this point, "housing" has been treated as a convenient term referring to a bundle of complex makeup, but there has been little discussion of what constitutes the bundle. It is clear, of course, that "housing" consists actually of a great many very specific items: copper pipes, forced air heating, brick facing, a dining room of particular size, and the like, but it is not clear that these are the features which concern households when deciding whether or not to purchase. It is quite plausible to suppose instead that households regard "housing" as producing certain kinds of general satisfaction, and individual items like doorknobs and chandeliers merely contribute to one or more of these general commodities.

The view that goods possess certain characteristics and that these characteristics—rather than the goods themselves—are the arguments of the utility function has been developed by Lancaster as his "New Theory of Demand" (1966, 1971). This theory can be expressed simply in the following propositions: define b_{ij} as the quantity of the ith characteristic supplied by a unit of the jth good. Then a quasi-production function B exists which "transforms" the goods purchased x's into characteristics z's; that is, $Z = BX$ where Z and X are vectors of characteristics and goods. The utility function is $U = U(z_1, z_2, \ldots, z_n)$ and is to be maximized subject to the two constraints $y = \sum_{i=1}^{m} p_i x_i$ and $Z = BX$.

The view that households are directly concerned with characteristics rather than goods is particularly satisfying when dealing with "housing." It is plausible and permits further simplification in the demand analysis, since there is no need to consider separately the interrelated demands for an enormous number of specific items. Accordingly, I shall adopt this approach in what follows and distinguish between "housing components," which are the specific items purchased, and "housing characteristics," which are what the household

given market are constant for all buyers and do not vary with income or work place. Another distinction is that I assume implicitly that any desired combination of housing characteristics can be obtained in a market at the prices prevailing there, whereas Quigley attempts to define a limited number of dwelling types (that is, combinations of characteristics) for households to choose among. The contrast between the models in this respect is that between variable and fixed-proportion models.

One important advantage of Quigley's approach is the explicit attention given to the choice between types of dwellings: apartments, multi-family units, and single-family; the present model considers only single-family housing purchases, but with a more extensive data base, this limitation could be removed.

gains utility from. One difficulty raised by this approach is how to distinguish and measure the quantities of housing characteristics embodied in each bundle. The solution to this is described briefly in the next section and more fully in Section VI.

C. An Informal Description of Housing Demand: A Postscript

The model of household behavior in the choice of location and purchase of particular dwellings has, I believe, considerable intuitive appeal; interestingly, it is possible to cite some simple informal evidence that households do behave in this way. Consider, for example, this advice from a leading consumer magazine to persons buying housing:

Step 1: Analyze your needs. Taking into account your age, family prospects and way of life, you can probably tick off your basic demands without any trouble. Do it . . . before you start those weekend wanderings. . . . notice that you can deal with any of these questions without getting into matters of price or plan or style or type of construction.

Step 2: Figure what you can pay. . . . two figures tell the tale . . . the amount of cash . . . for a down payment . . . (and) how much of your monthly income you can allocate to a monthly mortgage payment. How much can you spend? . . . First determine your net average monthly take-home pay. . . . Next, add up your monthly expenses for non-housing items. . . . Subtract. . . . What's left is your average monthly income available for *housing* expenses. Add the size of the mortgage your monthly payment will support to the amount of your down payment and . . . you've got the magic number, . . . the price category for you to shop.

Step 3: Now Hunt and Pick.[7]

The advice certainly suggests that the separation of decisions implied by the formal model is quite reasonable.

III. PRICING IN THE HOUSING MARKET

The housing market has a long-standing reputation for inscrutable workings:

The absence of a market place, the private and secret nature of transactions, the want of comprehensive market data, all combine to deprive the housing market of the benefits of a visible price structure. Both buyers and sellers, in varying degree, operate in the dark. . . . The ultimate uniqueness of every house makes it impossible to establish uniform sales units or standards of values (Twentieth Century Fund, 1944, p. 209.).

[7] "How to Buy a House in Five Easy Steps," *Changing Times* 27 (February 1973): 6–11.

Recent empirical research has demonstrated, however, that pricing in the housing market is not the capricious process long assumed but exhibits quite strong regularities of a very reasonable sort. What might superficially appear to be the quirks can generally be explained as the consequences of special housing characteristics or of circumstances involved in the transactions (Musgrave [1969], Kain and Quigley [1970], King and Mieszkowski [1973], King [1973a]).

When the housing bundle is well specified, it is possible to estimate the price relationships in a single housing market by applying a "hedonic price" equation of the following sort to observed housing transactions

$$\text{Sales Price (or rent)} = \sum_{i=1}^{m} \alpha_i SC_i + \sum_{j=1}^{n} \beta_j LC_j + \gamma L \qquad (3.1)$$

where

SC_i is the ith structural component (number of rooms, quantity of insulation) and α_i the price per unit;

LC_j is the jth location component (accessibility to the CBD, neighborhood quality) and β_j the price per unit;

L is the quantity of land purchased and γ the price per unit.

Provided that the transactions are genuine "arms-length" transactions and the components of the bundle known in detail, such an equation will explain a large fraction of the observed variation in sales prices as a function of the individual items purchased.[8] Moreover, the individual hedonic prices are often quite reasonable. In Section VI, for example, fireplaces will be found to add about $1,000 to the sales price of a dwelling, an amount approximating construction cost, and municipally provided garbage collection to increase the value of a house by about $300, a reasonable capitalization of the cost of privately contracted services in the area studied.

It is not to be expected, of course, that a single hedonic equation will describe all housing markets, for the prices in each will naturally reflect the interplay of supply and demand for the various bundle components. What is important for the present study is to observe that a metropolitan area of even moderate size may well consist of a number of linked but distinct submarkets, each needing its own hedonic price equation to describe the price patterns.[9] The subdivision of the metro-

---

[8] Typically, the R^2 of these equations exceeds 0.60.
[9] This is emphasized by Straszheim (1975).

politan area reflects fundamental characteristics of the supply and demand conditions for housing; and because of the importance of the resulting price variations for this study, it is useful to set these out clearly.

If the housing in a metropolitan area were built anew each year in accordance with the latest technology and prevailing wages and prices for material inputs, and if the composition of the bundles reflected a uniform pattern of demand throughout the area, there should be no reason for similar housing bundles to sell for dissimilar amounts. But in few areas is this a good description of either the supply or the demand functions for housing. Instead, on the supply side, the housing stock is built little by little over many years, during which input prices and technology both change. Once constructed, the housing remains, subject always to remodeling and somewhat limited possibilities for new construction, but with the essential characteristics of the stock in each area fixed by the nature of the original construction.

On the demand side there are essentially two problems. First, relative preferences for components of the housing bundle will change over time, so that a housing bundle of 1910 would not be judged an optimum bundle today, even at the old set of relative prices. In general, some components of the 1910 bundle have little value as a part of the 1910 bundle, though they might be valued as components of a different, more modern bundle. The consequence, of course, is that component prices which clear the market in the 1910 part of town will differ from the prices in the newly constructed sections. Second, the tendency toward such price differences will be strengthened to the extent that purchasers examine only the bundles in a limited geographic area. Reasons for this are manifold: reluctance to move from an ethnic neighborhood, racial discrimination, desire to be close to friends or work, a wish to live in a particular school district. Whatever the cause, such behavior eliminates the competitive pressure for price uniformity throughout the metropolitan area.

The consequence of inflexible, unadjustable supply within limited geographical areas and of fragmented demands will be the division of the large metropolitan area into discrete submarkets for housing bundles. Within each, there should be a regular relationship of sales price to bundle composition, but the relationship may differ from one submarket to another.

The variation of prices for identical components throughout a metropolitan area is critically important to this study because it provides the setting and means required to implement the model of household behavior set out. First, the model of housing purchase contained as a primary element the proposition that households would tend to search out and locate in those places with particularly advantageous sets of relative prices. Obviously, for this to happen, it is necessary that price variation occur and be discernible. Second, the model predicted that wherever they actually locate, households will alter their purchases in response to the housing prices in that place; consequently, by observing what consumers purchase in the different submarkets it should be possible to deduce how they respond to price variations in the usual sense. Third, the hedonic prices provide the means to treat housing as a bundle of Lancastrian characteristics. If one is able to determine which characteristics each component supplies (that is, the b_{ij}), the hedonic price for that component permits one to measure the expenditure on each characteristic by adding together the expenditures on appropriate components.

IV. DATA SOURCES

The data used in this study were obtained from two sources. First, the basic data are a set of detailed physical descriptions,[10] and the prices of some 1,800 single-family houses sold in the New Haven, Connecticut, metropolitan region from 1967 to 1970.[11] With a few exceptions, these 1,800 houses include all the single-family houses sold through the Multiple Listing Service (MLS) of the Greater New Haven Board of Realtors during this period.[12] These data plus additional information on neighborhood amenities and services, described below, provide the base for estimation of hedonic price equations like (3.1) for each housing submarket.[13]

The second data set, needed to examine choice of location and demand functions, was obtained as the responses to a mail survey di-

[10] The exact physical details used in this study are discussed in Table 3 below.

[11] This is defined to include New Haven, Hamden, North Haven, West Haven, East Haven, Woodbridge, Orange, Cheshire, and Wallingford. Essentially, this is the New Haven SMSA, except that four small outlying areas are excluded (Branford, North Branford, Guilford, Bethany) and Cheshire and Wallingford are added. All these towns lie within a semicircle of about ten miles radius centered on New Haven.

[12] The cooperation of the Board of Realtors in making these data available for this and other studies is gratefully acknowledged.

[13] It is important to emphasize that careful examination of these data found no significant evidence of inaccuracies in reporting either the sales price or the components. Furthermore, there was little evidence that homes sold through the MLS were distributed differently geographically from the total housing stock or were unrepresentative of its values in each census tract. This evidence is presented in King (1973a, Chapter III).

rected to each purchasing household. The questions covered such things as income, family size, education, place of work, and the like.[14] Somewhat more than 45 percent of the questionnaires were returned with usable information; however, some of these were rejected following internal consistency checks or because of failure to provide complete information. In addition, no responses from Cheshire are used. Responses for the remaining 683 households are examined in the demand analysis of this study.[15]

V. MEASURING NEIGHBORHOOD QUALITY

The set of physical descriptions for houses and the responses of purchasers to the survey questionnaire provide two exceptionally rich data sources for housing market analysis. They provide information explicitly for the hedonic price equations, and for demand analysis, and with some manipulation, for the model of location choice. The household's work site, of course, is obtained directly from the questionnaire, while the hedonic price equations provide the means for calculating price variations across the metropolitan area. Though some information on the third goal of residential location—neighborhood quality— was readily available as information on public services, to gain a more complete index of quality by neighborhood a novel procedure was developed and is described in this section.

Measuring neighborhood quality so that comparisons between places are possible is an extraordinarily difficult task for which two alternative approaches have been suggested. Some studies have attempted measurement by assembling so-called objective data: school achievement test scores, crime rates, fire damage, particulate matter in the air;[16] other studies have argued that the quality of a neighborhood is largely a matter of perception: the fear of crime will make a neighborhood undesirable regardless of whether crime actually occurs. Per-

[14] The exact household characteristics used in the demand study are defined in Table 7 below.

[15] It should be noted that the responses to the survey have been carefully examined for biases and accuracy. Rather good tests were possible; and although these suggested the presence of biases normally associated with mail surveys (toward overrepresentation of high-income, educated households), the biases were slight and not statistically significant. For a complete description see King (1973a, Chapter III).

[16] The outstanding example of this approach is Kain and Quigley's study of St. Louis which assembled data for some 32 neighborhood characteristics (1970). Other less ambitious studies have used such measures as average family income or education in the neighborhood, reasoning that high-income and highly educated families would choose high-quality neighborhoods.

ceptions may be based upon objective differences, but it is not certain that the relationship will be very exact.[17]

To my knowledge, despite the general recognition that use of perceptions is potentially a very desirable way to describe quality variations, the New Haven MLS data set is the only one for which this is actually attempted. For this collection of housing data, perceived neighborhood quality was obtained in the responses to a special set of questions in the mail survey of purchasers. Each respondent was asked to evaluate various neighborhood aspects on a scale of 1 (excellent) to 5 (bad); these included such things as the quality of the neighborhood elementary school, amount of air pollution, and danger of crime.[18]

To make use of these, I have defined neighborhoods by the attendance boundaries of each public elementary school in the metropolitan region. These had the advantage of being physically compact; and because they were twice as numerous as census tracts, were on the average smaller. The evaluations from respondents in each neighborhood, so defined, were averaged to yield an overall rating for each neighborhood characteristic.[19]

As might be expected, the evaluations of specific characteristics within each neighborhood proved to be correlated. Principal component analysis of the subjective evaluations revealed that more than three-fourths of the total variance could be accounted for by just two components.[20] None of the remaining six components individually accounted for more than eight per cent of the total variance, nor, as will be explained, was it possible to interpret any of them. Accordingly, this study will use just the first two components to describe the variation in perceived neighborhood amenity levels.[21]

As shown in Table 2, the first component is highly correlated with six of the original variables: *ELEMSC, HIGHSC, TRAFIC, FIRE,*

[17] For a discussion of this see Oates (1969) or King (1973a).

[18] The questions and responses used in the analysis are indicated in Table 1.

[19] Whatever the merits of perceptions, on abstract grounds, it is important to understand that the uses to which these are put in the present study involve the assumption that data obtained from an ordinal scale can be treated as cardinal. Clearly this is not always acceptable; however, certain theoretical arguments, experience with these data and their transformations, and comparison with various objective alternatives persuade me that for this study at least the assumption is reasonable. For a more complete discussion of this issue, see King (1973a, Chapter IV).

[20] For a complete discussion of this technique see M. G. Kendall, *A Course in Multivariate Analysis* (New York: Hafner Publishing Co., 1968).

[21] The decision to use only the first two components accords with the rule sometimes suggested of using only the components which have eigenvalues greater than 1.0, as the eigenvalue for the third component is 0.64.

TABLE 1

Correlations of Subjective Measures of Neighborhood Quality

ELEMSC	1.00							
GARBGE	−.12	1.00						
LIGHTG	.13	.57	1.00					
HIGHSC	.82	−.17	.12	1.00				
TRAFIC	.44	−.17	−.07	.53	1.00			
FIRE	.74	−.11	.27	.63	.51	1.00		
AIRPOL	.67	−.37	−.02	.77	.63	.65	1.00	
CRIME	.79	−.36	.01	.74	.56	.76	.80	1.00

NOTE: Definition of Variables
  ELEMSC: quality of local public elementary school.
  GARBGE: quality of garbage collection.
  LIGHTG: quality of street lighting, sweeping, and maintenance.
  HIGHSC: quality of local public high school.
  TRAFIC: amount of traffic on neighborhood streets.
    FIRE: danger of fire.
  AIRPOL: amount of air pollution.
  CRIME: danger of crime.

TABLE 2

Correlations of the First Two Components
and the Original Variables

	GEN Q	*SERVCE*
ELEMSC	.87	.17
GARBGE	−.32	.84
LIGHTG	.06	.91
HIGHSC	.88	.10
TRAFIC	.69	−.10
FIRE	.84	.25
AIRPOL	.89	−.12
CRIME	.92	−.06

Eigenvalues for first two components: 4.45, 1.66.
Percentage of total variance accounted for: 76.4.

NOTE: Responses were aggregated by elementary
public school district. The means calculated for each
variable were used in this analysis.

AIRPOL, and *CRIME,* and the second component with the remaining two; thus, the components distinguish what appear to be two separate aspects of neighborhood quality. Because of the high correlation with variables which seem to measure "goodness of life" or "pleasantness of surroundings," I consider the first component to be a measure of the general quality of the neighborhood and refer to it as *GEN Q.* The second component, on the other hand, seems to reflect the provision of specific urban services and is named *SERVCE.*

To confirm the identification of the components, I have examined the scores attained by specific neighborhoods of the region. As one would expect, those areas favorably rated on the first component are high-income neighborhoods, not densely settled, with local reputations as pleasant places to live.[22] The badly rated neighborhoods are in poor, slum regions of New Haven. Similarly, the areas rated worst by the second component are parts of East Haven, which is notorious as a poor provider of public services.

VI. THE PRICES OF HOUSING BUNDLE COMPONENTS

The empirical task in this section is the estimation of hedonic price equations like (3.1) for each housing submarket in the New Haven region. These will both describe price surfaces and permit the construction of gross housing characteristics.

A. Defining Submarket Areas

Before the hedonic prices can be estimated, there is one difficulty to be resolved: How should the limits of each submarket be determined? If the component prices were known at each point, it would be a simple matter to group places with identical or very similar prices into homogeneous market areas. But, of course, it is precisely because prices are not directly observable that the hedonic estimates are required.

I suggested previously that the extent of submarkets with uniform internal prices would depend on the nature of supply and demand functions. Following the model of residential location choice set out above, it seems likely that a major cause of geographically fragmented demand should be the variations between towns in public services, taxes, and location amenities. Location of work should also play a role, but in this small, compact region, accessibility should be relatively good everywhere, and its influence correspondingly reduced. Accord-

---

[22] Recall that a high score (5) on the subjective evaluation indicated that the neighborhood was undesirable. Thus, a favorable rating corresponds to a low score. This is important in evaluating the hedonic prices estimated in Section VI.

ingly, for this study, submarket boundaries will be defined by political boundaries; specifically, each town will be treated as a separate submarket.[23]

It might be suggested that whole towns are still too large to possess uniform housing prices—perhaps something smaller, like census tracts, would be more appropriate. This was considered but rejected for several reasons. First, the varieties of combinations of housing bundle components are not markedly different among the census tracts of each town. The average or most common bundle differs from place to place, but to a surprising extent the range of choices in each tract is quite wide. Thus, from the supply side of the market there is little reason to expect much within-town price variation. Second, and more pragmatically, the data requirements for satisfactory estimation of the hedonic price equations simply precluded work on markets much smaller than towns. As will be seen, even at the town level, limited variation in some characteristics have made it difficult to obtain reliable hedonic prices.[24]

B. Empirical Estimates

Given that housing submarkets will be defined by town boundaries, I can proceed to study the price variations among them in a straightforward manner. For each town, a hedonic price equation like (3.1) is defined, in which the observed sales price for the bundle is a function

[23] The only exceptions are the towns of Orange and Woodbridge, which are adjacent and very similar, sharing, for example, a common high school. They are combined and treated as a single unit.

[24] For this same reason, I have not adopted the method of using the data to determine submarket areas. In principle, it is correct to argue that submarkets could be distinguished by estimating separate equations for small areas and then making an F test for significantly different price patterns. However, because the housing bundle is so complex, the data requirements and the costs of meaningful tests are enormous. As a first prerequisite, it is essential that the hedonic equation be very fully specified. If not, it is virtually certain that correlations with improperly omitted variables will bias the estimates of those included. An F test between submarkets might then indicate a change in hedonic prices for bedrooms when what actually was occurring was a change in the correlation of bedrooms with swimming pools. It would be improper to conclude from such a test that the bundles are in separate markets, as the true prices of bedrooms and swimming pools taken separately might be identical. If the data base is sufficiently detailed to avoid this problem—as in the present case—it may still be that limited sample size results in inadequate variation of some component within some submarkets. This will result in price estimates that are spurious though strongly significant. In sum, the sample must be quite detailed, very large and exceedingly varied. The data set used in this study is one of the best now available for housing market analysis, but even it cannot meet these conditions fully. The solution adopted in this paper is to define submarkets following plausible a priori boundaries and thereby make the demand estimates contingent on the market definitions chosen.

of the various Structural Components—rooms, floor space, insulation, and construction materials; Location Components—measures of perceived neighborhood quality and certain public services; and Land purchased. The estimated coefficients for this equation will be the dollar value for units of each component, given the supply and demand relationships in the market.

The variables used in the hedonic equations are defined in Table 3, and the prices, estimated by ordinary least squares (OLS), appear in Table 4. In general, the equations are quite satisfactory; a large part of the variance in sales price is accounted for, and though individual coefficients vary among markets, the range of values often seem plausible. Note in particular the values for *HARDWD*, *GARG*1, *GARG*2, *FIREPL*, 2 + *BATH*, and *LAVTRY*, for which there may be a sense of construction costs to aid in evaluation. The reader will also observe that each equation includes several constrained values; this is one aspect which requires more extended comment.

As explained in note 24 above, the data requirements for satisfactory estimation of a hedonic price equation for housing are uncommonly severe because of the extraordinarily complex nature of the bundles. Improper specification of any regression equation will create biases in the estimates for included variables if correlations exist between the included and the improperly excluded variables. For housing, the penalty for using an inadequately detailed base will be erroneous implications for the component price surfaces across the metropolitan area.

While the data base available to this study is large by most standards and is uniquely rich in detail, it lacks sufficient variation of some characteristics in some markets. In New Haven, for example, though the total number of observations is quite adequate, only three houses had no basements. The coefficient for this variable reflected the overall departure of these observations from the regression and was significantly positive, rather than negative as expected. As another example, 2 + *BATH* had a strongly significant negative coefficient in East Haven; examination of the sample found that only one house in this generally low-income market had a second bath.

When hedonic prices for the individual town regressions took sizes and magnitudes contrary to reasonable a priori expectations, and when examination showed this to result from too few observations, it seemed best to reject these results. If accepted uncritically, they would lead to false conclusions about the budget constraint which households face in the market.

TABLE 3

Definitions of Variables for Hedonic Price Equations

FULLIN	0–1 dummy, 1 if house has full insulation. (S)
*GARG*1	⌠0–1 dummies, 1 if house has a one-car garage or a
*GARG*2	⌡two-car garage.
2+BATH	0–1 dummy, 1 if house has two or more baths.
LAVTRY	0–1 dummy, 1 if house has a partial bath.
BLAUND	0–1 dummy, 1 if house has a basement laundry area with drains and spigots.
HARDWD	0–1 dummy, 1 if house has hardwood flooring. (S)
FIREPL	Number of fireplaces in house.
75+AMP	0–1 dummy, 1 if house has wiring to supply more than 75 amperes.
STEAM	0–1 dummy, 1 if house has a steam heating system. (S)
EXCLNT	⌠0–1, 1 if realtor's evaluation of house
VGOOD	⎰quality was excellent, very good, or fair; relative
FAIR	⌡to good. (S)
FACBSS	⌠0–1 dummies, 1 if house had facing respectively
FACASB	⌡of brick, stone, or stucco; or of asbestos shingles. (R)
AGE	⌠
AGESQ	⎱Age and age squared of home in decades. (S)
SQFT	⌠Floor space and floor space squared in house in thousands
SQFTSQ	⌡of square feet.
SQFT/R	Average room size in thousands of square feet.
SMROOM	Number of small, special purpose rooms.
FINBMT	⌠0–1 dummies, 1 if house had a finished basement or no
NOBMT	⌡basement.
2STORY	0–1 dummy, 1 if house had more than one story. (S)
SIZLOT	⌠
SIZLT2	⎱Lot size and lot size squared in thousands of square feet.
DISCBD	Natural logarithm of distance from house to New Haven Green multiplied by lot size.
GEN Q	A measure of the quality of the local elementary school and high school, danger of crime and fire, amount of heavy traffic on neighborhood streets, and severity of air pollution. This measure is constructed from the perceptions of

(continued)

TABLE 3 (concluded)

	the purchasers of houses in each neighborhood. A high-quality neighborhood will receive a *negative* score on this measure; consequently, a negative hedonic price is expected. The measure is scaled by the lot size of the house.
SERVCE	A measure of the quality of local street lighting, sweeping, and maintenance, and the quality of garbage collection service. Like *GEN Q*, this measure is constructed from the perceptions of purchasers, and again, a high-quality neighborhood will receive a *negative* score. The measure is scaled by the lot size of the house.
GARBGE	0–1 dummy, 1 if house receives municipal garbage collection.
CSEWER	0–1 dummy, 1 if house has connection to city sewer.
PRICE	Sales price of house in thousands of 1967 dollars.

NOTE: An (S) or (R) following the variable definition indicates that values are scaled by the square feet, or the square root of the square feet, of living space.

The problem arose then of what values should be used to replace the rejected estimates. The choice has been to estimate the same hedonic equation, pooling the observations for the entire metropolitan sample. Rejected values were replaced by the estimates from the pooled equation, and the individual town equation was reestimated incorporating these constraints. It might be objected that this procedure also implies something incorrect about the price set confronting households in each market, since goods apparently virtually unobtainable are assigned a price relevant only to the entire region. Would some very high price not be more appropriate? The proper response to this, I believe, is to note that the sample of homes for which the price equations are estimated includes only a small fraction of all homes in the submarket. The problem, then, is more likely one of sample size than of actual inability to purchase some component.

Estimates from the pooled sample were used also to constrain values for neighborhood qualities — *GEN Q* and *SERVCE* — and the municipal services — *CSEWER* and *GARBGE* — in most submarkets. This was done for two reasons: first, the model of residential location choice implied that differences in neighborhood quality would be an important factor in the household's choice of location. It seems likely that

TABLE 4

Hedonic Prices for Housing Bundle
(thousands of dollars)

	All Towns	New Haven	Hamden	North Haven
INTERCEPT	11.0299 [a]	.8079	12.9907 [a]	15.2437 [a]
FULLIN	.6517 [a]	.6465 [b]	.9557 [a]	*.6517
GARG1	.9693 [a]	.3736	1.0724 [b]	.9710
GARG2	2.9139 [a]	1.2129 [c]	3.0659 [a]	3.4264 [a]
2+BATH	2.4398 [a]	1.0889 [c]	*2.4398	2.4735 [a]
LAVTRY	1.0045 [a]	1.0026 [b]	.9081 [b]	1.5998 [a]
BLAUND	.5467 [b]	1.7545 [a]	−.1908	.5323
HARDWD	.8791 [a]	1.2939 [a]	*.8791	.7210
FIREPL	.8488 [a]	.9662 [b]	1.1845 [a]	1.1183 [b]
75+AMP	.3868 [b]	.8676	1.1500 [a]	.8021 [c]
STEAM	.6080 [a]	.7886 [b]	.3396	*.6080
VGOOD	.5411 [b]	1.2916 [a]	.1337	.6380
EXCLNT	1.3412 [a]	1.1213 [a]	1.1233 [a]	1.7103 [b]
FAIR	−1.0926 [b]	.3951	.2036	−3.5326 [b]
FACBSS	1.5686 [a]	2.5228 [a]	.7144 [c]	1.4319 [b]
FACASB	−1.8922 [a]	−.8831	−1.5611	*−1.8992
AGE	−1.1324 [a]	−1.2323 [a]	−.1958	−.3541
AGESQ	.0545 [a]	.1033 [a]	−.0917	−.0250
SQFT	6.6966 [a]	7.7909 [a]	3.6654 [b]	1.0753
SQFTSQ	.8491 [a]	.1476	1.5856 [a]	2.0239 [a]
SQFT/R	−28.6988 [a]	12.2736 [c]	−32.6113 [b]	−25.1213 [b]
SMROOM	.6047 [a]	−.0448	.6858 [a]	.7522 [a]
FINBMT	.6834 [a]	−.7349	1.2947 [b]	.9674
NOBMT	.2351	*−1.5000	1.1513	−1.1198
2STORY	.1100	−1.3043 [a]	−.1830	.5729 [c]
SIZLOT	.2305 [a]	.7128 [a]	.3707 [a]	.0513
SIZLT2	−.0005 [b]	−.0028	−.0014 [b]	.0002
DISCBD	−.0662 [a]	−.1870 [b]	−.1523 [a]	−.0424
GEN Q	−.0678 [a]	−.2164	*−.0678	*−.0678
SRVCE	−.0192 [a]	*−.0192	−.1041	−.0456
GARBGE	.3068	*.3068	*.3068	*.3068
CSEWER	.4684 [b]	*.4684	*.4684	*.4684
$\bar{R}^2$	.82	.86	.71	.75
Standard Error	4.10	4.06	3.88	3.98
Number of observations	1,802	300	407	217

(continued)

TABLE 4 (concluded)

	East Haven	West Haven	Orange Woodbridge	Wallingford
INTERCEPT	8.5135 [a]	14.2757 [a]	17.4090 [a]	15.9887 [a]
FULLIN	.2762	.7213 [b]	*.6517	*.6517
GARG1	.4952 [c]	1.1068 [a]	1.4759	.7683 [c]
GARG2	2.1016 [a]	1.0102 [b]	2.6323	2.9629 [a]
2+BATH	*2.4398	2.5510 [a]	1.2516	.2508
LAVTRY	.9623 [a]	1.1976 [a]	.3671	.7036 [c]
BLAUND	.6251 [c]	1.2807 [a]	−1.1041	.7952
HARDWD	*.8791	.9237 [b]	.6756	.4902
FIREPL	.2953	1.3380 [a]	1.0454 [c]	1.1416 [a]
75+AMP	*.3868	.3791	.4057	.7243 [c]
STEAM	*.6080	.3000	*.6080	*.6080
VGOOD	.4956	.2385	1.2719	.2181
EXCLNT	.8055 [b]	1.1681 [a]	1.5848 [b]	1.1563 [c]
FAIR	−2.7934 [a]	−3.6185 [a]	*−1.0926	*−1.0926
FACBSS	2.5600 [a]	*1.5686	1.5740 [b]	*1.5686
FACASB	*−1.8922	−.5186	*−1.8992	*−1.8992
AGE	−1.0615 [a]	−1.5280 [a]	−1.0247 [a]	−.6772
AGESQ	.0819 [a]	.1343 [a]	.0513	.0366
SQFT	10.9198 [b]	4.4838 [c]	8.5781 [b]	6.8369 [b]
SQFTSQ	−3.0565 [b]	.5098	.8184	.4724
SQFT/R	−13.2051 [b]	−29.2845 [a]	−40.7100 [a]	−47.2890 [a]
SMROOM	.3592 [b]	.1295	.6697 [c]	.0027
FINBMT	.7400 [c]	1.2089 [b]	1.1308	1.3726 [b]
NOBMT	−1.2208	−.4199	2.0493 [c]	−.7944
2STORY	.0969	.6859 [c]	−.4962	1.0454 [b]
SIZLOT	.3053 [a]	.1853 [b]	−.0815	.1303 [b]
SIZLT2	−.0045 [b]	.0015 [c]	.0014	.0015 [c]
DISCBD	−.0430	−.0625	−.0059	*−.0662
GEN Q	*−.0678	−.2358	*−.0678	*−.0678
SRVCE	*−.0192	−.0667	*−.0192	*−.0192
GARBGE	*.3068	*.3068	*.3068	*.3068
CSEWER	*.4684	*.4684	*.4684	*.4684
$\bar{R}^2$	.54	.64	.62	.85
Standard Error	1.95	2.60	5.42	2.13
Number of observations	166	217	193	112

NOTE : Asterisk denotes constrained values (see text). Significance levels: [a] $t > 2.33$; [b] $t > 1.65$; [c] $t > 1.28$.

this would tend to promote a common price, since the demand for neighborhood quality would not be fragmented but metropolitan-area-wide. Consequently, in the absence of strong evidence that it was inappropriate, the market-wide price was imposed.[25] Second, for some services there was no within-town variation and therefore no possibility of calculating separate hedonic prices. All the homes in a town might, for example, receive municipal garbage collection, in which case the hedonic price equation for that town could not identify a value for the service. Yet to omit the variable in such towns would bias coefficients of included variables and lead to incorrect comparisons across towns.

C. Constructing the Housing Characteristics

To convert the observed housing components into gross Lancastrian housing characteristics, I make some important simplifying assumptions. The housing bundle is regarded as divisible into four gross characteristics: basic structure (*BSTRUK*), interior quality (*QUAL*), interior space (*SPACE*), and land, public services, and neighborhood quality (*SITE*).[26] These four characteristics are what the household actually demands. To get them, however, it must purchase specific housing components, a garage, a fireplace, a basement, and land. I assume that each component supplies only one characteristic, making it a simple matter to calculate the total expenditure on each characteristic by adding together the hedonic prices for all appropriate components. The assignment of components to characteristics is indicated in Table 5.

It must be recognized explicitly that the characteristics I define are arbitrary in several respects. First, there is no certainty that households do perceive the housing bundle as consisting of exactly these four components, put together in exactly this way, although the combinations seem quite reasonable. Second, Lancaster's theory implies that households will demand something like Interior Space, but the

[25] The constraints are not imposed for *GEN Q* in New Haven and West Haven or for *SERVCE* in Hamden, North Haven, and West Haven. In these towns preliminary work found the neighborhood quality to be especially high-valued. This appeared to reflect the existence within the town of a limited number of high-quality neighborhoods. If, for whatever reason, a family felt compelled to live in, say, New Haven, it would face keen competition for a dwelling in the superior neighborhood.

[26] Public services and neighborhood quality are incorporated into *SITE* because their capitalized values will be reflected in the cost of land. This does not mean that households can increase their purchase of, for example, good public schools by buying more land. A better quality school is available only by choosing a different location.

TABLE 5

Elements of the Housing Characteristics

Basic Structure (BSTRUK)	Interior Quality (QUAL)	Interior Space (SPACE) [a]	Site (SITE) [a]
FULLIN	HARDWD	SQFT	SIZLOT
GARG1	FIREPL	SQFTSQ	SZLOT2
GARG2	75+AMP	SQFT/R	DISCBD
2+BATH	STEAM	SMROOM	GEN Q
LAVTRY	EXCLNT	FINBMT	SRVCE
BLAUND	VGOOD	NOBMT	GARBGE
	FAIR	2STORY	CSEWER
	FACBSS		
	FACASB		
	AGE		
	AGESQ		

[a] The intercept term is allocated 80 per cent to SPACE and 20 per cent to SITE.

construction here adds the additional constraint that Interior Space is amalgamated entirely from items purchased as part of the housing bundle. Conceivably, items like room dividers or mirrors are also a part of Interior Space. Third, what to do with the equation intercept is a problem in constructing these gross components. Here it has been allocated 80 per cent to SPACE and 20 percent to SITE, in accordance with the ratio of structure to site value suggested by Housing and Urban Development (HUD) statistics (1970, p. 198). This can be justified by observing that the intercept is the value of structure and site after all special quality features and location advantages are stripped away. Admittedly, this is not entirely satisfactory, but there is no alternative which seems clearly better.

The price indexes for the four gross characteristics in each town are shown in Table 6. To obtain these, I have specified a standard housing bundle and have then calculated the cost of characteristics by summing the costs of the individual elements as given in Table 4. Finally, each entry has been normalized by dividing by the cost of SPACE in New Haven.

TABLE 6

Price Indexes for Housing Components [a]

	New Haven	Hamden	North Haven	East Haven	West Haven	Orange/ Woodbridge	Walling- ford
BSTRUK	.37	.79	.79	.57	.53	.55	.48
QUAL	.88	.78	.77	.48	.86	.81	.66
SPACE	1.00	1.22	1.44	1.21	1.06	1.82	1.49
SITE	1.63	.85	.42	.66	.99	.36	.47

[a] The standard bundle from which these were derived included *FULLIN, GARG2, 2+BATH, 2STORY, HARDWD, FIREPL, 75+AMP, EXCLNT* condition, 1 decade *AGE*, 1,420 *SQFT*, 20,000 *SIZLOT, GENQ*, and *SRVCE* of −.5 each. Distance from the CBD is an approximate median distance for the town as a whole. In the demand functions of Section V, the price of *SITE* is calculated for each house, according to the distance of that house to the CBD. Thus, the entries for *SITE* here are only illustrative.

VII. THE DEMAND FOR HOUSING CHARACTERISTICS

Using the hedonic prices obtained in the previous section to describe housing price surfaces in the metropolitan area and to construct the gross housing characteristics, I can now inquire whether household behavior corresponds to that predicted. The first question is whether households appear to view housing as a bundle of characteristics and modify their purchases in response to price and outlay variations. If they do, I can continue to the second aspect and investigate location choice as an interaction of prices, work site, and neighborhood quality.

To study the household's purchases of housing characteristics, I use the Rotterdam differential demand model of Barten (1964, 1967) and Theil (1965) with slight modifications as required for application to cross-sectional data and a single demand branch.[27] The resulting equations are of the form

$$w_j^* Dq_{ij} = \mu_i D\bar{m}_j + \sum_h S_{ih} Dp_{hj} + u_{ij}$$

$$h, i = 1, 4$$
$$j = 1, n \text{ households}$$

[27] The material in this section draws heavily on my paper "The Demand for Housing: A Lancastrian Approach" (1973b) and the reader is referred to it for additional details.

Here the q's and p's are the four characteristics identified in the previous section and their prices. The term $\bar{m}$ is the real outlay on the housing bundle and replaces an income term because of the assumed separability. The operator D indicates the logarithmic difference $\ln x - \ln \bar{x}$ where $\bar{x}$ is the mean value of the particular data series. Finally, $w_j^* = [(w_{ij} + \bar{w}_i)/2]$, where w_{ij} is the ith budget share $p_i q_{ij}/m_j$ for the jth household and $\bar{w}_i$ is the mean value of the ith budget share.

The "outlay" and price elasticities indicating household behavior are readily obtained from the parameters μ_i and S_{ih}. The former is defined as $\dfrac{\partial q_i}{\partial m} \dfrac{m}{q_i} \dfrac{q_i p_i}{m}$; the latter, as $\dfrac{\partial q_i}{\partial p_h} \dfrac{p_h}{q_i} \dfrac{q_i p_h}{m}$. Thus, deflating both by the budget share will yield the derived elasticities.[28]

The u_{ij}'s are random disturbance terms for which we assume $E(u_{ij}) = 0$ for all i and j; $E(u_{ij}, u_{hk}) = 0$ for $j \neq k$; but $E(u_{ij}, u_{hk}) \neq 0$ for $j = k$; $i, h = 1, 4$. That is, the errors are uncorrelated across observations but correlated for the purchases of each household as a consequence of the overall restriction on the housing outlay. It follows from this restriction that the covariance matrix of the error terms is singular, and all four demand equations are not independent.

The assumption of separability permits the demands for the four housing characteristics to be studied as a small, independent demand system. As is well known, classical demand theory implies certain restrictions on the parameters of such complete systems: symmetry of cross-price terms in real-income-compensated functions, homogeneity, and negative own-price elasticities. One of the great advantages of the Rotterdam model is the ease with which these restrictions may be imposed (Brown and Deaton, 1972, p. 1190), and because this increases efficiency, I impose symmetry and homogeneity.[29]

To impose restrictions across equations, parameters of the demand system are estimated simultaneously in a "stacked" equation, using the iterative Zellner estimation procedure (1962) to allow for the nonzero covariances of the error terms. Because the error covariance matrix is singular, only three of the four individual demand functions need actually be estimated; parameters of the other are recovered from these, using the budget constraint, symmetry, and homogeneity.[30] The estimated parameters are given in Table 7 and the elasticities at the mean budget shares in Table 8.

[28] The elasticity is, of course, not constant but depends inversely on the budget share.

[29] Negativity, as an inequality constraint, is not readily imposed, but the condition may be used to evaluate the estimates.

[30] The estimates obtained are invariant with respect to the equation omitted.

TABLE 7

The Demand Parameters for Housing Characteristics

Independent Variables	Dependent Variables			
	BSTRUK	QUAL	SPACE	SITE
OUTLAY	.2400	.3415	.3163	.1022
	(31.94)[a]	(36.11)	(35.73)	(19.06)
PSTRUK	−.0172	.0076	−.0343	.0439
	(1.77)	(.86)	(4.15)	(10.32)
PQUAL	[b]	−.0370	.0096	.0198
		(1.85)	(.71)	(2.52)
PSPACE			−.0712	.0959
			(1.49)	(16.37)
PSITE				−.1596
				(13.29)
R^2	.56	.67	.68	.85

NOTE: Definition of variables:

BSTRUK
QUAL
SPACE   } These are the four Lancastrian characteristics defined in Table 5.
SITE

PSTRUK
PQUAL   } These are the prices for the four characteristics. The method of calcula-
PSPACE { tion is explained in Section VI and sample values are shown in Table 6.
PSITE

OUTLAY This is the real value of the outlay on the housing bundle.

All variables are measured in natural logarithms and used as deviations from mean values as required for the Rotterdam model.

[a] t values in parentheses.
[b] Values below the diagonal are obtained from the symmetry condition.

TABLE 8

Elasticities at Mean Budget Shares

	BSTRUK	QUAL	SPACE	SITE
Outlay	2.06	1.71	.65	.52
Own-price	−.15	−.19	−.15	−.82

As evidence that households perceive housing as a bundle of components and modify purchases in response to prices and outlay, these results seem quite satisfactory. The R^2 for each demand function is quite high, especially considering that units of observation are individual households in cross section. All own-price elasticities are negative; cross-price coefficients indicate *BSTRUK* and *SPACE* to be complements, *QUAL* and *SPACE*, and *SPACE* and *SITE* to be substitutes, all of which seem reasonable. Purchases of quality and special structural features are highly responsive to increased outlay and thus, by implication, to income. Interestingly, the marked increase in *SITE* purchases in the outlying markets of the area appears to result more from decreased prices than from increased income.[31]

VIII. TRADING OFF COMMUTING COSTS, PRICE STRUCTURES AND NEIGHBORHOOD QUALITY

I come now to consider evidence relevant to the first part of the housing demand model set out in Section II. There it was suggested that because location is an integral aspect of a dwelling unit the decision to purchase would involve considerations of the implied journey-to-work costs, the neighborhood quality obtained, and the set of relative prices for housing characteristics. While the evidence for this portion of the model is still incomplete, there are certain regularities discernible even in simple examination, which are quite encouraging.

The method in this section will be the examination of the actual locations chosen by households for evidence that they can be explained as optimal compromise locations given the work sites, neighborhood qualities, and price patterns. From the previous section, it appears that households behave as though they perceive price variations for housing characteristics among the various submarkets. Thus, if place of work and neighborhood quality were no consideration, it would be reasonable to predict that a household would purchase its dwellings in that submarket where the particular combination of characteristics is lowest priced. To test this, I have calculated, for

---

[31] There are, however, reasons to doubt the precise accuracy of the estimates despite the generally high t statistics. First, the determination of prices in hedonic equations will create some problems of measurement error resulting in bias. Second, the households have the alternative of selecting their budget constraint by moving among markets; thus, the estimates of price response cannot be treated as exactly comparable to the parameters in most demand studies. It should be emphasized, however, that households are not likely to choose a location on the basis of prices alone, since location will affect the journey-to-work and neighborhood quality also. These latter two influences will help reduce bias from this second source.

TABLE 9

Distribution of Housing Purchases by Relative Cost of Market
(per cent)

Town	Low Cost ← 1	2	3	4	5	→ High Cost 6	7
New Haven	24	16	18	11	7	13	10
Hamden	20	26	18	11	6	10	9
North Haven	20	26	18	11	6	10	9
East Haven	18	12	14	18	18	19	2
West Haven	33	19	12	9	10	11	6
Woodbridge-Orange	2	18	9	25	22	16	8
Wallingford	19	20	13	18	18	7	5

NOTE: The entries in this table show for each submarket (town) the percentage of purchases for which this market was the cheapest, second cheapest, etc. For example, of the houses purchased in New Haven, for 24 per cent New Haven was the cheapest market for this type of dwelling; for 10 per cent, it was the most expensive. Percentages may not add to 100 because of rounding.

every dwelling actually purchased, its cost in every submarket at the prices prevailing there.

The results are shown in Table 9 as the number of times a dwelling purchased in, e.g., New Haven was purchased in the cheapest, second cheapest, and so on, market in the area. Without making any formal tests, it is apparent that households do not concentrate to any extent in the lowest cost market for their particular dwelling. There is some tendency to buy in the cheaper markets and only rarely do households buy in the highest-cost market. An indication of this is that the mean excess of actual price over lowest possible price is $3,700, while the mean excess of highest price over actual price is $6,100. Overall, however, it is apparent that predicting household location on the basis of where the observed dwelling is cheapest would be quite unsatisfactory.

The question now becomes whether the tendency of households to locate in other than the cheapest market can be explained in terms of the additional goals of low commuting costs and neighborhood quality. The tradeoff of a lengthier work trip for lower housing prices has a venerable standing in the urban economics literature. Although the cost variations for housing examined in this study arose for different

FIGURE 1

Plot of Additional Miles Traveled to Work
against Additional Housing Cost

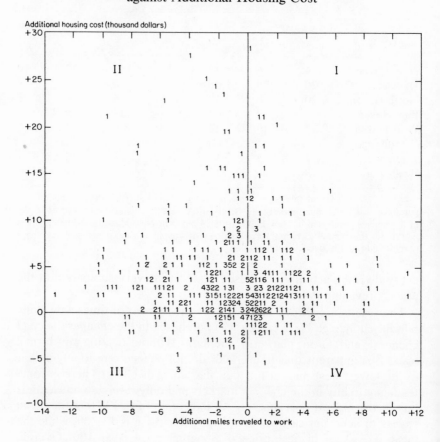

Additional housing cost (thousand dollars)

Additional miles traveled to work

reasons than are usually suggested, the rationale for the tradeoff is the same, and I begin by looking at this.

In Figure 1, the additional dollar cost incurred by purchasing in other than the lowest-cost market is plotted against the difference in the journeys-to-work from the two markets.[32] If households recog-

[32] The number of households examined in Fig. 1 and subsequent Table 10 is only 538 compared to the 683 studied in the demand analysis. For some households, job sites were unknown or outside the area studied; in addition, efforts were made to

nize low-cost markets but accept higher prices to achieve a more desirable commuting trip, the points should lie in quadrants II and IV.[33] It is evident that this clustering does not exist, though more observations lie in II and IV — 292 — than in I — 199. (In addition, there are 60 observations enjoying the double bonus of quadrant III.) [34]

At this point it appears that the hypothesis of an exchange of commuting cost for housing cost must either be abandoned as a rather imprecise description or amended by the introduction of a third goal, the search for neighborhood quality being that suggested. To examine this possibility, I show in Table 10 average excess commuting trips, excess costs, and excess neighborhood quality [35] by income classes for the observations in each quadrant of Figure 1.

The results are quite remarkable. In comparing quadrant I to II, notice that in every income class the neighborhood quality obtained by households in I (henceforth "I's") exceeds that of II's by a wide margin. With one exception where it is equal, the quality available to I's in the low cost market is substantially less than that available to II's. Thus, whereas II's in their choice of location have sacrificed little if any quality (the entries in the "Excess GEN Q" are usually small), I's have obtained much greater quality by foregoing the low-cost market. The cost of this to I's appears to be the longer commuting trip both in absolute distance and relative to the commuting trip from the low-cost market.

For the entries in quadrants III and IV, one's expectations from the hypothesis of tradeoffs are not so clear. There would seem to be no reason why the double bargains in III might not be triple

exclude all self-employed persons who might work in their own homes and such persons as traveling salesmen.

The calculation of the hypothetical work trip from the low-cost market is somewhat crude. Whereas the actual work trip was calculated quite precisely, the hypothetical trip was assumed to begin from a central location in each market. Markets are small (rarely more than two miles in diameter) but in future work this calculation will be refined.

[33] Quadrants III and IV exist because households are sometimes able to buy a dwelling for less than the price predicted for the cheapest market. This might reflect special bargaining skills, seller urgency, or the like. Households in IV can be regarded as trading off their "bargain savings" against a longer commuting trip, while those in III have obtained a double bargain: a shorter commuting trip and a lower price than in the low-cost market.

[34] There is some slight double counting in these figures, as observations lying exactly on an axis are counted as belonging to two quadrants.

[35] Excess commuting trips, costs, and neighborhood quality are all calculated by subtracting these items in the low-cost market from what is actually received. The neighborhood-quality measure is based on GEN Q only.

TABLE 10

Housing Costs, Commuting Costs, and Neighborhood Quality

	Income (Thousands of Dollars)						
	0–7.5	7.5–9.5	9.5–13	13–17	17–21	21–25	25+
Quadrant I							
Excess cost	2.20	2.62	3.66	4.68	10.34	11.11	10.30
Excess miles	2.19	2.85	2.35	2.01	1.66	.78	2.40
Excess GEN Q	.26	.36	.59	.56	.61	.50	.67
Value	19.09	19.78	23.10	24.33	32.00	44.71	40.11
HValue	16.90	17.16	19.44	19.65	21.67	33.61	29.81
Dwork	5.41	6.32	6.13	4.99	5.47	4.11	6.51
HDwork	3.22	3.46	3.78	2.98	3.81	3.33	4.12
GEN Q [a]	.27	.44	.51	.40	.71	.44	.74
HGEN Q [a]	.01	.08	−.08	−.17	.10	−.06	.07
Observations	25	44	70	31	12	7	10
Quadrant II							
Excess cost	2.35	3.24	3.74	5.00	8.43	10.92	12.87
Excess miles	−3.44	−3.26	−3.31	−2.81	−3.43	−2.73	−2.72
Excess GEN Q	.06	−.02	.00	−.07	.10	−.15	−.24
Value	17.02	20.56	22.20	26.38	33.29	37.68	46.23
HValue	14.68	17.32	18.46	21.38	24.86	26.75	33.37
Dwork	2.54	3.49	3.02	2.99	3.46	3.94	2.87
HDwork	5.95	6.75	6.34	5.80	6.89	6.66	5.60
GEN Q [a]	.06	.30	.26	.21	.35	.20	−.03
HGEN Q [a]	.01	.31	.26	.28	.25	.35	.21
Observations	42	57	65	38	24	7	22
Quadrant III							
Excess cost	−1.27	−1.50	−1.73	−1.96	−2.47	−6.07	–
Excess miles	−2.10	−2.28	−3.62	−2.95	−2.92	−4.71	–
Excess GEN Q [a]	−.30	−.54	−.07	.35	.13	.05	–
Value	13.60	16.72	19.26	24.04	27.63	26.98	–
HValue	14.87	18.21	21.00	26.00	30.10	33.05	–
Dwork	1.99	3.65	3.25	4.88	4.16	2.21	–
HDwork	4.03	5.93	6.87	7.83	7.08	6.92	–
GEN Q [a]	−.42	−.51	.17	.57	.38	.70	–
HGEN Q [a]	−.12	.04	.24	.21	.25	.65	–
Observations	20	13	12	8	6	1	0

TABLE 10 (concluded)

	Income (Thousands of Dollars)						
	0–7.5	7.5–9.5	9.5–13	13–17	17–21	21–25	25+
	Quadrant IV						
Excess cost	−.70	−.98	−1.30	−1.16	−.75	−4.93	–
Excess miles	1.44	1.95	1.57	1.19	.65	1.06	–
Excess *GEN Q* [a]	.62	.42	.37	.03	.63	.51	–
Value	17.55	16.60	17.87	21.88	23.09	15.91	–
HValue	18.25	17.58	19.17	23.05	23.84	20.84	–
Dwork	3.86	7.57	5.75	3.76	5.22	6.63	–
HDwork	2.41	5.61	4.18	2.57	4.57	5.58	–
GEN Q [a]	−.09	.44	.40	.55	.68	.91	–
HGEN Q [a]	−.71	.03	.03	.53	.05	.40	–
Observations	5	8	17	4	2	1	0

NOTE: Households are classified by quadrant from Figure 1 and by income class (in thousands of dollars) as shown in each column heading.

> *Value:* value of housing bundle (thousands of dollars) in market of purchase.
> *HValue:* hypothetical value of housing bundle calculated at the set of prices in the lowest-cost town.
> *Dwork:* journey-to-work in miles from actual dwelling.
> *HDwork:* hypothetical journey-to-work from low-cost town.
> *GEN Q:* neighborhood quality.[a]
> *HGEN Q:* hypothetical neighborhood quality, an average value for the low-cost town.[a]
> Excess cost: *Value − HValue*
> Excess miles: *Dwork − HDwork*
> Excess *GEN Q: GEN Q − HGEN Q* [a]

[a] To provide an easier, more intuitive understanding, I have multiplied the scores for *GEN Q* by −1 *in this table only.* Consequently, a *positive GEN Q* is desirable and a *positive* deviation indicates a better neighborhood. Differences in *GEN Q* of less than about .10 are not meaningful.

bargains as well, offering lower costs, shorter commuting trips and better neighborhood qualities. Still, one might expect that households would sometimes accept lesser quality to obtain the other two bargains, so the net effect is not certain. It appears, in fact, that for the majority of III's, quality is lower than that of I's or II's; moreover, for the same cases, it appears to be lower than that available in the low-cost market. Thus, there is some evidence that for the lower-income families a sacrifice in quality was accepted in order to obtain the dollar savings and the shorter commuting trip.

For quadrant IV, one's expectations are once again uncertain. However, it appears that the main influence on the location choice must have been the possibility of superior neighborhood quality, since the saving of housing cost is rather trivial and the extra commuting trip not great. In contrast, the neighborhood quality is high relative to that obtained in other quadrants for similar income levels, and the excess neighborhood-quality figures are (particularly for low income) among the largest in any quadrant.

IX. CONCLUSION

Housing markets have long been described as erratic, unpredictable, or even chaotic. Hopefully, the investigations reported here will help dispel some of this. The evaluation is incomplete and certain assumptions used in this analysis are clearly open to question; nevertheless, there can be no doubt that household behavior in purchasing a single-family dwelling and choosing a location conforms quite well to the model set out. Choice of location is surely complex, but it is not a random process; place of work, neighborhood quality, and optimal prices seem to shape the decision. To obtain a superior neighborhood, households will travel further and pay more than they would have to if the house itself were their only concern; conversely, the chance to save on housing costs and work trips will induce households to settle for less neighborhood quality, particularly lower-income families.

If one considers only the choice of dwelling type within a particular market, the evidence of economically rational behavior is unmistakable. Prices and outlay both influence purchases just as would be expected. One particularly interesting implication of these results is that an important heterogeneous good like "housing" can usefully be treated as a collection of fairly specific characteristics. Since the purchases of these different items respond quite differently to price and outlay changes, it is clear that suppressing these, as do the usual studies of "housing demand," will reduce understanding of consumer behavior in a very important market.

Finally, though much of the attention in this paper has been directed toward the model of household behavior, the fundamental role of hedonic price estimation must not be overlooked. Contrary to an established opinion, it appears that housing prices are not chaotic and randomly set; they may vary in relation to components but regularly and over discernible areas. Significantly, choice of dwelling type and location both indicate the price patterns to be sufficiently apparent to households so that decisions bear their marks. When detailed information regarding housing transactions is available, it seems that hedonic price estimation can usefully be employed to indicate to the outside observer the price patterns needed in the investigation of housing market behavior.

REFERENCES

Alonso, William. *Location and Land Use*, Cambridge: Harvard University Press, 1964.
Barten, A. P. "Consumer Demand Functions Under Conditions of Almost Additive Preferences." *Econometrica* 32 (January-April 1964): 1–38.
_____. "Evidence on the Slutsky Conditions for Demand Equations." *Review of Economics and Statistics* 49 (February 1967): 77–83.
Brown, A., and Deaton, A. "Models of Consumer Behavior." *Economic Journal*, 82 (December 1972): 1145–1236.
Kain, John F., and Quigley, John. "Measuring the Value of Housing Quality." *Journal of the American Statistical Association* 65 (June 1970): 532–548.
_____. *"Housing Markets and Racial Discrimination: A Microeconomic Analysis.* New York: NBER, 1975.
King, A. Thomas. *Property Taxes, Amenities, and Residential Land Values.* Cambridge: Ballinger Press, 1973a.
_____. "The Demand for Housing: A Lancastrian Approach." Processed, 1973b.
King, A. Thomas, and Mieszkowski, Peter. "Racial Discrimination, Segregation, and the Price of Housing." *Journal of Political Economy* 81 (May-June 1973): 590–606.
Lancaster, Kelvin J. "A New Approach to Consumer Theory." *Journal of Political Economy* 74 (April 1966): 132–157.
_____. *Consumer Demand: A New Approach.* New York: Columbia University Press, 1971.
Musgrave, John C. "The Measurement of Price Changes in Construction." *Journal of the American Statistical Association* 66 (September 1969): 771–786.
Muth, Richard F. *Cities and Housing.* Chicago: University of Chicago Press, 1969.
Oates, Wallace E. "The Effects of Property Taxes and Local Public Spending on Property Values." *Journal of Political Economy* 77 (November-December 1969): 957–971.
Paldam, Martin. "What is Known About the Housing Demand." *Swedish Journal of Economics* 72 (June 1970): 130–148.
Pollak, R. A. "Conditional Demand Functions and the Implications of Direct Separable Utility." *Southern Economic Journal* 37 (April 1971): 423–433.
Quigley, John. "The Demand for Urban Housing." Processed, 1973.
_____. "The Influence of Workplaces and Housing Stocks Upon Residential Choice: A Crude Test of the 'Gross Price' Hypotheses." Paper prepared for Toronto Meetings of the Econometric Society, December 30, 1972.
Straszheim, Mahlon. *An Econometric Analysis of the Urban Housing Market.* New York: NBER, 1975.
Theil, Henri. "The Information Approach to Demand Analysis." *Econometrica* 33 (January 1965): 67–87.
Twentieth Century Fund. *American Housing: Problems and Prospects.* New York: Twentieth Century Fund, 1944.
U.S., Department of Housing and Urban Development. *1970 HUD Statistical Yearbook.* Washington, D.C.: Government Printing Office.

Winger, Alan R. "Housing Space Demands: A Cross Section Analysis." *Land Economics* 28 (February 1962): 33–41.
Zellner, A. "An Efficient Method of Estimating Seemingly Unrelated Regressions and Tests for Aggregation Bias." *Journal of the American Statistical Association* 57 (June 1962): 348–368.

Comments on "The Demand for Housing: Integrating the Roles of Journey-to-Work, Neighborhood Quality, and Prices"

GREGORY INGRAM

HARVARD UNIVERSITY

STUDYING the demand for housing is conceptually very similar to studying the demand for other goods. There are quantities demanded and prices paid; presumably the quantities can be related to the prices and other household characteristics within the traditional framework of demand analysis. As King points out, however, it is often difficult to obtain information on the prices and quantities of the goods that comprise a dwelling unit. Although the quantities of the physical attributes of housing can be measured, the prices of these individual attributes cannot be observed directly. The only price observed in the housing market is the selling price or rent for the dwelling unit as a whole.

These data problems led many early empirical studies of housing markets to assume that dwelling units produce a homogenous good, "housing services," that sells at a constant price per unit at all locations in a metropolitan area. Since price differences are assumed away by these studies, expenditures are often used as a proxy for the quantity of housing services in demand analyses that relate the expenditure on housing to the income and other characteristics of households.

More recently, hedonic indexes for housing have been estimated so that prices can be imputed to individual housing attributes and the homogeneous housing services assumption can be relaxed. These hedonic indexes also constitute an empirical test for the constant price assumption imbedded in the homogeneous-good approach. Many of the hedonic equations that have been estimated, including those reported by King, suggest that the prices of housing attributes vary significantly within a metropolitan housing market. If attribute prices do differ, variations in housing expenditures include these price differences as well as possible quantity differences, so housing expenditures cannot be used as a pure measure of the quantity of housing consumed.[1]

Whereas a lack of price information inhibited housing market analysis in the past, the estimation of hedonic prices for large numbers of housing attributes has made the abundance of price information a problem for housing demand studies now. For example, King estimates prices for more than twenty attributes of a dwelling unit. These twenty-odd prices could be used in a simultaneous-equations framework to estimate the demand for each attribute, but the estimation problems would be severe. Some simplification is obviously called for to solve this multitude-of-attribute-prices problem.

In addition, different hedonic attribute prices are typically estimated for spatial subareas of a metropolitan housing market; King has estimated hedonic attribute prices for each of seven subareas in the New Haven region. Having different hedonic prices for several subareas may at first appear merely to exacerbate the multitude-of-attribute-prices problem by increasing the number of prices to be considered. However, the spatial stratification actually creates a new problem because a household must buy all of its housing attributes in only one subarea as a spatially tied purchase. This spatially tied purchase requirement differentiates the analysis of housing demand from that of most other consumer goods.

Analyses of housing demand based on hedonic prices differ principally in the way in which they resolve the multitude-of-attribute-prices problem and the spatially tied purchase requirement. King solves the multitude-of-attribute-prices problem by aggregating his

---

[1] King does not statistically test his individual equations to see if attribute prices differ significantly between towns in the New Haven area. Such tests assume that the specification of the hedonic indexes is correct. It has been argued that specification errors largely explain the spatial differences in attribute prices found by housing market studies; see George Peterson, "The Capitalization of Fiscal Variables," Urban Institute Working Paper 1207-25 (January, 1973).

numerous housing attributes into four "Lancastrian" housing characteristics. This number of characteristics presents few problems of estimation. King then satisfies the spatially tied purchase requirement by assuming that households have no opportunity for substitution among the seven subareas in the New Haven region. For example, if a sampled household has originally chosen a unit in East Haven, only the East Haven prices are allowed to influence that household's chosen quantities of the four housing characteristics. The demand equations are then estimated, using the seven sets of relative prices of the four aggregate housing characteristics as independent variables.

Although these procedures readily permit the estimation of demand equations, they are not without problems. Thus, reducing the number of housing attributes by constructing four aggregate "Lancastrian" characteristics places a strong condition on household utility functions. To be able to use a composite of price-weighted quantities of several housing attributes as an index of the quantity of an aggregate housing characteristic, households must be indifferent to the combination of attributes that comprise a constant expenditure on an aggregate characteristic. That is, a household's indifference curves in attribute space must be coterminous with the price surfaces defined by various expenditures on the attributes that make up each aggregate characteristic. The likelihood of this condition holding for the four aggregate characteristics is doubtless low.

Furthermore, restricting the choice set of households to a particular subarea for purposes of demand estimation severely limits households' substitution possibilities. If households actually do make substitutions among spatial subareas, their opportunity set is defined by the envelope of price surfaces in the seven subareas rather than by the price surface in a single subarea. Of course, using the envelope of price surfaces in demand estimation is not possible with the model put forward by King, because all households would face the same envelope of market prices. These prices would not vary across households; and without price variation, it would not be possible to estimate demand equations. The envelope of prices could only be used in a demand model that allowed the price envelope to vary by household, for example by adding household-specific travel costs to the market prices of housing.

One important housing attribute incorporated in King's demand framework is neighborhood quality, and his analysis in the final section of the paper suggests that neighborhood quality is an important determinant of a household's location choice. This analysis also implies that neighborhood quality cannot be combined with the other attributes in the *SITE* characteristic, because household location is explained or rationalized only when a household's choice of neighborhood quality (*GEN Q*) is included as a separate attribute in the travel cost–housing price tradeoff. King's paper represents an interesting attempt to integrate the choice of housing attributes, neighborhood quality, and travel costs, but he correctly warns the reader that in this area, much work still remains to be done.

Part IV
Measurement and Policy Issues
in Consumption Analysis

Risk Measurement and Safety Standards in Consumer Products

V. L. BROUSSALIAN

NATIONAL BUREAU OF STANDARDS *

I. INTRODUCTION

STATISTICS of injuries arising in homes and playgrounds are particularly distressing, since those involved are usually either helpless or unaware of the dangers. Few of these injuries are inevitable in any reasonable sense of the term, so that there is also a great sense of waste, both material and emotional. Yet is is obvious that injuries cannot be entirely eliminated. What we wish to do then, and what presumably the new Consumer Product Safety Commission (CPSC) would like to do, is to determine *when* injury statistics, such as those collected by the National Electronic Injury Surveillance System (NEISS), suggest the need for some public action (such as the setting of a physical standard), and *when* they do not.

There are two different but related issues. One is conceptual, namely, formulating a theory of accident occurrence for a specific product. The other is measurement. Clearly, the latter cannot be done independently of the theory. Nonetheless, in this paper, we shall be concerned primarily with the measurement aspect. The reason is a practical one: the CPSC is faced with the gigantic and difficult task of establishing some priority among hundreds of products on the basis of the injury data reported to it through NEISS and other sources. The initial need is for the CPSC to impose a semblance of order out of this mass of data, even though no theory of accident causation has been developed.

* [The author is a member of the Technical Analysis Division.] For helpful comments, I am indebted to Peter Colwell, Walter G. Leight, and Donald Corrigan who also provided research assistance. None of these individuals nor the National Bureau of Standards should be held responsible for the views expressed here.

Most safety-related legislation, and certainly the Consumer Product Safety Act (P.L. 92-573), does not aim at eliminating *all* hazards, but only the unreasonable ones. Yet none, so far as I am aware, has attempted to define operationally what an unreasonable hazard is.

In Section 2, a formal criterion for identifying unreasonable hazards is presented. In Section 3, measurement procedures implied by the criterion are discussed with reference to an actual case. The primary intention there is to assess and demonstrate the operationality of the criterion.

2. HAZARDOUS PRODUCTS AND THE MARKET

2.1. Definitions and Preliminaries

We shall give an economic definition of an unreasonable hazard which does not depend on, or presuppose, any particular rule of legal liability. An unreasonable hazard may be defined as the possible occurrence of an undesirable event in the course of normal use or consumption of a good, where the expected cost of the event is greater than the cost of avoiding it. There are three basic elements in the definition: (1) an undesirable event, the occurrence of which gives rise to loss of wealth or income, the enduring of pain or suffering, or death; (2) the probability of occurrence of the event; and (3) an action which may be taken to avoid the loss. The expected cost is defined as the likelihood of occurrence of the event multiplied by the loss sustained if the event should occur. Unless the context indicates otherwise, the definition will relate to society, so that, ordinarily, costs will include all costs of the injury, and avoidance will relate to the set of all possible avoidance actions.

2.1.1. Product Use.
The uses to which a product may be put are many, but we have to exclude from our purview those uses which are in some sense illegitimate. Thus, a hunting knife might be used as a nail extractor, or an ashtray to hammer a nail. The injuries that can conceivably result from such activities cannot provide a rationale for social intervention. Since such hazards can be avoided only by banning the product, the cost of avoidance must include all benefits derived from its legitimate uses. The cost of avoidance will then be inflated to the point of exceeding the cost of injury.

The question of what constitutes abnormal use is not merely of academic interest. The courts are continuously called upon to determine whether an injury is the result of misuse of a product, whether the manufacturer should have foreseen the danger which his product posed, or whether a consumer assumed the risk of injury entailed in the use of a product. All of these notions have their analogs in economics. Thus, a court will probably consider the risk of entrapment of a child in an abandoned refrigerator a foreseeable danger. In economics, it would be reasonable to consider such risk as one of the attributes of the product. On the other hand, if a refrigerator is used (criminally) as an entrapment device, then injury resulting from such misuse will neither in law nor in economics be attributed to the product. Finally, some injuries incurred in accidents on the speedway would not in law be attributed to the product, since the driver of the car will be considered to have assumed the risk, just as in economics we would assume that he valued the characteristic of high speed much more than other characteristics of the car. Although the dividing line between legitimate and illegitimate uses is quite blurred, the distinction is nonetheless important.

2.1.2. The Hazard. With any consumer product we may associate a hazard, $H(I)$. It can be viewed as a probability distribution of various types of injuries, denoted by I, arising in the course of normal consumption of the product. It depends upon the type of product, the technology and quality of materials and workmanship embodied in it (all usually summarized by the term "design"), and the information utilized by users.

2.1.3. The Cost of Injury. With the hazard, $H(I)$, we need a weighting function, $J(I)$, which assigns to each type of injury, I_k, a dollar weight J_k representing its severity. $J(I)$ thus stands for the cost of injury. It includes the decrease in wealth, both physical and human, and also pain and suffering. For simplicity, we assume that J is the same for all individuals. Alternatively, J_k may be viewed as the average cost of injury type I_k over all individuals.

For the purpose of our analysis, it does not matter that all injuries have to be monetized. Monetization means that individuals take risks involving bodily harm in return for money. It does *not* mean that individuals would necessarily accept a sum of money in return for submitting to *certain* bodily injury. There is overwhelming evidence to support the former; there is little to support the latter. Thus, the "monetary value of a child's life" does not mean that his parents, or for that matter, society will accept such an amount of money in return for his life. Such a tradeoff is not implied by the term monetization. The tradeoff which is implied is between money and the risk of life, which is hardly unusual.

In this connection we should note three points: (a) Society's and individuals' risk valuations may differ. (b) Although some people knowingly take risks involving bodily injury, many would probably not take such risks if they knew their real magnitudes. However, the issue here is merely whether risks of injury *can* be monetized, not whether the procedure would always yield the "correct" valuation. (c) Finally, a jury award may also be considered an indication of the money value of injury (or life). So may an out-of-court settlement. Even so, these do not imply that a plaintiff would consider such compensation sufficient for him to submit voluntarily to the same injury. Whatever it means to the plaintiff, it does have the effect of a price to potential defendants — a "controlled" price of injury, so to speak.

The product JH thus represents the expected cost of injury sustained by an individual in consuming a unit of the product. If the total quantity of the product consumed by consumers over an appropriate unit of time is denoted by X, the rate of social cost of accidents is given by XJH.

2.1.4. Avoidance of Injury. Injury avoidance covers a wide range of possible actions, but as a rule one should consider the least costly action first, and then proceed to more expensive ones, including the extremes of nonconsumption and nonproduction. It would include product design changes, the provision of technical information (say through labeling or advertising), and the gaining of experience and knowledge by consumers, all of which may conceivably affect the probability of injury occurrence, H.

An avoidance action has the effect of shifting the probability distribution H such that JH is reduced. If we assume that J is an increasing function of I, then JH will necessarily decrease when H is shifted to the left. Since it was observed earlier that H depended on such factors as product design and use information, any change in these factors which decreased JH would be tantamount to avoidance action. Avoidance actions thus can be taken by both producers and consumers. It is a commonplace observation that many consumers do not read instructions, or often seem not to understand what they read. To make headway with our analysis, however, we assume that consumers will follow instructions faithfully and utilize all the information provided with a product. We also assume that they can and do supply additional information of their own. If they are thereby able to shift the distribution H in the right direction, they would in effect be taking avoidance action. We categorize avoidance actions into two groups: alpha-actions, denoted by α, are those taken by consumers, and beta-actions, denoted by β, are those taken by producers. H is a decreasing function of α and β.[1] $J(\partial H/\partial \beta)$ and $J(\partial H/\partial \alpha)$ represent the costs of injury avoided when β and α avoidance actions, respectively, are taken.

Let $C(X; \beta)$ denote the average cost of a competitively produced quantity, X, of a consumer product of a given safety-related quality. The quantity X is equal to the sum of the consumption of all individuals, n, who consume the product, i.e., $X = \sum_{i}^{n} X_i$. As we have indicated, the parameter β refers to the class of safety-related characteristics of the product. We may think of β as a shorthand descriptor of the physical characteristics of a product, such as its flammability, shatter, and thermal qualities. For simplicity of manipulation, we shall treat β as one-dimensional rather than as a vector. The partial $\partial C/\partial \beta$, which will occasionally be written as C_β, is taken to be positive.[2]

The avoidance actions α cause a reduction in the occurrence of injuries (i.e., H) by affecting the behavior of consumers, as, for example, when they acquire or are provided with product information.[3] As with β-action, an α-avoidance action is not costless. Let $V_i(\alpha)$ refer to the cost of α-avoidance actions taken by individual i and assumed to be independent of the amount of consumption of X. The marginal cost $dV_i(\alpha)/d\alpha$ is taken to be positive.

2.1.5. Reasonable and Unreasonable Hazards. A hazard that can arise during the normal use of a product can be said to be unreasonable if it can be reduced through some action by producers or by consumers, or by both, and if the cost of doing so is less than the consequent reduction in its social cost.

This definition can be stated implicitly by the following inequality

$$[X \frac{\partial}{\partial \beta} C(X, \beta) + \sum_{i}^{n} \frac{d}{d\alpha} V_i(\alpha)] < -[XJ \frac{\partial}{\partial \beta} H + XJ \frac{\partial}{\partial \alpha} H] \quad (1)$$

More conveniently, the above expression can be written in a somewhat different notation, as follows

---

[1] Note that α and β refer to actions, not financing. A set of instructions, an α-action, may be provided by producers. And a safety device, a β-action, may be purchased separately by a consumer.

[2] For simplicity of representation, we have assumed that only costs of production are significant. However, increased cost of maintenance, diminished efficiency, reduced benefits, etc., have to be added to C_β if they are significant.

[3] To what extent, and why, consumers do not exercise care or utilize all the information provided are matters that perhaps a discipline such as psychology has more valuable things to say about than does economics. Here we assume that the information provided or available is correct and that it will, in fact, be utilized.

$$[XC_\beta + \sum_i^n (V_i)_\alpha] < -[XJH_\beta + XJH_\alpha] \qquad (1')$$

In (1'), the first term on the left-hand side denotes the cost incurred to provide a β-type avoidance action, such as installing a metal shield in every TV set to intercept harmful radiation. The second term denotes the cost incurred by consumers in taking an α-type avoidance action. An example is the purchase of skid-proof shoes for wearing when using a lawn mower. Note that α may also be in the nature of operating instructions, warnings, or informative labeling, in which case it has some of the characteristics of public goods.

Coming now to the right-hand side of the inequality, the minus sign preceding the expression in the brackets is necessary because H_α and H_β denote *reductions* in the hazard. The term XJH_β represents the savings in accident cost realized from the introduction of the β-type avoidance action. Similarly, XJH_α represents the savings in accident cost realized from the adoption of the α-type avoidance measure. Thus, inequality 1 represents the tradeoff that is possible, in principle, between avoidance cost and injury cost. When no further *net* gains can be realized from accident reduction, i.e., when expression 1 becomes an equality, the hazard still remaining is reasonable.[4]

Since at this stage we are only conceptualizing, the functional forms are to be understood only in their logical, rather than mathematical, connotations. Note that the inequality defining unreasonable hazards depends on each of H, J, and X. An unreasonable hazard may exist because of high probability of injury (e.g., sporting equipment and fireworks), or high cost of the injury (e.g., nuclear contamination and lead poisoning), or the large quantity of the product in use (e.g., processed food and automobiles). The above definition from society's viewpoint may be modified to represent unreasonable hazards from the points of view of consumers or producers by appropriate modification and interpretation of the terms of the inequality.

2.1.6. The Consumption of Unreasonable Hazards. In a competitive market, the individual consumer takes as given the physical safety features of the goods offered for sale along with their other characteristics. However, α-avoidance actions are a different matter. He must supply these himself or have them provided to him by the seller, such as in the case of a "free" training course or literature which accom-

---

[4] In principle, it is possible that there are products that are too safe. The inequality in (1) can be, in other words, reversed. Unreasonably safe products, however, do not seem to be a public issue.

panies the product. From his point of view, an unreasonable hazard exists if, by taking some avoidance action, he can reduce the expected cost of the range of possible accidents by more than the cost of avoidance, that is, if $(V_i)_\alpha < X_i J H_\alpha$.

Consumer behavior involves complicated phenomena and, therefore, we do not pretend that the above criterion "explains" very much. The following three observations, however, are relevant: First, though not explicitly accounted for in $V_i(\alpha)$, risk-taking behavior is reflected in it. Second, even were $V_i(\alpha)$ to reflect risk-taking behavior explicitly, $V_i(\alpha)$ is as subjective as any demand function. Thus, we face the same measurement problems in estimating this function as we would encounter in estimating individual demand functions. Third, it should be noted that $\sum^n X_i J_i(H_i)\alpha$, the total reduction in the cost of injuries directly realized by individuals through their own actions, need not equal XJH_α, the total reductions in costs of injuries experienced by society through the actions of its members. If there is an externality (e.g., if injuries to third parties are likely to occur for which the individual consumer is not made fully responsible), then the two expressions will not be equal. To illustrate, suppose that the rate of accidents involving bystanders increases indirectly due to bad driving habits, then refresher driver education will reduce accident costs more than might be foreseen by individual drivers, since they do not ordinarily perceive the hazards to which they expose bystanders. Also to be noted is the possibility that the overall cost of α-actions when provided by consumers is greater than when they are provided by the seller. For example, if automobile buyers were each to perform a thorough inspection of steering mechanisms to determine whether they are free of defects, the total cost to them of this avoidance action would most probably exceed the cost of an equivalent quality control provided by the manufacturer. The manufacturer is not only probably more adept at such inspection, but he may institute a sampling scheme which would be both effective and substantially cheaper than the inspection performed by the average buyer.

Consideration of what would constitute an unreasonable hazard from the producer's point of view will be discussed in detail below, along with other related topics.

2.2. Competition and Product Hazards

2.2.1. The Optimal Level of Product Hazards. The cause of injury may be a defect in design or manufacture (e.g., shoddy materials or workmanship, concealed sharp objects in toys, radiation or electrical leaks in appliances), lack of maintenance not equivalent to misuse, or normal material failure.

The social cost S of consuming X units of the hazardous product is given by the expression

$$S = XC(X, \beta) + XJH + \sum_{i}^{n} V_i(\alpha)$$

where the right-hand members represent production cost, including producer avoidance actions so identified; expected cost of injuries; and cost of consumer avoidance actions so identified.

For any given level of consumption of X, the social cost S is minimized when the following two necessary conditions are satisfied

$$C_\beta = -JH_\beta \tag{2}$$

$$\sum_{i}^{n} (V_i)\alpha = -XJH_\alpha \tag{3}$$

Simultaneous solution of (2) and (3), if possible, indicates how unreasonable hazards can be eliminated by joint actions of both producers and consumers. Furthermore, for any given β-action, equation 2 shows that producers should improve product quality so long as the reduction in the cost of injuries exceeds the cost of making the improvements. Correspondingly from (3), for any given α, avoidance actions by the consumer should also be taken as long as the reduction in cost of injuries exceeds the cost of the improvement.[5]

2.2.2. The Competitive Market and Product Hazard. How does the competitive market satisfy the above optimality conditions? Provided that there is voluntary exchange between producers and consumers and that transacting costs between them are negligible, then by the Coase theorem [Coase 1960], as discussed below, the market will bring about the optimal avoidance actions and product quality, regardless of who is made liable for injuries from consumption.[6]

A producer who can introduce a change in the physical characteristics of his product at a unit cost (C_β) that is less than the resulting reduction in expected accident cost to the consumer $(-JH_\beta)$ can be "bribed" by the consumer to do so. If safety is a product characteristic which is desired by the consumer (who will be assumed to be able to

---

[5] The foregoing formulation focuses on the hazard and its elimination. Hence the quantity X produced and consumed in the economy was assumed as given. However, full optimization conditions would ordinarily be expected to affect X.

[6] See also Demsetz (1972).

discriminate between greater or less safety), he would certainly be willing to bear the cost of the improvement via a higher price. If there is competition among producers, it will act as a spur for a producer to introduce the change, whether or not the law holds him liable for the cost of accidental injury, for otherwise he would lose his customer to those of his competitors who do. The process will come to a stop when condition 2 holds.

The producer may also be motivated to provide information and other α-type avoidance measures. He may be able to provide some (but not all) of these more cheaply than the consumer, either because of his superior knowledge of his product, or because of his ability to distribute the cost over all units produced. If transacting costs are negligible, a consumer will be willing to "bribe" the producer to supply these avoidance measures rather than doing so himself. But competition among producers, if present, will independently tend to bring about the same result. The process will come to a stop when condition 3 holds, with producers providing α-type avoidance measures in which they have a comparative advantage, and consumers taking avoidance actions (as explained in 2.1.6) in which they have comparative advantage.

Thus, what is economically efficient will eventually be adopted, regardless of who, by law, is held liable for accidental injuries, provided either competitive conditions obtain or transacting costs are neglible (voluntary exchange being possible).

If third parties suffer accidental injuries (externalities) because neither producers nor consumers consider the costs they impose on third parties in their decisions, and provided that transacting costs are negligible, the three groups can together ensure that the party which can most efficiently reduce these externalities will do so.

In a recent paper "The Economics of Product Safety" (Oi, 1973), Oi shows that in a competitive market where products of the same kind but of different degrees of riskiness are available, a consumer maximizes his utility by buying that product whose "full price" (i.e., market price plus expected loss from injury) is minimum. If the liability for injury is assigned to the consumer, we would expect him to buy insurance or to self-insure, and thereby cover his expected loss. In such a case, the full price of the safe product would consist of its market price plus the insurance premium, the latter depending on the expected damage which the individual will suffer. On the other hand, if liability for the loss were placed on the producer, he too may self-insure or buy product liability insurance. Provided he has full freedom to sell to whomever he pleases at whatever price he pleases (i.e., transacting costs are zero), the full price offered to the consumer will be the same as in the other case. Of course, the producer also has the option of changing the quality of the product, but that decision does not essentially change the conclusion that liability does not affect the level of utility of the consumer under our assumption.[7]

2.3. Unreasonable Hazards in the Economy

The main purpose of the discussion in 2.2 has been to show that voluntary exchange and especially the competitive market, under certain specified conditions, would eliminate unreasonable hazards but allow reasonable ones. We want to address now the conditions under which we might, on the basis of economic theory, expect the economy to tolerate the presence of unreasonable hazards. These conditions are implied in our previous discussion. For convenience of exposition, they are grouped below under five main headings: uninsurable risks, high transacting costs, high litigation costs, consumer sovereignty, and third parties.

2.3.1. Product Liability Insurance and Self-Insurance. If for various reasons, actuarial risk cannot be determined, a product-related accident insurance market is not likely to emerge. Currently, there are only a few types of product-related accident insurance available to the consumer, the most familiar being automobile accident insurance. And though we have home accident insurance, such insurance is not related to specific household products, as, for example, ladders, floor waxes, and ovens. As for product liability insurance for the producer, the current unsettled situation is an indication of the difficulty of forecasting the liability of producers with respect to injuries associated with their products.[8]

The main factors which are inimical to the determination of actuarial risk are lack of valid data and "moral hazard."

---

[7] Note that avoidance action on the part of the consumer in Oi's model consists of his purchase of a safer product, which is distinguished by an insurance cost that is smaller than that of the less safe product. For this, he pays a higher market price. Likewise, the producer's avoidance action consists in manufacturing a safer product, which is distinguished by a product liability insurance cost which is lower than that of the less safe product. For this, he incurs a higher cost of production. In terms of our model, the insurance cost is JH, whether incurred by the individual consumer or by the producer. Any savings in this cost, $-(\partial(JH)/\partial\beta)$, would be realized by the producer at the cost of $\partial C(X, \beta)/\partial\beta$, which is equivalent to $\partial P/\partial\beta$, the increase in price to the consumer, where P is the market price, assumed equal to $C(X, \beta)$.

[8] See Forrest C. Mercer, "Product Liability Law in the 1960's — The Insurer's View," Paper presented at the Product Liability Prevention Conference, August 22–24, 1973, Newark College of Engineering, Newark, N.J.

Dearth of good data may be due to their cost. The circumstances surrounding a consumer product-related accident may, for obvious reasons, be expensive to investigate and establish *relative* to the cost of the injury. A second reason which tends to keep hazard information from becoming public knowledge is one that is often discussed in a different context, namely, consumer education. Consumers are often alleged to be unable to estimate hazards correctly, or to understand information provided on hazards and to cope with these hazards when they actually occur.[9] Whatever the truth about consumer comprehension and response to hazards, a manufacturer may find that it does not pay to be too explicit about the hazards related to his products, unless such explicitness is likely to reassure an already frightened consumer. For example, if consumer hostility toward nuclear power generation is based upon misinformation concerning the true hazards of nuclear contamination, consumer education will probably increase acceptance of this type of power plant. On the other hand, if the location of an automobile's gas tank is a potential cause of fiery explosion in a collision, a manufacturer who announces that he has reduced this hazard by as much as fifty per cent may succeed only in causing prospective buyers to favor alternative modes of transportation. In such a case, industry will not volunteer such hazard information; nor will it encourage governmental provision of this type of hazard information.[10]

But there is another aspect to consumer comprehension of hazards which is not sufficiently appreciated. It is often stated in terms of consumers' inability to estimate hazards correctly. We should recall, however, that in theory it is not important under the Coase conditions that consumers be able to estimate hazards correctly for the emergence of optimal safety levels for consumer products. They no more need to know about hazard estimation than they need to know about the intricacies of modern production methods. Risk estimation may be an activity that is most efficiently provided by producers, rather than by consumers. And if a question of credibility arises, producers have, theoretically, recourse to independent testing laboratories (Underwriters Laboratories [UL], Consumers Union [CU], and others) to persuade consumers that their safety claims are genuine. But if the measurement of risk depends on properties of a product that are themselves complex (e.g., burn properties of foam plastics), consumers are

---

[9] Cf. the statement of Corwin Edwards before the National Commission on Product Safety (NCPS), *Hearings,* Vol. 9A, p. 138.
[10] This of course does not imply that manufacturers of substitutes, e.g. battery-driven cars, will not point out this hazard to consumers.

not likely to be able to estimate expected losses. Without this information, the consumer cannot make a rational decision. If *caveat emptor* prevails, the consumer obviously cannot self-insure, and if *caveat venditor* prevails, the consumer would still not be in a position to choose intelligently between two products that included, in their prices, estimates (by the producer) of expected damage claims.[11]

The second main reason which inhibits the emergence of a product-related insurance market is "moral hazard," that is, the impact of insurance on consumer behavior or producer behavior resulting in an increase in demand for compensation and even in higher injury rates.[12] If consumers are insured against costs of injuries, total claims are likely to increase, even if injuries did not, because small claims which formerly would not have been presented are now pressed, and because consumers will be inclined to be less concerned with the costs incurred, such as for medical care. Similar type problems arise in products liability insurance sold to producers.[13] Furthermore, the presence of insurance may induce more risk taking, however slightly; that is, it will affect α-type and β-type avoidance actions, including the purchase and sale of lower-quality products. In the aggregate, these may result in higher injury rates. As premiums are increased to cover these higher costs, better-than-average-risk consumers will forgo insurance, driving premiums still higher. Under these circumstances, insurance ceases to be a profitable business, unless discriminatory pricing policies are practiced, a procedure which is likely to run afoul of public regulatory agencies. If, for the reasons cited, no adequate product-related accident insurance is available (and self-insurance cannot be effectively practiced), then the consumer is not in a position to treat risk as an objective datum but rather as something entering directly into his preference function. The risk-averse consumer in such a situation may reduce his consumption below what might be socially justifiable. That is, he may consider unreasonable what from society's point of view would be a reasonable hazard.[14]

[11] It does not help much here to have government or industry assure uniformity in the measurement of risk or in test procedures. Uniformity per se is more likely to help manufacturers cut costs than help consumers make better decisions. The problem is that "safety," though a desirable good, is often conceptually difficult to measure. To say that consumers prefer more safety to less begs the question of whether they would recognize an increase in safety. Indexes of risk are not easy to interpret.

[12] On "moral hazard," see Arrow (1963, 1968), Grubel (1967), Pauly (1968), and Ehrlich and Becker (1973).

[13] Mercer, "Product Liability Law . . . ."

[14] The foregoing discussion does not provide a rationale for a standards-setting role by government. If the unintended effect of a standard in connection with a highly com-

2.3.2. High Transacting Cost. A critical assumption which is fundamental to the Coase theorem is that transacting costs are negligible.
Most consumption occurs over a period of time, whereas the buyer-
seller relationship usually ends with the completion of the act of sale-
purchase. The consumer is in a better position to monitor his consumption, while the seller is in a better position to appraise the qualities of
his merchandise. The efficient method of ensuring safe consumption
is to make the consumer responsible for the *manner* of his consumption.
At the same time, competition among sellers acts to reduce the consumer's lack of knowledge about product characteristics. It would be
inefficient to assign responsibility to sellers inasmuch as sellers will
find it difficult (though not impossible) to influence the way purchasers will consume products. Firearm dealers, for example, might
require annual psychiatric and police reports from purchasers of fire-
arms, or appliance dealers might require customers to buy inspection
and maintenance contracts. Such requirements might even be tailored
for specific customers, the cost varying on the basis of use and the
customer's educational background and income level. Though the
cost of thus monitoring the activities of consumers would be included
in the price, it is likely to be greater than if consumers acted on their
own responsibility.

It is unlikely, of course, that producers would be allowed to resort
to these cost-reducing devices designed to minimize their total liability
for accidents sustained by their customers.[15] These prohibitions can
be viewed as further escalation of transacting costs. Oi (1973) has
shown that where producers are required to charge uniform prices, the
full price of the product will include its production cost plus a premium representing the average expected claim for damages arising
from accidents sustained by consumers in general during consump-

---

plex product is the creation of a sense of security for the consumer which is not justified by the necessarily limited class of risks on which the standard is based, he would
continue to make his decisions in an uninformed way. The result is that: (a) even though
products will tend to become more homogeneous with respect to safety, they may be no
safer on the average than before; and (b) if more consumption is induced, the cost of
accidents may rise. To the extent that the government standard may not be significantly
more stringent than the lower end of the previous product spectrum (i.e., it is a minimum
standard), the social cost of accidents may increase. It thus follows that consumer education, one way or another, cannot be ignored as a practical matter in favor of physical
standards, as the National Commission on Product Safety (NCPS) seemed to imply in its
Report (1970).

[15] Mortgage institutions which might require some of their mortgagors to practice
family planning would similarly find that such a cost-cutting device is "socially" unacceptable.

tion.[16] The result of this uniform pricing policy is that those consumers whose expected cost of injury is greater than average (usually the more well-to-do) will realize a gain and those whose expected cost of injury is less (usually the less well-to-do) will experience a loss, compared to the alternative of full discrimination among customers. In other words, some wealth redistribution, most probably from the poor to the wealthy, will take place.

To what extent does high transacting cost allow unreasonable hazards to remain in the market? The answer, one would suspect, is "very little." Competition in the market is a far more important factor for safety than low transacting costs. Suppose that the prevailing rule is *caveat emptor,* and that a manufacturer markets a commodity (say, a play tent) which poses an unreasonable hazard to children because (a) the material of which the tent is made is flammable, (b) the very shape of a tent favors sudden conflagration, and (c) children like to light candles inside a tent. Assume that treating the material with flame retardant or changing its shape reduces the hazard far more cheaply than constant vigil by parents, and assume further that the manufacturer's avoidance cost is less than the expected cost of injuries. How is the manufacturer to be induced to introduce the safety feature?

If consumers could band together, it would surely be economical for them to "bribe" the manufacturer to use nonflammable material, since the amount of the bribe is less than the alternative avoidance cost (by assumption) and is also less than the avoided injury cost. But the total costs of identifying parents who are potential buyers of the tent, of organizing and representing them, of undertaking investigative studies, public relations, negotiations, etc. — all covered by the term "transacting cost" — would probably exceed the benefits that such a group of concerned parents might derive. Therefore, this course of action is not likely to be taken.

Most of these burdensome activities would, however, be unnecessary if there were competition among manufacturers of tents, *and* if parents indeed wanted safer tents and were willing to pay the extra price for them. Some producers would discover this latent demand and attempt to satisfy it. Expressing this result in a different way, competition among producers will reduce transacting costs so drastically that little overt action by consumers will be necessary, other than their acts of purchase.

By way of contrast, consider the case of a public utility supplying a

[16] In the terminology of our model, this premium is JH.

residential community with natural gas. Suppose that its installation practices occasionally resulted in gas explosions involving personal and property losses. Because the public utility is a monopoly, considerable time may elapse before it decides that an increase in gas rates to finance improved installation practices, greater supervision, and better materials can be justified to the general public and to the cognizant regulatory agency. The process would have to be impelled by periodic newspaper accounts of such tragedies, an aroused public, letter-writing campaigns, public hearings, and so on.

High transacting costs are thus akin to "noise" in a system, but they are not as serious as absence of competition or lack of information.

2.3.3. High Litigation Costs. Claims against producers or sellers are not costless. The NCPS considered the cost of litigation to be a principal reason for the ineffectiveness of products liability law in eliminating unreasonable hazards, especially where the cost of litigation exceeds the cost of injury.

Although an injured consumer may receive less than he deserves, the award, or the possibility of it, will act as an incentive for the manufacturer to improve the safety of his product. While it is true that the manufacturer is likely to be wealthier than the injured consumer, he will nonetheless consider the settlement option if he is an income maximizer. Moreover, on the basis of financial consequences of adverse publicity, a settlement is preferable to possible loss of suit.[17] The cost of defending a suit is no less onerous to a manufacturer than to the consumer. And though a lost suit may not by itself cripple a manufacturer, considerable pressure can be exercised on him to the benefit of the consumer by retailers, wholesalers, and distributors who are also vulnerable to suits.

Where the cost of litigation (including attorney's fees) exceeds the cost of the injury, the consumer will not exercise his right to sue. The situation is essentially equivalent to transacting costs being significant. However, in addition to legal devices designed to reduce litigation costs, such as small claims courts and class action suits, the market influences described earlier (namely, good reputation and business pressures of intermediaries) are still operative. In other words, the problem is not as bleak as it is usually described. We should realize that a court of law is not a liability-dispensing machine which is activated whenever rights and liabilities are to be assigned. It is rather a

---

[17] Scares resulting from isolated instances of food poisoning have been known to result in millions of dollars of losses and even in bankruptcies. See *Forbes*, April 15, 1972. pp. 55–57.

settler of *doubtful* claims, at a price. If the rules of liability are clear and the facts admit of no uncertain interpretation, the law is obviously quite effective. The role of the courts can easily be exaggerated.

Nevertheless, the high transacting cost represented by litigation leads to some market imperfection, and to that extent some unreasonable hazards will not be "filtered" by the market. Fortunately, these are not likely to include major hazards which are uppermost on the agenda of public agencies. Since the high costs of litigation are themselves the object of concern, we can expect eventual adoption of innovative measures directed to the heart of this problem.

2.3.4. Consumer Sovereignty. Suppose that a particular product is banned because, say, in the opinion of the new Consumer Product Safety Commission, it represents an unreasonable hazard, and another product which is less hazardous but more expensive is favored. Assuming that the marginal cost of the safer product does not change as a result of the shift toward it, then the decline in the social (or aggregate) cost of accidents should exceed the decline in the consumer utility (due to the additional cost of safety). This follows from the fact that the banned product is *unreasonably* hazardous. However, some consumers must have believed otherwise, since before the ban was imposed they had the option of consuming the safer product but preferred to consume the other. Therefore, they were either systematically wrong in their assessment of the hazard — a possibility which we have already considered — or they are not the best judges of their own welfare. Although this latter inference is contrary to the fundamental ethical principle of consumer sovereignty, many statements by consumer advocates unfortunately imply this view of the consumer. Granted that such views often result from honest misreading of the facts, and granted that often they are reinforced by particular instances where consumers did not seem to have a good rationale for their choices, nevertheless in large part they are expressions of basic values. Since this is not a political or ethical investigation, no more will be said here on the subject.

2.3.5. Third Parties. A special case of high transacting costs occurs where the victim is not a party to the transaction which has led to the injury. Such an individual is commonly referred to as a "third party" or innocent bystander, and the injury as a disutility or negative externality. Third parties exert little influence on the transaction; it is too costly for them to do so, since they would have to identify the parties to a transaction and anticipate its nature. By the same token, parties to a voluntary transaction would not, in the process of arriving at their bargains (say, to produce, sell, buy, or consume), consider the costs they are likely to impose on others.

An example of a third party is a pedestrian who is injured in a highway accident due to a defect in a passing car.[18] Another example is an accident where the automobile driver is under the influence of alcohol. The public has little chance to ensure that a habitual drinker will demand, or that the manufacturer will install, a device to prevent operation of the car when the driver is intoxicated. A third example where different basic values could lead to different conclusions is the purchase by parents of hazardous toys for their children. While parents act in the interest of their children in various degrees, children have no independent influence on the safety of toys made and purchased for them.

If a transaction between a producer and a consumer, or seller and buyer, creates an externality in the form of a hazard imposed upon a third party, the terms corresponding to $X_i J(\partial(H)/\partial\beta)$ and $X_i J(\partial(H)/\partial\alpha)$ inequality 1 will appear to the transactors to be less than their true social value by the value of the externality. It is therefore possible for the inequality to hold from *society's* point of view, signifying the existence of an unreasonable hazard, while simultaneously conditions 2 and 3 hold.

To recapitulate, five major conditions were reviewed which gave rise to market failure. Most of them turned out to be special cases of high transacting costs. Technological reasons seemed to give rise to case 1 (excepting complexity of hazard), and cases 2 and 5. Legal and social considerations gave rise to case 3 and partially to case 2. Even where consumers were allegedly irrational (case 4), it was a case where those who knew better found it costlier to reason than to legislate. Yet, as was implied in the discussion, in the perspective of market performance, competition was the single most dominant force in reducing transacting costs.[19]

3. IMPLICATIONS FOR MEASUREMENT

3.1. Introduction

Since injury data are collected in order to help decide whether public action is indicated and, if so, whether a physical standard would be

---

[18] The manufacturer's liability is primarily to the car owner, not to the pedestrian.

[19] In an unpublished paper entitled "Reasonable and Unreasonable Hazards in Law and Economics," presented at the Western Economic Association Conference (August 15–17, 1973), I have argued that legal rules of products liability are quite consistent with principles of economic efficiency, as discussed in this section.

justified, it is necessary that measurement procedures be appropriate for the task of discovering the presence of an unreasonable hazard.

Assuming that obtaining adequate data about a certain hazard presents no problem, the question I wish to address is, What sort of data do we need? In answering this question, I make use of the theoretical apparatus of Section 2. In order to prevent the following discussion from moving at an abstract level, I shall draw most of my illustrative material from one particular hazard for which a physical safety standard has actually been set. This is the hazard of death by entrapment in a household refrigerator. It is not, however, my intention to evaluate the standard here. I start with a brief history of the present refrigerator magnetic-door standard, which is to serve as our illustrative case. A short description of a potentially major source of hazard data on household products, namely NEISS, will also be given.

3.2. Refrigerator Hazards and Magnetic Doors

Between 1946 and 1955 inclusive, 114 cases of deaths of young children trapped in household refrigerators, iceboxes, and freezers were reported. These children had apparently entered the enclosures during play, and subsequently the doors were somehow closed. Because entrapment was in an airtight compartment, asphyxiation resulted within the first hour [20] (Table 1).

The tragic nature of these deaths prompted the Congress of the United States to pass a law (P.L. 84-930) on August 2, 1956, requiring safety devices to be installed on household refrigerators shipped in interstate commerce.[21] These devices were to allow the doors of refrigerators to be opened easily from the inside. The task of prescribing such a device, called also a safety standard, was entrusted to the Department of Commerce, which in turn assigned the National Bureau of Standards the task of developing it.

One year later, on August 1, 1957, the National Bureau of Standards published specifications for two alternative safety devices, to take

[20] This view has been disputed. A research team at the University of Louisville School of Medicine claimed that it had "proved conclusively" that deaths in refrigerators were the result of heat stroke rather than lack of oxygen. (See the *Courier-Journal*, February 21, 1970.) This theory may explain some puzzling but largely ignored observations scattered in police reports to the effect that the victims were warm, soaking wet, or dehydrated at the time they were discovered.

[21] The Senate Committee on Interstate and Foreign Commerce stated in its report on H.R. 11969, which bill later was enacted into law, that neither publicity nor state laws and local ordinances forbidding the abandonment of refrigerators were adequate to ensure safety.

Table 1

Recorded Deaths in Refrigerators [a]

Year	Deaths	Incidents	Year	Deaths	Incidents
1946–55	114	N.A.	1964	44	30
1956	11	8	1965 [b]	22	13
1957	14	8	1966	31	19
1958	17	11	1967	31	19
1959	15	10	1968	26	14
1960	6	4	1969	20	11
1961	25	16	1970	17	11
1962	35	22	1971	10	10
1963	21	12	1972	10	6
			1973 [c]	10	N.A.

NOTE: Difference between incidents and deaths is due to multiple deaths. N.A. indicates not available.
SOURCE: Refrigerator Service Engineers Society, Des Plaines, Ill.
[a] Includes freezers and iceboxes, United States and Canada.
[b] Adjusted for 2 deaths and 1 incident of homicide.
[c] First nine months.

effect on October 30, 1958, as required by the Act. The device which was eventually adopted universally by the industry required that a force of not more than 15 lbs.[22] be sufficient to open the door when applied from within the refrigerator. Present day magnetic-closure devices on refrigerators and freezers are supposed to be in conformity with this standard.[23]

3.3. *The National Electronics Injury Surveillance System (NEISS)*

NEISS, operated now by the Consumer Product Safety Commission, came about through the merger of two separate data-collection programs: the Hospital Emergency Room Injury Reporting System (HERIRS) set up by the former National Commission on Product Safety, and the National Injury Surveillance System (NISS) set up by the Food and Drug Administration (FDA) in 1969. NEISS be-

[22] Supposedly, a child can comfortably exert this much force against the door of a refrigerator.
[23] It is interesting to note that, perhaps in anticipation of the mandatory standard, industry and the Department of Commerce had worked out, prior to the legislation, such a device which could have been adopted on a voluntary basis.

came fully operational on July 1, 1972, when the last hospital of a statistically selected sample of 119 (out of 4,906 hospitals across the United States) began reporting. Participating hospitals report daily on injuries treated in their emergency rooms. Not included in NEISS are, therefore, injuries treated in doctors' offices (estimated by CPSC at 41 per cent of the total), at home (18 per cent of the total), and by direct hospital admissions (3 per cent).

NEISS groups products into 19 general categories. Injuries are summarized and tabulated monthly showing, for closely related products within each category (e.g., electric dryers), total incidents classified by age and sex of victim. A mean severity index is calculated for each product group, based upon a system of weighting applied to 9 categories of injuries.[24]

The Bureau of Epidemiology, which has management responsibility for NEISS, also conducts in-depth investigations of some injuries, selected on the basis of their severity and frequency. *All* cases of death, as well as injuries related to flammable fabrics, are investigated.

On September 30, 1973, the CPSC issued a ranked listing of product categories based on an index of severity and frequency of injuries associated with them, as reported through NEISS.[25] The topmost ten included, in descending order, bicycles, stairs, doors, cleaning agents, tables, beds, football-related products, playground equipment, liquid fuels, and architectural glass. Refrigerators and freezers ranked seventy-third on the list. However, victims of refrigerators and freezers are not ordinarily routed through hospital emergency rooms, since they would already be dead on arrival. Since we know that during the first nine months of 1973 ten children were victims of refrigerators, the ranking of this product category should shift at least to somewhere within the thirty to forty rank class.[26]

3.4. Market Failure

At a fundamental level, an empirical issue to be settled is whether there is evidence of market failure. The five aspects of market failure discussed in Section 2 should be examined.

Investigation of market failure requires some evidence of a kind not directly related to hazard data. In other words, the problem is not

[24] CPSC, *NEISS NEWS*, Vol. 1, No. 6, August 1973.
[25] Ibid., Vol. 2, No. 4, December 1973.
[26] Bearing in mind that the same rate of accidents was considered intolerable by Congress in 1955, it is rather astonishing that there are so many products today that appear to be even more hazardous.

so much one of hazard measurement as of the theory of accident occurrence. Nonetheless, data on hazards should, as far as possible, shed light on the presence of market failure.

3.4.1. Third Parties. The data collected should indicate separately injuries to third parties, including children. In terms of our basic illustration, the victims of refrigerator hazards are children. Since the majority of these children belong to the households owning the hazardous appliances, and as we shall see presently, the hazard can easily be comprehended by consumers, the transaction between the principal parties may be considered to give rise to no externality (see Section 3.4.5 below).

3.4.2. Complexity of the Hazard. Injury data should distinguish between hazards which are easy to comprehend and those which are complex. As far as potential hazards from refrigerators are concerned, there is a single major hazard of interest, namely, death by entrapment. On one hand, the victim most likely does not comprehend it; on the other, the consumer is certainly able to understand it easily but may have to be reminded of it. (See 3.5.3)

3.4.3. High Transacting Costs. Whether transacting costs are high is not a question into which data on hazards can offer any insight. Nonetheless, we shall consider this issue, and the following two which are similar in this respect, because they provide an opportunity to evaluate the practical utility of the theory developed in Section 2.

Are transacting costs between manufacturers of refrigerators and consumers so high as to permit an unreasonable hazard to exist? Considering that competition among manufacturers of refrigerators has always been quite keen and that the hazard faced by owners' children is not less than that faced by nonowners' children, the market should have no difficulty transmitting, or revealing, latent demand for safety, if it exists, to the manufacturers.

As between those who might abandon refrigerators and those whose children might be endangered as a result, negotiations are quite costly. However, criminal liabilities[27] are imposed on the former group in most states;[28] many counties have similar ordinances.

3.4.4. Cost of Litigation. We consider next the effect of the high cost of litigation on the level of the hazard. By and large, the available socioeconomic evidence indicates that the majority of those responsible for abandoning the refrigerators which caused death to children

---

[27] Possibly civil as well.
[28] See for example, Section 334 of the *Annotated Code of Maryland*, entitled "Iceboxes: Abandoned and Discarded."

came from relatively low-income classes. Therefore, an action in tort for negligence is not likely to net significant damages to the plaintiff after litigation costs are defrayed. The disincentive effect of civil liability is thus attenuated, and the degree of hazard from abandoned refrigerators is to that extent higher than otherwise. However, deaths in *abandoned* refrigerators constitute a small proportion of total deaths in refrigerators. A survey of 146 such deaths between 1959 and 1969 shows that only about 30 per cent (45 deaths) occurred in *abandoned* refrigerators, freezers, and iceboxes.[29]

3.4.5. Consumer Sovereignty. It is conceivable that the underlying assumption of Public Law 84-930 was that consumers were taking chances which, in the opinion of the lawmakers (and other supporters of the bill), they should not be allowed to take. In other words, the welfare of children here, as on other occasions, could not be left entirely to their parents. The Committee on Interstate and Foreign Commerce stated (Senate Report No. 2700): "No doubt publicity campaigns to make parents alert to the dangers of deaths in refrigerators are helpful, but they are inadequate to meet the problem. . . . The bill here being reported is essential to protect the lives of the innocent children of this nation." However, we should note that an example of an inexpensive but effective informational campaign directed at adults (including parents) is the action of those manufacturers whose instructional materials accompanying new refrigerators and freezers now include a reminder to the buyer of the potential danger to children of the old unit being replaced.

In conclusion, clear evidence of market failure is absent. As a matter of fact, the publicity given to this hazard in the mid-fifties led to the development of a number of patented workable devices. Indeed, one major manufacturer of applicances adopted a magnetic closure device for one of his models even before P.L. 84-930 was passed.

3.5. Establishing Unreasonableness of the Hazard

3.5.1. Foreseeability, Assumption of Risk, and Abnormal Use. Not all accidents arise in the course of normal use of a product. Some are totally unforeseeable; others are the result of risk assumption by the victim (reflecting his particular preference function); and still others are neither of the above, but constitute misuse of the product. It is not difficult to design an injury information system which distinguishes these from the rest. As examples, football injuries arising profession-

[29] See Appendix B.

ally may be separated from those occurring on school playgrounds; auto accidents on race courses from those on ordinary highways; injuries to fingers caught in meat grinders from those resulting from cases of "assault" with a meat grinder.

Reverting to the refrigerator illustration, the hazard posed to children is foreseeable; no risk-taking behavior on the part of the children can be reasonably assumed; and no cases of misuse have been reported, with the exception of one case of homicide (Pennsylvania, 1965) and one case of suicide (by an adult, Michigan, 1954). (The data on deaths in refrigerators can be adjusted for the former instance.)

3.5.2. The Hazard (H). After injury statistics are corrected for unforeseeable injuries, for those arising when unusual risks are assumed, and for those occurring in abnormal use, the need to assess the hazard probabilistically still remains.

Referring again to refrigerator hazard, available data on deaths through entrapment in refrigerators are given in Table 1 on an annual basis, by number of deaths and by number of incidents. Available statistics on sex and age of victims and on month of accident are not presented here.

Given the above data, how should the probability of death in a refrigerator be measured? To what population, that is, should the frequency of recorded deaths be related? Such a population might be associated with the total number of refrigerators in existence, those abandoned, the total number of deaths within the age group 1 through 12 years, or some other aggregate.

The choice of the "denominator" is a matter of definition of the hazard, to depend initially on whether it accords with common sense, but ultimately on whether it proves to be useful. Transporting ourselves back in time to 1955 and 1956, when Congress was considering HR 2181 and HR 11969 (later to become P.L. 84–930), it would have seemed reasonable, considering that a physical device was the focus of attention, to define the hazard as "the probability that a refrigerator in existence in 1956 would be involved in the accidental death of a child." One might refine this measure of the hazard by separating the following three component conditional probabilities: the probability that an abandoned refrigerator will be the cause of death, the probability that a refrigerator *not* in use but not abandoned will be the cause of death, and the probability that a refrigerator in use but temporarily out of service will be the cause of death. Each might be expected to vary over time as the denominator changes. One might even wish to distinguish between refrigerators and freezers.[30] Nevertheless, for other purposes, alternative definitions might conceivably be more appropriate. For example, the hazard might be defined as the probability that the death of a child of a particular age group will be due to a refrigerator rather than to some other cause.

Ideally, the proper sequence in the measurement of a hazard would be to develop a theory of accident occurrence relating to the product in question and then, in light of the theory, to define an appropriate hazard or set of hazards. For example, it may be hypothesized that refrigerator deaths are causally related to the following independent variables: number of refrigerators in existence in different use-states (in storage, operating, abandoned); the number of children in different socioeconomic classes; employment of mothers (at home, not at home); sex; age; geography (urban/rural); presence of siblings; and time of year. If verification of the hypothesis by, say, a multiple regression analysis, indicates some of the factors to be statistically significant, the hazard should be defined accordingly.

To appreciate the importance of this procedure, consider the impact of the large number of state laws and local ordinances imposing criminal sanctions on those responsible for abandoning refrigerators. The evidence shows that more than twice as many deaths have occurred in nonabandoned refrigerators than in abandoned ones. It would have been of little value to define the hazard solely in terms of abandoned refrigerators. Furthermore, even if the standard were to eliminate refrigerator deaths entirely, the presence of other significant factors might cause injuries associated with *other* hazards to go up as a result; i.e., there is no reason to believe that the standard would cause a *net* reduction in death rates, or other injuries, taken over all types of hazards.[31] Funding considerations have precluded pursuing this line of analysis.

---

[30] Public Law 84-930 applies only to household refrigerators; freezers are subject only to voluntary safety standard, to which most manufacturers seem to adhere (Underwriters Laboratories [UL 250], 1971]). I am not aware of the reason for Congress's neglect of freezer doors, given that children have frequently died in freezers. However, a number of bills have been introduced, but not passed, to extend coverage to home freezers and combinations.

[31] The 1958 standard on refrigerator doors did not, of course, eliminate the hazard in subsequent years, as Table 1 shows. This is probably due to the fact that stocks of old-type refrigerators were not eliminated. If we assume the life of an old-type refrigerator to be about fifteen years, peak displacement by new-type refrigerators will occur in the late sixties. The 1969 survey, mentioned earlier, and a telephone survey of police departments in late 1973 concerning accidents occurring between 1963 and 1973 turned up no instance of death in a new-type refrigerator or freezer. However, not enough time had then elapsed for new-type refrigerators to be discarded or stored away in significant numbers.

Without recourse to an expensive survey, it would have been extremely difficult to obtain reliable estimates of the numbers of refrigerators and freezers in use, in storage, or abandoned (but not scrapped) for any year, let alone over a period of time. Thus, it is not possible to calculate the three probabilities that a refrigerator or freezer in use, in storage, or abandoned will be involved in a fatal accident. However, our purpose is not to evaluate the 1958 standard but to illustrate how product hazard might be measured for the setting of safety standards. Hence, we shall be content with only three alternative estimates and quite rough orders of magnitude.[32]

To estimate the probability that a household refrigerator would have been involved in the accidental death of a child in 1956, we relate the number of such incidents in 1956 (i.e., 8) to the total number of household refrigerators in existence during that year. By means of linear interpolation between 1952 and 1960, for which years there are estimates of total households equipped with electrical refrigerators and freezers, an estimate of 50 million units for 1956 was obtained.[33] This number was repeatedly mentioned during the 1955 hearings on H.R. 2181 as the estimated total number of units existing in 1955. The probability of fatal involvement may therefore be computed as 8/50,000,000, or one in 6,250,000. This probability estimate, however, is clearly too crude an estimate for the hazard in question.

Since Congress in 1956 was thinking of the problem in terms of a physical standard on *new refrigerators* (and since it eventually did set such a standard), the relevant measure of hazard would have been the probability that a refrigerator (but not a freezer) sold in 1956 would be involved in a fatal accident during its lifetime. Such a measure could, at that time, have been based only on previous history. Taking the average life of a unit to be fifteen years, and interpreting this (heroically, to be sure) to mean that all refrigerators sold in 1941 were displaced in 1956, we relate deaths involving only refrigerators to this number and obtain an estimate of 7/3,374,000, or about one in 480,000.[34] (For comparison purposes, we may relate the number of incidents in

---

[32] Sources of the data on sales of refrigerators and freezers used in this section are principally: Miller (1960), Burstein (1960), and *Statistical Abstract of the U.S.*, annual volumes. See Appendix A.

[33] 1950: Refrigerators – 37.8 million; freezers – 4.9 million
1960: Refrigerators – 49.6 million; freezers – 11.2 million
Source: *Statistical Abstract of the U.S.*, 1971. Unless otherwise emphasized, the term "refrigerator" will include "freezer" as well.

[34] We know that in 1959, 60 per cent of deaths involved refrigerators. Applying the same percentage to 1956, we estimate 11 × 60 per cent = 7 refrigerator deaths. In 1971, out of the ten deaths reported, 7 involved refrigerators.

1971 to the number of refrigerators sold in 1956, a ratio of 7/3,382,000, or about one in 450,000). Estimates for years prior to 1956 can also be computed, but that is not necessary for our purpose.

Finally, given that state and local governments were concerned primarily with *abandoned* refrigerators and freezers as sources of hazard, a measure of the hazard should be the probability that a refrigerator or freezer abandoned in, say, 1956 would lead to a fatal accident.[35] On the assumption that 80 per cent of the 3.382 million refrigerators sold in 1956 were destined to be replacements (Miller, p. 197), whereas only 10 per cent of the 1 million freezers sold were for replacement, we estimate total displacements in 1956 as 2.806 million units,[36] to which we relate the 11 deaths. This yields a probability estimate of about one in 255,000. This estimate is, of course, much too rough, since not all displaced refrigerators and freezers are *ordinarily* abandoned; some are kept as second units and others are scrapped immediately. The hazard from abandoned refrigerators and freezers is therefore higher than indicated. On the other hand, since the numerator includes incidents in "nonabandoned" units, which probably account for more than half the cases, the hazard is considerably overstated.

3.5.3. Hazard Avoidance (H_β and H_α). The mandatory physical standards adopted on October 30, 1958, for refrigerators, and the similar, but voluntary standards adhered to since then by most manufacturers of home freezers, are examples of β-type avoidance measures. The evidence, insofar as it has been possible to ascertain,[37] shows no deaths of children caused by units complying with these standards. Such evidence is certainly heartening. However, in the fourteen years from 1959 till 1972, 313 deaths were reported, more than twice the number of deaths reported in the thirteen years prior to 1959. It appears that the long-term solution which Congress sought to bring about has indeed been achieved, but no solution for the short-term has been realized.[38]

[35] Since the U.S. Congress could have jurisdiction only over sales of refrigerators and freezers, states and municipalities were left with the responsibility for hazards arising from the existing stocks. By 1955, most states had already passed criminal liability laws with regard to abandonment.

[36] This is close to 2 million units estimated to be discarded annually, as mentioned in the 1955 hearings on HR. 2181.

[37] See Appendix B.

[38] I have seen no reports of incidents where children emerged from magnetic-door units after being inside them. The fear has been expressed that children who enter refrigerators, magnetic or otherwise, in play might be overcome by lack of oxygen before

As for α-type avoidance, three measures may be identified with respect to refrigerator hazards: (a) The warning literature (published by the Association of Home Appliance Manufacturers) which now accompanies new refrigerators and freezers, and the various warnings stamped on such units, as specified in UL250, the voluntary standard for safety, required by Underwriters Laboratories; (b) the varied literature on refrigerator and freezer hazard published by the Department of Health, Education, and Welfare — Public Health Services (DHEW-PHS) and the National Safety Council, among others; (c) the state criminal codes and local ordinances relating to abandonment and outside storage of refrigerators and freezers.

How much have these α-measures contributed to safety? It is difficult to assess the impact on consumer behavior of these actions; I am not aware of any studies which have attempted to make this assessment. However, we may accept as reasonable the Congressional view that additional public information of the kind provided in 1955 would have had no significant lasting effect on consumer behavior.[39]

3.5.4. The Cost of Injury (J) and the Costs of Avoidance (V_α, C_β). Since the outcome of an accident in our illustrative case is either death or no-death, the problem of estimating J is somewhat simplified. Though the life of a child can never really be exchanged for money, society surely has on occasions made decisions which imply a value placed on life.[40] Funds for this study, however, did not permit an estimation of the value of a child's life by inference from any particular social decision.

An alternative approach is to take the valuations placed on children by juries or judges in cases of wrongful death. Ordinarily, such awards include the present value of a child's monetary contributions to his parents, compensation for pain and suffering and loss of companionship, and occasionally punitive damages. Again, for budgetary reasons, a thorough review of awards over, say, the past ten to twenty years was out of the question. However, reference was made to 49 *American Law Reports* (*ALR*) 3d 934 under "Damages — Death of a Minor,"

---

attempting to come out. In experiments conducted in 1955 — clearly far from approximating the real situation — some children made no attempt to come out once entrapped (Bain, 1958).

[39] If one were evaluating the current standard, it would be legitimate to ask whether its adoption in 1958 dampened the enthusiasm with which α-actions of different kinds might have been pursued.

[40] It is often claimed that our society values children more than adults. If so, this is some compensation for their lack of the vote. It is interesting to note that in the weighting scheme of the CPSC, the severity index of an injury is doubled if a child is involved.

518 *Measurement and Issues in Consumption Analysis*

which contains annotated cases dating back to 1941 in which the courts were called upon to consider the excessiveness or adequacy of awards of damages for personal injuries resulting in the death of minors. No instance was found of an award, considered not excessive, above $75,000 for a child under six years of age. It thus seems that an estimate of $100,000 would be rather on the high side as an average value of a child's life, and therefore quite a conservative estimate for our purpose.

The safety standard which the National Bureau of Standards, Department of Commerce (NBS−DOC) promulgated on August 1, 1957, pursuant to the 1956 Act, resulted in the universal adoption by industry of a magnetic door-closure device. This device, though effective, appears to have been the least expensive of the devices known at that time. Cost estimates presented in 1955 for all such devices, including some similar to the current one, ranged from 85 cents to $10. I am told by knowledgeable individuals whom I have consulted that the average cost of manufacturing the current device is actually less than the average cost of the mechanical devices that were replaced by it.[41] Taking into consideration developmental and administrative costs, it seems reasonable to assume that the net marginal cost (C_β) of adopting the present safety device is very small or even zero. I have been unable to determine, however, whether maintenance cost and food-keeping efficiency have changed.

As for the cost of avoidance (V_α) by consumers/parents, it depends on the base from which increases in α are made and obviously on the nature of these additions. Although in 1956, educational and informational campaigns might have been escalated at a moderate cost, the impact (H_α) would probably have been barely noticeable. Putting the matter differently, to produce a significant effect on the hazard, the cost of this kind of α-action would have been extremely high. However, I am aware of no studies which have attempted to determine to what extent consumers were aware of refrigerator hazards, how efficiently such knowledge might be transmitted to them, how long it might remain in their consciousness, and so on. This does not mean that current α-actions, as for example, the first one mentioned in 3.5.3, are not effective as far as they go.

As alternative α-actions which might have been considered, municipalities could have offered to haul away old refrigerators, or to secure those in storage, at zero price, the cost of the operation to be covered

---

[41] Not, however, less than the average cost of the "burstable" devices which were coming into use in the early fifties on cheaper model refrigerators and freezers. The cost differential there might have been in excess of 60 cents.

by taxes. The *net real* cost to society may not be great. This line of inquiry will not be pursued here.

3.5.5. Is Refrigerator Entrapment an Unreasonable Hazard? In addressing this question, we shall follow the accident "theory" implicit in the deliberations that took place in the mid-fifties prior to enactment of P.L. 84-930. According to this theory, two main hazards were to be distinguished. One hazard was associated with refrigerators and freezers which would be added to the then existing stock and over which Congress could exercise jurisdiction. The other hazard was associated with the existing stock, over which states and municipalities had jurisdiction. A secondary distinction was also made between refrigerators and freezers, perhaps on the ground—since found to be unjustified—that a closure device suitable for refrigerators would not be suitable for freezers.

With regard to the hazards from refrigerators yet to be acquired, the class of β-actions under consideration was expected to eliminate the hazard entirely. Thus, the injury cost avoided per unit, $-JH_\beta$, discounted at, say, 6 per cent over fifteen years, would be approximately $100,000 \times .41726 \times 1/480,000 = 9$ cents.[42]

Since the cost of avoidance, C_β, was assumed to be zero, this hazard was unreasonable and the β-action contemplated justified. Had C_β been in excess of 9 cents, the hazard would have been judged reasonable and the β-action unjustified. However, it should be recalled that at the time of legislation, the estimate of this cost exceeded 9 cents.

With regard to the hazard from the existing stock, it was pointed out earlier (3.5.3) that a marginal increase in the level of α-action known then would have produced no practical effect on H, i.e. $H_\alpha = 0$. Obviously, this implies that the hazard was reasonable and nothing could be gained by expending resources at a higher rate on α-type avoidance actions.

The above determination of the reasonableness of the hazard is crucially dependent on the estimates of probability and other parameters. Hence, the illustrative nature of the computations should again be emphasized. Furthermore, it should be noted that "reasonableness" is a relative concept, and depending upon our technical capabilities, our inventiveness, and our familiarity with the hazard, what might have appeared reasonable twenty years ago may conceivably be regarded as unreasonable today, and vice versa.[43]

---

[42] The present value of one dollar at 6 per cent discount rate, for $n = 15$, is $.41726.
[43] For a similar view of the law, see my "Reasonable and Unreasonable Hazards in Law and Economics."

3.6. Summary and Conclusion

I set out to examine the problem of measuring risk when the primary purpose of the measurement is to decide whether a safety standard can be justified. Since the standard would be required only if the hazard was judged to be unreasonable, it was necessary to develop a criterion of reasonableness. Although it *assumes* some theory of accident occurrence which is necessary for the selection of relevant alternative injury-avoidance measures and for assessing their impact, this criterion is formally economic.

In order to demonstrate the operationality of the criterion, it was applied to an illustrative, but actual, case. It was pointed out that measurement procedures, especially with regard to risk of injury, had to be explicitly designed with this criterion in mind and implicitly in accordance with the underlying theory of accident occurrence. Finally, although the discussion did not purport to show how standards should be set nor how to evaluate them once set, the implication was clear that an analysis of the kind illustrated was essential for public action in the product safety area.

APPENDIX A

TABLE A.1

Estimates of U.S. Sales of Refrigerators and Freezers 1946–1957
(thousands)

Year	Refrigerators (2)	Freezers (3)	Refrigerators (4)
1946	2,100	210	1,997
1947	3,400	607	3,126
1948	4,495	690	4,495
1949	4,284	485	4,284
1950	6,020	890	6,000
1951	3,731	1,050	3,698
1952	3,195	1,141	3,196
1953	3,650	1,090	3,287
1954	3,425	975	3,135
1955	3,825	1,100	3,896
1956			3,382
1957			3,164

NOTE: Data are net of exports. Gas units are not included.
SOURCE: Columns 2 and 3 are from Burstein (1960). Column 4 is from Miller (1960).

APPENDIX B

According to a memorandum on file at NBS, the Office of Engineering Standard Services (OESS) conducted a survey in 1969 of incidents of refrigerator entrapment deaths occurring in the preceding decade. Police departments were contacted in cities where incidents were reported to have happened. This information was obtained from the Refrigeration Service Engineers Society, Des Plaines, Ill. Responses were received regarding 104 of these incidents, representing a total of 154 deaths.[44] Of these incidents, 69 involved refrigerators or refrigerator-freezers, 16 involved portable picnic coolers, 14 involved freezers, and 7 involved iceboxes. None involved magnetic door closures.

A check of the files in the OESS showed that they still had the survey responses for 79 of the 104 incidents. The 16 cases concerning the picnic coolers were apparently removed and used in the development of the current voluntary safety standard for picnic coolers. The other nine could not be accounted for. Tables B.1 and B.2 present a summary of the information presently in the OESS file.

In order to bring the 1969 OESS survey up to date, a list of the names, dates, and locations of all reported incidents from January 1969 through June 1973 was obtained from the Society's international headquarters in Des Plaines, Illinois. I then obtained telephone confirmation that 29 of the 31 incidents in the U.S. during that time period did not involve magnetic doors. In one case, there was no information as to the type of closure in the police file, and in the other, the file could not be located. The following tables (B.3 and B.4) provide a summary of the information concerning only accidents in the U.S.

[44] Over the period of this survey, 130 incidents were reported by the Refrigeration Service Engineers Society. Therefore, coverage of the tabulation exceeds 75 per cent. It should be noted that the Society relies on its members to report incidents in their areas. It is therefore possible that some incidents have not been reported.

TABLE B.1

		State of Use				Kind of Unit Involved		
Year	Incidents	Abandoned	Storage	Used	Unknown	Refrigerator	Freezer	Icebox
1968	1	1	0	0	0	1	0	0
1967	17	6	10	1	0	14	3	0
1966	10	5	3	2	0	7	1	2
1965	10	3	3	2	2	9	1	0
1964	16	4	10	2	0	14	2	0
1963	5	1	3	1	0	3	0	2
1962	8	2	4	2	0	5	2	1
1961	8	2	3	3	0	6	2	0
1960								
1959	6	1	2	2	1	4	1	1

TABLE B.2

Year	Deaths	State of Use				Kind of Unit Involved		
		Abandoned	Storage	Used	Unknown	Refrigerator	Freezer	Icebox
1968	1	1	0	0	0	1	0	0
1967	28	9	18	1	0	21	7	0
1966	17	8	3	6	0	12	3	2
1965	20	7	6	3	4	18	2	0
1964	25	8	14	4	0	21	3	2
1963	8	1	5	2	0	6	0	2
1962	13	2	4	2	0	7	4	2
1961	12	2	3	3	0	7	3	2
1960								
1959	8	2	3	2	1	5	1	2

TABLE B.3

		State of Use				Kind of Unit Involved			
Year	Incidents	Abandoned	Storage	Used	Unknown	Refrigerator	Freezer	Icebox	Unknown
1969	7	4	3	0	0	6	1	0	0
1970	10			2	8	7	3	0	0
1971	6	2	4	0	0	4	2	0	0
1972	4		1	2	1	3			1
1973	4	2	2	0	0	3	1	0	0

TABLE B.4

		State of Use				Kind of Unit Involved			
Year	Deaths	Abandoned	Storage	Used	Unknown	Refrigerator	Freezer	Icebox	Unknown
1969	12	4	8	0	0	11	1	0	0
1970	17			2	15	12	3		2
1971	8	2	6	0	0	6	2	0	0
1972	7		2	3	2	3			1
1973	8	4	4	0	0	3	1	0	0

REFERENCES

Arrow, K. J. "Uncertainty and the Welfare Economics of Medical Care." *American Economic Review* 53 (December 1963): 941–973.

——. "The Economics of Moral Hazard: Further Comments." *American Economic Review* 58 (June 1968): 537–539.

Bain, Katherine; Faefre, Marion L.; and Wyly, Robert S. "Behavior of Young Children Under Conditions Simulating Entrapment in Refrigerators." *Pediatrics* 22, Part I (October 1958): 628–646.

Burstein, M. L. "The Demand for Household Refrigeration in the United States." In A. C. Harberger, editor, *The Demand for Durable Goods.* Chicago: University of Chicago Press, 1960, pp. 99–145.

Coase, Ronald H. "The Problem of Social Cost." *Journal of Law and Economics* 3 (October 1960): 1–44.

Demsetz, H. "When Does the Rule of Liability Matter?" *Journal of Legal Studies* 1 (January 1972): 13–28.

Ehrlich, I., and Becker, G. S. "Market Insurance, Self-Insurance, and Self-Protection." *Journal of Political Economy* 80 (July/August 1972): 623–648.

Grubel, H. G. "Risk, Uncertainty and Moral Hazard." *Journal of Risk and Insurance* 38 (March 1971): 99–106.

Miller, H. Laurence. "The Demand for Refrigerators: A Statistical Study." *Review of Economics and Statistics* 17 (May 1960): 196–202.

National Commission on Product Safety (NCPS). *Final Report of the National Commission on Product Safety.* Washington, D.C.: Government Printing Office, June 1970.

Oi, Walter Y. "The Economics of Product Safety." *Bell Journal of Economics and Management Science.* 4 (Spring 1973): 3–28.

Pauly, M. V. "The Economics of Moral Hazard: Comments." *American Economic Review* 58 (June 1968): 531–537.

Comments on "Risk Measurement and Safety Standards in Consumer Products"

JOHN P. GOULD

UNIVERSITY OF CHICAGO

IN this paper, V. L. Broussalian is concerned with the important practical problem of determining when safety hazards are "unreasonable" in the sense that they justify public action by governmental agencies such as the Consumer Product Safety Commission. As I understand it, a major objective of the paper is to direct the attention of governmental policymakers to the salient conceptual and empirical issues surrounding this kind of regulation. In this perspective, Broussalian's paper deserves credit on a number of points. First, he shows that in a well-functioning market, there is no reason to suppose that any "unreasonable" hazards should exist.[1] He then identifies the kinds of market imperfections, such as transactions costs, possible difficulties in establishing product liability insurance, high litigation costs, and third-party effects that might lead to products with unreasonable hazards. One clear implication of Broussalian's discussion in my judgment is that the existence of unreasonably hazardous products cannot be assumed a priori and the burden of proof is appropriately assigned to those who would maintain that the market is not working well. Broussalian is also correct in emphasizing that the issue of the existence of unreasonable hazards is essentially an empirical matter that raises a variety of difficult measurement problems. By conducting much of the analysis in terms of a concrete case — refrigerator hazards — Broussalian is able to convey vividly an understanding of the nature of these empirical problems.

Despite my generally favorable reaction to this paper, there are several specific issues on which it can be challenged. The central theme of the paper is to devise a reasonable way of deciding when an unreasonable product hazard exists. Broussalian's definition of an unreasonable hazard is given by equation 1, which says that a hazard is unreasonable if the marginal gain from reduced injuries and deaths exceeds the marginal cost of reducing the hazard. This is basically a cost-benefit criterion which, like most such criteria, is easy to accept in principle but much harder to implement in practice. In the usual cost-benefit situation, it is relatively easy to identify costs and extremely difficult to define and measure benefits. In Broussalian's specification, there appear to be serious measurement problems on both the cost and benefit side.

The evaluation of benefits requires estimation both of the monetary value of injury and for human life, as well as the *marginal* effect of accident-avoiding actions on the probability of distribution of injury or death. These are difficult measurement tasks but are presumably within the scope of economic analysis.[2] Evaluation of the costs of avoiding

---

[1] Much of Broussalian's discussion makes reference to the nonexistence of unreasonable hazards in perfectly competitive markets. It can also be shown, however, that a profit-maximizing monopolist would not have an interest in producing products that impose unreasonable hazards on consumers.

[2] For example, at this Conference, Rosen and Thaler have presented a paper that takes up the question of evaluating human life.

accidents raises problems that are not so easily resolved. Broussalian rather casually introduces the function $V_i(\alpha)$ to represent the cost of accident-avoiding activities for individual i. According to equation 1, the aggregate cost for consumers is obtained by summing $V_i(\alpha)$ across individuals. It is far from clear that any meaningful interpretation can be given to this procedure. For example, what set of individuals should we sum over to get this measure of cost: current users, potential users, or some other group? Should the existence of a small fraction of users with high marginal cost of accident avoidance be the criterion for deciding whether a product should be eliminated from the market or modified in any substantial way? Is it reasonable to treat excessive caution on the part of individual A as a perfect substitute for foolhardy behavior on the part of individual B, as the summation in equation 1 implies? By stating the criterion function as he does, Broussalian implicitly makes interpersonal utility comparisons. This is a far more subjective basis for assessing the reasonableness of product hazards than the paper seems to suggest.

Another serious problem with Broussalian's specification is the assumption that the output of the commodity, that is, X, is fixed. Instead of maximizing social welfare, Broussalian uses the criterion of minimizing social cost for a given level of consumption.[3] The difficulty here is that a governmental policy that increases costs is likely to lead to a decrease in the quantity of the good consumed. This decrease in quantity will lead to a reduction in consumer welfare that may be of substantial magnitude. The importance of this kind of welfare loss has been made clear by recent work of Sam Peltzman, which assesses the net benefits of the 1962 amendments to the Food, Drug, and Cosmetics Act.[4]

It may be objected that the conditions given by equations 2 and 3 of Broussalian's paper should be fulfilled at *every* level of output if we are to satisfy efficiency criteria. The problem is harder than this, however, because the practical tradeoff may be between a low level of output where (2) and (3) are satisfied and a higher level of output where (2) and (3) are violated. It is entirely possible that net social welfare is greater in the latter case.

In view of these problems, one may have serious doubts as to whether any significant headway can be made in empirical implementa-

---

[3] See section 2.2.1 of Broussalian's paper.
[4] Sam Peltzman, "An Evaluation of Consumer Protection Legislation: The 1962 Drug Amendments," *Journal of Political Economy* 81 (September/October 1973): 1049–1091.

tion of Broussalian's model. Unfortunately, the case of refrigerator hazards dealt with in his paper does little to dispel these concerns, because it does not require one to face the really difficult questions. Broussalian notes that the cost of the magnetic door-closure device is less than the cost of the mechanical device that it replaces. Given this cost advantage of the safer device, we do not have to worry very much about the accuracy of our assessment of the expected marginal gain. The new device would be preferred even if all we could claim for it is the avoidance of an injury that would cost a nickel 100,000 years from now. Similarly, Broussalian asserts that the marginal gain H_α of greater caution by consumers is negligible, so that we never really face the problem of how to assess the vaguely defined marginal cost of avoidance function V_α.[5]

In summary, I wish to emphasize that my reservations about this paper are not meant to detract in any way from the great merit I see in this line of research. The general problem Broussalian raises is significant and he has made a heroic effort to come to grips with the hard questions. I hope that he and others will be encouraged to continue the search for answers to these questions.

---

[5] However, Broussalian's arguments about H_α raise the possibility that consumers are *excessively* cautious with respect to refrigerator safety and we are then faced with the problem of welfare loss of the opposite kind.

The Concept and Measurement of
Product Quality *

E. SCOTT MAYNES

UNIVERSITY OF MINNESOTA

I. INTRODUCTION

QUALITY is a topic which economists, by and large, have swept under the rug.[1] This paper faces up to the problem by proposing, and arguing for, a concept of product quality, and by showing how it might be measured empirically.

The plan of this paper is first to excite your interest by presenting a sample of actual measurements of product quality in local consumer markets. A discussion of the uses to which quality may be put follows, along with an effort to distinguish my work from that of other toilers in the same vineyard — namely, those working on hedonic price indicators, and Kelvin Lancaster, with his characteristics approach to consumer demand theory. The heart of the paper will deal with the conceptualiza-

* The long gestation period of this paper has given birth to a large number of critics/creditors. My debt is heaviest to Edward M. Foster, and W. Keith Bryant of the University of Minnesota. But I am also deeply indebted to Marcel K. Richter, Leonid Hurwicz, Herbert Mohring, and Neil Wallace of Minnesota; Richard D. Emmerson, J. Edward Russo, Harold Nelson, and Lucille Thompson of the University of California, San Diego; Arthur J. Rolnick of the Federal Reserve Bank of Minneapolis; and Christopher Babb of Cornell. The residual responsibility for accepting or rejecting criticisms so generously given rests with the author.

[1] A survey of the major economic journals during the postwar period yields about twenty articles dealing directly with quality. Most of these belong to the hedonic price index literature, discussed in Section IV of this paper. Several deal with the selection of quality level as a factor in product differentiation. See [10] as an example. Several deal with the proposition of accepting price as an indicator of quality [e.g. 27, 12]. One, Theil's [31], by accepting the mean price as an index of quality, seeks to estimate the demand for quality.

However none essays the task of this paper — conceptualizing and measuring quality per se. Nor has any word about quality reached economic undergraduates if Samuelson's text [26] is representative. One will look in vain to find "quality" in the index. And the closest one comes in substance is a discussion of product differentiation and

tion and measurement of product quality in full detail. A final section will suggest some research possibilities opened up by this essay.

This paper is infused with the view that economic theory and concepts should be the servants of intelligent consumers and handmaidens to empirical research. Accordingly, the concepts presented here represent the simplest possible formulations and have been shaped with empirical measurement in mind.

II. PRICES, QUALITY, AND QUALITY-DEFLATED PRICES IN LOCAL CONSUMER MARKETS: SAMPLE RESULTS

The results reported here are typical of those obtained from a series of investigations made under my direction by upperclassmen and graduate students at the University of Minnesota since the spring of 1970. In all these investigations, students were instructed to obtain estimates of variations in money prices, quality, and quality-deflated prices for a variety of products on the local markets in which consumers would normally purchase. (These markets included mail-order outlets.) The samples of brands/models and retail outlets were selected purposively rather than by probability methods. However, students were urged to take special pains to cover those brands and/or retail outlets whose prices or qualities were expected to be unusually high or low.

Quality may be assessed for either a *variety* – a product/brand/model combination – or, when the characteristics of a seller are also taken into account, for a *specimen* as well. In the sample results reported here, quality was assessed for both varieties and specimens of sofa beds.

The *quality* of a *specimen* was defined as "the subjectively weighted

---

the factors accounting for it. The identical observation applies to graduate theory texts if [15] is taken as representative.

There is evidence of much earlier interest in the problem of quality. Stigler reported [28, page 315] that John Bates Clark "became preoccupied with a problem to which he could not find a useful solution: how to apply marginal analysis to variations in the quality of goods."

Evidently, the difficulty of the subject has put off many. In his classical article on "The Economics of Information," George Stigler commented: "The search for knowledge on the quality of goods, which has been studiously avoided in this paper, is perhaps no more important but, certainly, analytically more difficult. Quality has not yet been successfully specified by economics, and this elusiveness extends to all problems in which it enters" [29, page 224].

Georgescu-Roegen [13, pages 97–105] asserts gloomily that despite the quantification of some aspects of reality, there will always remain a "qualitative residual" which will defy measurement.

Psychologists and marketers have devoted considerable attention to quality. But their focus has been upon *perceptions* of quality rather than on the conceptualization and measurement of quality. [17] is representative.

average of characteristics," *characteristics* being in turn defined as the "services giving rise to utility," such as safety, durability, and beauty.

The sofa-bed investigation reported here presents data for ten specimens on sale at four different retail outlets. This particular study was selected for presentation on the basis of its representativeness and the care invested in its execution.

In assessing the quality of *varieties* of sofa beds, the investigator identified and weighted the characteristics of the good itself as follows:

Characteristic		Weight
Aesthetics		.50
Comfort:		.15
As sofa	.10	
As bed	.05	
Durability:		.15
As sofa	.10	
As bed	.05	
Convenience		.10
Warranty		.06
Safety		.04
	Total:	1.00

As for the retail outlets or sellers, their characteristics were identified and weighted as follows:

Characteristic	Weight
Sensitivity, pleasantness	.35
Convenience	.25
Knowledge of product	.20
Reliability	.10
Warranty (retail seller's expected performance with respect to his responsibility)	.10
Total:	1.00

In combining the characteristics of the good itself and of the seller to obtain the quality of a specimen, the investigator assigned a weight of .85 to characteristics of the good and .15 to characteristics of the seller.

Results from this sample investigation are presented in Table 1. Three outcomes are salient: the wide range of money prices, the wide range of quality,[2] and perhaps even more significant, the fact that the

---

[2] Since the boundaries of the quality index are defined precisely, 0.00 representing a total absence of desirable characteristics and 1.00 representing the quality of the ideal specimen, differences in this scale are meaningful and not arbitrary. See Section V for further discussion of the concept of quality.

TABLE 1

Variations in Money Prices, Quality, and Quality-Deflated Prices
in a Local Market: Sofa Beds in Minneapolis [a]

Retail Outlet (1)	Brand/Model (2)	Varieties [b]			Specimens [c]	
		Money Price (3)	Qual- ity (4)	Quality- Deflated Price [d] (5)	Qual- ity (6)	Quality- Deflated Price [d] (7)
1	A	$230	.49	$ 469	.52	$ 440
	B – Sale price	250	.61	410	.63	398
	– Regular price	339	.61	556	.63	540
	C	260	.63	411	.65	402
2	D	450	.70	643	.92	488
	E – Sale price	399	.98	407	.98	408
	– Regular price	460	.98	469	.98	470
	F – Sale price	269	.64	420	.68	395
	– Regular price	380	.64	594	.68	558
3	G	499	.84	594	.86	580
	H – Sale price	560	.63	889	.68	828
	– Regular price	702	.63	1,114	.68	1,033
4	I	385	.60	641	.62	623
	J	269	.59	456	.62	434
Means:		$389				
The range:		$230 to $702	.49 to .98	$ 407 to $1,114	.52 to .98	$ 395 to $1,033
Ratio of highest to lowest:		3.06	2.00	2.76	1.88	2.62

[a] These data were collected by Kathryn S. Hochsprung, a senior at the University of Minnesota. The work was done in the spring of 1973. All dollar figures are rounded to the nearest one dollar.

[b] A *variety* of a product is a product/brand/model combination. The assessment of the quality of a variety does *not* take account of characteristics of the seller.

[c] A *specimen* is a product/brand/model/seller combination. Its quality assessment does take account of characteristics of the seller.

[d] The quality-deflated price P^* equals P/G where P = money price and G = quality.

deflation of money prices to take account of quality did not appreciably reduce the range in quality-deflated prices.

These results are not singular but, rather, are typical of the results obtained in more than thirty such investigations. It should be noted that these thirty or so investigations embrace a most diverse set of products, ranging from color TV sets to bicycles to food blenders to auto insurance to wigs, but not including foods.

The reactions of the investigators to their own efforts, though informal in character and necessarily inconclusive, are suggestive. All found the task of assessing quality both tractable and meaningful. When queried, all felt strongly that their quality assessments were both valid and reliable.

The skeptic can find much in the results above and in results not presented here about which he may properly be skeptical:

1. The investigations were carried out by students, not by professional social scientists. (The assessment of quality is, we shall argue, a matter for individuals. However, the students may err in their handling of data as compared with knowledgeable professionals.)
2. Were all the relevant characteristics considered in arriving at the quality measure? (The skeptic may be able to think of other characteristics he would seek in that product.)
3. Is the "product" class on which measurements were performed too broad or too narrow? For example, are there some sofa beds included in the sofa bed comparison which the critic would not consider an acceptable substitute for others in the class? [3]

Despite these doubts, I suggest that the sample results above have two "messages" for us:

1. The measurement of product quality along these lines is feasible.
2. More definitive measurements are likely to confirm the existence of wide ranges of money prices and of the quality-deflated price in local consumer markets. [4]

It is now time to state clearly the uses to which quality may be put.

[3] At the Conference, several discussants voiced doubts that Specimen *H* should be included in the "product" class for Table 1. When this issue was posed to Kathryn Hochsprung after the Conference, she reaffirmed her judgment that Specimen *H* was sufficiently similar in characteristics to the other sofa beds viewed as to warrant "serious consideration" for possible purchase. And there was no question that the seller of Specimen *H* was easily accessible and hence a part of the relevant "market."

[4] The number of brand/models sampled in the sofa bed example was small. Evidence from other investigations with larger samples of models suggests that the wide ranges found in money prices and in quality-deflated prices is not attributable to outliers.

III. THE USES OF QUALITY

An acceptable, empirically measurable concept of quality should have three major uses: (1) as an *index of possible payoffs* to searching (shopping) by consumers, (2) as an *index of the "informational effectiveness"* of markets, (3) as a *building block in economic theory,* facilitating the development of market demand/supply relationships for differentiated products. Each of these requires further explanation. We now turn to this task.

An Index of Possible Consumer Payoffs

Should an intelligent consumer ask an economist how much consumers should shop (or "search").[5] The economist would naturally, correctly, and perhaps fervently (!) recite the marginal rule: "Keep searching (shopping) as long as the expected gross payoff from searching exceeds the expected cost of an additional search." [6] This "answer" at once begets two other questions: (1) What is the nature of a "payoff"? (2) How does one estimate the value of the expected gross payoff?

A *payoff* may be defined as "any gain resulting from searching." A moment's reflection will disclose that gains may take the form of a lower money price (quality equal) or better quality (money price equal) or both. What the marginally calculating consumer would find highly useful is a measure of quality which renders money prices and quality commensurable. The instrument which will perform this task is a cardinal measure of quality. And it is just such a measure which is proposed in this paper.

Figure 1, depicting the data of Table 1, conveys price-quality information relating to sofa beds in a choice-facilitating manner. Assume for the moment that the consumer has access to Figure 1 and also to the identity of Specimens A, B, C, and so on. Assume further that all consumers would make uniform assessments of the quality of various

---

[5] A *search* is defined as "each attempt to secure and to act on information regarding the price and/or quality of a product." Thus, search, as used here, would include all of the following: "shopping," consultation of publications giving product information, telephoning retailers to ask if they carry a given brand, getting information from the "yellow pages," consulting a mail-order catalogue, and — very important — bargaining.

[6] *Costs* include "anything which is undergone or forgone in order to attain a given end." Thus, the dollar equivalent of someone's distaste for shopping may be a "cost" of shopping. Alternatively, the dollar equivalent of the activity forgone in order to undertake shopping, e.g., an afternoon's sailing, represents another type of cost. The more common varieties of costs, such as transportation costs, are naturally included.

FIGURE 1

Price and Quality in a Local Market: Sofa Beds in Minneapolis

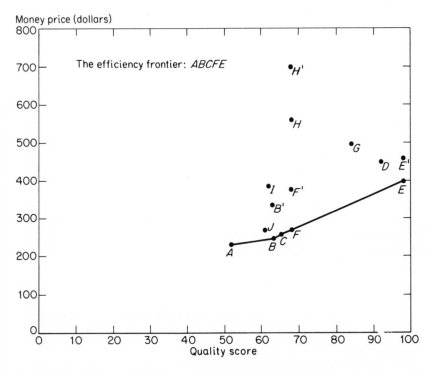

NOTE: Letters represent various specimens. Where an identical letter appears twice, the primed designation, e.g., *H'*, represents a "regular" price while the unprimed designation, e.g., *H*, represents a sale price.

SOURCE: Table 1.

specimens. (The assumption of uniform assessments of quality will be discussed later.) For the choice-maker the dominant and most useful feature of Figure 1 is the *efficiency frontier, ABCFE*. The efficiency frontier consists of the set of points and the line segments connecting them, for which a given level of quality may be purchased at the lowest price.

In choosing among the specimens available,[7] the rational consumer would proceed along the efficiency frontier from left to right. His first inclination would be to consider Specimen *A* with a money price of $230. Should he purchase more quality? Figure 1 (and the supporting data from Table 1) would reveal that by purchasing Specimen *B* for a sale price of $250 he could achieve a 21 per cent increase in quality (.11/.52) for only a 9 per cent increase in money price paid ($20/230). Or, to consider another alternative which would be attractive to someone with a taste for the "best," by purchasing Specimen *E* at the sale price of $399, he could achieve an 88 per cent increase in quality as compared with *A* (.46/.52) for a 74 per cent increase in price ($169/230). Which should he do? Only the consumer himself can say whether the marginal improvement in a particular comparison is "worth" the additional money outlay. But one thing is certain: the choice of the rational consumer would lie on the efficiency frontier.

But, supposing our prospective purchaser had access to Figure 1, but *not* to the identification of the brand/model/seller represented by *A*, *B*, *C*, etc. Under these conditions four pieces of information would be particularly useful: (1) the range in quality, given on Figure 1 by the distance on the horizontal axis from *A* to *E*; (2) the visual correlation, if "high," between price and quality; (3) the average slope of the efficiency frontier, $\Delta P/\Delta G$, where G = quality (a mnemonic for "goodness"); (4) the ratio of the maximum price to the frontier price, here approximately H'/F. But why should these four be singled out as important? The question is answered below in terms of the data of Figure 1.

The large range in quality, *E* being approximately twice as "good" as *A*, poses a major choice for the purchaser: Should he opt for more or less quality? If the correlation between price and quality is "high" meaning "visually obvious," then price becomes a proxy for quality and the purchaser, with a knowledge of the average slope of the efficiency frontier, $\Delta P/\Delta G$, can obtain the quality he desires by focusing on the money price asked.

When the correlation is low, the intelligent consumer should shift his attention to the discovery of the efficiency frontier. At this point, he will be interested, too, in the ratio of the maximum price to the corresponding frontier price. The greater this ratio, the greater the amount he should search for a lower money price.

---

[7] Careful definitions of *product* — needed to identify the specimens properly counted as part of the product class — and *market* — needed to determine which sellers and which buyers are properly part of the class — are given in Sections VII and VIII. For the moment, we assume that satisfactory definitions of product and market are at hand.

But suppose our prospective purchaser had access to only a single statistic from Table 1. What would be most useful? My candidate would be the range in quality-deflated prices P^*. If this range was small, it would suggest that price was indeed closely associated with quality, and that the searcher should concentrate on price. If this range was large, considerable searching would be appropriate and considerable payoffs might be expected. For specimens of sofa beds, this range was $395 to $1,033, suggesting very large payoffs, indeed.

It is useful to recall that, in this discussion, we have assumed that consumers make uniform assessments of quality. If, and as, quality assessments by different individuals become increasingly less uniform, then different consumers are likely to identify different efficiency frontiers, and variations in P^* as assessed by one individual would become increasingly meaningless to other individuals. In mentioning the issue of uniformity versus nonuniformity in quality assessments, it is worth recalling the informal judgments of the student investigators: they felt that others undertaking the same quality assessments would achieve highly similar results. Obviously, a test of the congruity of quality assessments and of efficiency frontiers is an important topic for future research.

A Measure of the "Informational Effectiveness" of Markets

Economists will naturally be interested in the extent to which different buyers achieve the best possible terms offered in a given market. As a first approximation, we will designate as *informationally effective* any market in which all buyers purchase specimens situated on the efficiency frontier, assuming uniform assessments of quality. And we will propose variations in the vertical distance of prices from the efficiency frontier for any given level of quality (the excess of the price actually asked over the price on the frontier) as a measure of the informational effectiveness of markets: the greater the variation in distances from the frontier, the less informationally effective a market.

Note that this concept applies only to *informational* effectiveness and not to overall effectiveness. The single price charged in a market which is perfect from the informational viewpoint might be the "high" price of the perfect monopolist.

We might check the working of the proposed measure against the sofa bed data presented in Figure 1. Here the most distant price, H', exceeds the corresponding price on the efficiency frontier, F, by $433 ($702 minus $269). Other points are also considerably removed from the efficiency frontier, though not as extremely as H'. It is clear that the market for sofa beds is a long way removed from the zero variation from the frontier which we would expect to find in an informationally perfect market. The culprit in this case is undoubtedly the fact that efforts to obtain information regarding price and quality are costly and imperfect, as are efforts to act on the basis of such information, e.g., bargaining, or a visit to another seller.

Why do we propose the variation in the distance from the efficiency frontier only as a first approximation measure? First, the validity of the measure rests on the assumption that, within product classes, different consumers make identical quality assessments. If consumers differ in their assessments of quality, then it may be perfectly reasonable for Consumer I to prefer Specimen A over Specimen B at the same money price, while Consumer II prefers B over A. This event, generalized, would yield variations in the distance from the frontier, as measured by either I or II, which would be consistent with an informationally *effective* market.[8] For this reason, too, the extent of congruity in quality assessments is an important topic for future research.

A second qualification arises from the prevalence of price discrimination based upon objective factors. Suppose—and this is an actual case—American Airlines offers a two-thirds reduction in fares between certain cities to dependents traveling with a family head and returning within a specified period. This example of price discrimination will increase the distance from the efficiency frontier, but need not imply informational ineffectiveness. Such would be the case if advertising and/or airline clerks succeeded in informing all eligible persons of this favorable fare. If, however, the efforts of advertising and airline clerks failed to inform all of those eligible, then the observed variation in the distance from the efficiency frontier would be attributable, in part, to an informationally ineffective market.

It should be noted that much price discrimination arises from the very fact that consumer ignorance makes possible the separation of markets. An example would be the different prices paid, as a result of bargaining, by different purchasers of identical new cars. To the extent that it results from differences in information and *not* from differences in bargaining skills (knowledge equal), this kind of price discrimination contributes to the informational ineffectiveness of the market in which it occurs.

Summing up, economists should be interested in the informational

---

[8] The task will be simpler if it turns out that individuals, similarly situated, tend to make uniform judgments regarding the delineation of "markets," "products," and quality. If individuals' judgments on these matters differ, the analysis will become more complex and less general but not impossible.

effectiveness of markets. The assessment of quality is a necessary ingredient in the evaluation of this facet of market performance. Just how much variation in the distance from the efficiency frontier is required to justify a verdict of "informational ineffectiveness" is rendered uncertain, due to the possibility of differences in quality assessments and also to the existence of price discrimination based on objective factors.

A Building Block in Economic Theory

With respect to the theoretical treatment of quality, Edward Chamberlin's legacy, Chamberlin [5, 6], is at once laudable and lamentable. It is laudable because—although he rarely used the word *quality*—Chamberlin successfully explained why producers/sellers seek to incorporate real or imagined quality differences into their products and thereby "differentiate" their products. The successful product differentiator, as all of us know, is not a "price taker," but is, in some degree, a "price maker."

Chamberlin's legacy is lamentable, however, because instead of developing the concept of quality, he moved in the dead-end direction of defining each product variant as a separate "product." And this ineluctably led to the well-accepted conclusion in economic theory [9] that the development of *market* demand/supply relations for sets of closely related "products" is inadmissible.

It is my contention that the deflation of money prices by an acceptable measure of quality—the P^* cited earlier—plus appropriate definitions of "product" and "market" will provide us with the necessary building blocks from which market demand and supply relationships for differentiated products may be constructed.

It is my hope that the concepts of quality, product, and market presented in this paper will prove up to the task. And it is my belief that the task is both important and feasible. Most of the purchase decisions consumers make involve the assessment of quality as an important ingredient. If economics is to be helpful and relevant in this sphere, there must be developed models which incorporate quality differences. If the concepts proposed in this paper—or their successors—are found acceptable, then the task of moving to market demand/supply relationships for differentiated products should be relatively straightforward.

---

[9] This conclusion is "well accepted" in economic theory but not in the domain of applied economics and econometrics, as witnessed by various studies of the demand for automobiles, refrigerators, houses, and food.

IV. THIS PAPER AND THE EXISTING LITERATURE

The central task of this paper is to conceptualize and measure product quality. It is this emphasis on quality per se which distinguishes this effort from Kelvin Lancaster's pioneering work on the characteristics approach to consumer demand and from the hedonic price literature. For those with a taste for taxonomy, this paper probably fits best in the economics-of-information literature. We shall consider each in turn.

For the contributors to the hedonic price index literature, quality [10] is a "pain in the neck." Their primary objective is to purge time-series price data of quality effect so that they can obtain valid measures of "pure" price changes.

Their view of quality is highly similar to that proposed in this paper. Adelman and Griliches [1, page 539] propose that "the quality of a commodity be regarded as a composite of different characteristics." However, since they wish to obtain measures of *average* money prices over time, the hedonists confine their attention to the *average* effects of *only* those characteristics which have a measurable influence on money prices. By contrast, our formulations will embrace *all* characteristics entering the utility function and will be concerned with individual, as well as with average, assessments of quality.

It is ironic, considering the length [11] and strength [12] of the hedonic literature to note that none of its practitioners has sought to generalize the measurement of quality as this paper does.

Though my work could have been inspired by the hedonic approach, it was, in fact, stimulated by Kelvin Lancaster's seminal work on the characteristics approach to consumer demand.[13] But the approach here differs from Lancaster's in several important ways.

First, in two articles and one book, Lancaster never felt it necessary or desirable to develop a measure of quality. By contrast, it is my view that the concept of quality is essential for the pursuit of the three objectives set forth above—the estimation of consumer payoffs, the assessment of the informational effectiveness of markets, and as a building block in economic theory. In addition, it is my expectation that the concept of quality will be helpful, both normatively and positively,

---

[10] For a succinct summary of the hedonic approach, cf. [32]. Landmarks in the development of the hedonic approach include [7, 1, 11] 1971. See Griliches [14], 1971, for a set of papers covering most aspects of the literature.

[11] The hedonic approach dates back at least to Court's paper in 1939 [7].

[12] The quality of both the papers and the contributors to the volume edited by Griliches [14] testify to the strength of the hedonic literature.

[13] The basic paper is [19]. But many of Lancaster's ideas are spelled out more fully in his 1971 book [21]. For a simpler version of the paper, see [20], and for trenchant criticism, see [4].

in dealing with the problem of consumer choice among products whose quality differs. The stress which subscribers to *Consumer Reports* place on the quality ratings supports this view.[14]

A second major difference between this paper and Lancaster's work concerns the assumptions which each makes regarding the properties of characteristics. Lancaster assumes that characteristics are both *objective* and *universal,* whereas this paper rejects both assumptions, and instead takes the view that characteristics may be subjective and nonuniversal. The significance of these different assumptions will be discussed later. Here, it is our intention to alert the reader to the fact that this paper departs from, rather than follows, Lancaster in major respects.

As has been said, this paper probably fits best into the economics-of-information literature. Indeed, it deals with a problem *not* taken up by Stigler in the classical and seminal 1961 paper which launched the economics-of-information literature. In that paper Stigler wrote [29]:

> The search for knowledge on the quality of goods, which has studiously been avoided in this paper, is perhaps more important but, certainly, analytically more difficult. Quality has not yet been successfully specified by economics, and this elusiveness extends to all problems in which it enters.

The central task of this paper, to which we now turn, is to take up the challenge which Stigler eschewed: the successful specification of quality.

V. THE CONCEPT OF QUALITY

Some Preliminary Definitions

Before proceeding to the concept of quality per se, we must pause to define again, or to define in at least a preliminary way, the closely related concepts of *specimen, variety, characteristic, product,* and *market.*

A *specimen* is a "product/brand/model/seller combination," for

---

[14] Of the subscribers to *Consumer Reports* who purchased a given product, the following proportions reported that they had bought a "top-rated model":

Hair shampoo	81%
Color TV set	75
AM/FM radio	48
TV or FM antenna	51
Coffee maker	77
Sewing machine	64
Record changer	62

Source: Benson and Benson, Inc. "Survey of Present and Former Subscribers to *Consumer Reports*" (Consumers Union, mimeographed, 1970), Tables T21 and T22.

example, a 1971 Buick Sports (i.e., station) Wagon purchased from Fairways Buick. (A more careful specification of a specimen would require the listing of the motor type, the accessories, and other features which distinguish this class of Buick from other Buicks.) If we dropped the seller designation ("Fairways Buick") and spoke of *any* 1971 Buick Sports Wagon, we would be dealing with a *variety*. Though it is appropriate to conceptualize and measure the quality of either a specimen or a variety, we shall deal below with the quality of a specimen.

For purposes of understanding our concept of quality, the preliminary definition of a characteristic used earlier will suffice: A *characteristic* is "any service giving rise to utility," such as safety, durability, beauty. A full discussion of characteristics, their specification and the measurement problems they pose, will follow our delineation of the concept of quality.

Bear in mind the uses to which the concept of quality is to be put. We will wish, for example, to estimate the range of quality of a given "product" in a given "market." Or we will wish to draw a demand curve, with the money price deflated by quality, for some differentiated "product." Thus, we need a definition of *product* to decide *which specimens* will be appropriately included in the class for which quality evaluations and comparisons are to be made. And, analogously, we will need a definition of *market* to decide *which sellers and which buyers* (consumers) are to be appropriately included in the evaluation/comparison class. For now, we will provisionally assume that satisfactory definitions of product and market are at hand. The actual definitions proposed and argued for in this paper will be taken up after we have dealt with quality per se.

The Concept of Quality

Verbally *quality,* by the definition proposed here, consists of:

> "the extent to which a specimen possesses the
> service characteristics you desire."

Formally, the *quality* of the kth specimen, $G_k{}^{ij}$, is given by

$$G_k{}^{ij} = \frac{\sum_{l=1}^{L} (W_l{}^{ij} \cdot Ch_{kl}{}^{ij})}{\sum_{l=1}^{L} W_l{}^{ij}} \tag{1.0}$$

where

G_k^{ij} = the quality of the kth specimen of the jth product class as assessed by the ith individual.

W_l^{ij} = the weight assigned to the lth characteristic in the jth product class by the ith individual.

Note that for different specimens of the same product class the weights assigned to a particular characteristic are identical.

Ch_{kl}^{ij} = the characteristic score assigned to the lth characteristic of the kth specimen in the jth product class by the ith individual.

Characteristic scores range from 0.00 to 1.00 with two alternative interpretations, giving rise to two alternative models for quality:

Model A: The Proportionality Model. Here 0.00 denotes a total absence of the characteristic and 1.00 denotes the amount of this characteristic in the "ideal" specimen, k^o. Values between 0.00 and 1.00 denote the ratio of the amount of the characteristic possessed in the kth specimen to the amount possessed in the ideal specimen.

Model B: The Direct Measurement Model. Now the characteristic score Ch_{kl}^{ij} refers to the *marginal utility* conferred by whatever amount is possessed by the specimen under consideration. A score of 0.00 denotes zero marginal utility, 1.00 the marginal utility of the ideal specimen (with respect to that characteristic), and other real numbers the ratio of MU_k to MU_{k^o} where k^o is the ideal specimen.

For convenience, weights will be assigned so that they sum to 1.00 for each specimen. This assumption, coupled with the convention adopted for characteristic scores, implies that G_{k^o}, the quality of the ideal specimen, will equal 1.00.

For some purposes it may be helpful to normalize the quality score of a specimen, G_k^{ij}, by expressing it as a ratio to the mean quality for that product. Then, $\hat{G}_k^{ij}$, the normalized quality index would be

$$\hat{G}_k^{ij} = G_k^{ij}/\bar{G}^{ij} \qquad (2.0)$$

where

$\bar{G}^{ij}$ = the mean score for all specimens in the jth product group as assessed by the ith individual.

And, of course, we can utilize G_k^{ij}, the normalized quality index, along with the money price of a specimen, $P_k{}^j$, to obtain the P_k^{*ij}, which we encountered earlier

$$P_k^{*\ ij} = P_k{}^j / G_k{}^{ij} \tag{3.0}$$

Variation in P_k^{*ij} among the various specimens in a product class provides a convenient index to possible payoffs to consumer searches.

And, as we shall now show, P_k^{*ij} is exactly equivalent to $P_k{}^j / MU_k{}^{ij}$, or the ratio of price to marginal utility for that specimen.[15]

Quality and the Utility Function: Two Models

We turn first to the Direct Measurement Model and then to the Proportionality Model.

Direct Measurement Model. The proof (dropping the i and j superscripts as unnecessary here) that G_k is equal to marginal utility follows immediately from our assumptions:

a. As specified above, the characteristic score, Ch_{k1} measures the marginal utility conferred by characteristic number l.

b. We assume that the total increment to utility provided by specimen k (MU_k) is a weighted sum of the utility provided by each characteristic

$$U(k) = \alpha_1 Ch_{k1} + \ldots + \alpha_L Ch_{kL} \tag{4.1}$$

c. It is apparent that if the weights, W_l, are appropriately chosen to be equal to the α_l, the quality index $G_k = W_1 Ch_{k1} + \cdots + W_L Ch_{kL}$ is identical to the utility specified in (4.1).

The Proportionality Model. Here the proof is the same, but requires a somewhat stronger assumption concerning the utility provided by each class:

a. We once again need to assume that

$$U(k) = \alpha_1 Ch_{k1} + \ldots + \alpha_L Ch_{kL} \tag{4.1}$$

Given that assumption, the proof is again immediate.

b. Since in this model the characteristic score measures the quantity possessed rather than the utility provided, (4.1) now says that utility provided is directly proportional to the quantity possessed of each characteristic. That is, if we let $U(Ch_{kl})$ represent the amount of utility provided by characteristic l in specimen k, we are assuming that

---

[15] In this paper "marginal utility" refers to the utility summed over a discrete step, namely the increment resulting from going from zero to a single specimen of a product.

$$U(Ch_{kl}) = \alpha_l \cdot Ch_{kl} \qquad (4.2)$$

This assumption is not required for the Direct Measurement Model.

In the Direct Measurement Model it is assumed of course that each individual will make the judgment required.

The essential difference between the two models is that the Direct Measurement Model allows for declining marginal utility as more of a characteristic is found, or is thought to be found, in a particular specimen.

A property the two models share is the assumption of cardinality.

Knowledge and Quality

Quality assessments are knowledge-dependent in several respects. In the first place, the weights assigned to a characteristic will depend upon the knowledgeability of the assessor. For example, in an area where sanitation practices are poor, the assessor who understands bacterial theory is likely to assign greater importance (a larger weight) to cleanliness of food preparation in assessing the quality of restaurant meals than is an assessor who does not understand bacterial theory.

In the second place, the knowledgeability of the assessor is likely to affect the assignment of characteristic scores. In both the Direct Measurement Model and the Proportionality Model, characteristic scores are assigned with reference to "ideal" specimens. The assessor's perception of the "ideal" will depend upon his general knowledgeability. The assessor of the characteristic, automobile "performance," who is familiar with the performance of the Wankel motor, is likely to have a higher reference standard for "performance" than an assessor who is not. Hence, the base on which the characteristic score depends will differ between these two assessors.

Sometimes assessors may omit a characteristic which they "really" believe relevant. That is, if someone asked them — after a quality assessment had been completed — what weight they would have assigned to a particular omitted characteristic, they may answer with a nonzero value.[16] The effect of omitting a characteristic which "should" have been included is to produce errors in the quality score.

Finally, assessors may be unaware of the existence of particular

---

[16] Morris Kaplan, the late longtime Technical Director of Consumers Union, stated — on the basis of many episodes — that ordinary consumers identify fewer relevant characteristics than test engineers and, further, that, when prompted, acknowledge that they would accept "as their own" most of the missed characteristics. (Personal conversation with Morris Kaplan, August 12, 1971.)

brands, models, or sellers who are properly part of a given product/ market set. Such omissions would produce errors in estimates of parameters of quality over a given product/market set, e.g., estimates of variation in P^*.

Since the state of knowledge varies over time, operational use of quality measurements may require the use of a time subscript. A reading of *Consumer Reports* or the driving of a new car may change one's quality index for that model.

Quality: Objective or Subjective?

If my reading of the "message" of several seminars on "quality" is correct, our fraternity yearns for an *objective* measure of quality. Unfortunately, such cannot be: quality is intrinsically subjective.

To see why, let us assume provisionally that (1) the characteristic scores in equation 1.0, the definition of quality, are provided "objectively" by (say) Consumers Union, and that (2) these scores are accepted as correct by all consumers. Then, assuming the Proportionality Model, the only source of variation in quality assessments of identical specimens comes from the weights assigned by different individuals, the W_{j1}^{ij}, to the various characteristics.

Whence cometh these weights? They come from a time analysis a la Becker [3] of alternative utility-maximizing activities, which give rise to a derived demand for characteristics. The latter then lead to the planned purchase from a particular product set. Understandably, different individuals will prefer different activities, and this may lead to different preferences for characteristics, even within a product set.

All of which makes sense, as an example may make clear. Consider two individuals, A and B, both contemplating the purchase of an FM radio receiver. For convenience, let us assume that the product/market set of specimen is identical for both. We will further assume that the quality of these FM sets is a weighted average of but two characteristics, sensitivity and selectivity. Sensitivity denotes the ability of a receiver to pick up distant signals while selectivity refers to the capacity of a receiver to reproduce a signal without interference from other signals in adjacent bands. It makes sense and should come as no surprise that A, who lives at the very fringe of a metropolitan area should assign a heavy weight to sensitivity and hence high "quality" to receivers judged high with respect to sensitivity. By the same token, B who lives in the heart of the metropolitan area beset by many competing FM signals assigns a heavy weight to selectivity. Thus, their quality assessments are at once different and subjective.

But what of Consumers Union and its weights? Are they not "objective"? The answer is, "No, of course not!" CU's product testers, whose quality-scoring system closely corresponds to that proposed here, seek to estimate weights appropriate to an "average" user of a product. But this part of the process is unavoidably judgmental and subjective. The reason: the taste for characteristics comes only from the utility functions of individuals.[17]

Subjectivity can arise also from the *characteristic score* component of the quality measurement. Even if Consumers Union or other testing agencies can devise satisfactory objective tests of characteristics,[18] the individual is free to accept in whole, in part, or not at all CU's assessments. This freedom to choose for himself endows the characteristic score with subjectivity.

The discussion of characteristic scores above pertains only to the Proportionality Model. In the Direct Measurement Model, the individual is required to make an intrinsically subjective assessment of the rate at which marginal utility declines as the amount of a characteristic produced by a specimen increases. So, here, too, the objectivist is thwarted.

The only possible consolation for the objectivistic is the hedonic approach, which, in the view of some of its exponents, converts subjective notions of "quality" into a combination of objectively measurable or "rankable" traits.[19] The hedonist, using a statistically reproducible method, regresses time-series or cross-section data on a set of objective characteristics in order to ascertain the implicit prices of the characteristics. By summing these implicit prices, he obtains an estimate of the *average* quality of a given *variety* (but not a specimen). However, the objective measure of quality here exists only as a mean estimated over an entire product/market set.

Uniformity versus Nonuniformity in Quality Assessments

The formulation of quality proposed in this paper permits, but does not impose, nonuniformity in quality assessments. This is the reason

[17] Recognizing this essentially subjective element, many people argue—like a University of California colleague of mine—that Consumers Union should not publish quality ratings per se.

[18] As footnote 14 indicates, about 50 per cent to 75 per cent of subscribers to *Consumer Reports* reported that they had purchased "top-rated" models for a varied set of products. The remaining 25 per cent to 50 per cent of subscribers either were unable to follow *Consumer Reports'* ratings (due perhaps to the nonavailability of the top-rated model) or chose not to do so.

[19] Adelman and Griliches [1, page 539] claim the conversion of "subjective" notions of quality to something objective as a property of the hedonic approach. Using the "quality" of milk as an example, they assert: "Note that, in this process, the subjective notion of the 'quality' of a particular type of milk has been quantified by a specific combination of objectively measurable or rankable traits."

for including an "*i*" superscript in the formula for quality. Three reasons support this procedure. First, as argued above, knowledgeability affects quality assessments, and knowledgeability will probably differ among individuals. Second, as just argued, the weights attached to characteristics come from the utility function, and individuals' tastes for various characteristics may differ sufficiently to produce different quality assessments of identical specimens. Finally, even if these two reasons were not compelling, the spirit of consumer sovereignty would support the notion that individuals should be permitted to make different quality assessments.

The possibility of different assessments raises a most important empirical question: To what extent, in fact, do different individuals make different quality assessments over identical sets of specimens? We may recall that the student assessors cited at the outset of this paper felt that the quality assessments of other individuals of the identical set of specimens would be closely similar to their own. On the other hand, we have substantial evidence that many readers of *Consumer Reports* buy models other than those top-rated by *Consumer Reports*.[20] Some acting in this way may do so because their weights, or tastes, differ from those adopted by CU's testers.

Additivity

The definition of quality in equation 1.0 embodies additivity on the grounds that (1) additivity is intuitively attractive, and (2) a simpler formulation is preferable to a more complex one. Only after strong evidence is offered regarding the unacceptability of the simpler formulation should one move toward a more complex formulation.

VI. RELATED CONCEPTS: (1) CHARACTERISTICS

Some of the points made below have been hinted at earlier. Clarity, however, demands that they be dealt with explicitly, even at the cost of redundancy.

Characteristics As Services

Characteristics, repeating our earlier definition, are the "*services giving rise to utility.*" [21] But why should they be defined in terms of

---

[20] See footnote 18.

[21] One of the leading hedonists, Triplett, also opts for the definition of characteristics as services [32, pages 9–10].

Lancaster does not state whether characteristics are services or things. But an extensive example in which the characteristics of an automobile are analyzed deals mostly

services rather than the more objective factors—inputs—which "produce" them? There are several reasons.

First, it is the services, we believe, which consumers really want, not the means which produce them. They want the cool air and the comfort resulting from the operation of an air conditioner, not the air conditioning apparatus itself. Similarly, consumers want safety, not disc brakes per se.

Second, because (sometimes) many different inputs are required to produce a given service, the definition of characteristics as services will reduce the number of characteristics to be considered and thus render measurement easier. For example, a characteristic such as the "safety" of an automobile might have the following inputs (and more!): brakes (stopping distance, fade resistance, lack of "pull"), tires, interior layout (effect on crash survival), locks, emergency handling, layout of controls, visibility (location, size and reflection properties of glass areas). As we shall see a few pages hence, sixty-one or so inputs (or subcharacteristics) in a modern automobile reduce to eleven service characteristics. If individuals assign characteristic scores for the characteristic as a whole without separately evaluating each input or each subcomponent of a characteristic, then a reduction in the number of characteristics will render measurement easier.

A third reason for preferring to view characteristics as services is that the process of producing a desired service may be complex, marked by nonlinearities or perhaps multiplicative relationships. Under such circumstances it may be easier and more accurate to measure the output (the service rendered) than the inputs.

In some cases, there may exist a rather simple and dependable relationship between inputs and the service outputs. In such cases, it becomes a matter of convenience as to whether the assessor seeks to measure the characteristics directly, or by the inputs which produce them. The assessment of the quality of a mattress provides a convenient example. One assessor identified four "characteristics": (1) spring construction, (2) handles, (3) firmness and edge support, (4) surface conformity to body. It seems clear that "spring construction" was thought to be closely related to the service characteristic, "durability"; that "handles" were proxies for "portability"; that "firmness" and "surface conformity" were both viewed as components of "comfort."

It should be noted that the product-testing organizations such as

with characteristics which are services [21, page 170]. However, Lancaster is adamant in asserting that characteristics are objective and that, therefore, intrinsically subjective characteristics, such as beauty lie outside his domain of analysis [21, page 114].

Consumers Union frequently utilize the measurement of inputs as a proxy for service characteristics. But it should be remembered that their taste is necessarily different from that of the ordinary consumer. In order to protect the organization's reputation and financial integrity, they must confine themselves to products for which reproducible information provides an acceptable approximation to quality. Their reproducible information may include the results of product tests, or reports of experience (frequency of repair data, satisfaction with insurance settlements), or judgments (taste tests for beers or foods) from either panels of experts or from probability samples of a relevant population.

Characteristics Subjective, Nonuniversal

We will assume that the amount of a characteristic associated with a particular specimen is subjective and nonuniversal. By this, we mean that each individual will decide for himself, on the basis of whatever information he possesses, the extent to which a particular specimen possesses a given characteristic. This assumption does not preclude the possibility that for some characteristics of some specimens, objective evidence regarding the amount of the characteristic exists and is so compelling that it is universally accepted.

What we do argue is that objective data regarding characteristics are unusual and that for most characteristics of most products, individuals will not possess such objective evidence. Or, even if they do possess it, they may choose to accept it wholly, in part, or not at all.

Consumer Reports, with a current circulation of 2,100,000 and a maximum estimated audience of approximately ten million, is the most important producer and distributor of objective data on characteristics and quality.[22] Still, it reaches at most but one out of six families. And, in a year, it tests about 120 products.

The Optimal Level of Abstraction

A vexing problem in the measurement of characteristics is the determination of the optimal level of abstraction. Consider the performance of a soprano. Should we consider "beauty" as the characteristic? Or, assuming that beauty in a vocal performance has as its components such things as "color" and "range," should we consider *each compo-*

[22] *Consumer Research Magazine* also provides objective data on a wide variety of products. Its circulation is approximately 100,000. Other publications such as *Motor Trend* (circulation of 610,000), *Car and Driver* (circulation of 619,000), and *U.S. Camera* distribute both subjective and objective information to specialized audiences.

nent of "beauty" as a separate characteristic? My recommendation is that each assessor use that level of abstraction or aggregation at which he feels he can make the most accurate judgment, overall. My guess would be that more knowledgeable assessors would be aware of more components and would feel that greater accuracy would be achieved by judging each component separately and then combining assessments on the various components.

Negative Characteristics

Some characteristics, which we denote as *negative characteristics,* are undesirable. Ugliness, which goes well beyond the absence of beauty, would be such a characteristic. In the quality formula, we would attach to such a negative characteristic a negative weight, but a positive characteristic score.

The Characteristics of an Automobile

Perhaps nothing communicates as effectively as a concrete example. In this spirit, an illustrative set of service characteristics for an automobile are presented in Table 2. Several comments are in order.

Even for a good as complex as an automobile, the number of characteristics is "small" enough to be easily manageable. However, the example does not include the characteristics of the seller (reliability, convenience, etc.) although our theory calls for this. As a rough guess, seller characteristics might double the number of characteristics to be dealt with.

The information required to score each subcomponent separately is considerable. Little wonder that so many better-educated consumers turn to *Consumer Reports!* Given these considerable information requirements, it is only realistic to expect that most consumers will assess quality in a very rough, nonquantitative way.

Table 2 represents one person's supposedly exhaustive set of characteristics for an auto. It seems highly likely that the reader might be inclined to partition the characteristic space differently: to use different names, or assign different components to the same major component. Additionally, it seems likely that the reader may conceive of major characteristics or components which he feels relevant, but which were omitted from this set and hence given an implicit weight of zero. In practice, the partitioning of the characteristic space by one individual will necessarily be arbitrary and omissions of relevant characteristics will be inevitable.

The clear implication is that most consumers do not have access to

TABLE 2

The Service Characteristics of an Automobile:
A Tentative Taxonomy [a]

Characteristic	Characteristic Component or Input
1. Economy-Durability [b]	Operating Costs: Gas-oil use Repairs — Frequency and average bill (parts and labor) Parts cost and accessibility Geographic access to servicing Insurance costs Capital Costs: Depreciation — Expected loss of market value due to obsolescence Wear Deterioration due solely to passage of time (not use) Warranty Security against theft Time off the road for repairs
2. Comfort	Temperature control and ventilation (heating, air conditioning) Noise levels Ride Space (legroom, etc.) Seating: Comfort (padding, shape, angle, adjustability) Height
3. Performance	Maneuverability (size) On the road versus local Acceleration: From stop Passing Control Shifting Handling Speed

TABLE 2 (continued)

Characteristic	Characteristic Component or Input
4. Convenience	Steering (ease and precision)
	Ease of entry and exit
	Access to controls
	Storage:
	Baggage
	Glove compartment
	Ease of cleaning
	Ease of starting
	Application of power shifting
	Opening and closing of windows (manual versus electrical operation)
	Ease of parking:
	Steering
	Size
5. Safety	Collision absorption
	Visibility:
	Forward
	Side
	Backward (rear window defogger)
	Day/night
	Brakes:
	Stopping
	Fade resistance
	Emergency characteristics
	Tires
	Layout – effect on crash survival
	Locks
	Emergency handling
	Layout of controls
	Structural strength and rigidity
	Size
6. Aesthetics	Lines
	Color
	Finish
7. Status	Technical virtuosity
	Opulence
	Scarcity
8. Carrying Capacity: People	Number
	Effect on handling characteristics (an interaction)

(continued)

TABLE 2 (concluded)

Characteristic	Characteristic Component or Input
9. Carrying Capacity: Things	Usable cubic footage
	Flexibility for carrying odd shapes
	Durability of carrying surfaces
10. Pollution Effect	Noise
	Exhaust fumes

[a] Compare this set of characteristics with those used by Lancaster [21, page 106] in an illustrative computation of his technical efficiency approach: accommodation (size and comfort of seating, etc.), ride qualities, handling and steering, engine (quietness and performance), brakes, frequency of repair record (based on model of previous year), manufacturer's suggested retail price. Lancaster abstracted his characteristics from *Consumer Reports*.

[b] From a more sophisticated view, the durability of a specimen might be more carefully defined as "the weighted average of the rate at which characteristic scores do *not* decline over time" or, equivalently, as "the subjectively weighted average of quality over time." That is, if a specimen continued to provide service characteristics at the initial rate, it would be perfectly durable. By this interpretation each characteristic would have its own weight which might or might not have a time subscript. Each characteristic score — see equation 1 — would have its own time subscript.

In the author's view, this more sophisticated definition is too complex to be operational. For this reason, economy-durability is defined more judgmentally, as above.

objective data on characteristics even if they desired it. They must perforce make subjective judgments regarding the extent to which specimens possess a given characteristic. Until empirical research suggests otherwise, it would be fatuous to *assume* that characteristics are objective and uniform.[23]

VII. RELATED CONCEPTS: (2) PRODUCT

It may be helpful to repeat background assumptions made earlier. We assumed that the consumer has already undertaken a personal "survey" of the activities in which he might engage, and that this "survey" has resulted in a commitment to purchase some specimen in a given product class, subject to a maximum outlay. The quality assessment will help determine *which specimen* to purchase, *not whether to spend* on this product category.

[23] Nonetheless, this is the assumption adopted by Lancaster in his technical efficiency approach. Lancaster declares [21, page 114]: "It is essential that the characteristics be an objective, universal property of the good (or activity)." This assumption was criticized by John S. Chipman [4, page 46] who asserted "that this assumption is a postulate and not a consequence of Lancaster's scheme."

The product class consists of *all* of the goods from which the consumer might choose for a particular purchase. Estimates of $P*$ (the quality-deflated price) will be made over this entire population or, more likely, a sample which is representative of this population. Realistically, the purchasing consumer is likely to be aware of and to purchase from only a small subset of this population.

The concept of *product* is needed to decide which specimens are appropriately included in the population for which quality evaluations and comparisons of $P*$ are to be made.

We define a *product* as "the set of goods which, assuming perfect information regarding their characteristics and money prices, would in the consumer's judgment serve the same general purpose for some maximum outlay." Again, clarifying comments are in order.

This concept is personal and subjective. Each individual must decide for himself which specimens are sufficiently similar to be seriously considered for possible purchase.

The perfect-information assumption enables us – the economist or the empirical researcher – to identify *all* specimens which are *potentially* relevant to this consumer's purchase decision, even though, realistically, this consumer may remain unaware of some of them.

Presumably, different specimens within a product class would possess rather similar characteristics.

The maximum-outlay specification effectively keeps the consumer from possibly violating a self-imposed budget restraint which he has adopted at an earlier stage of the purchase process. For example, on grounds of size, maneuverability, and other characteristics, a Mercedes sedan might qualify as a "compact sedan." For some consumers, however, the $7,000 plus price of the Mercedes would exceed their budget constraint and thus effectively purge the Mercedes from the "compact sedan" product group.[24]

In practice, it would appear that the delineation of product classes has posed few problems. None of the thirty or more student investigators undertaking quality assessments in 1970 reported any difficulty in determining which specimens were appropriately included, and which were appropriately excluded, from the relevant product classes.

---

[24] It is interesting to see how the related literature deals with the concept of "product." Lancaster [19, 21] does not define a concept of "product."

Not surprisingly, in the hedonic literature, the *product* is market determined. Triplett places different varieties in the same product class if (1) they share the same set of characteristics, and (2) the implicit characteristics prices are the same [31, page 14].

VIII. RELATED CONCEPTS: (3) MARKET [25]

While the concept of *product* enables us to say *which specimens* are appropriately included in the evaluation/comparison class, a concept of *market* is needed to say *which sellers* and *which buyers* are appropriately included.

In terms of its functioning, a *market* may be defined as "the area within which the price of a commodity tends to uniformity, allowance being made for transportation costs" [30, page 85]. Substitute "quality" for "transportation" and acknowledge that prices must be adjusted for quality, and we have a *functional* definition which is suitable for our purposes.

Our problem is to operationalize the above conception by developing a further definition which enables us to decide which sellers and which buyers are appropriately included in the same "market."

What we need is the population of sellers from whom a particular consumer *might* have purchased, not the set which he actually considered. In seeking to identify the "from-whom-might-buy" population, we assume that our sample consumer possessed perfect information regarding the probability distribution of the net payoff, i.e., the gross payoff less the cost of the search. We assume further that he followed the marginal rule: "Undertake additional searches as long as the expected gross payoff from a given search exceeds the expected cost of that search." Any seller "discovered" by an infinite number of repetitions of this rational search process would be appropriately included in the market. This procedure gives us the set of sellers in the market defined for a particular consumer.

Now we seek to identify the buyers appropriately included in this market. Any consumer who, by applying the same marginal search rule, might have "discovered" *any* of the above-listed set of sellers would be counted in the same "market."

Summing up, a *market* may be operationally defined as "the set of sellers which might be 'discovered' by Consumer A in applying the rational search rule *plus* the set of buyers who, pursuing the same rule, might have purchased from A's set of sellers. In identifying relevant sellers and buyers, it is assumed that all consumers possessed perfect information regarding the probability distribution of net payoffs to search."

[25] Neither the hedonists nor Lancaster define a *market*. In practice, however, the hedonic approach has been applied to removing quality effects from price indexes for entire economies. In effect, therefore, means are estimated over the aggregate of all local markets.

It would have been most gratifying to report that we succeeded in specifying an acceptable set of search procedures which readily identified the particular sellers and buyers to be included in a market.

Unhappily, such was not the case. Despite much racking of brains and consulting of colleagues, we were unable to specify an acceptable set of search procedures beyond the general statement of the marginal rule.

Ironically, as in the case of the concept *product,* practice has proved easier than theory. Student investigators reported no problems in determining which sellers should be included or excluded from a particular market. And they were strongly confident that other investigators would decide as they had.

Some "qualitative" observations may prove useful. Like the concept of product, this concept, too, is personal and subjective. However, it is our guess that the set of sellers and buyers assigned to the same market by different, but similarly situated, consumers will turn out to be highly similar.

As an example of the market concept, it may be useful to examine the illustrative market for sofa beds cited at the beginning of the paper. The sellers included four retail outlets in Saint Paul (where the investigator lives): the dominant department store, a local mail-order outlet for a national chain, a local discount-type store, a local "high-class" home furnishings store. Since each establishment or branch has the authority to modify prices and choose the brand/models it offers, it is the establishment or branch's customers who make up the buyer side of the market. In this case, this outlet of the dominant department store may attract customers from several hundred miles away. Thus, the consumer side of this market would be more geographically dispersed than the seller side. Note, however, that the market would not include *all* people within a given radius of Saint Paul. Instead, it includes only those who might actually have purchased a sofa bed from the four retail outlets *while following the marginal rule.*

A final observation concerns the application of the search rule. One must differentiate between purchases in which the product in question bears the full marginal cost of the search versus a purchase which rides piggyback on some other "more important" purchase(s). An example of a full marginal-cost-bearing purchase might be the toothpaste purchased by someone who had just arrived at a hotel or motel late in the evening, toothpasteless. By contrast, a partial-marginal-cost purchase would occur when a person engaged in a major shopping trip added toothpaste to his shopping list. Which of these situations yielded the larger "market" (more sellers) would depend upon the number and geographic clustering of sellers relative to the location of the consumer for whom the market is defined.

IX. AN AGENDA FOR FUTURE RESEARCH

The concepts proposed in this paper were formulated explicitly with an eye to future empirical measurement. Set forth below are my priorities regarding alternative research projects which might stem from the conceptual framework proposed in this paper. This listing is made without testing the reader's patience by specifying how the proposed research might be carried out.

My first-priority candidate would be a large number of "demonstration" measurements, seeking to assess the quality of widely variegated products. The purpose would be to demonstrate the feasibility of measuring quality along the lines proposed here and to ferret out problems associated with it. Any such measurements should include follow-up interviews with the quality assessors to ensure that they understood the relevant concepts and that the measurements taken conformed to the model specified.

In case a quality assessor purchased a specimen of the product under investigation, one would want to know whether he purchased a specimen on the efficiency frontier. An off-frontier choice would seem to call for an explanation.

Of almost equal importance would be research designed to ascertain the extent to which quality assessments of an identical set of specimens are "uniform." In its strongest form, "uniformity" of quality assessments would call for the designation of identically sited frontiers by different assessors. Next strongest (but still highly satisfactory) would be the designation of efficiency frontiers consisting of identical specimens in the same left-to-right sequence, but with different widths. Less pleasing, but still interesting, would be an efficiency frontier consisting of the same set of specimens, but containing some reversals of order.

Even if different individuals differ in their quality assessments, it would still be interesting and useful to obtain some measure of the extent of variation of prices from one individual's frontier.

A fallback position on the uniformity-of-assessment front might center on the distinction between "primarily objective" and "primarily subjective" characteristics. *Objective* characteristics would be those which are subject to reproducible tests, e.g., the durability of a sofa bed. Objective characteristics might also include characteristics for which judgments by panels result in "little" variance. Subjective characteristics would include all others. In the sofa bed example, the "aesthetic" aspects of a sofa bed might represent a subjective characteristic. The objective of this fallback research would be to ascertain through correlation techniques the extent (if any) to which reproducible measurements of objective characteristics dominate overall quality judgments. (Research in this direction was suggested to me by Richard Emmerson of the University of California, San Diego.)

Two other potential projects depend upon a finding of considerable uniformity in the making of quality assessments. *If* extensive research shows a considerable degree of uniformity in quality assessments for informed consumers, then these two tasks assume relevance: (1) an attempt to assess the "efficiency" of consumption of low-income versus high-income households; (2) the development of market demand/supply relationships taking account of quality.

Embodied in the first is the notion that low-income households, being less amply endowed – both genetically and culturally – on the average, may, in purchasing, use their income less effectively than high-income households. More specifically, it might be hypothesized that low-income households while spending in a given product category may obtain less quality per dollar of outlay. If such a finding should be confirmed, it would suggest that current data on the distribution of money income understate the "true" degree of inequality.

REFERENCES

[1] Adelman, Irma, and Griliches, Zvi. "On an Index of Quality Change." *Journal of the American Statistical Association* 56 (September 1961): 535–548.

[2] Akerlof, George A. "The Market for Lemons: Quality, Uncertainty, and the Market Mechanism." *Quarterly Journal of Economics* 84 (August 1970): 488–500.

[3] Becker, Gary S. "A Theory of the Allocation of Time." *Economic Journal* 75 (September 1965): 493–516.

[4] Chipman, John S. "Discussion of Lancaster's 'Change and Innovation in the Technology of Consumption.'" *American Economic Review* 56 (May 1966): 45–49.

[5] Chamberlin, Edward H. "The Product as an Economic Variable." *Quarterly Journal of Economics* 67 (February 1953): 1–29.

[6] ———. *The Theory of Monopolistic Competition*. Cambridge: Harvard University Press, 1933.

[7] Court, A. T. "Hedonic Price Indexes with Automotive Examples." In *The Dynamics of Automobile Demand*. New York: General Motors Corporation, 1939, pages 99–117.

[8] Dawes, Robyn M.; Coombs, Clyde H.; and Tversky, Amos. *Mathematical Psychology: An Elementary Introduction*. Englewood Cliffs, N.J.: Prentice-Hall, 1970.

560 *Measurement and Issues in Consumption Analysis*

[9] Dhrymes, Phoebus J. "Price and Quality Changes, in Consumer Capital Goods: An Empirical Study." In Zvi Griliches, editor, *Prices Indexes and Quality Change.* Cambridge: Harvard University Press, 1971, pages 88–175.

[10] Dorfman, Robert, and Steiner, Peter O. "Optimal Advertising and Optimal Quality." *American Economic Review* 44 (December 1954): 826–836.

[11] Fisher, Franklin M., and Shell, Karl. "Taste and Quality Change in the Pure Theory of the True Cost-of-Living Index." In Zvi Griliches, editor, *Price Indexes and Quality Change.* Cambridge: Harvard University Press, 1971, pages 16–54.

[12] Gabor, André, and Granger, C. W. J. "Price as an Indicator of Quality: Report on an Enquiry." *Economica* 33 (February 1966): 43–70.

[13] Georgescu-Roegen, Nicholas. *Entropy as an Economic Process,* Cambridge: Harvard University Press, 1971.

[14] Griliches, Zvi (ed.). *Price Indexes and Quality Change,* Cambridge: Harvard University Press, 1971.

[15] Henderson, James M., and Quandt, Richard E. *Microeconomic Theory: A Mathematical Approach,* 2nd ed., New York: McGraw-Hill, 1971.

[16] Hirshleifer, Jack. "Where Are We in the Theory of Information?" *American Economic Review* 63 (May 1973): 31–39.

[17] Jacoby, John: Olson. Jerry C.; and Haddock, Rafael A. "Price, Brand Name, and Product Composition Characteristics as Determinants of Perceived Quality." *Journal of Applied Psychology* 55 (December 1971): 570–579.

[18] Krantz, David H. "Measurement Structures and Psychological Laws." *Science* 175 (March 31, 1972): 1427–1435.

[19] Lancaster, Kelvin J. "A New Approach to Consumer Theory." *Journal of Political Economy* 74 (April 1966): 132–157.

[20] ———. "Change and Innovation in the Technology of Consumption." *American Economic Review* 56 (May 1966): 14–23.

[21] ———. *Consumer Demand,* New York: Columbia University Press, 1971.

[22] Maynes, E. Scott. "Consumerism: Origins and Research Implications." In Eleanor Sheldon, editor, *Understanding Family Behavior.* Philadelphia: J. B. Lippincott, 1973, pages 270–294.

[23] ———. *Decision-Making for Consumers.* New York: Macmillan, 1976.

[24] ———. "The Power of the Consumer." In Burkhard Strümpel, James N. Morgan, and Ernest Zahn, editors, *Human Behavior in Economic Affairs,* Essays in Honor of George Katona. Amsterdam: Elsevier, 1972, pages 399–420.

[25] Morris, Ruby Turner, and Bronson, Claire Sekulski. "The Chaos of Competition Indicated by Consumer Reports." *Journal of Marketing* 33 (July 1969): 26–34.

[26] Samuelson, Paul A. *Economics.* 9th ed. New York: McGraw-Hill, 1973.

[27] Scitovsky, Tibor. "Consequences of Judging Quality by Price." *Review of Economic Studies* 12 (1944–1945): 100–105.

[28] Stigler, George J. "The Development of Utility Theory, I." *Journal of Political Economy* 58 (August 1950): 95–113.

[29] ———. "The Economics of Information." *Journal of Political Economy* 69 (June 1961): 213–225.

[30] ———. *The Theory of Price.* 3rd ed. New York: Macmillan, 1966.

[31] Theil, Henri. "Qualities, Prices and Budget Enquiries." *Review of Economic Studies* 19 (1951–1952): 129–147.

[32] Triplett, Jack E. *The Theory of Hedonic Quality Measurement and Its Use in Price Indexes.* Bureau of Labor Statistics, Staff Paper 6. Washington, D.C.: Government Printing Office, 1971.

Comments on "The Concept and Measurement of Product Quality"

F. THOMAS JUSTER

NATIONAL BUREAU OF ECONOMIC RESEARCH
AND UNIVERSITY OF MICHIGAN

SUMMARY OF THE MODEL

IN this paper, Maynes essentially argues the case for a cardinal scale of overall quality measurements, designed to achieve these objectives:

1. to measure the informational effectiveness of markets;
2. to measure the payoff to search; and
3. to create a building block for demand theory.

The cardinal measurement of quality is derived from essentially ad hoc judgments of individuals, using a fixed weighting scheme to determine the relative importance of product characteristics and individual consumer judgments about the extent to which different products embody specified characteristics. Quality scores for characteristics are then combined into an index, defined as ranging between 0 and 1. Finally, the quality scores are used to estimate deflated or quality-adjusted prices.

The basic philosophy behind Maynes's concern with quality measurement and with the construction of quality indexes is an essentially normative presumption that markets function very imperfectly, and that development of quantitative information on quality would permit consumers to make different choices that would come closer to optimizing their welfare, given the budget constraint. But to prove that case, it is necessary to show that the observed variation in money prices cannot be attributed to variation in quality, or alternatively, that there is significant variation across products in quality-adjusted prices. That is, in order to demonstrate that quality measurement is important, it is essential to show that existing market decisions reflect significant imperfections resulting from lack of knowledge about quality.

The alternative model of consumer markets, which is widely accepted by economists, is, of course, that differences in prices for functionally comparable products at a single point in time simply reflect differences in quality as perceived by buyers. Hence, we usually proceed to use price differences in cross section to measure changes in average quality over time, as in the hedonic price index literature.

To me, there seem to be two basic flaws in the measurements that Maynes provides, and in the inherent structure of the way he proposes to go about inquiring whether markets function with serious imperfections. Suppose that, as the data in his Table 1 show, there is a significant positive association between the quality rankings and the money prices. Then, whether the quality-adjusted prices show a significant amount of variation across products or only small random variation will depend largely on the scaling used to measure quality. Taking the extreme case, suppose that the rank correlation between price and quality were perfect. Then, there must be some way of scaling the quality variable so that the observed variation across products would be zero, and any other way of scaling would provide either a positive or negative association between the original money prices and the quality-adjusted prices.

If price and quality scores are not perfectly correlated, then no utility transformation of the quality scale will provide the result that quality-adjusted prices are equal across different specimens. Instead, it must be true that some consumers are buying less quality than they could get at the same price, or more generally, paying a higher price for less quality. That provides prima facie evidence of imperfect functioning of markets and suggests that gains in social welfare would accrue as a result of an index of product quality.

However, even a less than perfect ranked correlation between price and quality indexes cannot be interpreted as necessarily reflecting market imperfections if one assumes that the relative importance (weights) of certain characteristics vary across households. In terms of invariance among households it is far more plausible to suppose that judgments about the quantitative differences among products in quality or characteristic dimensions is invariant among households than to suppose that the relative importance attached to certain characteristics is also invariant. As Maynes himself points out, there are solid reasons for supposing that the circumstances of particular individuals (location, age) are very likely to result in differential importance for particular product characteristics and, hence, in a weighting scheme which is not universally applicable to all groups of individuals or households. For example, relatively high-income households are quite apt to place quite heavy weight on product characteristics which minimize shopping time and provide insurance against malfunction, rapid and convenient delivery and/or installation, and so on. Specimens which are relatively high priced because they include substantial components of these types of sellers' services would not, in Maynes's scheme, show up with a higher quality rating than a specimen with more of the desirable product characteristics but very little desirable seller characteristics. And in that case, the rank correlation between price and quality would be far from perfect.

Unless one is willing to make strong assumptions about the cardinality of characteristic scores (or utility derived from characteristics), and about invariance among the population in weights assigned to characteristics and in the assessment of characteristic scores, the model in Maynes's paper will not have any empirically verifiable content. The paper actually contains two models: one described as the Direct Measurement Model, the other described as the Proportionality Model. The only difference between them is that the Proportionality Model says that quality is proportional to the weighted quantity of characteristics of different specimens, while the Direct Measurement Model says that quality is proportional to the weighted sum of the utilities conveyed by these same quantities of characteristics. The Proportionality Model, being more objective, is less subject to differences in individual judgments about the value of additional units of a given quality characteristic. For example, the Proportionality Model might have as an ingredient the horsepower of automobiles – or perhaps more appropriately, the time it takes to accelerate to a given speed during a fixed time span. However, the Direct Measurement Model would require consumers to judge the gain in utility from having more acceleration, not just the objective facts of differences in acceleration among vehicles. While it is no doubt true that proportional differences in a characteristic like acceleration do not provide proportional differences in utility, it is also true that there must be substantial differences among people in the relative importance ascribed to acceleration – the middle-aged shopper is not likely to value that characteristic very highly, whereas the teen-age hot rodder might regard it as the dominant characteristic of automobile quality. There seems to be no solution to this problem and, hence, as Maynes himself recognizes, no uniform solution to the quality measurement problem.

Despite these difficulties, Maynes argues that it is useful and important to construct comprehensive quality indexes, and moreover, that they can be constructed via weighting with marginal utilities rather than by quantities of different characteristics. However, on the basis of the evidence and argument presented in his paper, I am not persuaded that there is a great deal to be gained from pursuing the work of producing and refining a broad-gauge index of average product quality.

SOME SPECIFIC COMMENTS AND QUIBBLES

1. In the data shown in Table 1, Maynes notes that the range of quality-deflated prices is about as large as in original prices. However, the rank correlation between money price and quality is significantly positive, and the coefficient of variation in quality-adjusted prices is less than that in original prices. If one clear outlier is ignored, the coefficient of variation is cut by more than a third.

2. In the weighting schemes presented for both product and seller characteristics, the inherently subjective nature of the characteristics is their dominant characteristic. For product characteristics, aesthetics gets half the weight. In seller characteristics, sensitivity and pleasantness gets a third of the weight, while convenience gets another quarter. No weight is apparently given to such significant dimensions of seller characteristics as the range of models available for comparison; the time it takes to be served; whether or not delivery is available, and if so, at what cost; how long it takes to obtain delivery for a purchase; and so on. Presumably some of these characteristics are buried in the convenience terms, but that is not clear from the discussion.

3. The importance of Maynes's cardinal measurement assumption should be underlined — ordinal ranking will not suffice for his purposes. Only if all consumers assess characteristic quantities as the same across all products, have identical marginal utility functions for characteristics, possess perfect knowledge of market alternatives, and have uniform weights for all characteristics will it be true that the variations in p^* will be zero. While one can easily conceive of uniform judgments about the relative importance of various quality dimensions or about the marginal utility of increased amounts of characteristics, a consumer with a low wage rate and consequently a low value of search and shopping time is not going to place a high premium on retail establishments which minimize both, but at substantial cost. Nor does it seem plausible that aesthetics will receive the same relative weight as durability and serviceability for consumers with different levels of income.

4. A related point is the meaning of the end points on the Maynes quality scale. Is there really a zero point where the characteristic has

zero quantity or zero utility? Or a unity point where the characteristic reaches a limit that cannot be exceeded?

If not, and if the absolute *differences* in the observed quality scale are more accurate than the levels or the proportional differences, the observed results could be reversed: in the data, the maximum and minimum quality observations are in a 2:1 ratio on the present scale if seller characteristics are ignored, and on a 3:2 ratio if seller characteristics are included. But the price range has a maximum to minimum ratio of 3:1, hence one obtains a substantial range of quality-adjusted prices. But adding or subtracting a constant from the quality scale is capable of reducing the variation in p^* so long as there is a positive rank correlation between price and quality.

5. Re: market functioning and knowledge. Efficient functioning doesn't depend on complete knowledge for all units: it requires only sufficient knowledge to make inferior products unprofitable.

6. Re: other forms of empirical evidence that could be used. Suppose that buyers were shown to have typically visited x outlets in the process of acquiring a given product, or to shop typically at y different outlets for purchases of sundries? Would that not mean that any observed differences in p^* are more likely due to differences in judgments about quantitative characteristics or differences in the weights given to characteristics rather than to lack of knowledge about alternatives? In short, what does the empirical evidence look like regarding actual consumer search and experimentation?

7. Re: structure. Is additivity of characteristic scores plausible a priori? I submit not, since there must be threshold effects of essential characteristics without which large amounts of other characteristics are useless: a well-designed piece of furniture that won't last more than a month under normal usage isn't worth anything, whereas a well-designed article that has better durability characteristics may be worth a great deal.

8. Re: research strategy using the quality scale. How are quality characteristics correlated across commodities? If the correlations are high enough and positive, the whole measurement problem becomes enormously simplified. Maynes presents no data here, and does not even discuss the problem.

As a way of determining whether the notion of aggregate quality measurement is meaningful, why not test it by application to areas where one expects differences in the informational effectiveness of markets a priori? For example, there may be a lot or a little informational effectiveness *generally,* but there should be less than average where: (a) the market area has a high degree of mobility among consumer units, and word-of-mouth judgments are therefore less important. (b) the market area has a relatively large fraction of poorly educated consumers, whose ability to process information is on the average less than that of consumers in other market areas. In these situations, the variance in quality-adjusted P should be higher than average.

An alternative strategy which would reach one of Maynes's objectives—increasing the informational effectiveness of markets—although it would not contribute to either theoretical developments or to measuring the payoff to search—would be to concentrate on the development of a better information system by which consumers could assess relevant data as an input into rationalizing purchase decisions and, indirectly, improving the functioning of markets. As I see it, the basic difficulty with existing consumer information systems is that, ordinarily, they are not relevant to the decisions that consumers actually have to make. To the extent that information about product characteristics and performance is available, it is subject to a substantial time lag between the time the data are collected and the time they can be used. Such data are quite apt to be product- and area-specific and of limited relevance to many potential users, and they are only available in a form which entails going through substantial amounts of nonessential information in order to find out what one would like to know.

CONCLUDING COMMENTS

Although the general tenor of most of these comments is critical of the notion that quality change can be measured in an effective way using the techniques described by Maynes, it should be noted that the presence of formidable conceptual difficulties does not necessarily warrant the conclusion that the procedures and measurements lack economic or social utility. It is one thing to argue, as I have above, that differences in the characteristic weights among the population make it difficult or perhaps impossible to draw conclusions about the efficient functioning of markets from the sort of data that Maynes has provided, and another to say that these differences are quantitatively important enough to make the information useless for the purpose of improving consumers' decision making. Most attempts to measure conceptually complex phenomena can be subject to the same type of critical comment, but it is not until someone has attempted to make the measurements, and then tried to use them, that the issue can be fully resolved. Hence, although my own judgment is that aggregate measures of product quality along the lines described by Maynes will not really prove to be useful, it should be recognized that judgments of this sort are apt to be biased on the conservative side, and that there is some detectable proportion of cases in which they will prove to be wrong.

Comments on "The Concept and Measurement of Product Quality"

JACK E. TRIPLETT

BUREAU OF LABOR STATISTICS *

MAYNES commends his proposal for measuring quality for a number of purposes and asserts that it is different from alternative procedures, such as the hedonic method. His argument for the usefulness of his proposal for economic analysis consists merely of a recitation of problem areas where *some* way of dealing with the quality problem is needed; moreover, he makes no attempt to show how his proposal is related to, or exactly how it differs from, Lancaster's "New Theory of Demand," on the one hand, and the hedonic technique on the other.

I intend to compare Maynes and the alternatives, and will in the process also consider the usefulness — to economists — of his proposal. I agree fully with Juster's points, which deal mainly with the question of whether Maynes's proposals are likely to be of use for constructing better consumer information systems, and will therefore ignore that aspect of Maynes's paper.

Maynes assumes that "quality" is a concept that is inherently measurable, so that a suitable approach will yield a *scalar, nonmonetary* measure of quality. He also asserts that his measure is cardinal.

My own view of "quality" — and this view is explicitly advanced as the concept that underlies the hedonic method — is that quality itself is not a measurable concept, in the sense of obtaining a *scalar, non-*

---

* The views expressed are those of the author and do not represent an official position of the Bureau of Labor Statistics.

monetary quality indicator. Under this view (which I will henceforth refer to as the "hedonic" viewpoint), when we use the word *quality*, what we really are doing is making a kind of shorthand reference to the several quantities in a *vector* of characteristics. Under the hedonic view, there is no measure of quality, as such, because there is no way to combine directly the various elements of the characteristics vector — the problem is exactly analogous to adding apples and oranges. However, provided we can find an appropriate (implicit) price for each of the characteristics, it is possible to obtain a measure of the *value* of the vector, by valuing the quantity of each characteristic by its implicit price, and then combining the results (the most natural way is simply to add them up).

To reiterate the distinction in another form, under Maynes's view there is, in principle, a measure of quality comparable to the quantity measures which we are accustomed to use in measuring inputs and outputs — a scalar measure whose formation requires no monetary valuation. Under the hedonic view, a measure of "quality" can only be obtained by a process comparable to the construction of GNP — we can combine the apples and oranges (characteristics) into an aggregate called "fruit" (quality) only by valuing quantities of the individual fruits (characteristics) by market prices. We may speak of the resulting aggregate (be it "fruit," real GNP, or quality) *as if* it were a physical measure, and we often do so; but this should not disguise the fact that it has properties which are different from the properties of a purely physical measure of quantity.

Maynes's view and the hedonic view of the economic concept of "quality" are two very different ways of looking at the matter. It is of no value to argue which one is a better or more accurate perception of reality — possibly neither is very good.

But there is a straightforward answer to Maynes's plaint that those of us who have been working within the hedonic framework have failed to put forth a concept of measurable quality along the lines he proposes: for purposes of economic analysis and measurement, a scalar notion of measurable quality simply is not necessary. Even if we conceded that quality is intrinsically representable as a scalar, and even if we believed that Maynes has found the tool for measuring it (which I do not believe), we would have to find a way to attach a value to the quality index anyway. What we require — and, really, *all* we require — is a measure of the *value* of quality, and that, in the hedonic view, is feasible *without* a scalar quality index.

Moreover, the measurable quality view has some built-in limitations that are avoided by the approach inherent in the hedonic or characteristics analysis. One of these is the tastes problem.

Consider two individuals (I and II) who are asked to choose between two different varieties (call them A and B) of a product which has only two characteristics (*r* and *s*). Suppose further that the proportions of characteristics *r* and *s* in variety A are different from the combination found in variety B, though both A and B sell at the same price, and that individual I prefers A to B, while individual II prefers B to A.

Maynes explicitly states that under his proposal, A is judged higher quality by I's assessment, but by II's, variety B is higher quality than variety A. Hence, nothing can be said, unless interpersonal comparisons can be made. Differences of taste of this kind make consistent quality measurement impossible under his system, and, moreover, no analysis of the situation can be carried out. This is a serious defect for economic uses, for the situation he describes must be regarded as an empirically pervasive one.

In contrast, the hedonic view does not require that tastes be anywhere near so uniform across consumers. Under the hedonic way of looking at quality, the situation described above could result from the preferences mapped in Figure 1. Given the relative implicit prices of *r* and *s*, and their respective indifference curves (I and II), individuals I and II locate at points A and B, which points correspond to the proportions of characteristics *r* and *s* contained in varieties A and B. There is nothing particularly surprising or perplexing about the situation diagramed. Budget allocations for goods and services as conventionally defined are frequently found to differ, and pose no massive problems for the analysis of consumer behavior. No greater problems are posed when the same thing occurs with respect to budget allocations for characteristics.

I would certainly agree that if we *have* to confront the issue of taste differences, little is really gained by evading the question. But that does not alter my preference for systems — when the choice presents itself — in which taste differences play a lesser, rather than a larger, role. Under the hedonic view, taste differences present major difficulties only for a small number of situations (for example, if individual I were to regard characteristic *r* as desirable, while II would pay to get rid of it).

I turn now to the question of whether Maynes is doing hedonics (or Lancastrian analysis) by another name. I think not, but a clear resolution of the question is impeded by the lack of precision in Maynes's specification.

FIGURE 1

Budget Allocations in a Goods World and in a Characteristics World

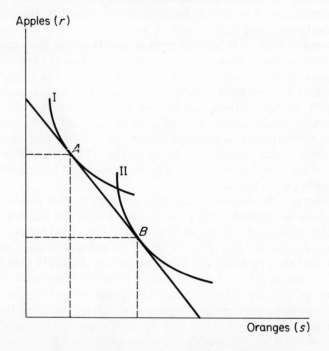

Maynes's quality definition is set forth in his equation 1.0, on p. 542. This can be written (dropping the superscripts)

$$G_k = \frac{\sum_l (w_l \cdot ch_{kl})}{\sum_l w_l}$$

where G_k is the quality of variety k of some product, w_l is the weight assigned to characteristic l (the weights "for convenience" sum to unity), and ch_{kl} is the "characteristic score assigned to the lth characteristic of the kth specimen" (Maynes, p. 543). Interpretation of what is meant by these weights and by the term "characteristics scores" is greatly hampered by persistent ambiguity in Maynes's text.

Maynes gives two specifications (pp. 543–544) for the Ch's: (a) the "characteristic score" is the *quantity* of characteristic l (expressed as an index); (b) the "characteristic score" is the *marginal utility* of the total quantity of characteristic l found in variety k. The weights are spoken of in the paper as "subjective" or "assigned," without a clear specification of what is meant. In discussion, Maynes has suggested two alternatives: (a) the weights are marginal utilities for characteristics (which interpretation is consistent with the example of radio receivers, discussed on p. 546); (b) the weights are the proportions of total expenditure on characteristics allocated to the various characteristics (the latter definition is probably the proper interpretation to place on survey responses, if one were to establish the weights by asking consumers to rate the importance of various characteristics in the purchase of a particular product).[1]

Some combinations of these various possible definitions of weights and characteristic scores are unreasonable. For example, characteristics definition (b) and weight definition (a) require us to weight marginal utilities by marginal utilities. Moreover, I cannot see any meaning to weighting characteristic scores (however defined) by expenditures on characteristics, so I rule out combining weight definition (b) with anything.

This leaves a relatively simple and familiar interpretation for Maynes's equation 1.0. Quality (at one point he writes "utility") is defined as the summation of quantities of characteristics, each of which is assigned an appropriate weight. Equation 1.0 is thus equivalent to a "branch" utility function, assumed to be additive, defined on characteristics as arguments—and, of course, with the simple additive form, the w_l's are marginal utilities.

In this form, Maynes's proposal may be contrasted with Lancaster's "New Theory of Demand" (1971), and with the hedonic quality measurement technique. Lancaster proposed that consumer theory be reformulated by entering characteristics, rather than goods, in the utility function (the utility function could be a very general one), and

---

[1] To revert to the grocery-cart simile advanced elsewhere, suppose a cart contains X pounds of corned beef and Y pounds of cabbage, and the total price of the grocery cart of food consists of the sum of expenditures (made at that purchase) on corned beef and on cabbage—i.e., $p_b X + p_c Y$ (where the p's are implicit prices of corned beef and cabbage, respectively). If one asked the purchaser of this cart to assign a "subjective" weight to the importance of the two characteristics corned beef and cabbage in determining the value (or "quality") of the cart of food, the most likely answer would probably be based on the relative sizes of expenditures (i.e., on $p_b X$ and $p_c Y$). Some consumers, however, might have the number of pounds (X and Y) in mind, some the relative prices p_b and p_c and some may well be referring to something else. This underscores the problem of trying to evaluate consumer survey or opinion data of this particular type. One wonders exactly how the students in Professor Maynes's classes interpreted their task of determining weights.

explored the differences this would make to theory, and some of the implications to be drawn for empirical work. What Maynes has done is similar to Lancaster's approach in that both have written a utility function defined on characteristics. But where Lancaster correctly and properly wrote the utility function in a very general form (in the absence of any information that could specify its form), Maynes assumes a very specific utility function defined on characteristics – a utility function which, moreover, has severely restrictive properties.[2] And he proposes it, not as a theoretical or analytical tool, but as a measurement device! Hence, the connection with Lancaster's work is, as Maynes says, rather remote, but hardly for the reasons Maynes gives.

The hedonic technique is employed as a measurement tool, so in terms of function, it is directly comparable with Maynes's proposal. In the hedonic technique, the price of a product variety (or "specimen" to use Maynes's term[3]) is viewed as simply a sum of expenditures on characteristics. That is, given the implicit price of characteristic l (p_l), and the quantity of characteristic l embodied in a particular product variety (Q_{lk}), then (assuming for simplicity a strictly linear specification of the hedonic function) the product ($p_l Q_{lk}$) represents the expenditure on l when variety k is purchased, and

$$p_k = \sum_l p_l Q_{lk} \qquad (I)$$

equals total expenditure on all characteristics when variety k is purchased.[4]

It is a mistake to assume, from the superficial similarity of the form of equation I and Maynes's equation 1.0 that they are indeed similar. Characteristics (Q_{lk} in equation I, or Ch_{lk} in Maynes's equation 1.0) are measurable, in principle, if the right kind of data are available. The

---

[2] Such as additivity, which Maynes finds "intuitively appealing"; economists who have worked on consumer demand models regard the implications of additivity as a serious liability. As Goldberger (1967, p. 31) remarked: "Direct additivity may be a plausible specification when goods are defined broadly, but not when one works with a fine classification of consumer expenditures."

[3] Many hedonic studies have not considered store services as an attribute or characteristic, mainly because they have been carried out using list prices or some other data source which contains no information on store services, or on store-to-store price variation. In principle, however, the hedonic technique would encompass such factors where appropriate, and where data were available.

[4] Other forms of the hedonic function require modification of this statement, but the basic nature of the disaggregation described in it holds for most forms which have been used in the hedonic literature.

hedonic method and Maynes's proposal both require this. But in addition to measurable characteristics, the hedonic technique requires only that prices for different varieties be available, and from this the implicit prices – the p_i's – are estimated. Maynes, on the other hand, requires information on the *utilities* of characteristics.

In other words, if cardinal utility exists, and if someone invents a "utilometer" to measure it, we could implement Maynes's proposal. Of course, then we wouldn't have to, because we could also measure the utility of variety k directly, without recourse to characteristics at all, and without bothering about establishing a functional form for the branch utility function linking characteristics to goods.

In short, the Maynes proposal contains nothing that has measurable implications, and the "measures" he purports to have made cannot be interpreted as anything but ad hoc judgments, without scientific validity either as numbers or as a procedure.

Finally, I think it important to reiterate the distinction between the idea that quality is intrinsically measurable in a scalar, nonmonetary form (which is the premise that Maynes labors under), and the opposing view – namely, that what we mean by the term "quality" is no more than a nonspecific and nonquantitative shorthand reference to a vector of characteristics. I would like to be as conservative as Juster in eschewing "impossibility theorems." But I really believe that pursuing any notion of scalar, nonmonetary quality measurement is following a will-o'-the-wisp, for the reason that it will inevitably lead right down the road that Maynes has followed – a road which ends in a tollgate labeled "measurable, cardinal utility."

We have, it is true, notions that consumers assess the quality of different product varieties, and decide that one is higher or lower quality than another; moreover, we often think of situations where a consumer decides that, even though one product variety may be higher quality, it is not worth the price differential asked for it. It is therefore tempting to assume that these actions must imply behavior in reaction to some unique, scalar measure of quality inherent in varieties of goods – a scalar measure that can be set against price in the consumer's decision-making process.

These consumer decisions, however, can be given an interpretation within the framework of behavior toward characteristics (using the analytic tools of Lancaster); the characteristics interpretation of consumer behavior dispenses with a measure of quality as such, in favor of an optimization process similar to the standard theory of consumer behavior, but conducted over the characteristics of goods (rather than on the goods themselves, or the "quality" of goods). If we have data on characteristics of goods (required under Maynes's proposal, as well as for Lancastrian analysis and hedonic estimation), we can study demands for characteristics directly (as King has done, in the paper in this volume), without finding it necessary to "deflate" prices by a "quality index."

One of the major accomplishments of the characteristics approach to consumer behavior is that it has relieved us of the necessity for producing a scalar quality measure in order to analyze the phenomenon we call "quality." The characteristics approach to consumer behavior — and to the interpretation and measurement of quality — has, it is true, ambiguities and inchoate aspects of formidable magnitude. But even though that path is not yet thoroughly explored, and though the measurements it yields are no doubt imperfect and inadequately understood, still it seems to me to have much more promise than attempting to implement any notion of a scalar quality index. Imperfect or not, the characteristics approach to quality has yielded both measurement and analysis, and has advanced our understanding of the quality phenomenon. The scalar quality measure approach has no accomplishments to recommend it, even though it has been around far longer. I doubt if it will yield anything of value even if much more work is expended upon it.

REFERENCES

Goldberger, Arthur S. "Functional Form and Utility: A Review of Consumer Demand Theory." Social Systems Research Institute, University of Wisconsin, Systems Formulation, Methodology, and Policy Workshop Paper 6703 (October, 1967).

Lancaster, Kelvin. *Consumer Demand: A New Approach.* New York and London: Columbia University Press, 1971.

Reply to F. Thomas Juster and Jack E. Triplett

E. SCOTT MAYNES *

SENSING economies of scale, I have framed a single reply to Juster and Triplett. The two of them direct three major criticisms toward my paper:

1. *Juster doubts that local consumer markets are informationally imperfect,* contrary to Maynes. It follows therefore that "differences in prices for functionally comparable products at a single point in time simply reflect differences in quality as perceived by buyers."

2. *Juster expects different individuals to have varying preferences for different characteristics.* Hence, different individuals will make differing assessments of the quality of an identical specimen and, for this reason, one individual's overall measure of "quality" will not be useful to another.

3. *Juster doubts and Triplett denies that the measurement of quality,* according to the cardinal formulation proposed in my paper, is *useful or meaningful.*

I shall deal with each in turn.

THE INFORMATIONAL IMPERFECTIONS OF LOCAL CONSUMER MARKETS

It is in fact my view that, informationally, many local retail markets function very badly indeed. Due to costly price/quality information and imperfect searches by consumers, there coexist high and low money prices, high and low quality, and — worst of all — high and low quality-deflated prices. Price in many of these markets is *not* an indicator of quality. Indeed the difficulty of assessing quality contributes to the informational imperfection of these markets.

The desire to test this view carefully and validly has been a major

---

* In view of the conspicuous references to Consumers Union, it should be noted that the author, though Treasurer of CU, is speaking as an economist and *not* as an officer of CU.

factor in motivating my efforts to formulate a theoretically acceptable and empirically measurable concept of *quality*.

But, as a challenger to accepted views, hopeful of exciting interest, I would seek to provide at least preliminary evidence of the informational imperfection of markets. Three pieces of evidence are adduced.

The first evidence comes from calculations by Morris and Bronson [8] of rank correlations between price and quality for 48 sets of products, mostly consumer durables. The sample consisted of all the product tests conducted by Consumers Union (CU) in the 1958–1967 period for which defensible price and quality data were available. The results were emphatic: for only 12 out of 48 tests, or 25 per cent, were statistically significant correlations obtained (5 per cent level of significance, one-tailed test). For 10 of the same set of 48, the correlation coefficients were negative, though not statistically significant. The Morris-Bronson analysis is subject to several limitations: (1) It assumes that Consumers Union's placement of brand/models into ordinal ratings groups would be accepted by all consumers; (2) it utilized list prices instead of more realistic "bargained" or "discounted" prices; (3) its quality measure pertains only to varieties and then only to the testable characteristics of these varieties.

In defense of the wide acceptance of Consumers Union quality ratings, it may be noted that subscribers to *Consumer Reports* reported that they purchased "top-rated models" from 48 per cent (AM/FM radios) to 81 per cent (hair shampoo) of the time [1].

Consider, next, five-year term life insurance policies. In the language of my paper, its predominant characteristic is "after-death income protection for survivors." Since consumers tend to purchase life insurance in large multiples and the same purchase price (or set of prices) applies for a long period in the future, consumers should be strongly motivated to search for a low price. Surely, in an informationally effective market, the prices charged by different sellers to an identical purchaser would exhibit only small variations. (As Juster so helpfully reminds us (page 565): "Efficient informational functioning of markets doesn't depend on complete knowledge for all units: it requires only sufficient knowledge to make inferior products unprofitable.")

The facts contrast starkly with the prediction. They come from a careful study, reported in the January, 1974 issue of *Consumer Reports*. CU reported the "interest-adjusted" prices charged by 125 companies, including the 20 largest. Separate prices were obtained for potential insurees classified by three variables: age, size of policy, whether the policy was participating or nonparticipating. This gave rise to 18 estimates of the ratio of the highest price to the lowest price as follows:

Age	Face Value of Policy	Ratio of Highest to Lowest Price [a]	
		Nonparticipating	Participating
25	$ 10,000	1.89	1.55
	25,000	1.85	1.42
	100,000	1.84	1.42
35	$ 10,000	1.60	1.35
	25,000	1.58	1.37
	100,000	1.54	1.41
45	$ 10,000	1.49	1.35
	25,000	1.49	1.59
	100,000	1.44	1.39

[a] Companies whose policies are available only to specialized clientele, e.g., Teachers Insurance and Annuity Association of America (TIAA), are excluded from these calculations.

My question for doubters: Are these the results you would expect for an informationally effective market?

A third example, so hoary that it has become a consumerist cliché, is aspirin. Despite declarations by consumer product testing organizations,[1] the Federal Trade Commission, and eminent pharmacologists [see 2, page 69] that "aspirin is aspirin," the Bayer brand of aspirin sells for $0.78 per 100 tablets, whereas an equivalent amount of unbranded aspirin on the same shelf sells for $0.18 [6, page IV-7]. A second question for doubters: How long does it take for the word to get around?

These three examples suggest—but do not establish—that local retail markets are informationally ineffective. The conceptualization and empirical measurement of quality are necessary for a careful and persuasive test of the informational effectiveness of markets.

[1] *Consumer Bulletin* stated in its February, 1973 issue (page 13): "A government agency [FTC] holds [as Consumers Research did many years before] that one aspirin is about as good as another, in spite of advertising to the contrary for Bayer and other aspirins. . . . there is no persuasive scientific evidence that one brand is more effective for the relief of headaches than another."

UNIFORMITY OF QUALITY ASSESSMENTS AND THE CONCEPTS OF "PRODUCT" AND "MARKET"

Economists have been remarkably cavalier regarding the delineation of "product" and "market" sets. Juster scrupulously honors this tradition. (A possible exception to the generalization is the analytically useful, but nonoperational, device of separating "products" on the basis of cross elasticities.)

And, in so acting, Juster may have rendered one of his major criticisms of my paper partially invalid. Juster asserts, on a priori grounds, that differing preferences for a given set of characteristics on the part of different individuals would tend to make uniform quality assessments unlikely. He cites two examples:

1. ". . . high-income households are quite apt to place quite heavy weight on product characteristics which minimize shopping time. . . ."

2. ". . . the middle-aged shopper is not likely to value that characteristic ["acceleration" in an auto] very highly whereas the teenage hot rodder might regard it as the dominant characteristic of automobile quality."

Juster concludes: "There seems to be no solution to this problem and, hence, . . . no uniform solution to the quality measurement problem." Juster's speculations regarding the two examples seem plausible. And, unquestionably, they give rise to differing assessments of the quality of identical specimens.

But a crucial issue is the delineation of product/market classes within which quality comparisons might appropriately be made. My paper devotes two major sections to problems of delineating product/market sets, an investment which went unremarked in Juster's criticisms. It would be my contention, with references to the above examples that:

1. Otherwise similar high-income and low-income households might include (exclude) different sellers in "their" market set—due to possible differences in search cost, high-income households tending to view shopping as more costly;

2. Middle-aged shoppers would tend to exclude "high-performance" models from their product set while teen-age hot rodders might include only high performance models in theirs.

If my contentions are correct, these examples contain an important lesson: the confinement of quality comparisons to appropriate and carefully delineated market/product sets should eliminate a major source of nonuniformity in quality assessments. Nonetheless, the possibility of nonuniform quality assessments will continue to exist and should, of course, be investigated empirically.

THE USE AND USEFULNESS OF CARDINAL UTILITY

In an apt turn of language, Triplett states (page 573): "I really believe that pursuing any notion of scalar, nonmonetary quality measurement is following a will-o'-the-wisp, and the reason is that it will lead right down the road that Maynes has followed – a road which ends in a toll-gate labeled 'measurable, cardinal utility.' "

This is indeed the road on which I am traveling. But, contrary to Triplett, there exists strong evidence – from the market! – that the road exists and, further, that the benefits of the road exceed the tolls. Millions of American consumers have paid the tolls and have taken repeated trips on this highway since 1936 when it was first opened. Though the toll authority has not usually allowed users to travel at the high speeds for which the road was designed, there is strong evidence that users are pleased with the services provided. Let me explain.

The "highway" is *Consumer Reports* published by Consumers Union, the services provided are quality ratings (and other relevant consumer information), and the toll is presently $11.00 per year. Currently about two and one-quarter million subscribers are paying the toll. "Passengers" in these "vehicles" – using the road, but not paying a separate toll – are estimated at about ten million.

With some qualifications the quality scoring system employed by Consumers Union conforms to my Proportionality Model. The weights, or relative marginal utilities associated with a given characteristic, represent the consensus judgment of CU's testers. The characteristic scores are based on reproducible tests or on the reproducible judgments of panels of users, sometimes "experts." CU's quality assessments take account of only those *characteristics* for which such reproducible measurements may be obtained and its quality assessments are restricted to products for which such "objective" characteristics are judged to be dominant.

In *form,* CU's quality scoring system is cardinal. But in presentation and in textual interpretation, CU has for the most part acted conservatively and taken an ordinal posture. In this way, CU has permitted less than maximum "speeds" on its "highway."

CU does not publish the implicitly cardinal, numerical quality scores. Instead, it divides the varieties tested into "rating groups" in which quality differences are implicitly nonexistent (as reflected in alphabetical listing) or are described as small ("closely ranked models differ little in overall quality"). Differences between groups are assigned verbal labels, e.g., Very Good, Acceptable – Good, Acceptable – Poor, Unacceptable.

Cardinality manifests itself in CU's ratings in the form of a "Best Buy" designation. "Best Buys" come *only* from the highest quality rating group and should, in CU's words, "provide more quality per dollar." In my usage a "Best Buy" would lie on the efficiency frontier.

To illustrate CU's handling of quality scores, consider the hypothetical data in Figure 1. CU might designate varieties *NOPQ* as "Acceptable – Very Good," *F* through *M* as "Acceptable – Good," and *A* through *E*, as "Acceptable – Fair." Then, cardinally, CU might designate *N* and *O* as "Best Buys."

Let me spell out the limitations of CU's ratings and the differences between what it does and what is proposed in my paper. CU's product tests are restricted to nationally or regionally distributed products and

FIGURE 1

Consumers Union's Largely Ordinal Treatment of
Cardinal Quality Scores

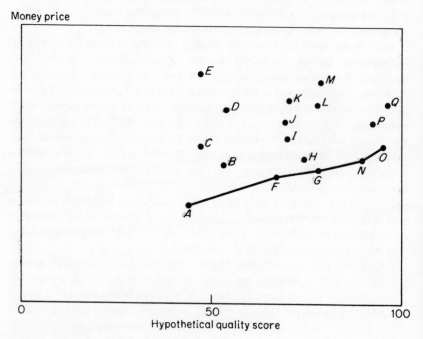

NOTE: Letters denote various specimens.

brands and, largely, to products for which "objective" characteristics dominate. My product set, by contrast, would be all-inclusive. CU confines its attention to characteristics for which reproducible measurements may be devised, whereas, again, mine would be all-inclusive. CU's reports of prices are list, or those encountered in a variety of cities, whereas mine would be those found in a single, local market.

CU's basically additive model is sometimes modified by the use of thresholds for certain characteristics. Specifically, a subthreshold value of some desirable characteristic, safety, for example, or an above-threshold value of some undesirable characteristic will automatically map the quality score of that variety to zero or to a verbally equivalent "Unacceptable" rating. This practice of CU's—which corresponds exactly to a suggestion by Juster (page 565)—is one which I should be pleased to follow.

In my empirical investigations stemming from my proposals, I would also plan to follow CU's path in interpreting results ordinally until convincing evidence is obtained in support of the stronger, cardinal interpretation.

Juster and Triplett address themselves to particular problems which they identify with the quality measure proposed. Juster asks (pages 564–565): Is there really a zero point or a unity point [on the scale for the characteristics score]? His doubts seem to rest not with the definitions offered, but rather with the question of whether these points can be identified by the users of the scale. My answer, on the basis of ex post discussions with students using the scale, would be that they understand the scale and make appropriate use of the end points and the cardinal (ratio) interpretation of the characteristic scores.

Juster laments (page 563) the absence of "any empirically verifiable content." While I have not been able to devise any empirical test of the structure of the measure, I would argue that for a quality assessor, whether he purchased a specimen on the efficiency frontier would constitute a strong test of the consistency of this model with observable behavior.

Triplett observes correctly (page 573) that there exists no universally acceptable measure of utility along the lines of, say, a kilometer for measuring distance. Does acceptance of this proposition imply the acceptance of the opposite proposition—that utility and other similar "subjective" variables are not susceptible to useful measurement? I believe not.

Consider, for example, "consumer attitudes," a variable which seems, if anything, more nebulous than utility. Yet Juster's research career has centered upon largely successful efforts to demonstrate the predictive usefulness of such subjective variables as "consumer attitudes" and "subjective purchase probabilities" [4, 5]. The use of such subjective variables is plagued by the need to calibrate the apparently different implicit scales which each individual uses. (See [7] for a discussion of this problem.) Yet it would be my judgment that calibration is feasible and that success in this endeavor would yield very large payoffs.

A last comment relates to economists' rather schizoid views of what individuals can and cannot do by way of data assimilation and calculation. I am struck by the readiness of many economists to assume that individuals can perform prodigious feats of data assimilation and complex calculation, *as long as this behavior is "well buried" in a theoretical model.* And I am equally struck by the readiness of many economists to doubt individuals' capacities in this respect when the research requires—as in the case under discussion—actual data assimilation and calculation. Let me illustrate the point.

To utilize wage differences as measures of accepted risk, Thaler and Rosen, in a paper presented at this Conference, had to assume that in selecting an occupation and accepting a wage rate, workers in a risky occupation had access to and were able to digest data of the sort contained in Thaler and Rosen's Table 1. Or, alternatively, that "somehow" they could absorb these "facts." This, despite the fact that an audience including many professional data collectors were fascinated by some unexpected data in the table. For example, who would have thought of elevator operators as accepting a risky occupation?

Another example is the life-cycle hypothesis of saving. "All" that this theory requires of an individual is that he: (1) estimates the probability distribution of his employment income for each year up to and including the year of his death (but not beyond!); (2) select an appropriate discount rate; (3) discount the stream of expected income back to the present; (4) adjust his consumption—interpreted as "services enjoyed"—to this present value of labor income, and to net worth as well.

Our profession seems to have accepted the assumptions of data assimilation and calculation implicit in these two examples. By contrast, the task implicit in assessing quality seems like child's play.

THE MEANING OF WEIGHTS AND CHARACTERISTICS

Triplett (page 570) found my definitions of "weights" and "characteristic scores" ambiguous. Let me clarify my intentions.

The weights are intended to represent the relative importance, or relative marginal utilities, assigned to each characteristic in a product. The characteristic scores are scalars, denoting the marginal utility conveyed by this characteristic in a given specimen as a ratio to the marginal utility provided by the "ideal specimen." Thus, for the "ideal specimen," the weight represents the share of the total marginal utility of that specimen which would be conferred by a given characteristic. Thus, too, the overall quality score of the ideal specimen would be 1.0.

REFERENCES

[1] Benson & Benson. *Survey of Present and Former Subscribers to Consumer Reports.* Princeton: Benson & Benson, 1970.

[2] Burack, Richard. *The New Handbook of Prescription Drugs, Revised Edition.* New York: Pantheon, 1970.

[3] Fellner, William. "Operational Utility, The Theoretical Background and A Measurement." In W. Fellner, editor, *Ten Economic Studies in the Tradition of Irving Fisher.* New York: Wiley, 1967.

[4] Juster, F. Thomas, and Wachtel, Paul. "Anticipatory and Objective Models of Durable Goods Demand." *American Economic Review* 62 (September 1972): 564–579.

[5] ———. "Uncertainty, Expectations, and Durable Goods Demand Models." In Burkhard Strumpel et al., editors, *Human Behavior in Economic Affairs: Essays in Honor of George Katona.* New York: Elsevier, 1972.

[6] Maynes, E. Scott. *Decision-Making for Consumers.* New York: Macmillan, 1976.

[7] ———. "The Power of the Consumer." In Strumpel et al., editors, *Human Behavior in Economic Affairs* (see 5 above).

[8] Morris, Ruby Turner, and Bronson, Claire Sekulski. "The Chaos of Competition Indicated by Consumer Reports." *Journal of Marketing* 33 (July 1968): 26–34.

Measuring Real Consumption from Quantity Data, Canada 1935–1968 *

DAN USHER

TIME series of real consumption may be constructed by deflation or by revaluation. To measure real consumption by deflation, one divides the value of consumption in current dollars by the value of an appropriately chosen price index. To measure real consumption by revaluation, one collects time series of quantities consumed and evaluates the quantities of each year by the prices of some arbitrarily chosen base year.

In principle and subject to the appropriate choice of index number formulae, deflation and revaluation ought to give identical measures of real consumption, because quantity is equal to the ratio of value and price for the aggregate of all goods, as well as for goods taken one at a time. Suppose the year 0 is chosen as a base year in the double sense that real consumption in the year 0 is set at 100 and that prices in the year 0 are used as weights in the quantity index. In each year t, real consumption assessed by revaluation is given by the quantity index

$$Q_0^t = \frac{\sum_{i=1}^{n} p_i^0 q_i^t}{\sum_{i=1}^{n} p_i^0 q_i^0} \times 100 \tag{1}$$

where p_i^0 is the price of the good i in the year t, q_i^t is the quantity

* I appreciate the able assistance of Robert Lippens and Mrs. Wiktoria Kierzkowski in collecting and processing the data. Malcolm Urquhart and Joel Diena of Statistics Cànada have read drafts of this essay and have made helpful suggestions. The project was financed in part by the Canada Council and in part by Statistics Canada.

consumed of the good i in the year t and so on. Real consumption assessed by deflation is the ratio of an index $Y_0{}^t$ of consumption in current dollars

$$Y_0{}^t = \frac{\sum\limits_{i=1}^{n} p_i{}^t q_i{}^t}{\sum\limits_{i=1}^{n} p_i{}^0 q_i{}^0} \times 100 \tag{2}$$

and a Paasche price index

$$P_o{}^t = \frac{\sum\limits_{i=1}^{n} p_i{}^t q_i{}^t}{\sum\limits_{i=1}^{n} p_i{}^0 q_i{}^t} \tag{3}$$

We see at once that the two measures of real consumption are the same,[1] that is

$$Q_0{}^t = Y_0{}^t / P_o{}^t \tag{4}$$

The two series are not the same in practice because the world does not present us with neat time series of prices and quantities of n distinct goods which together constitute the whole of real consumption. In the course of this paper it will be shown that the rate of growth of real consumption assessed by revaluation is typically less than the rate of growth of real consumption assessed by deflation, and that the ratio of the two series provides a measure – a crude one but the only such measure we possess – of the rate of quality change implicit in the official national accounts. The time series obtained from the revaluation of quantity data also provides a link between growth rates of consumption of particular goods and services and the growth rate of consumption as a whole.

Deflation is preferred to revaluation for measuring real consumption in the official national accounts in every country in the world. There are cogent reasons for this preference, but there has to my knowledge been no systematic analysis of the relative merits of the two series. Nor has there been any attempt to measure real consumption by revaluation to compare the growth rates of the two series and draw out the

---

[1] As is well known from the theory of index numbers, a base-weighted Laspeyres quantity index may be a biased indicator of the extent to which people are becoming better off in the course of time. The index is sufficient for the limited purpose of contrasting deflation and revaluation.

extra information the second series provides about the process of economic growth. That is the purpose of this paper.

I attempt to construct a time series of real consumption from quantity data for Canada over the years 1935 to 1968. The paper begins with a statement of the reasons why national accounting offices choose to measure real consumption by deflation rather than by revaluation of quantity data. There follows a discussion of the kind of information one might hope to obtain by measuring real consumption by revaluation as well. There is a discussion of problems in collecting and processing quantity data. Finally, there is a brief description of the results.

THE ADVANTAGES OF DEFLATION

The advantages of deflation are these:

(i) The data on value and prices required for measuring real consumption by deflation are more readily available than the quantity data required for measuring real consumption by revaluation. Data required for deflation are consumption in current dollars, which can be got from financial statements of firms, and a sample of prices. We need not have a complete enumeration of prices because competition can be trusted to keep price differentials among firms within a narrow range. By contrast, quantity data can only be obtained from a complete enumeration of firms or from a very large and detailed sample of households. At present there are many items of consumption, including books and furniture, for which we have no quantity data at all.

(ii) Deflation makes it possible to measure real consumption without having to account explicitly for the full diversity of goods and services in the economy. In measuring real consumption by deflation, one can get by with a price index of a few representative goods in each category of expenditure, in the hope that prices of goods in the index change at about the same rate as the average of prices of all goods in the category. In measuring real consumption by revaluation of quantity data, we must somehow come to grips with the fact that there is an infinite variety of goods and services, and that no two goods are really identical in every respect. Some goods, such as pounds of flour bought at different times, are similar enough so that we are content to treat them as amounts of the same commodity. Other goods are so nearly unique that we hesitate to combine them into quantities presumed to persist in some homogeneous form for the whole duration of the time series. Novelties, such as hulahoops, clackers, and yoyos, are goods of this sort, and as a matter of practice, one has little option but to assume that prices of novelties rise at about the same rate as prices of some other class of goods. One deflates values of novelties by, for instance, the consumer price index to obtain a time series of the real output of novelties, on the assumption that, whatever novelties may be, the efficiency of labor and capital in producing them is rising at about the same rate as the efficiency of labor and capital in producing other things. Since one cannot construct a genuine time series of the quantity of novelties, the validity of the assumption cannot be checked, and we can never know whether the estimate of the quantity of novelties is accurate or not. As an alternative, we could derive a quantity series for novelties by assuming that consumption of novelties increases at the same rate as consumption of some other class of commodities. This assumption is probably less satisfactory than the assumption that the relative price of novelties and some other class of commodities has remained constant.

(iii) Devaluation entails an automatic correction for quality change. Think of value, v, as being the product of price, p, quantity, q, and quality, m. We would like a time series of real consumption to reflect changes in quantity and quality but not price. We get this result if we deflate value by a price index, as long as the price index represents the value each year of a bundle of goods of a given quality and design; the price index would be a true reflection of p, and the deflated series would be $v/p = qm$, which is exactly what we require. If consumers consider one good suit to be the equivalent of two poor suits no matter how many good suits and how many poor suits are put onto the market, then the dollar value of expenditure on suits deflated by the price of one kind of suit or by a price index with fixed weights is an ideal measure of real consumption of suits, while a quantity index of the number of suits purchased would be inappropriate.[2]

These advantages of deflation over revaluation, the availability of data, the ease of accounting for the diversity of goods and services, and the automatic correction for quality change, provide some justification for the preference for deflation in the official national accounts.

THE ADVANTAGES OF REVALUATION

It would be difficult to argue for the replacement of deflation by revaluation as the principal method of measuring real consumption in

[2] This example shows that deflation may give us a correct measure of real consumption inclusive of quality change, but it does not prove that quality change is always accounted for correctly. In the course of this paper, we shall consider examples where quality change is overlooked or is imputed erroneously.

the national accounts, but I think a case can be made for measuring real consumption both ways. A supplementary series constructed by revaluation of quantity data can be useful in several respects:

(i) The principal reason for wanting a time series of real consumption derived from quantity data is to connect our measure of aggregate consumption with information about particular goods and services we enjoy. One would like to think of national income statistics as constituting the last chapter and summation of an imaginary statistical abstract. Each preceding chapter shows change, improvement or deterioration of some aspect of the economy — food, clothing, transport and communication, health, education. The final chapter combines changes in all aspects of the economy into one measure of the progress of the economy as a whole. The accounts as they are now set up do not serve that purpose because one cannot link time series of real consumption to more detailed and specific information about the economy. Measures of real consumption based directly on quantity data forge the link automatically.

For example, the Canadian national accounts show that food consumption per head has increased at a rate of 1.4 per cent per annum between 1935 and 1968. Broadly speaking, Statistics Canada arrives at that figure by dividing the value of retail sales of food by the food component of the consumer price index. Let us consider this 1.4 per cent and ask what information it contains about food consumption in Canada. One might ask what the growth of 1.4 per cent in food consumption implies about the Canadian diet. Can we infer from the 50 per cent increase in food consumption that Canadians are enjoying an adequate or more than adequate diet, that diets in 1935 were on the average inadequate, or that Canadians are eating more or better food in 1968 than in 1935? Of course, one can only speak of averages in this context because nothing in the national accounts indicates, or is intended to indicate, whether consumption is evenly distributed; but one might ask whether all Canadians would have adequate diets if food consumption were evenly distributed. To all of these questions, the answer is the same. We do not know and cannot find out, even by examining the primary data that enter into the construction of the national accounts.

Food consumption as measured in the national accounts may have increased for a number of reasons: Canadians may be consuming more food of all kinds, more bread, cheese, fish, milk, and so on. Canadians may be switching from less nutritious to more nutritious food — from bread to meat, fruit, and fresh vegetables. The increase in food consumption may reflect a change in the seasonality of our eating habits; we may be paying a premium for fresh fruits and vegetables out of season. The quality of food may have improved. Bread may be richer in vitamins, apples less likely to be rotten or wormy, flour less likely to be dirty or to contain impurities. Increased food consumption has many dimensions, but nothing in the national accounts as they are now constructed permits us to apportion the total increase among the contributing factors or even to say with confidence which factors are accounted for and which are not. Worse still, the measured increase in food consumption may reflect factors which are quite separate from the amount and quality of the food we eat. Part of the measured increase in food consumption is factory preparation of TV dinners, cloth for tea bags, tin for cans, ice for freezing, paper for packaging, or labor cost of washing, peeling, grinding, or mashing food before it enters the home. Factory preparation of food may improve its quality as food, or it may be a convenience for housewives, in effect, a labor-saving device comparable to home freezers or automatic mixers. Food and packaging are both goods, and increases in both have a place in the national accounts, but one would like to know which is which. One would like to know what proportion of the 1.4 per cent increase is food and what proportion is paper and tin. On this matter, the accounts are silent. The increase might be food, packaging, or any combination of the two.

The argument for connecting aggregate consumption with the detail of quantities consumed is reinforced by the recent revival of interest in the welfare implications of the national accounts. It is felt that social indicators of justice, equality, education, health and other non-economic aspects of well-being should be compiled and, if possible, combined with economic statistics into aggregates which might signify progress or retrogression. The measurement of real consumption from quantity data fits particularly well with these developments, because social indicators are themselves like quantity data in the sense that they could serve as arguments in the utility function. Crime rates, hours of leisure, proportions of eligible age groups attending school, age-specific mortality rates, pollution indexes, or Gini ratios of the income distribution can be arranged in time series and might be incorporated like ordinary quantity series into the body of the accounts if appropriate prices could be found or imputed. These imputations can be introduced more easily and naturally when real consumption is initially developed from quantity data than when real consumption is measured as a value deflated by a price index.

A case can be made that the increase over time in urban site rents should be counted as a cost of progress and should not be included in consumption. To exclude site rents, one must limit consideration of housing to the physical characteristics of the house and its grounds — number of rooms, floor space per room, area of the lot, facilities, and so on — and ignore advantages of location. This correction comes automatically when real consumption is measured by revaluing quantity data.

(ii) An index of quality change in consumption goods can be obtained as the ratio of real consumption assessed by deflation and real consumption assessed by revaluation, because the former includes quality change while the latter does not. This measure of implicit quality change is a crude one, for the two time-series of real consumption may diverge for a variety of reasons, not the least of which is that the index number formula employed in measuring real consumption from quantity data differs substantially from the formula employed in the construction of the national accounts. Nevertheless, this measure of quality change is the only such measure we possess, and it is possible on occasion to bring general knowledge to bear on the question of whether the rate of implicit quality change is reasonable or not. For instance, it is shown below that of the 1.4 per cent annual increase in real food consumption per head in the national accounts, only 0.6 per cent can be accounted for by the increase in quantity, leaving 0.8 per cent that must be explained by quality change. That seems to me to be a very high rate of quality change in food and suggests that the sources of quality change ought to be examined closely. The work of Griliches and others on hedonic price indexes has tended to suggest that quality change has been imperfectly removed from the price indexes used in the national accounts so that the growth rate of real income is underestimated. By contrast, the growth rate of our quality series seems unreasonably large for some categories of expenditure, suggesting that the overall bias in the growth rate of real consumption may go in either direction.

It should be stressed that the measure of real consumption assessed by deflation will only capture quality change if all quality change is eliminated from the price index, and that complete elimination of quality change from the price index may prove difficult or impossible. There are situations where quality change cannot be measured at all because similar items cannot be identified as different amounts of the same stuff. One can say that a 1920 model automobile and a 1970 model automobile are both members of the genus "automobile," but a Pierce-Arrow of 1920 is better than a Volkswagen of 1970 in some respects and worse in others. Even when quality change can be identified, the spread between the prices of two qualities of goods may vary over time because of relative scarcity or changes in tastes. Suppose that red salmon is preferred to white salmon for buffet lunches, but that white salmon is preferred to red salmon in salmon sandwiches. In 1935, red salmon was rare and costly relative to white salmon, and statisticians considered red salmon to be the higher quality item. In the interval between 1935 and 1968, red salmon became more plentiful, and by 1968 a great deal of red salmon was used in salmon sandwiches and white salmon was relatively expensive. The statistician who based his quality classification on the year 1935 would overestimate the improvement in welfare resulting from the increased consumption of salmon, while the statistician who set his quality classification on the year 1968 would underestimate it. The index number problem in this example is not different from index number problems that arise when time series of ordinary commodities are combined, but problems of this sort might easily be overlooked in the procedures for constructing price indexes to deflate values in the national accounts.

Deflation may also give rise to spurious quality change when the price of a commodity varies from place to place or when part of the price of a good is payment to avoid externalities which have emerged since the first year of the time series. An example of spurious quality change is provided by the valuation of "natural" foods in the national accounts. Today we pay a substantial premium for foods guaranteed to have been grown on farms that use only natural fertilizer. Perhaps the ill effects of chemical fertilizers ought to be reflected somewhere in the accounts, but there is surely something peculiar in the present practice of implicitly counting that premium as extra food in a comparison with an earlier year when natural fertilizers were used as a matter of course. A similar problem arises from the effect of urbanization on the value of housing services. The quantity of housing in the national accounts is measured by deflating the value of rents paid or imputed by a price index of rents, with farmhouses and city houses treated as though they were separate commodities. Since rents are generally higher in the cities than on the farms, the identical house is counted as more house if it happens to be in the city than if it happens to be in the country. Consequently, an increase in the proportion of city houses to farm houses causes the national accounts to show an increase in housing services per head even if no one is better or more comfortably housed than he was before.

(iii) All commodities, even those we call goods as opposed to services, are really bundles of goods and services. A pound of cheese purchased at the grocer's is more than just cheese; it is the convenience and aesthetic appeal of the shop where it is sold, the length of time one has to wait at the cash register, the delivery from the shop to the purchaser's home, the extent to which it is processed, cooked, or cut to save the purchaser time in preparation at home. These services, ancillary to the purchase of a piece of cheese, are included in real consumption measured by deflation but excluded from real consumption measured by revaluation, and any increase over time in services provided per unit of goods is reflected as part of the growth rate of one series but not the other. A strong case can be made that an increase in services per unit of goods ought to be counted as part of economic growth, but enough exceptions can be found to this general rule to justify the creation of a supplementary series of goods exclusive of their service component. A large part of the improvement in the service component of goods consists either of a substitute for housework or of some other labor-saving arrangement. Since housework is excluded from the national income, substitutes for housework might be excluded as well. Alternatively, if real income were to include an imputation for leisure, it would be double counting to include labor-saving increases in the service component of goods. Time series of quantities of goods exclusive of their service components are what is required for linking the data in the accounts with investigations of special aspects of welfare such as diets or housing conditions.

(iv) Time series of quality might have some interesting uses in the theory of demand. In every attempt to compute a set of demand elasticities for all commodities simultaneously that has come to my attention, the authors have used real expenditures by commodity group in the national accounts as if these series were quantity data. It may be that the quality series implicit in each of the national accounts series have more in common with one another than with the series of quantities to which they are attached. "Quality of food" and "quality of clothing" may be more like one commodity in their response to changes in income or to changes in prices of other goods than "quality of food" is like "quantity of food" or "quality of clothing" is like "quantity of clothing." I have not attempted to test this conjecture. In view of the biases and approximations that enter into the construction of the two series of real consumption, and of the fact that the quality series is a residual, it is doubtful whether this conjecture could be tested with the available data.

A TIME-SERIES OF REAL-CONSUMPTION-BASED QUANTITY DATA: CANADA, 1937 TO 1968

I have assembled all the relevant quantity data I could find into a time series of real consumption by revaluing quantities at 1961 prices. The main results of this computation are presented in Table 1, which is a comparison of my estimates of the growth rates of real consumption and its components with the estimates in the official national accounts. The aggregated commodities in Table 1 are food, alcohol, tobacco, housing, automobile services, purchased transport, communication, appliances, health services, and clothing. Several hundred time series of quantities from which the aggregates were derived are presented in Table 2. The main results of the study are presented at the end of the paper in a series of charts, one for each aggregate commodity and one for real consumption as a whole. Each chart is a comparison of time series of real consumption as assessed in the national accounts, of real consumption as we have estimated it from quantity data, and of implicit quality change defined as the ratio of the two series in every year.

The tables are largely self-explanatory, and the sources of data are indicated in the notes. In discussing this material, I will first consider a number of empirical and conceptual problems that emerged in the course of preparing the data, and will then comment briefly on some of the results.

(i) Missing data. The data are incomplete in two respects. There are whole categories of expenditures for which we have no quantity data or so little that it is not worth attempting to construct a quantity index, and there are some items missing from every category of expenditure. For the categories of "recreation" and "miscellaneous," where we have virtually no quantity data at all, I have treated the time series of real consumption in the national accounts as though they were quantity data, and have included these series with genuine time series of quantities in computing the overall rate of real consumption as assessed by revaluation. For all other categories of expenditure, I have adopted a procedure equivalent to assuming that the rate of growth of the missing series is equal to the rate of growth of the series included in Table 2. The procedure is to weight growth rates of the principal categories of real consumption not by the 1961 values derived from the prices and quantities in Table 2, but by the corresponding values in the official national accounts. Consider, for instance, the growth rate of food consumption of 0.6 per cent in the far right-hand column of Table. 1. This figure is the growth rate of the value at 1961 prices of

TABLE 1

A Comparison of Growth Rates of Consumption per Head:
Canada, 1935–1968

	From the National Accounts		Recomputation from Quantity Data	
	Values in Dollars per Head in 1961 (1)	Growth Rates (Per Cent) (2)	Values in Dollars per Head in 1961 (3)	Growth Rates (Per Cent) (4)
Food	266.37	1.4	266.37	0.6
Alcohol	51.49	3.8	51.49	3.2
Tobacco	40.79	2.9	40.79	2.9
Clothing	124.79	1.8	124.79	0.9
Housing	} 355.96	2.8	{ 329.09	0.6
Appliances			26.87	6.8
Health services	56.80	2.2	108.62	1.7
Purchased transport	34.27	2.6	34.27	0.1
Automobiles	126.38	4.6	126.38	3.6
Communication	20.67	4.2	20.67	3.1
Education	13.82	4.9	138.23	2.2
Recreation	63.44	3.5	63.44	3.5
Miscellaneous	222.56	3.5	207.30	3.1
Total real consumption	1,377.34	2.8	1,538.31	1.8

NOTE : The values in column 1 and the growth rates in column 2 are from unpublished and preliminary estimates by Statistics Canada of personal consumption expenditure. The categories of expenditure are the same as those in the national accounts except that "housing" includes "gross rent, fuel, and power" and "furniture, furnishings, and household equipment and operation," with the exception of appliances. The category of recreation in Table 1 consists of the national accounts categories of "recreation, entertainment, and education" less education, which is included separately. Column 3 is the same as column 1, except for "health" and "education," which include public current expenditure as estimated in Table 3; for "appliances," the value of which is taken from *National Accounts: Income and Expenditure, 1965*, Dominion Bureau of Statistics (DBS), 13-201, Table 47, item 23; and for "miscellaneous," which excludes some provincial sales tax, originally put into the miscellaneous category because it could not be allocated among commodities. The growth rates in column 4 are from Table 2. The growth rates for consumption as a whole in columns 2 and 4 are computed according to the formula:

$$G = \sum_i V_i G_i \div \sum_i V_i$$

where

G is the growth rate of total real consumption;
i refers to a row in the table;
G_i is the growth rate in the ith row; and
V_i is the value in the ith row.

TABLE 2

Quantity Data: Canada 1935–1968

A. Food: Domestic Disappearance, Lbs. per Capita, Calendar Year or Crop Year Commencing:

	1935	1940	1945	1950	1955	1960	1965	1968	1961 Price ¢ per Lb.
Meat (carcass weight)									
Beef	53.6	54.5	67.0	50.6	71.5	69.2	81.7	86.8	81.7
Veal	9.8	10.8	12.5	9.4	8.7	7.6	8.4	6.4	90.9
Mutton and lamb	6.0	4.5	4.3	2.2	2.8	3.2	2.8	4.2	71.2
Pork	39.3	44.7	52.7	54.9	57.6	55.3	49.2	53.6	79.3
Offal	5.5	5.5	5.7	4.9	5.7	4.9	3.6	3.8	10.0
Canned meat	1.3	1.1	3.4	4.0	4.5	6.4	4.3	4.3	47.2
Total meat	115.5	121.1	145.6	126.0	150.8	146.6	150.0	159.1	
Eggs	34.6	30.8	33.0	30.1	36.4	36.7	32.0	32.0	26.4
Poultry (edible weight)									
Chicken	8.6	9.0	11.5	9.2	12.6	15.1	19.2	21.2	70.5
Other	1.8	2.6	2.7	2.3	4.1	5.6	8.0	8.2	70.9
Total poultry	10.4	11.6	14.2	11.5	16.7	20.7	27.2	29.4	
Pulses and Nuts									
Dry beans	4.3	3.8	3.8	4.8	3.7	2.9	2.4	2.2	11.1
Dry peas	6.3	5.1	2.9	1.8	0.9	1.4	1.6	0.2	11.1
Nuts	3.0	3.2	4.4	3.6	3.9	4.2	4.9	4.8	49.2
Cocoa	2.6	4.4	3.3	2.9	2.7	1.5	3.5	3.9	122.6
Total pulses & nuts	16.2	15.5	14.4	13.1	11.2	10.0	12.4	11.1	
Oils and Fats									
Butter	30.6	30.4	21.1	22.3	20.5	13.8	15.1	13.3	69.9
Lard	3.9	7.0	11.3	9.5	8.6	7.2	7.4	7.8	23.1
Margarine	0.0	0.0	0.0	6.8	8.0	7.6	7.0	7.6	31.0
Shortening	9.8	7.6	9.8	9.6	9.8	9.4	9.9	14.1	34.3
Other	(3.0)	(3.0)	(3.0)	3.0	2.4	4.1	4.7	5.9	42.1
Total oils and fats	47.3	48.0	45.2	51.2	49.3	44.9	44.1	48.7	

Item									
Potatoes									
White	198.6	213.0	162.9	180.8	150.6	158.9	156.0	170.2	4.8
Sweet	0.5	0.6	0.8	0.8	0.6	0.5	0.4	0.2	16.8
Total potatoes	199.1	213.6	163.7	181.6	151.2	159.4	156.4	170.4	
Cereals									
Flour:									
Wheat	179.2	164.2	197.2	158.3	147.8	135.2	142.6	130.1	24.9 (bread)
Rye	0.4	0.4	0.2	0.3	0.9	4.8	5.1	3.8	9.2
Total	179.6	164.6	197.4	158.6	148.7	140.0	147.7	133.9	9.2
Oatmeal & rolled oats	8.0	7.3	9.5	6.2	5.0	5.0	5.1	4.1	9.2
Pot & pearl barley	0.3	0.3	0.8	0.3	0.2	0.2	0.1	0.1	9.2
Cornmeal & flour	1.7	0.2	0.8	0.8	0.8	1.7	3.0	4.1	
Buckwheat flour	0.2	0.1	0.1	0.1	0.1	0.1	0.04	0.02	
Rice	4.0	3.7	3.3	4.1	4.5	4.5	6.1	4.5	20.8
Breakfast food	5.3	5.2	8.0	6.8	7.3	7.2	7.0		31.8
Total cereals	199.1	181.4	219.9	176.9	166.6	153.7	163.9	142.2	
Sugars									
Sugar	87.5	96.5	74.3	101.0	97.1	96.6	100.5	101.8	9.6
Maple sugar, etc.	2.8	2.7	1.1	1.6	1.1	0.8	0.4	0.5	30.0
Honey	2.9	2.2	3.1	2.3	1.7	1.4	1.8	1.4	30.3
Other	(7.0)	(7.0)	(7.0)	(7.0)	(7.0)	5.5	5.7	5.5	19.1
Total Sugars	100.2	108.4	85.5	111.9	106.9	104.3	108.4	109.2	
Coffee	3.2	3.5	4.5	6.0	6.6	9.0	8.7	9.7	120.0
Tea	3.2	3.6	4.2	4.0	2.7	2.4	2.4	2.5	74.0
Vegetables (fresh equivalent basis)									
Cabbage		13.6	18.9	14.1	12.4	10.2	9.0	9.3	8.9
Lettuce		5.2	6.2	7.2	8.2	8.4	9.7	10.5	19.0
Spinach		1.6	1.2	1.2	1.1	0.8	0.7	0.5	24.4
Carrots: fresh		9.6	12.0	15.6	13.2	16.9	14.1	15.1	13.4
canned	0.12	0.12	1.3	0.5	0.5	1.1	1.8	1.9	
Total		10.3	15.1	17.3	15.5	18.0	15.9	17.0	
Beans: fresh	.7	2.6	2.4	2.6	2.1	1.9	1.7	0.8	28.3
canned		1.1	2.0	1.8	2.3	2.3	2.4	2.7	
frozen							1.2	0.8	
baked canned	2.1	3.6	1.8	4.4	3.9	4.2	5.3	4.3	
Total	2.8	7.3	6.2	8.8	8.3	8.4	10.8	8.6	

(continued)

TABLE 2 (continued)

A. Food (continued)

	1935	1940	1945	1950	1955	1960	1965	1968	1961 Price ¢ per Lb.
Peas: fresh		1.5	1.0	0.9	0.7		0.1		26.9
canned		3.6	5.5	4.6	5.7	4.3	4.0	4.4	
frozen		0.3	1.1	0.9	1.0		2.2	2.7	
Total		5.4	6.3	6.3		4.3	6.3	7.1	
Beets: fresh		4.8	6.9	6.3	7.8	3.3	1.1	1.1	
canned	0.1	5.1	5.0	5.6	4.2	0.9	1.0	1.0	12.2
Total						4.2	2.1	2.1	
Cauliflower		2.3	2.9	2.6	2.4	1.6	2.0	1.8	34.4
Celery		5.2	7.1	6.6	8.2	6.6	6.4	6.7	15.5
Corn: fresh		4.0	5.1	3.1	5.4	3.9	4.0	3.5	10.1
canned		6.0	7.2	10.8	10.4	9.8	10.6	11.3	
frozen					2.0		2.4	3.1	
Total	6.4	12.1	14.3	18.0	16.3	13.7	17.0	17.9	
Cucumbers		(1.7)	(1.7)	(1.7)	(1.7)	(1.7)	1.4	3.0	15.0
Onions, not processed		10.5	13.2	14.2	13.0	11.8	13.0	10.3	11.5
Asparagus: fresh	0.3	0.4	0.3	0.4	0.3	0.3	0.2	0.5	33.6
canned		0.5	0.3	0.5	0.5	0.6	0.6	0.6	
frozen							0.1	0.1	
Total		0.6	0.6	0.6	0.7	0.9	0.9	1.2	
Turnips		(4.5)	(4.5)	(4.5)	(4.5)	(4.5)	7.2	7.7	7.3
Unspecified: fresh		0.3				13.9	1.8	2.2	15.0
canned				0.8	0.7	0.8	3.0	3.3	
frozen				0.8	2.7	5.5	1.3	1.2	
Total		0.3	0.4	1.6	3.4	20.2	6.1	6.7	
Total vegetables		81.8	103.8	106.6	105.1	110.6	113.9	115.1	

598

Fruit (fresh equivalent basis)									
Apples: fresh		29.4	12.8	24.7	31.6	14.7	27.4	27.1	18.4
canned		4.1	2.4	2.1	3.2	2.9	3.5	4.1	
juice		2.2	4.5	7.0	11.5	8.1	8.9	11.1	
frozen							0.6	0.6	
Total		37.2	25.6	37.3	45.5	25.7	40.4	42.9	33.6
Apricots: fresh		0.3	0.4	0.4	0.7	0.4	0.1	0.3	
canned		0.1	0.1	0.2	0.5	0.4	0.4	0.4	
Total		1.4	0.5	1.3	1.6	0.8	0.5	0.7	
Bananas	13.2	13.0	24.0	11.5	18.2	(16.7)	16.1	17.6	18.7
Cherries: fresh		0.4	0.7	0.5	1.4	0.2	0.6	0.9	29.1
canned		0.3	0.1	0.5	0.6	0.6	0.5	0.3	
frozen						0.1	0.7	0.6	
Total		0.8	1.0	1.3	2.4	0.9	1.8	1.8	33.6
Peaches: fresh		4.4	5.6	2.2	4.6	4.8	4.2	5.2	
canned		1.8	1.4	3.6	4.0	4.2	4.4	3.7	
Total		6.6	7.6	6.5	9.1	9.0	8.6	8.9	11.0
Pineapples: fresh		0.9	1.3	0.6	3.1		0.3	0.3	
canned		2.6	0.2	2.2	1.7		4.0	3.6	
juice		0.5	0.3	1.4	4.8		1.3	1.7	
Total		4.0	1.8	4.2		(5.7)	5.6	5.6	20.0
Plums, etc.: fresh		1.3	2.2	1.5	2.3	1.7	1.7	1.8	
canned		0.2	0.8	0.5	0.5	0.3	0.3	0.3	
Total		6.1	10.7	5.2	5.1	2.0	2.0	2.1	
Raspberries: fresh		0.9	0.6	0.6	0.4	0.1		0.1	
canned					0.1	0.1	0.1	0.1	
frozen		0.1		0.1		0.5	0.6	0.6	
Total		1.2	1.3	1.1	1.1	0.7	0.7	0.8	
Strawberries: fresh		2.3	1.0	1.1	1.4	1.5	0.9	1.8	56.1
canned		0.1		0.2	0.2	0.1	0.1	0.1	35.3
frozen						1.0	1.3	1.1	
Total		3.0	1.6	2.0	2.7	2.6	2.3	3.0	27.5
Grapes		21.1	23.9	24.7	22.4	8.7	11.9	10.5	21.1
Pears: fresh		2.1	3.9	1.8	3.0	2.6	2.1	2.7	23.2
canned		1.0	0.9	1.9	2.2	1.8	2.4	2.1	
Total		3.0	4.8	3.8	5.2	4.4	4.5	4.8	

(continued)

TABLE 2 (continued)

A. Food (concluded)

	1935	1940	1945	1950	1955	1960	1965	1968	1961 Price ¢ per Lb.
Unspecified: fresh		2.9	3.4	0.4	0.7		7.9	7.2	25.0
canned				0.3	1.1		5.1	5.3	
frozen							0.4	0.1	
juice				11.2	15.6		3.9	5.7	
other	23.2	19.2	25.6	19.2	27.0		21.7	20.7	
dried					20.1				
Total	23.2	22.1	29.0	31.1		37.7	38.4	38.0	
Citrus: fresh lemons		2.7	3.4	2.1	2.0				
fresh oranges		21.9	37.8	24.0	27.1				18.2
fresh grapefruit		4.5	9.7	6.7	8.4				26.8
fresh total		29.1	50.9	32.8	37.5	31.7	25.0	23.3	20.0
juice		3.4	4.0	13.0	31.5	31.7	21.6	28.1	
Total		22.5	54.9	45.8	69.0	66.0	46.6	51.4	
Tomato (fresh equivalent)		42.4	52.8	53.9	55.9	59.3	60.9	61.6	
Total fruit		194.4	239.5	229.7	263.1	240.2	243.1	252.5	25.1
Fish									
Fresh & frozen		6.1	6.8	6.8	7.3	7.7	9.0	8.3	48.0
Smoked, salted, pickled		1.7	1.6	2.3	1.8	1.8	1.6	0.9	30.3
Canned		3.8	2.6	4.6	4.5	3.1	2.9	3.0	35.9
Total fish		11.6	11.0	13.7	13.6	14.6	13.5	12.2	
Milk & Cheese									
Fluid milk & cream: retail wt.	400.7	387.6	468.8	401.1	397.7	393.2	318.5	294.7	11.7
milk solid	45.7	44.2	53.4	45.7	45.3	44.3	36.3	33.7	102.3
Cheese									
Cheddar: retail wt.	2.7	2.2	2.4	2.3	2.8	5.9	3.4	3.4	73.0 (all cheese)
milk solid	1.8	1.5	1.6	1.5	1.9	3.8	2.2	2.2	121.7
Processed: retail wt.	1.0	1.5	2.9	2.5	2.9		3.8	4.3	121.7
milk solid	.6	.9	1.7	1.5	1.7		2.2	2.5	
Cottage: retail wt.		0.2	0.4	0.6	0.9	1.3	1.6	1.7	121.7
milk solid		0.1	0.1	0.2	0.2	0.3	0.4	0.4	

Other: retail wt.	3.0	4.9	7.2	8.6	10.4	1.3	1.9	2.7	121.7
milk solid	.4	.6	.9	1.1	1.3	0.8	1.2	1.8	
Ice Cream: retail wt.						39.1	27.4	35.8	233.0
milk solid						4.7	3.4	4.5	
Whole Milk									
Evaporated: retail wt.	4.3	8.3	11.4	17.5	18.4	17.7	16.1	14.3	10.1
milk solid	1.1	2.1	2.9	4.4	4.6	4.6	4.2	3.7	64.4
Condensed: retail wt.	0.7	0.6	0.8	0.8	0.8	0.8	1.0	1.2	35.3
milk solid	0.2	0.2	0.2	0.2	0.2	0.2	0.3	0.3	141.2
Powdered: retail wt.		0.1	0.5	0.4	0.2	0.3	0.2	0.2	35.5
milk solid		0.1	0.5	0.4	0.2	0.3	0.2	0.2	35.5
Skim Milk									
Evaporated: retail wt.	0.0	0.1	0.2	0.9	0.6	0.2			16.8
milk solid		0.02	0.03	0.2	0.1	0.1			87.1
Condensed: retail wt.	0.4	0.4	0.3	0.3	0.2	0.1			17.4
milk solid	0.1	0.1	0.1	0.1	0.07	0.3			52.7
Powdered: retail wt.		2.3	2.6	3.4	5.6	6.9	7.1	7.6	34.1
milk solid		2.2	2.5	3.3	5.4	6.6	6.9	7.4	35.5
Buttermilk									
Condensed: retail wt.	0.0	0.0	0.2	0.2	0.1				17.4
milk solid			0.1	0.1	0.0				52.7
Powdered: retail wt.						0.4	0.4	0.6	34.1
milk solid						0.4	0.4	0.6	34.1
Whey: milk solid							2.1	1.8	(100)
Miscellaneous: milk solid							0.8	1.0	(100)
Total milk	49.9	52.0	64.0	58.7	61.0	66.4	60.5	59.7	
Soft Drinks (gallons)		4.7	4.3	7.5	8.0	9.0	10.3	12.5	94 (per gallon)
Alcoholic Beverages									
Spirits (proof gallons)	.65	1.09	.89	.83	.98	1.16	1.38	1.76	2,017 (per proof, gal.)
Beer/ale (gallons)	5.04	6.35	10.24	12.37	13.30	13.20	14.21	14.97	250 (per gallon)
Wines (gallons)	.34	.46	.36	.38	.39	.50	.61	.67	923 (per gallon)
Tobacco									
Cigarettes (number)	491	682	1,422	1,277	1,599	1,952	2,223	2,263	2 (per cigarette)
Cigars (number)	11	15	17	15	16	18	26	21	
Tobacco (lbs. smoking, chewing, snuff)	2.2	2.7	2.4	2.2	1.6	1.3	1.0	0.9	1,000 (per lb.)

TABLE 2 (continued)

B. Food Indexes (1961 = 100)

	1935	1940	1945	1950	1955	1960	1965	1968	Value in Dollars 1961
Meat	83	87	105	90	108	105	109	116	107.73
Eggs	102	91	97	89	107	108	94	94	8.94
Poultry	45	50	61	50	72	90	118	127	16.31
Pulses & nuts	127	174	152	132	125	96	156	162	4.58
Oils & fats	144	143	117	131	124	99	106	111	18.73
Potatoes	125	134	103	115	95	88	99	107	7.69
Cereals	130	119	144	117	110	101	107	92	37.07
Sugars	104	110	89	111	105	100	104	104	11.00
Vegetables	(74)	74	89	95	96	100	97	97	17.39
Fruit	(84)	84	107	103	116	107	107	111	51.6
Fish	(91)	91	89	106	107	102	111	101	5.27
Milk & cheese	77	78	95	86	88	102	87	88	67.31
Coffee	36	39	50	67	73	100	97	108	10.80
Tea	133	150	175	167	113	100	100	104	1.77
Food index	89	91	104	96	103	102	104	106	366.37
Soft drinks	(43)	51	47	83	89	99	116	138	9.07
Alcohol	47	69	77	84	93	100	113	130	61.03
Tobacco	59	76	98	88	90	97	104	102	56.38
Food index including soft drinks	88	91	102	96	103	102	104	107	375.43

TABLE 2 (continued)

C. Appliances

	1935	1940	1945	1950	1955	1960	1965	1968	1961 Price (Dollars per Unit)
Stoves									
Electric (no. per th. of pop.)	2.2	2.8	1.8	11.9	14.1	12.5	15.1	15.9	137.85
Gas (no. per th. of pop.)	2.2	3.0	2.2	4.3	3.8	2.8	2.5	2.2	123.06
Vacuum cleaners (no. per th. of pop.)	3.3	5.1	1.4	15.5	15.3	15.6	20.9	26.5	47.70
Refrigerators (no. per th. of pop.)	3.1	6.9	0.3	16.6	23.8	16.7	18.0	22.5	172.72
Radio receiving sets (no. per th. of pop.)	17.6	43.3	4.2	57.4	72.6	77.0	120.2	169.6	42.27
T.V. sets (no. per th. of pop.)				2.4	51.7	20.0	26.8	37.6	164.66
Washing machines (no. per th. of pop.)	7.3	11.5	4.8	21.1	19.4	17.9	21.0	23.0	120.30
Home freezers (no. per th. of pop.)					3.9	5.6	8.6	8.8	173.92
Toasters (no. per th. of pop.)	11.4	15.0	11.8	23.8	21.8	16.7	33.2	33.3	8.54
Electric flat irons (no. per th. of pop.)	16.2	20.5	14.9	37.8	38.3	22.2	38.3	39.7	9.05
Clothes dryers (no. per th. of pop.)					3.1	7.7	10.3	11.5	135.05
Th. of incandescent lights (no. per head)	2.1	2.5	3.7	5.1	5.4	5.0	5.6	6.0	0.19
Water heaters (no. per th. of pop.)		4.8	7.6	19.9	25.6	30.8	36.5	37.3	48.00
Value per capita	3.13	5.95	1.99	12.64	24.03	18.23	23.78	29.25	
Index (1961 = 100)	17	32	11	68	129	98	127	157	

603

TABLE 2 (continued)

D. Clothing: Shipments by Canadian Manufacturers

	Unit	1935	1940	1945	1950	1955	1960	1965	1968	1961 Price Dollars per Unit
1. Aprons	No./Person	.0842	.1814	.2685	.2093	.2128	.1777	.1442	.1084	.62
2. Bathing suits	"	.0616	.0757	.1037	.1263	.1203	.1602	.1830	.1346	2.81
Shipment + import − export								.1902	.1571	
3. Bathrobes	"	.0532	.0957	.1423	.0837	.0880	.1207	.2129	(.2873)	4.25
4. Blouses	"	.0918	.1160	.5119	.5587	.6726	.6818	.7650	.5898	1.87
Shipment + import − export								1.0412	.8911	
5. Regular model coats	"	.2080	.2004	.2609	.2338	.2189	.1707	.2013	.1906	21.30
Shipment + import − export								.2217	.2369	
6. Fur coats	"	.0078	.0113	.0173	.0146	.0135	.0116	.0092	.0092	229.87
7. Fur-lined coats	"	.00005	.00035	.00031	.00037	.00024	.00004	.00010	.0000	103.18
8. Jackets	"	.0075	.0064	.0572	.0065	.0773	.0728	.1017	.0863	10.59
Shipment + import − export	"							.1307	.1699	
9. Raincoats	"	.0572	.0731	.0519	.0571	.1155	.0716	.1199	.1531	8.88
Shipment + import − export	"							.1564	.2767	
10. Short coats	"	.1140	.1179	.1690	.2097	.2904	.3584	.5351	(.5868)	6.84
Shipment + import − export	"							.5365	(.5875)	
11. Dresses	"	1.124	1.134	1.382	1.190	1.077	0.870	0.892	0.957	6.78
Shipment + import − export	"							.9179	1.0167	
12. Footwear	Pair/Person	3.378	4.070	4.737	3.578	3.249	3.1512	3.462	2.921	4.18
Shipment + import − export	"							3.860	4.581	
13. Foundation garment	No./Person	0.277	0.319	0.599	0.728	0.895	0.970	1.293	1.269	1.82
Shipment + import − export	"							1.318	1.288	
14. Gloves & mittens	Pair/Person	.989	1.148	2.105	1.659	1.384	1.165	1.278	1.567	0.76
Shipment + import − export	"							2.282	1.646	

Item	Unit									
15. Headwear	No./Person	1.3937	.9728	1.1819	.9408	.8675	.7305	.7417	.7620	1.71
Shipment + import − export	"							1.6360	1.2356	
16. Hosiery	Pair/Person	6.849	8.641	8.442	8.086	7.051	9.122	10.632	10.538	0.34
Shipment + import − export	"							10.533	10.558	
17. Nightdresses, nightshirts	No./Person	.1447	.1522	.1782	.1841	.2339	.2071	.3119	.3557	1.82
18. Pants	"	.2467	.2646	.3886	.3613	.3276	.3204	.5009	.4684	4.75
Shipment + import − export								.8349	.9937	
19. Playsuits		.1015	.0322	.1752	.0829	.1208	.1026	.1722	.0177	1.27
20. Pyjamas		.2128	.2245	.3353	.3356	.3871	.5254	.5313	.5339	1.74
17. & 20. Sleepwear								.8432	.8898	
Shipment + import − export								.9842	1.1334	
21. Scarves	"	.0862	.1599	.2455	.2625	.2490	.2015	.1920	(.8989)	0.75
Shipment + import − export	"							.2836	(.1650)	
22. Shirts	"	1.270	1.466	1.277	1.498	1.887	1.764	1.7139	2.2815	1.85
Shipment + import − export	"							1.1683	3.1089	
23. Ski suits & snowsuits	"	.0108	.0211	.0538	.0456	.0367	.0867	.1179	.0604	3.09
24. Skirts	"	.0365	.0485	.1256	.1846	.3205	.3231	.2809	.2593	3.40
Shipment + import − export	"							.2832	.2627	
25. Slacks and jeans	Pair/Person	.0246	.0115	.0621	.1371	.2852	.4195	.7475	.8210	2.12
Shipment + import − export	"							.8676	.9846	
26. Sport shorts	"	.0132	.0132	.1310	.1375	.1438	.1503	.2075	.2542	1.32
Shipment + import − export	"							.2906	.4122	
27. Suits	No./Person	.1722	.1716	.3594	.2120	.1717	.1369	.2293	.2221	31.27
Shipment + import − export	"							.2336	.2334	
28. Sweaters	"	.3657	.6923	.8330	1.1086	.8123	1.0125	1.2273	1.0356	3.10
Shipment + import − export	"							1.3937	1.0876	
29. Underwear	"	3.268	3.796	4.133	4.242	4.716	4.666	5.005	4.9584	0.67
Shipment + import − export	"							5.146	5.3567	
Clothing index (1961=1.00)		.83	.93	1.24	1.05	1.02	.97	1.16	1.14	

TABLE 2 (continued)

E. Housing

	1931	1941	1951	1955	1960	1965	1968	1961 Price Dollars per House
Number of dwellings								
1 room(s)	84	65	64	51	55	51	56	2,180
2	151	151	166	143	120	119	138	5,200
3	198	255	344	373	386	389	466	8,250
4	312	422	669	787	858	845	932	11,504
5	343	438	673	856	1,060	1,260	1,363	14,851
6	418	508	662	803	967	1,097	1,176	17,617
7	286	310	371	408	466	531	621	18,685
8	213	218	239	252	263	305	358	21,050
9	250	209	221	199	229	259	284	26,591
Total	2,253	2,576	3,409	3,872	4,404	4,853	5,394	
Number of dwellings with running water								
hot and cold			1,940	2,530	3,472	4,243	4,907	
cold only			584	532	468	312	272	
total		1,559	2,524	3,062	3,940	4,555	5,179	
Number of dwellings with flush toilets		1,450	2,187	2,751	3,469	3,820	5,044	
Number of dwellings with installed bath or shower		1,270	1,938	2,483	3,375	4,171	4,861	

Dwellings per thousand people							
1 room(s)	8.09	5.6	4.6	3.2	3.1	2.6	2.7
2	14.55	13.1	11.8	9.1	6.7	6.1	6.7
3	19.08	22.2	24.6	23.8	21.6	19.8	22.5
4	30.07	36.7	47.8	50.1	48.0	43.0	44.9
5	33.06	38.1	48.0	54.5	59.3	64.1	65.7
6	40.29	44.1	47.3	51.2	54.1	55.8	56.7
7	27.56	26.9	26.5	26.0	26.1	27.0	29.9
8	20.53	18.9	17.1	16.1	14.7	15.5	17.3
9	24.09	18.2	15.8	12.7	12.8	13.8	13.69
Total	217.17	223.8	243.5	246.7	246.4	247.7	260.1
Value of dwellings in 1961 dollars per head	3,385	3,413	3,646	3,701	3,743	3,828	3,738
Index of value of housing per head	85.8	90.3	96.3	98.8	100.0	101.2	106.4
Quality of housing							
% running water (P_1)		.64	.74	.79	.89	.94	.96
% flush toilet (P_2)		.56	.64	.71	.79	.79	.94
% bath & shower (P_3)		.49	.57	.64	.77	.86	.90
Quality index [a]	.83	.83	.87	.89	.93	.95	.98
Revised housing index [b]		78.9	88.2	92.5	97.9	101.3	109.8

[a] Quality index $= .6 + 1P_3 + 1P_2 + 2P_1$.

[b] Revised housing index $=$ housing index $\times$ quality index (based 1961 $=$ 100).

TABLE 2 (continued)
F. Health

	Unit	1935	1940	1945	1950	1955	1960	1965	1968	1961 Price Dollars per Unit
Physicians in active fee practice	No. per 1,000 people	.7184	.7434	.7463	.7445	.7687	.8102	.8379	.8795	26,000
Dentists in active fee practice	No. per 1,000 people	.3572	.3474	.3495	.3183	.3217	.3068	.3025	.3017	24,000
Graduate nurses in hospitals	No. per 1,000 people	.6415	.7097	.8087	1.2757	1.5321	1.8931	2.1914	2.5248	25,000
Hospital beds	No. per 1,000 people	8.526	9.952	9.381	10.179	10.688	10.345	10.478	10.220	3,590
Value	$ per head 1961 = 100	73.80 68	80.26 75	81.74 75	95.51 88	104.45 96	112.73 104	121.53 112	129.85 120	

608

TABLE 2 (continued)

G. Education

	1935	1940	1945	1950	1955	1960	1965	1968	Cost Inclusive of Forgone Earnings 1961 Dollars
Number of students ('000s)									
Primary	1,877	1,818	1,735	1,956	2,184	3,234	3,818	4,127	300
Secondary	277	329	307	349	387	715	1,150	1,324	1,600
Undergraduate	33	36	38	69	65	95	164	237	3,600
Graduate	1.5	1.6	1.7	5.3	4.9	9.1	21.9	35.2	8,000
Students per 100 people									
Primary	17.31	15.97	14.39	14.26	13.91	18.43	19.44	19.89	
Secondary	2.55	2.89	2.54	2.55	2.47	4.00	5.85	6.38	
Undergraduate	.30	.32	.31	.50	.41	.53	.83	1.14	
Graduate	.0138	.0141	.0141	.0387	.0312	.0509	.1115	.1700	
Expenditure $ per head at 1961 prices	104.85	106.68	96.32	104.71	98.57	4.52	190.96	216.55	
Index (1961 = 100)	69	71	64	69	65	95	127	144	

TABLE 2 (continued)

H. Transport and Communication

	Unit	1935	1940	1945	1950	1955	1960	1965
Transport								
Civil aviation	⎰Passenger miles per capita	.732	3.617	13.184	42.577	81.622	159.318	257.865
Railroad		146.11	191.24	528.51	205.38	184.21	126.68	135.71
Motor buses	⎰Passengers carried per capita	5.24	5.73	8.26	9.81	5.10	3.43	2.65
Urban transport		103.39	116.14	127.57	113.80	77.47	57.59	50.11
Automobiles (stock)	⎰Number per capita	.091	.108	.096	.139	.187	.230	.269
Motorcycles (stock)		.0010	.0012	.0012	.0032	.0023	.0019	.0038
Communication								
First-class letters	Number per capita	(34.87)	(34.87)	(34.87)	38.00	(41.06)	45.40	45.20
Telephones		.057	.064	.078	.110	.145	.221	.270
Telegrams		.882	.989	1.305	1.351	1.139	.768	.587
Cablegrams		.120	.145	.182	.123	.143	.142	.155
Automobile & motorcycle								
Value	(1961 = 100)	40.36	47.90	45.58	61.77	82.95	101.95	119.36
Index		38	46	41	59	79	97	114
Purchased transport								
Value	(1961 = 100)	28.97	32.37	45.06	37.09	26.96	23.17	25.91
Index		127	142	198	163	118	102	109
Transport inclusive of automobiles								
Value	(1961 = 100)	69.32	80.26	87.65	98.86	109.91	125.12	144.27
Index		54	63	69	77	86	98	113
Communication								
Value	(1961 = 100)	9.96	11.01	13.44	15.97	18.02	22.53	25.57
Index		42	47	57	68	77	96	109
Transport & communication								
Value	(1961 = 100)	79.29	91.27	101.09	114.83	127.93	147.66	169.84
Index		52	60	67	76	85	98	112

	Unit	1968	1961 Price Dollars per Unit	Percentage Not attributable to Business Use	Imputed Price Dollars per Unit
Transport					
Civil aviation }	Passenger miles per capita	388.273	0.0557	67	0.0371
Railroad }		123.10	0.0312	75	0.0234
Motor buses }	Passengers carried per capita	2.89	0.81	100	0.81
Urban transport }		50.81	0.20	100	0.20
Automobiles (stock) }	Number per capita	.302	553.32	80	442.66
Motorcycles (stock) }		.0068	92.22	80	73.78
Communication					
First-class letters }	Number per capita	50.33	0.05		
Telephones		.302	75.63		
Telegrams }		.426	3.90		
Cablegrams		.196	3.90		
Automobile & motorcycle					
Value		134.19			
Index	(1961 = 100)	128			
Purchased transport					
Value		29.79			
Index	(1961 = 100)	131			
Transport inclusive of automobiles					
Value		163.97			
Index	(1961 = 100)	128			
Communication					
Value		27.78			
Index	(1961 = 100)	118			
Transport & communication					
Value		191.76			
Index	(1961 = 100)	127			

TABLE 2 (continued)

I. Quantity Indexes for the Main Categories of Expenditure

	1931	1935	1940	1945	1950	1955	1960	1965	1968	Value in 1961 $ per Head	Growth Rate
Food (including soft drinks)		88	91	102	96	103	102	104	107	375.43	0.6
Alcohol		47	69	77	84	93	100	113	130	61.03	3.2
Tobacco		59	76	98	88	90	97	104	102	56.38	2.9
Housing (no. of rooms)	86										
Housing (with quality index)		(73)	(78)	(83)	(88)	93	98	101	110		0.6
Automobiles		38	46	41	59	79	97	114	128	105.05	3.6
Purchased transport		127	142	198	163	118	102	109	131	22.79	0.1
Communication		42	47	57	68	77	96	109	118	23.54	3.1
Appliances		17	32	11	68	129	98	127	157	18.68	6.8
Education		69	71	64	69	65	95	127	144	150.79	2.2
Health		68	74	75	88	96	104	112	120	104.48	1.7
Clothing		83	102	127	105	102	97	116	114	59.56	0.9
Total Consumption		67	74	84	85	94	99	111	120	1,538.30	1.8

NOTE: All time series are from other parts of Table 2. The value shares used in computing total consumption on the last line are not those in this table but are, instead, taken from the national accounts and reproduced in the first column of Table 1. In estimating total consumption, index numbers of recreation and miscellaneous are incorporated from the national accounts because there are no quantity data on these items.

TABLE 2 (continued)

J. Quality Indexes (1961 = 100)

	1935	1940	1945	1950	1955	1960	1965	1968	% Growth Rate
Food (including soft drinks)	78	86	97	96	93	100	100	100	0.8
Alcohol	70	63	85	101	101	99	99	90	0.8
Tobacco	64	63	86	92	91	100	100	97	1.3
Housing					81	97	115	127	1.5
Automobiles	84	91	29	122	115	102	121	114	0.9
Purchased Transport	41	44	58	68	84	98	102	94	2.5
Communication	83	83	91	100	103	100	110	119	1.1
Education	59	60	76	89	100	89	127	142	2.7
Health	92	102	120	121	127	152	127	107	0.5
Clothing	71	68	82	83	89	104	90	94	0.9
Total Consumption	76	80	87	95	98	103	104	103	0.9

NOTE: All quality indexes are ratios of "Quantity Indexes Implicit in the National Accounts" and "Quantity Indexes for the Main Categories of Expenditures."

613

TABLE 2 (concluded)

K. Quantity Indexes Implicit in the National Accounts (1961 = 100)

	1935	1940	1945	1950	1955	1960	1965	1968	Value in $ per head	Growth Rate
Food	69	79	99	93	96	102	104	107	266.37	1.4
Alcohol	33	44	66	85	94	99	112	118	51.49	3.8
Tobacco	38	51	85	81	82	97	105	99	40.79	2.9
Housing (inclusive of fuel, rent, furniture, appliances, household operation)	51	57	60	71	85	97	117	130	355.96	2.8
Actual and imputed rents	48	50	58	65	81	97	117	135	248.77	3.2
Automobiles	32	42	12	72	91	99	139	146	126.38	4.6
Purchased transport	52	63	115	112	100	100	112	124	34.27	2.6
Communication	35	39	52	68	79	96	120	140	20.67	4.2
Education	41	43	49	62	65	85	162	205	13.82	4.9
Health	63	76	90	107	122	159	113	129	56.80	2.2
Clothing	59	70	103	88	91	101	105	107	124.79	1.8
Recreation	45	55	64	81	104	96	116	126	182.38	3.1
Miscellaneous	44	45	73	70	91	99	118	138	222.56	3.5
Miscellaneous (minus unallocated sales tax)	47	48	77	71	94	101	114	129	207.30	3.1
Total consumption	51	59	73	81	92	102	115	124	1,377.34	2.8

Further Notes to Table 2

The numbers in parentheses are quantities per head which, for the want of data, are interpolated or extrapolated from the rest of the series of which they form a part. Except where stated otherwise, prices are either from records of Statistics Canada or are current prices deflated to 1961 by a component of the consumer price index. Publications of Statistics Canada are identified by the letters DBS, standing for Dominion Bureau of Statistics, which was the name of Statistics Canada when these publications were released.

Food: The quantity data are from *Food Consumption in Canada,* DBS 32-226. This publication presents the data as pounds per head of domestic disappearance, and only minor adjustments were necessary in transferring the data to Table 2. For the years prior to 1955, eggs were converted from dozens to pounds at a rate of 1.53. Chickens are converted from dressed to eviscerated weight at a rate of .76 and from eviscerated to edible weights at a rate of .71; these conversions are made for other poultry at rates of .85 and .79; and prices are adjusted accordingly. Though Table 2 contains data on fresh, canned, frozen, and dried vegetables separately, all quantities are expressed in "fresh equivalents," and all prices are "fresh equivalent" prices; that is, either prices of fresh vegetables or prices of other forms of vegetables adjusted by the same factors used to convert pounds of canned, frozen, or dried vegetables to a fresh equivalent basis. Conversion factors between canned, dried, or frozen vegetables and fresh equivalents are contained in *Food Consumption in Canada.* The same principle is applied in converting quantities of fruit to fresh equivalents and in converting quantities of dairy products into pounds of milk solids. Quantities of flour were evaluated at the price of bread because most flour is consumed in that form. The apparent fall in the quantity of grapes consumed between 1955 and 1958 is due to the fact that the early figures refer to the fresh equivalent of grapes consumed in all forms—as fresh fruit, jams, preserves and raisins—while the later figures refer only to fresh fruit, and grapes consumed as jams, preserves, etc., are included as "unspecified."

Alcohol, Tobacco, Soft Drinks, Clothing, Appliances: Quantities consumed of alcohol, tobacco, soft drinks, and appliances are estimated as domestic disappearance, shipments of domestic firms plus imports minus exports, and the sources of data are indicated in Table 4. However, consumption of clothing is estimated from domestic shipments alone because data on international trade in clothing are unavailable for the years prior to the revision of the trade classification in 1961.

Prices of clothing and appliances are unit values of shipments. These are satisfactory surrogates for retail prices if wholesale prices of imported and exported items are the same as prices of items domestically produced, and if retail margins are the same for imported items as for domestically produced items. If these conditions hold, it does not matter that items are valued at wholesale prices because growth rates of consumption in each major category are aggregated by value shares of expenditure in constructing the total growth rate of real consumption in Table 1. Prices of alcohol, soft drinks and tobacco were obtained from local distributors in Kingston.

Transport and Communication: Quantities of transport and communication in Table 2 are estimated from these sources: DBS publications 51-202, 52-210, 53-215, 53-D-20, 53-216, 53-219, 56-203 and 56-201. Data on passenger-miles ought to refer to miles traveled by Canadians but they do not; they refer to passenger-miles supplied by Canadian carriers. I have made rough guesses as to shares of the different means of transport attributable to business and personal use. Urban transport includes buses, trolley cars, streetcars, charter buses, and subways. Unfortunately there are no data on number of fares prior to 1946; the numbers in the table were gotten by supposing that total use of urban transport is proportional to nonagricultural employment (M.C. Urquhart and K. Buckley, *Historical Statistics of Canada,* series C59 and C66). The estimate of the number of pieces of first-class mail is based on data supplied by the Post

Office supplemented by data from Urquhart and Buckley, *Historical Statistics of Canada*. There are no data on amounts of first-class mail in the first decade of our period but estimates for the years 1900 to 1915 in Urquhart and Buckley suggest that we are not too wide of the mark in guessing that the number of letters sent grew in proportion to population.

Prices of purchased transport and communication are unit values, revenues divided by quantities, in the year 1961. Use prices of automobiles are imputed by dividing the estimate of total private expenditure on automobiles in the national accounts by the number of automobiles in the year 1961. In this calculation motorcycles are counted as sixths of automobiles.

Medicine: Numbers of physicians and dentists are from Urquhart and Buckley, (B108 and B111) p. 44, supplemented for the years after 1960 with data from *Earnings of Physicians in Canada,* Health Care Series #21 and #25, Department of Health and Welfare, and *Earnings of Dentists in Canada,* Health Care Series #26, Department of Health and Welfare. The number of graduate nurses in hospitals (DBS 83-212, Hospital Statistics III, Hospital Personnel) is combined with the number of hospital beds (DBS 83-210) to serve as a surrogate for the remainder of medical expenditure. Consequently, the imputed price of nurses is not the actual wage but a substantially higher figure, and the value imputed to hospital beds is the total value of medical services over and above the imputed value of doctors, dentists, and nurses in 1961. This measure of real consumption in medicine shares with the measure in the national accounts the defect that it is of inputs to medicine rather than outputs of health.

Education: The number of students are from Urquhart and Buckley, Section 5, with additional information supplied by S. Zsygmond of the education division of DBS and some interpolation to fill in gaps in the data. Estimates of cost are based on communications from Barry Lacombe of the Economic Council and David Dodge of the Ministry of Finance, Ottawa.

Housing: The data on numbers of dwellings subdivided according to numbers of rooms and on numbers of houses with running water, flush toilets and installed bath and shower are from *Household Facilities and Equipment,* DBS 64-202 for the years from 1953 to the present. The earlier data are from the census: *Census of Canada, 1931, Volume I, Summary,* Chapter XX, p. 329; *Census of Canada, 1941, Volume IX, Housing,* Table 6b, p. 20; *Census of Canada 1951, Volume III, Housing and Families,* Table 12, p. 12. Prices of new houses are used as surrogates for rents. These prices are supplied by Dev Khosla of Statistics Canada and they are from a so far unpublished survey of house characteristics and house values. The surrogates are adequate if rents are proportional to house prices.

In principle, a quality index could be devised along the lines followed in constructing hedonic price indexes. I have instead constructed an index with arbitrarily chosen weights and designed to be multiplied with the index of housing based on number of rooms. The index gives a value of 1 to a house with running water, flush toilets and installed bath and shower, and a value of 0.6 to a house of the same size with none of these.

Table 2 as it stands is a condensation of a larger table in which quantities are presented for every available year from 1935 to 1968. The full table is available from the author on request. See Tables A and B for sources of data.

TABLE A
Sources of Data: Alcohol, Tobacco and Appliances

Commodities	DBS Catalogue Number	Table Name (1935–1951)	DBS Catalogue Number	Table Name (1952–1960)	DBS Catalogue Number	Table Name (1961–1968)	1935–1960 in Trade of Canada		1961–1968 in Trade of Canada	
							Import Number 65-203	Export Number 65-202	Import Number 65-203	Export Number 65-202
Alcohol Spirits	32-206	Production	32-206	Production & Sales Excluding Sales Tax and Other Duties	32-206	Production & Sales Excluding Sales Tax & Other Duties	1511-1516	1020, 1030, 1040	17360, 17310, 17320, 17330, 17340	17320, 17340, 17399
Wine	32-207	Production of Wine	32-207	Shipments of Own Manufacture (Matured Wines)	32-207	Shipments of Own Manufacture (Matured Wines)	1530, 1531	1060	17230, 17250	17299
Beer	32-205	Statistics of Products Made in Brewing Industry	32-205	Shipments of Goods of Own Manufacture	32-205	Shipments of Goods of Own Manufacture	1501	1010	17220	17220

(continued)

617

TABLE A (continued)

Commodities	DBS Catalogue Number	Table Name (1935–1951)	DBS Catalogue Number	Table Name (1952–1960)	DBS Catalogue Number	Table Name (1961–1968)	1935–1960 in Trade of Canada		1961–1968 in Trade of Canada	
							Import Number 65-203	Export Number 65-202	Import Number 65-203	Export Number 65-202
Tobacco										
Cigarettes	32-225	Production of Domestic Cigarettes	32-225	Factory Shipments of Domestic Cigarettes	32-225	Factory Shipments of Domestic Cigarettes	1785	1560	18330	18330
Cigars	32-225	Production of Domestic Cigars	32-225	Factory Shipments of Domestic Cigars	32-225	Factory Shipments of Domestic Cigars	1784	1550	18350	18350
Appliances										
Electric Stoves	43-201	Number & Selling Value of Stoves Made in Canada	43-201	Factory Shipments of Stoves Made in Canada	43-204	Factory Shipments of Stoves Made in Canada	5716		66115	
Gas stoves	43-201		43-201		43-204		5717		66211	
Washing machines	43-201	Production of Domestic Washing Machines	43-201	Factory Shipments of Domestic Washing Machines	43-204	Factory Shipments of Domestic Washing Machines	5450, 5451	5611	69805, 69809	69809

Product		Production		Factory Shipments					
Vacuum cleaners	43-201	Production of Electric Vacuum Cleaners & Parts	43-201	Factory Shipments of Electric Vacuum Cleaners & Parts	43-203	5590	5442	69209	65054
Refrigerators	43-201	Production of Electric Refrigeration Equipment	43-201	Factory Shipments of Household Refrigeration Equipment	43-204	9079, 9080	9190	65541, 65543	63038
Radio sets	43-201	Production of Complete Radio Receiving Sets	43-201	Factory Shipments of Complete Radio Receiving Sets	43-205	6175	6450	63035, 63036	63037
TV sets	43-201	Production of Television Sets (Commences in 1949)	43-201	Factory Shipments of Television Sets	43-205	6174	6174	63937	
Home freezers	43-201		43-201	Factory Shipments of Home Freezers	43-204	9092		65546	
Toasters	43-201	Production of Electric Toasters	43-201	Factory Shipments of Electric Toasters	43-204			66159	
Electric ironers	43-201	Production of Electric Flat Irons	43-201	Factory Shipments of Flat Irons	43-203	5454		69835	
Clothes dryers	43-201		43-201	Factory Shipments of Clothes Dryers	43-204	5448		69829	

(continued)

TABLE A (concluded)

Commodities	DBS Catalogue Number	Table Name (1935–1951)	DBS Catalogue Number	Table Name (1952–1960)	DBS Catalogue Number	Table Name (1961–1968)	1935–1960 in Trade of Canada		1961–1968 in Trade of Canada	
							Import Number 65-203	Export Number 65-202	Import Number 65-203	Export Number 65-202
Incandescent light bulbs	43-201	Production of Electric Lamps (Bulbs)	43-201	Factory Shipments of Electric Lamps (Bulbs)	43-210	Factory Shipments of Electric Lamps (Bulbs)	6148		68202	
Water heaters	43-201	Production of Electric Water-Tank Heaters	43-201	Factory Shipments of Domestic Water-Tank Heaters	43-203	Factory Shipments of Domestic Water-Tank Heaters	5732		65353, 65369 65371	
Soft drinks	32-208	Production of Carbonated Beverages (All Industries by Province)	32-208	Shipments of Own Manufacture	32-208	Shipments of Own Manufacture		17199	17199	17199

TABLE B

Sources of Data: Clothing

DBS Catalogue Number		Title of Source		Table Name		Imports Vol. III *Trade of Canada* (65-203) Annual (1961–1968: Table 3)	Exports Vol. II *Trade of Canada* (65-202) Annual (1961–1968: Table 3)
1935–1960	1961–1968	1935–1960	1961–1968	1935–1960	1960–1961		
31-201	31-211	Manufacturing Industries of Canada	Products Shipped by Canadian Manufacturers	Alphabetical List of Products Manufactured in Canada–Year	Products Shipped by Canadian Manufacturers–Year	Underwear & sleepwear No. 78119-78199 Outwear No. 78304-78390 Outwear knitted No. 78404-78489 Apparel Accessories No. 78921 Hosiery No. 78522-78549 Headwear, Gloves and Mittens No. 78618-78635; 78649-78683 Footwear No. 79012-79099	Underwear No. 78009 Sleepwear No. 78019 Outwear No. 78022, 78037, 78045, 78093, 78094 Hosiery No. 78055-78059 Headwear, Gloves and Mittens No. 78065-78069 Footwear No. 79012-79099

all items of food consumption included in Table. 2. However, the list of foods in Table 2 is not quite complete. It excludes salt, spices, and I do not know how much else. To compensate for the missing items in Table 2, I have assessed the share of food in the growth rate of Total Consumption in the last row of the right-hand column of Table 1 by weighting the estimated growth rate of food consumption by the value share of food consumption in 1961 in the national accounts, rather than by the corresponding value share derivable from Table 2. This procedure would yield the correct result if consumption of items of food excluded from Table 2 grew at the same rate as consumption of the items included in the table.

A much more important instance of missing data is that the quantity of clothing is measured by shipments of domestic producers rather than by shipments plus imports minus exports, because the data on quantities exported and imported are only available for the final decade of the series. My weighting procedure compensates for the missing data on exports and imports if, and only if, the proportion between shipments and consumption of clothing has remained constant over time. As we have no quantity data on fuel and furniture, I assume the growth rates of consumption of fuel and furniture to be the same as the growth rate of consumption of the services of houses; the value of housing in Table 1 includes fuel and furniture, but the quantity data pertain to housing alone.

Missing data for particular years within a time series were interpolated or extrapolated; interpolated or extrapolated data are put in parentheses to distinguish them from genuine quantity data.

(ii) The choice of the base year. The year 1961 was chosen as the base year because it is the most recent base year in the Canadian national accounts and because Statistics Canada has a good deal of price data for that year. Though it would be interesting to compare my measure of real consumption with one constructed from prices of an earlier year, I have not done so because prices have proved difficult to obtain. An attempt to measure the rate of growth of food consumption using 1935 prices, obtained for the most part from advertisements in newspapers, showed that the change of base year had no appreciable effect. The choice of the base year has a significant effect on the measure of the growth rate of the quantity of purchased transport, because there has been a substantial shift over time from trains and buses to airplanes, and a gradual fall in the relative price of air transport and surface transport.

(iii) Public and private consumption. The attempt to specify outputs of health and education gives rise to two interesting problems in pure accounting. The first problem is one which is latent in the measurement of real consumption by deflation, but which is brought into the open when one measures consumption from quantity data. The issue is simply that health and education are provided partly in the public sector and partly in the private sector. Expenditure on health is not looked upon as a unity in the national accounts, because the first and fundamental division of expenditure in the accounts is between the public and private sectors, and as it turns out in the Canadian accounts, private expenditure on health and education is included in personal consumption, and public expenditure on these items is included in total government consumption but not presented separately anywhere in the accounts. One can discover from the accounts how much private individuals spent on health and education in current dollars or in 1961 dollars, but one cannot find out how much was spent in total or whether society's total real consumption of these items is increasing or not. For growth accounting, one needs statistics of gross national expenditure subdivided in the first instance by commodities, objects or purposes, rather than by agents, so that public and private expenditure on the same or closely connected objects might be combined. The need is especially acute when the dividing line between the public and private sectors is changing over time. This information is not now provided in the Canadian national accounts.

The second accounting problem concerns the distinctions between consumption, investment, and intermediate products. It is a convention in the national accounts that with certain exceptions which need not concern us here, all public expenditure is counted as final product, and any public expenditure that does not lead to the creation of tangible capital is counted as public consumption. This convention evolved at a time when the main purpose of the accounts was to serve as a tool of stabilization policy, and the convention is reasonable in that context. The convention is less reasonable in the context of measuring economic growth, for as has often been observed, a large part of what the accounts classify as government consumption might be classified instead as public cost of production. No one derives direct enjoyment from the activity of the Ministry of National Revenue. The collecting of taxes is not a consumption good. It is intermediate, and its contribution is as a prerequisite to the production of goods and services already included in the accounts.

A very crude classification by purpose of combined public and private expenditure is presented as Table 3. The first column entitled "cost of

TABLE 3

Expenditure by Purpose, 1961
(Millions of Dollars)

	Cost of Produc-tion (1)	Consump-tion (2)	Gross Invest-ment (3)	Consump-tion + Gross Investment (4)
Food, alcohol, and tobacco		6,541		6,541
Clothing		2,276		2,276
Housing				6,329
Rents & imputed rents		3,656		
Fuel		412		
Electricity		347		
Gas		122		
Residential construction			1,792	
Furniture		1,955		1,955
Recreation		1,157		1,157
Miscellaneous consumption		4,059		4,059
Transport [a]				2,130
Purchase and use of automobiles	1,138	1,137		
Other (private)	208	417		
Construction of roads and bridges			874	
Public current expenditure	214			
Communication [b]				598
Telephone (private)		324		
Post and telegraph (private)		53		
Public expenditure	116	221		
Education [c]				2,877
Private expenditure	⟵——— 252 ———⟶			
Forgone earnings of students	⟵——— 1,053 ———⟶			
Public current expenditure	⟵——— 1,248 ———⟶			
Public capital expenditure			356	

TABLE 3 (concluded)

	Cost of Production (1)	Consumption (2)	Gross Investment (3)	Consumption + Gross Investment (4)
Medicine [d]				2,159
Services of doctors, etc.	←———	580	———→	
Hospital care (private)	←———	207	———→	
Drugs (private)	←———	310	———→	
Other (private)	←———	39	———→	
Public current expenditure	←———	845·	———→	
Public capital expenditure			178	
Research [e]				859
Government			135	
University			51	
Business			141	
Government n.e.s. [f]				409
Defense	1,647			
General government	571			
Natural resources	605			
Public safety	489			
Foreign aid		67		
Public investment n.e.s.			342	
Industrial Investment [g]			6,619	
Total (with current expenditures on education and health included as consumption)		27,327	10,489	38,833

NOTE: Entries in column (1) refer only to costs of production borne by consumers or by government and counted as final product in the official accounts.

Further Notes to Table 3.

Except where stated otherwise, the data are from unpublished and preliminary estimates by Statistics Canada of personal consumption expenditure and of capital formation in the public sector. The reader should be warned that my attempt to apportion public expenditures among purposes is crude, that some items of expenditure may have been overlooked, and that there may be some double counting.

[a] To convert transport to work from a final product to an intermediate product, one-half of private expenditure on automobiles and one-third of other private expenditure on transport are attributed to cost of production rather than consumption. Public expenditure on road maintenance is counted as cost of production, a procedure consistent with the treatment of maintenance and repair in the private sector. Ideally the accounts should include as part of consumption an imputation for the services of roads. Public current expenditure on transport in Table 3 is the difference between total public expenditure on transportation (1,088 million) as estimated in *A Consolidation of Public Finance Statistics 1961*, DBS 68-202, Table 2, and total gross capital formation on roads and bridges.

[b] Public expenditure on communication is estimated from the source cited in *a;* one-third is assumed to be the cost of production.

[c] Public current expenditure in education is the residual when private expenditure (252 million), scholarships (12 million), current expenditures on research in universities (65 million), and capital formation in schools and universities (356 million) are deducted from total expenditure (1,913 million) as estimated in *Survey of Educational Finance 1961*, DBS 81-208, Table 1. Expenditure on research in universities is included elsewhere in Table 3.

[d] Total public expenditure on health is from *A Consolidation of Public Finance Statistics 1961*, DBS 68-202, Table 2. Public current expenditure is this total less capital formation in hospitals.

[e] *Industrial Research and Development Expenditure in Canada*, DBS 13-532, Table 2 of Section 4. Values for 1963 are reduced by 22 per cent, for it has been estimated that expenditures on research have been growing at 11 per cent a year.

[f] See note *a.*

[g] Total investment by firms less capital expenditures by firms on research (27 million dollars).

production" includes only those intermediate products (or what I choose to call intermediate products) which are counted as final products in the accounts. It is supposed that half of private expenditure on automobiles, one-third of other transport, all public expenditure on transport, and all of defense and "general government," are costs of production, in that they contribute to welfare indirectly through the intermediary of other goods and services. Similarly, both current and capital expenditures on research are counted as investment, because benefits from these expenditures accrue in the future and not in the current year. Health and education are not classified as cost of production, or as consumption, or as investment exclusively, because they share attributes of all three categories. Education is net investment when it leads to an increase in the stock of human capital. Education is cost of production (analogous to maintenance and repair of physical capital) when it preserves the stock of human capital by replacing skills of men who leave the labor force. Looked at from a different point of view, education is consumption, like going to the movies or reading a newspaper or hiring a baby-sitter. I have been conservative in adjusting values of consumption in Tables 1 and 2 because I wished to em-- phasize the contrast between deflation and revaluation, and not accounting problems per se. No private expenditure was shifted from consumption to cost of production, but private consumption was enlarged to include current public expenditure on health and education, for the quantity series pertain to health and education as a whole.

(iv) Quality and quantity. This distinction is by no means absolute, for the rate of quality change depends on what aspects of a good or service one is able to, or chooses to, record as quantity data. The shift over time from cereal consumption to meat consumption is quality change if the quantity of food is measured in calorific equivalents but not if cereals and meats are treated as separate goods. In Table 2, the shift from cereals to meats is recorded as an increase in the quantity of food consumed, but any improvement over time in the processing of food is unaccounted for in the quantity data and thereby assessed as part of quality change.

The available data on education would seem to permit us to measure the quantity of education either as numbers of students or as numbers of teachers and other inputs to the educational process. In conformity with its general procedure for expressing services in real terms, the national accounts deflate the value of education by a price index of inputs. We have chosen instead to measure the quantity of education by the number of students, subdivided into primary, secondary, undergraduate, and graduate, and evaluated at the cost per student in 1961 dollars inclusive of earnings forgone. Numbers of students has the advantage as a quantity indicator that it is an aspect of output rather than input, but it has the disadvantage that it fails to account for improvements in the quality of education resulting from changes in student-teacher ratios. Neither measure of the quantity of education captures the really important quality change manifested in the expansion of knowledge over time. Since we have no data on the output of health comparable to numbers of students as measures of the output of education, we follow the accounts in assessing output by input. The quantity index of health contains four items: numbers of doctors, numbers of dentists, numbers of graduate nurses in hospitals, and numbers of hospital beds. Services of doctors and dentists are evaluated at their gross incomes. Graduate nurses in hospitals and numbers of hospital beds are together considered as surrogates for all other aspects of medicine, including drugs and services of medical equipment. Nurses' services are evaluated in Table 2 at a price substantially higher than the nurse's wage, and the value of the services of hospital beds is measured as the difference between total expenditure on medicine and estimated expenditure on doctors, dentists, and nurses. This measure of real consumption of medicine has little to recommend it other than the availability of data. But it is important to recognize that the problem of choosing measures of real output of health and education is not circumvented when real consumption is measured by deflation, for difficulties inherent in the choice of quantities are also inherent in the choice of a price index, and a true price index cannot be constructed unless one can specify exactly what it is that is being priced. The quantity indexes of health and education in Table 2 may not be much worse than corresponding quantity indexes implicit in the Canadian national accounts.

Housing is the one category for which I have adjusted original quantity data for what might be called quality change. The original data are numbers of dwellings subdivided according to numbers of rooms and evaluated according to the purchase price of dwellings in 1961, on the assumption that house rents are proportional to house prices. This time series of the quantity of housing is then adjusted for the percentage of dwellings with running water, flush toilets, baths, and showers to obtain the series used in measuring real consumption in Table 1. It is significant that the rate of quality change, the difference between real consumption assessed by deflation and real consumption assessed by revaluation, is much higher for housing than for any other category. This may be genuine quality change or it may be the outcome of errors of measurement in one or both of the time series.

(v) Stocks and flows. Ideally, real consumption should be a flow of services, and the increase over the year in the stock of consumer durables should be counted as investment. Housing is treated in this way in the national accounts, for rent is counted as part of real consumption and the purchase of new houses is counted as investment. Purchases of durables like automobiles, furniture, and appliances are counted as consumption rather than as investment, and no attempt is made to impute values of the services of these items. In measuring the quantity of services of automobiles, we assume that the flow is proportional to the stock, but we follow the national accounts in treating purchases of appliances as consumption, and in not imputing for services of the stock. In connection with its forecasting models, the Bank of Canada has attempted to revise the measures of consumption and investment in Canada by treating the purchase of consumer durables as investment.

A COMPARISON BETWEEN THE TWO MEASURES OF REAL CONSUMPTION

The principal result of my calculations, as shown on the bottom line of Table 1, is that the rate of growth of real consumption per head is a full percentage point less when measured by revaluation of quantity data than when measured by deflation, 1.8 per cent per year as against 2.8 per cent per year in the national accounts. Part of the 1.0 per cent difference is undoubtedly quality change, part is due to conceptual differences between the series, and part is due to errors of measurement. Though we cannot apportion the 1.0 per cent among these factors, some insight can be obtained from the time series of quality change at the end of Table 2 and in the accompanying charts. A substantial improvement in the quality of food has been concentrated in the period prior to the end of World War II. Quality change ceased abruptly in 1947, and since then the deflated and revalued time series of real consumption have grown at about the same rate. I would be inclined to speculate that the apparent quality change before and during World War II is spurious, and that the revalued series is a fair representation of what should have been measured in the deflated series. The food series is the best of the quantity series. The coverage is detailed and comprehensive. The choice of 1961 as a base year does not seem to make much difference to the growth of the series; in fact, contrary to expectation, a very crude attempt to weight quantities at 1935 prices actually lowered the overall rate of growth. There may have been some improvement in the processing of food prior to World War II, but it is hard to see why the improvement should have been greater before the war than afterwards, considering that the introduction of frozen food occurred in the latter period. Tobacco and alcohol show a very rapid rise in quality between 1940 and 1945, and one cannot help suspecting that these quality changes are spurious too. On the other hand, the obviously spurious zigzags in the alcohol quality series prior to the war are transmitted from the quantity series, where they probably reflect my failure to adjust for changes in inventory. The rate of growth of quality of housing seems high, but it may be that there was a steady improvement over and above the qualities already incorporated into the quantity index. Part of the growth of the quality of housing is a consequence of the gradual movement of people from farms and small towns, where housing is cheap, to the city, where housing is dear. This shift is counted as an increase in real consumption of housing in the deflated series but not in the revalued series. One can have very little confidence in the quality index of clothing because the coverage of the revalued series is incomplete. The quality indexes in medicine and education are almost meaningless, because the deflated series refer to private expenditure and the revalued series refer to total—public and private—expenditure. The bump in 1961 in the deflated and quality series is a consequence of a reclassification of certain hospital expenditures from the private to the public sector.

The very rapid growth of quality of purchased transport is implausible, but it is difficult to compare the accuracy of the deflated series and revalued series because of some very serious index number problems that arise in any attempt to construct real series in this category. From 1935 to 1968, air transport increased rapidly while urban transport, rail transport, and bus transport all declined. A crude attempt to reweight the time series of the components of the index of purchased transport at 1947 prices increased the rate of growth of the revalued series but not nearly enough to account for the growth in quality. Except for the war years, the deflated series and the revalued series for automobile services grew at about the same rate, so that the overall growth of the quality series is negligible. The apparent decline in quality of automobile services during the war is a consequence of our decision to measure the flow of automobile services by the stock of cars. The corresponding series in the national accounts includes purchases of new cars as well as operating expenses. During the war, the flow of new cars was cut off and gasoline consumption was reduced sharply, but the decline in the stock of cars was only moderate by comparison. The surprising feature of the automobile chart is that improvements commonly believed to have taken place in the quality of automobiles—improvements such as the automatic clutch, larger engines, and safety features—are not reflected in the quality series. It should perhaps be stressed that the quality series in automobiles, as in every other category of expenditure, is strictly a relation between the two quantity series. A genuine quality change not reflected in the time series of real consumption assessed by deflation would be excluded from our quality series as well.

Though the task of data collection in preparing this paper was considerable, the work itself is no more than a pilot study designed to elucidate the relation between indexes of real consumption, and to illustrate in a very rough way the orders of magnitude of their growth rates. I doubt whether a really good set of quantity data will emerge until Statistics Canada takes a hand in creating it and makes an effort to attach quantity series to as many as possible of the items in the accounts.

[Appendix figures begin on the following page.]

APPENDIX: GRAPHS OF REAL CONSUMPTION AND
QUALITY CHANGE

FIGURE 1

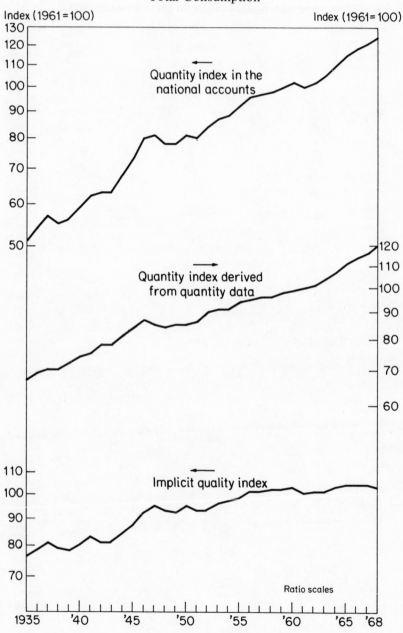

Total Consumption

FIGURE 2

Food

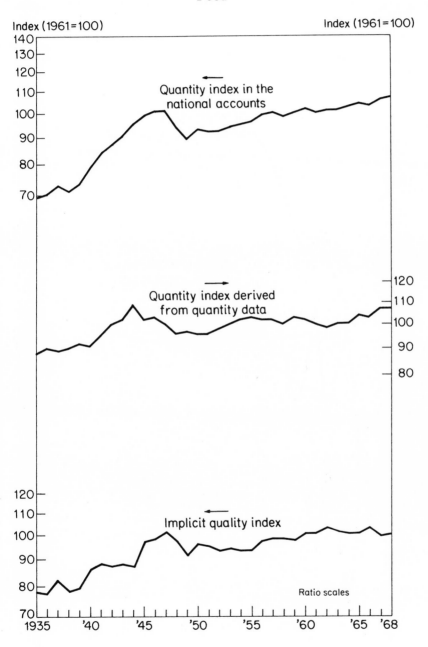

FIGURE 3

Alcohol

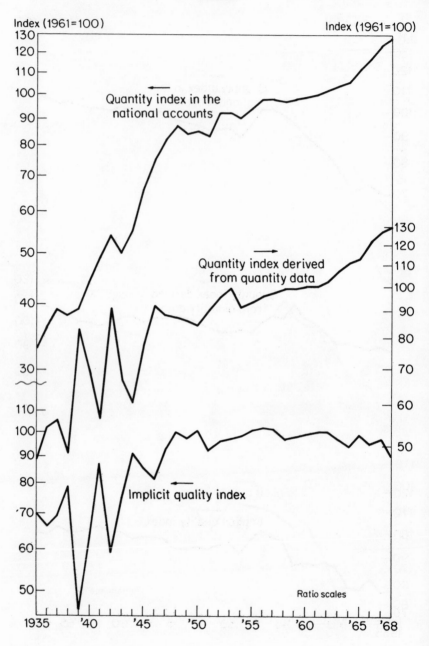

FIGURE 4

Tobacco

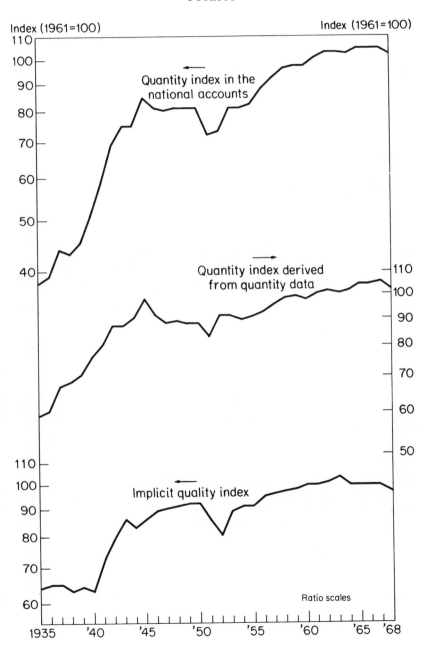

FIGURE 5

Clothing

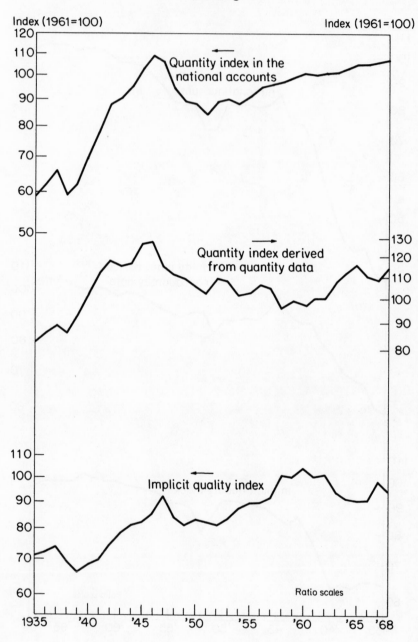

FIGURE 6

Housing

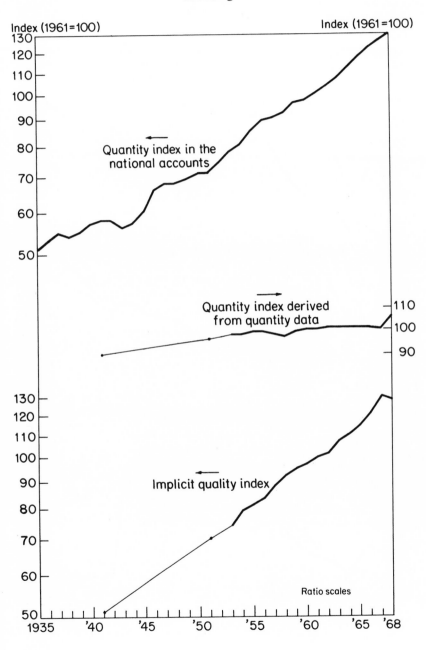

FIGURE 7

Medical Services

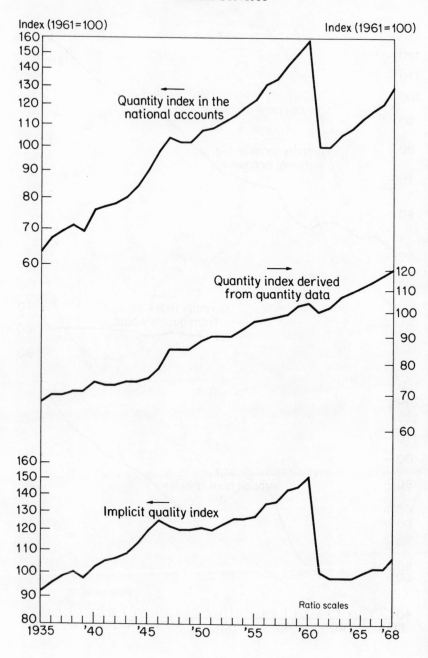

FIGURE 8

Purchased Transport

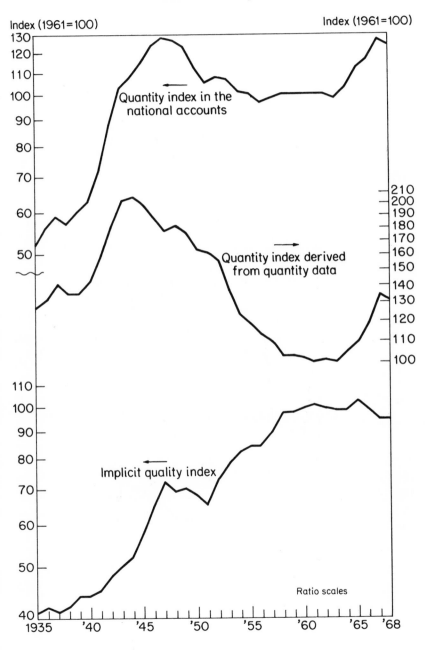

FIGURE 9

Automobiles

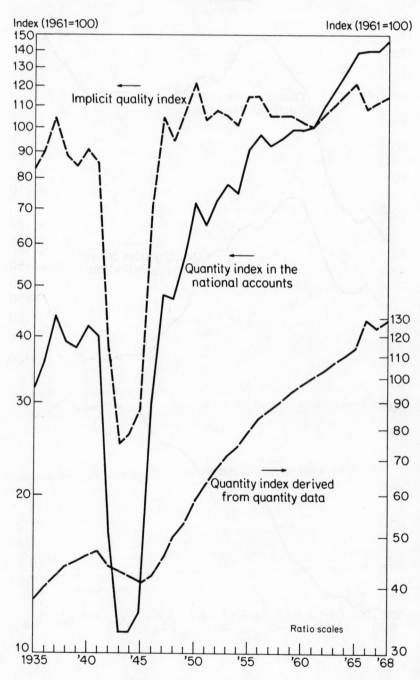

Index (1961=100)

Index (1961=100)

Implicit quality index

Quantity index in the national accounts

Quantity index derived from quantity data

Ratio scales

FIGURE 10

Communication

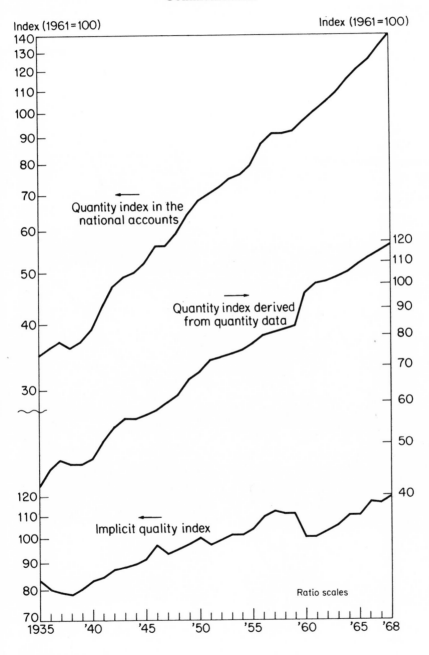

FIGURE 11

Education

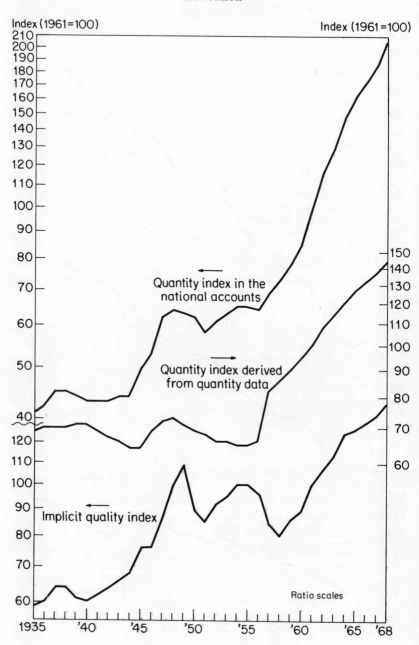

Comments on "Measuring Real Consumption from Quantity Data, Canada 1935-1968"

MARGARET G. REID

UNIVERSITY OF CHICAGO

DAN USHER is to be commended for the attention he has given to the shortcomings of data available for estimating secular change of total quantity of consumption. His review of them provides a useful introduction to prospective users of annual estimates of national consumption expenditures. At the same time, it seems likely to assure agreement with his doubts "whether a really good set of quantity data [for Canada] will emerge until Statistics Canada takes a hand in creating it and makes an effort to attach quantity series to as many as possible of the items in the accounts" (p. 631).

The estimates presented are likely to stimulate discussion along several lines. My comments will deal with a few of these. I must at the outset confess that I have only limited knowledge of the national accounts of Canada and my knowledge of the construction of corresponding accounts of the United States is far from complete. I am a user of consumption data, not a compiler, and am more acquainted with their imperfections than with techniques for their improvement. Usher's discussion does, however, deal more with their imperfection than with improvement.

The title of this paper refers to measuring real consumption from quantity data. Indexes of "quality" of categories of consumption and of "total" consumption are, however, presented and receive considerable discussion. These represent change of price-deflated consumption expenditures not explained by the quantity indexes developed. Quality indexes, thus, are subject to the errors of the expenditure series, of the price indexes used to deflate them, and of the estimated quantity indexes. Usher notes that the elimination of the quality change from the price index is still a matter of considerable concern. This is only one of the biases affecting the measures presented that are relevant to their interpretation. How is a quality index to be interpreted that aggregates addition to expenditures due to "factory preparation of TV dinners, cloth for tea bags, tin for cans, ice for freezing, paper for packaging, or labor cost of washing, peeling, grinding, or mashing food before it enters the home" (p. 590). There will, however, be agreement with Usher that "One would like to know what proportion of the 1.4 per cent increase is food and what proportion is paper and tin. On this matter, the accounts are silent. The increase might be food, packaging, or any combination of the two" (p. 590). The accounts are likely to remain silent until the quantity index is derived from characteristics of food that identify the marketing services utilized.

Stimulus for improvement of estimates of quantity of products consumed will come from an awareness of their contribution to knowledge of demand and welfare. Improvement of many series of quantity of products and their prices seems likely. There seems less reason to expect an increase in demand for quantity indexes of broad categories or products. Presently, demand appears to be for less, rather than more, aggregated quantity series.

Usher seems to regard quantity indexes of the type he describes as being more indicative of welfare than are price-deflated expenditures, because they fit better with the social indicators of justice, equality, education, health, and other "noneconomic" indicators of welfare. His discussion presents meager support for this argument. It leaves untouched the matter of what we would have to know about the association between average and distributive change. Surveys of food consumption and dietary adequacy do make such a contribution. Aspects of food consumption associated with adequacy of diets are, however, represented more by Usher's indexes of quality than quantity.

He notes, for example (p. 589), that price-deflated expenditures for food per head show an increase of consumption of 50 per cent between 1939 and 1968. He inquires whether we can infer that Canadians are eating more or better food in 1968 than in 1935. His answer is that "nothing in the national accounts indicates, or is intended to indicate, whether consumption is evenly distributed; but one may ask whether all Canadians would have adequate diets if consumption were evenly distributed." He continues to point out that to all of these questions the answer is the same. "We do not know and cannot find out, even when examining the primary data that enter into the construction of the national accounts." Information on consumption is, however, not limited to the national accounts.

Usher's quantity index of food shows an increase of about 20 per cent between 1939 and 1968. He does not dwell on its relevance to the quality of diets but does note that the quantity index of food excludes the additional cost of out-of-season fruits and vegetables, prices of which tend to be relatively high, and also the cost of chemical enrichment of foods, much of which was of flour, bread, and milk. Consumption of out-of-season fruits and vegetables tended to increase the consumption of vitamin C, and the chemical enrichment of flour and bread added appreciably to the consumption of iron and the B vitamins, nutrients below recommended allowances in many diets, as indicated by dietary surveys of the United States of the mid-thirties. The effect of enrichment is apparent in average consumption of nutrients added to flour and bread, products of greater quantity in low- than high-cost diets. This enrichment by itself seems likely to have had little effect on the quantity of flour and bread consumed, its percentage addition to cost was small, its effect on flavor and texture of products insignificant, and mandatory enrichment restricted consumer choice. Between 1935 and 1968 per capita consumption of the chemical nutrients added to flour and bread increased about 30 per cent (statistics of the U.S. Department of Agriculture); and dietary surveys of the mid-fifties indicated an appreciable increase in the proportion of adequate diets, in spite of a decrease in the consumption of flour-bearing enriched foods. A weighted index of nutrients per capita of the national food supply would have greater relevance to welfare than a quantity index of foods. Knowledge of this relevance would, however, be increased by information provided by surveys on the distribution of foods and their nutrients among consumers.

Indexes of average consumption, no matter how perfected, will not contribute to knowledge of distributive change unless they are supplemented by microdata that reveal the conditions that generate it, and that can be shown to be associated with average consumption. We are very far from knowledge of this type.

Much of the discussion of this paper implies that the quantity indexes describe real consumption. There is surely need for more specificity of terms for the analysis of consumption. Precise thinking and measurement call for precise concepts. To consumers, quality is a component of real consumption. Usher notes that quantity of products, such as number of units, may be substitutes for less or more units, depending on the combination of their characteristics. His quantity indexes will thus be biased by change in such substitution. The theory of consumption of characteristics of products developed by Lancaster provides a frame of reference for interpretation of real consumption. Usher recognizes this, and his indexes of quantity of housing and education identified some of their characteristics. Their identification is, however, very crude compared to that of many cross-section studies of housing and education. Such investigations may provide better identification of characteristics of housing and education in time series to come.

Broad categories of products, such as food, clothing, and others, differ greatly in the extent to which their quantity indexes represent a constant mix of characteristics. This mix is more homogeneous for food than for transportation, appliances, and clothing; or for housing and education, for which some identification of characteristics was made. Increase of consumption with income is chiefly a substitution of a product of higher for one of lower quality. A quantity index is homogeneous in characteristics if these are identified by the items priced, or if their mix in the items priced changes little. Many of the food items of Usher's series identify the substitution associated with increase of income; and for others, little change occurred in the mix of characteristics. Meats, such as beef and pork and lamb, include a wide range of qualities, but their joint production ensures little change in the mix of characteristics: the ratio of sirloin steak to pot roasts tends to be stable.

An important aspect of real consumption has been overlooked by Usher; namely, the contribution to real consumption of the household economy. The distribution of productive resources between the household and the market has been changing. How is this change to be represented? That increase of food expenditures due to increase of processing, including TV dinners, represents an increase in the quality of food seems likely to be doubted by many persons, even when they agree that a shift of the provision of meals from the household to the market has occurred. Many other substitutions of productive resources between the household and market economies have occurred and further shifts seem likely. Increase of women in the labor force has been, and seems likely to continue to be, a powerful stimulus.

Price-deflated expenditures accurately measured should yield indexes of change in real consumption identical to the quantity-weighted consumption of the products represented. Usher reported no such correspondence. Conditions contributing to their disparity are many. Some are more easily corrected than others. Greater correspondence of the two series will come from improvement in the estimates of deflated expenditures or in those of the quantity of consumption they represent. At best, many questions raised by Usher will remain unanswered. A balance may best be achieved by improvement of price-deflated series of consumption expenditures, and supplementary estimates of interactions between the money and household economies, and of welfare series of average and distributive change.

The Conference on Household

Production and Consumption:

A General Comment

RUTH P. MACK

INSTITUTE OF PUBLIC ADMINISTRATION

THE hallways of this conference room seem to have been haunted by an uninvited guest, one bearing the insignia: tastes, value systems.

I do not mean to say, of course, that value systems have been entirely excluded in the sense of being locked into the ceteris paribus attic. Indeed, this is not at all typical of recent work in consumer economics. Direct consideration has been given to the values implicit in attention to permanent income and to wealth. These are primarily economic. But even psychosocial values have been recognized as influencing spending. The relative-income hypothesis is a case in point, in which community standards are recognized; this notion of a social norm is likewise implicit in regional and national differentiation in consumption and saving patterns. The most far out of these concerns are, perhaps, those reflected in "attitudinal" variables, which are recognized (with notable lack of unanimity) as influencing when, if not what, people buy. In general, this rather gingerly recognition of the fact that man does not live by bread alone is understandable when concern focuses on how man earns and acquires his bread.

But bread is a dwindling proportion of the diet of twentieth-century Americans. Affluence brings not only cake but television dinners. These other interests will range over all the things (not merely material goods and services) which people find desirable and of value—the desire for intimacy; for social belonging and participation; for intellectual, religious, or aesthetic experience; joy in the out-of-doors; and so on—such interests and desires can influence both how much income people earn and how it is divided among material goods and services, as well as between these and noneconomic goods.

If noneconomic values can thus influence the shape of the standard collection of Engel curves in affluent societies, how much more likely are they to influence subjects discussed in these conference papers: the demand for children, or for health, and its relation to schooling; nonmarket aspects of real wages; desired characteristics of housing; product quality; safety and risk.

Necessarily, how families spend time and money for each of these desirables will be influenced by differences in their view of well-being, broadly defined.

Such differences will, at a minimum, increase the *variance* in the functional relationship between the dependent and independent variables isolated in statistical analysis. If this were all, perhaps my concern for serious attention to the value systems that are relevant to choice would not be justified. We have learned to live with extremely wide variance in cross-sectional analysis, though one laments the potentially useful information which remains unidentified in the pool of ignorance (variance).

But, I submit, that it is not all. For one thing, within the sample that is studied there may be people having *different life styles,* the nature of which is lost and thus *misinterpreted in the parameters.* For example, Maynes proposes "variations in P^* as a measure of informational effectiveness of markets." But, the validity of the measure rests in the assumption that within product classes, different consumers make identical quality assessments (p. 537). Yet quality assessments for the product illustrated, sofa beds, assign over half the total weights to the convenience and pleasantness of the vendor and the aesthetic characteristics of the product (list of weighted characteristics, p. 531). Certainly there would be many conscientious long-term types of homemakers for whom durability, comfort, convenience of operation, and trustworthiness of the vendor would be deemed of dominant importance, thereby violating Maynes's basic assumption. It would mean that variations in $P*$ would be consistent with informationally effective markets and no longer a measure of such effectiveness. Realizing this, he says, "the extent of incongruity of quality assessments is an important topic for future research" (p. 538). I doubt that one would get very far studying congruity in such assessments without very specifically and inventively studying precisely *incongruity* due to different value systems or life styles, and accommodating the theory of this provocative and valuable work to what is thereby learned.

Another possible, though highly conjectural example, is in the Michael-Willis paper and concerns the puzzling finding that the likelihood of using the pill is less for women marrying at later rather than earlier ages, ceteris paribus. Could this suggest that later marriages may be partly motivated by the intention to stack up a family promptly — "the time has come for that kind of thing"? If so, the negative coefficient for the pill actually reflects a difference in *desired* timing of family formation. Also, it is possible that interpreted in this fashion, the age-at-marriage variable may be sufficiently correlated with the wife's education variable to grab away some of the latter's usual strong inverse influence.

We have been speaking of how differences in value systems within the sample studied can condition and distort the meaning of the measured variables. This can also occur as a result of the way in which such *value systems relate to institutional characteristics.* For example, how would Heckman's interpretation of his findings change if people's investment in on-the-job training during the life cycle was less an expression of their willingness to invest in skill-capital than an impressed investment in seniority-capital consequent to the nature of the job structure within and among firms (including union rules). Insofar as this structure gives workers little opportunity voluntarily to buy more training by accepting a lower wage, continuity of choice between schooling and on-the-job training is called in question, as is the homogeneity of the value system of those who rely primarily on each of the two sources of capital formation.

Values not only differ among individuals at a given time; they also *change over time.* Certainly, some of the differences in measuring real consumption by inflating quantity data rather than deflating dollar data consists of such shifts in what people desire. Quantity data, as Usher points out, "could serve as arguments in the utility function," and he shows how their weights on the total utility vector change over time. It is most encouraging to find that ingenious hard work seems capable of displaying and quantifying such change and that it appears to be substantial.

A dramatic example of a changed value system in this country, indeed perhaps the most extraordinary one in social history, was the shift in fertility rates in the late fifties and sixties from about the highest to the lowest in the century. This astonishing change in an aspect of behavior typically regarded as most deeply rooted and predictable must certainly have reflected fundamental aspects of the social scene — resentment of the Vietnam war, awareness of world population and ecological problems, generation gaps, social malaise. No doubt the pill may have helped to effectuate intentions but it certainly could have been no more, whatever its price advantage, than, shall we say, a drop in the whole causal bucket.

The data that Michael and Willis used to examine "diffusion of the pill" applied to women who began their first, second, or third pregnancy interval in the period 1960–1964. The authors say, "Note that the 'date the interval began' operates as a time trend in the analysis, so it is assumed to be negatively related to the information cost of pill adoption" (p. 83). I cannot judge just how many and which years are covered by typical observations, but clearly whatever they are, they fall in this period of dramatic social change. Certainly insofar as the coefficients label as a process of diffusion (or cost of information bearing on the "price" of the pill) any of this broad social change in the desirability of children, the label is incorrect. In any event the point illustrates how time trends in values could distort econometric findings. In studies in which data from sequential cross-section samples are combined, the potential distortion would, of course, be bound to be present.

In summary, differences in value systems among individuals or from one time to the next can distort measured parameters and their ostensible meaning. Such distortion blemishes the usefulness of the evidence concerning the groups studied. More seriously, it can mean that application of conclusions to other groups, subcultures, cultures, or times is truly perilous.

Value systems and tastes appear to have been stalking around the

Conference, whether or not they are listed as legitimate guests. What would happen if they were dealt with more openly? The answer, I fear, is that it would not be at all easy to do so, and could only be done, at best, at the cost of considerable loss of precision of measurement. Nevertheless, the usefulness of such measurements as were achieved would be greatly increased.

The Conference has itself contained hopeful signs of progress. Grossman's explorations of the relation of health to schooling, in his sensitive attention to multi-directional causal relationships (e.g., health to schooling, schooling to health via wives' schooling, past schooling to schooling, past health to current health) and his successful use of subjective variables (visual perception, job satisfaction, and self-rated health status) seem to suggest ways that value systems might be identified. Maynes, Usher, and King were all trying to salt the tail of birds of the "fashion" feather; at least their measurements did not concentrate on the narrowly economic aspects of individuals' utility systems. And it is in these more general well-being arguments of the total utility vector that many important differences in value systems are likely to reside.

However, if we are to deal explicitly with "evaluative activity" in a parallel manner to which we are now, thanks to the Lancaster-Becker model, dealing with "productive activity," [1] investigations will need to be addressed, among other things, specifically to identifying life styles. Anyone can think of possible approaches — parallel analysis of selective samples; multi-directional analysis of groups of independent and dependent variables; interviews, games, and experiments designed to exhibit tradeoff functions. But to invent and utilize such approaches requires another hard and large step forward in the analyses of "Household Production and Consumption." However, I must say, in view of the large step forward that the Conference papers represent, the next step seems, in the light of our present social concerns and situation, exciting . . . and inevitable.

---

[1] I sketched such a modified model in "Values, Social Indicators and Priorities," a paper presented at the Twentieth International Meeting of the Institute of Management Sciences, June 1973.

Index

tive method, 75–76; and fertility, 5–6, 34, 36, 36n, 44, 44n, 45, 102, 104, 105n, 112, 133, 143; variations in, 35, 84n, 120

Sheps, Mindel C., 32, 32n, 33n, 104, 112n, 122n

Shnelvar, Ralph, 99n, 130n, 227n

Sibley, David, 115n

Silver, Morris, 147, 153n

Simon, Julian L., 100n

Smallwood, Dennis E., 246

Smith, Adam, 10, 266, 267, 269

Smith, James P., 147n, 197, 227n

Smith, R., 287n

Society of Actuaries, Occupation Study of, 10, 187

Specialization, periods of: investment of time during, 236n, 239, 241, 242; leisure during, 239, 242; number and timing of, 239, 241; wages during, 239, 241–42; work and, 239, 242. *See also* Life cycle stages

Specimens, product: definition of, 541–42; product class of, 554–55; quality of, 530–31

Stafford, Frank, 227, 228, 229

Statistics Canada (Dominion Bureau of Statistics), 589, 595n, 615n, 626n, 631, 643

Stephan, Paula, 227, 228, 229

Sterility: and contraceptive behavior, 63, 80, 136n; period of, 32–33, 34, 35, 36, 54

Stigler, George, 530n, 541

Stockwell, Edward G., 147, 153n

Stone, Richard, 316n, 406n

Stotz, M. S., 386n

Strazheim, Mahlon, 451n, 458

Strotz, R. H., 315n

Stuart, Alan, 125n

Substitution: among housing submarkets, 16, 486; among meats and produce, 403, 404, 430, 431, 449; among observed and unobserved attributes, 393, 397; between household and market economies, 646, 647; between expenditures on children and other budget items, 30, 39, 41, 100; between income and job risk, 277, 278, 299–300; between quality and quantity of children, 30, 41, 97; between quality and quantity of goods, 588, 645–46; in cost-of-living indexes, 3, 13–14, 22, 397, 399, 444; in quality of purchases, with increased income, 646; relative prices as marginal rates of, 311

Survey of Economic Opportunity (SEO), 10, 143, 286, 288

Taeuber, Irene B., 27n, 29n

Tastes, consumer. *See* Preferences

Taubman, Pau J., 163, 200n, 265n

Taylor, Lester D., 14

Terleckyj, Nestor, 305n

Thaler, Richard, 9–11, 297n, 298–301 passim, 582

Thangiah, S. G., 400, 442

Theil, H., 403, 473, 529n

Thompson, Lucille, 529n

Thorndike, NBER-, sample. *See* NBER-Thorndike sample.

Thorndike, Robert L., 163n, 164n, 172, 173n, 200, 203

Tietze, Christopher, 34, 37n

Time: allocation of, 8–9, 214, 227, 228, 233–34, 235; as constraint on family size, 4, 40; as cost of fertility control, 44; as household input, 39, 96; illness-free, 150, 166, 167–70, 214, 215, 216, 222; as input to health, 151–52, 214; investment of, 8, 9, 155n, 228, 229, 231–32, 234–37, 239–41, 242, 244–45, 250–53, 254, 259–60, 262, 263; leisure, 227, 228, 229, 230, 232, 235; as output of health capital, 7, 150, 154; preference, in lifetime utility functions, 106, 234, 237, 260; price of, 228, 234–35, 260; at work, 7, 18, 235

Tornqvist, L., 13, 442–43, 447

Training, on-the-job: cost of, 230; effect of health on, 190; as investment in human capital, 8–9, 155n, 228, 234–37, 251–57, 263, 649; and job structure, 649; relationship to working time, 230; variation in, 230–31

Transaction costs: of avoiding risk, 16, 499, 504, 507, 511; of fertility con-